Praise for *Brotherton's Travels*

Spanning three continents and half a century, *Brotherton's Travels* is the story of life on the edge, the proverbial struggle to make art matter in a world that works against it. Greg Boyd's work with Asylum Arts Press was nothing short of heroic, a lifeline for hundreds of innovative writers. But beyond that, Boyd's carefully crafted memoir is a portrait of a man unwilling to settle for a dull existence. As a poet, fiction-writer, editor, teacher, and visual artist, Boyd was an ongoing source of inspiration to people he worked with. And it's fitting that his memoir ends with "Planet Hazmat," a stunning and insightful condemnation of the socio-economic forces that are turning our planet into a toxic waste land. Though Greg Boyd has a great absurdist sense of humor, *Brotherton's Travels* is not light reading. Instead, it's a book to read carefully, a book to savor and learn from.

— Stephen-Paul Martin,
author of *TwentyTwenty* and *The Ace of Lightning*

If you're into contemporary literature and small press publishing, this splendid memoir is for you. In *Brotherton's Travels*, author and visual artist Greg Boyd details what it takes to swim against the current as a writer and publisher of avant-garde literature in America. I hope he's found his asylum at last.

— Paul Rosheim,
editor and publisher of Obscure Publications

Greg Boyd is, like his great-great grandfather, "a handsome, bold, and entertaining fellow." Moreover, a headbanger of the first order, Boyd was Baudelaire in the battle scarred San Fernando Valley when the Left Coast renaissance was in its mid-century infancy. Boyd's memoir *Brotherton's Travels* recounts what earthlings now realize was the halcyon age of the boho California *coup de foudre*. Reading Greg Boyd's work makes me want to wave my hands and pound on the table. I can't get caught inside without him.

— Susie Bright,
author of *Big Sex, Little Death: A Memoir*

Greg Boyd's *Brotherton's Travels* is so rich in details, personal histories, literary reminisces, and chronicles of Boyd's often dysfunctional family romance that writing a blurb for it is harder than describing the mating rituals of one-eyed, two-toed inhabitants of a yet-to-be discovered alien planet. In short, one must bring both one's intellect and imagination to the task. One should start, of course, by dealing with Boyd's claim that his memoir isn't even about him, but instead concerns his alter-ego, whom he names Brotherton. In a sense, the creation of an alter-ego allows him to look objectively at his real self, which, in turn, frees him from the self-indulgent psychic bloodletting that characterizes most memoirs. In *Brotherton*, Boyd sometimes resembles James Boswell recounting Samuel Brotherton Johnson's peregrinations. Other times, when Boyd's unflinching idealism keeps him afloat, he resembles Don Quixote kicking the crap out of windmills, accompanied by his wife Donna, herself a much wiser version of Sancho Panza. Now all of this in a 500-page memoir might be boring, but Boyd the writer, using short sections of clear yet musical prose, somehow creates a memoir that ends being a page-turner. But what really makes this memoir special is Boyd's authentic voice, one whose hopefulness constantly battles with his clear-eyed disappointment in the human condition. This contrast is most evident in the two endings the book offers: one at the end of the penultimate chapter, the other which closes the book and presents a possible apocalyptic vision of the future. Being familiar with Boyd's work and sensibility, I lean toward the former ending. There, while at home in Spain, Boyd describes how, after he and Donna awake from a nap, she points to a little sailboat moving across the ocean—an image reminding Boyd of a tiny red, plastic sailboat he owned as a child, a memory that makes him "recall a dream in which [he] once caught a glimpse of eternity." This "glimpse," so often gifted to us through imagery, is what makes life worth living. It's one of those archetypal moments Boyd has always doggedly pursued in his life and work—one that we all crave. Perhaps Boyd states this communal experience best when explaining the etymology of his alter-ego. "Call me Brotherton," he proclaims, "for we are all brothers, and for better or worse, this world we inhabit together is both our tribe and our town." In this sense, *Brotherton's Travels*, like all great memoirs, is as much our story as it is Greg Boyd's.

— Peter Johnson,
winner of the James Laughlin Award and author of
While the Undertaker Sleeps: Collected and New Prose Poems

Also by Greg Boyd

Circus Deluxe (Jump River Press, 1982)

La Fanfarlo by Charles Baudelaire, translated and with an introduction and notes by Greg Boyd (Creative Arts Book Company, 1986)

Balzac's Dolls and Other Essays, Studies, and Literary Sketches (Légèreté Press, 1987)

The Masked Ball: Prose Poems and Prints (Unicorn Press, 1987)

More Lies, and Other Stories (Europa Media, 1988)

Puppet Theatre: Prose Poems and Prints (Unicorn Press, 1989)

Water & Power: Stories (Asylum Arts, 1991)

Carnival Aptitude: Being An Exuberance in Short Prose and Photomontage (Asylum Arts, 1993)

Sacred Hearts: A Novel (HiJinx, 1996)

Modern Love and Other Tall Tales (Red Hen Press, 2000)

The Double (Doppelangelgänger): An Annotated Novel (Leaping Dog Press, 2002)

Three the Hard Way: Erotic Novellas (with William Harrison and Tsaurah Litzky, Touchstone, 2004)

The Nambuli Papers (Leaping Dog Press / Blue Rain Films, 2004)

Horny: Stories Selected & New (Leaping Dog Press, 2012)

BROTHERTON'S TRAVELS

Brotherton's Travels: Memoirs

Greg Boyd

Brotherton's Travels: Memoirs. Copyright © 2025 Greg Boyd

Cover and interior illustrations © 2025 Greg Boyd

All rights reserved. No part of this publication may be reproduced, stored in a retrieval system or transmitted in any form or by any means, electronic, mechanical, photocopying, recording or otherwise without the prior permission of the publisher.

Library of Congress Control Number: 2024949935

ISBN Paper 978-1-58775-054-0
      E-Book 978-1-58775-055-7

1 3 5 7 9 10 8 6 4 2

Coyote Arts LLC
PO Box 6690
Albuquerque, New Mexico 87197-6690
www.coyote-arts.com

For Donna, who has walked beside me.

Contents

Brotherton	3
Raised by Wolves	15
Scissors on the Beach	69
It's a Wonder (I Can Think at All)	
Part 1, Education	103
It's a Wonder (I Can Think at All)	
Part 2: Literary Apprenticeship	151
The Last Unicorn	209
Do-It-Yourself Asylum	235
Literary Road Trips	289
Almost Paradise	325
Living in the Past	359
Sore Feet and Miracles	389
Santa Ana de los Cuatro Rios de Cuenca	415
Vista del Mar	485
Addendum	511
Planet Hazmat	513

Thus, gentle reader, I have given thee a faithful history of my travels… wherein I have not been so studious of ornament as of truth. I could, perhaps, like others, have astonished thee with strange improbable tales; but I rather chose to relate plain matter of fact, in the simplest manner and style; because my principal design was to inform, and not to amuse thee.

— Jonathan Swift, *Gulliver's Travels*

Brotherton

"Call me Ishmael." The hostess looked up from her clipboard and asked, "How do you spell that?"

— *The Double (Doppelangelgänger)*

C ALL ME BROTHERTON. It's how I sometimes think of myself. He's my double, my alter-ego, a character who sometimes appears in my books. A silent film comedian, a sleight of hand huckster, a failed artist, a literary trickster, he surfaces under various guises and names: George Body, Edouard Jouvret, Aristide Nambuli, and, of course, Brotherton. Yet despite these fictions, Brotherton really does exist, albeit as a family history lost to deception several generations ago. It's complicated, but what I'm trying to say is that while Brotherton is not my name, it could or even should have been.

In *Romeo and Juliet,* Shakespeare famously asked, "What's in a name?" It's a good question, and not so obvious as it first appears. After all, "That which we call a rose / By any other name would smell as sweet." Yet though the names Montague and Capulet led to tragic consequences in the play, those of us who are not star-crossed lovers probably take our names more or less for granted.

When I was a young child, my parents told me that Gregory meant "watchman." They also told me I was descended from a Scottish king. In time, I came to understand that my father had been named after my grandfather. In fact, the two of them shared the same appellation, which automatically made my father into a lesser version manifested in the "Jr." that always accompanied his name. I didn't fancy the idea of being a junior, so I was glad that my parents had not resorted to such royally uninspired duplication as to christen me "the third." Instead, they hung Charles around my neck as a kind of booby prize middle name. At any rate, what my parents told me must have assuaged my curiosity enough that for many years I didn't give much thought to my name. Having been assigned to me at birth, it seemed as constant as the color of my eyes and hair (both of which changed as I matured), and it never occurred to me that I could call myself something else or legally change my name to better match my current circumstances. Nor did I ever consider that there were strangers who shared my name.

In school, having a name that starts with a letter near the beginning of the alphabet is an unearned perk, a bit of luck that puts one at the front of the line or the front of the class. I was also fortunate that my name didn't immediately bring to mind something comic nor rhyme with a scatological expletive. Most importantly, since Gregory already ended in the letter "y", the shortened form did not, so I wouldn't be stuck with a little boy's name later in life. That's not to say I particularly liked my name nor that I didn't sometimes wish I'd been christened Mick or Nick Valent, or Ulysses McGregor or Aloysius Charpentier. However, it wasn't until my last year of college, when I began to write with publication in mind, that I first thought carefully about my name and how to present myself to the world.

In those days, I considered myself a poet, so I wanted a serious, decisive, and memorable moniker. I wanted it to be as smooth as marble, as durable as granite. William Butler Yeats and W. H. Auden seemed like good names for a poet. Even T. S. Eliot had some traction. G. C. Boyd, on the other hand, sounded more like an accounting firm than a fount of poetry. It thuds off the front of the rim like a missed free throw in a tied playoff game. So instead, I opted for balanced syllables: Gary Snyder, Allen Ginsberg, Hart Crane, Tom Clark, Ted Jones, Aitch Dee (that is to say Hotel Delta, or H.D., the pen name poet Hilda Doolittle sensibly employed when publishing her work). So I shortened Gregory Charles Boyd to Greg Boyd, the name that has since appeared on all of my books. While it's not flashy, I've always thought it looks good in print. Typography abounds with handsome letter "G" majuscules. By the time I considered another person sharing my name, I had published over a hundred poems and stories in magazines, authored several books, translated a novella by French poet Charles Baudelaire, edited a literary and arts magazine called *Asylum*, published and exhibited my block prints, and established a literary press called Asylum Arts Publishing. By then, increased use of personal computers and access to the Internet had resulted in a reshuffling of the deck of relative celebrity. I remember the first time I entered my own name in a search engine, I came up at the top of the list. Other Greg Boyds included an ex-professional football player, a theater director, and the owner of a store selling vintage guitars and other musical instruments. For a while, we were an interesting little clan.

According to *Wikipedia*, the term "egosurfing"—which means to check the entries associated with one's own name on a search engine—was coined by Sean Carton in 1995 and first used in print that same year by Gareth Boanwyn in his "Jargon Watch" column in *Wired*. Well, thanks, Sean, for minting new linguistic currency. In Ecuador, I met an American writer who liked to point out that he had coined the term "steampunk." It seems that was his claim to fame. From time to time, he'd be invited to steampunk conventions to remind people in funny costumes that he'd invented a name for what had by then evolved into an imaginary lifestyle. Anyway, back in the early days of the world wide web, Internet searches could be revelatory and bizarre. Today it's not particularly unusual for people, even those who don't write books or play professional football, to "Google" themselves and others in order to check on the relative health of their public personas or to see if people they've recently met online really exist.

A few years later, I again typed my name into a search engine, hoping to discover some as yet unseen reviews of my books. Instead, I found that I had disappeared from the top pages of the listings, eclipsed by a new star with the same name. A theologian, author, and pastor of a mega-church in St. Paul, Minnesota, this Greg Boyd had been featured in a front-page profile published in the *New York Times* after losing twenty percent of his congregation because he had refused to support conservative political causes and had instead criticized the hypocrisy of the politicized nature of evangelical Christianity. His most popular books include *The Myth of a Christian Nation* and *Letters from a Skeptic*, both of which I've since read. Normally, I object to the dogma associated with organized religion, but my theologian namesake's books seem thoughtful and well intentioned.

On the other hand, I read recently that Greg Boyd the ex-professional football player has been sentenced to nearly three years in prison for tax fraud, while Greg Boyd the theater director has also suffered a decline in reputation. *The Houston Press* reports that a local theater paid $388,000 in severance pay for him to leave his job as its director, after thirty years in the position. According to one source, "the man's tenure… was considered by those who worked with him, almost unanimously, as a reign of terror" of verbal and psychological abuse.

More disturbing still, there's at least one other Greg Boyd whose criminal tendencies have affected me personally. About twenty years ago, I briefly and unwillingly shared a small part of his life, when I suddenly began receiving aggressive and disturbing phone calls from a collection agency. Several times a week, at all hours of the day or night, a disembodied male voice chastised me for being a scoundrel and a thief. "Don't you feel bad for cheating people out of money?" the voice would ask, "aren't you ashamed of yourself?" Actually, I wasn't, I told him, though I would be if I were the one getting paid to call strangers in the middle of the night to accuse them without proof of things they didn't do. Still, he persisted. I realized that talking to him was a version of hell in which you played endless Sisyphean games of tic-tac-toe that always ended somewhere around 3:00 in the morning, in an exhausting and mutually unsatisfying draw.

After several calls, I learned that someone named Greg Boyd had purchased an expensive ring on credit from a jewelry store in a city I had never visited and failed to make payments on it. Once I had established the facts, I thought it would be easy to correct this case of mistaken identity. I told the caller from the collection agency that I had never set foot in the store he mentioned, nor the mall, nor even the city. He didn't believe me and the calls persisted. In vain, I suggested a comparison of identification, but he refused. By now, I'd grown weary and annoyed. The more I tried to help resolve the confusion, the nastier he became. When he began calling my wife at her job, I searched the Internet for advice, then wrote a cease and desist letter to the collection agency and the jewelry store, with a copy indicated for my (imaginary) attorney. The calls ended immediately upon receipt of the letters.

A few years later, my wife and I began to hear from friends and acquaintances in our rural California community, and even read in the local newspaper, disturbing stories about our son breaking the law and being arrested. Clearly this was yet another case of mistaken identity by a secret name-sharer, as by this time our son was in the Air Force, stationed in Alaska. Identity theft teaches us that we are nothing but a composite of numbers attached to a name. It's a bit disconcerting to realize that something so essential to our personal identity, our reputation, and our financial health is not reliably our own. To add further irony, even the names we *think* are ours, though perhaps not uniquely ours, may not be entirely reliable or accurate either.

Such is the case with Brotherton. It's a good English name, I think, though perhaps rather too self-important and upright. It reminds me of one of the bumbling nincompoops that sometimes populate the novels of Charles Dickens. Appropriately, like some minor Victorian novel, the story of Brotherton unfolds within a suffocating milieu of coal dust and horse shit, lust and deception.

Thomas Brotherton, it seems, was my great-great grandfather. Sire of a large brood of unruly newcomers, Thomas was the founding patriarch of my family name. The long-rumored circumstances of his having become a Boyd remained for many years a somewhat sordid family secret. While I'm not sure exactly how much my father, Charles Boyd, Jr., knew about his great-grandfather, I imagine my grandfather must have told him something about the roguish reputation of the old man he remembered from his childhood in the isolated hills of Pennsylvania.

What I do know is that in his sixties my father became interested in genealogy and spent a good deal of time and money researching and investigating both sides of his family tree. His mother's family was easy to trace. The historical record included births, deaths, marriages, property acquired, and even some charming old photos of a large group of rough looking bearded men holding saws, levels, hand planers, and other tools of the trade, who made up the family contracting business. The Wexlers were a family of carpenters and masons who had built hundreds of houses and buildings in Pittsburgh. Earlier heroes had fought in the Civil War, owned a toll road, helped rid the colonies of the Mad King, or played some role in building the Erie Canal. Early records pointed back to a German town in Saxony. Temporarily seduced by his latest obsession, my father traveled to Germany, where he uncovered a trove of municipal documents that pushed the family origins back to medieval times. Or at least that's the story. If we trace our past back far enough, we're likely to find that we're all related to someone powerful and famous, perhaps even the Roman emperor Caligula.

On the other side, his father's tree proved to be of denser wood. There was no rich and detailed history connecting the Boyds to Scottish royalty, as in the genealogical fairy tale my sister and I had been told as children. There were no faded sepia photographs of Gilded Age toddlers seated on velvet pillows, no records of the family castle being sold or mortgaged, no formal garden with a brick path leading back to the Old Country. Instead, the trail ended just a few steps into the Pennsylvania woods. Birth, death, marriage and census data all came to a sudden and unexplained halt after only a few generations. Nevertheless, in the course of his dogged research, my father managed to track down or reconnect with enough chatty distant relatives to piece together a kind of oral history based on scandal-mongering and undisciplined whispers. The common thread that held together the collective tongue-wagging was a juicy and unforgettable tale of betrayal and abandonment.

The story begins with Thomas Brotherton, a young family man who worked for a Pittsburgh coal distributor, delivering chunks of black carbon to nearby rural areas. Thomas drove a horse-drawn wagon, probably a flatbed rig of medium capacity, loaded with pre-bagged coal for heating houses. Because his weekly route circulated through towns and villages a day or two distant from the Pittsburgh coal yard, he was often absent from home. Thus, he normally spent two or three consecutive nights on the road, lodging in various taverns along his route. No doubt the roads were bumpy and dusty, or else wet and muddy, and the routine monotonous. One might wonder how he passed the hours. Did he sing to himself as he drove? Did he make up dirty limericks and jokes to entertain fellow teamsters in the tavern over flagons of ale at the end of the day? Did he conjure up the image of his wife's shy smile as she stood at the stove in the morning, or picture his children sleeping together like mice in their little bed at home?

Because he was a regular customer and a handsome, bold, and entertaining fellow, Brotherton, who always signed the ledger with the name of the coal company that employed him, struck up cordial relations with the tavern owners along his route. Like most working men, he enjoyed his drink. No doubt he also played cards and told stories, though he neglected to mention his wife and children, for, as it happened, one of the tavern owners had an attractive, unmarried daughter. We'll call her Molly (or Maggie or Elizabeth).

Though we can't know how many months or years it took for the mutual flirting to finally come to fruition, eventually Molly found her way to Thomas' room and bed. For a while thereafter, they enjoyed their weekly trysts, in spite of the risks and the need for near complete silence. We can imagine that Molly's heart raced when she saw the coal wagon pull into the yard. We can imagine the wink Thomas would give her on the sly as she served him his ale and plate of stew. There's no need to dwell on the details of reproductive biology, which haven't changed even a bit since prehistoric times. Suffice to say that eventually Molly became pregnant.

Times being what they were, and with guns as prevalent a part of American culture as they remain to this day, the two lovers decided to marry as quickly as possible. Thomas taxed his brain for a pseudonym and came up with the most obvious choice: the name painted in large white letters on the coal wagon parked in the yard below, which happened to be Boyd. He told Molly his name was Thomas Boyd, and that he was the nephew of the owner of the company. Due to poor pay and his uncle's shabby treatment, he had no intention of staying forever in his employ. Instead, the newly self-minted Boyd proposed a move to the country. Molly was delighted with the entire proposal. After Thomas introduced himself to her perplexed parents, the wedding was arranged for the following week, as Thomas needed to return the coal wagon to his employer and collect his final pay.

After the wedding, Thomas and Molly disappeared into the hill country of Pennsylvania, where Thomas bought some land and a worthless house from one of his wife's distant relatives. There he and Molly fucked like rabbits and produced a sprawling, half-feral brood that lived more or less contentedly, scratching in the soil and hunting deer in the forests until they were called away to war or to work in the Pittsburgh steel mills.

When my sister and I were pre-teens, my parents needed time to themselves for the unsuccessful marriage counseling and the epic emotional turmoil that preceded their impending divorce. So they shipped us off to spend part of the summer in Pittsburgh with our Boyd grandparents. Like his great-grandfather, my father would soon abandon his wife and his two children to marry his divorced secretary, who already had a child from her previous marriage. After the divorce, my grandparents would cease to acknowledge my sister and me, and we would have no further contact with them. Cold people those Brotherton-Boyds and Wexlers.

That summer, however, my grandparents treated us well. They took my sister and me to see Fort Necessity and Gettysburg, as they knew that I was keen on history. They also took us to places normal children would go, like Kennywood Park to ride roller coasters, and the demolition derby to see cars smash into each other. I also spent a good deal of time with my uncle Darrell, who let me borrow a low-resistance bow and taught me how to target shoot at his archery club. One weekend, we all went to meet some of my grandfather's relatives, who owned a cabin built along the banks of a green, algae-tainted creek filled with leeches. I remember how my sister and I sat together on a wooden picnic table off by ourselves, away from the beer-guzzling, hee-hawing adults. We watched our distant cousins dunk each other's heads under the water of the vile creek. When they came out dripping algae and dotted with dark spots, their parents picked off the leeches and laughed, while the younger kids, some still in diapers, played unsupervised with a set of deadly lawn darts.

So what turns out to be the most memorable event in my illustrious family history is that the Boyd family was founded by a polygamist who abandoned his first wife and children to begin a second family with a new wife under an assumed name. Though not much was said about his earlier life, at least one person my father talked to remembered hearing the name and relative age of Thomas' first wife, the unfortunate Mrs. Brotherton.

Armed with this new information, further searches yielded a match for Brotherton and his first wife, listed as a widow on later documents, as well as birth records for several children, data which seems to confirm the rumor of Thomas' polygamy. However, no information exists about Thomas Brotherton's parents nor his siblings. Perhaps he had been an orphan, as he'd no doubt told his new wife and family. At any rate, the trail had gone cold. Still, some births had been recorded: unlike the Mohicans, the Brothertons survived, though no thanks to their faithless sire.

My reference to Cooper's clunky novel provides an even clunkier transition to another set of Brothertons. As unlikely as it seems, there actually exists a tribe of Native Americans called The Brothertons. How and why they chose that name is a matter of speculation at this point, though the Christianized tribe members may have been influenced by the rather ironic—given their treatment by their neighbors of European descent and the American government—notion of the brotherhood of man.

The tribe was formed in New England in 1785 as The Brotherton Indian Nation, from remnants of disappearing Algonquian-speaking tribes, mainly Christianized Mohegan, Pequot, Montauk, Narragansett, Niantic, and Tunxis. Pressured by American farmers and settlers who lusted after their land holdings after the Revolutionary War, the tribe moved to Oneida land in New York state, where they stayed until they were again pressured to sell their land and move west to Wisconsin. After the Brothertons cleared their Wisconsin land for farming and built the town of Brotherton there, the federal government again proposed to move the tribe further west to present day Kansas under the Indian Removal Act. By then the Brothertons had had enough of forced relocations. In 1834, the tribe asked to become United States citizens and convert tribal holdings into individual land allotments as a legal strategy to avoid being forcibly moved west yet again. In 1839, Congress passed an act granting them citizenship and they stayed in Wisconsin.

Nevertheless, the tribe was still a tribe and to this day continues to be one. They are, after all, brothers. Sadly, the Brotherton tribe is currently unrecognized by the United States government, which claims the Brothertons gave up their status as an independent nation when they signed the agreement to accept citizenship. It's a ridiculous argument and an absurd and arbitrary decision, as nearly all decisions regarding Indian affairs tend to be. Yet the decision stands, in spite of the fact that the Bureau of Indian Affairs itself confirms that citizenship and sovereignty are not mutually exclusive and all Native Americans are United States citizens. Oh, brother, what have you done to the Brothertons?

Along with the horrors of the slave trade and the racism spawned by the institution of chattel slavery, there is nothing more shameful in U.S. history than the destruction and betrayal of the indigenous peoples of America. If you think those days are behind us and those attitudes have changed, think again. The violent, humiliating, and militaristic tactics used by local law enforcement agencies, private security firms hired by oil interests, and police sent to Montana by six neighboring states, against the Standing Rock Sioux in 2016, illustrate the lasting power of our collective disdain for the original Americans. The use of attack dogs against peaceful Standing Rock Sioux Dakota Pipeline protesters in 2016 and the subsequent arrest and mistreatment of Native American medical doctors and tribal leaders demonstrates how little has changed in the prevailing attitude toward the people the government has historically displaced and abused.

May the Brotherton Nation, along with the Standing Rock Sioux and all other indigenous people on the planet, thrive in spite of the devils in Washington. May their children flourish and the bison return. May the Ghost Dance bring back the grass and the streams. Pequoit, Montauk, Narragansett, Brotherton, all of them sounds the wind makes blowing through the trees.

If I could join the Brotherton tribe, I surely would, though apparently neither it nor I exist according to the law. Yet we are both outlaw Brothertons, which makes us perfect for each other.

So what's in a name?

For ten years I edited a literary magazine called *Asylum,* and, for another ten years after that, books I published under the Asylum Arts imprint. During those years, I received many bizarre submissions, proposals, and letters. I used to keep a file of the most improbable, humorous, or just plain crazy. On one occasion, I received a submission of five remarkably bad poems, along with a stilted cover letter which began, "Dear George Body."

Although I didn't publish the poems, I did put the name to use as an ironic pseudonym. I even published a long story called "The Conference," in which I parody myself. In the story, a writer named George Body, who lives in the fictional city of San Sebastian, California, and publishes a magazine called *PapaDadaBlastFurnace,* operates a writer's workshop called The Suburban Writer's Conference out of his tract home in a working-class neighborhood.

When Donna and I lived briefly in France after our wedding, people called me Gregoire or Grégory, as they couldn't twist their mouths around the pronunciation of Greg, which always ended up sounding like *Grec,* or Greek, in French. During the years I lived in Ecuador, people called me Gregory Charles rather than Greg Boyd, as Spanish speaking countries use both maternal and paternal family names instead of assigning a second given or "middle" name, like Charles. I got used to it quickly, though I preferred the woman who sold fruit in the *mercado* who simply and ironically called me *"Joven,"* though my expiration date for "young" was, even then, long past.

In Spain, where we live now, people seem less concerned with names. Unlike the more formal Spanish speakers in Latin America, they address all but the most elderly and esteemed members of society in familiar terms. Instead of using names, they often call each other *"Guapo"* or *"Guapa."* Since foreigners, mostly from other European Union countries with different naming conventions, make up ten percent of the population, names don't play a big role in conversation. We live in Andalusia, close to the beach, where people wear anything and everything, and even sometimes nothing. Nobody cares. In a place that relaxed, one really doesn't need a name.

In the end, I don't really care what people call me—Gregory Charles Boyd, Greg Boyd, Gregory Brotherton, Gregory Charles, Brother Greg, George Body, or even Groyd, which is what my son and his high school friends called me. To me they are all aliases, legal jargon, or simply nonsense, though some are clearly more imaginative than others. We may think we know who people are, but a name is nothing more than a label on a bottle. Who can be certain what's really inside?

So you may call me Timmy or Zimmy, it's all the same to me. Better still, you may call me Brotherton, for we are all brothers, and for better or worse, this world we inhabit together is both our tribe and our town.

Raised by Wolves

Rollie could recall, from the time he was a young child, his mother yelling, slamming doors, and rattling pots and pans in the kitchen while his father sat silently at the kitchen table, his chin resting on his hand, his eyes focused on something far in the distance.
   —"What's Wrong With This Picture?" from *Water & Power*

"It's not our fault," they'd tell each other as they grew older, "it's us against them."
   —"What's Wrong With This Picture?" from *Water & Power*

MY FIRST MEMORY involves a borderless liquid field of transparent black-and-white membranes dividing and multiplying. It looked like a film shot under a microscope, projected onto a wall somewhere within a darkened room inside my brain. Not precisely a memory, it was instead an awareness of my own consciousness coming into existence, a vapor trail of mitosis. These images recurred in my dreams for years throughout my early childhood. Did the moving pictures constitute a memory of the formation of my brain, perhaps within the womb, or did they occur in real time as I continued to grow? Who can know such things? All I can say about it now is that the experience was at once hypnotic and terrifying in its otherworldliness, as my waking consciousness provided no point of reference for what I saw in my dream. It was as if I were watching a live stream of my own brain cells multiplying. Some dreams are so disturbing that they force you to wake up in an agitated state. While this dream was surreal and unsettling, it was also strangely beautiful. I woke from it feeling overwhelmed and perplexed. Though I lacked the tools to define or even describe it, the dream connected me to larger concepts and to an expanded consciousness I couldn't possibly understand and still can't fully describe or explain.

And so it begins.

While I didn't have this recurring dream every night, or even very often, it nevertheless made a big impression on me and became one of my strongest memories of early childhood. Of course, I never told anyone about the dreams, as I lacked the vocabulary with which to describe them. When I learned to read in first grade, the dreams suddenly stopped.

I've retained other memories of events from my earliest childhood as well. Though I don't remember falling down a flight of steep wooden stairs at my grandmother's apartment building in Pittsburgh, when I was able to crawl but not yet walk, I do remember being in my crib. My parents later told stories about how I used to put myself to sleep by positioning myself on all fours and then rocking back and forth so that my head banged against the headboard of the crib, causing it to roll forward. My sister told me that she has vivid memories of my head-banging as an infant. Those memories distress her to this day. "The noise was not soft and rhythmic," she told me, "It was loud and disturbing. Frequently you moved your crib across the room in front of the door, making it almost impossible to enter the room. I felt compelled to rescue you, but I was afraid of getting in trouble."

When I researched infant head knocking on the Internet, I found that it's fairly common and almost always goes away in time. Of course, my parents could and should have protected my head by installing pillow bumpers around the crib, and anchored the crib in place to keep it from moving and making such a disturbing racket. Strangely, I distinctly remember feeling compelled to do it—or at least I think I do. Experts in child development would likely doubt the validity of such pre-verbal memories. Still, I believe I did it to overcome boredom. My mother would routinely put my sister and me to bed whenever she got tired of us. I think I just needed stimulation and I found moving the crib around the room entertaining. I liked that I could affect such a change. It may have also been a protest, a cry for attention, a way to exert some control over my surroundings. My sister also worries that my head-banging might have caused damage to my developing brain. If it did somehow lower my intelligence, I'm glad, as it seems high enough as it is. I certainly wouldn't have wanted to be burdened with the freakishly high IQ my father possessed. At any rate, it's impossible to know why I head-banged in my crib.

My strongest uncontested early memory, however, concerned a book. Though I never read Kenneth Grahame's novel for children later in life to my own son, I had always loved *The Wind in the Willows*, which my mother read to me as a child. I recalled the story, read serially in afternoon installments, over several weeks, as one of my fondest memories of time enjoyed with my mother. However, forty years later, when I talked to her about my recollection, my mother could hardly believe me when I told her how much I had always loved the animal characters of Mole, Rat, Toad, and Badger and their wild adventures, how afraid I had been of the weasels and ferrets. "I never read that book to you," she told me. "I read it to your sister. You weren't even talking yet. I held you on my lap to keep you quiet as I read the story to Linda."

* * *

One morning during the time I lived on Sawmill Road in Paradise, California, I had a strange and unexpected encounter. Driving home after dropping my son off at his junior high school, I noticed something in the road ahead of me. A low, thick morning fog obscured the trees on either side of the street, transforming the familiar scene into a murky dreamscape. I couldn't discern exactly what I was seeing through the windshield. From a distance, it looked like a deer, or even a large dog, milling in the center of the road. Because of the thick fog, I had been driving slowly. Now, I covered the brake pedal with my foot. As I approached, I saw a human toddler take form.

Dressed only in a diaper, he stood alone in the street, his arms extended in front of him. For a brief moment, we stared at each other.

Leaving the engine running, I turned on the emergency flashers and set the parking brake. Then, I hurried out to pick up the child, hoping other vehicles that might happen along the road would approach with caution. I carried the curly-haired blond boy in my arms back to my truck and set him on my lap as I pulled off the street and onto the shoulder, then shut off the engine. I set the little boy on the seat next to me and tried to reassure him, but he was too young to answer my questions or speak at all. His skin felt cold, but he appeared to be in good health and seemed happy to be picked up, carried, and held. He didn't make a sound.

For the next five minutes or so I walked up and down the street with the child wrapped in my arms, calling out in the hope that someone in the fog was searching for a little boy who had accidentally wandered off in a brief moment of inattention. I walked along both sides of the street. Then I listened carefully to the silence; the fog around me had muffled every sound. Not a single car passed by. No distraught, sobbing parent or caregiver appeared suddenly out of the fog. For some reason I thought of William Stafford's poem "Traveling through the Dark." I wondered what to do.

In those days, very few people had cell phones. Finally, it occurred to me to take the child to the local market at the next intersection, where Pentz Road met Sawmill Road, about a quarter of a mile away. The women who worked in the market could call the police and care for the child with me until they arrived and took over the search for the missing parents.

When the police arrived, I told them what had happened and they thanked me. They said they would go house to house and try to get more information. They took my phone number, but never called me. At home, I felt uneasy. What if someone had simply abandoned the child on the side of the road, like a dog or cat they couldn't afford to keep or no longer wanted? Somehow I felt responsible for the boy, and I wanted to know what had happened to him, but I found no information in the newspaper or on the local television news. I thought of calling the police, but decided against it. There's so much sadness in the world, almost all of it far beyond our control. Finally, I let it go.

I still think of that child occasionally. I hope that he reunited with loving parents who provided him with a stable environment in which to grow and thrive. I hope he has had a good life. But what kind of parents would abandon or allow, through neglect or by accident, a child to wander alone in the middle of a foggy road? What effects do the random circumstances of our birth manifest throughout our lives? We don't get to choose where on the planet we will appear, nor into what financial, physical, nor emotional circumstances. Equally important, we don't get to choose our parents.

* * *

My parents met in junior high school in Pittsburgh. My father, a year younger than my mother, had already skipped a grade. He would skip others as well, and would begin his university studies at Carnegie Tech at the age of sixteen. "He followed me around like a puppy dog," my mother used to tell my sister and me. Apparently, neither she nor her best friend Shirley liked Charles very much. "We wanted to be left alone, but we couldn't get rid of him." One of the earliest photos I have of my father shows him dressed in some kind of uniform holding a French horn. My mother played the violin. At least they had that much in common. Another old photograph shows my parents together in their first year of high school. My father looks like a little boy, while my mother holds her friend's dog in her arms and forces a faint, enigmatic smile.

From the time I was a young child, my mother and grandmother always described my father as a genius. "How can someone with a genius-level IQ act like such an idiot?" my mother would ask my sister and me. My mother told us that as a boy our father was so smart that it drove his mother Gertrude crazy, which in turn drove him crazy. That was my mother's explanation, anyway. She told us how my father had watched his mother throw a temper tantrum in response to something he had done as a toddler. Seeing her on the floor kicking her legs, beating her fists, and crying in front of him at that age had somehow warped his psyche. At a very young age he detached from his mother, which arrested his emotional development. As a young child, he would take himself to the Pittsburgh public library, riding the trolley by himself. He didn't relate well to others. When invited to a party, he brought a book, which he would read alone instead of socializing. He lacked empathy and could never connect with children, including his own.

For a while, my father had wanted to be a minister, but he outgrew God before he was out of short pants. He resented his parents because they refused to buy him a Monopoly game. He knew they could have afforded to buy the game, if only they had cared enough about him. In high school and college, he worked as a caddie at a golf course, catering to the rich, which he found demeaning. He resented their position in society and learned nothing from his contact with the elite. Instead, it inspired in him an overwhelming, competitive desire for wealth and status. A musical prodigy, he played the French horn so well that his teachers told him he could have been a professional, right out of high school. However, his father, who worked in the steel mills, insisted that he study engineering instead. Though he hated math and could whistle, hum, and break entire symphonies down into parts, my father set aside his French horn and accepted a scholarship to Carnegie Tech, where he studied electrical engineering. When he graduated from college, he got a job at General Electric in Columbus, Ohio. In the end, however, he'd have a harder time giving up music than he did earlier giving up God.

I have a few photographs of my mother at various stages of her life—as a young child, as a teenager on my grandparents' farm in Pennsylvania, as a bride, as a young teacher, as a mother, as an old woman. In most of the unposed and candid photos of my mother, she has a haunted, rigid look. In the earliest pictures, her expression reflects the terror and pain she must have already felt. At any rate, by the time she became an adolescent, she had learned how to smile and soften her face in the presence of a camera.

My mother attended Duquesne University on a music scholarship, where she played second violin in the orchestra. Her father, August Pusateri, had operated his own fruit stand in the public market most of his life, and her mother Margaret worked as a baker and cook at the YWCA. Like my paternal grandparents, they had struggled through the Great Depression and they resisted spending money on a frivolous college education. During the 1930s they had been so poor that a rich, childless relative once offered to raise my mother in their place, providing for her and offering her every advantage. My mother categorically refused, so the rich couple extended their offer to one of her cousins instead. Throughout her life, my mother competed with and resented the advantages and eventual inheritance her cousin Mary Jo had received.

One of my mother's friends from school claimed to be a Russian princess whose family had escaped to America during the Russian Revolution. When the girl died tragically from a childhood disease, her family gave my mother one of her expensive German dolls as a keepsake. It was a Shirley Temple doll that my grandmother considered too precious to be handled, so she put the doll on display on a high shelf and forbade Marjorie to play with it. My mother reacted against the injustice and never forgave her mother, who she considered controlling and unwilling to accept her for who she was. Late in her life, my mother began collecting antique dolls. She spent thousands of dollars on them and kept the collection in a specially constructed closet. The most expensive ones she displayed in wooden cases with glass, so that her house resembled a creepy doll museum. When she died, she left the dolls to my sister, who discovered that the Shirley Temple doll had been repaired where the neck had been broken.

My grandmother had grown up on a farm and was the youngest of twelve siblings. Consequently, she'd been used as a servant at home by both her parents and her older siblings. Unfortunately, she carried forth this abusive Old World attitude in her relationship with her own child, who she expected to take care of her, in turn. As an adult, I eventually learned that my mother had an older brother who died in his infancy. The building in which my grandparents lived had been fumigated, and they didn't realize that it was dangerous to spend the night there. The baby boy had been asphyxiated in his sleep. Uneducated and unskilled, my grandparents struggled financially and their only remaining child represented their last, best hope for a better life.

My grandfather's parents immigrated from Sicily. Like my grandmother Margaret, August Pusateri came from a large family and had nearly as many brothers and sisters as she did. One old photo shows him, along with seven of his brothers and one sister, at the beach in Atlantic City around 1920. They look like a rough bunch, like teenage Italian-American gang members from a Scorsese film. I also remember hearing how my mother used her violin to manipulate and control her father and his rough friends and brothers when they came to the apartment in Pittsburgh. The sad tunes she played on her violin calmed them when they drank and raged. Her melancholy violin melted their Frankenstein hearts and made them so maudlin they wiped their eyes with the back of their hands.

Some of these people, August's brothers included, had clear connections to the mafia in Pittsburgh and were busy stuffing ballots in local elections, while August ran his fruit stand in the public farmer's market. One of his brothers was a self-destructive alcoholic. At some point, my grandparents tasked little Marjorie with walking home with him from work each day; with a little girl in tow he would be less likely to succumb to the temptations of the many bars along the way. Growing up during the Great Depression, poverty, deprivation, and adult responsibilities robbed my mother of a normal childhood.

I never met my grandfather August, as he died before I was born. Because neither my mother nor my grandmother ever talked about him, all that's left of him is a drawing he made with colored pencils—a pretty good likeness of a pig. He had given the drawing to my mother, and she had let me frame it and put it up in my room as a child. I've still got that damned pig.

Throughout my mother's childhood, my grandmother entertained unrealistic fantasies about Marjorie and pressured her to be more feminine. She twisted little Marjorie's long hair into ringlets, causing her to scowl in the photos in which she appeared. My grandmother had wanted her child to be a perfect little doll, a talented Shirley Temple who, violin tucked beneath her chin, would charm the world and propel them out of their poverty and their miserable existence. So they scraped up the money to pay for her music lessons, which they considered an investment in the future. Eventually, my mother's hard work, talent, and desire to transcend the limits of her home life resulted in a scholarship that seemed like it might offer her some degree of control over her destiny.

While her parents wanted her to continue living at home and support them financially, or perhaps marry an older, connected, or even "made," Italian man from the neighborhood, my mother instead planned her escape. She had talked Charles into rescuing her with an offer of marriage. As he'd always been openly infatuated with Marjorie, it was his chance to finally possess her. He showed up at her parents' apartment with a big box of new pots and pans—a gift for his would-be mother-in-law—and boldly asked the green grocer for his daughter's hand. Such condescending treatment by a German boy he'd always thought harbored homosexual tendencies enraged August. He never spoke to his daughter again.

My parents married in a civil ceremony. The two photos I have of the joyless event look like pictures from a shotgun wedding. Marjorie wore a matching skirt and jacket rather than a wedding dress. Though my father mustered a thin smirk, my mother couldn't quite force a smile. Nevertheless, she had escaped to Columbus, Ohio and was soon pregnant with my sister. Only a few weeks later, my grandfather August died suddenly and prematurely in Pittsburgh of a massive heart attack. Guilt-ridden and overwhelmed, my mother felt lost and abandoned. Years later, she told my sister that she spent much of her pregnancy crying.

A few days after giving birth to my sister, my mother suffered a dangerous postpartum hemorrhage that nearly killed her. For some reason, she'd had trouble getting to the hospital. For years afterward, she irrationally blamed my sister for both the death of her father and the hemorrhage. Though typically spontaneous in her emotional reactions, my mother at times planted a grudge from seed, watered it with tears, and fertilized it with the bitterness of accumulated years until it produced, like the tree in William Blake's poem, poisonous fruit.

* * *

When my sister and I were still very young, our mother still practiced and played her violin several times a week. Linda and I hated the sound of the instrument because it hurt our ears, but also because it was so sad. Though she knew that it made us cry, she played anyway. If I'm completely honest, I'd have to say that she even weaponized the instrument against us. I remember her telling us throughout our childhood that we needed to "toughen up."

Though my father had given up his French horn, he bought a beautiful set of wooden German block flutes for himself and my mother, so they could play duets. I remember that they played Bach's Brandenburg Concertos together on Sunday mornings while my sister and I watched television in the next room. My father worked as an electrical engineer at the General Electric research lab in Syracuse during the days and studied for his Ph.D. at Syracuse University at night. We saw him only on Sundays. After breakfast and a musical interlude, we usually took a long drive in the country, where my parents liked to look at antiques in the little country stores.

Once, on one of our Sunday drives, we stopped at a big field of tulips. Workers had just finished picking the flowers, and the most perfectly formed tulips had already been packed and shipped off to florists. A sign proclaimed that members of the public could take whatever flowers remained before they plowed them under. So the four of us walked among the fields of partially picked flowers, gathering a big bouquet to bring home with us. In the car on the way home, I realized that I had lost my little hippo stuffed animal. I remembered I'd set the toy down in the field when I picked a flower to hand to my mother. Somehow, in all the excitement, I'd forgotten about my hippo. At that time, Little Hippo was my favorite toy, the stuffed animal I took with me to bed at night and carried with me wherever I went.

I begged my father to turn the car around and go back for my hippo, but he kept driving. "They've probably already plowed the field, so we'd never find it," he said.

"Please," I pleaded, but my father ignored me. When I kept whining, my mother told me I should have been more careful and taken better care of my toy. Now that I had lost it, no one could do anything about it. "Why can't we go back and find it?" I pleaded. I couldn't stand the thought of my hippo disappearing under the ground, buried alive. Though I cried all the way home, my parents did their best to ignore me. Later, my mother bought another, identical little hippo toy, which she hid in her closet for a Christmas present. However, when I became very ill well before the holidays, she took pity on me and gave it to me early.

My mother found the story of Little Hippo to be iconic in some way, and she repeated it endlessly throughout my life, telling it to my girlfriends, buying me hippo-themed Christmas gifts, and refreshing everyone's memory of the story at family gatherings. No matter what she did, I shrugged it off, never giving her the satisfaction of a strong reaction, hoping she would tire of it. Nevertheless, for some reason she couldn't let it go. I found her obsession with the story indicative both of her lack of empathy for me as a child, as well as her continuing lack of respect for me as an adult.

I remember sometimes taking naps with my mother as a very young child. I would try to time my breathing so that it coincided with hers. However, such intimacy didn't last, as she was in a hurry for her children to grow up, become independent, and leave her the hell alone. Once we were no longer toddlers, she disliked it when we called her name, held onto her, or tried to cling to her legs. Linda, two years older than me, had already broken the habit by then, so my mother singled me out for ridicule. "Mother, Mother, Mother, pin a rose on me," she would sing, mocking me whenever I craved her attention and affection.

In our backyard in Syracuse, we had a crab apple tree that came to symbolize unpleasant behavior. Whenever we appeared tired, grumpy, or unhappy, our mother would call us names. Her favorite was "Crabby Appleton," which we knew from the cartoon villain we'd seen on Captain Kangaroo. "Crab-by Apple-ton, rot-ten to the core," she'd sing at us. If my father happened to be around, both my parents would laugh when, right on cue, one of us burst into tears in their Punch and Judy show.

My mother made Boston cream pies, rhubarb pies, and a coconut cake shaped like a lamb for Easter. She also made chipped beef on toast, fried Spam, and scrambled eggs burned black in butter. In Syracuse, we had a big summer vegetable garden and my mother fed us a constant supply of cooked vegetables, including squash, which I couldn't seem to choke down. I remember that it would stick in my throat, threatening to asphyxiate me, and causing me to gag and retch or spit it out onto my plate. Though eating squash literally brought tears to my eyes, my mother did not give up. She tried serving it with marshmallows on top, which did nothing to alleviate the problem. I simply could not eat the squash, which of course disappointed her and made her angry.

* * *

My mother spanked us. Because she struggled with a personality disorder that made her unpredictable and emotionally volatile, she had a strong tendency to react impulsively to the world around her. Throughout our childhood, my sister and I walked on eggshells. Like prisoners watching their jailer's every move, we regulated our emotional responses and shaped our behavior in accordance with her moods. We asked for nothing. The more we asked, the less we got. It was a game and we learned how to play it.

My mother tended to compartmentalize her life, dividing it into realms in which she could exert absolute control and others where she must relinquish control. While more passive in social situations with strangers or at work, for example, she dominated and controlled absolutely everything at home. As an adolescent, I remember her coming home from work enraged at the parents of a pupil who had complained about her teaching or her treatment of their child, or at administrators or the school's principal. She sometimes raged for hours. Because such out of control behavior was not tolerated in the outside world, she took advantage of her family to vent her anger, frustration, and powerlessness. She directed her temper at whatever surrogate was on hand, including her children, until it finally burned itself out. There was nothing rational about her reactions.

Likewise, I'm not sure she really thought much about why she spanked us, or even if what we had done justified such punishment. Instead, she acted in the moment as a way to control and channel her rage. The worst spankings happened in public places, which added an element of humiliation and shame to the physical pain. She'd pull down our little pants and give it to one or both of us with her bare hand. I remember once I had a crazy idea to hide while she shopped for groceries at the market. I wasn't really lost, just playing hide and seek with my sister. But my mother didn't find anything playful about our game and spanked my bare bottom in the front of the store, just past the checkout lines, where everyone could see.

Sometimes she grabbed whatever was handy and used that instead. Once, when I was about four years old, my mother spanked my sister and me with a two-by-four. My parents had been remodeling the attic of our little house in Syracuse, and they left us alone downstairs while they worked. We took advantage of our freedom to use a bed as a trampoline. Our mother must have heard our wild jumping and exuberant screaming. She came downstairs and caught us at it. As usual, unamused at our joyful antics, she gave us a hard look and told us to stop. After issuing a further stern warning, she disappeared back upstairs. Though we feared her, the temptation overwhelmed our judgment. Safely out of her sight, we looked at each other and smiled. Then we began to jump on the bed again, though quietly now, without the screaming and laughter. Suddenly, mother appeared again in the doorway, a short, sawed off section of two-by-four inch board in her hand. My sister and I froze in place. I still remember the terror I felt seeing her there. I still remember her rage. We had disobeyed her. I still remember the beating she gave us.

Despite a vast body of scientific research that discredits the efficacy of corporal punishment, despite the American Academy of Pediatrics warnings against spanking, despite a United Nations treaty that recommends banning "all forms of physical or mental violence" against children, despite studies that show adults who were spanked as children die younger of cancer, heart disease, and respiratory illnesses, at least two thirds of Americans still accept spanking as appropriate parental behavior. While more enlightened countries now treat spanking, even in the home, as a form of child abuse, and a violation of children's human rights, the United States, along with Somalia, remains one of only two countries in the world that have failed to ratify a United Nations treaty protecting children.

As we grew, my sister and I developed strategies to avoid such punishments, though we continued to live in fear. We became experts at interpreting our mother's moods and we hid from her whenever anger threatened to overwhelm her. The smallest details provided clues: the look on her face, the burned eggs she served for breakfast, the chipped beef and toast. Even her choice of clothing could be like a warning flag run up the mast of a man-of-war. So we read by ourselves, played quietly in our rooms, shut ourselves in the closet, left the house whenever she put on the hideous blue or brown seersucker suits with short pants she wore when deep cleaning. We learned that we must never draw attention to ourselves, lest it result in an unwanted response. If we had a problem, we hid it, or talked to each other about it instead of going to our parents. We could not trust them to comfort or reassure us. Their irrational responses and their tendency to ridicule rather than nurture destroyed our faith in them.

My sister Linda protected and reassured me as best she could. Despite our irrational parents, neither of us felt completely alone. At least we had each other. Though we certainly could not have had the words to express our feelings and our terror at that time, we somehow knew that we were not the cause of our parents' problems. Though bad things happened around us constantly, together we determined and proclaimed our innocence. We helped each other whenever we could. We talked together about our parents and tried to make sense of the emotional chaos.

My mother directed much of her anger at my father, who, because he felt no genuine emotions, simply ignored it, a result which only served to increase her rage. Sometimes, she directed her anger and frustration at her mother, instead. She accused her of ruining her life at every turn. I loved my grandmother, who was the kindest person I knew, and it hurt me to see her abused. Though Gram was clearly hurt by the attacks, she loved her daughter unconditionally, and she did little to defend herself. Sometimes, my mother directed her anger at my sister, who represented a rival for my father's very limited attention. Sometimes, though rarely, I think, she directed her anger at me, mainly because I reminded her of my father.

I realize now that, by intention or otherwise, my mother had trained my sister and me from the time we were little to be the perfect surrogates to whom she could direct her occasional emotional meltdowns and fits of uncontrollable anger. We were always available and could absorb large doses of abuse. Anger-eaters, we swallowed her invective in silence, lest it be directed at us instead. Powerless children, we had no choice.

* * *

Because we were too young for school, my mother took Linda and me to the Syracuse China factory, where she would spend hours looking through big bins of "seconds" for a particular pattern of dishes she collected. While she sorted through the bins, we had to stand or sit quietly. It bored us to watch her pick up and put back cups, saucers, dinner plates, salad plates, and dessert plates for what seemed like hours. We hated going to Syracuse China.

At some point, my parents decided it might be fun to go camping. So they bought an inexpensive canvas tent, a Coleman stove, and some folding cots. They drove us to a state campsite in the Adirondack Mountains, where we camped for two nights. The first night no one slept much, as we spent hours shivering under blankets my mother had brought from home. The next day, my parents drove into the nearest town and bought two pairs of quilted long underwear and two sleeping bags for themselves. That night, they pinned my sister and me inside blankets and piled the rest on top of us. Though I imagine my parents slept better, I remember I still shivered in the cold. Nevertheless, my sister and I loved camping. Whether we slept well or not, we enjoyed having an adventure.

My favorite place in Syracuse was the French Fort, a big log stockade that overlooked Onondaga Lake. The fort had blockhouses, catwalks, a cannon, and even an underground escape tunnel that led from one of the houses into the woods beyond. For some reason, I loved history and even the old things I saw in antique stores. When we visited the fort, I pretended to be a soldier or frontiersman. Once, we went to Watkins Glen, where we walked along a trail that followed the narrow gorge above a river. Though I was only five or six at the time, the woods transformed me into Hawkeye Natty Bumppo. At one point I yelled, "Look, an Indian!" which startled my mother and caused her to twist her ankle.

I also remember wandering around the campus of Syracuse University, where both my parents had gone to graduate school. In the fall, workers raked giant piles of leaves on the grass lawns and my sister and I would jump into them. Sometimes, when we went downtown, we got to see a movie. I remember we saw *Swiss Family Robinson, 101 Dalmatians, Lady and the Tramp, Mary Poppins* and *The Incredible Mr. Limpet*. We also saw *Bambi* at the drive-in theater, dressed in our pajamas and lying in the back of our car.

Whenever my mother grew tired of watching us, she put us to bed. With experience, we learned that the schedule of our naps depended largely on her level of patience or exasperation. We also learned, like Pavlovian puppies, that if we played quietly after lunch, or even went to our rooms to play by ourselves, she might forget about us so that we could avoid a nap altogether.

Worse than the threat of naps was having to go to bed before dark during the summer months. Every evening, the ice cream man would drive his truck down our street, music blaring. The neighborhood kids would flock to him. Sometimes, if my parents were outside working on their garden, they would give Linda and me each some small coins with which to buy a Buried Treasure—a combination of vanilla ice cream and frozen orange sherbet on a plastic stick. Best of all, a plastic figurine hid beneath the ice cream. These toys, the buried treasure, came in many colors and could be anything from an animal, a member of a dwarf band, a locomotive or caboose, a pirate, a clown, an Indian chief, a baseball player, or a cowboy. Sixty-five different collectible toys, each of them in different colors, kept kids coming back for more.

I remember lying in bed in the fully lit downstairs bedroom listening to the ice cream truck arrive. I could hear the excited voices of my friend next door and the kids down the street just outside the window as they lined up to buy their treats. It didn't seem fair to me that I had to go to bed when the rest of the world played outside, ate ice cream, and collected Buried Treasure toys. The hot tears rolled down my cheeks. Though my parents would have called me Crabby Appleton, I didn't care.

When I was old enough to attend Bear Road Elementary School, my sister and I rode on a bus that stopped in front of our house to pick us up every morning. Once, I came home from school with lice on my head. Since my mother lacked the patience to look for the nits, she took me to a barber shop to have my hair cut so short that I was nearly bald. She told me that it was the only way to get rid of the lice.

* * *

I was a sickly child. Like all small children, my sister and I contracted the major childhood illnesses: measles, mumps, chicken pox. I constantly suffered head colds, chest congestion, and sore throats as well. When my sister had her tonsils removed, she spent a night in the hospital, which terrified me. The pediatrician suggested my parents have mine taken out as well, but for some reason they resisted. The year I went to kindergarten, my mother told us we could play outside in the snow after school. She must have forgotten us, for we stayed outside well after dark, playing in our homemade igloos and having a snowball fight with the neighbor kids.

The next day, I had a high fever and congestion. Over the coming days and weeks, my condition did not improve. I lost weight and didn't have much energy. Eventually, the pediatrician, Dr. Maglioni, or Dr. Macaroni as we called him, diagnosed me with walking pneumonia. I hated needles and having my blood drawn, which is something the doctor did once a week for many months. Though I eventually recovered, I missed much of the school year, and it took several years for my lungs to become stronger.

My mother had little patience for dealing with a sick child. She lacked empathy, and she openly admitted that she disliked caring for others. When I could, I hid my injuries from her because I feared her rough and unsympathetic treatment. Once, I fell off my bicycle and ripped open my knee. I tried to clean the wound myself, but I nearly fainted from the pain and couldn't remove all the small pieces of gravel embedded in the flesh. When the wound became infected, my mother soaked it twice daily in nearly boiling water laced with Epsom salt. A few years later, I cut out the planter's warts that had grown on the bottoms of my feet with a pocket knife I sterilized over a flame and stuffed toilet paper into the bleeding holes rather than tell her about the warts. Miraculously, my surgeries succeeded and the warts never grew back.

Another time, I fell during a street football game and broke my arm in two places. When I returned home cradling my mangled limb, my mother told me to go to my room and rest. "You'll feel better in the morning," she said. "If it's not bleeding, I don't want to hear about it," she often used to tell us. I remember reading a biography of Harry Houdini as my broken arm got hotter and hotter and swelled to nearly double its size. We ended up in the emergency ward of the hospital later that night.

Despite my absences during the time I was ill with pneumonia, I had a kindergarten girlfriend named Sally. I remember she had blond hair and wore a checkered sky-blue-and-yellow dress. We liked each other and agreed that we should get married. Once, I drew a picture of her in her blue-and-yellow dress and hid it under the carpet in my bedroom. When I looked for it later, the picture had disappeared.

In 1964, my parents took us to New York City to see the World's Fair. I don't remember much about the trip except for the eerie audio animatronic dolls in the "It's a Small World" Disney attraction that premiered at the fair before moving to Disneyland in Anaheim, California. I also remember the Monsanto "House of the Future," which Disney also recreated in Anaheim, and which I saw later when we moved to California. I got two souvenirs from the trip: a subway token and a twenty-five-cent green plastic Sinclair Brontosaurus created in a machine at the fair.

One summer, my father drove us south on a low-budget family vacation. We spent a week in Virginia Beach, where my mother stepped on some broken glass and badly cut her foot. After a trip to the emergency room, she spent the rest of the vacation on crutches. At the beach, we saw large Navy vessels offshore conducting a training operation. We stayed in a run-down cabin at a cheap motel. Every night, we ate at a hamburger stand called Piggly-Wiggly. Since we never got to eat food like that at home, my sister and I enjoyed eating hamburgers and french fries wrapped in paper. Next, we went to Myrtle Beach in South Carolina. I remember seeing moss hanging from the trees as we drove along the back roads. I also remember seeing signs for segregated restrooms and drinking fountains, which my parents condemned, though in whispers.

On the way home, we drove through Richmond, which had a big museum devoted to the Civil War housed in a distinctive round building. For some reason, I was obsessed with everything having to do with the conflict between the Union and the Confederacy. Given my young age, I have no idea where I had learned about the war or why it fascinated me. By the time we arrived, however, the museum had already closed for the day. Though I begged my parents to spend the night so that I could visit it the next day, instead we piled back into the car and drove through the night back to Syracuse. Years later, when Donna and I moved to Virginia, I visited several museums in Richmond, though I could never find anyone who remembered a

Civil War museum existing in a round building. Ironically, when I asked my father, he confirmed my memory.

As unlikely as it seems, even as a preschool aged child I exhibited a strong fascination for the past. Old places, buildings, and objects seemed to whisper their secrets to me. I loved historical places and antiques, as well as the costume dramas and period adventures I sometimes saw on television. Once, I found a misshapen wooden trunk with an arched top for sale at an antique store. I was certain that it had previously belonged to a pirate and I begged my parents to buy it for me so that I could use it to store my toys. Though the shop owner had ticketed the lopsided wreck for $5.00, my mother offered him half that amount, which he gladly accepted.

At the age of four or five, I became obsessed with the "War Between the States." Years later, when my parents grew weary of fielding my questions, they finally gave me a book called *The American Heritage Golden Book of the Civil War* as a Christmas present. The book was heavily illustrated and crammed full of Mathew Brady photographs of dead bodies and bearded officers and men, along with hypnotically attractive color battlefield maps populated by tiny rows of blue and grey uniformed soldiers. I spent countless hours over the next several years committing much of the text to memory and reenacting specific battles with armies of miniature plastic soldiers.

* * *

Sometimes we drove to Pittsburgh, where we stayed in my grandmother Margaret's apartment downtown. Gram was my mother's mother, and she lived by herself in an old walk-up apartment near a big park that had buildings full of exotic birds. A man in the park sold hot nuts and popcorn from a cart. The back of the park overlooked railroad tracks that Gram warned us were very dangerous. "Once, a little boy climbed over the fence and his shoe got stuck on the tracks," she said. "It was terrible." Of course, we imagined the worst. In addition to our walks in the park, sometimes we went to a museum to see dinosaur skeletons.

Gram always knew how to keep us entertained. She told us stories about her childhood on a farm. She told us how she spit cherry pits at a bull that had chased her up a tree and how a rooster had pecked at the beads on her dress. She told us about her many brothers and sisters. She took us to Sears and Roebuck to visit her sister Mary, a friendly, smiling woman who gave us hugs and gifts.

When we visited her in Pittsburgh during the summer, Gram took us out to the tiny screened-in back porch connected to the fire escape that overlooked the yard behind her apartment building. She gave my sister and me each a little pail of water and a paintbrush and asked us to paint her porch for her. We spent many happy hours "painting" the walls and floor. To this day, I've always found house painting to be satisfying work.

Gram also let us "fish" for watermelon on her porch. First, she filled a metal wash basin with water. Then, she cut up pieces of watermelon and put them into the basin. She gave each of us a piece of wire with a bend at the end and we'd try to catch the watermelon fish that she moved around with her hands. Eventually, she'd attach a piece to the hook and we would catch a salmon to eat.

Gram worked in the kitchen at the YWCA as a cook and a baker. She knew how to make *povitica*, a Croatian sweet bread, as well as cream puffs, petit fours, crêpes, custard, rice pudding, and all kinds of cookies. She loved to watch others eat food she prepared. Because she had worked in a commercial kitchen, Gram never liked to eat in restaurants. "It's not clean," she'd say. Whenever we did eat out with her, she always ordered a grilled cheese sandwich.

Sometimes when Gram baked at home, she left a little flour on the counter and made a trail of tiny "footprints" in it. "Look," she'd say, "Jimmy's been here." She told us that Jimmy was a pixie who lived in her house. Whenever something got lost or misplaced, she blamed Jimmy for the mischief. Gram somehow managed to catch sight of Jimmy with amazing frequency. "There he is!" She'd say, pointing, but my sister and I could never look fast enough to see him.

The year before I began kindergarten, my mother went to Syracuse University to study for a Master's degree in Education and prepare for a career as a teacher. Linda had started the school year as a first grader, but I was still too young for kindergarten, so my mother arranged to pay the next door neighbor to look after me during the day while she was gone. She made a deal with me that if I behaved myself and made it successfully through the year, she would buy me the one thing in the world I coveted most: a toy musket. At the end of the year, she delivered on her promise. My father took a picture of me standing guard in back of our house wearing short pants and a grey hat with a Confederate flag on it, the toy musket slung over my shoulder.

The following year, when I started kindergarten, Gram came to live with us in Syracuse. My mother had started work as a teacher that year and Gram stayed at home to watch us after school or if we missed school due to illness. Of course Jimmy came with her. Gram said he must have snuck into one of her suitcases when she wasn't looking. Soon he was up to his old tricks, moving things around and playing with our toys while we were at school. Sometimes I'd come home from school to find a tower made of wooden blocks on the floor of my room. "Come look what Jimmy made," I would say. Since Linda could read by herself, sometimes Jimmy left little fingerprints in her books. Whenever Gram made cookies, she'd always leave one out on a plate for Jimmy. "That way he won't steal them all and hide them," she'd say.

One morning when I wasn't feeling well before school, my mother said I could stay home with Gram that day. Gram served me crêpes with maple syrup for breakfast and told me stories. Then she let me watch television while she set up the ironing board and started to press the clothes. She had already folded some clean towels into a neat stack and set them aside. Suddenly she cried out, "Oh my God, that's my brother Claude's face on the wall. Come look!" The sun was shining brightly through the window behind us. When I looked where Gram pointed, I saw a man's profile projected as a shadow on the wall. Gram seemed very upset and sad. Later that evening, she received a phone call from her sister Mary, who told her that their brother Claude had died of a heart attack.

My best friend was our dog Frisky, a Shetland Sheepdog my parents bought from a breeder. Wild and energetic, Frisky liked to herd children by nipping at their heels. I wrestled with her, but she fought back and always escaped my hold. Then she'd back away from me and bark. Another game I played with her was bullfighting. I'd get a towel from the bathroom and wave it at her. "Toro, toro," I'd say, until she charged at the towel like a bull. Sometimes I swooped the towel up and to the side just before she arrived and she'd crash into the couch. She'd charge at me until she finally managed to grab the towel out of my hands. Then she'd shake it in her jaws and strut around the house with it.

My favorite toy at that time was a big stuffed teddy bear. I used to like to fight and wrestle with him on the floor. When I watched *The Lone Ranger* or *Flash Gordon* on television, I'd pretend my bear was one of the villains and I'd fight with him just the way Roy Rogers or The Lone Ranger would beat down the bad guys.

One day, I came home from school to find my bear missing from my bed where I'd left him. There was a note on my pillow that said some robbers had taken him. They wanted me to pay a ransom to get him back. I didn't have any money and I was really angry and upset that someone had taken my bear. Gram seemed upset, too. The next day, when I came home from school I found my bear back on my bed. "The mafia took him, but Jimmy outsmarted them and got him back," Gram told me.

* * *

I always imagined that my mother must have been a very stern and strict teacher, the kind of teacher the other kids in school warned you about, the kind of teacher that could easily ruin your life for a year. My grandmother told Linda and me stories about how as a young child my mother had arranged her dolls into a classroom and then spent hours giving them lessons. "She always wanted to be a teacher," Gram said. "Sometimes she'd pick up one of the dolls and discipline it for not learning its lessons." We imagined our mother doing the same thing at work.

Years later, when I was teaching English at California State University, Northridge, I visited my mother's classroom to work with her students on writing poetry. I was surprised to see the easy rapport she had with the class. I could see that they trusted in her calm and professional guidance. After school, she showed me stacks of unused new textbooks she had stored in the closets of her classroom. "They change the curriculum and the books every three years and the textbooks only get worse and worse. If I used these books, the kids wouldn't learn a thing, so I just put them in here and keep using sets of the best old textbooks I've collected over the years. That way the kids leave here knowing what they're supposed to know."

The best thing my mother did for me was take my sister and me to the library. She brought us regularly to the big public library in Syracuse before either Linda or I could read and let us pick out books for her to read to us at home. Later, she let us pick out books we wanted to read ourselves. When we moved to California, my mother drove us after school nearly every week to the West Valley Branch of the Los Angeles County Library in Winnetka. I had my own library card and I could already read well enough that I rarely used the children's section. Instead, my mother allowed me to browse everything that interested me throughout the library. Though she generally gave us an hour to pick our new books, I would have gladly spent the entire day looking through the stacks and sampling the books, seated at one of the long tables.

Each week I scrambled to narrow down my choices. I always left with the maximum number of books one could check out at a time. My favorites included history, biography, and novels. Though I read eclectically and without any guidance, I often delved deeply into subjects that sparked my interest. I particularly liked military history. I also read novels. At first I read books in series like *Danny Dunn and the Donut Machine*. Later I read *Treasure Island* and *Robinson Crusoe*, along with books by John Steinbeck and Jack London. More importantly, I fostered my natural intellectual curiosity, gained a love of knowledge and books, and established a reading habit and connection to and love of books that has been one of the touchstones of my life. From a young age, I knew that I wanted to be a writer.

* * *

My father was a stranger who sometimes lived among us. I had learned as a young child that he seemed disinterested in most people and particularly in children. He was busy at work or at the university and we rarely saw him. When he did come home, we had to be quiet so that he could study in his office or translate technical papers from Russian. On Sundays, he took us on long drives. The rest of the week he usually ignored us.

We lived on a big corner lot fifteen minutes by car to downtown Syracuse. Our house had two bedrooms, a basement, and an unfinished attic. There was a porch in the back and a detached one-car garage. Later, my father designed and built a staircase that led from the living room to the attic. Then he built a big dormer window and added a bathroom and three tiny bedrooms upstairs. The front of the little house faced Buckley Road. Across the street lived a German Shepherd dog that terrified my sister and me. The side of the house and the garden faced Rita Lane, a street that dead-ended into a wood. At that time, there may have been a dozen houses on the street. On the other side of our house, a farmer with a tractor tended a big rhubarb field. The other kids who lived on Rita Lane told us that the farmer would shoot buckshot at anyone who went into the field. If you searched for them, there were plenty of places to pick wild blackberries in the woods and fields nearby.

When my parents remodeled our house in Syracuse, my father set aside the leftover scraps of soft pine wood. He cut and sanded them, and fashioned a set of building blocks for me. Some of the blocks were square and others rectangular. One had an arch cut into it. A couple others were cylindrical. Though unpainted and simple, I loved those blocks and played with them for years. He also helped my mother plant a big vegetable garden during the summer months and built my sister and me a playhouse in the backyard.

One day, my parents took us to downtown Syracuse to go swimming at the YMCA and YWCA indoor pools, which were in the same building, but with separate facilities for men and women. Linda went with my mother, while I had to go with my father to the men's locker room and pool. I wasn't used to being alone with my father. In fact, I had probably never been alone with him before at that point. Though I can't remember what creeped me out about the experience, I do remember that I refused to get undressed in the locker room. My father put on his swimming trunks and encouraged me to do the same, but I would not budge. When he tried to lift my shirt over my head, I began to scream and cry. He told me I would have to sit near the side of the pool and watch as he swam, but I refused to go near the pool. Finally, he gave up in frustration, and we waited in silence in the car for my mother.

The woods at the end of Rita Lane represented a wild and uncivilized place. By the time we had started school, my mother allowed us to go into the woods with our friends, but only for a short walk. I remember the path crossed over a meadow with crackled mud before entering a thicker wood. We never went very far, as we'd been warned about copperhead snakes. Also, someone had told us once about some bad kids who had tied another kid to a tree. Clearly, the woods were full of danger. For protection, I once smuggled a kitchen knife out of the house to take with me. My mother discovered it and punished me.

Even in those days, my father lived a double life. Though I didn't know anything about it at the time, my mother knew he was unfaithful to her. She later told my sister that he'd had girlfriends throughout their marriage, from nearly the first day. Sometimes, on our Sunday drives, we stopped for dinner at a German restaurant. My father had studied German in high school and at Carnegie Tech, and he needed to pass language exams in German and Russian for his Ph.D. My mother never liked going to that restaurant, though I didn't know why. Nearly twenty years later, when I was dating Donna and studying French, my father told me that he'd improved his German because he got himself what he called "a sleeping dictionary."

Syracuse is part of the Lake Ontario snow belt, which stretches from Rochester, to Syracuse and Utica, to Watertown. The average snowfall per year in the area is 116 inches. I remember snow drifts as high as the roof of our house, and icicles four feet long. The winters lasted from mid-November through late March. Most of that time we spent indoors. Fortunately, we had enough space in our basement to ride our tricycles around in a circle. Because of the low ceilings and lack of windows, even remodeled basements can be spooky places. I remember ours had a black upright piano at the bottom of the stairs leading down from the kitchen. My mother plunked at the piano a little and taught Linda how to play some simple songs.

My father taught my mother how to drive. When she got her license, they bought a second car, a Volkswagen Beetle that my father usually drove to work. One snowy night on his way home from work, he hit a patch of black ice, lost control of the car, and collided with another vehicle. He broke his leg in the accident. His leg in a cast, he hobbled around on crutches for several weeks. After his accident, my sister began having nightmares about something bad happening to him. She would wake herself up crying. I remember everyone being awake together until she would calm down enough to go back to sleep.

My father played ball with me exactly twice in my life. The first time was in our house in Syracuse. One Saturday, my mother had gone somewhere by herself, leaving my father in charge of us. I was sitting on the lower landing of the stairs and my father on the couch across the living room. We had a tennis ball that we tossed between us as Frisky chased the flight of the ball back and forth. Of course, my mother would never have allowed us to throw a ball in the house had she been home. My father was so rarely around that he didn't know the rules.

One Saturday morning, Linda and I went with our father to ride our sleds at a park that had once been a strip mine or quarry. Though the park was close to our house, we were too young to carry the heavy wooden sleds, so we piled into the car. The scooped out quarry had been partially filled in on the sides to create slopes. The ride was fast and terrifying.

My sister and I loved the excitement of Christmas. We got to look through the H & S Green Stamps and Sears and Roebuck catalogs to make a list of gifts we hoped Santa might bring us. The supermarket displayed the best toys in big boxes on ledges above the food, but Santa never delivered any of those boxes to our house. We did, however, have a big Christmas tree with lots of decorations and lights. We also had a little electric train that ran in a circle under the tree. I remember putting animals from the nativity scene onto the flatbed car of the train and taking them for a ride. Later, my father bought a bridge and some extra track and attached them to a sheet of plywood, so that we could play with the train all year long in the basement. He made a papier-mâché mountain with a tunnel, added little buildings and trees, roads and cars. My mother painted everything so that it looked almost real.

One year, my parents drank so much on Christmas Eve that they mislabeled all the Christmas gifts. When my sister and I woke up early the next morning, eager to open our presents, we found a pile of barely wrapped boxes, most of which had no labels. I remember my parents were still dressed in their pajamas and bathrobes. They seemed more relaxed than usual. "It looks like Santa got drunk last night," my mother told us.

* * *

At school on Friday, November 22, 1963, I remember our teacher calmly informed us that we were being dismissed early because the president had died. At home, my parents watched television all weekend. My mother didn't return to work until after the funeral. I remember reporters interviewing Lee Harvey Oswald's teachers and I believe I saw Jack Ruby shoot Oswald on live television. Though very young at the time, I have a distinct memory of these events.

The following summer, some kids in the neighborhood decided to raise money to donate to the Kennedy Presidential Library. My sister's friend lived down the street and had older siblings, including a brother in junior high school who helped us organize and stage a neighborhood carnival. Their parents brought us some big cardboard appliance boxes, which we fashioned into booths for games like ring-toss, bean bag toss, and balloon popping with darts. We sold tickets to the games and shows we staged and gave away Popsicles and snack cakes for prizes. At the end of the day, we had made eight dollars, which seemed like a pretty good donation. Later, we learned that the brother had used the money to take his family out to dinner.

* * *

After he received his Ph.D., my father began searching for a new job. The lifestyle and weather in California attracted him, as did the aerospace industry, which blossomed around Los Angeles after Sputnik and Kennedy's promise to land a man on the moon by the end of the decade. With his newly minted credentials, he landed a job near the San Fernando Valley, in the City of Los Angeles. My parents made plans to move after the end of the school year, though for some reason we didn't actually leave until August. I was eight years old and had just finished second grade.

I believe Gram stayed in Syracuse to oversee the sale of the house there, then lived with her sister in Pittsburgh until we were settled in Los Angeles. I remember we drove across the country with our dog Frisky and a few toys in the back seat of the car and our suitcases packed full of clothes in the trunk. My parents placed the rest of our belongings onto a commercial moving truck.

We drove through Washington, DC, where my father detoured in a circle around the Mall and pointed out the Washington and Lincoln monuments, though he didn't stop the car. Instead, he drove like a maniac across the country, barely stopping for meals or bathroom breaks. We saw Chicago, also from the car. We suffered the boredom of interminable cornfields in Iowa and Nebraska. Though we begged to stop at one of the giant "Indian" emporiums, my father kept his foot on the gas pedal. Then, when we got to Denver, for some reason he decided to drive to the top of Pikes Peak, bouncing for hours over a rutted dirt road with dangerous hair-pin turns.

Next we drove across a vast desert. Though we must have passed through Las Vegas, I don't remember it. Instead, a sign on the side of a bleak and desolate strip of highway welcomed us to California. I recall tumbleweeds, cactuses, and vast, empty expanses of sun-baked desert leading to dry mountains in the distance. My mother sobbed and cried in the front seat. The previous day, the Watts Riots had erupted in Los Angeles. When we checked into a motel in the San Fernando Valley that afternoon, we watched on television as parts of the city burned. The reports told us that snipers were shooting at the firefighters as they drove their trucks through the streets. Though the rest of us were frightened and unsettled, my father seemed exhilarated to finally be in California.

We stayed in a motel in Encino for a month, while my parents looked for a house to buy. I remember going to look at a beautiful, newly constructed house in Thousand Oaks, a short drive from where my father would work. My sister and I loved the house, as it had everything we had hoped for, including a swimming pool. We went as far as to decide which bedrooms we would like to have. Instead, my mother insisted on buying a filthy, run-down tract house in a working-class neighborhood in Canoga Park—a ubiquitous, cookie-cutter ranch-style dwelling with geometric wooden ornaments on the garage door. Unhappy with the cross country move and suspicious of my father's intentions, she punished him in the most hurtful ways she could, by denying him the status he so desperately needed, making him drive for forty minutes to work and return each night to a dingy house without a pool or even air conditioning, set in a blue collar neighborhood and surrounded by people who didn't like or respect him. If my mother wasn't happy, then she didn't allow anyone around her to be.

Meanwhile, my father began working in Calabasas, at Rantec Microwave Systems, a manufacturing and engineering company specializing in microwave antennas for military applications. At Rantec he met people who he would eventually recruit to work for him at Microwave Applications Group, a company my father founded with a partner in Chatsworth several years later.

During our first year or two in California, my parents seemed as out of place as American retirees on a guided bus tour of Europe. They wandered around with their mouths open in wonderment. My father personified the stereotypical socially awkward engineer: prematurely balding, dressed in a short-sleeved button-up shirt with a skinny tie and a pocket protector, a slide rule in a holster on his belt. Nevertheless, he embraced the changes in social norms, whereas my mother resisted and resented the casual southern California lifestyle and the sixties youth culture. I remember how she returned home one day from grocery shopping enraged that she'd seen a woman in shorts, sandals and a bikini top at the market. "Back east we wore white gloves to go out in public," she reminded us.

We went to Disneyland and Knott's Berry Farm, took the tour at Universal Studios, drove around Beverly Hills. We went to Olvera Street and the Farmers Market. We went to the San Fernando Mission, then eventually visited every mission up and down the coast. We went to beaches and tide pools, where my sister collected shells. We drove to Hollywood to see the hippies outside the Whisky a Go Go on Sunset Boulevard. My father brought home records by Simon and Garfunkel and The Beatles, then later albums by Bob Dylan and The Doors. The Vietnam War raged on television each evening at 6:00, as Walter Cronkite reported the daily body count.

One of the engineers my father worked with at Rantec owned a beach house in Oxnard Beach, about an hour's drive from the San Fernando Valley, where we lived. We had gone to visit this man and his wife and my parents decided that they, too, should invest in one of the small houses on the beach, as it would provide a good escape from the heat of the valley in the summertime.

The neighborhood had once been called Silver Strand Beach and had been connected to a development called Hollywood-by-the-Sea. In the 1920s, real estate developers sold building lots to Hollywood movie stars like Clark Gable and Rudolph Valentino, who built vacation homes there. Other famous actors and actresses, such as Charlie Chaplin and Greta Garbo, were also said to have spent time there on vacation. During World War II, the Navy built a huge base adjacent to the development, where they trained Seabees to construct air fields and forward bases. In the 1960s, the beach community was a sloppy mix of modest frame houses of all kinds and military surplus Quonset Huts made of corrugated galvanized steel with arched roofs.

My parents eventually bought a small, two-bedroom house on San Fernando Avenue, a block away from the wide, sandy beach that stretches half a mile between the rock jetties of Port Hueneme and Channel Islands harbor. The previous owners had painted the stucco exterior pink. On a clear day, we could see Anacapa Island offshore, eleven miles away. Later, my parents also bought a sixteen-foot motorboat with a seventy-five horsepower outboard motor, but only after my father had finished his sailboat phase.

For some reason, my father decided that he wanted to take up sailing. Instead of enrolling in a class or hiring someone to teach him privately, he read a book. Convinced of his mastery of the subject, he began renting sailboats at the Channel Islands harbor on weekends. As the boats he rented grew in size and complexity, he needed me to help crew them, as boats with two sails required extra attention. Though he eventually figured out how to keep the boat from ending up "in irons," and managed to tack out of the narrow channel of the harbor and bring the boat more or less gently to dock again, his poor seamanship always put dozens of other pleasure boaters at risk. Whenever my father sailed, people seemed to yell at us from every conceivable angle. His short career as a skipper ended when he ran a twenty-eight-foot sailboat into the rock jetty at the harbor during a storm warning. Though such irresponsible behavior was typical of my father, I'm surprised that the rental agent let a landlubber with a pocket protector take his children sailing in gale force winds that day.

Meanwhile, my father was furiously building a Sabot, a tiny, eight-foot-long sailing dinghy with a Dutch wooden shoe class insignia on the sail. He had bought a pre-made fiberglass hull for the boat and a set of blueprints for the wooden internal frame, which he built in the garage in Canoga Park and in Oxnard. I remember doing a lot of finish sanding on the mahogany rudder and daggerboard pieces. In the end, however, his interest waned and it took two years to complete the project. Then my father took his list of running gear and rigging to a boat outfitter and bought the lines and blocks, brass cleats and pulleys, and the sail. After so much hard work and so many delays, I was excited that we would finally get to sail the boat.

Unfortunately, the beautiful little Sabot with the bright red hull and the mahogany beams gleaming under ten coats of marine varnish would never sail. Though we put the boat on the rack of the Ford station wagon and launched it from the public wharf at the harbor, my father never figured out how to rig the boat properly. It sat for hours in the water as he worked on it. Finally, he gave up. We took the boat out of the water, disassembled the mast, and mounted the hull on top of the station wagon. We brought it back to the beach house, and stowed it in the garage. Instead of asking someone for help, my father never touched the boat again. In time, I realized that my dream of sailing the boat had sunk in the turbulence of my father's psyche.

* * *

My father disappointed me at every turn. It often seemed to me that he was incapable of finishing anything he started, fulfilling any promise he made, or doing anything I asked, no matter how simple. He dressed weirdly and acted strangely. He was a poor communicator, didn't relate well to others, and had little patience. He seemed awkward and abrupt. I got the feeling that no one had much liked him as a child and they still didn't. He hurried manically through public places. When we went shopping, usually at a discount department store called White Front, he walked so fast I almost had to run to stay with him.

After the sailboat failures, he took up fishing and bought his co-worker's used motorboat. We went to White Front, where he bought himself a deep sea fishing rig, a surf fishing rig, and a huge tackle box that he stuffed full of hooks, leaders, spools of line, lead sinkers, and lures. Though we planned to fish in the ocean, he bought me the cheapest toy fishing rod and reel he could find. It came pre-assembled, shrink-wrapped on a cardboard backing. A crappy rig designed for lake fishing, it proved to be useless in the ocean.

We fished from the rock jetty at the harbor and we fished in the open ocean from our boat. We surf fished from the beach near the house in Oxnard and also by the power plant near the Ventura River, where the warm water attracted the fish in the early evening. My father was an unlucky fisherman who rarely caught anything, except when we paid to go out on the deep sea fishing boats that left from the harbor on half day excursions. Using their rented equipment, we'd both come home with a big sack of red snapper and rock cod filets to give away or put in the freezer.

As my father soon grew bored with fishing from the beach, I appropriated his surf fishing rig. The big tackle box was too heavy for me to carry when I walked by myself to fish at the beach or from the rock jetty. I asked my parents to buy me a lighter, smaller plastic tackle box of my own, but they ignored me as they always did when I asked for something. Tired of stuffing the hooks, sinkers and leaders into my pockets, or carrying them in plastic bags, I fabricated a box of my own, using whatever scraps of wood and hardware I could find lying around the garage at the beach house. I was ten years old and had never handled tools before. Given my age and lack of experience, and having only poor and mismatched materials to work with, as well as access to only the most primitive hand tools, the box I created turned out to be nearly perfect in its failure. At the same time, it served as a tribute to my stoicism and determination. Though pathetic as a tackle box, I used it anyway, and I kept the box long after I realistically evaluated it as junk. It was among the very few possessions I took with me when I moved out of my mother's house at the age of eighteen. When I was in college I painted a Cubist face, along with other odd motifs, and wrote *"Tout est Rien"* on the box with acrylic paints. When we left the United States to live abroad, we sold, gave away or discarded almost everything we owned, including my personal library. I still have that box.

Meanwhile, in our neighborhood around Acre Street, I was the only kid who didn't have a bicycle. Even my sister had a lime green Schwinn step-through bike with whitewall tires my parents had bought her for Christmas. Of course, like every boy in southern California at the time, I desperately wanted a Schwinn Stingray with pullback handlebars, a banana seat, and a sissy bar. My father, who had his own English Raleigh Sports three-speed bike, hated the absurd and pandering design of the Stingray. "You can ride my bike when you're older," he said, which meant I'd never get a Stingray with a banana seat. And that was the end of that, as my mother was fond of saying.

During this time, my friends must have taught me to ride their kid-sized bikes, as I have no home movie in my head of my father holding onto a bicycle as I pedaled then suddenly letting go. More to the point, there was no way for me to properly straddle his bike with 27-inch wheels. Nevertheless, one day I took the English three-speed from the garage and set it on the street by the curb. Then I climbed onto the curb and from that height I was able to sit on the bike with my left foot on the pedal and my right foot on the curb, which was eight inches above the wheels. I took off riding down the street, peddling with the tips of my toes. In order to dismount, I slowed down and swung my leg over the crossbar, stepping onto the ground as I glided the bike to a stop. It was awkward at first, and I took a couple of spills, but with practice I mastered the technique. Eventually, I also learned how to mount the bike in the same manner, pushing off with one leg, then swinging over the frame once the bike was rolling. Suddenly, I had a bike, and a pretty good one at that. My parents didn't say much about it, though they must have wondered how I'd learned to ride at all.

Aside from a bicycle, the one thing all boys at that age wanted back then was a good baseball glove. For years I played ball on the street, at school, or at the park without my own glove. Though I was usually able to borrow a glove from a player on the opposing team when it was their turn to bat, sometimes I had to play with my bare hands or even not play at all. My father had never participated in sports and had almost no interest in them, particularly baseball, so he couldn't understand why I thought I needed my own mitt. Though he was unreceptive to my pleas, I nevertheless lobbied him whenever I found him at home. I worked overtime on my mother as well. Finally, she ordered my father to take me somewhere to buy a glove.

In the sporting goods section of White Front, I showed my father the first baseman's glove I coveted. My favorite positions were first and third base, and I wanted a tall glove with a deep, high pocket. Instead, my father picked up the least expensive model he could find, a lightweight outfielder's glove with a small pocket and almost no padding for the hand. Though leather, it was not well made, and I never managed to break it in properly. Every glove I had ever borrowed had been better. Still, though a disappointment, at least I didn't have to hand this one back to its owner between innings.

Though all of my friends at school played on Little League teams, my parents saw no apparent value in team sports, so again my lobbying failed. Instead, I got to join the Cub Scouts. I don't remember anything significant about the Cub Scouts, except for the time I attended a meeting and the Den Mother had to run to the market. While she was gone, the unsupervised cubs shot at birds out the window with a BB gun. My parents didn't own guns, had never, in fact, touched them. While the other kids argued at school about which caliber hunting rifles were superior, I pretended to tie my shoe. It was like they were speaking another language.

When I began playing basketball seriously in my last year of elementary school, I begged my father to put up a backboard and hoop above the garage so that I could practice and play on our driveway. Surprisingly, my mother supported this idea. She told me that she had played basketball on her high school women's team. One weekend, my father bought some two-by-fours and measured and cut them into supports for the backboard we'd bought pre-made. He did a reasonable job of following the instructions and soon had the supports bolted to the rafters. Unfortunately, he had not bothered to measure the distance from the driveway to the lip of the rim, so the finished basketball court was nearly a foot lower than a regulation court. At first it didn't matter much, especially because the slope of the driveway brought the height close to regulation on shots greater than fifteen feet. However, when I grew to my full height in the eighth grade, I could easily perform acrobatic dunks on shots under the basket.

When he'd finished work on the driveway basketball court, my father stayed to take a few shots with me to try it out. His first shot bounced off the backboard with a loud thud, missing the rim altogether. His next was an airball that missed everything. Meanwhile, I was sinking jump shots from all over the court and showing off my reverse layups. He made a couple more attempts without coming close, then left me to my game. That was the second and final time he played ball with me.

Some people, foremost among them my father, should be barred for life from operating boats. While the sailboat experience had been bad, the motor boat wasn't much better. Once, he launched the boat without putting the drain plug back in after washing the saltwater from the interior. My father had backed the trailer with the boat into the water at the launch ramp and I was on the dock making the boat fast as he pulled the station wagon up the ramp and toward the parking lot. I noticed that the boat was filling up with water. Somehow I had the presence of mind to jump inside and search for the drain plug, which I found on the floor under a couple inches of water. The water was shin high in the boat before I could screw the plug back into the drain.

Though we had no backup motor and no radio, my father sometimes took the open sixteen-foot boat all the way to Anacapa Island, eleven miles off shore. Lucky for us, when the Murray outboard engine eventually blew up, we were on a lake in Oregon rather than on the blue expanses of the Pacific Ocean.

* * *

A year after we arrived in California, my mother got a job as an elementary school teacher in the Los Angeles Unified School District and Gram came to California to live with us again. My parents shuffled Gram between the beach house and the house on Acre Street in the San Fernando Valley, depending on their own needs. A vital person with near endless stamina, Gram was heavy on her feet and as strong as the bull at which she'd spit cherry pits as a child. My parents used her as a baby-sitter, caretaker, cook, cleaning woman, and gardener in much the same way her parents and siblings had made her into their servant when she was a child. Whenever she cooked for the family, Gram stayed in the kitchen, in case there was something someone needed. "Sit down," my mother would order her, repeating the lines of their long-playing Ionesco comedy. Instead, Gram would set to work preparing dessert and brewing coffee. Only after everyone else had finished eating did she allow herself a small plate of food and a cup of coffee. "You can't do anything with her," my mother would then say.

There were many secrets in my mother's family. Neither Gram nor my mother ever talked about my grandfather. I wondered why he had objected so strongly to my mother getting married and what kind of relationship he had had with his wife and daughter. From time to time, other buried secrets bubbled to the surface in conversations my sister and I overheard. Gram had grown up on a large farm in Pennsylvania, in a big family where she was the youngest of twelve brothers and sisters. Her father owned many acres of fields and forest, along with a lumber mill and stone quarry. The men in the family looked after the horses and bulls and oversaw work at the large, planted fields, the mill and the quarry, while the women worked around the house and tended the kitchen garden and the chickens, cows, and pigs. Gram's mother often spoke Croatian at home and she regaled her daughters with earthy talk as they prepared food in the kitchen. "Your father has a big one, like this," she'd say, holding up a giant sausage and laughing as they blushed. "Twelve children," she'd remind them, "twelve."

Before coming to America, my great grandfather had been an absentee landlord in the Austro-Hungarian Empire. After the First World War, the Empire collapsed and the family lost most of their overseas wealth. Until then, my great grandfather had traveled by ship once every few years to meet with family and check on his holdings. He usually brought back a young girl who would work around the house for a year or two in exchange for passage to the United States. As there's little doubt a man who fathered twelve children had an enormous sexual appetite, one can only imagine what happened to those young girls he brought home with him from the Old Country. Another scandal involved one of Gram's older sisters, who had married a man who became a traveling salesman. Whenever he was away, she placed a blue light in the front window of her house. Many local men were known to visit the house at these times.

Though a practicing Catholic, Gram sometimes dabbled in fortune-telling, astrology, folk tales, and home remedies. She also loved ghost stories. In her cosmology, competing belief systems coexisted effortlessly. Because of her playful attitude toward fortune-telling, I always suspected an unacknowledged Roma connection buried somewhere in her eastern European roots. While some of Gram's fascination with fortune-telling no doubt resulted from background, culture, and traditions, growing up in a large family on an isolated farm also must have exposed her to alternative forms of entertainment. Social life at that time consisted largely of conversation, music, print media, and games. Families often gathered in the evening to sing and play instruments together, read aloud, discuss politics and ideas, or play cards or other games. As Gram's parents had been raised in the late nineteenth century, a period during which fortune-telling and occult parlor games were hugely popular both in Europe and America, no doubt they passed on some of those games to their children.

Whenever the phone rang at unexpected times, Gram would jump in her seat and exclaim, "Who died?"

"Holy Christ," my mother always grumbled in response, shaking her head as Gram rushed to pick up the receiver.

Strange things were always happening around Gram. Most of the people on her side of my family have what we would call a highly developed sense of "intuition," which is to say the ability to sense that something is going to happen before it actually does. Gram had this gift and we usually listened to her when she said she had a strong feeling about something. Though it's difficult for a well-educated and logical person to accept, I have learned through experience in the course of my life to trust my intuition and I try to take such warnings seriously. More than a few times I'm glad that I did.

Throughout our elementary school and junior high school years, my sister and I took turns inviting a friend to accompany us on weekend visits to the beach house. In the summer months, our friends sometimes stayed up to a week. During this time, my friends and I swam and body-surfed, built castles and forts on the beach, and fished for perch from the shore or crabs at the rock jetty. We got up early to comb the beach for sand dollars and sea glass, then came home to eat dozens of Gram's crêpes with syrup or jam. In the afternoon or evening, when we were sunburned and tired, Gram would tell everyone's fortune, using a regular deck of playing cards. Sometimes she'd use a Tarot deck, but she didn't seem as comfortable with the symbols. Our friends were amazed at how much she seemed to know about them and how accurately she could sense their hopes and dreams for the future. Though the fortunes were always rather vague and short on details, they were satisfying nonetheless. Mostly they made us laugh. Sometimes Gram read people's fortunes in the leftover tea leaves in the bottom of their cup. In the morning and late afternoon, she usually brewed a pot of strong coffee in a percolator on top of her stove, which gave her a chance to read fortunes in coffee grounds as well.

Due to poor reception, a lack of local channels, or simply because there were more interesting things to do, we never watched television at the beach house. In fact, I don't even remember us having a television there. Instead, we played cards and other games like Bunko. When we played Bunko, we didn't keep score according to the rules. In fact, I never knew Bunko was a real game until years later. In our family version of the game, players sat around the table and took turns rolling five dice. Whenever someone rolled a triple, everyone would scream, "Bunko!" and try to grab hold of as many of the dice that showed the triple as they could. For each die a player grabbed, he or she got a point. A player who grabbed a die that was not part of the triple, lost a point. In the event that a player called out "Bunko" when there was not a triple, he or she would lose a point, as would anyone who touched any of the dice. In short, Bunko was a game of anticipation that required fast reflexes and advanced hand-to-hand combat skills.

Gram also enjoyed teasing and scaring our friends. At night, she liked to tell ghost stories. Some of them, like the story about the cedar chest our mother had in the closet at home, were even true. The chest had belonged to a distant relative. No one in the family had much cared for this man while he was alive. After his funeral, Gram had taken his cedar chest because none of his children wanted it and she needed a safe place to store wool blankets in the summertime. After the funeral, Gram set the chest against the wall in a corner of the room. She went into the kitchen to prepare food for the guests. As people relaxed, they began to talk about the deceased man. Some of them said that he was mean-spirited and avaricious, which was true. Suddenly, the chest began to shake violently and move noisily around on the floor. Then everyone stopped talking and stared at the cedar chest. Someone suggested that perhaps they shouldn't say anything further about the dead man. Everyone agreed that they would never speak ill of him again. Only then did the cedar chest stop shaking and thumping. And since that day it has never moved again.

Another game that scared our friends was what I later learned was called "table turning" or "table spinning," a pastime popular in the Victorian era. We called it "making the table talk," because the table would rise up onto two legs, then tap out yes or no answers to questions about the future. To make the table rise, a group of at least four people would sit around a table with their fingertips lightly touching the top. Then, everyone would chant, "rise table, rise," in a slow and rhythmic voice. We usually used a light folding card table, but when we had extra people we used the massively heavy solid maple dining room table. It could take a long time and a lot of patience and concentration to build enough energy to lift the table. Eventually, participants would feel a slight electrical current running through their fingertips. Suddenly, the table would begin to rise up on one end, then bump back on the floor. After two or three bumps, it would rise up higher and everyone would stand and back away from their chairs until the table was standing completely balanced on two legs.

Then one of us would instruct the table to answer our questions, one tap for yes and two for no. We learned quickly to ask only silly questions like, "Will Linda have more than five children?" or "Will Greg be a famous writer?" It was an eerie feeling when the table quickly lowered and raised itself to answer our questions, then returned to its position balanced on two legs. Once, we raised the table with my friend Dave who had said it was just a trick and couldn't be done. When the table came off the ground he was so scared we thought he might faint. Suddenly Gram pulled her hands off the table and the table immediately crashed to the floor. Gram's face looked pale gray, the color of ash. "What's wrong?" we asked.

"I don't want to do this again," she said, shivering slightly. "I felt someone's cold hands around my neck." And that was the end of the talking table.

* * *

After two years at Rantec, my father took a job as an assistant professor of engineering at the University of California, Los Angeles. From all indications he was an excellent and popular professor, which in that environment is perhaps the best way to insure professional failure. He had accepted the job on the condition that he progress to associate professor after three years, but when the time came for him to be considered for the promised faculty promotion, a key member of the committee that considered such promotions devoted himself to undermining him. Due to professional jealousy and his own insecurity, this tenured professor resented the fast-tracking my father had insisted on when he took the job. In the end, the committee shamed itself and embarrassed the university by not recommending my father for the promotion. Instead, the chairman of the department told him he could remain an assistant professor and try for promotion again after another three years. My father resigned on the spot and instead founded his own microwave technology and manufacturing company.

Despite the predictable bad ending, my father's three years at UCLA represented a relatively calm and normal period for our family. Though it was impossible to obtain tickets to see the UCLA basketball team play at Pauley Pavilion—as this was the period during which basketball legend Lew Alcindor, later Kareem Abdul-Jabbar of the Lakers, played for coach John Wooden and won three consecutive national championships—he did manage to secure season tickets to see UCLA's football team play their home games at the Los Angeles Memorial Coliseum. For three years, my father and I attended the Saturday home games. Though the Bruins were always nationally ranked and had dominant, winning seasons, they always managed to lose at the last second to cross town rival USC and miss going to the Rose Bowl. Though the drive to and from the games usually passed in silence, the football games themselves were the best memories I have of my father.

My parents also took my sister and me to a performance at a round theater in Encino, where we saw Dick Van Dyke in *Bye Bye Birdie*. Hollywood was just around the corner and it was easy and affordable to see comedians and actors perform live. My parents also went to see *Hair*, a rock musical famous at the time for its many popular songs, its controversial themes, and the full nudity of actors on stage. They also took my sister and me to see folk singer Joan Baez perform at Pauley Pavilion in 1969. I remember the astounding clarity of her voice and how the crowd applauded when she talked fondly about her relationship with her ex-boyfriend Bob Dylan. Though there were thousands of people in the audience, it seemed like a small gathering of friends.

Later that same year, we drove to San Francisco, where we rode the cable cars, visited the wax museum at Fisherman's Wharf, and ate ice cream sundaes at Ghirardelli Square. We walked through the Haight Ashbury district and saw the hippies. My mother let us buy some love beads from a hippy girl on the street. It was the summer of love, but it would all soon blow up.

One of the few books my parents kept on the shelf in the living room near the console record player and the new color television was called *The Velvet Underground*. The cover featured a whip and a pair of Victorian women's lace-up boots with spike heels. Written by journalist and sexologist Michael Leigh and first published in 1963, the book detailed, through interviews with participants, sexual deviance in contemporary American culture, with chapters devoted to swinging, key parties, sadomasochism, transvestism, drug abuse, homosexuality, pedophilia, bestiality, and pornography. Because it was on the shelf, I read this book at a young age. I also read the novel *Portnoy's Complaint*. If someone left a book around, I would read it. I read everything, whether I understood it all or not.

With my mother we went to movies, usually musicals, which I hated: *The Sound of Music, Oklahoma, Oliver!, The Singing Nun, Funny Girl, Georgy Girl,* and the abysmal *Finnegan's Rainbow.* Fortunately, we also saw other movies: *Planet of the Apes, Cat Balou, True Grit, 2001: A Space Odyssey, Romeo and Juliet, A Man for All Seasons, The Taming of the Shrew, The Pink Panther, The Prime of Miss Jean Brodie, Klute, The French Connection, American Graffiti, Butch Cassidy and the Sundance Kid, Five Easy Pieces, M*A*S*H, The Sting, The Last Picture Show, Patton,* and *Serpico.* I remember some of these films fondly, others less so.

Perhaps the most memorable movie experience I had with my mother was when she dragged us out of the theater after the first fifteen minutes of a film starring Kirk Douglas and Yul Brenner. Called *The Light at the Edge of the World,* the film was about pirates who take over an island with a lighthouse so that they can lure ships onto the rocky shore in order to loot what is left of the shipwrecks. My mother railed against the amorality of the theme and screamed at the ticket sellers and theater manager that the whole production was vile and offensive. Though they refunded the cost of the tickets, nothing anyone could do or say would calm her down. Once lit, her anger burned until the fuel was spent.

Despite her occasional emotional melt-downs, my mother seemed relatively content during this period. She disliked engineers, who she said were all social misfits, so she was pleased when my father took a teaching job. She enjoyed having a connection to education and university life. More than anything, she wanted my father to succeed in his teaching career and embrace the academic lifestyle. She wanted us to move to a more upscale neighborhood in Westwood, west Los Angeles, or Santa Monica, and to enjoy the cultural connections and educational opportunities the university would offer us all. My father, however, was restless. Already, he had begun planning his escape and had worked up a design for an improved version of microwave phase shifters for radar applications. He wanted to form a company that would build and sell these devices. The house in Westwood didn't interest him. It was someone else's dream.

* * *

My father launched his business, which he called Microwave Applications Group, in 1969, using money my mother had saved from her teaching jobs. She helped him file the paperwork to incorporate the company and typed up the first proposals on the kitchen table of the house in Canoga Park. Initially, he had two partners, though one was a young engineer with two kids still in diapers, who decided very early in the process not to quit his day job. That left my father and another electrical engineer he'd worked with at Rantec, this one with a special talent for fabrication, as equal partners.

My father's partner was a tall, thin, rakish-looking man with a big handlebar mustache. He had an aura of physical danger about him, perhaps because he'd been a marine who'd survived fighting against the Chinese in the bitter cold at the Chosin Reservoir during the Korean War. Apparently, he was an extremely clever fabricator. So he was the one who would translate my father's mathematically based theoretical engineering designs into the physical prototypes that could be used to demonstrate military-specification functionality to Westinghouse, Raytheon, and other government contractors.

My mother disliked this man from the first minute she met him. "I don't trust him and I don't like him," she told my father. It was clear to her that he was a trickster, a deceiver, a predator, and a con artist. Nevertheless, at first she forced herself to at least tolerate him, as he was an essential part of what looked to be part of her future. Later, she labeled him "evil." Though his name was Bob, she always referred to him as "the Devil." Ironically, his dark haired good looks would later remind me a lot of her second husband, an electrician, also a Korean War veteran, who she'd met in a bowling alley several years after my parents' divorce.

It was easy to see why my mother despised "the Devil," as he encouraged my father's worst tendencies and quickly pulled him deeply into the swinging 60s world of "free love," group sex, and unrestrained excess. My father tried his best to get my mother to agree to an "open marriage," one in which she would ideally become a willing participant. When she refused, he simply pursued his desires in spite of her, living a thinly veiled double life.

My mother knew from the beginning that my father had been unfaithful in their marriage. As socially awkward as he was, for some reason he never lacked for extramarital partners. The proof of his infidelities had been evident everywhere. He fooled no one but himself with his lies and deceptions. Set loose in the permissive atmosphere of 1960s southern California and surrounded by negative role models and influences, he felt free to create his own reality. He became even less reliable and less willing or even capable of telling the truth or controlling his desires.

I remember getting into the back seat of our station wagon one day. My father had just started the car and was letting the engine idle as it warmed up. My mother sat next to him on the bench seat in front. Suddenly my sister pulled a small jewelry box from the crack between our seat and the back rest. 'What's this?" she asked. My mother turned around and reached back for box. When she opened it, she found a necklace with a diamond insert on a gold chain. "Oh, Charles," she said, sarcastically, as she slipped the necklace over her head, "how nice of you to think of me." Nobody said anything. My father backed the car out of the driveway. We drove for a few minutes and then my mother hissed, "You're such a bastard." In my imagination, I see her throw the necklace out the window as we speed down the freeway, but that's not what happened. Instead, she sobbed, filling the car with her pain as we drove. For many years, she kept the necklace as a symbol of her martyrdom. Though my father was incapable of feeling shame, she nonetheless wore it as a badge of honor with which to chide and punish him. Just as Nixon would secretly bomb Cambodia and a stoned Jim Morrison would perform a song so gritty that the owner of the Whisky a Go Go would terminate The Doors' contract as the house band, my father would continue to pour gasoline on the dumpster fire of his marriage. Such deceit and destruction was in the air. It was the end.

During that time, we got a gray toy poodle named Angel. The dog had been meant as a gift for Linda, but the neurotic animal growled and snapped at everyone but my mother. Angel would be the first in a long line of aggressive, insane toy dog breeds my mother cultivated as pets. Since my mother forbade Angel to sit in her lap when she drove, whoever was unlucky enough to ride "shotgun" on her stagecoach had to do so with a lip-curled, growling poodle sitting on their lap. I remember how I used to hold Angel with both of my hands wrapped around her neck to keep her from attacking me. I often fantasized about throwing her out the window of the moving car.

At this stage of my life, I had a recurring dream in which I wandered around a big department store, like Macy's or May Company at the Topanga Mall, where my mother sometimes took us shopping for school clothes. In the dream, I carried a big sledge hammer or a baseball bat, which I used to destroy the glass counters and display cases, the cash registers, the mannequins, the dressing rooms and clothing racks. It was an exhilarating dream, though a confusing one. I couldn't understand why I felt so good, so free and happy, when I'd done something so forbidden and destructive.

My parents began to argue even more than usual and my mother's emotional swings intensified. Though they could not get along, my parents were nonetheless addicted to each other. When, at my mother's insistence, they attended a couple's therapy session, my father left the initial meeting in a fit of narcissistic rage. After my father had stormed out of the office, the psychiatrist told my mother that she should get away from him as soon as possible and not let him near her children.

Instead, she helped him plan a two-week family vacation to Oregon and Washington. I wrote about this disastrous vacation in a story I published called "What's Wrong With This Picture?" in my collection *Water & Power,* a book I ironically dedicated to my father. Though I changed the names and narrated from a third-person point of view, the details of the story are all true. My father really did leave us in a roadside diner while he drove six hours round trip to retrieve the airline tickets he suddenly remembered he'd left at home. My father really did manage to upend the dining table each morning, spilling restaurant coffee all over himself. In an unconscious murder-suicide attempt, my father really did try to take our little boat through high incoming surf at the mouth of the Columbia River with my mother, my sister, and me all on board.

My sister and I returned from the trip shell shocked and happy to go back to the relative safety and emotional calm of junior high school. A few weeks later, my parents separated and my father got an apartment and moved out of the house for good. In our back room, on the stereo, Jim Morrison's hypnotic voice droned on, slowly building to an explosive Oedipal climax. My father left a hideous purple V-neck sweater and a coffee mug that I sometimes used. When my mother told me he'd left, I didn't respond. I had no opinion that I was willing to share, though I figured that if he wasn't around, then my mother couldn't fight with him. I also knew that his presence at home would eventually make my own life more difficult. In truth, I was glad to see him go. I didn't mind taking out the trash or cutting the grass. I put myself to work painting the house and then started painting the houses of the other divorced teachers who worked with my mother.

* * *

In junior high school I took electric shop. While I didn't build anything cool or useful in the class, I got the schematics for a shocker game and a light organ that I wanted to build on my own over the summer. I started the shocker in class, cutting a maze pattern into a piece of sheet metal and making the metal wand that the player would use to attempt to pass through the holes, spirals, and zig zag patterns without the metal tip touching the edges. I asked my father if he could provide the capacitors and resistors and power supplies I needed for the two projects, as his company had a large electrical lab with all kinds of electronics components. While I did get the parts I needed to build my projects, the schematics came back altered to fit whatever parts the electrical lab had on hand. Instead of operating off a C-size battery, my completed shocker game worked off a giant dry cell battery. If you touched the sheet metal you'd get a strong shock, which made the game more fun by raising the stakes. Though grounding the circuit produced a strong jolt, I slowly became acclimated to it to the point where I sometimes I shocked myself intentionally in the morning when I woke up, just to get myself going. The light organ I built also produced significantly more power than the original design. Instead of converting the audio frequency signals from music into rhythmic effects by lighting up a string of tiny, colored lights appropriate for home use, the one I built would have been better suited to a commercial discotheque.

I hooked this light organ up to the Harman Kardon stereo receiver we had in our spare bedroom, which my sister and I had converted to a place where we could hang out with our friends and listen to music. We furnished the room with two low yellow and black plaid couches that doubled as single beds, a couple of bean bag chairs, and some psychedelic black light posters. We started buying albums with whatever money we made doing odd jobs. Soon we had a collection that included Black Sabbath, The Beatles, The Who, The Doors, Santana, The Rolling Stones, Jimi Hendrix, Simon and Garfunkel, Bob Dylan, Cream, Cat Stevens, Carole King, Janis Joplin, Bread, Iron Butterfly, Steppenwolf, Neil Young, Pink Floyd, The Eagles, Creedence Clearwater Revival, Led Zeppelin, Steely Dan, The Yardbirds, Ten Years After, Bad Company, and Chicago.

At the height of the Sexual Revolution, society in general was more open and tolerant of frank discussions of human sexuality. I remember I took a health class at Chatsworth High School the summer before I began there as a student. Though I had never before volunteered to go to summer school, the class was a prerequisite for driver's training, and I wanted to be certain I could get my driver's license on my sixteenth birthday. Devoted entirely to human sexuality and reproduction, the class surprised me, as the teacher placed no limits on discussions of the theme. She addressed all questions matter-of-factly. She also addressed sexual pleasure with startling clarity and detail. She presented the class with the full range of birth control options and discussed homosexuality and alternative sexual lifestyles without moralizing or judgment. While most of the students spent the summer pretending to be jaded experts on all things sexual, no one left the class ignorant.

After my parents divorced, my father bought a house in an upscale neighborhood in Northridge. My mother used to take us over to his house to use the pool during the summer, when she knew my father was at work. Once, we found him on the back porch practicing his new French horn with another horn player, who was clearly gay. My mother finally stopped invading his property when my father came out of the house dressed only in a bathrobe one day. He was not happy to see us, as he had been enjoying some "afternoon delight" with his secretary.

Nevertheless, he sometimes invited his children to his house, but only when he planned in advance on seeing us. I remember, for example, that I spent many summer afternoons sitting at a table on the back porch of that house by myself, soldering hundreds of electronic components to circuit boards. A friend in the neighborhood had shown me the FM radio tuner he'd built from a kit in just a few days, and I thought it might be fun to build one myself and have it in my bedroom. I foolishly asked my father if he'd consider helping me. Instead he bought a kit for a portable color television. After months of tedious work, I finally finished building the kit. I plugged it in and ... nothing. It didn't work.

My father didn't have time to fix the television, so I suggested we send it to the manufacturer, Heathkit, which is what the instructions said to do, after you'd tried all the troubleshooting steps without success. By this time I was something of an expert on following Heathkit directions, having wasted several months building the television. However, my father ignored me, and the television stayed in a box at his house for a year. Then he gave it to the head of the electronics lab at his company, a smart guy who was writing his Ph.D. dissertation in mathematics. But the math whiz couldn't fix it either, so it stayed in the box. I guess my father must have thrown it away when he remarried. After all, who in their right mind would want a useless television cluttering up their house?

When my sister was sixteen, my father offered to take her with him on a trip to Paris. He'd begun traveling to Europe regularly, as his company had a contract to build radar parts for a French company called Thomson-CFS. I don't know why my mother agreed to let Linda go off with him alone, especially given the advice she had already received from the psychiatrist. While in Paris, my father took my sister to both the Louvre and to Pigalle. He walked her at night through the red light district at Saint-Denis. She told me he also took her to a sex museum. Then he took her to Galleries Lafayette, where he bought her a skimpy French bikini that he made her try on and model for him.

* * *

After a week, my father took Linda to the airport in Paris and put her on a plane for the twelve-hour flight back to Los Angeles, while he continued his exploration of the City of Light. I went with my mother to LAX to pick her up. When we got to the airport and checked the arrivals board, we learned that the flight had been delayed by a couple of hours. Then, when the plane finally landed and passengers began to debark and exit from customs, we waited for over an hour and still she had not appeared. My mother became increasingly agitated and tried to ask the customs agents inside if they had seen my sister, but they ignored her concern and told her that only exiting passengers could enter the customs area.

These days, even a distraught mother would be wrestled to the ground and arrested, if not shot, for disregarding the instructions of armed customs officers at the airport. Even then, it seemed foolhardy if not maniacal when, yelling at the customs agents, and screaming for them to get out of her way, my mother pushed through the exit doors and burst into the secure area. Once inside, she spotted my sister, who had been detained and was being questioned because she could not produce receipts for the gifts my father had bought her in France. In the end, the wrath of my mother was so intense, so furious, that the agents let Linda leave the area immediately without any further discussion of customs duties.

Ever since my father left home, I'd been living in a household of women. All around me, emotions and hormones constantly boiled over. I wore myself out on the basketball court and started smoking marijuana with my friends. Occasionally, one of my sister's friends would show up at our house to hide from her parents for a day or two while some storm blew over. Linda told me about one of her friends from school who wanted to get even with her father for cheating on her mother and had slept with all of her father's friends, one after the next. The world was spinning so fast it seemed as if the center might not hold. One day, Linda told me about a phone conversation she had overheard, in which my mother told one of her schoolteacher friends how my father had described his participation in orgies where a group of men would all have sex with one or two young girls or prostitutes over the course of an evening. These social club events took place at an apartment specifically rented for this purpose and furnished with wall-to-wall mattresses.

My mother never bothered to guard her feelings or keep her conversations private. Some time later, my sister found out about a girl who had participated in one of these gang bangs and had later committed suicide. Apparently suffering from a guilty conscience and looking for some kind of absolution, my father had told my mother about the tragedy. "You want a mother, not a wife," I remember my mother having told him on many occasions. It's easy to see why.

* * *

When my sister was seventeen, my father once gave her the following nugget of paternal advice: "It's okay to have lots of sex with whomever you want, just try not to do it with too many different people in the same day." Many years later, my mother shared some details about her relationship with my father: She told my sister that he had been an exceptionally skillful lover. That such admissions and advice constituted both too much and the wrong kind of information from parents seems obvious, though the thought didn't seem to occur to either of them. Though they constantly seemed to drag my sister into their psycho-sexual labyrinth, for some reason they left me alone.

I recall that my parents both had some kind of strange attraction to gay culture and female impersonators, which they'd gone to see together various times when they were still married. For unknowable reasons, they later took my sister with them to such a show. Perhaps my mother thought it was educational. When my sister turned eighteen, my parents took her to see the pornographic film *Deep Throat*. Though they'd been divorced for a couple of years, and each was dating someone else, that didn't seem to inhibit them from sharing such a special outing with their daughter on her birthday. At the time, I thought it was strange and wrong on so many levels. Today, I just think they were both batshit crazy.

* * *

I've often said, half-jokingly, that I was raised by wolves. I'm not sure, however, that wolves are an appropriate metaphor. There's a man in Spain, named Marcos Rodríguez Pantoja, whose parents sold him to a hermetic goat-herder as a young child. When the hermit died in the Sierra Morena mountains, the boy was discovered and nurtured by a pack of wolves, who saved his life by bringing him food. The boy lived among these animals for the next eleven years. Eventually, he abandoned human language. At the age of nineteen, police found him and brought him back to civilization bound and gagged, to keep him from howling and biting.

Nuns and a priest in Fuengirola taught him to speak once again. They showed him how to walk upright, dress, and eat at a table, using cutlery. Over time, he slowly adapted to life in society. After military service, he worked for a while in the hospitality industry, though he proved to be ill-suited for a normal life. He lived in a cave for a while and preferred animal companionship to people. The subject of studies and documentaries, to this day he believes that living with animals in the wild is better than being stuck with humans in society. Like everyone else, his experiences define him.

Though my parents did not sell us to a goat-herder, they still did irrevocable damage to my sister and me. Perhaps every parent inadvertently unbalances their children and it's just a matter of degree. For years, I told myself my parents did the best they could, given their own past experiences and their personality problems. I told myself it could have been worse. Even now, it's difficult for me to accept that I suffered neglect and abuse as a child. Writing about my parents' failings seems like a betrayal, like an admission of my own failings. The past is a powerful influence, though it is also what we make of it. Though for most of my adult life I distanced myself from my past, it eventually caught up with me. If we grow up among wolves, we must acknowledge them for what they are in order to leave them behind. We must try our best not to repeat our parents' mistakes. Though we will also fail, we must do the best we can.

Scissors on the Beach

> As for himself, Rollie saw a tall, skinny boy in a white t-shirt, long shorts, and blue deck shoes, a boy with curly hair that rejected its forced part. As best he could define it, the expression he wore was one of astonishment.
> — "What's Wrong With This Picture?" from *Water & Power*

> what if the gods (temperamental
> as they are) had made Sisyphus
> ride a tricycle up the hill forever?
> — "Sisyphus as Sword Swallower" from *Circus Deluxe*

W<small>E WERE SITTING</small> around our campfire on the beach passing quart bottles of Miller High Life and joints, when some crusty dude appeared suddenly out of the darkness. He wore jeans and a hooded sweatshirt, and behind his blond beard he looked ancient, maybe thirty. Hooked in his finger was a one gallon Carlo Rossi wine bottle filled with a murky brownish liquid. "Hey," he said, holding up the jug, "you guys want some jimsonweed tea?"

Like many other Saturday nights, we were camping out at County Line, a wild and unclaimed stretch of beach on the border between Los Angeles and Ventura counties, a kind of no-man's land that, due to some bureaucratic dispute, neither county's Sheriff's Department patrolled at that time. Because of its unique status, County Line was the only non-developed beach in our part of southern California where it was possible to make a fire, pitch a tent, or enjoy life without the fear of being rousted, hassled, or arrested. Though we sometimes stayed at state beaches with campgrounds, the high fees and need for advance reservations made spontaneous trips impossible. Worse, the rangers made minors show written parental permission. Sometimes they even insisted on speaking to parents by phone before approving an overnight stay.

The stranger sat down next to the fire and someone passed him a joint. "I'm gonna get everyone on this whole beach wasted tonight," he explained, setting the jug down between his feet. "I brew this tea from *toloache* that grows in the canyon." His hands moved constantly as he talked, as though he were signing to deaf people. "It's my mission in life, you know." He chuckled at the depth of his own wisdom. "A shaman in New Mexico turned me on to the recipe." We nodded our heads and passed the joint as he talked. "The Navajo used this tea in their ceremonies to alter consciousness," he said, waving the joint in the air in front of him like he was writing zeros on a chalkboard. "It gave them access to their spirit guides." He held up a finger as he paused to take another hit. "I shit you not," he exhaled, "you drink from this bottle and in the morning you'll be talking to Abe Lincoln."

Most of us politely declined when the Locoweed Piper passed the bottle around the fire. Luckily, the hippie didn't insist, though he seemed pleased when Dave gave it a try, then passed the bottle to Randy and some kid we'd met on the beach, who both took a long pull. "Tastes like shit," said Randy, wiping his scruffy mustache on the sleeve of his army surplus jacket. When the bottle had made its way around the fire, its owner stood up. "Gotta book," he said, disappearing again into the darkness. "Party hearty."

According to an article on Belladonna intoxication published in the *American Journal of Therapeutics*, intoxication from jimsonweed (*datura stramonium*), typically produces, among other physiological effects, delirium, hallucinations, and bizarre behavior that can last several days. Amnesia is another commonly reported effect.

In the morning, we made baloney sandwiches for breakfast. For some reason, we always ate baloney on sliced white bread when we camped. If the trip was longer than one night, we'd usually buy some hot dogs and buns, big bags of potato chips, cookies, and snack cakes as well. I'd tried making pancakes on the Coleman stove my parents had bought when they took my sister and me camping in the Adirondacks Mountains back in New York, but it was too much work to prepare them and clean up, so I never bothered again. Instead I used the stove to heat up solvent to clean motorcycle chains in the garage at home. Once, the butane flared up as I was lighting the burner and singed off most of my eyebrows.

The next morning, after everyone had finally crawled out of their sleeping bags, we located Dave, standing by himself at the edge of the water. Randy was missing in action. The other kid from the night before had disappeared as well, but no one cared about him. After a few minutes, Dave wandered back to our camp, complaining of cottonmouth. He had sand plastered to his cheek. Randy was still nowhere in sight, so once we'd finished eating our sandwiches, we decided to organize a search. Fred climbed up the cliff to Pacific Coast Highway and looked in the parked cars, while Dave, Frank, and the rest of us fanned out along the beach. There were a couple of tents pitched close by and we asked the handful of campers we saw if they'd noticed a strange kid our age wandering around. One of them pointed at a blue nylon backpacking tent.

We wandered back to our camp and sat down. A few minutes later, we saw Randy crawl out of the tent, followed by a hippie chick a few years older than us. We watched as he wandered down to the ocean and stood at the shore, staring aimlessly out to sea. Finally, somebody went down and fetched him back to our camp, where we tried to feed him a baloney sandwich. "Who was that chick?" we asked. "How'd you end up over there with her? Did you jump her bones?"

"Na, na, na," is all he said. Aside from that, he wasn't talking. Though he hadn't touched the baloney sandwich, he sat down on the beach and began eating pinches of sand he held between his thumb and forefinger.

"What the fuck are you doing?" we yelled at him, losing patience.

"So many scissors," he explained, shaking his head in wonder. "There are all these scissors on the beach. Millions and millions of scissors." Then he began to laugh hysterically. When we slapped the sand out of his hands and washed his mouth with a bottle of water, he sat passively like a small child and didn't offer any resistance.

After breakfast, we decided to pack up and head north. The ocean was already choppy, blown out with no real swell, so we opted to camp where we'd told our parents we'd be, north of Oxnard, at McGrath State Beach. The plan was to pitch a big wall tent and get stoned inside on bong loads while we waited for the surf to improve. We carried our sleeping bags, the ice chest, and our surfboards up the cliffs at County Line and loaded them into Fred's van.

Meanwhile, Randy had disappeared again. When we saw him wandering in the middle of the highway, a couple of hundred yards from where we'd parked, we stopped traffic and escorted him off the road. It was clear that Randy was seriously tripping and to keep him safe we needed to appoint a full time babysitter. One of us, in rotating shifts, would have to watch over him day and night.

Named Jamestown weed by the original English settlers of Virginia, *datura stramonium* is a dangerous, sometimes fatal plant. Some soldiers sent to quell the rebellion at Jamestown in 1676 mistakenly boiled and ate it. In 1705, Robert Beverly, Jr. published a contemporary account of the incident in his book *The History and Present State of Virginia, Book II: Of the Natural Product and Conveniencies in Its Unimprov'd State, Before the English Went Thither*, in which he wrote "… they turned natural fools upon it for several days: one would blow up a feather in the air; another would dart straws at it with much fury; and another, stark naked, was sitting up in a corner like a monkey, grinning and making mows [grimaces] at them; a fourth would fondly kiss and paw his companions, and sneer in their faces with a countenance more antic than any in a Dutch droll. In this frantic condition they were confined, lest they should, in their folly, destroy themselves… and after eleven days returned themselves again, not remembering anything that had passed."

The following two days at McGrath State Beach passed in a blur of beer, bong smoke, and baloney. When we ran out of supplies, we made a run to the liquor store or mini mart to buy bread, peanut butter, and more beer. In those days, especially in beach communities, minors had few problems acquiring alcohol. Just park beyond the line of sight of the cashier, then send someone in to shop while you asked the first longhair that pulled into the parking lot to buy you what you wanted. Back then, most people under thirty despised "The Man," which is to say authority and regulations in whatever form they took. They were happy to help burn it all down.

During this time, Randy remained mostly quiet. Sometimes he would say something profound and disturbing, though mostly he remained silent or babbled nonsense to himself. He seemed to spend most of his time focusing on details only he seemed capable of seeing. It was as though he had entered another dimension and had discovered the place where lost things are temporarily housed. Once, when the rest of us were struggling to start a campfire on which to cook our hot dogs, he suddenly stood up and walked over to a large bush, where, to our amazement, he reached in and pulled out a half-full can of lighter fluid. The following morning, when we walked down to the beach to check out the surf, he suddenly stooped down to pick a five dollar bill off the sand.

It was a long couple of days. The swell was too small to surf, we'd already spent most of our money, and we were running out of weed. Like sailors becalmed at sea, we could only wait it out, for we all knew we couldn't abandon Randy or let him go home to his mother until he was capable of more or less normal interaction. On the third day, to our great relief, he finally emerged, his mind nearly intact, out of the maze of his stupor. "Wow," he said, looking around to get his bearings, "how's it going?" He shook his head and rubbed his eyes like a young child who has just awoken from a long nap. We asked him what he remembered and he replied, "absolutely nothing." When we told him about the girl in the tent, he couldn't believe it. "Are you shitting me?" he asked, half-smiling, and shook his head again.

* * *

My parents had been separated or divorced for roughly—in every sense—three years by the time I started high school. Any pretense of normal parental responsibility had long disappeared. Meals prepared and eaten at home were meager and unreliable, progress in school unmonitored, rules forgotten or abandoned within a vortex of chaos and personal disintegration. My mother was barely around. She rarely shopped for food and never cooked. I remember I was often hungry during this period. I ate many meals and snacks at the houses of friends and neighborhood kids. My sister recalls me asking her, "what's for dinner?" We both knew the cupboards and refrigerator were empty. "I remember in junior high looking at you standing at the bus stop," she told me recently. "You were emaciated, with dark circles under your eyes. You looked like a photo of a prisoner in a concentration camp."

The most poignant memory I have of junior high school was putting my head on my desk and falling asleep during my classes. At home I slept little and only fitfully, as my parents, though technically separated, frequently engaged in a kind of emotional hand-to-hand combat that resonated throughout the house, especially late at night, when they thrashed together in the bedroom across the hall. Shielded by a closed door, a pillow wrapped around my head, I tried to block the opera of confusing and contradictory noises that kept me awake. The scenario usually began with angry whispers that became shouted out accusations, followed by hysterical crying and sobbing, then a tense silence, followed by coital moans and orgasmic release, progressing next to heart-rendering fits of post-coital weeping, followed again by semi-whispered accusations. Finally a door would slam and my father, battered but still unbeaten, would leave for the night.

After a year of high drama, my parents slowly began to wean themselves off their obsessive and self-destructive attraction to each other. Finally, they divorced. Nevertheless, they continued to see each other for years thereafter. Even after they had both remarried, they used my sister and me as an excuse to meet. Years later, I briefly dated a girl who took me to a screening of the film *Bad Timing* at a theater on Santa Monica Boulevard. "It's my favorite film," she told me. The film was about sexual obsession, jealousy, and the profound damage caused by uncontrollable desire and emotion. Though I didn't make the connection at the time, I later recognized in the film behavior that had been part of my parents' relationship. I remember I left the theater feeling numb and wondering what in the hell I was doing dating someone who found the dramatization of such a theme so engaging.

At some point my father bought an expensive house for himself on a big corner lot in Northridge, a property with the swimming pool my sister and I had always coveted. He even told us he liked to go skinny dipping at night, the thought of which instantly triggered a gag reflex. He put me to work demolishing and hauling away a treehouse in the backyard and digging deep holes that I filled partway with gravel for the little vineyard he planted in order to make his own wine. During this period, he started playing the French horn again and successfully auditioned for a chair in the Burbank Community Orchestra. We sometimes saw him in the company of younger women and openly gay men. My mother constantly complained to my sister and me about him.

"Men are all like that," she repeated, like some kind of mantra. "He was always obsessed with me, from the time he was a boy. I should have never married him." She hated that he had always refused to fight openly with her. "He just sits there, drifting off into space. He doesn't have any emotions. He used to go to parties and read a book. Engineers are all like that." She blamed his mother: "When he was a toddler his mother couldn't handle him. She threw a fit in front of him. After that, he never developed normal emotions." Like a witch constantly stirring a cauldron, she cursed him at every opportunity. She dangled his image in her mind as she stuck pins in his eyes at the dinner table. She rent her clothes and ground her teeth as she spit acid on him from her distant lair. My sister and I looked at each other and rolled our eyes.

Meanwhile, my mother banked her alimony payments and used the money to take Linda and me on a summer trip to Hawaii one year, and to Florida, Jamaica, and Puerto Rico the next. In Hawaii I surfed for the first time, tearing up my feet on the coral and riding the white water on a rented board at Waikiki Beach. My mother bought us firecrackers, which were legal there, for the fourth of July. I remember that the hotel detective came to our room to tell us to stop throwing them off the balcony. I bought a bright orange t-shirt that showed an American soldier firing an M-60 machine gun. "Saigon, City of Enchantment," it said. In Puerto Rico we took a tour of the Bacardi Rum distillery. I was bored and asked if I could stay at the visitor center and read a book while I waited for the tour to end. When my mother and sister returned, they found me drinking rum and coke while I waited. Though I was only fourteen, I was tall. I guess I must have looked older to the *puertoriqueños*.

At home, my mother went out to drink and dance with the other divorced teachers from her school. She met an off-duty cop who showed her his gun in the nightclub. Then she started taking vacations by herself during her summers off from teaching, where she had a fling with an opportunistic officer on the cruise ship. She showed us a picture of the two of them together. In the photo she looks at the camera with sad, exhausted eyes, while an Italian man in a white uniform beams at her side. Back on dry land, she joined a boozy bowling league in Mission Hills filled with middle-aged singles, where she met Phil, a divorced electrician who sometimes got into fights when he drank.

My sister Linda, who'd always been my best and only real ally and support against our parents, had more trouble adjusting to the changing circumstances than I did, mainly because she was two years older and more emotionally vulnerable. Unlike me, she felt devastated and abandoned when my father left. Irrationally, my mother blamed Linda for everything. A long bout of mononucleosis added to her alienation, as she missed most of her junior year of high school. When she did go to school, she hitch-hiked home in hot pants. Once, my father drove past her without stopping, his secretary—later his second wife—sitting close by his side in the car. Minutes later, a long-hair in a stolen yellow Corvette offered her a ride. On the lam after escaping from jail in Canada, her new boyfriend used to write her long letters from prison after he was arrested and sent back.

Despite her misadventures, Linda had always been a top student. Though she had been absent much of the school year, she had already passed all the available Advanced Placement courses. Exhausted, alienated, depressed, and desperate for love and attention, she decided to drop out of high school. When she confessed her intention, our mother barely reacted to the news. "Okay," she responded. Fortunately, a counselor recognized Linda's irrational decision as a plea for help and talked her into staying in school. "You need to be there," he told her. "Just come whenever you feel like it. Don't worry about grades or attendance. We'll make sure you graduate." Senior year she signed up for a special practical nursing course that met for three hours each morning. She worked four hours each afternoon as an aide at a nursing home.

In nursing, Linda found her calling and decided to attend Mount Saint Mary's College, one of the best professional nursing programs in the country. While a number of her similarly talented friends opted for med school, my sister felt a strong pull toward nursing instead. An idealist who wanted to make a difference on a personal level, she said that she wanted to ease people's suffering. Disappointed that Linda would choose to waste her potential and make plans to attend such an expensive private college, my mother insisted that she put off her studies for a year and instead continue working at the nursing home after graduation. "Empty bedpans for a year and then decide if that's really what you want to do with your life," she said.

My mother's new boyfriend Phil moved in with us. He had three children of his own, all of them younger than me. In addition to his neglected kids and his drinking problem, Phil's baggage included his ex-wife, a belly-dancing, red-haired nurse named Lee. Recently re-married to a doctor, she nonetheless kept her lover, an Hispanic pool boy, living on-site in a trailer parked in the driveway of the doctor's big house in Chatsworth, just down the street from the residence of Los Angeles Police Chief Ed Davis. Meanwhile, Phil's kids cycled in and out of our house after being kicked out by their mother or running away from the hell she created. There was always one living with us and they changed places frequently, almost as if they'd agreed amongst themselves to take turns. Eventually, however, they learned that there was no escape, as my mother's personality defects, though different from Lee's, occasioned similar levels of drama.

Such chaos seemed normal to me. Almost everyone in our working-class neighborhood in Canoga Park had multiple kids, cars, and dogs, and with the good southern California weather most of the younger kids spent a lot of time riding bikes in the street, or playing ball on front lawns or improvised driveway basketball courts. When they were home, the teenagers hung out in garages with doors open to the street, where they pumped iron, drank beer from Styrofoam coolers, and listened to "Aqualung" by Jethro Tull or "Baba O'Riley" by The Who, as they worked on their cars and motorcycles. The adults didn't bother much about a gathering of kids, as they all had offspring of their own.

One of the nearby houses on Acre Street was owned by a couple who worked in the circus. Some kids in the neighborhood repeated a rumor that the wife performed an act with a boa constrictor snake. Other kids claimed they'd spied on her sunbathing nude in her backyard. The man who lived across the street from us was an electrician who had escaped from communist Poland by hiding himself in the wheel well of an airplane. That was the story, anyway. We believed it then, though it sounds far-fetched to me now. His wife played the piano and prayed while she waited for The Rapture. Next door to them lived a woman who sewed costumes for a movie studio in Hollywood and next door to us on one side a man with three daughters, but only one lung, who died while we were living there. On the other side of us lived a broken man who had fallen in love with his secretary and married her, but in the process lost his children, his successful car dealership business, and his health. The house my parents bought had originally been owned by a deaf couple, whose children were able to hear but communicated with their parents in sign language.

At the beginning of my junior year of high school, a strange-looking kid suddenly appeared in the neighborhood riding a loud Huskavarna dirt bike. Dressed in jeans and a white t-shirt, his long blond hair fanned out from his shoulders. He made a fast, noisy pass around the block, then whipped around the corner again, slowing down to pop a wheelie in front of us, which he rode down the street for an impressive distance. We listened as the two-stroke engine carried him around the corner and down the next street, where the engine noise stopped. The rider appeared again five minutes later on the back of a beat up Stingray bicycle, again riding a wheelie.

"Hey," he said, "I'm Richard, but people call me Richard." He laughed at his own joke. "I just moved in around the block." For much of the next school year I drove Richard to high school. His father was a hulking Mexican who sprayed "popcorn" acoustic ceilings in new construction projects. His mother was Norwegian but had disappeared long ago. Richard's father had married a woman who had a kid Richard's age from an earlier marriage, and though his stepbrother was allowed to ride in his friends' cars, Richard was not. It was a forty-five minute walk to the high school and there was no bus available, so Richard begged me to pick him up each day on Nordhoff Street and drive him the rest of the way to school. He was terrified that his father might see him, so he usually huddled down in the passenger seat, his head lower than the dashboard, puffing on a joint that he shared with me.

One day late in the school year, some kids came tearing up the street with the news that Richard's father was beating the crap out of him on the lawn in front of his house. Without thinking, I jumped on my motorcycle, rode around the block and up onto the grass. Richard was on the ground, with his father above him, punching his head. I revved the engine of my bike until he looked up at me. Then he walked away toward the house, leaving his son crumpled in the grass like a crushed and discarded paper cup.

During those years, I spent a lot of time hanging out at my friend Dave's house. The oldest of four kids, Dave was always big for his age. In high school he measured six feet, four inches tall. He was also big-boned, strong and muscular, well coordinated, fast, and nimble on his feet, which meant he excelled naturally in team sports, especially football and basketball. Because he had so much potential, much was expected of him. His mother encouraged him to read and study, while his father coached him from an early age. He was a star player wherever he went, a semi-reluctant action figure whose personality was better suited to contemplation than competition. We first met in the third grade and we'd been friends ever since. Though I drifted into and out of participation in Pop Warner football and summer league and high school basketball teams, our relationship had always been based more on intellectual compatibility than sports.

With Dave and his two brothers all in high school at the same time, his house was a place where the phone never stopped ringing and kids naturally gathered. Unlike my house, David Sr. and Marcia, Dave's parents, kept their house well stocked with food. If you were hungry and his mom was cooking, you were welcome to stay for dinner. David Sr. had played college football at the University of Nebraska and he was famous for his many years of coaching Pop Warner football teams to undefeated seasons. Like my own mother, Dave's mom was a teacher in the public schools. I enjoyed talking about books with her, or watching football in the den with Dave's dad. To me their home seemed lively and chaotic, but in a good way.

* * *

Given the instability and tension at home, I began to plan my escape at an early age, knowing my mental health and perhaps my survival were at risk. By the time I was fifteen, I'd found a job as a dishwasher on weekends at a Japanese restaurant. I saved everything I earned working at the restaurant, as well as money I made painting houses for the teachers my mother worked with. By the time I was fifteen and a half, old enough to get my Learner's Permit for driving, I had saved enough money to buy a motorcycle. Though my father had stipulated that I could only buy a new motorcycle with a four-stroke motor, thinking that I'd be too lazy and uninspired to ever come up with enough money to meet his criteria, I bought a street legal 100cc Honda Enduro bike the day after I passed my Learner's Permit test.

Less than a week later I put on my helmet and rode my Honda around the S curves on Nordhoff Street, then up DeSoto to Chatsworth for my first day of high school. The breeze on my face tasted of freedom.

Now I could ride my motorcycle through winding canyon roads and up dirt paths in the hills surrounding the San Fernando Valley. I could get a job painting houses, washing dishes, parking cars or doing janitorial work. I could collect aluminum cans on the beach, crush them with a flat rock and sell them by the pound for gas money. I could eat donuts at all hours, hamburgers from McDonalds, Tommy's, or Bob's Big Boy, tacos from Taco Bell or Jack in the Box, fried chicken from Pioneer, hot dogs from Cupid's. I could skip school and instead go to the beach as long as I counted my absences carefully enough to avoid missing more days in the school year than the law required to progress to the next grade. I quickly learned that by being careful and smart, with a wink to the law, I could largely operate within my own ethical and moral framework, and go anywhere and do anything I wanted.

My second year of high school, Linda used the money she had saved working at the nursing home to buy a Volkswagen our father helped her pick out. Though it looked fine on the outside, it was in a deplorable state mechanically. The car broke down constantly and spent more time in the shop on Parthenia Avenue owned by a German mechanic than parked in front of our house. Once, when I'd gone with my sister to retrieve the Beetle and she paid him cash for fixing the brakes, the mechanic pulled a huge wad of bills from his pocket in order to make change. I'd never seen so much money in one place. "You should be careful about flashing so much cash," I volunteered. The mechanic slowly turned his head to look at me, like a Tiger tank turret swiveling to lock in on a flimsy Sherman. He spoke with a thick accent.

"I'm not afraid," he said. "I was in the war. Since then, I'm not afraid of anything."

Drunk on freedom, a couple of times I borrowed my sister's Volkswagen and drove with friends to far away destinations and back just because I could. The first time I drove through the desert to Yuma with a neighbor. We snuck out of our houses in the middle of the night and pushed the Beetle down the street a ways before starting it up and heading toward the freeway. We both left notes on the kitchen table for our parents. "I've run away from home," I wrote. "I borrowed Linda's car but promise to bring it back tomorrow." To her credit, for once, my mother chose to find the humor in the situation, though she made me promise not to cross any more state lines on my own.

Another time, Randy and I took the Volks and headed north, driving up the 101 to Santa Barbara, then winding along Pacific Coast Highway all the way to Big Sur. We slept for an hour or two in the car on the side of the road, then ate breakfast and headed back, passing a hundred or so Hell's Angels on their Harleys going the opposite direction. On the radio Mick and the Stones played "Angie," The Allman Brothers Band "Ramblin' Man," and Led Zeppelin "Ramble On." In Santa Barbara we stumbled onto the site of some amateur motocross races, which we watched for a couple of hours. Finally, we arrived home hungry and exhausted, but full of stories to tell our friends.

When my sister finally purchased a more reliable car, I got the Volkswagen, which extended my range considerably. I was free to disappear for days at a time on surfing expeditions, or attend the Rose Parade in Pasadena on New Year's Eve. Now that the car belonged to me, I could fix it myself, which meant no more expensive trips to see Fearless Franz. Once, when my friend Butch invited me to camp and ride motorcycles in the desert with his family, but there wasn't room for my bike in the back of their truck, I removed all the seats except the driver's seat from the Volkswagen. Then I took the front wheel off my bike, crammed the whole thing into the car and drove across the desert to the Colorado River. I was proud of myself and my little car, but Butch's dad Jerry was less impressed. "I don't like those cars," he told me, "because Hitler created them." Though I didn't believe him, I kept my mouth shut.

Later I learned that he was right. Hitler had himself conceived of an affordable "people's car" *(volkswagen)* that would be economical and practical enough for common people to own. In 1934, he commissioned Ferdinand Porsche to design a mass produced car with the following specifications: the vehicle must be able to transport two adults and three children at 100 km/h (62 mph), with a fuel economy of at least seven liters of fuel per 100 km (32 mpg). The engine must be capable of sustained cruising on Germany's new highway system. The design must allow for parts to be quickly and inexpensively exchanged. The engine had to be air cooled, to make winter operation more practical. While never released in great numbers until after the war, the Volkswagen went on the become the most produced car of a single platform ever made, with nearly 22,000,000 cars manufactured.

In the spring of 1974, during the height of the oil embargo and ensuing gas crisis, drivers were still suffering through even-odd gas rationing in California. As I desperately wanted a muscle car with a big V-8 that I could build into a street-racer, I decided it would be a good time to sell the Volkswagen. I advertised the Bug for sale at "best offer" in the classified section of *The Valley News and Green Sheet*, a local paper named for the distinctive pale green color of its front page. The calls began coming in the night before, when savvy car shoppers picked up the Sunday morning edition from the news rack in front of the publishing facility in Van Nuys.

The morning of the sale, dozens of potential buyers swarmed around the driveway. I'd detailed the entire car, tuned it up, and changed the oil. I began taking bids, but told people I was waiting until 3:00 to determine the best offer. A bidding war ensued and I finally closed bidding at $800.00, a small fortune at that time and at least double the car's real market value.

With the proceeds of the sale, I bought a custom-built '55 Chevy hot rod for $600.00. A couple months later, Dave's dad gave me a Corvair Monza as payment for painting their house, and I bought a new distributor and a set of tires for it. Now I had two cars, along with my motorcycle, now stripped down for dirt bike riding, and a 50cc Honda I'd bought for $7.00, which my friends and I used to stage street drag races by running it on high octane pure kerosene until its engine finally seized up. My mother's garage, which she'd ceded to me in order to keep my friends out of the house, now resembled a junkyard. My friends and I had filled it with old surfboards, weights and a bench press, and coolers stocked with beer. Crisscrossing chains constructed of beer can pull tabs hung from the rafters. I remember one lazy summer afternoon Dave and I sat talking in the garage while we split a case of beer. Though the future loomed large, for the moment I was living a carefree existence, an existence that made me, as Peter Johnson titled one of his collections of prose poems, "pretty happy."

* * *

The first time I got really drunk was on a camping trip to Ensenada, Mexico with my friend Butch and his family. I was fifteen years old. I'd been on camping trips with them several times before and it was always an adventure. Butch was named after his father, Gerald, a six foot-five Texan with a huge belly and a short temper, who'd played defensive tackle for a couple of years on the Dallas Texans, the original NFL expansion team that later became the Dallas Cowboys. Like my friend Dave's father, Jerry was a fine and generous man who also coached Pop Warner football teams. He had a dry sense of humor that rolled out with his Texas accent and he was a pleasure to be around, once you got used to him.

"Goddamnit, Butch!" he'd bellow dozens of times each trip. Depending on the circumstances, Butch would either roll his eyes, ignore him completely, or sheepishly ask, "what?" in his high-pitched voice. Sometimes we'd camp at Lake Cachuma, in the mountains between Santa Barbara and Solvang. Jerry's old truck would usually break down on the steep road leading to the lake. "Goddammit!" he'd scream from under the hood.

The best thing about these weekend camping trips was riding motorcycles, both around the campgrounds, on the long trails through the surrounding hills, and sometimes even on the public roads, all without a driver's license. Though Jerry was clearly a "Law and Order" kind of guy, he wasn't the least bit concerned about the California Vehicular Code.

Another great feature on these trips was that they provided proximity to Butch's older sister, a foul-mouthed eighteen-year-old hippy goddess, who entertained me with her bad attitude and her spirited arguments with her father over politics, social norms and everything else. She also helped educate me with her street smarts and her playful flirtation. Sometimes she brought one of her boyfriends along on these trips, which always resulted in a kind of Texas-flavored Shakespearian comedy.

In Mexico we stayed at a campground close to the beach. The first night Butch and I wandered off to have a look around and discovered a little building where campers could purchase food and drinks out of vending machines. There were picnic tables nearby. One of the vending machines sold cans of beer in addition to cans of soda, so we fed it some coins and watched as it burped back ice cold Tecate. We drank until we ran out of coins and started back to the campsite.

I remember feeling happy and relaxed. Everything seemed pleasant and funny, though I hadn't realized I was physically impaired until we arrived at the campfire and sat down with Butch's family. Everyone was sitting on folding camp stools, and for some reason I made a big circle in front of mine before I stumbled forward and tried to sit. I must have missed the stool because I ended up on the ground. I don't know what happened to Butch, but someone helped me up and put me to bed. The next morning, along with the usual chili cornbread, bacon and eggs, Jerry placed two cans of cold beer in front of our plates. "Morning, boys," he said, "drink up." He wasn't kidding, so we did.

For many people high school can be a difficult time. For whatever reason, they don't fit in, don't have any friends. There was a kid who lived in the next block up from me who'd been mercilessly teased on the bus to junior high for his big ears, which were always a ready target for flicking fingers or what the kids then called "limpies"—strikes delivered to an unsuspecting ear lobe from behind with a limp ring finger. In junior high everyone called him "Ears" and the name had stuck, though eventually he'd grown his hair long so that it covered his ears completely. Though he tried in high school to reinvent himself, he still wore nerdy black-rimmed glasses and black pointy zip up boots. He still had a grating voice and an annoying laugh. Though he wanted to be funny, he wasn't. Though he wanted to be cool and even tough, he was neither.

One weekday night, Richard was plaguing me with his company. He finally persuaded me to accompany him to see a girl who lived nearby, a girl he said was "in heat." We took off on foot. I was glad when she wasn't home. On the way back, we ran into Ears and Richard struck up a conversation with him about something stupid. I was about to head back alone, when Ears invited us to his house to drink some malt liquor. "My mom doesn't care if I drink," he said. "She buys Old English 800 for me because that's what I like. It's the strongest beer you can buy, stronger than Colt 45. I bet you can't drink three pints."

"I could drink three pints of paint thinner," said Richard.

"Well, we'll see then. If either of you can polish off three talls, you don't have to pay me for the six pack. Otherwise you do."

We entered his house, where we met his mother, a small, neat-looking woman who seemed pleased that her son had company. After she excused herself and went into the den to watch television, we popped open the copper-colored cans. It's not easy to describe the taste of Old English 800 Malt Liquor. I imagine rubbing alcohol mixed with Gatorade might result in something similar, though even that would probably be more agreeable. "This stuff tastes like shit," said Richard after his first pull.

"Yeah, but it gets you really fucked up," said Ears.

When we were done drinking, we left the house. Richard and I were both pretty slammed after only three each and it didn't cost us anything aside from having to listen to Ears talk shit for an hour. I went home and put myself to bed. The room was spinning, which I knew was a bad sign.

In the morning, I woke up covered in vomit. The bedclothes were a mess. I opened up the window to air out the room, which smelled as bad as I felt. Then I stripped off the bedclothes and rolled everything up in a ball, which I shut inside my closet. Somehow I managed to talk to my mother from behind the closed bedroom door. She was about to leave for work and wanted to make sure I got up for school. I took a shower, then drove to school to look for someone who would ditch classes with me so that I could hose down my ruined bedclothes in the backyard before taking them to the laundromat. My friend Rob was glad for an excuse to cut class.

Though it didn't begin well, the day turned out okay after all.

* * *

Like most adolescent males, I had girls constantly on my mind. As my voice changed, so did the frequency of my erections, which seemed to happen without my consent, even at inopportune moments, the biological imperative jousting constantly with socially acceptable behavior. During junior high, I had thousands of burning questions, millions of fantasies, a handful of touchy-feely touch football encounters with girls whose names I barely knew, and two lovely, innocent girlfriends.

The first one I talked with on the phone most nights for months, though neither of us had much to say. I suppose we just wanted to learn about what it was like to be together with someone in a safe and familiar way. She was a tall, very thin girl named Bobby-Jo with a huge, bushy mane of beautiful, curly blond hair. She was so thin and as yet undeveloped that she seemed to be less forceful than the air she encountered, so that she leaned back slightly as she walked, like R. Crumb's "Keep on Truckin'" comic. I finally took her on a date to go bowling. Our mothers each drove us to the bowling alley on DeSoto Avenue, then picked us up a couple hours later. We both had fun and I don't know why we didn't do it again. Eventually summer ended and we stopped calling each other. A few years later, after she'd grown up and matured, she was perhaps the most beautiful girl in high school.

Diane, my second junior high girlfriend, was a shy, quiet girl who sat at the desk in front of me in biology class. She had long, straight brown hair and sad eyes. Once, she came to school with a black patch over her eye. She told me her father's belt buckle had injured her when he beat her for burning incense in her bedroom. Apparently, he thought she'd been smoking marijuana. The day before graduation, ninth graders got to go home after half a day. For some reason, the school had not informed parents of the change in schedule, so we took advantage of a few hours of freedom and walked to my house. We drank a little bottle of cooking wine I found in the back of one of the kitchen cabinets. Then we listened to music and awkwardly embraced, kissed, and groped for a few minutes. Neither of us had any idea what we were doing, which, as it turned out, wasn't much. Then I walked with her back to Chatsworth, all the way to Mason Park, where she lived in a big house on the corner. Excited and embarrassed, I thought about her all the way home. I didn't see Diane over the summer and I quickly lost track of her in high school. I talked with her once a couple years later and she politely invited me to attend a Bible study group. I told her I'd think about it, though we both knew that wasn't going to happen.

As soon as I could drive a car, I took girls to the movies, though usually only once. In those days "good girls," were respected and liked, though they were not particularly popular, as they made poor girlfriends. After the initial encounter, my date and I would agree either to be friends and quit dating, or we'd move on to something more interesting. Instead of the movie we'd told our parents we were going to see, we'd park the car in a dark place and do everything possible to destroy any vestige of self control that might keep us from fulfilling our biological destiny. Eventually, the gods would wink and nod. Then, after much experimentation and a little luck, tab A would find its way into slot B.

I lost my virginity in the parking lot of a pizza parlor, on the front seat of my sister's Plymouth Duster. The next day, I showed up at Zuma Beach with a smile on my face that wouldn't go away. My friends took one look at me and knew I'd got laid. It was always obvious to everyone when something of that magnitude occurred.

Those lucky enough to have steady partners who were sexually active in high school entered into a realm of bliss, a tunnel of love that temporarily kept the world and the future at bay. Suddenly they could channel their raging hormones and spiking emotions into acts of physical intimacy and release, the pleasures of which they could never, even in their most intense marathons of teenage masturbation, have imagined. Fucking was like diving head-first into a pool of warm vanilla pudding. It was like rolling on the floor with a room full of puppies. It was like driving down the freeway at 120 mph while simultaneously jerking off, eating ice cream, and listening to Jim Morrison sing "Light My Fire." Except that it was way better. It was a waking wet dream in which you're surfing naked with a huge erection and ejaculate as you get fully tubed. But unlike a dream, at that age you can catch your breath and do it again and again.

Young couples with this kind of synergy ache when they're apart. They live to be alone together in their Garden of Eden, the private place where the two of them have miraculously invented human sexuality and everything else that's good. To say my partners and I lacked discretion, self-control, common sense, or even common decency would be an understatement, for collectively we were caught in compromising circumstances by both parents and the police. One of my sister's genius friends wrote a hilarious pornographic novella called "Horny in High School," which passed through the school from hand to hand in mimeograph form like an illegal Samizdat copy of *The Master and Margarita*. The title says it all.

*   *   *

Though I didn't start surfing until I was in high school, I learned to read the waves and bodysurf during the summers I spent at the house my parents owned a block from the ocean at Silver Strand Beach in Oxnard. Ironically, though my grandmother lived in the house during the time I was in high school and I'd practically grown up there, I couldn't surf at Oxnard Beach because of the territorial locals who did not tolerate intruders on their turf. Any car with surf racks that wasn't familiar to them was subject to a broken radio antenna, flattened or slashed tires, or worse. The waves between Port Hueneme and Channel Islands Harbor were very powerful and thick, making for fast rides that required a high level of skill that the local surfers had acquired and uninitiated outsiders usually lacked. Like the beaches of Orange County, it was an unfriendly surfing destination, one my friends and I avoided.

Instead, I learned to surf at Sunset, a bikini-thin strip of sand near the intersection of Sunset Boulevard and Pacific Coast Highway. A kid in one of my classes had recently started surfing and it was all he could talk about. He'd just got his driver's license and his father had helped him rebuild a funky little red Opel. He told me he could drive to the beach after school twice a week, as long as he took his little brother along. He invited me to go with them if I could find a surfboard to borrow.

My sister had been dating an airplane mechanic named Marcus who surfed. I asked him if I could borrow a board and he let me use his diamond-tail Hobie, a short, fast stick that was a horrible choice for a beginner. Nevertheless, I strapped it onto the surf racks on the Opel and soon I was wiping out at Sunset and loving every minute, despite the numbingly cold water. The following week, I visited a surf shop, where I looked at surfboards and instead used the little money I had to buy a shorty wetsuit.

Unlike snowboarding, which can be learned in a day, it takes practice and a fair amount of time to learn how to surf. Though the basic technique seems simple, the waves themselves present the biggest challenge. Even at the same spot, conditions vary from day to day, or even hour to hour. Reading waves is an important skill, for there's no point in dropping in on a wave that's about to close out.

Paddling for the right wave and timing the take off correctly is another challenge. Too early and you pearl. Too late, you're over the falls. Either way you're eating ocean. Like a toddler learning how to walk, it takes practice, commitment to building skills, and a willingness to fail many times in order to eventually succeed. Standing up also happens in stages. Beginners usually try getting onto their knees first, which simply doesn't work. Through trial and mostly error, I eventually learned how to "pop up" in one fluid motion as the board dropped at an angle that put me on my feet within touching distance of the steep wall of the wave. I still remember my first successful rides as pure exhilaration.

By the time I'd learned how to stand up and ride the white water straight in to the shore, Marcus, my sister's boyfriend, called to say he wanted his Hobie back. Since I didn't know where he lived, my sister went with me to deliver it to his apartment. I remember it was awkward when she caught him with another girl there. "You should have called, first," I told her.

"Fucking bastard," was all she could say. So I took her to Bob's Big Boy for milkshakes and we split a plate of french fries. A week later, another friend gave me a longer but battered board with a round nose, which I tried to repair with fiberglass and epoxy. Though it was waterlogged and slow, it kept me in the water.

The next time I visited the surf shop, I saw Marcus' Hobie there for sale on consignment. The owner let me take it home after I agreed to some cash up front and monthly payments. Like an Italian sports car, that board got a lot of looks. Eventually, I learned to ride it. Later I took to riding longer boards. Marcus eventually regretted selling the Hobie and I sold it back to him and bought an eight-foot Infinity big-wave board, which I kept until I graduated from college.

Surfing engages the senses. The rush of water that fills your wetsuit on a winter morning, water so cold it gives you a headache when you first duck under, and the warmth of pissing into that polyurethane longjohn as you wait for the first set. The hoot of your friend warning you off the wave he just caught to your left as he drops down and cuts back, crossing in front of you. The view from the cliffs of big sets lining up off of San Onofre. The laughter of a girl who came along for the day. The feel of her lips and body under a blanket at sunset. The pleasure of peeling out of a slimy wetsuit and dressing in soft, warm flannel and jeans, lighting up a smoke and pulling onto PCH. The way my shoulder ached after the paddles back from the long rides at Leo Carrillo, the taste of potato chips, cookies, Hostess Twinkies and sodas from 7-Eleven at Sunset or the liquor store in Ventura. The hamburgers, French fries, and tacos from Jack in the Box in Malibu. The warmth of the sun, the taste of salt, the sound of waves crashing,

Driving through twisting canyons in a '65 GTO, a '66 Mustang, a Volkswagen, an Opel, my '63 Corvair, listening to *Who's Next, Houses of the Holy, Dark Side of the Moon, Bad Company, Blind Faith,* and *The Low Spark of High-heeled Boys* on the eight track, "Maggy Mae," "Imagine," "Black Magic Woman," "Born to Run," "No Woman, No Cry," "Tangled up in Blue," "Superstition," "Free Bird," "Rocket Man," "Money," "Nutbush City Limits," "Angie," and "Take it Easy," on the radio. And then there were the smells: The rubber stench of wetsuits saturated with urine and saltwater, the umbrella drink aroma of coconut surfboard wax, the sweet, pungent smell of burning rope, of blackened popcorn, of Mary Jane's leafy skirt gone up in smoke.

My friends and I surfed up and down the coast from Sunset to Tankers in north Ventura County. Occasionally, we made a safari to the San Diego area beaches, particularly San Onofre. We avoided all the Orange County beaches. In those days, everybody had their own favorite spots. If you drove, you got to pick the destination. Bob liked Sunset, while Lorne, who surfed goofy foot, preferred Leo Carrillo. Dave often went to Zuma or Tankers up north, while I liked Topanga or the point break at C Street near the Ventura Fairgrounds.

Despite the consistent, well-formed point break, none of us liked to surf at Malibu, because it seemed like a parody of itself, like some kind of bad trip *Beach Party Bingo*. In reality it was hard to find a place to park and always crowded, with hot doggers and nose-riding long-boarders snaking every wave and kooks wiping out in front of you. You couldn't sit on the beach for more than five minutes without some grom asking, "can I borrow your stick?"

Like the Fountain of Youth or Shangri-la, surfers are always searching for a "Secret Spot," an unknown and inaccessible section of coastline where perfectly formed waves break, though no one is around to catch them. While these mythical surfing destinations exist mainly in the minds of surfers, stories nonetheless circulate about tiny coves under sheer cliffs only accessible from the ocean by boat, or secret paths far from any road that pass through fenced off private property and lead to pristine private beaches or point breaks.

In high school I wrote a short story for one of my English classes called "The Secret Spot." In my narrative, a group of young surfers, seduced by old tales of perfect but unattainable waves, ignores the barbed wire fences and warning signs to sneak onto a coastal military base just before dawn. As the sun comes up, they launch themselves into the water and paddle toward a set of thick, right breaking waves, which they ride for what seems like hours, as if in some idyllic dream. Then they paddle back and sit on their boards to wait for the next set. On the empty beach behind them, they see their own footprints in the sand. Suddenly, a loud, unexpected sound crashes over them. They swivel around to catch sight of something they were not meant to see—a pair of silver flying disks screaming toward them low and fast. The story ends with the sound of gunshots and red stains in the water.

* * *

For some reason, I always had friends who were also named Greg. At Limerick Elementary school, where I met Dave in the third grade, the only black kid in the school was in our class and was also named Greg. We were friends and I remember him as a bright, sensitive, kind and articulate child. In junior high, I met another Greg, a loud-mouthed beanpole the other kids called Linker because of his long arms swung like an ape when he walked. Thus he became The Missing Link, which quickly got shortened to Linker. When my mother got to know him, she renamed him Greg Two. He was a sharp kid who was in my seventh grade experimental "Columbia Math" class. One of only a handful of students who grasped the concepts and passed the tests, he nonetheless displayed an even greater interest in subverting the class.

Mrs. Holman, our math teacher, was famous for wearing the same two dresses over and over. Most days she stood at the blackboard with her back to the class and wrote out a stream of math symbols that only she, Greg, and a couple of genius nerds could interpret. Every few weeks we took a test. There were no letter grades, but it was clear from the beginning that most of the students were getting at best five or six correct answers out of thirty questions. I doubt I was doing even that well. All of us had been placed in this experimental math program developed at Columbia University because we had displayed a high aptitude for mathematics on standardized tests we'd taken the year before. Now, however, in my case at least, that aptitude had been forever destroyed.

As anyone who has ever worked a meaningless, unchallenging job can tell you, a year can be a long time to spend doing nothing. To prove that our creativity had not yet been completely snuffed out, and to keep ourselves from dying of boredom, the students in the class collectively invented a number of subversive games. Our favorite, at least in the row in which I sat, was a kind of "tug-of-war" played while seated in our desk chairs. The row would be split into equal numbers of participants down a center line. The object of the game was to push the desks ahead of or behind you to the front or back wall of the classroom. Greg and I were on opposing teams. He sat at the head of the row and I anchored the row at the back. Rarely did either team actually achieve a clear victory, though on at least one occasion Greg's chair came even with Mrs. Holman at the black board. Most of the time she didn't notice, though once she stood for a moment with the chalk in her hand and her mouth open, staring in disbelief. Then she turned back to the blackboard and continued her scribbling.

In high school, Greg quickly developed a passion for cars. Like most male high schoolers, he dreamed of having a fast ride. When the film *American Graffiti* came out in 1973, it reminded us of our own lives, though the police had long ago shut down any stoplight races on Van Nuys Boulevard and done everything in their power to ruin the traditional Wednesday night cruising scene. Somehow, Greg saved up the money to buy a jacked up 1965 Pontiac GTO coupe with a four-speed manual transmission, modified exhaust headers and gears in the differential, glasspack mufflers and a set of fat Mickey Thompson rims and tires. It was a fast car to begin with, and he set out to make it even more impressive. Greg made friends with every mechanic he could talk to, as well as the owners and clerks of the auto parts stores in Chatsworth. He learned how to rebuild the Holly carburetor, how to tweak the suspension. He searched the local junkyards for coil springs and missing trim parts, sewed up the leather bucket seats and headliner.

Greg was also famously stingy. Though he always had a job and would flash a roll of bills from his pocket at every occasion, he hated to spend a dime. He made friends with a girl who worked at Earl's Donuts, a favorite hangout, and fixed her car without charge so that he always got free donuts. His GTO had come with an eight-track tape deck and two tapes, which he played over and over for years. He had a homemade green surfboard he'd bought at a garage sale for $5.00. Unlike his two eight-track tapes, which actually played, the "The Green Monster" was famous for being ugly and nonfunctional and was the subject of many jokes. Nevertheless, Greg stubbornly stuck with it. Dozens of times I rode with him to Zuma, his favorite beach, with the monster strapped to the racks of his GTO. Inevitably, he would paddle out with us, pearl on a dozen waves, then spend the rest of the day bitching about the shitty waves, though no one else had trouble riding them. From time to time, I'd test my skill by borrowing the monster. Like a bucking bronco in a rodeo, it was all you could do to hang on for a moment.

Another talent Greg displayed was an uncanny ability to spell any word correctly, even words he'd never heard before and whose meaning completely eluded him. Though I had always been a prolific reader of books, I didn't master spelling until college, when I forced myself to check the spelling of every word I wrote until I finally memorized them. Greg's unnatural and completely unearned ability irritated me, especially when I was the one writing his essays so that he could graduate early from Grover Cleveland High School after being expelled from Chatsworth the previous semester. His troubles had begun when he'd nearly run over the school principal, who had been directing traffic in a parking lot after a football game. Greg had thought that someone was trying to back out from a parking space in front of him. So instead of stopping, he continued forward and nudged the principal out of the way with his car. His poor judgment, lack of basic courtesy, and his near homicidal impatience resulted in his expulsion from Chatsworth High School.

It always seemed to me that he was his own worst enemy. I never completely understood nor accepted Greg's constant angst and deep seated anger. He genuinely despised all authority figures, including his parents and grandparents. Though his behavior was often intentionally provocative and confrontational, he nonetheless felt personally mistreated and victimized by the police, school officials, girls that rejected him, and even local businesses. While his paranoia made him hysterical, unpleasant, and even dangerous, it also produced a comic effect. When his friends teased and imitated him, uncharacteristically, he accepted the ribbing good-naturedly.

Driving with Greg was always an adventure. A road warrior and motorized duelist, he frequently engaged in street races and high speed highway antics. Once, on the way to the beach, another car entered an on-ramp in front of him, forcing him to brake. What ensued was a dangerous game in which Greg and the other driver took turns passing and cutting each other off at increasingly high rates of speed. Though we could see that there were two young children in the other car, I couldn't make Greg listen to reason. "Be cool," I kept saying. "Why the fuck can't you just be cool?" Instead, he downshifted to third gear, stomped on the accelerator, and passed the other car on the right hand shoulder of the freeway, the GTO's 400 cubic inch engine screaming as we approached an overpass. He shifted into fourth gear and cut in front of the other car just moments before we would have hit the concrete wall of the overpass. Then, laughing hysterically, honking the horn, and flipping the other driver the bird out the window, he continued to accelerate to 120 miles per hour. Part of me wanted to rip Greg's head off his scrawny, sociopathic shoulders, while another part, high on adrenaline, thought it was just the kind of story I'd want to write about some day.

Greg was jumpy and couldn't sit still for very long. He preferred to be busy working on something, preferably with his hands. He used his fast and powerful car as an extension of himself. Another time, Greg got a speeding ticket on Plumber Avenue. He slowed down because he saw a car coming up fast behind him in the rearview mirror and thought it was another hot-rodder who wanted to race. Even the cop had to laugh when Greg told him what he'd done, though he wrote the ticket anyway.

I spent a lot of time working on cars with Greg, and even got good enough at rebuilding Holly carbs that I made money repairing and tuning up other people's cars. I took classes in auto mechanics at the high school and more specialized auto mechanics classes over the summer at West Valley Occupational Center. The latter classes bored and depressed me so much that they finally persuaded me that I was not well suited for a career as an auto mechanic.

In the spring of 1974, I bought a yellow 1955 Chevy with a modified 327 Corvette engine, custom headers, a racing differential, and cut out rear fenders with huge back tires, which my mother's boyfriend immediately named "The Screaming Yellow Zonker." The car ran on high-grade fuel and got about eight miles to the gallon. I couldn't afford to insure it, so it mostly sat in the garage while I drove up and down the coast looking for surf in a beat up Chevy Corvair. The previous owner had built the '55 Chevy to be a twelve-second quarter-miler. I'd never lost a street race in the '55 Chevy until the clutch blew out at a traffic light against a stock El Camino pickup truck.

Greg and I were in my garage replacing the clutch that same evening when an idiot named Mark, who was a year older than us and lived up the street from me, came buzzing by in his blue with white racing stripes Camaro Super Sport 396. Mark was the kind of kid who acted like his car was the fastest quarter-miler in the valley, but always found some excuse not to run against my '55. We hated this cocky punk and were glad when he stopped to ask if my car had broken down again. To shut him up, Greg offered to run his car against the Camaro. We were surprised when he accepted.

Greg fired up the GTO and quickly uncorked the headers. Then the two cars drove the few blocks to Mason Avenue and Nordhoff Street, where Mason dead-ended at the railroad tracks, a wide, level stretch of blacktop a bit more than a quarter mile long. Because it was not yet a through street, it was always completely devoid of traffic. We used the traffic light in the distance to signal the start. In a few seconds it was over: the Camaro had been shut down and its owner shut up.

During high school, Greg had a job as a parking lot attendant in a building on Ventura Boulevard in Encino, where his father worked as a property manager. Because he had hair down to the middle of his back, Greg tucked his locks underneath a cheap looking wig when he went to work. When he finally quit his job at the parking lot, he wore the wig to school the next day.

Our history teacher, Mr. Benevidez, a gruff man who never shared anything personal or expressed emotions of any kind, smiled and chuckled to himself when Greg came into the class looking hang-dog depressed and telling other students that his parents had made him cut his hair as a punishment. Then suddenly Greg stood up and with a flourish that would make any high school thespian proud, whipped off the wig and shook his long hair out. "Quit my pissant job, so I won't be needing this anymore," he said as he walked to the front of the class and tossed the wig into the trash next to Mr. Benevidez's desk.

Ironically, after graduating from California State University, Northridge, Greg became a high school teacher.

* * *

On the day I turned sixty-one, my friend Dave, who I'd been out of touch with for many years, sent me an email. He reminded me how throughout high school I used to quote Pete Townshend's lyrics from The Who's 1965 song, "My Generation." He wondered about the irony of a sixty-one year old man looking back on the words, "I hope I die before I get old."

"Nothing really changes," I wrote back to him, "except for the aches and pains and the bad teeth that come when the warranty on our bodies expires. The rest is unchanged… or at least until we stop ticking. Thus I have no doubt that no matter the condition of my body, I will certainly die before I get old."

In 1989, an interviewer for the television show *Good Morning America* asked Townshend about his famous line. He replied that, at the age when he wrote the lyrics, "old" meant for him, "very rich." In his autobiography Townshend claims the lyrics were inspired by the Queen Mother, who had once ordered his 1935 Packard hearse towed off the street in Belgravia because the sight of it offended her as she drove through the neighborhood.

In the 1970s, I could never afford to buy tickets for The Who concerts when they came to Los Angeles on tour, but I finally got to see them play at an outdoor amphitheater in Sacramento in June of 2002, a few days after their fifty-seven year old bass player John Entwistle died in bed with a stripper in a Nevada casino hotel. The cause of death was a heart attack induced by an overdose of cocaine. He had been diagnosed with heart disease, yet had continued to smoke twenty cigarettes a day.

After cancelling two concerts, The Who hired Pino Palladino to fill in for Entwistle on bass guitar. The band then launched their tour at the Hollywood Bowl, playing on in honor of their fallen band mate. "My immediate mission is to complete this tour in good heart, and to remember John in my quiet and private times," Townshend wrote on his web site. "We are musicians, entertainers. We can do it. We have the right tools. No worries."

Townshend still jumps in the air and windmills his guitar when he performs. Roger Daltrey still swings the mic on its cord, and tosses it into the air and catches it on stage. Even minus Keith Moon's manic drumming and Entwistle's commanding baseline and calm presence, Townshend and Daltrey gave it everything they had. The crowd in Sacramento was mostly people in their 50s and 60s, dressed in jeans and The Who maximum R & B, Spitfire target, or Union Jack t-shirts. They stood up to dance and sang along with the lyrics. No worries, indeed. Daltrey and Townshend still rocked, still captivated. They had the right tools. They did it.

Years later, I stumbled upon a video on YouTube of a group of ancient Brits in a retirement home singing "My Generation." Some of them display a remarkable degree of swagger. After a bit of investigation, I learned that the group had been put together in 2007 by Tim Samuels, a documentary film-maker working for the BBC on a feature about the social isolation of elderly pensioners in Britain. After the success of the Samuels' documentary and the popularity of the YouTube video of "My Generation," the group branded themselves The Zimmers, after the Zimmer frame, the UK term for a mobility aid known in the U.S. as a walker. Some of the forty people in the original video went on to record an album of rock and roll covers and perform live on *Britain's Got Talent*, making it to the semi-final round.

When I was a senior in high school, my creative writing class was assigned to come up with "most likely to..." tributes for each graduating student. That final semester, I disliked that easy elective course even more than my required government class. The other students were mainly thespians or musicians. To me they seemed like a flock of preening peacocks. They ceaselessly fawned over the teacher and exhausted me with their enthusiasm and pretension. In protest, I submitted a tongue-in-cheek short story about an old lady who fed her cat raw meat. When the woman died, leaving her pet locked inside the house, the cat ate her body. Ironically, though my high school teacher dismissively—and perhaps appropriately—evaluated my creative efforts as barely average, twelve years later I'd be teaching Advanced Narrative Writing at the university.

While the other students teased each other with "most likely to marry a doctor," "most likely to win a Nobel Prize," or "most likely to be a millionaire," they described me as "most likely to be a bum." Like Keith Moon, I suppose I wasn't expected to live a long or productive life. Like Keith Richards, whose surprising longevity is the source of long-running jokes, thus far I have. Outraged at our classmates' casual cruelty, a girl stood up with her fists clenched at her sides and scolded them. "You don't know him at all," she said, slamming a book on her desk in disgust. I watched in amused silence.

I didn't give a shit what the idiots thought of me. *Why don't you all f-f-fuck off?*

* * *

It's forty minutes to sunset at Topanga Beach, late August, 1975. A light offshore Santa Ana breeze stiffens the waves as the swell breaks steadily off the point in small, well-formed sets. Surfboards under our arms, Dave, his little brother Sam, a couple other surfing buddies, and I walk barefoot down the dirt path from the makeshift parking lot on Pacific Coast Highway, jog across a stretch of sand, wade a dozen careful steps along the rocky bottom, then launch ourselves onto the surface of the water.

This is a farewell of sorts, for in the weeks to come life will change forever. Some of us will take up studies at distant universities and others will log the first hours of a lifetime of work building houses, solving problems, managing accounts. Some of us will go on to attempt to teach other discontented and disinterested teenagers, kids just like us, something about science, math, literature, or foreign languages. But we don't know any of that now. We only know that a part of our lives is over and another part about to begin.

Just the week before, two of us had been hassled by the cops for trying to sneak into Six Flags Magic Mountain, using the expired employee identification card of a friend who had a summer job there. I told the security guards that I'd found the ID card on the ground in the parking lot and thought I might as well try the employees' entrance. He didn't believe me, so we stayed there a couple hours until our friend finally came to claim us. He lost his job and we got to drive away with him.

Back in the Valley, we stumbled onto a house party in Chatsworth and someone on the street handed Dave a cold beer. A minute later a big guy asked for a sip of the beer. Dave handed it to him and watched as he upended the can, pouring its contents on the ground. "Hey, what the fuck?" Dave said, but the big guy just pointed at the badge on his belt. Both he and his buddy suddenly looked a lot older. Then we all went home. It felt as though our luck, along with everything else, had just changed.

Someone hoots past as we paddle out, riding a zig-zag seam along the face of a crisp wave. On the flat rooftop of a dilapidated beach house, two guitarists, a bass player, and a drummer jam under the red-orange sky. A toddler dances naked on the sand, as his mother sways topless at the water's edge. Over and over we drop in, sweep along the shore, then kick out, paddle back, and do it again. In the distance, the sun dips into the ocean. Then the breeze begins to chop the surface of the water as darkness gathers. Fifty yards off the point, we collapse onto the decks of our boards and pull toward the bumps in the distance—the closing set on a perfect evening, the last day of summer.

 The Topanga Beach I remember doesn't exist anymore. These days the surf bums and hippies are gone, along with the ratty beach houses the county bulldozed years ago to make a parking lot. There are lifeguard towers and metal trash bins and signs warning against dogs, glass containers, and alcoholic beverages. These days no one sleeps on the beach at night or dances naked at sunset. Though the waves still break slowly off the rocky point, the rest is gone forever.

It's a Wonder (I Can Think at All)

Part 1, Education

> For some reason we shake hands. I learn that he's a high school English teacher, divorced, no kids. I still don't know his name. When I tell him what I do, he suddenly acts interested, even though he's never seen my books. "They're a little hard to find," I tell him. He smiles in an arrogant high-school-English-teacher way that burns a hole in my gut. I finish my drink in one big gulp and feel the ice cubes clink against my teeth. Then he wants to talk about different authors. I tell him I hate them all, that I wish I had dropped out of college before my teachers had sucked away most of my originality and replaced it with insights into Henry James.
> — "A Nick Adams Story" from *Water & Power*

> Once, laughing you said
> your hand was a cracked mirror,
> and showed me the broken line
> you cupped in your palm.
> — "Bareback Rider," from *Circus Deluxe*

WHEN I TAUGHT classes in literature and writing at California State University, Northridge in the late 1980s, I used to park my old Volvo on the street a half a mile from the university and walk to campus. I'd bought the car from a traveling salesman for $300. The transmission shuddered and the brakes had a weak grip. The leather seats had come apart, so I dressed them in my old t-shirts. Since I was an adjunct instructor, that was the kind of car I could afford.

Though considered a "part time" instructor, I nevertheless taught the same number of courses as the tenured faculty, but for a quarter of the pay. The university allowed my contract to end each academic year, then renewed it for another year a week before classes began again in the fall. Since the English Department made offers to adjunct faculty based on enrollment, I never knew what classes I'd be teaching or if I'd even have a job. Because I could not afford to pay hundreds of dollars each semester for a parking permit in the faculty lot, I walked.

I've never minded traveling by foot. In those days, I found that walking gave me time to breathe deeply and mentally prepare for my classes. One advantage of walking is that pedestrians can, like water, find the most direct route, instead of flowing along the cement channels created for vehicular traffic. My path usually took me directly through the massive student parking lots, where I saw thousands of shiny new cars owned by undergraduates.

A commuter campus, California State University, Northridge served over a million people who lived in the San Fernando Valley area of the city of Los Angeles. One day, I asked the eighteen- and nineteen-year-old students in one of my sections of Freshman Composition to raise their hands if they had traveled to the university that day on the bus or other public transport. Not a single hand went up. When I asked how many had walked or rode a bicycle, I counted two. The remaining twenty students had traveled alone in their own cars.

In those days, tuition fees for California residents to attend a state university cost about $200 per semester. While buying textbooks added to that cost, it was still possible to receive a university education for considerably less than the cost of a compact foreign car. I could never understand why so many young people voluntarily chose to begin their lives in debt. While in theory we are free to form our own values and live in whatever manner suits us, in practice, advertisers and social norms create a population of uncritical consumers. As Noam Chomsky has pointed out, in contemporary America, advertising and student debt have combined to create a powerful means of indoctrination and wage-slavery.

Traditionally, exposure to literature, history and philosophy helped readers develop what used to be called "critical thinking skills" that helped inoculate them against the propaganda, lies, and political manipulation of the ruling class and monied interests. Studies of the reading habits of people in England in the late 1800s suggest that working-class people had read more widely in classics than better educated upper-class people. In the United States, in 1920 most people had only an eighth grade education, yet there was half as much illiteracy as today.

I always urged my students to read widely on their own and foster their own intellectual interests. "Your college courses are just a shallow introduction to a subject," I'd tell them. "If you continue to rely on others to educate you, you will simply memorize and parrot back a few tidbits of preselected information that you will soon forget, the way you did in school for the past twelve years. Instead, you must educate yourself according to your own interests and passions. That's why there's a library on campus with over a million books. That's where you should spend your time. If you learn to love the library, you will never lack for entertainment throughout your life and it will not cost you a penny." Though a reluctant academic, I was clearly an idealist. No doubt I was also a fool, for my students stared back at me with blank faces.

* * *

My first memory of formal education neatly encapsulates my experience in public schools. I distinctly remember how my kindergarten teacher reprimanded me—gently but with absolute authority—for not forming the number eight correctly. She insisted that I write the figure by forming a fluid, upright infinity symbol, whereas I preferred to make a snowman out of two zeros stacked one on top of the other. Though the end result was virtually the same, she insisted that what I was doing was incorrect and unacceptable. Though I had no choice but to alter my orthography, I never saw a reason why I should. 88888888.

I missed school often my first year, as I'd come down with a bad cold after playing in the snow after dark. I woke up the next day with a fever and a sore throat. My lungs were congested and I had a cough that wouldn't go away, even after several weeks. My parents took me to see a doctor, who gave me a series of weekly blood tests. Though no one really knew why the symptoms continued over several months, they nonetheless referred to it as atypical or "walking" pneumonia. In photographs from that time, I look pale and weak. My head usually leans to one side or the other, as though the weight of it was too heavy for me to hold in place.

The following year, I learned to read. I remember the excitement I felt working through the Dick and Jane primers and my frustration with the slow pace of the class. I wanted to go on to the next book in the series, but the other students were holding us back. The "look-say" approach to reading instruction used a combination of whole word learning and phonics popular at the time. When a student would struggle to pronounce a word, the teacher would encourage the student to "sound it out."

I was good at recognizing words and at sounding out new vocabulary. My love of stories and books allowed me to quickly master reading. Throughout school, I always read at a level far above my grade. However, for many years creative spelling plagued my written expression. Like an Elizabethan typesetter prior to Dr. Johnson's dictionary, I continued to spell words the way they sounded, using my own personal phonetic transcriptions. Perhaps my teachers and the authors of the Dick and Jane books should have introduced us to the International Phonetic Alphabet at the same time they taught us to read. Throughout elementary school, my teachers had me read my stories out loud to the class. At the time I thought it was because I was a gifted storyteller, but now I realize it was likely the only way they could make sense of what I'd written.

Once I had mastered reading and could select my own books from the library, school became less interesting for me. Even in New

York, which had much better schools than California, the pace of instruction was measured to keep the slowest students from being left behind. School emphasized memory, repetition, and what was called "Good Citizenship," for which we received a grade on each report card.

For most of us, our school years pass in a blur of bus rides, line-ups, roll calls, seating charts, and weekly desk cleanings with gritty detergent and brown paper towels. In this factory, clocks tick, bells ring, whistles blow, books open and close, mats cover the floor for obligatory after lunch naps. Everything smells of peanut butter and disinfectant. Each morning, we salute the flag and pledge our little allegiance.

In my school, we sometimes ducked and covered, hiding under our flimsy plywood desks in a modified fetal position from the cataclysmic mutually assured destruction of thermonuclear bombs, or else marched outside in military order when the fire bells rang. We memorized spelling lists and multiplication tables. We learned of the wisdom and goodness of our Presidents and about something called Manifest Destiny. We made handprints for mother's day and tempera paintings of fierce-looking Indians and smiley-faced pilgrims in hats with buckles to illustrate the first Thanksgiving. At some point, a teacher told me I wasn't good at drawing, so I stopped making art for the next fifteen years.

On Friday afternoons, our teachers separated us by religious denominations and herded us into yellow buses that took us to the church of our parents' choice for religious indoctrination. A few kids stayed behind at school and painted zoo animals, read books from the library, or worked on their citizenship. Though my father was an atheist who refused to have anything to do with religion, my mother insisted on raising her children in the Catholic Church. By the time I started school, she had already begun dragging my sister and me to church, where she dropped us off for Sunday school while she attended the service. On religious holidays or special occasions, my sister and I also attended mass. In those days, priests still performed the mass in Latin, which gave the ritual a dreamlike quality. However, the didactic homily, delivered in English, quickly broke the spell.

Despite my young age, the classes in Catholic dogma must have terrified and inspired me, for I sometimes talked with God at home in my bedroom when I was alone. I told him that I knew that I needed to try harder to be a better person. In those days, I also sometimes compiled mental lists. Once, I tried to keep track of all the small physical pains and discomforts I felt—stomach aches, headaches, ear aches, colds, fevers, rashes, insect bites, hangnails, skinned knees and elbows, bad dreams, fears, and as yet impossible to understand or define psychological stress. I wondered if there would ever be a time when I would feel perfectly healthy and happy. I abandoned the project after a week or two, when it seemed that the answer would be no. At the same time, I made a list of my faults: I was selfish, a baby, and a bad person.

In second grade, I began taking Sunday classes to prepare for my First Confession and my First Communion. While my mother and sister went to mass, I went to a room with other children my age to learn about the Sacrament of the Eucharist. Everything about God, the bloody death of Jesus, and the impossible to fathom Holy Trinity, confused and overwhelmed me. What exactly was a Holy Ghost, I wondered but didn't ask. Each Sunday I felt as though I were being abducted by aliens who took me to a strange room where they drugged me with their hallucinogenic mythology and excised parts of my brain. One day, a priest arrived in his black robe and disappeared into a closet, where we were taken, one by one, to confess our sins. The catechism teachers called us by name and no one noticed when my name was never called. I was too shy and too afraid to say anything. I didn't want to go into that closet anyway.

The following week, the children in my class and I attended our First Communion. The church heaved with organ moans and smoky incense. As we kneeled at the altar, the priest mumbled something in Latin and placed a paper thin wafer of tasteless bread on our tongues. It was supposed to be the body of Jesus. We made our parents happy and proud when we gobbled it up and swallowed the Son of God like hungry little cannibals.

I remember that I had to wear a stiff white shirt with a white bow tie to the mass, and that I received a ceremonial white Bible. Though there must have been some kind of party afterward, I felt dread rather than excitement, as I expected to be struck dead by lightning at any moment for the sin of taking the Eucharist without having first confessed. For years, I had feared the creepy, omniscient God who could read my mind and know what was in my heart. Like the Hobbit, Frodo in *The Lord of the Rings,* the thought of existing under the constant gaze of the Eye of Sauron terrorized me. But as the days and weeks passed without incident and my anxiety slowly lessened, I began to realize I'd been deceived.

I didn't tell my mother anything. Reluctantly, I continued to attend Sunday mass for the next five years. Sometimes my mother dragged me along to confession with my sister. When it was my turn to tell the priest about my sins, I made up stories about playing with matches, disrespecting my parents, or taking the Lord's name in vain, none of which I'd actually done. Though I couldn't think of anything sinful that I *had* done, I'd been taught that it was a greater sin not to have anything to confess. I hated Easter most of all and wondered why they would tell children such a disturbing and detailed story about what could only be described as sadistic torture and execution. Finally, I told my mother I'd had enough. "I don't want to go to church and I don't want to be confirmed. I'm like Dad," I said, though I was nothing like my father, "I don't believe in God."

Though I was done with religion by the age of twelve, as a child and adolescent I continued to evaluate myself and my surroundings from a moral, ethical, and spiritual perspective. The perceived faults I had listed as a young child came from others instead of from self-analysis. As I got older, I continued to review and analyze my own behavior and motives. I identified in myself a capacity for persuasion that allowed me to manipulate others, particularly my peers, and make them do what I wanted. Over time, I trained myself not to misuse this ability.

When I was eight, my parents moved from Syracuse, New York to Los Angeles, California. My mother enrolled me at Limerick Elementary School, a pleasant walk from our house in Canoga Park. Unfortunately, I'd already mastered the entire third grade curriculum the year before in New York. Though unchallenged at school, the weather allowed me to play outside for the first time throughout the winter months. Slowly my lungs got stronger, and I became more physically fit and athletic.

During that first year in California, I met Dave, one of the other pupils in my third grade class. He has been a friend ever since. Dave's family had moved from Nebraska and arrived in California only a few weeks before my own. At that time, he lived a couple of blocks away, in a rented house with a big tree in front that I would climb with him and his younger brother after school. Already tall and gifted athletically, he was a good friend to have. Even as a child, his passion and vitality seemed balanced by his humility as well as a deep sense of wonder and a natural curiosity. I admired his confidence and liked him for his intelligence. Unlike most of the other children, he was capable of engaging in meaningful conversation. Over the years, he's managed to retain these qualities. Today, I'd describe him as a soulful person.

In fourth grade, for some reason my class read about Japanese culture and history, listened to Japanese songs, and learned to sing "Sakura," a song about cherry blossoms, in Japanese. Our teacher also introduced us to haiku poems, which she read to us. One day, she told us we were going to write our own haiku. She reviewed the five-seven-five syllable format and the nature conventions inherent in haiku. She talked to us for a few minutes about something called Zen. I wrote my first poem in a couple of minutes, then started writing more. Around me I could see that some of my classmates were struggling. Occasionally, a student would crumple a paper into a ball and start over on a new sheet. I looked forward to reading mine out loud when the others finished. As I waited, I wrote several more.

It usually took me about fifteen minutes to walk to school. My first year I walked with my sister, then later with Dave or other kids from the neighborhood. However, on days when homeowners left their trash cans at the curb to be emptied, the commute usually took longer, as my friends and I often found something of interest along the way. We carefully examined the trash as we passed by and took anything of interest home with us. Though we called the practice trash-picking, we nonetheless took pride in the books, comics, board games and puzzles with missing pieces, broken toys, cigar boxes, rusty tools, and other junk we found.

Though my parents had lost interest in the antiques, they had sometimes shopped for in New York, going to flea markets and antique stores as a young child had given me a love of old and pre-owned items. To me such goods felt invested with history and prior experience. That they were no longer shiny and new didn't make them less appealing. Sometimes these unexpected finds pulsed with arcane knowledge that bordered on magic. Once, my friends and I found a plastic bag full of lace garter belts, bras, and girdles. Another time, we stumbled upon a stash of nudist magazines that had been left in one of the empty fields down by the railroad tracks. The black and white photos of naked people seemed both magnetic and dangerous. Though none of us had any idea why we wanted them, I remember we divided up the magazines and each took a couple home with us. I hid mine behind the rough-framed tar paper walls of the garage. That my parents didn't give me an allowance or access to my own money as a child no doubt increased my interest in scavenging and trading possessions with my friends. I remember trading a worthless trinket to a new boy in my class at school for an expensive leather soccer ball. By the time I was ten years old, I'd already become an accomplished scavenger and horse trader.

By sixth grade, I was playing basketball with a group of friends each morning before school on the driveway of a classmate named Daryl, and with Dave and his brother Jody after school at the court in the backyard of the house his parents had bought on Parthenia Street. One day, the ball bounced high off the backboard, over the cement block wall, and into the alley behind the house. When Dave opened the gate and went to retrieve it, some kids from the junior high, who were passing through the alley after school, called him some bad names, then threw the sharp metal top of a tin can they'd found lying on the street at him. Though he was big for his age, Dave's tormentors were at least two years older. Nevertheless, my friend had already learned the importance of holding his own against would-be bullies. I watched, deeply impressed, as he gave the older boy who'd thrown the sharp metal object a quick and precise beating.

One of my friends had a mother who stayed at home during the day. He lived just up the street from the school and walked home for lunch. Sometimes he invited me to join him. His mom fed us chicken noodle soup and toasted cheese sandwiches. Most of my friends watched *Batman* and *The Monkees* on television. Some kids in my class wore pointy black Beatles boots to school. Many played on Little League baseball teams. A few were already gun nuts who argued about the best caliber of ammunition and bragged about their fathers' rifles and hand guns.

On the playground, boys competed in softball, tetherball, handball, volleyball, and foursquare. However, our favorite team sport was dodgeball, or socco as we called it. Socco matches more often than not resulted in hurt feelings, bad falls, minor injuries, personal rivalries, and fist fights. Most of the brawling lasted only a few seconds, with solid punches rarely landed. After school, depending on the season, I usually played football, basketball, or baseball with the kids in the neighborhood. We measured off and spray-painted hash lines in the street to form a football field. At least two of our houses had basketball courts. Baseball, or more specifically batting, presented a bigger challenge, due to the high risk of broken windows.

While in elementary school, I also tried to learn how to play the guitar. My parents were both accomplished musicians, and my sister, talented and brilliant in everything she pursued, took flute lessons and played in the school orchestra. Since everyone in my family played a musical instrument, I eventually asked if I could take guitar lessons at the music store where my sister had her flute lessons. My mother agreed and the store sold her a cheap instrument with nylon strings and a hard carrying case. I was paired up with a young instructor for weekly half hour sessions.

My teacher taught from Mel Bay method books. I learned some musical notation and scales so that I could play the melodies of simple songs. My hands barely fit around the neck of the instrument and the nylon strings often buzzed or sounded fuzzy. I also learned to strum a few chords, but they were difficult to form and didn't make sense, as I didn't sing along. The only song I remember learning was "House of the Rising Sun." Even that was disappointing, as the sounds I produced sounded nothing like what I heard on the radio. My teacher could play in a way that produced music, but apparently the techniques he used were too advanced for me to learn. I needed more practice, he said, always more practice. Later, in junior high, my wood shop teacher would say the same thing in a different way: "more sanding."

I disliked practicing at home by myself. The repetition bored me. After learning scales and fingering notes, I still didn't know how to play a single riff. I felt uninspired, which made me lazy, which in turn made me guilty, insecure, and unhappy. After a while, I quit practicing... I could hear a ball bouncing and kids' voices yelling outside. I put down the guitar and went out to play. My mother knew I wasn't applying myself and asked if I wanted to continue. I hated to admit that I had failed and instead hung on a while longer. She talked to my teacher after my lessons, but nothing helped. Finally, I gave up. I laid the instrument to rest in its carrier coffin and buried it behind my closet door.

When my parents bought a set of World Book Encyclopedias and put them on the bookshelf in the living room, I poured over the volumes. I spent many happy hours reading articles at random and feeding my intellectual curiosity. Eventually I got tired of walking between my bedroom and the living room every time I had a question, and I asked my mother if I could move the encyclopedias to my room where I could refer to them whenever I wanted. By the time I got to junior high school, I'd turned over the pages so many times that I knew where all the photographs of snakes were in each of the volumes. I avoided those pages if I possibly could.

I also discovered classic films, though I didn't really know what they were at the time. When my grandmother stayed at the beach house, I sometimes wheeled her black and white portable television into my room and watched random programs late at night when I was supposed to be sleeping. Sometimes I watched boxing matches broadcast live from the Olympic Auditorium in Los Angeles. I also remember tuning in to a program on the public television station that showed old films. I watched in horror as a runaway baby carriage rolled down the Odessa Steps in the film *Battleship Potemkin*. I thought it was footage from a newsreel. I also remember feeling sad and confused by a film about an old man, a film I later learned was Ingmar Bergman's *Wild Strawberries*. However, the film that affected me most was one I've never been able to identify. It was a black and white film with voice over narration in a language I didn't understand. I recall reading the subtitles. The film concerned a man who could not seem to accept that everything in life changes, deteriorates, decays, and dies. Beauty fades and leaves fall to the ground. Termites attack the new house he has built. I don't know how the film ends, only that it overwhelmed me at the time. Though a recent search led me instead to the astounding work of Bill Morrison, a filmmaker who uses decaying nitrate film stock to make avant-garde films such as *Decasia,* I still have not identified the film I saw as a child.

My mother played an important part in my early education by facilitating weekly visits to the Los Angeles Public Library. Though she had brought my sister and me to the public library regularly when we lived in Syracuse, when we moved to California she was concerned that we would be bored in school, so she encouraged us to use the year to educate ourselves at the library, a habit I have continued throughout my life. I remember how proud and excited I was to receive my own library card in the third grade, and how I would leave the library each week with books piled high in my arms. I never bothered with the children's section. Instead, I read everything that attracted my interest: history, biography, literature, science fiction. No one thought to review or censor my selections. Though my reading was totally undirected, I followed my interests and curiosity, which led me to make unexpected discoveries.

* * *

In seventh grade, I left Limerick Elementary School to attend a newly-built junior high school in Chatsworth, only a few miles from the Santa Susana Field Laboratory, where Atomics International operated experimental, unshielded nuclear reactors and Rocketdyne tested rocket engines. Half of these reactors suffered failures, including the first core meltdown of a nuclear reactor in 1959. The collective failures resulted in periodic massive radiation dumps into the atmosphere above the San Fernando Valley from 1957 to 1981. Appropriately, the new junior high school was named after Ernest Lawrence, a nuclear physicist who won the Nobel Prize in 1939 for inventing the cyclotron, which sounds rather like a self-propelled bicycle or a carnival ride that spins around like the rinse cycle in a washing machine, pinning people to its sides with centrifugal force, but is in fact a kind of enclosed racecourse for accelerating charged atomic particles. Lawrence, bless his heart, is also known for his work on the Manhattan Project, which ultimately resulted in the atomic bomb, and for founding the Lawrence Berkeley National Laboratory and the Lawrence Livermore National Laboratory, the latter of which is tasked with overseeing the "safety" and reliability of America's Pandora's Box full of nuclear weapons. To bring the story full circle in the narrative cyclotron, during the initial stages of the construction of Ernest Lawrence Junior High School, halfway around the world the United States Air Force was occupied with its own little construction and cleanup project, after a mid-air collision resulted in four thermonuclear bombs falling on the Spanish village in which I now live.

My sister, now in ninth grade, had been among the first to attend Lawrence Junior High School, which had opened only the year before. I vividly recall how we rode a bus to school half an hour each way. On the bus, the older kids routinely bullied the seventh graders, whom they labeled "scrubs." A carnival atmosphere of sexual tension, threat, laughter, screams, and minor acts of violence prevailed on board these big yellow school buses. The drivers were often unable to control the chaos well enough to drive safely. Their only recourse was to pull the bus to the side of the road, shut off the engine, and threaten not to continue until the accelerated particles calmed down. Some of the kids considered these forced stops a victory, for they'd be late to school and their tardiness would be excused due to the school's own unreliable transportation. Typically, bus drivers quit after only a few weeks, or even a few days, though in the ninth grade we had the same driver for the entire year. He'd cut a deal with some of the most disruptive kids that he'd blast Creedence Clearwater Revival at full volume on the way to school and Deep Purple on the way home. In exchange, they'd at least stay in their seats and refrain from fighting or throwing things out the window.

In those days, young people were at war with authority and rebellious behavior was gaining momentum. Rock music, the anti-war movement, and the growing counter-culture influenced everything from fashion to philosophy. My junior high school tried to enforce a strict dress code. Boys were required to wear shirts with collars and were restricted from having hair that touched the collar in the back. Girls could not wear pants to school and the hems of their dresses or skirts had to be longer than their fingertips when they stood with their arms hanging at their sides, hands open and fingers extended. They could not wear sandals or open toe shoes, nor heels of any height. Makeup was also technically forbidden, though tolerated if discreetly applied. Most importantly, if a girl had a developed bust, her breasts had to be locked up as tightly as possible to avoid becoming a distraction.

Female students often found creative ways to subvert both the dress code and their parents' attempts to limit their self expression. Prior to the bell that signaled the beginning of the school day, it was common to see girls in front of their hall lockers pull off clothes they'd left their houses wearing only a few minutes earlier to reveal the mini skirts and tight blouses with lace ruffles they'd worn underneath, or exchange staid shoes for the more extravagant pair they kept in their school locker. Fashion magicians and quick-change artists, these girls used their lockers like theatrical wardrobes for inter-act costume changes. Each morning hundreds of frumpy schoolgirls transformed themselves into Mod sirens dressed in micro minis and white patent leather go-go boots. They teased long, straight hair so that it stood up in the back and applied mascara to their eyelids. Once they'd achieved the desired effect, they slammed shut their lockers and strutted into homeroom to start the school day.

Most of our parents were young enough to be caught between two worlds. Many of them enjoyed or at least tolerated our music. My parents, though both trained classical musicians, bought my sister and me albums by the Beatles, The Doors, and Bob Dylan. They talked about the lyrics to Simon and Garfunkel songs and noted the Beatles continuing improvement as a musical ensemble. At the same time, our parents couldn't understand or condone the chaotic rejection of existing social values. Though they may have come to the conclusion that the Vietnam War had been a mistake, they weren't ready to protest it in the street. Nor were they enthusiastic about their children being disrespectful, or looking and dressing like "hippies."

By eighth grade, the dress code seemed a distant memory. Straight-leg Levi 501 blue jeans and t-shirts with pockets were the de facto uniform for virtually all young men in secondary schools, at least in Southern California. During the summer between eighth and ninth grade, almost everyone I knew refused to get a haircut. A few even showed up to school with shoulder-length hair and whatever sideburns and scruffy mustaches they could grow. While the official dress code had not changed, social norms had. No longer did teachers and administrators suspend girls for wearing skirts they deemed too short, or boys for having hair that was too long. Vice principals even stopped administering swats with a wooden paddle. Nevertheless, discipline and control never go out of style.

Three kinds of teachers existed at my junior high school. The first were authoritarians who ruled the classroom with an iron tongue and depended upon threats and psychological intimidation to break the will of even the most unruly students. Middle aged men with permanent scowls, who generally taught physical education or shop classes, the maximalists among them yelled each word at ear-bleeding volume like boot camp drill sergeants, while the minimalists spoke rarely and with as few words as possible, in a quiet, measured tones that somehow conveyed so much pent-up testosterone and threat that students scarcely breathed or moved in their presence. These wardens and prison guards were more interested in keeping order in their classes than in teaching. Given their responsibility for the safety of their students and the proximity to power tools and neck breaking gymnastic apparatus, I suppose they had little choice. Despite their efforts, I remember that a print shop student at the school ignored the constant warnings against crossing the thick yellow lines painted on the shop floor surrounding the monstrous machinery. When he stuck his finger into a hole in the hungry printing press, it promptly amputated and consumed the curious digit.

Despite the potential whine of the band saw and the clouds of sawdust, I remember wood shop as a clean and silent place. The teacher, an unassuming middle-aged man with a flattop haircut, wore short-sleeved button-up plaid shirts and carried a wooden ruler, which he sometimes tapped in his hand. A super-minimalist, he expressed himself more through his coiled body language and piercing stares than through words. In fact, he rarely spoke. When he did, he uttered the words so slowly and softly that students had to lean forward in their chairs to hear him. We spent most of the time in class cleaning the shop, which was always already cleaner than the kitchen of any five-star restaurant. The ten minutes he typically allowed us to work on our projects we spent sanding pieces of wood with what seemed like an infinite number of grades of sandpaper. We were required to ask the teacher's permission before advancing to the next step of the project. Each time a student asked, the teacher ran his finger over the wood, or measured with his ruler. "More sanding," he said. It's taken me fifty years to fully understand and appreciate such deceptively simple, Zen-like wisdom. In retrospect, I see that "more sanding" was one of the most profound lessons I learned in school.

Another teacher who made a strong impression was Mr. Fair, a six-foot-three-inch ogre who, due to his massively wide shoulders and tiny bald head, appeared, even dressed in his gray business suit uniform, more like Dick Butkus, the famous middle linebacker for the Chicago Bears, than a teacher. With a booming voice and a cruel and withering sense of humor that crushed dissension and obliterated teenage spirit, Mr. Fair taught a subject called Social Studies, a mystery meat course which turned out to be a year of political indoctrination and brainwashing. In the class, we learned to fear and hate Communism, Socialism, and anything that disrupted a free market economy, while studying how horrible it was to live in the U.S.S.R., the Eastern Block, and perhaps even the land of wine-swilling, surrender-monkey frogs. Mr. Fair was the perfect delivery system for such an intercontinental ballistic missile of hyperbole, over-simplification, and propaganda. "You may not like me," he taunted us the first day of class, "but you can't say I'm not fair."

Mr. Fair modeled his classroom on a prisoner-of-war re-education center. The first week of school he yelled constantly, terrorizing students to the point of tears. Once they'd been properly broken, passive students sat straight at their desks and listened silently to his monologues. As a reward for our compliance, our guide sometimes entertained us with street theater antics that happened offstage, just outside the door to the classroom. In the oft-repeated scenario, Mr. Fair waited for an unsuspecting student to slam shut a locker after the bell had rung. Then he burst outside and harangued his victim with a barrage of abuse and threats while we whooped and applauded unseen from inside the classroom. By the time Mr. Fair walked back into the classroom again, you could hear a pin drop. During these performances, I sometimes detected the faint trace of a smile on his face.

As bad as the authoritarian, prison guard teachers were, they understood that anarchy did not facilitate learning. Though they sometimes overcompensated, they did, at least, keep control of the classroom. The second type of junior high school teacher lacked this essential skill and left it to the students to self-regulate and determine for themselves what kind of learning environment they would share.

While they would occasionally draw a class devoid of the worst troublemakers and chaos agents, an unusual circumstance which would allow them to transmit information normally, more often they would operate in a protective bubble of their own making, ignoring the distractions around them. In extreme cases, their dedication to the subject matter turned them into deaf, dumb, and blind pinball wizards with no audience. Then decorum unraveled, along with the teacher's authority, and the class descended into bedlam.

In eighth grade, I had an English teacher with a Ph.D. in literature. I have no doubt she had many interesting insights into the books she wanted us to read and discuss. Unfortunately, the students in her class chose not to read these books. Nor did they allow her to lecture or discuss them, as they were otherwise engaged in climbing in and out of the windows, throwing all manner of trash around the room, shouting, laughing, wandering around to talk with their friends, leaving unexcused to smoke in the bathroom down the hall, and opening and slamming the door. After only a couple of weeks, poor Mrs. Ph.D., who had never previously taught in a junior high school, decided that instead of reading and discussing Charles Dickens' *Great Expectations,* it might make more sense to shut the window shades, darken the room completely, and show her classes an old film interpretation of the novel instead. Thus she sat, stooped in her chair, her body shaking slightly in the dark, her glasses on the desk before her, her eyes closed, her hands sometimes covering her ears. For the next few months, we watched a lot of black and white films and even a few cartoons. Mrs. Ph.D. didn't return for the spring semester. Everyone said she'd had a nervous breakdown.

Fortunately, a third type of teacher also existed. These teachers knew how to balance the need for authority and civilized behavior in the classroom with respectful and enthusiastic presentation of subject matter. They also understood the difference between shoveling propaganda and helping students learn to think for themselves. I remember a few of these teachers actually taught me something of use: how to read and analyze a short story by O. Henry, Faulkner, or Saki, how to view America within the historical context of Twain's classic novel

The Adventures of Huckleberry Finn, how to plan, structure, and write a five-paragraph essay, how to use a typewriter and format a business letter, how to understand something about electricity, genetics, and human reproduction, how to interpret Greek mythology and Homer's great epic poems as both literature and the foundations of psychology.

Unfortunately, I did not learn any math in junior high nor high school. In fact, I never learned any mathematics at all aside from the basic arithmetic I mastered in elementary school. Though I was competent in math as a young child, I never felt I was particularly good in the subject nor did I have much interest in numbers. I remember that learning to use an abacus was the most interesting and fun part of my study of math. So I was surprised when I received the news, just prior to starting junior high school, that I had tested so highly in mathematics that I was one of 2,500 "gifted" students in California who were being placed into the Secondary School Mathematics Curriculum Improvement Study, an experimental program developed at Columbia University. I was so surprised that at first I thought my teacher must have mixed up my test score with that of one of my classmates.

Building on the "New Math" movement of the 1960s, the goal of "Columbia Math" as my teacher called it, was to introduce students to "fundamental concepts and structures" within a unified program of study that eliminated the traditional separate studies of algebra, geometry, trigonometry, pre-calculus, and computer programing. Columbia math included many topics that even today I don't recognize, including modular arithmetic, algebraic inequalities, Boolean algebra, abstract algebra (it's all pretty abstract to me), bases other than 10, and symbolic logic, along with statistics and probability. The program offered six years of material, from grades seven through twelve, though I can only comment on the first year, as that's as far as I got with it. Honestly, I don't think I really progressed beyond the second week. The textbook we used was called *Unified Modern Mathematics.* Nationwide, about 25,000 students had been pressed into service aboard the ghost ship launched by the Secondary School Mathematics Curriculum Improvement Study during the late 1960s and early 1970s.

I've written elsewhere about the games students in my seventh grade Columbia math class played to amuse themselves while Mrs. Holman, our teacher with only two dresses, dripped, splashed, and threw numbers and symbols at her abstract expressionist blackboard, talking with her back to us. Of the twenty students in the class, only a handful were able to correctly answer more than eighty per cent of the questions on the exams. The rest of us were lucky if we got ten per cent right. Given that only two students really gave a shit and fifteen students were sleeping with their eyes open, calculate the average success rate.

At the end of the school year, I begged my mother to call the school and ask that they put me into a regular math class. I had had all I could take of Columbia math. As it turned out, I was pretty much finished with math altogether, for the wizards of Columbia's experiment had altered my brain forever. I took algebra in junior high school and passed the class, though I knew that I had not understood anything. I repeated the class in high school with the same result: I left knowing I'd understood nothing, learned nothing, failed completely, though I passed the course with ease. I remember asking our neighbor's grown daughter, an accountant, to help tutor me in junior high. There were times when even she struggled to make sense of the "word problems" that I'd been assigned to puzzle out. Though she patiently tried to help me translate the words into equations, my brain short circuited and shut down all mathematical functions.

I remember one moment of sublime beauty that happened in junior high school. It must have been during the spring semester of my first year. My sister, who was a ninth grader, played the flute in the school orchestra. She had been taking private lessons for several years and she was a naturally gifted musician. In fact, Linda was good at everything she did. Anything I struggled with, she could do with ease. She could spell any word and got perfect grades on her report cards. She could do algebra, geometry, trigonometry, and calculus. She could draw and paint and make sculptures. She was a top student, a perfectionist who routinely stayed up all night to work on a class project.

One afternoon, my English class was cancelled and the class instead walked to the auditorium for a concert by the school orchestra. When the orchestra performed Debussy's *Prelude to the Afternoon of a Faun,* my sister played the hauntingly beautiful flute solo. The stage lights were shining on her as she stood on stage. I remember how I struggled to keep myself from crying. I wiped my eyes on my sleeve and trembled in my seat. I had never felt so overcome with emotion. Sadly, neither of our parents had bothered to come to the concert.

During my three years in junior high school, my parents were consumed by their separation and divorce. I threw myself into sports as a way to exhaust myself physically and distract myself from negative thoughts. Each day I played pick-up basketball during the lunch break at school. At home I practiced with kids in the neighborhood, playing on driveways with backboards and rims mounted above garage doors. In the fall, we played football in the street, where we'd marked off and spray painted yard markers. For years I'd begged my parents to let me play Little League baseball, but they had no interest in sports. Now that they were separated, I increased the pressure and changed the sport to football.

During the summer before ninth grade, my mother signed me up to play Pop Warner football on one of the Chatsworth Chiefs teams, which were assembled from players with similar ages, heights, and weights. I was tall for my age and very thin. Since I wanted to play on the same team as other kids from my age group and class, I was forced to limit my weight during the season, even though I was still growing and always hungry. Players were weighed before every game, and if they exceeded the limits they would not be allowed to play. I remember times when I had to starve myself and show up to games dehydrated in order to play.

The Chiefs were a relatively new organization that operated within an already well-established league. We played against teams fielded by other communities in the San Fernando Valley: Canoga Park, Granada Hills, San Fernando, Burbank, and Northridge among them. We also played against teams from farther away, including Lancaster and Simi Valley.

My coach was an impossible to please, cigar-smoking man with a beer belly, who yelled constantly. His sons and their friends, all of them ex-high school and junior college players, acted as the assistant coaches. Though I respected them at the time, in retrospect, I see how their own experiences had conditioned them to become sadists who relished our suffering as they put us through one "hell week" after another. They had learned to accept and foster a culture of mindless belittlement, violence, and domination from their own coaches, which they in turn passed on to us under the guise of "building character." In game situations, blame was widely distributed and praise reserved for the occasional great catch on a post pattern that turned into a long touchdown. Players were also commended for a particularly brutal tackle, quarterback sack, or body block. "Use your helmet as a weapon," they told us, over and over, and I did.

I played defensive end effectively and with zest. On offense I played tight end, but with less enthusiasm, as our team didn't pass the ball much. I remember the exhilaration I felt busting up a sweep, forcing the ball carrier to turn inside and then making a tackle. I was particularly good at rushing the passer and occasionally sacked opposing quarterbacks for a loss, blocked their passes, or forced a fumble.

Near the end of the season, a new kid showed up one evening at Chatsworth Park, where the team practiced. He was dressed in one of our practice uniforms and helmets, but wearing tennis shoes instead of cleats. Normally, kids were not allowed to join the team midway through the season, as they were not properly conditioned and risked injury, so we were all surprised to see him. Like me, he was a big kid, and I later learned that his father had been having discipline problems with him at home and had asked our coach if he could bring him onto the team and "take him down a peg."

Because I was one of the biggest and most physical players on the team, I was pulled out of practice and pitted against the newcomer in a series of one on one tackling drills that lasted the better part of an hour. As it was clear that the new kid had never played contact football before, at first I tried to make technically correct, clean, and effective tackles that spared him from getting the wind knocked out of him, but the coach got in my face and yelled at me. "Put a hit on him," he screamed. "What is he, your girlfriend? Quit dancing and show him how to play football. You can make out after practice." It was already dark and getting cold under the weak overhead lights in the park, as I relentlessly punished the kid, flattening him with my helmet or running straight through him when I had the ball. Fortunately, he was a tough kid and picked himself up again and again. When the coach asked him if he'd had enough, he glared back and slowly shook his head no. Though he never said a word, it was clear that he refused to be broken. I remember his nose was bleeding badly and we had to stop at least once for him to wipe the blood from his face. When we were finally done, his white practice uniform was soaked with wet mud and his dark, rusty blood, as was mine. Finally, I was told I could go back to regular practice. "Good job," I said to the kid. What I really meant was, "I am so sorry."

"Thanks," he said, avoiding my eyes.

After that experience, I could never bring myself to participate fully in the game again. Though I still showed up to practice, I let myself exceed the weight limit for the last league game of the season, and watched my team win from the bench dressed in street clothes. I didn't bother to show up for the team's postseason game or the team banquet. When someone called later to tell me where I could pick up my team trophy, I told them I didn't want it. Nor did I try out for the high school football team the following year. I was done with football.

Instead, I played high school basketball, though again my career was cut short. The second week of practice, the coach of the B team, a math teacher named Mr. Davis, spoke privately to each player. I remember he told me at that time, before having ever seen me play, that my role would be as a member of the scrimmage team to help prepare the regular players for the teams we would face in league play. Shocked at the unfairness and absurdity of what he said, I left without responding. I determined that I would prove him wrong, but nothing I did got his attention. He'd made up his mind, picked his team in advance, and had no capacity to make creative adjustments along the way.

Halfway through the team's mediocre season, we played against our own undefeated junior varsity team, whose players included my friend Dave, another six-foot-five forward, and a six-nine center who later played backup on Duke University's national championship team. We were losing thirty-six to eight when the coach put me into the game, hoping I could at least lean into some of their much taller lineup. To everyone's surprise, against bigger, more talented, and better coached players, I excelled. Since our set offense was laughably ineffective against the Junior Varsity players, I ignored it and resorted to the kind of creative and instinctual street play I knew best. I'd played for years against many of these players and I scored half of our team's points, though we still lost by a wide margin. Afterward, a couple players suggested the coach utilize me in league games. Despite their efforts, I continued to ride the pine.

For the remainder of the season, I did my best to display how little I cared about team sports in general and basketball practice in particular. I made jokes, honed the already sharp edge of my sarcasm, and vaguely went through the motions. Once the coach asked to see me after practice. "I can't tell if you're just lazy or you really are that slow," he said to me. For the next three days in practice I finished first in every set of "lines" the team ran, answering his question. Then I went back to my dogging and jogging. The season dragged on. At one game someone stole my clothes from a locker at an inner city gym. Later I was suspended for some minor infraction and attended a game in street clothes. I didn't care about any of it. I was used to dead dreams. The following year, I didn't show up for basketball practice. Over the summer, I'd grown my hair long and quit shaving. I enrolled instead in a badminton class to satisfy my physical education requirement. The varsity basketball coach shook his head at me in disgust.

I channeled my enthusiasm instead into girls, cars, parties, and surfing. In general, school didn't interest me, though I remember reading a few good books in English classes and I once wrote a long poem in the manner of Bob Dylan's song "Lilly, Rosemary, and the Jack of Hearts" called "Ballad of a Bad Man," which my teacher insisted I read aloud to the class. Nevertheless, I was usually just a body seated at a desk, though a body that was frequently absent. In the three years I attended high school, I can't remember having had a single personal conversation of substance with any teacher. No one asked for my opinion or offered guidance. No one offered encouragement. Students who didn't take Advanced Placement classes, play team sports, participate in student government, write for the school newspaper, help design the yearbook, play in the marching band or orchestra, or perform in plays or musical theater were of little consequence. We were invisible.

While my high school classes usually bored me, my U.S. history class enraged me. After reading the introduction and the initial chapters, I refused to open the textbook again. Throughout my childhood, history had always interested me and I had read *American Heritage* magazine and as many books as I could find at the public library on the American Revolution and Civil War. I had also read Jack London, Sinclair Lewis, John Steinbeck, Mark Twain, Ray Bradbury, Kurt Vonnegut Jr., and J. R. R. Tolkien. I had studied the Romans, the Russian Revolution, and the great conflicts of the twentieth century on my own. From my reading, I knew that the U.S. history textbook was an absurd collection of propaganda and lies.

A gruff little man who never deviated from the textbook nor shared his own thoughts, opinions or experiences, the teacher sometimes called on me to answer questions. Over time he realized that, depending on my mood, I would either shrug my shoulders and say, "don't know," or else provide a detailed answer. Because I wrote well and passed the exams with ease, he eventually left me alone. Many years later, I learned that Mr. Benevidez had been a soldier in the Philippines during the Second World War and had survived the Bataan Death March. After the American and Philippine defenders of Bataan surrendered to the Japanese in April of 1942, around 70,000 prisoners were forced to walk seventy miles without food or water under brutal conditions. At least 6,000 men died during the forced march. Toward the end of my senior year of high school, hundreds of helicopters flew desperate people out of the American Embassy compound during the fall of Saigon. I remember watching the televised images of sailors pushing helicopters off the decks of Seventh Fleet aircraft carriers into the South China Sea. How I wish Mr. Benevidez would have thrown away the textbook and talked to us instead.

Throughout high school, students were required to attend a never-ending series of school-wide events called "assemblies," held in the gym. These mandatory gatherings were usually for the purpose of forcing students to attend didactic lectures by former heroin addicts who came to the school to warn of the dangers of substance abuse, using the train wreck of their own life experiences to illustrate and prove their thesis. Sometimes, however, there were surprise performances by minor celebrities such as The Village People, who I remember performed their song "YMCA" to a somewhat bewildered audience years before it became a hit. Once we owned cars, my friends and I usually left campus during the assemblies and staged our own gatherings at Earl's Donuts a few blocks away.

One morning, teachers from several classes herded their students into the library and showed them Alain Resnais' 1954 film *Nuit et Brouillard (Night and Fog)*, in the original French, with English subtitles. I remember walking around school afterward in complete silence, stunned by what I'd just seen. I don't think we ever discussed the film in any of my classes. What I do remember is that I was so overwhelmed by what I'd seen that for the next couple of days I raised my hand to cut off my friends whenever they tried to speak to me. The images of piles of naked, emaciated dead bodies being bulldozed into mass graves were beyond words, and for a time everything else seemed trivial and unworthy of discussion. "I don't want to talk," I said. Though it had been presented to me without interpretation or even discussion, Resnais' documentary on the Nazi death camps of the Holocaust and man's inhumanity to man taught me the only real lesson of consequence I learned in high school. Even at the time, it was clear to me that I had learned more in a half hour of watching a film than in three years of sitting in classrooms.

Given my lack of interest in school, it's not surprising that I figured out how to limit my exposure to it. The first time I was absent from high school, I wrote my own excuse and signed it with my mother's name. Since that initial letter was the one the Attendance Office at the school kept on file as an example of my parent's signature, all subsequent absences went unquestioned, though I always wrote the excuses and signed them myself. I took pains to be careful and consistent; even when I really had been ill and my mother wrote my excuse, I copied the letter into my own handwriting and signed her name to it before destroying the original.

I also learned how to gain access to my private student file, where I discovered my IQ score. I didn't have much faith in the test results, since my father, who was a super genius according to the test, was at the same time awkward, asocial, and foolish. I was relieved to see that my own score, while high, fell well short of my father's. In addition to checking my IQ, I also altered the attendance records in my student file from time to time. Once I even changed a grade from a C to a B, just to see if I could get away with it. I really had no reason to change my grades, as I always maintained slightly higher than a B average, even though I did the minimal work possible and often skipped classes. In addition to the mandatory English, History, Government, and Math classes, I selected as electives courses in Art, Co-Educational Cooking, Auto Mechanics, Badminton, Bowling, Creative Writing, and Film Study. I also took Spanish, where in two years of classes I learned how to say, *"Hola, me llamo Gregorio. ¿Qué tal? Gracias. Adiós."* That much I mastered the first year. I don't recall learning anything at all the second year. *Qué coño pérdida de tiempo fueron mis días en la secundaria.*

Gaining access to and altering my school records was amazingly simple. Each semester, students who needed to transfer out of a course during the first two weeks of classes could go to the Counseling Office and wait in line to see their assigned academic advisor, who would review the proposed change and then approve the transfer from one subject or class to another. To facilitate this process, the counseling staff divided all the students into four groups, separated by grade and last name. One counselor dealt with all the students with names starting with A through F, and so on. The records for these students were placed in banker's boxes on a table outside each of the four counselors' offices. As each student entered, he or she told their academic advisor their last name and the advisor would go to the appropriate box and pull the student's cum file so that they could write in the new information. I noted that they used liquid paper to make these corrections.

Instead of waiting half an hour in line to see the counselor, I went to the main office and asked to borrow a little bottle of liquid paper. "I'll just be a couple of minutes," I reassured the secretary. Then I went to the boxes, pulled my file, brushed over my current class and then neatly printed my new class onto the line on the card. After glancing at my file, I returned it to its place in the box. Then I returned the liquid paper to the secretary. The next day I returned with my own bottle of liquid paper and adjusted my grade. In the spring semester I again pulled my file. This time I lowered my days absent the previous semester in order to increase my available vacation days for the new semester. Though I never considered what I was doing to be wrong, I did not share my strategy nor encourage others to similarly undermine the system. I figured that the record belonged to me, and concerned only me, and if I was smart enough to reclaim ownership of it, then that initiative also presented an example of my learning potential that the record might as well reflect.

Because high school was so boring and pointless, I took classes over the summer in auto mechanics at West Valley Occupational Center. I also painted houses and worked after school at various jobs: dish washer, bus boy, parking garage attendant, janitor, and truck driver, delivering desks and filing cabinets for an office furniture company. These early work experiences made me question the validity and ethics of the economic system. I saw how owners and employers overworked and underpaid their workers, as well as treating them as inferiors. I soon realized I was happiest when painting houses as an independent contractor or collecting and recycling aluminum cans on my own. I felt sorry for anyone who worked at McDonalds, Taco Bell, or Jack-in-the-Box. "I don't want to be a cog in the wheel," I said to my friends. I simply couldn't envision a life of mindless, soulless work that only served to concentrate wealth and power in the hands of a self-serving elite.

I was eighteen by the time I finished high school, which meant my mother could legally kick me out of her house, which she promptly did. A few days after graduation, she burst into my bedroom unannounced while I was sleeping and banged a howling vacuum cleaner repeatedly against the leg of the bed frame. Like many of my friends, I had no plans for the future beyond enrolling in classes at the local junior college and continuing to waste my time as I had in high school. I had not taken the SAT, spoken with an academic advisor in high school, nor consulted with my parents about further educational opportunities. No one had expressed much interest in me. No one expected me to succeed. I left home after packing my MG sports car with my surfboard and a plastic trash bag full of clothes.

For months prior to graduation, I had tried to find a friend who would accompany me on one of my ill-conceived adventures. One involved staking a mining claim on public land in the Sierra Nevada mountains and operating a placer mine. The other was more simple but just as intimidating: pick crops with migrant farm workers. Years later, I thought how different my life might have been if I would have known more about the French Foreign Legion. I had always known that I wanted to be a writer, but I had no life experience and thus nothing to say. I figured I needed to have adventures that would provide me with stories I could write about. However, none of my friends expressed much interest in accompanying me. I was on my own.

After my expulsion, I quickly realized that I had exactly two options: talk to a military enlister and get on the next bus to Boot Camp at Fort Confederategeneral, or talk to my father, who I'd barely seen for the past three years. I figured I might as well start with my father, as I really had nothing to lose. So, I drove to Microwave Applications Group, the company he had founded in Chatsworth several years earlier, where I sat across a big desk from him and told him what had occurred. As I talked, I noted that my father now sported an elaborate and ridiculous comb-over with which to hide his baldness. As a teenager he'd had a terrible case of acne that his doctor had treated with radiation. The treatments resulted in early hair loss.

My father understood my mother's capacity for theatrics. He proposed that I live at his house in Northridge while I sorted out my future. Since he was my father, his offer included a list of conditions: I must apply immediately for admission to California State University, Northridge, take a full load of courses, and work afternoons in the microwave test lab at his company. He left me to make calls to the university for information about tests and admission procedures, then took me on a tour of his company, introducing me to some of the employees along the way. I noted that he still walked unnaturally fast. Over the years he'd gained weight and as I followed behind him, his waddling reminded me of a cartoon duck hurrying around a farmyard.

Somehow, the stars snapped into alignment. I learned that I could still take the SAT college admissions test, though the final testing date prior to the fall semester was less than a week away. That same afternoon, I drove to the university, where I signed up for the test and paid the fees. The following Saturday morning, I took a seat in a sterile classroom in Sierra Hall along with a dozen other late test takers and waited for the proctor to signal that we could begin the exam. Aside from questions requiring basic arithmetic, I left the rest of the math section blank. I had researched the Scholastic Achievement Test briefly and learned that unanswered questions somehow scored higher than wrong answers. Though the rest of the test seemed easy enough—questions designed to measure reading comprehension and vocabulary—I nevertheless left the classroom feeling as though I had little chance of success.

A few weeks later, I received a letter with my test score. Apparently, my strong performance on the verbal section of the test produced a combined score high enough to gain admission to the university in spite of my near complete lack of knowledge of mathematics. After I received the test scores, I studied the university catalog and listed all the majors that I could pursue without taking math. From that list I chose a double major in English and history, then mailed in my application to the university. A couple weeks later, I received a letter of acceptance.

After years dodging flying knives in my mother's three ring circus, living with my father, his wife, and her young daughter in a house filled with imposing, dark furniture seemed surreal and otherworldly. Heavy drawn curtains covered the windows and the dark interior seemed deathly quiet. Standing in the kitchen, I could hear the faux antique grandfather clock ticking in the next room. I named the house "The Mausoleum." The inhabitants ate meals in silence, and conversed in muted tones or whispers, if at all. Even the cat skittered silently away whenever I appeared. After I'd parked my surfboard in the garage next to Paula's Volvo and my father's BMW, my father told me I could sleep in the den, where I crashed for a year on a fold out couch. After a few weeks, I gave up unfolding and folding the bed and simply stretched out on the sofa, which was more comfortable anyway.

Since I had to fill out a massive and detailed application for a government security clearance, which took months to process, investigate, and issue before I could work in the restricted test lab at Microwave Applications Group, my father had told me I could enjoy what was left of the summer and start work and classes at the same time when the semester began in September. Meanwhile, he put me to work painting the outside of his house and gave me a copy of Ayn Rand's novel *Atlas Shrugged* to read. Most days I drove to the beach to surf with friends and painted in the evening when it was cooler. As for Ayn Rand, though I dutifully read the book, I was already immune to that virus. As the summer advanced, even surfing seemed bittersweet, for I knew that soon my life would change forever.

My first class at the university met at 7:00 am on Mondays, Wednesdays, and Fridays. The professor, a revisionist historian, spoke in a tedious monotone. As an incoming freshman, I'd had last pick during registration and barely managed to find five available classes that met mornings and didn't have prerequisites. Despite the early hour and the uninspired delivery, my introductory U.S. history course nonetheless provided the spark that flamed my interest in higher education. The first thing the professor told us was that much of what we'd been taught about the history of our country in school was inaccurate or untrue. He spent the next several months systematically debunking the propaganda we'd been force fed in school. I remember thinking to myself after class one day that, for the first time in my life, someone in a position of authority had entrusted me with the truth. Grateful and relieved, I resolved to sharpen my tools and get to work.

A bearded graduate teaching assistant only a few years older than his students taught my Freshman Composition class. He assigned essays based on rhetorical modes. In my first paper, I compared and contrasted the challenges British forces faced during the American Revolutionary War with those faced by American forces during the recently ended Vietnam Conflict. I was pleased when my professor returned the paper with the comment, "You write well for a freshman." Near the end of the semester, I went with another student from the class to talk with our professor in his office in Sierra Tower. He seemed happy to converse with us and eagerly shared his own struggles in graduate school. I remember he told us how one of his professors viewed all literature through the lens of Freudian psychology. "He reduces everything to phallic symbols and vaginas with teeth," he said. "Sometimes I think I'm going to have a nervous breakdown."

I also took a class in logic my freshman year. The instructor, yet another young, bearded man, wore his hair in a long ponytail that hung to the middle of his back. Because he chain-smoked during his lectures, he kept the windows in the room open wide and encouraged students sensitive to the smoke to sit by them. "I'm sorry," he told us the first day, "but without the cigarettes, I can't teach. I'm just too nervous." Though he gave students the opportunity to change classes, I can't remember anyone leaving. An excellent teacher—funny, engaging, and challenging—he gave the subject depth and connected it to real life. He made me aware of the various ways ordinary people, politicians, and corporations use language to deceive, sell, and manipulate. The last week of class he showed up to class with short hair and no beard. I could hardly recognize him. "I just passed the bar exam," he explained.

During this time, I worked four hours each afternoon in the microwave test lab at Microwave Applications Group (MAG). Many of the engineers there seemed as socially awkward and creepy as my mother had always insisted they were. One of them, a squat, bald man in charge of fabrication and production, enjoyed dazzling the poorly educated assemblers who worked for him with his elevated diction. I sometimes caught him reading a dictionary at his desk, which he would quickly conceal in the drawer whenever someone entered his office. Like many of the people surrounding my father at the time, the production manager had an unsavory, reptilian aspect that I found disturbing. Once he told me that he liked to drive by the high school and ogle the young girls on his way home for lunch. "I like to check out the coming attractions," he explained, staring at me intently. I felt sorry for his son, an unpopular kid I knew from junior high and high school.

My first weeks of work, several employees at the company told me how much I resembled my father. I suppose they were just expressing a fact or registering their initial impression. Nevertheless, the likeness they noted wasn't something I wanted to acknowledge. In my mind I wasn't anything like my father and I didn't want others to falsely assume there was a close connection between us, no matter what I looked like. It always disturbed me as well that throughout my life people had trouble distinguishing my speaking voice from my father's. Over the phone, we sounded identical, so close in fact that even my wife had trouble knowing who was on the line when my father called and I wasn't home. Of course, my father's verbal mannerisms were so bizarre that he gave himself away almost immediately.

At first, I worked in various capacities as a general helper in the production area or machine shop, or else ran errands in the company van. When I finally received my security clearance, I began work in the microwave lab, where I ran a series of quality assurance and military specification tests on units to be shipped to Westinghouse or other vendors assembling finished radars for the Navy or Air Force. Following written regulations, we locked the doors to the lab during tests in order to ensure that Russian spies grinding ceramics to spec in the machine shop or driving the taco wagon that visited the parking lot outside twice a day didn't wander inside and gain access to the secret frequencies known by tens of thousands of workers and military personnel around the country. Two teenaged technicians performed the tests, which a group of well-paid ex–Air Force and ex-Navy officers observed and monitored. In truth, these consultants would sit on stools and talk for hours about football games and vacations, their hands folded across their beer bellies. I never once saw them look at the data, the test set-up, or even check the frequency or power level. I remember signing my name to the cover sheets of thick stacks of test certifications for phase shifters and other parts that would go into B-1 bombers or AWACs radar arrays.

One of the tests involved bolting a large AWACs phase-shifter to microwave couplers and running high amounts of power through it for forty minutes. On loan from Westinghouse, the high-voltage power supply looked like something out of Fritz Lang's *Metropolis*. A massive gray unit the size of a small elephant, it had dozens of buttons and dials, none of which made any sense to me. When running, the machine generated a deafening level of noise. My job was to sit on a stool near the unit being tested and make sure it didn't begin to smoke, melt, or burst into flames. In such an event, I needed to immediately shut down the power supply by hitting the red panic button. I usually read books for my literature courses during the tests. Does my memory fail me, or did I drape a lead blanket over myself as I pondered works by Shakespeare, Milton, and John Donne?

At Christmas, I ate a Cornish game hen my father's wife had prepared. It was one of two meals she knew how to cook. Since I'd broken up with my high school girlfriend a few months earlier and lost contact with most of my high school friends, I had nowhere else to go. I avoided my mother, who I'd not quite forgiven. Besides, I was content to spend some time alone. Though my Spartan lifestyle sucked eggs, I could see myself evolving. After dinner, my father opened another bottle of wine and poured us each a glass. "How about a game of chess?" he offered. It was the first and last game I ever played with him.

Throughout my childhood, my father maintained a near mythical reputation as an expert though occasional player. He'd played chess competitively in high school, then against fellow graduate students in Syracuse. Later he played against family friends and visiting engineers. In all that time I'd never seen him lose. I wondered why he would suddenly insist on playing against me. Aside from a basic knowledge of how the pieces moved on the board, I knew nothing about chess, as I'd always preferred more active sports.

Because my father never did anything without calculation, I suspected he was toying with me to demonstrate his intellectual superiority. So I determined to concentrate fully and try to give him a good game. After the second bottle of wine, I was surprised to find myself holding a queen, rook, knight, and two pawns, while my father had only two pawns and his king left. Still, he wouldn't give up. In the end I had trouble trapping his king and closing him out. Suddenly, my father told me the game had ended in a draw and started putting the pieces away. I laughed at him and asked how. He explained that the threefold repetition rule states that if a position arises three times in a game, either player can claim a draw during that position. At the time I thought he was making up new rules to keep from losing. "I didn't know about that rule," I said, "but it doesn't matter because we both know who won."

My co-worker in the lab was a compact and athletic looking young man with long blond hair and a mustache. A year older than me, he had been the senior class president at Chatsworth High School the year prior to my graduating class. Though he never formally studied engineering nor held any degree or certification beyond a high school diploma, he was an eccentric, self-taught engineer who became an expert in the field of microwave design. He later ran a successful consulting business. According to my father, who many years later hired him to consult on several projects, Ken proved to be a capable and highly professional problem-solver.

Though Ken had been a top student, class president, and the captain of the Chatsworth High School Cross Country running team, I also knew him to be a problem drinker. His religious fanatic parents had raised him in a self-realized hell of guilt, denial, and restriction. Ken mocked their intolerance constantly. Among his many other talents, he had a comedian's sense of timing, body language, and understatement. Ken was a naturally gifted storyteller. Along with poet Richard Martin and poet and performance artist Bob Flanagan, I remember him, at that stage of his life, as one of the funniest people I had ever met.

During our shared time working in the lab, Ken and I spent many hours discussing matters of faith, belief, ethics, and morality. An atheist studying literature, history, and philosophy and a fundamentalist Christian testing the limits of his independence from his parents' dogmatic and inflexible worldview, our opinions and beliefs rarely meshed. Nevertheless, in spite his codified beliefs, Ken had a supple mind and a finely tuned sense of irony at that time, and we both enjoyed our mental sparring.

One afternoon, our supervisor asked us to go to his house in Chatsworth to help move a piece of heavy furniture. While we were waiting, Ken sat down at a piano in the living room and slowly and carefully placed his hands on the keyboard, as though he were testing the burner on a hot stove. At first, I thought he was going to bang out "Chopsticks" or "Twinkle-Twinkle Little Star," but instead he leaned into a long section of a difficult piano concerto, playing from memory with the kind of self-assurance and flair only present in professional musicians. When he'd finished, he stood up and laughed like Tom Hulce's Mozart in the film *Amadeus*.

From the time he was a small child, Ken's parents had forced him to study and practice the piano, and for several years he had competed in junior piano competitions around the country. "I quit playing when I left home," he told me, getting into his royal blue Chevy Chevette 396 Super Sport. He fired up the engine and made the glass packs growl. "I never really liked that shit, anyway." Then he pushed an Electric Light Orchestra tape into the eight-track player on the dashboard, chirped the fat tires, and drove us back to work.

I worked afternoons at my father's company for a year and a half. Donna, who I'd met in a freshman religious studies class and had begun dating late in the spring semester, remembers how I complained about the job, both because of the boredom and absurdity of it, but also because I was ethically and philosophically opposed to the work that was being done there. I didn't approve of the military-industrial complex and hated being even the tiniest part of it.

A speech communications major, Donna was a friendly girl with a thick mane of long brown hair who sometimes talked to me for a couple minutes before the professor arrived to begin class. One day, she asked me if I could do her a favor and meet her near the benches outside of Sierra Hall after we'd both finished our morning classes. She told me that some creepy older guy had been approaching her and making her uncomfortable as she walked across campus on her way to her car. She wondered if my presence might help deter him in the future. When I arrived, I found Donna sitting on one of the concrete benches. We sat together for an hour and talked. Then I walked her to her car. Though no creepy guy ever showed up, we did get to know each other better.

When we realized that we were also both enrolled in the same journalism class, which met just prior to our religions in America class, we began walking across campus together from one classroom to the next. As the spring weather improved, one day I suggested we ditch the religion class. Instead, we spent the hour lounging in the sun on the grassy hill next to Sierra Tower. I think it may have been the first time in her life that Donna ever ditched a class in school.

A couple weeks later, we went out on our first date. I had planned to take her to a restaurant in Malibu, but the engine in my dependably unreliable English sports car quit running in Topanga Canyon and I barely managed to coast the car down the winding road to within several hundred yards of Pacific Coast Highway. From a gas station at the intersection, I called my sister for a ride and she showed up an hour later, my mother riding shotgun. After dropping them off in Sepulveda, I borrowed my sister's car and took Donna for a late dinner at an all-night coffee shop on the way back to her parent's house in La Crescenta. From the beginning, it was clear to me that Donna was a good sport. No doubt it was equally clear to her that life with me would be an unpredictable adventure.

To everyone's relief, I moved out of my father's house after my freshman year, and for a short time shared a small rental house with my friend Greg. That arrangement quickly became unsustainable, as Greg was an impossibly bad roommate. One night, he stormed into my bedroom without knocking and accused me of wearing and stretching out one of his goofy polyester button-up shirts. As he talked, he pushed his face closer and closer to mine until I finally pinned him by the neck to the wall and told him to back off.

At that point, my mother, who claimed to be helping my sister with her tuition at Mount Saint Mary's College, called my father and told him that he should at least help me with my rent while I was an undergraduate. So, my father signed the rental agreement for an apartment in Chatsworth in the same building where my co-worker Ken lived. Even with my part-time job, I could barely afford to eat and buy gas to drive to school and work. I didn't have a phone. I remember eating mostly pancakes, *huevos rancheros,* boxed macaroni and cheese, and fresh bread with peanut butter or honey from the supermarket bakery.

The following year, I told my father that I needed more time to concentrate on my studies. Consequently, I didn't want to continue working part-time at his company. He agreed to continue paying my rent but offered only a tiny stipend in addition. Though a millionaire owner of an engineering and manufacturing company with seventy employees, he'd never been generous with his children. I determined I'd look for work painting houses during the summers, when I didn't have classes, and save money to last throughout the school year.

After I quit working at MAG, Donna and I continued to socialize with Ken and his girlfriend Pam, who would soon become his wife. Eventually, we drifted apart. After their wedding and the birth of the first of their many children, they moved to Northern California. We visited them years later, when they lived on a large plot of land with horses and other animals and a big house near Placerville. After a while, Ken began to talk seriously about religion and then bitterly complained that the public schools were teaching devil worship to his children in the form of Native American creation myths.

Like many adult survivors of rigid and abusive parents, he'd become just what he'd rebelled against when I knew him as a teenager. A few years later, my father told me that Ken had died of cancer in his early fifties. I remembered the many times I'd seen him leading the pack of cross-country team runners along the streets of Chatsworth and how the team had trained on the steep, winding canyon roads around Bell and Box canyons, along property that bordered the toxic Santa Susana Field Laboratory.

In school, I made the Dean's List every semester after my freshman year. During our sophomore year, Donna's cousin Kathy came to study for a year at CSUN. The two of them got an apartment on Reseda Boulevard, where I spent much of my time and ate many of my meals. Kathy had grown up in France, where her father taught in a private college, so she was a native speaker of both English and French. Donna had lived with her cousin's family for a year and attended the college there between high school and university, so she also spoke French fluently. Their constant conversations in French soon persuaded me to begin studying the language as well. Unlike my experience in high school Spanish classes, my university French classes were completely immersive. The class met five times per week, and from the very first day, the professor, skilled at pantomime and chain-smoking in class, spoke only French.

Studying French was yet another revelation for me. I loved how empowering it felt to speak another language. My studies expanded my mind in important ways and gave me new approaches to understanding linguistics. French quickly became a passion for me and after I completed my first year of study, I continued taking two courses each semester until graduation.

Because my high school education had been so poor, I had a lot of catching up to do. I remember hearing other English literature students talk about Wordsworth, Keats, and Shelly before class. I had no idea who these people were, though I correctly imagined they were writers. My experience with poetry was nearly nonexistent at that time. I'd studied and written some haiku poems in elementary school and read "The Raven" by Edgar Poe and a prose version of *The Iliad* in junior high. In high school, my English teachers never presented poetry to their classes.

At the same time, I'd grown up listening to lyrics by Bob Dylan, Paul Simon, Leonard Cohen, John Lennon and Paul McCartney, Pete Townshend, Jim Morrison, Joni Mitchell, Neil Young, Mick Jagger and Keith Richards, and Jackson Browne, which inspired me to compose, during my senior year in high school and first year of university, a fat notebook full of words without music that I mistook for poems. Though I didn't share these first efforts at poetry, my eventual exposure to the work of historical and contemporary poets insured the rapid destruction of my collection of doggerel.

Of the Romantic poets I studied in my university survey course, I liked Coleridge and William Blake best. In other courses, I remember connecting with the poems of Thomas Hardy and D. H. Lawrence. However, at that time in my life, perhaps the most impactful work I read was Matthew Arnold's poem "The Buried Life." For some reason, I hadn't yet figured out that I wasn't the only person in the world with a rich and sometimes unsettling interior life. The poem gave me a sense of connection that I'd lacked previously. Though I struggled a bit with that first English literature course, I managed to bring my grade up to a "B" by writing an extra credit research paper on Coleridge's poem "Christabel."

Despite my lack of background, I became a serious and dedicated student. I read constantly. If a professor mentioned a book in class, I noted the author and title, then went to the library and read it. I always began work on my term papers soon after they were assigned. Instead of cramming for tests, I took notes throughout the semester and read secondary source materials. Though my professors never discussed how to make sense of the disparate facts and information they presented, I tried to put what I had studied and learned into a larger context, to make connections and draw conclusions.

After adding French to my studies, I dropped my dual major in history, changing it to a minor instead, which freed up extra time for additional French classes. I took the required mix of English courses designed around historical periods in English and American literature, writing and rhetoric, critical theory, linguistics, and courses devoted to the work of a single, major author. In retrospect, the required course of study for my major in English made no sense. It was at once overly broad and too specific, and the emphasis on randomly selected survey courses made it difficult to make connections that would allow students to view literature holistically. If I had not spent the years after graduation filling in the holes in my reading of major texts and adding books from world literature before returning to graduate school, I would not have had sufficient background in literature nor the critical perspective to write intelligently about it.

The summer between our sophomore and junior years, Donna and her cousin traveled together to France for six weeks. I had no money for trips and instead worked as a house painter. Though it was hot, exhausting, repetitive work, I liked being self-employed. Working "under the table," I made good money and didn't pay taxes. Most of my earnings I set aside to supplement my income over the coming school year. When Donna came back from France, she came to my apartment wearing a pretty yellow dress with a floral pattern. I was so glad to see her that I'll always remember her in that French dress.

My first house painting partner was my high school friend and ex-roommate Greg. In spite of our problems as roommates, neither of us harbored any lasting bad feelings. By now he had begun studying business administration at CSU Northridge and he also needed to earn money to support himself during the academic year. We called our business "On the Wall House Painting." Though we were non-union painters without a contractor's license, outlets for the best professional paints, anxious for our repeat business, offered us deep professional discounts. As college students who worked cheap, and had excellent prior references, we had no trouble arranging jobs in advance. Typically, we lined up a whole summer's worth of painting jobs by word of mouth referrals and by canvassing residential neighborhoods.

Since our rates were a third of what a painting contractor would charge, our customers were always satisfied. Normally we required half the money for a job up front, in order to cover the cost of buying our materials. Greg was in charge of accounting. He carried around a thick wad of cash in his pocket, which he counted each day. One morning he crashed his car into a car parked on the side of the road. He'd been counting the wad of cash while driving. Ironically, a homeless person was sleeping in the car at the time. I don't know what arrangements Greg made with the other motorist, but I'm sure he must have sacrificed a large portion of his share of the profits that summer.

Donna and I spent nearly all of our free time together. We enjoyed each other's company and never argued. At some point we decided to plan an extended trip together in Europe after graduation. We opened a bank account in my name that we called "the E fund" and added small amounts to it whenever we could. Donna saved some of the money she made working part time and summer jobs at a veterinary clinic, Busch Gardens, and a small company that made fancy cakes for restaurants. Each summer I also deposited over a thousand dollars I'd made painting houses into the "E fund."

Though we never had much money for entertainment, Donna owned a dependable car, which meant we could take long drives. Back then, we both enjoyed cruising down the highway. We loved the sense of adventure, and for us the idea of the journey was more important than the destination. Since we had no budget for overnight lodgings, we limited ourselves to how far we could drive in a single day. Sometimes we got up early and drove through the desert to Mammoth Lakes, a ski resort on the east side of the Sierra Nevada mountains, a six-hour drive from where we lived. When we arrived, we'd stretch our legs, have something to eat, then turn around and drive back home. Eventually these drives evolved into backpacking trips, where we camped in the mountains for several days. We bought some used equipment for a few dollars at garage sales, and invested in a light two-person tent. It was a way to extend our adventures without adding much expense. The summer between our junior and senior years we hiked up Duck Pass and made a big circle in the high mountains above and behind the town of Mammoth Lakes. We wore paratrooper pants we bought from the Army surplus store in Reseda and ate peanut butter and freeze-dried meals.

During our junior year, Donna and I, along with another student in the Foreign Languages Department, went to UCLA to see French singer Georges Moustaki perform a concert at Pauley Pavilion. Donna knew his music from the year she had spent in France and we already owned a couple of his albums. As the French language had become something we shared and which helped bind us together, Moustaki's intimate folk music felt like our own private sound track. The small francophone community in Los Angeles centered largely around the Alliance Française and a bookstore in Westwood that sold French books at insanely inflated prices, mainly for use by students at the many colleges and universities in the area. The Moustaki concert represented a rare opportunity for us to experience a French cultural event.

While Donna and I knew each other throughout our college years, our relationship was constantly evolving, which is another way of saying that we experienced a number of breakups. I instigated all of these emotional cataclysms, as I was restless, uncertain of the future, and unwilling to commit myself to a lifelong relationship at such a young age. Halfway through our senior year, I told Donna that the limits of our relationship were too confining and I needed room to grow. I didn't want to be unfaithful or disloyal, yet I wasn't ready to be married at the age of twenty-two. Though she was devastated, we remained friends. At the time we were all but living together and our lives were already deeply intertwined: shared friends, shared books and records, shared interests, plans and life goals. For years we'd been planning to travel together in France after graduation, and perhaps even live there a while if we could find work. Now I'd blown up all those dreams and I really didn't even know why, as we were soulmates who in spite of everything were still growing up together. Since Donna had generously shared everything she possessed with me, cooked meals when I was hungry and broke, and paid for me when we went out, I gave her half the money in the E Fund, though the better part of it had come from my house painting work.

In addition to my English and French classes, during my senior year I also studied Japanese history and tutored students in writing, both in classrooms and in the university's writing lab. In the lab I met some of the graduate teaching assistants and began to participate in more outside activities. I wrote poems and went to a few poetry readings, both on campus and at local bookstores. I read works by Jack Kerouac, Alan Ginsberg, Gregory Corso, Gary Snyder, and other writers and poets of the Beat Generation. I pondered an anthology of contemporary American poets and hung out more with students who were studying literature. I thought about going to Japan to teach English.

My senior year I also worked on the university literary magazine *Angel's Flight.* I had published one of my poems in the magazine the previous year and a friend from class invited me to participate on the editorial staff of the magazine. There I met a graduate student named Rachel Sherwood, who was already an accomplished poet. She had studied at a university in Wales and possessed a weariness of the world that seemed impossible in someone so young. A precocious worldliness and a mysterious sense of impending doom informed her work. The force of her intellect and her opinions, the surety of her tastes, the way she wore scarves and tucked her jeans into her boots, and the aggressive and playful manner in which she tossed her hair at once attracted and intimidated me. I remember that her apartment, even her messy car, impressed me with their chic aura of chaos. Because she burned so brightly, she was never indifferent: she either loved something or someone or she hated it, him, or her. She listened to punk rock and opera. She hated her father, who she told me worked for the CIA and had facilitated unspeakable horrors in Vietnam.

Immediately after graduation, I threw myself into house painting jobs so I would have enough money to fund my extended travels abroad. Two weeks before my scheduled departure, I went backpacking in a place called Lost Canyon in the mountains behind Sawtooth Pass in Mineral King over the July 4 weekend. When I returned from my four days in the wilderness, I learned that Rachel had been killed by a drunk driver whose car had crashed head-on into her car. I don't remember who told me, only that the news came via a phone call. At that moment the whole world stopped making sense. I attended the memorial service in a complete daze. There was really nothing meaningful anyone could say to lessen the hurt. I carried that sadness and sense of loss with me when I left for France a week later.

Donna had gone to France as well, though weeks earlier, on a different flight, and with different plans and friends. Unexpectedly, we met up again in Paris, where we both stayed for a while in student housing on rue de Vaugirard across from the Jardin du Luxembourg. Donna took a photograph of me sitting on a green wooden bench in the park, my hands behind my head, my legs spread out straight in front of me. I was overwhelmed, yet at the same time relieved to be in Paris. One of our mutual friends from the university, a French major named Rose, had already been living in Paris for two months, and she had given both of us the tip about the cheap lodgings she had found.

I remember a small group of us cooked and ate meals together at the pension, went to museums, shopped for books, and ate crêpes, ham sandwiches, and *pommes frites* on the street. Since I was planning to write the Great American Novel while I was there, at one point I went off to look for a portable typewriter to buy. I also found a shop that sold men's hats, where I bought myself a *beret Basque*. Donna and her last college roommate had been traveling together in Europe and by this time their relationship had come unglued to the point where they could hardly be together in the same room. Some of us decided to go on the train, along with some Australian students we'd met, to see the cathedral at Chartres. Donna and I spent the night together there in a dingy hotel near a canal.

Donna told me she was returning to the U.S. in less than three weeks. I had originally planned to travel alone, then meet up with a friend in southern France, where I'd arranged to rent a tiny house in Fréjus. Since I'd just learned that my friend had decided at the last minute not to come to France, and instead had taken a job as a technical writer, Donna and I decided to spend the next couple of weeks traveling together. We went to Strasbourg and stayed with Donna's friend Anne's family. Next, we went to visit other friends she had in Switzerland. Then we traveled on the night train all the way to Rome.

In Rome, we suffered from the August heat. I remember walking around the ruins of the ancient Roman Forum under the midday sun, then buying multiple cans of ice cold Coca-Cola from a street vendor and drinking them on the sidewalk. We stayed at a cheap pension near the train station. One night we sat beside the window of our room and watched a man eating alone on the outdoor patio of the restaurant across the street. There was no one with him and no one at any of the nearby tables, yet he talked and gestured for hours during his meal. I was reading plays by Ionesco at the time and I recall thinking the diner's performance was one of the strangest things I'd ever seen. Now, of course, with cell phones and headsets we wouldn't think twice about seeing someone sitting alone having an animated conversation, but in those days, it was truly strange.

Before we got on the train to return to France, we bought cheese and tomato sandwiches and pizza to take with us on the seventeen-hour trip to Carcassonne. On the train we met a French man who was traveling home from Greece, where the sailboat he'd built by hand had burned to the water while he was ashore. He hadn't slept or showered in days. We shared some of our lunch with him. In the evening, we crossed the border and shared a compartment with some young men returning to their French military service from leave and a young Spanish philosophy instructor, who orchestrated the conversation in what seemed to us shockingly informal French.

By the time we arrived in Carcassonne at 3:00 in the morning, I had the cold sweats and was feeling very ill. We got off the train and I went into the station bathroom and vomited. Then I lay down on the grass outside the station, too sick to move. Donna carried our backpacks, one at a time, a long distance up the hill to a youth hostel in the old town. We both took a shower, but when they told us we couldn't sleep there during the day, Donna went off to look for a hotel back in the lower part of the city. Somehow we made it to the hotel, where I stayed in bed ill for three days, unable to eat and too weak to move. The owners brought me tea and toast on a tray. We left Carcassonne when I was well enough to travel.

We took a train to the Côte d'Azur, where striking railway workers stranded us in Toulon. Each day we went to the beach and swam in the ocean. At night mosquitos that came through the open window of our cheap hotel room kept us awake. When the strike finally ended, we returned to Paris, where Donna caught a flight home, while I met up with Rose. The two of us traveled together through other parts of France for much of September, until she left for her job as an au pair in Germany.

We were all in flux in those days, living a romantic, nomadic existence where nothing lasted more than a few hours, days, weeks, or months. We shared meals and wine with complete strangers. We sat on the floor in train stations, leaning against our luggage. Everywhere we went, we saw young people dressed in shorts and sandals, carrying backpacks. Together we traveled, trusting in our youth and our luck. We gave ourselves over to the moment, planting memories to harvest in the future, in times of boredom, routine, deprivation, and need.

In Fréjus, I lived alone in a tiny cottage set in a garden behind my landlord's house. It was a long walk to town and to the market, and an even longer walk to the ocean. I bought and read novels by Zola, Balzac, Stendhal, Proust, and Flaubert. I discovered the prose poem in work of Rimbaud and Baudelaire, and celebrated the absurd in Ionesco, Camus, and Sartre. I marveled at Micheaux's tiny horse. I also read the novels of Dostoevsky in French translations. I wrote long letters in French, which I mailed to Donna in California. I wrote an amateurish novel about a house painter struggling to become an abstract expressionist painter, and a series of poems based on freak show performers in a circus. I learned to speak French.

Because I was by myself, in a place where no one understood any other language, I made good progress. After weeks of living alone and in isolation, I craved human contact and sought it out everywhere. I conversed with my landlady, who repaired and built mattresses in an open-air shed in her garden. I talked to the postman and the shopkeepers in town. I asked questions and started conversations with bartenders, waiters, and strangers in the cafe. The following month, I rented an apartment in Juan-les-Pins on the coast near Antibes. By the time I returned to Paris in December, I was eager to talk to people my own age, and I remember having long conversations with the Muslim engineering students from Indonesia who were my roommates in the pension.

In Paris, I went back to the Jeu de Paume to look at Monet's haystack and cathedral series. I stared at paintings through the windows of galleries. I boxed up my French books and sent them book rate to my mother's house in California. I talked about writing with some students selling their literary magazine on the Boulevard Saint-Germain. I drank Guinness and flirted with a pretty French bartender in an Irish pub off the rue des Écoles.

Eventually, I took the ferry to England and the train to London. The first person I spoke to there was an old man dressed in a shabby but clean suit. With great dignity, and what seemed to me to be a distinct sense of entitlement, he asked me to buy him a cup of tea. I agreed and he took me to his favorite shop, where he told me about his experiences in the war. Somehow it took him a good forty minutes to drink his little cup of tea. When he finally finished, he set the spoon back on the saucer, and stood up. "Well, then," he said, "goodbye." I wandered around London for a week, where I explored the British Museum and the National Gallery. I bought a facsimile copy of William Blake's *Songs of Innocence and of Experience* in a big bookstore, along with a Penguin edition of selected poems by Charles Bukowski and Harold Norse. It was early December and the weather had turned cold. I considered going back to Paris, but instead bought a one-way ticket to California.

It's a Wonder (I Can Think at All)

Part 2: Literary Apprenticeship

> "Hear, hear," someone said, as he started to run toward the open window, "you can't do that." But by then he was already soaring upward, above the rooftops and over the towers and halls below.
> —"Escape from the Academy" from *Carnival Aptitude*

THE NEXT COUPLE of years passed in a blur of experiences. I entered a graduate program in French, got a job tutoring writing at the university, and painted houses. For a while I lived with other students in a rented room in a house in Granada Hills owned by a science fiction writer named John, who had a weak heart and hair nearly down to his waist, with a beard to match. I traded my rent for labor and painted the inside and outside of the house, which was in a deplorable state of disrepair. I enlisted a student named Patrick, one of the other roommates in the house, as a helper, and together we cut grass, trimmed trees and bushes, removed beer can tab curtains, repaired windows so they could again be opened, painted, and scrubbed away fifteen years of collected filth and grease splashed nightly from John's deep fryer in the kitchen.

Our landlord reacted like an exposed cockroach when someone unexpectedly switches the lights on in the kitchen in the middle of the night. A prolific but unskilled science fiction writer who had published two pulpy paperback novels with rocket ships on the covers, he worked part time as a secretary for a commercially successful science fiction writer. Though he could be inventive and entertaining in person, John was also delusional.

The bedroom I rented shared a wall with John's room, or rather with the closet of his bedroom, a space he had converted to serve as a bed for his seven year old daughter on weekends, when he had custody of her. His wife, Carmella, would call the house at all hours, anytime during the week. She was always rude to whoever answered the phone. Though divorced, John seemed terrified of her, and did his best to calm her down whenever she called. When we asked him why he put up with her abuse, he told us her father and family were in the mafia and he'd never see his daughter again if he showed Carmella any disrespect.

Strangely, this fear of mafia hit men did not keep John from physically punishing little Nicole. Most Saturday mornings I woke up to an absurdist drama in which a child torments and manipulates her father, and the father in turn threatens the child. The taunts and warnings escalate, in a kind of choreographed sequence, until the father finally makes good on his promise to "get the belt." After receiving a severe beating, the child wails for ten minutes, followed by fifteen minutes of whimpering in her closet. Finally the father comes back to say he's sorry and tell her how much he loves her.

Years later I heard from one of the other roommates, a social worker who directed a juvenile halfway house and worked for the municipal court, that Nicky, by then a teenager, had ended up in the court system as a teenage prostitute. John continued to collaborate as an editor of science fiction anthologies and to grind out his sociopathic dystopian novels. I remember how he'd gauge his own self worth by the number of pages he'd been able to write that day. Sometimes in the evening, he'd rub his hands together as he sat in his ratty recliner in the living room and pulled on his long beard. "Fourteen pages," he'd announce. On a bad day, he'd stand hunched over his electric fryer stirring his potatoes. "Three pages." A recent Internet search reveals that at some point John moved east and reinvented himself as a successful writer, scholar, and publisher. The incongruities inherent in his online biography and the associated links demonstrate how easy it is to manipulate open knowledge systems in order to create a fictional online persona.

During the time I lived in Granada Hills, I studied modern French novelists, including Marcel Proust, André Gide, François Mauriac, Samuel Beckett, Alain Robbe-Grillet, Nathalie Saurraute, and Michel Butor, among others. I surveyed the history of French theater and examined the theory of comedy. I also discovered Abraham H. Maslow's *Toward a Psychology of Being*, which had a profound impact on me, as it gave me permission to "self-actualize," which is to say to nurture and accept my creativity.

I also began publishing my first poems in literary magazines, including the newly re-named university literary magazine *The Northridge Review*, which published some of my circus-themed poems. A selection of those poems won that year's Academy of American Poets student writing prize at the university, for which I received a cash award of a hundred dollars. As a challenge to myself and a possible future literary hoax, I wrote 900 lines of rhyming verse in the manner and style of Samuel Taylor Coleridge. These verses extended, but still left incomplete, "Christabel," the English Romantic poet's unfinished gothic masterpiece. I also founded a new literary magazine called *Amputated Fingers*, which I funded through house painting. I advertised a call for submissions in *Beyond Baroque* magazine, an avant-garde poetry magazine with a national reach. Within a week, submissions began to overwhelm my post office box. Through these submissions I first made contact with several writers who would later become mainstays of *Asylum* magazine, among them Eric Basso, whose work would also figure prominently in the list of books I would eventually publish.

Over the next three months, I chose the work I liked best and asked a few poets I admired for work to publish. Among them was a young Los Angeles poet named Kate Braverman, who had recently published a book of poems and a novel called *Lithium for Media* with Harper Collins. Younger poets in Los Angeles admired Braverman for her work's combination of raw emotion and lyricism. She was the Patty Smith of Silver Lake. When I told her how I had chosen the name

Amputated Fingers from a line in one of her poems, she sent me two new poems for the magazine.

Once I had selected work for my magazine, I learned how to set type for offset printing on the Compugraphic phototypesetting equipment at the NewComp Graphics Center at Beyond Baroque Foundation in Venice. At this time a lot of local poets, writers, literary editors and publishers hung out at Beyond Baroque Foundation, which was rather appropriately located in the old Venice Jail building. There I encountered Jack Skelly, Dennis Cooper, and Bob Flannagan, among other young poets who, along with David Trinidad, formed the vanguard of the Los Angeles poetry scene at that time. Though all of these poets were under thirty, they were a good deal more sophisticated, accomplished, self-assured, and ironic than me. At twenty-three and just out of college, I was out of my depth—enthusiastic, earnest, and completely clueless. I remember I once composed a suite of short poems called "The Existential World of Jacques Cousteau," which I typeset and laid out as a poetry broadside, with one of my early linocut prints as an illustration. When I gave my broadside to several poets I knew at Beyond Baroque, Dennis Cooper pointed out that I had misspelled Jacques in the title. "I think it's J-a-c-q," he said. Though not prone to blushing, I remember feeling a hot wave rush up from my toes all the way to my face. The remaining copies of the broadsides went into the dumpster outside my apartment.

I'd always been a poor speller. Whenever I wrote a paper for my classes in college, I routinely looked up every word with more than two syllables. Gradually, over four years, I memorized the correct spellings of common words. With practice and frequent reference to the dictionary, my spelling improved, though even today I find myself mystified by some of the words spell checkers flag as incorrect. "How do you spell stapler?" I asked Donna a few minutes ago. I can't imagine what possessed me to become an editor of literary magazines and books. Certainly, I worked very hard at proofreading.

Around this time, David Trinidad approached me with the idea of publishing a book of poems by Rachel Sherwood. He told me he wanted to form a press in her honor and begin by publishing her work. He asked if I'd co-publish the first book. Though I contributed half the money for the book, ultimately David did all of the design and production work. He had been a very close friend of Rachel. Also, he had been badly injured as a passenger in her car the night of her fatal accident. Nearly a year later, he was still recovering from his physical and psychic injuries. The book was something he needed to do for his recovery.

As the semester came to an end, I advertised myself as a house painter on the university job listings. One day a lawyer with a huge house in the Encino hills called me about a job. I drove my van up to his fenced property and gave him an insanely high bid, which he accepted on the spot. Pat was my partner in the house painting business that summer. We began work on the job as soon as we'd completed our final exams.

The owner had the strange distinction of having the same first and last name. He was also a passive aggressive jerk, who for some reason liked nothing better than looking over Pat's shoulder and complaining about how he was going about his work. I recall Pat telling me that Patrick Patrick was going to punch Stanley Stanley in the face if Gregory Gregory didn't get the double named asshole off his back. I asked the owner not to disrupt my crew. "If there's something troubling you, talk to me about it and I'll take care of it," I said. Though he left Pat alone after that, the attorney insisted next that we power wash his wooden fences before painting them. As we had not discussed this requirement earlier, I told him we'd do it if he would agree to pay for the cost of renting the equipment. By now Pat and I were getting tired of the job and even more tired of the owner. We hired another friend to work by the hour power washing and painting the wooden fences so that we could finish the work and get out of there with our sanity intact. It took just over two weeks to complete the painting job. When it was done, the three of us agreed that it looked first rate, but we were worried that the lawyer would try to stiff us on our payment.

The next day we showed up with a chain saw in the back of the van. We were seriously considering cutting down every tree on his property if he refused to pay us. Fortunately, the owner surprised us by writing me a check and complimenting us all on our excellent work. He even proposed that I give him a quote for painting the inside of the house next. I told him that I was very sorry, but we were booked up for the summer. "We'd rather work outside, anyway," I said, "as we're students who spend most of our time indoors with our noses in our books."

I had been in constant contact with Donna since she moved to the San Francisco Bay Area, where she was working as a teller in a bank in Lafayette. At some point, we decided to get together again, so I packed my books and clothes into my van and headed north. We rented an apartment in the Rockridge neighborhood between Berkeley and Oakland. It was a wonderful place full of big houses built in the 1920s and 1930s. There were shops and restaurants a block away, along Telegraph Road, extending all the way into downtown Berkeley. I made regular trips to Cody's and Moe's bookstores, and had long conversations with a young poet who had a tiny typesetting business in Berkeley. He was publishing small editions of slim poetry books by poets like Bob Kaufman and Steve Richmond. I asked him where I should get my magazine printed.

Our apartment overlooked a noisy self-service gas station. Nevertheless, it was cozy, romantic, and full of 1930s bohemian charm. Though we often awoke in the early hours of the morning to the sound of a tanker truck filling up the underground gas reservoir, we liked the view from above and the liveliness of the corner. The apartment had oak hardwood floors and wainscoting, and leaded glass French doors between the living room and bedroom. Our bed was a mattress on the floor. It was a quiet building, with only a handful of neighbors. The landlord, a soft-spoken, bald gentleman, lived downstairs with his elderly mother. For some reason we called him Mr. Muffin.

Unfortunately, the only employment I'd been able to find was working odd shifts as a security guard in downtown San Francisco office high-rises, mostly old buildings like the haunted Flood Building on Market Street. During those seemingly interminable white nights, I wrote poems and read Russian novels. Working as a security guard in San Francisco gave me insights into human nature and helped me solidify my values. Oddly enough, the job also led me to become a print-maker.

Though most of my work was on the graveyard shift, my schedule changed so frequently that my body clock never adjusted. Sleep deprived and clock-drunk, I could never quite get my bearings. I was constantly on call. If I wanted a paycheck, I needed to take any posting that was offered or there would be fewer opportunities to work in the weeks ahead. During the days that I didn't spend sleeping or getting ready to face another surreal night, I visited bookstores and museums.

Occasionally, I worked overnight shifts at convention centers and large hotels with convention facilities, among them the Hilton, which was located in the Tenderloin district, considered at the time to be the most dangerous area in the city. Since my shift began at midnight, I had to walk from the Market Street BART station through the Tenderloin to the hotel. One of my co-workers advised me to keep my hand in the pocket of my overcoat, finger pointed as if I were holding a gun, to walk erratically in fits and starts, and to talk and yell incoherently as I moved. I took his advice and no one came near me.

One of the conventions I worked at was the annual meeting of the American Medical Association. Each of the three nights of the convention my co-workers and I gorged ourselves on the left-over food piled high on the banquet tables in the lobby. Particularly attractive were the mounds of exotic fruit and giant wheels of imported cheese. Some of the rounds had barely been cut into. Yet each day caterers came to restock the tables with fresh mounds of fruit and new cheese wheels. When I asked what became of the leftover food, my supervisor told me it would be thrown into the dumpster in back of the hotel by the morning cleaning crew before the catering staff brought in fresh provisions. When I asked why this perfectly good gourmet food wasn't donated to a food bank or homeless shelter, he informed me that it was likely "more cost effective" to throw it away.

At the time, Donna and I barely had enough money to buy food or do our laundry at the coin-operated machines next to the Chinese take-out. So, at the end of my last shift at the AMA convention, I put twenty pounds of Swiss Gruyère under my overcoat and walked out of the Hilton Hotel onto the mean streets of the Tenderloin. I could see my breath in the cold morning air. I yelled out some gibberish and laughed maniacally as I walked toward Market Street, knowing that Donna and I would eat well for weeks to come.

I also worked at the Antiquarian Booksellers Convention. For four consecutive nights, I wandered among the empty booths, handling rare books and manuscripts. I examined a sheaf of original watercolor paintings by Henry Miller and a first edition of James Joyce's *Ulysses*. I read poems in little magazines published in the 1920s by small presses in Paris. I looked at old broadsides and chapbooks, struggled with the handwriting in letters, read aloud a poem by Baudelaire. But mostly I marveled at the price tags, for which I felt nothing but disgust, as I knew of the struggles and financial challenges most of these authors had faced in their lifetime. That a surviving copy of a literary masterpiece that had been banned shortly after publication, thereby depriving its author of any earnings from years of work was now fetching a hundred thousand dollars seemed a grim and ironic commentary on the value of literary artists. I felt disdain for the parasitic professionals who make a living off the work of others, and for the selfishness and greed of the wealthy, who compete among themselves to collect and hoard such artifacts.

Once my father visited us, or rather picked us up and drove us to a famous steakhouse for dinner. On the way to the restaurant and during the meal, he ignored Donna and barely said a word to her. He was rude to me as well. As was his custom, he ordered the biggest and most expensive cut of beef for himself, along with two bottles of expensive wine, most of which he guzzled himself. It soon became apparent that the purpose of his visit was to express his disapproval that Donna and I were living together "in sin." Such absurd and unexpected moralizing enraged me. After all, my father was an atheist who had abandoned his wife and children to pursue his serial infidelities, then married his secretary. When I told him he lacked the moral authority to lecture me on the subject, he accused me of being interested only in his money. I looked at his fleshy face and watched his jowls move as he chewed his meat. "How about you take your money and shove it up your ass and bury it there with you when you die," I said.

Meanwhile, my work situation had continued to deteriorate to the point where I was receiving few postings, most of which were awful. Over time, I began to turn down shifts at the worst locations, which gave me more time for museum visits, including an amazingly good exhibition entitled "Expressionism, a German Intuition, 1905–1920" at the San Francisco Museum of Modern Art. The paintings by Emil Nolde, Max Beckmann, Franz Marc, Wassily Kandinsky, Erich Heckel, Ernst Ludwig Kirchner, and others jolted me with an electric shock of inspiration. I immediately wrote a suite of poems based on seven different paintings. My friend Pat later set three of these poems to music and recorded them as art songs for baritone accompanied by a chamber music ensemble. Yet as great as the paintings were, the woodcuts affected me even more.

I remember that I returned to the museum each day for nearly two weeks, where I spent hours carefully studying the simple, bold woodcuts. I decided that I couldn't exist without owning at least one of these prints. Penniless and semi-unemployed, my only options were to attempt to steal one from the museum or try to make them myself.

The next day, I walked half a mile from our apartment to the California College of Arts and Crafts, where I used the last of my money to buy some linoleum blocks, cutting tools, a brayer, paper, and ink. At the time, I was still working on a sequence of poems based on circus acts that would later be published as my first book, *Circus Deluxe*. For my initial attempt at print-making, I decided to illustrate five of the poems that would be included in the book.

Donna made very little money at her job and I was being offered fewer days at work, so it became increasingly difficult for us to pay the rent, buy groceries, and put gas in her car. A kind of gloom descended over us and our happiness began to melt away like ice cream left too long in the sun. As an experiment, my friend Pat had grown some marijuana from seeds under a grow light in his closet. He'd given me a plastic sandwich bag full when I left Granada Hills, but neither of us believed it would be very potent. I hadn't smoked much pot since high school, so the bag sat forgotten and unused until one day Donna and I decided to bake brownies with it.

We were sad and needed something sweet to cheer us up. When the brownies came out of the oven, we both ate a couple and they seemed to have no effect. They tasted good, however, so we ate the whole tray of them. An hour or so later, I was humming loudly at my typewriter. We were both pleasantly high and we decided to go outside. We'd never been to the Carnation Ice Cream parlor on Telegraph Road, so we counted our pocket change and set off walking. Once there, we both ordered a hot fudge sundae. As we ate, we noticed that each of us said "um" without thinking every time we took a bite, which made us laugh. Soon we were laughing hysterically, our heads on the table. We wondered if we would be asked to leave before we were able to finish our ice cream, which only made us laugh louder.

When I had been hired, the owner of the security company, an ex-police detective, had promised me a significant raise after I had completed my probationary period. However, from talking to other guards I worked with, all of whom, like me, were college graduates struggling in the tightly union-controlled San Francisco job market, I knew that none of them had ever received their promised raise. We'd all been lied to and played for fools. One day, I put my freshly laundered polyester uniform into a paper bag and rode BART into the city. I went to the office of the security company and asked to speak to the owner. When a young vice president attempted to talk me down from my suicide mission, I told him he ought to be ashamed of himself for lying to and taking advantage of so many people. I told him I quit, then set the bag on his desk. Then I walked straight into the owner's office, told him he was a liar and a crook, and walked out of the building. When word got around what I had done, some of my guard friends pitched in to take me out to dinner.

Though I looked for work for the next few weeks, searching the help wanted ads in the newspaper each day and canvassing businesses in Berkeley, there were no openings. Once, when Donna and I were out together, we came home to find that someone had forced the lock on our door and broken into our apartment. Though we had nothing of value, they had rifled through all our drawers looking for non-existent cash. Nevertheless, they did take something of great sentimental value: a gold plated Huguenot Cross and chain Donna had got in France during the year she had lived with her aunt and uncle. We felt like our private space had been violated, and nothing there ever seemed secure or safe again.

As our poverty grew, our happiness waned. Donna and I both knew we'd failed again. We were broke and without prospects. I was uncompromising and self-righteous, and Donna too insecure in our relationship to make further sacrifices. So we closed up our apartment and handed the keys to Mr. Muffin. It was a sad day for everyone. Donna kept her underpaid bank teller job and moved back in with her old roommate, while I drove my Volkswagen van south on interstate 5. Despite its beauty, San Francisco can be a cruel place.

Back in Los Angeles, I lived briefly in my van until I got an apartment with my former roommate Pat, and took a job as a typesetter at a newspaper in San Fernando. By this time Pat, who was studying to be a professional singer, and had been playing leading roles in the Music Department's opera productions, had quit living in the house in Granada Hills and needed a place to live. Just a few days earlier, he had had a confrontation with John, the owner of the house, who had spent the previous few days attending a science fiction writers convention in Los Angeles. John dressed for the occasion in a blue velvet tuxedo, and was so manic by the time he finally came home, he was gesturing wildly and babbling nonsense. "I'm ten thousand years old," he told Pat, "and so are you." Then he threatened Pat with a large kitchen knife. When the police arrived, they took John to the psych ward for observation. Meanwhile, Pat gathered his possessions and moved out.

I began dating a girl named Gail, an English major at the university, who I had originally met a couple months earlier at the publication party for Rachel Sherwood's book *Mysteries of Afternoon and Evening*. Gail had met David Trinidad and they quickly became friends. As I got to know her better, I learned that Gail had been sleeping with all of Rachel's former lovers without knowing it, more or less in order.

Now it was my turn. Though she had never met Rachel and didn't even live in the same state at the time of the accident, somehow she'd assumed Rachel's identity for a while after her death. I dated Gail for several months. When I asked her about the identity switch, she told me that she'd known nothing of Rachel or her history, that things just happened that way without any intent on her part, that she had no control over it. Apparently, it was as strange for her as it was for everyone else involved.

I worked as a typesetter for a couple of months at the *San Fernando Sun,* a community newspaper with a long and distinguished history. While I was a very fast typist, accuracy was equally important, as there was no means of seeing what got keyboarded until the galleys were printed. The paper employed a full-time proofreader, who sent back long lists of corrections, which would be reset and cut into the stories before they were marked up again by the editor, then passed on to the crew laying out and pasting-up the actual pages of the newspaper. Though not accurate enough to be a career typesetter, I was a good worker and a quick study, so I moved to camera work and paste-up as well as ad design and make-up. In time, I became proficient in all aspects of pre-press production work and moved seamlessly between jobs, following the main thrust of the work flow as the newspaper made its way through the production cycle.

Two months after I began work at the paper, the owners of *The Sun* sold the paper to the Hearst Corporation, which owned newspapers and magazines all over the country, including *The San Francisco Chronicle, The Houston Chronicle, Cosmopolitan,* and *Esquire.* The Hearst name has always evoked strong images and reactions: William Randolph Hearst, the extravagance of Hearst Castle, Patty Hearst, and Orson Wells' famous film *Citizen Kane.* These days Hearst Communications continues to be a massive information conglomerate that also owns television stations, and parts of cable networks such as A&E and ESPN. In 1980, the corporation began to buy up community newspapers throughout Southern California. They consolidated the physical production of roughly a dozen of these weeklies in *The Sun*'s facility.

Though wages had been frozen during the long negotiations for the sale to Hearst, management had promised workers at *The Sun* a raise immediately after the sale was finalized. Unfortunately, the Hearst Corporation had acted in bad faith and blocked the promised pay raises. Three years later, after raising revenues by cutting jobs and sharing production costs, Hearst was able to sell the papers to other investors for big profits. As anyone who has ever worked in a job with deadlines knows, newspaper work is fast-paced and stressful, even under ideal circumstances. Holiday ads and inserts inflate the size of the paper, effectively doubling the workload. Suddenly, with the addition of only a couple of skilled part-time workers, *The Sun* was putting out a dozen newspapers instead of the two I'd been hired to work on. I was working sixty hours a week to get the papers out, while the raise I'd been promised had evaporated.

A few of the papers that survived and succeeded in the transition had editors who cared enough about their work and their papers to drive to San Fernando and personally direct the make-up of their pages. The others we threw together haphazardly, as we rushed to meet the printer's deadline. I remember standing at the long line of paste-up tables, utility knife in hand, with these editors literally looking over my shoulder as I made cuts to fit in the stories they cared most about or helped them redesign their front pages so that they looked the best they could before we put their paper to bed. These editors displayed loyalty and professionalism that made no difference at all to the Hearst Corporation. They had pride in their work, even though most of them earned little more than I did.

My roommate Pat had started his semester working nights as a waiter at twenty-four-hour diner. The schedule was killing him, as he worked all night, then attended his classes, came home to sleep for a few hours in the afternoon, then went back to work again. Lacking sleep, he had little patience for prickly, demanding customers who appeared like ghouls in the dark, early hours of the morning and left with complaints instead of tips. I suggested he apply at the newspaper, where he got a part-time job afternoons building ads.

The newspaper had hired several new people, including Pat, who collectively upset the already delicate balance of personalities in the shop. Overworked and underpaid, the workers had become increasingly high strung. One of the ad specialists fell off the stool at her drafting table and had an epileptic seizure. People made errors because they had too much to do and were working too fast. There were conflicts over what types of music people wanted to hear on the radio, which resulted in a tug of war between Country and Classical music. Finally, the Production Manager decreed, "No Specialized Music," which meant no classical music.

Meanwhile, I talked to everyone in the shop and tried to suggest that we should meet with management and present a unified front in regards to our promised raises, but the production manager was afraid for his job. The others who, like me, punched a clock, likewise didn't want to "rock the boat." Finally, only Pat and I met with the newspaper's managing editor. She looked us over carefully as we sat down across from her at her big desk. She listened quietly as we reminded her of raises we'd been cheated out of. Then she told us she was powerless, as the Hearst Corporation simply refused to authorize any raises. "I wish there were something I could do, but my hands are tied," she concluded.

I looked at her and spoke calmly. "If I were in your position, I would tell the people at Hearst that asking me to break a promise made to so many people in good faith is unacceptable, that my word and my good name mean more to me than their money. I would tell them that my values, my reputation, and my dignity are not for sale. I would tell them I quit." As I talked, the managing editor listened with her hands folded on the desk. At one point she nodded her head. Then she thanked us and walked us to the door. Two weeks later she was still the managing editor and we had all received our raises. Ironically, though everyone in the shop knew Pat and I were responsible for their raise, they resented us more than ever. Some lessons you have to keep on learning.

* * *

While I was a student and instructor at California State University, Northridge, I often used the Northridge branch of the postal service. Located on Reseda Boulevard, a couple of blocks from the university, the branch always seemed busy. Sometimes the line snaked through the inside of the building and extended onto the sidewalk outside. It typically took half an hour or more to finally reach one of the clerks working behind the counter. At first, the long waits annoyed me. Beside myself with frustration, I sometimes abandoned my place in line after fifteen minutes. Around me, people grumbled about the poor service and the waste of time. Everyone seemed to be in a hurry. Everyone seemed to be unhappy.

Eventually, I learned to use these long waits as a kind of weekly Zen seminar. I observed the human drama that I imagined played out at the post office each day: the nervous woman with the baby carriage, the foot-tapping business man in the pin-striped suit, the bored student who needed to buy postal money orders with which to pay his utility bills. I studied the facial expressions, the conversations, and the actions of people in line. I noted how their reactions affected others around them. I watched the clerks working behind the counter and thought about attitude, mindfulness, and patience.

One of the clerks, a slight, middle-aged woman with curly, shoulder-length, steel gray hair impressed me, so I began to study her more closely. Despite the tedious, repetitive work and the often miserable and indignant customers, she always wore a slightly bemused smile. She greeted each customer politely and maintained eye contact throughout the encounter. It was clear that she gave everyone her complete and undivided attention. She handled every task with good cheer and professionalism. Despite the long lines, she never hurried. She tamed even the most unpleasant customers with simple courtesy and good service. Whereas the other clerks I saw distanced themselves emotionally from the customers, answered questions curtly, sometimes unintentionally sighed in exasperation, the Zen master in the blue gray uniform remained fully present in each moment. Unlike the other clerks and the customers, she actually seemed to be *enjoying* her time at the post office.

* * *

For my twenty-third birthday, David Trinidad gave me an inscribed copy of Enid Starkey's biography of the French poet Charles Baudelaire. "Stay hungry," the inscription read. As I progressed through Starkey's text, I came across a reference to an early novella entitled *La Fanfarlo*, which Baudelaire had written when he was twenty-four and published in a magazine two years later. I was curious about this text, so I walked to the Oviatt Library, a short distance from my apartment on Darby Street, where I found the novella published in a volume of Baudelaire's complete works. The forty-two-page text seemed dense and sometimes difficult to understand, so I checked the book out and brought it home, where I began to puzzle it out with the help of a French-English dictionary. When I'd finished reading *La Fanfarlo*, I realized that I had already rendered about thirty percent of the original French into a rough English language translation. I decided to see how well I'd done by comparing my version to existing published English translations. When I returned to the library and searched, I could not locate any existing English language edition. Over the next few months, I completed my translation, then filed it away for the future. Though I knew that my translation was inadequate, I didn't know anyone I could ask for help with it.

For a couple of years, I'd been publishing my poems, many of them from the manuscript of *Circus Deluxe*, in little magazines like *Maelstrom, Scree, Poetry/L.A., Colorado-North Review, Poet Lore, Pinchpenny,* and *Wormwood Review*. I kept a hand written log of all my magazine submissions and agonized over the slow editorial responses. Still, the results encouraged me: though top tier magazines ignored my work, my overall acceptance rate was still close to twenty percent. An editor in Wisconsin had published some of my circus-themed poems in consecutive issues of his magazine *Jump River Review*. When he began to publish books as well, he asked to see the manuscript of *Circus Deluxe*. He sent me a contract for the book within a week of receiving it.

Though delighted to have found a publisher for my manuscript, I worried about the production values of the Jump River Press books I had seen. I had conceived *Circus Deluxe* with a strong visual component in mind. In addition to the five linocuts I'd done in Rockridge, I felt that the design should include, at very least, typography that reflected the circus. So I proposed to the editor and publisher that I design, typeset, and lay out the book myself at no cost. With permission from the management of *The Sun*, I did the work in the production shop after hours.

By this time, I'd grown tired of my literary friends, tired of driving to Venice for poetry readings, tired of Papa Bach's Bookstore and the NuArt theater, tired of drinking, tired of eating meals at 3 a.m. at places with names like "The Lair." While it had seemed at first entertaining and romantic to live between the covers of a bohemian novel about a group of young literary upstarts set in Los Angeles in the early 1980s, a novel in which one of the characters assumed the personality of a poet from their group who had died tragically at a young age, a novel in which characters actually speak lines like, "fuck the romance, just pour the wine," the reality was, in fact, unsustainable, unhealthy and unproductive. I'd had a rough childhood and it turned out that I didn't have much patience or talent for recreational neurosis.

In August, I took a week off from work and drove to Oregon with my mother to look at some property for sale. On the way, we stopped in Martinez and had lunch with Donna. As an adult, I had spent very little time alone with my mother, so the long drive gave us a chance to talk. I learned that she could be a charming, interesting person when she interacted one on one. Perhaps it was easier for her to control her emotions with only one person around her, whereas groups often seemed to overwhelm or upset her. She always felt a need to be the center of attention and control every situation, as she did in her job as a school teacher. If she couldn't dominate her surroundings, she retreated to a safe place inside herself and fed her resentment. Eventually, a kind of rage would overwhelm her and surge to the surface, like lava spewing from a volcano. I'd been conditioned from early childhood to do everything possible to keep that volcano from erupting and to run like hell whenever it did.

On the east side of the mountains in Oregon, we found some pristine semi-developed ten acre wooded lots for sale in a place called La Pine. I wished I had had the resources to purchase one, but I didn't have the means, nor any credit history to back up a loan. My mother asked my opinion of the property, and I told her how much I liked it. She bought two side by side lots for $12,000 each.

I'm not sure exactly when or how it happened, but suddenly I felt a kind of clarity of thought and purpose that had previously been lacking in my life. After seeing each other again briefly in August, Donna and I had been speaking regularly on the phone. As the weeks passed, I began to feel strongly that we should be together. I called her and said I wanted to see her, as I had something important to discuss with her. Though she didn't know what I would tell her, she arranged a weekend trip and flew down to stay with her parents in La Crescenta. When we got together, I remember that we took a walk on the campus in order to be alone. I spent a long time talking about our complicated history together, and I told her I was sure that we could make the relationship work if we both committed to it fully.

I told her that I wanted to be honest and forthright with her. For that reason, I wanted her to know that in order to be the person I felt that I was meant to be, it was vitally important for me to pursue my career as a writer. Because that basic fact would always be a constant in any relationship, I needed a partner who would understand, value, and agree to support this goal. In turn, I would help her realize her own goals and support her in whatever she wanted to do. I promised that we would have adventures together, and I told her I was ready for anything if she was, too. Finally, I asked her to marry me. Donna walked about fifteen steps without saying anything. Clearly my proposal had surprised her. Suddenly she stopped. "Yes," she said, "I will."

Just before Christmas, Donna quit her job at the bank and I helped her move back to Los Angeles. As she had run up some debt while living in the Bay Area, we agreed that she would work through a temp agency and live with her parents to save money and pay off the debts. I would continue to save what I could from working at the newspaper so that we would have enough to buy plane tickets and live for a while in France after the wedding. We wanted to be realistic and clear-headed, to learn from our past mistakes, even as we planned our next irresponsible adventure. Thus we were trying our best to learn about money and how to best manage it, for we both understood that ultimately the success of our shared life would be measured not by how much money we earned, but by how faithfully we adhered to our own values. We knew that we would need to find a balance between society's expectations and our own, between the time we traded for money and the time we needed to make art.

We planned the wedding for late April, a few months away. We wanted it to be a traditional but low-key celebration, free of church dogma. In addition to writing our own vows, we planned to incorporate readings of poems into the service. I would design the invitations based on a prose poem and accompanying linocut called "Jigsaw Puzzle." The service itself would be outside, in the garden at the Unitarian Church in Pasadena, where Donna's parents attended services. My mother and grandmother would prepare food for the reception, which we would hold at Donna's parents' house in La Crescenta.

On the morning of the wedding, I put on the gray pin-striped, three-piece suit my father had given me as a high school graduation gift. I had only worn the suit twice before, once to grad night in high school, and the other time to my mother's wedding, when she married Phil a year later. Luckily, it still fit. However, when I'd finished dressing, I realized that I'd given away the boots I thought I still owned and therefore lacked shoes to wear with the suit. I considered going to the wedding barefoot, but I didn't want to evoke the famous image of barefoot Paul McCartney crossing Abbey Road in the company of the other Beatles, along with its "Paul is dead" connotation. Finally, I squeezed my feet into a pair of my roommate Pat's black shoes, which were two sizes too small for me.

For me, the highlight of the wedding service was Pat's performance of Gregory Corso's poem "Marriage." The wedding guests got a good laugh out of Corso's ironic description of marriage, with the exception of my father-in-law Bob, who found the poem too avant-garde for his tastes. Of course, Bob didn't like Mahler's symphonies either, as they were "too modern," so I didn't worry much about his criticism. Though I had told the photographer specifically in advance that I preferred that he take candid shots of the wedding, and avoid cookie-cutter poses, he nevertheless tried to photograph me with my knee on the grass, holding the wedding ring aloft like the Holy Grail. Donna recalls that in response I told him to pack up his equipment and leave.

Though both my mother and her new husband and my father and his new wife showed up and briefly breathed the same air, the ceremony and the reception went off without any major disruptions. My mother did, however, blow up at my grandmother for sneaking off to appear in the photos that were taken of my father's family posing with the bride and groom. At the reception, it seemed to me that we ran out of food too early. I'd insisted on serving foreign beer, my only contribution to the planning of the reception. Though it was an off brand we got from Trader Joe's, at least it was better than Budweiser. I remember my friend Dave's parents, David Sr. and Marcia, came to the wedding, as did our old neighbors from Acre Street. Jerry brought his own booze and left the empty bottle in the ivy by the pool. Like the lines in Corso's poem, only a handful of my friends attended, "all scroungy and bearded / just waiting to get at the drinks and food." Donna and I left late in the afternoon to spend a couple of days at a hotel in Santa Barbara. We learned later that some of the unmarried members of the wedding party had paired up after the reception and had sex. Clearly the wedding had been a success.

Three months after our wedding, we were on our way to France, where we had arranged to stay in part of a big house owned by friends of Donna's aunt and uncle. Part of an old winery built in 1820, the property was located in the village of Langlade, fifteen kilometers from Nîmes. Inhabited by the daughter of the owners, the large two-story stone house looked onto a big courtyard, with a majestic palm tree in the center. Low winery buildings surrounded the courtyard and there was a giant underground cellar for storing casks. In back, a large formal garden, now in disarray, overlooked a narrow valley filled with vineyards. Our host, a medical student at the University of Nîmes, was named Lis.

With a history dating back to the Romans, Langlade first appeared in a historical record in 1125 as Anglata. Located close to the Via Domitia, the Roman road that ran between Nîmes and the village of Sommières, a small community of farmers and sheep herders grew around a modest church (Église Saint Julien). Documents from 1149 describe the village as having a presbytery, a hospital, and a cemetery. Though the village has more than doubled in population and spread out considerably in recent years, in 1982 it still had its original form: a narrow rectangle surrounded by parts of the remaining stone walls. When we lived there, most of the buildings in the original center of the village were uninhabited.

Over its history, Langlade gained a name for wine production. Louis XIV awarded Langlade a coat of arms in 1696 (three vine stakes with a bunch of grapes on a silver background) in recognition of the quality of its wines. In 1982 the Cavalier Windmill *(Moulin à vent Cavalier),* a famous historical mill which sits on the hill just above the village, was a roofless husk. It has since been repaired to fully working order. I remember that I once took a photo of Donna wearing the wool overcoat she had borrowed from her father for our trip. I was standing on the path leading up to the mill and caught her in an unintentional heroic pose. Whenever I saw the photo, I always referred to it as, "I came, I saw, I conquered," until one day the picture mysteriously disappeared from the photo album.

In 1982, half the hotel rooms in Paris did not have private bathrooms. Unless you were willing to pay extra for a nicer room, there was no place to take a shower and the toilet was down the hall. When we arrived in France, we stayed for a week in a hotel on the left bank, halfway between the Gare Montparnasse and Notre Dame. Though shabby and inexpensive, the hotel offered a convenient location and included breakfast. Each morning, the chambermaid brought coffee, bread, butter, and jam to the room on a tray, where we ate it in bed. At night, we often heard drunks and prostitutes arguing on the street outside and mice crawling inside the wall behind the headboard. After a week, we changed hotels so we could take a shower.

We traveled south and stopped briefly to look at the apartment in which I'd stayed on my earlier trip, across from the train station in Juan-les-Pins. Then we spent a week at the beach in Carnon. It was early September and the ocean was still pleasantly warm. One day, a storm blew in and we were stuck inside our tiny vacation rental apartment, which was about the size of a large closet. The apartment was in a seven-story building next to the harbor. Though it had a modern kitchen, the convertible couch was not comfortable enough for two people to sleep on, so we slept instead on the bunk beds recessed into the entryway. The next morning, we got up early and walked on the beach. The waves had churned up the sand so that the coins the tourists had dropped all summer long now rested on top of the sand. We gathered the silver-colored one- and five-franc coins and even a couple bronze-colored ten-franc coins as we walked and stuffed them into our pockets, just as I'd done in the recurring dream I sometimes had.

After lunch, we called Lis from the post office. She offered to pick us up the following day and drive us to Langlade, about forty minutes away by car. After eating breakfast at a cafe by the harbor, we waited for her to arrive. Then we tossed our backpacks into the hatchback of her old Renault and took off in the direction of Montpellier. When we got to Langlade, Lis gave us a tour of the house and showed us where we'd be staying, in a separate apartment, blocked off from the rest of the house by two locked doors. Aside from the rough-hewn rafters and roof beams in the attic, and the red tile roof, the entire structure was made of stone, including the uneven floors. We had our own small kitchen, with a gas water heater, a coal burning stove that vented out the huge fireplace, and a cramped bathroom with a miniature shower and a toilet crammed beneath the stairwell. Though there was just enough headroom to stand up straight in the shower, I saw that I would have to sit down to use the toilet.

The kitchen, dining area, and living room were separated from the bedroom by a small anteroom with a table and chair, where I set up the portable typewriter I'd bought in Paris on my previous trip. The bedroom offered a big bed, a dresser, and a window that looked out over the garden and the vineyards. The front part of the apartment had a round dining table with four chairs, a huge antique wooden sideboard, a window seat with a cushion, and an armchair. Everything was either well worn or an antique. There was little doubt that most of the furnishings, kitchen utensils, dishes, and cutlery had been used for several generations.

The next day, we explored the village, though there wasn't much to see, beyond the little church, the ruined mill, and a few winding streets full of mostly abandoned stone houses. Eventually, we found a tabac and a small, depressingly understocked grocery store. Every morning but Sunday, a baker's truck brought bread to the town square at the top of the hill, where a handful of old women lined up to buy their baguettes. Once a week, a butcher came to sell meat out of another truck and a vegetable grocer came with fresh produce. The big supermarkets, the cafés and restaurants, the bookstores and fancy shops, and the *pâtisseries* were in Nîmes, a day trip away.

Nevertheless, we settled in with gusto, happy to be together, to speak French and drink wine from the co-op, to cook and eat whatever was available, to read the few books that were on the shelf and to buy more on our weekly visits to Nîmes. Each morning, when we heard the baker honk his horn as he passed by in his van, Donna walked up the hill to buy bread and croissants, if there were any left, for our breakfast, while I brewed strong coffee in the French press coffee pot. We cut an entire baguette in half, then sliced it down the middle and spread butter and jam on it. After breakfast, I went into my little office and worked on the manuscript of a metafictional novel called "Novelties."

The manuscript concerned a novelist who was writing fiction about an assassin, and reading a Russian novel when he wasn't busy writing. Somehow, the events in his life began to merge with the plot in his novel, as well as the one he was reading, until it became increasingly difficult to sort out exactly what was happening to which character and in what story. For months I worked on the braided narrative without realizing how unreadable it had become.

In tiny Langlade, word got around quickly that a strange young couple was living in the Dufès house. First, we met the neighbors, a pair of octogenarian sisters known locally as *"les pommettes,"* who lived in a stone house without indoor plumbing. Soon thereafter, the next-door neighbors, a French military officer and his wife, whose families had come to France to escape the fascists during the Spanish Civil War, stopped by to introduce themselves. Madame Nomdedeo, a lonely, neglected, and rather unstable woman became a frequent visitor. Over the coming months, we met other people who lived in the village. Most of them were elderly and eccentric.

Each evening, after she returned from her long day of classes at the university and prepared and ate her dinner, Lis would come to our apartment to drink a cup of *tisane* and talk about the events of the day. Though she was born in the United States, where her parents had lived for several years when she was a child, Lis spoke only French with us. She had a lively intellect, an abundance of energy, and an opinion about everything. While Donna had little interest in sparring with her, I enjoyed the many spirited debates we engaged in, even though advancing my arguments in French put me at a disadvantage. Lis was also something of an eccentric. She kept her spiky hair cut very short, ate mostly pureed food like a baby, and sometimes wore fleecy, blue flannel pyjamas with feet when she did chores in the yard or came to visit us.

When we first arrived, we found a large pile of stones in the garden behind the house. Some time earlier, the fifteen-foot-high retaining wall that rose from the street below had partially collapsed. For several years, the repair and reconstruction of this wall had been an ongoing family project. Lis' parents lived in Geneva, where her father, Joachim Van der Bent, a social philosopher, worked as a researcher and librarian for the United Nations. Her mother, whose family had lived in Langlade for eight hundred years, had for many years worked as a nurse. Like her daughter, Eliane was a force of nature: intelligent, direct, and opinionated, she was a perpetual fount of stories, history, and gossip. Though she possessed a biting and sarcastic sense of humor and had little patience for fools, I always found Eliane to be a wonderful resource and a kind and generous friend. Clearly, she had a soft spot for intellectuals and poets.

One weekend, Eliane arrived unannounced with her two college-aged sons. She distributed old clothes and told us to put them on and get ready to work. Soon Lis was operating the cement mixer like a demented sprite, as the rest of us stacked stones between the wooden guides and troweled in cement. At one point, a curious villager came to inspect our work. Lis introduced me as "a young poet from America." He shook my hand eagerly. "The trowel and the poem go well together," he said. I agreed and we talked for a while. Though he was a farmer, he knew a lot about literature. Over the course of the next two days, the wall grew four feet. In a fit of sudden inspiration, Lis and I executed a "rosette" pattern of stones that only became visible from below after her brothers removed the wooden forms. It was a surprise for everyone, though I think Donna and I liked it best. When we returned to Langlade thirty years later, the wall, with its subtle rosette, was still standing. The trowel and the poem.

By late October, the weather had changed. There were no more lunches or *goutés* in the courtyard and the nights got progressively colder. A cold *mistral* sometimes blew for days. Lis called for a coal delivery and we fired up the stoves. At first, we were comfortable and basked in the heat during the evenings. But as the weather got progressively colder and the stone walls and floors cooled with it, our small coal stove struggled to heat the apartment. During the day, one or both of Lis' cats would come inside our apartment and sit on our laps while Lis attended her classes in Nîmes. We began to close the French door to concentrate the heat in the front room, which, over time, made the bedroom and bathroom as cold as an icebox.

In early December, a storm covered the village, the vineyards, and the valley beyond in a soft white blanket of snow. Having lived for years in snowless Southern California, Donna and I frolicked happily and wandered around the village like children home from school on a snow day. We climbed to the top of the hill above the village, next to the ruined windmill, where we took photos and marveled at the quiet beauty of the place. By now, our apartment was so cold that we usually wore multiple layers of heavy clothing inside. At night, Donna put a hot water bottle into the bed and shivered as I stayed up late to read French translations of novels by Milan Kundera. I pushed the armchair as close as it would get to the stove and turned the pages, my wool peacoat wrapped around me.

I had discovered the prose poem during the time I was writing *Circus Deluxe* and had incorporated some of my first efforts into the book. In Langlade I also wrote prose poems, some of which would later appear in *The Masked Ball*, including "Souvenir," "White Nights," "Intimate Gossip," and "A Train Trip." Every morning, I pounded away at my novel. When Madame Nomdedeo visited, I closed the doors between the rooms so I could concentrate over her voice. Evenings I read French novels and poems by Baudelaire. I thought about what to do with my translation of *La Fanfarlo*.

Meanwhile, we ate soup and bread, pasta with *lardon,* and *ratatouille,* drank strong coffee and red wine. On Thanksgiving Day, we baked a whole chicken and tried to make a pie out of a stringy *courge,* which was the closest vegetable we could find to a pumpkin. The main dish was delicious, but the pie turned out so bad we had to feed it to Lis' chickens. Occasionally, Lis invited us to meals she prepared, and fêted us with escargot or shrimp crêpes. During our time in Langlade, we learned that Lis is a very perceptive person. After our first conversation, she prophetically named us 'Les Marginaux.' Later, she also predicted that Donna and I would have a son that she would meet one day. All of us knew Donna and I couldn't stay in Langlade forever, so we tried to be fully present in the moment and not take our friendship for granted.

At Christmas, we planned a trip to visit friends in France and Switzerland. First we went to Geneva, where we stayed with Eliane and Joachim at their apartment. Then we went to Lugano to visit Donna's friend Mary, who had been an exchange student at Crescenta Valley High School. One night, Mary took us to dinner at her parents' house in the hills above Lake Lugano. An architect in the family had designed the octagonal house and we spent a wonderful evening there enjoying good food and conversation. Though Mary and her family usually spoke Italian, the entire evening unfolded in equally fluent French for our benefit.

Next, we went to Le Locle, also in Switzerland, where we celebrated Christmas with Donna's friend Michel and the rest of his family. His father, Eric Perrenoud, whom everyone called "Pink Floyd," was a minister who had been friends with Donna's uncle most of his life. Many of the people we visited on this trip had some connection to Collège Cévenol, where Donna had studied while living with her aunt and uncle in 1974. Some were friends her aunt and uncle had known since just after World War II, when they had all worked in France on reconstruction efforts. Later, Donna's uncle Jim had taught at Collège Cévenol and raised his family mostly in France.

After Christmas, we went to Strasbourg to visit our friend Anne, who Donna had met at a Collège Cévenol work camp. On New Year's Day, we had a round bundt style "king cake" with a plastic figurine hidden inside. While I can't remember who ended up with the slice with the figurine and was crowned the king of the feast, I do recall Anne's grandfather asking me if I would smoke a cigar with him. As we puffed, he told us how in his lifetime he had seen his home change from German to French control in 1918, then from French to German control in 1940, and back again to French control in 1945.

One day, Anne drove us to Natzweiler-Struthof, a Nazi concentration camp in the Vosges mountains about fifty kilometers from Strasbourg. Initially used as a labor camp to intern members of resistance movements in Europe, it later became a death camp. About half of its 52,000 inmates died from overwork, hunger, and disease, while some were also used in medical experiments or simply executed. Anne's father seemed very displeased when he learned his daughter had taken us there. "No one wants to see that," he said.

That evening, Anne drove us to a cottage her family owned in the Vosges, where some of her friends gathered to celebrate the new year. Among them was her boyfriend, Jeff, who was from what is now known as the Democratic Republic of Congo and was studying law in Paris. I remember Jeff gave me a detailed lesson about the history of the United States' economic involvement, interference, and political dirty tricks in his country. Years later, when I lived in Latin America, I would hear the same complaints from Ecuadorian friends. At that time, like most Americans, I knew nothing about the negative consequences the meddling of the CIA, the World Bank, and American corporations in the affairs of other countries around the world had produced. I was shocked by what Jeff told me and promised myself I would do some research and try to come to a better and more complete understanding of what my country really represented. When we came back to Nîmes on the train, Lis picked us up at the station. Donna climbed into the back seat with our luggage, and I sat next to Lis. As she drove, I talked for half an hour straight, eagerly telling Lis everything I could remember about our trip in as much detail as I could. I found myself talking faster and faster as I described sights we'd seen, recreated dialog from conversations, related a series of droll anecdotes. Suddenly, I stopped mid-sentence. *"Mon Dieu,"* I said, *"je me sens que je peux vraiment parler français!"*

Back at the house in Langlade, we found, along with a few letters that had come in the mail, five one-hundred-franc bills on our round kitchen table. It was the money we had given to Lis just before we left on our trip because we had wanted to be sure we paid our rent on time for the month of January. When Donna saw the money, she knew immediately what Lis had done. She shook her head, gathered up the bills, and took them next door. I wasn't surprised when she came back a few minutes later, the bills still in her hand: it wasn't easy to win an argument with Lis. "She wanted to give us a Christmas present and she knows that we don't have much money," Donna explained. Both of us were touched and grateful for Lis' generosity.

We wanted to do something for Lis, so we decided to make a book of black and white photographs of Langlade and her house. Donna had already shot several rolls of film that we planned to bring back to the U.S., where the processing cost a fraction of what it did in France. However, our idea meant we now needed to buy black and white film and have it developed and printed in Nîmes. On our weekly bus trips to the city, we gathered the materials we needed, including a small, bound photo album for the finished pictures. Unfortunately, in spite of the high cost, the quality of the processing was poor and our little photo book was not as handsome as we had hoped it might be. Still, it was a gift from the heart.

As with all of France, Langlade and the surrounding areas offered up constant reminders of its rich history. The city of Nîmes has a large and well preserved Roman arena, as well as the lovely Maison Carré temple. Lis had told us about the old Roman road that ran through the hills from Langlade to Nîmes, as well as the ruins of a pre-Roman settlement that could be found in the hills nearby. One sunny day, we followed her directions and walked to the Oppidum de Nages, where we took pictures of the foundations and walls of the settlement. Another day, we walked nearly twenty kilometers through scrub pine, olive trees, and goat pastures along a barely visible path through the wilderness, following the Roman road all the way to the industrial outskirts of Nîmes.

Since village life could be monotonous, and since we had no television, didn't spend much time listening to the radio, and read the newspaper only sporadically, our trips to Nîmes helped connect us to the larger world. The bus to Nîmes stopped at the unused railroad tracks a couple blocks down the hill from the house early in the morning, again just past noon, and for the last time around 6:30 in the evening. A successful trip to the city entailed both planning and patience, as there was always extra time to kill waiting for the bus to return in the evening. We usually took the midday bus and walked from the train station, which also served the local buses, past the Roman arena, and through the old part of the city. Invariably, we bought a couple *petit pans au chocolate* from a *pâtisserie* on the narrow walking street we favored, and snacked on them as we looked in the windows of the shops. Then we ate lunch at one of the less expensive restaurants or cafés in town. Afterwards, we would spend time looking at books and buy one or two for the coming week. If the weather was nice, we might sit on a bench in one of the parks. Sometimes we went to a museum, usually to look at the Roman artifacts and mosaics I found so attractive. Then we'd have coffee or wine and read in a café. Finally, we'd buy whatever groceries and specialty foods we needed or couldn't get in Langlade, then walk back to the station and catch the bus home.

Unlike the noon bus, the evening bus back was always crowded, mostly with students returning home from school. The bus snaked its way through Nîmes, making a lot of stops. By the time we arrived back in Langlade, exhausted and hungry, the fire in our stove would have gone out. Donna would reheat some soup as I relit the fire. We'd pour a glass of wine, put some butter on the bread we'd brought back with us, and think about how lucky we were.

In February, Eliane returned to Langlade and stayed two weeks. She had grown up in the big house and the village would always be her home. One day, while she was visiting with us, the postman brought a package for me. It contained copies of my first book of poems, *Circus Deluxe*. Eliane promptly ordered Lis to go in her car to buy croissants so we could have a breakfast celebration worthy of the moment. It always amazed me how much French people at that time honored literary and artistic workers. They treated even the most unimpressive of them with the kind of respect our culture reserves for celebrities, professional athletes, and business tycoons.

Though happy that it had finally appeared, I was disappointed by the quality of the book's production. I had designed and set the type myself, but the printer under-developed the photographic negatives. I noted also that the paper and cover stock were of poor quality. Nevertheless, I filed these complaints away for a time when I could do better. For the moment, I was in France enjoying my little spontaneous publication party.

By March, we were running out of money. Though Donna had talked to someone in Montpellier about working part-time in the schools, we had just enough cash left to buy our tickets back to California and pay the first and last month's rent on an apartment rental. If we spent that money moving to Montpellier with no cash reserves, we'd be in deep trouble if something went wrong. Also, we'd been planning to go to Oregon to help my mother's husband Phil build a house on the property they had bought in La Pine the previous summer. Still, it could have gone either way. Perhaps we flipped a coin, which is something we sometimes resorted to in those days, when faced with a big decision.

As it happened, we reluctantly left France. Back in Los Angeles, we stayed for ten days at Donna's parents' house. My father invited us to visit him in Santa Maria, where he had recently moved his company and built a large new facility in an industrial complex by the local airport. We drove up for the day and he gave us a tour of the sprawling facility. At that time he had 120 employees producing phase shifters for the B-1 bomber. He took us to lunch at a steak house, then asked me about my plans now that I was married. When I told him I was still weighing my options, he offered me a job as Vice President of Marketing. He told me I'd have a new company car every two years and said he'd help us get a house on nearby Shell Beach. As someone who had grown up surfing, owning a house a few steps from the ocean was my ultimate fantasy. With the cost of California real estate, such an offer seemed ridiculous. I imagined a sticky web of strings dangling from the ceiling as my father talked. "Thanks," I told him, and declined. "I don't have any training, experience or interest in marketing, and that's just not what I want to do with my life."

"He just wants you to feed his cat and take his trash cans out to the street for him when he's out of town," Donna said in the car on the way home. We both knew what he was up to. We didn't trust him.

When we visited my mother, she told us that she had decided not to build on the property in Oregon right away. Instead, Phil would remodel the two bedroom Spanish style house they owned next door to the house they'd bought in Sepulveda. They proposed that I work, along with Phil and Greg Two, who had recently quit his job as a sales representative at a beverage distribution company, remodeling the little house. Then, in a frenzy of activity, Donna landed a job at a bank in Toluca Lake, we bought an old Chevy pickup truck from Phil, and we moved into an apartment in Northridge.

I had to wait nearly two months to begin work on the house, as my mother had only just informed the renters they would need to find a new place to live. So I began work on a comic novel called "The Jester." I also began making linocut prints to illustrate my new prose poems, which had begun to appear in little magazines. One day, I went to speak with one of my former French professors about my translation of *La Fanfarlo*. I asked if she would be interested in working with me on revising the work. "What you're doing is certainly interesting and worth pursuing," she told me, "but I can only work with you on it if I get paid. The only way to do that is for you to come back to the university as a graduate student and sign up for an independent study." Though I was surprised that she would place such a condition on her participation, I told her I'd see what I could do. Maybe I'm naive, but I've always been disappointed when people base every decision on money.

Though not keen on the idea of returning to school, I knew that I needed help with my translation in order to produce a publishable version. As I had no interest in teaching French, I didn't see any point in pursuing the advanced degree I'd started earlier. Instead, I thought about designing a special major in literary translation. To submit such an application I needed to first get approval from the Dean of Graduate Studies. I made an appointment to speak with him the following week.

A former chairman of the Business Department, the dean was a practical man. He listened to my proposal, then told me that it made more sense for me to get a Master's Degree in English, which was something any future employer could understand. "It will be half as difficult as what you're proposing," he said, "plus you've already earned graduate units in French that the English Department will accept as literature electives within the degree program. You can revise your translation while you work in the writing lab and tutor within the English Department this year, and get a teaching assistantship next year. Those jobs will keep you afloat while you get your degree, and when you graduate, you can go on to a Ph.D. or get a junior college teaching job." I had to admit that what he said made sense. So I shook his hand, finished my application, and went to talk to the Chairman of the English Department about tutoring work.

When the house was finally empty, Greg and I gutted it completely. Then we put in a new bathroom and kitchen, new windows and doors, and sheet rock throughout the house, while Phil pulled new wires and updated the electrical system. We put in new fixtures and refinished the oak floors. I painted the entire house, inside and out while Phil and Greg put on a new roof. When it was finished, the house looked great. My mother said that Donna and I could rent the house for $300.00 per month until they were ready to sell it. Though the house was farther to the university, the rent was a bit less than what we were paying at the apartment and I'd have an extra room to use as an office.

In September, I began classes at California State University, Northridge. The first semester, I worked on my revisions of *La Fanfarlo* and tutored undergraduates in writing. In the spring, I began to look for a publisher for my translation. I took a class in bibliography and scholarly methods and wrote an in-depth biographical, critical, and textual introduction to *La Fanfarlo,* which I used for the seminar paper. I did most of the research at UCLA, which had much better primary resources in French literature.

Once, on our way to the library in Westwood, Donna and I narrowly avoided a bad accident. We were so poor back then that we made due with a series of junk cars we bought and drove until they quit running. We were driving the old Volvo I had bought from a traveling salesman. Though I usually didn't trust the car for long trips, I once drove it to Vasquez Rocks with Tom Miner, the editor of the little magazine *Pinchpenny,* who visited us from Sacramento. On our way to UCLA that Saturday morning I was behind the wheel, diving down Parthenia Street toward the entrance to the 405 Freeway, when suddenly the rear wheel assembly on the Volvo broke and the car skidded down the road on its axle, throwing up a shower of sparks. Though I maintained control of the car at thirty-five miles per hour, I wonder what would have happened if we'd been traveling at highway speed.

* * *

In the spring, I learned that Marvin Malone of *The Wormwood Review* had awarded *Circus Deluxe* the "Wormwood Prize" for the best neglected book of poetry of 1982. I had already reconciled myself to a life in which irony would reign supreme. Though even at the time such a dubious honor seemed like a portent, it nevertheless amused me to be publicly recognized for being publicly ignored. I saw recently that the complete list of Wormwood Award winners included Kurt Vonnegut, Jr. *(Mother Night)*, Russell Edson *(The Very Thing That Happens)*, Charles Bukowski *(Notes of a Dirty Old Man)*, and Thomas Wiloch *(Tales of Lord Shantih)*. Vonnegut, Bukowski, and Edson were all strong influences on my work and Wiloch a frequent contributor to my magazine. In fact, I later published all of these authors except Vonnegut in *Asylum*.

Marvin Malone, who edited *The Wormwood Review*, published a number of my poems over the years, some from *Circus Deluxe*, others from what would become *The Masked Ball*, and still more from a manuscript of comic poems I called "Trash Collection." The latter manuscript was a project I had undertaken in part as a reaction to the "Stand-up Poetry" being produced by other *Wormwood Review* poets like Charles Bukowski, Ronald Koertge, Gerald Locklin, Charles Webb, Fred Voss, and others. While I appreciated the humor, irreverence, spontaneity, energy and instant connection these poems offered, I also thought they could easily become facile and trite. To test these ideas, I wrote sixty short poems over the course of three or four days. Malone published half a dozen of these poems in *Wormwood Review* and others appeared in other little magazines. They weren't very good poems. In fact, they were garbage, as advertised by the title.

During this time, I also continued to publish a wide range of new work in magazines, mainly prose poems from a manuscript I was developing called "Intimate Gossip." My interest in the prose poem had begun earlier with Baudelaire and other French poets. I had incorporated several of my early prose poems into *Circus Deluxe*. More recently, I had discovered Michael Benedikt's classic *The Prose Poem: An International Anthology*, as well as Russell Edson's *The Very Thing*

That Happens, along with work by Robert Bly and other contemporary American poets.

Meanwhile, the initial responses to *La Fanfarlo* had been encouraging. While some of the presses with a history of publishing literature in translation did not think the manuscript was a good fit for them, they all agreed that it was an interesting work that should be published. Teo Savory at Unicorn Press, herself a translator of French poetry, wrote me a long, personal letter. She told me that the translation was very promising, though she thought it needed further work and revision. She urged me to seek out someone to help me improve the translation and to continue submitting the novella for publication. She also expressed interest in my own work and asked to see the manuscript of "Intimate Gossip," as Unicorn was very interested in publishing letterpress books of original work by poets in illustrated editions. That I was both writer and illustrator of my own work intrigued her.

I also received another long letter from a gentleman named Kendall Lappin, whose translations of poems from Baudelaire's *Les Fleurs du mal* I had read in the course of my research. I had sent his publisher my manuscript, and he had passed it on to Kendall for evaluation. Kendall's letter was direct and generous. He told me that my manuscript should not be published in its current state, but that he would be delighted to help me put it in order. He asked for nothing in return, as the pleasure of working on the text was its own reward. I could hardly believe my good fortune, as just the person I needed had appeared on cue, out of the ether.

A retired professor of French at the U.S. Naval Academy in Annapolis, Kendall was a first-rate translator. I jumped at the opportunity to work with him and told him I would gladly credit him as editor on the critical edition I was preparing. We began our collaboration immediately, and within a week the first set of corrections and questions arrived by mail. I was already working on the annotations to the book as well as the introduction, so suddenly I was completely immersed in the life and work of Charles Baudelaire.

Kendall turned out to be an excellent mentor. Though he'd never lived in France, nor even visited the country, he had a gift for languages. He had begun his study of foreign languages at the Defense Language Institute Foreign Language Center in Monterey, California as a young naval officer during World War II, where he mastered Japanese, French, and Russian. Because of his natural talent for languages, he had been assigned to the Naval Academy in Annapolis, where he continued to teach as a civilian professor throughout his working life. Kendall's insights into Baudelaire's sublime French surprised me at every turn. I developed a deep respect for his abilities as a translator of French literature, and an even deeper appreciation for his friendship, kindness, and generosity.

Over the course of the next year, Kendall and I batted the manuscript back and forth a dozen times. He helped me uncover the layers of irony inherent in the text and provided elegant solutions for Baudelaire's made up words or archaic expressions. We argued about individual words, enjoyed each other's insight, intelligence, and wit. In short, we had fun doing something meaningful together, even though neither of us expected to gain much else from it.

Meanwhile, I submitted a proposal to undertake a creative thesis for my M.A. degree. Because I knew that I had little patience for the passive-aggressive hoop-jumping so prevalent in academia, I had thought carefully about how to succeed in graduate school. My solution involved pursuing projects that aligned with my own esoteric interests, while ignoring the interests and specialties of my professors. By working on fresh and unusual material, my independence and expertise would inoculate me against intellectual bullying. Since my background in French literature had already led me to explore the prose poem long before most American poets and editors had adopted the form, I proposed to write a collection of original prose poems, illustrated by my original block prints. I would support my creative work with an essay in which I defined the genre and illustrated its characteristics by analyzing the work of Russell Edson and Robert Bly, two of the prose poem's earliest American practitioners. My preliminary research suggested that very little had been written on the subject in English. It pleased me that many of my primary sources would be in French, rendered into English in my own translations. The English Department accepted the proposal almost immediately and without qualifications. Over the summer, I researched and wrote the critical essay. I also completed my block print illustrations for "Intimate Gossip."

The following semester, I took a seminar in creative writing, my first and only class in the subject since high school. To be honest, I took the seminar not because it would further my education, but because it rewarded me with three units. While I had already published a collection of poems, I had also written three unpublished (and unpublishable) novels, as well as two other collections of poems. Writers learn by reading voraciously and by writing, not by sitting in a circle talking about each others' early efforts. I found workshops pointless for writers who had already published, and potentially damaging for those who had not yet developed a voice of their own. Consequently, I tried to be non-prescriptive about the work of the other students, while ignoring comments about my work.

Though I told him I believed writing was something best done alone, my professor, Benjamin Saltman, insisted I also attend a private writing workshop he hosted in his home. As he wouldn't take no for an answer, I finally agreed to go once and tell him what I thought afterward. While the people in the group—which included CSUN students and alumni Nicholas Campbell, Michael Newell, Jodi Johnson, Ron Pronk, and Ricardo Means-Ybarra—were talented and personable, I didn't change my opinion about workshops. I was married and had a job. I was translating French literature and writing my own work. I didn't have time for a writing club. After fulfilling my obligation, I told Saltman I wouldn't be coming back.

When I'd finished the illustrations for my collection of prose poems, I sent the manuscript to Teo Savory at Unicorn Press and submitted the thesis version, along with the essay on the prose poem to Professor Saltman, who was my thesis advisor. A few weeks later, Teo wrote back to say that Unicorn would like to publish the work as a letterpress book in an edition of 500 handset and hand-bound copies to be printed on their hand-cranked Vandercook SP-15. She asked that I change the title from "Intimate Gossip" to "The Masked Ball." I agreed and she sent me a contract for the book.

Having a letterpress book of my work published by a venerable press like Unicorn at such young age was a dream come true for me. That Teo, Alan, and the staff at Unicorn would invest themselves so deeply in my work validated everything I was doing. I felt as though I had just received a Pulitzer Prize and won the lottery. I wanted to share my success, so at the next meeting of my creative writing seminar when Ben Saltman told me during the break halfway through the three-hour meeting, that he planned to read through the manuscript of my thesis that weekend while he attended a faculty retreat, without thinking I blurted out, "I've had some good news along those lines. Unicorn Press has just accepted the manuscript for publication. They will publish it as *The Masked Ball.*" I watched Ben's face contort into a rictus. It was as if I had told him I was having an affair with his wife or had run over his cat on the way to class. He didn't say a word. Instead, he turned his back to me and walked away.

Perhaps the most bizarre experience I had in graduate school was a seminar I took in Critical Theory. The professor was a bearded man with a booming voice, a barrel chest and the libido of a satyr. As the course was mandatory for the degree and that professor the only one who taught it, for years the department had placed its students in an unfortunate situation. It was common knowledge that the professor talked complete nonsense for hours on end. His lectures were so intentionally obtuse and incomprehensible that students could not look at each other for fear of erupting into spontaneous fits of laughter. I remember that there were times when I had to bite my tongue hard enough to bring tears to the corners of my eyes as a way to distract myself so that I would not explode into laughter. Meanwhile, the professor continued babbling nonsense, oblivious to the students. He never asked questions. The students never talked. We just sat there in shocked, bored, or disgusted silence, hour after hour. In retrospect, I wonder how I was able to get through it. There's no doubt in my mind that the man was insane.

It was common knowledge around the department and the university in general that this professor was a serial sexual predator of young female students. There were several outstanding lawsuits against him and against the university for his abusive and unprofessional behavior. Female friends had told me that the women's bathrooms were full of warnings about him that students had scribbled on the walls. A rumor circulated that the department secretary had once entered his office using the master key, and found him with his pants around his ankles, furiously pumping a student bent over his desk. He placed ads in the "education" section of the classifieds in some of the local "Free Press" papers in which he advertised seminars in "advanced sexual pleasure" and related topics.

When I scrambled the footnotes from my translation of *La Fanfarlo* and arranged them into an incomprehensible stew of critic-centric nonsense for my seminar paper, the professor wrote across the top of my paper: "Clearly this course is nothing more than a footnote in your career." Bingo.

The following year, I worked as a teaching assistant and taught Freshman Composition classes. I enjoyed teaching from the first day and quickly found that I had a vocation for it. I tried to make each session an unforgettable experience for my students, even as I was teaching myself how to teach. Some of the other teaching assistants complained of stage fright and sometimes threw up before teaching their classes. Others had trouble conveying and maintaining their authority. When they asked me for advice, I reminded them that most of the freshmen they were teaching had little life experience and even less knowledge. "Just keep in mind that anything you tell them is probably news to them," I offered. I had also learned that it was important to prepare and have specific goals for each class, while maintaining flexibility and suppleness. Perhaps more importantly, I learned to throw myself into what I was teaching, to show my enthusiasm and love of the subject, to entertain as I educated. It seemed obvious to me that if I didn't believe in my own authority, then students would not waste their time listening to me. In the end, teaching was just rhetoric, and you had to find the right balance.

At some point that year, I finally heard back from City Lights Books about *La Fanfarlo*. Though they, too, returned my manuscript, they were also sympathetic towards the project and suggested I send the work immediately to a relatively new publishing house in Berkeley that was looking to build a strong, eclectic list. On their recommendation I submitted the newly revised translation, notes and introduction to Creative Arts Book Company. A few weeks later I received a letter from Donald Ellis, the publisher, accepting the manuscript for publication. He offered me a standard royalty arrangement with a $500.00 advance.

It was January and we were between semesters. I had gone to the university to use the library and to check my mailbox at the English Department, when I ran into one of my former professors in the hallway outside the department office. She had taught the seminar in Bibliography and Scholarly Methods, and I had used my introduction to *La Fanfarlo* as my seminar project. When I was an undergraduate, she had been my professor for a survey course in English Literature, as well as a course devoted to Shakespeare. I naively thought she would be pleased that my translation had been accepted for publication. Instead, she listened in silence, then turned her back on me and walked down the hall. I couldn't believe I'd triggered the exact same response in two of my professors in one year. Apparently, such rudeness and professional jealousy were normal in that environment. Another professor had witnessed the exchange. She told me not to take it personally. I wanted to respond, "how else could one possibly take it?" Instead, I smiled and muttered something nonsensically polite.

Despite my negative experiences with some of the faculty, there were some excellent teachers and fine people in the English Department at Northridge. I had a first rate seminar on the novels of John Steinbeck, taught by Louis Owens, a dynamic young assistant professor who went on to write novels of his own. Harry Stone, a renowned Dickens scholar whose classes I'd never taken, once visited one of my classes and wrote a wonderfully perceptive and thorough evaluation of my teaching, an act of professionalism for which I've always been grateful. Perhaps the most influential professor I knew at Northridge was Lawrence Stewart, who taught me how easy it was to be humble, gracious and kind to students. He was the graduate advisor and his door was always open. When students visited his office, he always offered them a cookie out of a round tin he kept in his desk drawer, as though they were special, valued guests. He treated everyone with dignity and kindness and displayed a wry sense of humor. While I was never a student of his, through his warmth, encouragement, and friendship, he nonetheless taught me many valuable lessons.

In late January, I received a letter from the novelist Barry Gifford, author of *Wild at Heart,* which David Lynch later adapted for his film by the same title. Gifford told me that Creative Arts, which was at the time his publisher as well, had brought him in as an editor to oversee several books, my own included. I don't recall him doing any editing, nor influencing the text in any way. Kendall Lappin had already done an excellent and thorough job of editing the book, and would be credited as the editor on the title page, as I had specified in the contract. Gifford did, however, insist on inserting his own bizarre "translation" of Baudelaire's title into my introduction. He wanted me to refer to it as "literally, The Boaster or Braggart—in this context, perhaps, The Flaunter." That there was nothing "literal" about Gifford's alternate titles must not have occurred to him. At any rate, despite my resistance, he would not budge. So I told him to put brackets around his interpolation, as I wanted nothing to do with it. Though the ink was barely dry on the contract and I had yet to receive my advance, already I was feeling less than satisfied with the publication process.

Meanwhile, I was deeply involved in the world of little magazines, as I read, supported, and published in dozens of them around the country. I began to research their history, along with the history of American literary presses like New Directions, Grove Press, as well as more contemporary innovative poetry publishers like Unicorn Press. I read an influential essay by Marvin Malone, editor and publisher of *The Wormwood Review,* in which he related that the average lifespan of most literary magazines was roughly three years, then provided a detailed blueprint for successfully publishing a literary magazine with longevity. I became increasingly interested in book design, letterpress printing, and publishing.

My last semester of graduate school, I decided to launch a new literary magazine called *Asylum*, which I planned to model on Malone's criteria for *Wormwood Review*. I would design the quarterly so that it would be economical to print and mail, and I would do all the editing and production work myself. Since the magazine would depend mainly on my own willingness to work on it without pay, in theory subscriptions would eventually cover production costs and it could be maintained for many years.

From my earlier experiences in publishing, I already knew a lot about pre-press production. I also had many contacts with magazine editors who listed calls for submissions for *Asylum*. I contacted a number of writers directly as well. I knew that editing and producing a magazine was the easy part. What vexed me most was paying for it. Since Donna and I were barely earning enough to survive, I needed to find another source of income to raise money with which to launch the magazine. Painting houses was not an option, as it didn't fit well with my teaching schedule. Finally, I took an early morning newspaper route delivering the *Los Angeles Times*. The job required me to get up at 3:00 a.m. and bag hundreds of papers, which I then threw into the back and passenger seats of my car. Then I spent hours driving around dark residential neighborhoods in the San Fernando Valley, throwing the papers onto the driveways of subscribers. After two months, I had saved enough to fund *Asylum* well into the future and quit delivering newspapers. Donna hated that I was gone at night and we were both glad when that particular nightmare ended.

The first issue of *Asylum* magazine came out in the spring of 1985. My first subscriber was Lawrence Stewart, who remained a subscriber for the ten years I published the magazine. Patrick Kelly was listed as the co-editor of the initial issue, which included work by Louis Owens, whose short story appears in the issue, Eric Basso, and Thomas Wiloch, among many others. I typed the first four issues on a proportionally spaced IBM Selectric typewriter and reduced the pages on a photocopy machine. I set the titles on one of the first generation

Macintosh computers in the campus computer lab and printed them out in galley form on an Apple LaserWriter. Then I pasted up the entire issue and made photocopies from the master. I collated the pages on the kitchen table and bound them with a saddle stapler. I used the same production method for the first year and a half of the magazine, then changed the pre-press to desktop publishing when I got my own computer. The premiere issue, the most rare of the entire ten year run, had a limited print run of only 150 copies. By 1995, *Asylum* had become *Asylum Annual,* a large-format, nationally circulated magazine with sewn bindings and a print run of 2,500 copies.

By the time I received my degree, Donna was nearly five months pregnant with our son Eric. I had applied to teach composition at Northridge in the fall and the Director of Composition had already told me that I would be offered classes based on enrollment numbers. Nevertheless, my impending fatherhood had brought on a heightened sense of responsibility. I decided to apply for part-time teaching jobs at some of the other local colleges as well. In the end, I accepted three classes at Northridge and two classes at College of the Canyons in Valencia, while turning down work at Pierce College, Valley College, and Loyola Marymount. Fortunately, a new system-wide contract for part-time faculty had just been negotiated at the California State University system, which included health care benefits for the first time. The timing could not have been better: suddenly, we had comprehensive insurance benefits which would cover the birth of our child.

That semester, I taught two sections of Freshman Composition and one section of Introduction to Literature at Northridge, and two sections of Basic Writing, a course for remedial students, at the junior college in Valencia. I was teaching at Northridge three days a week and driving to Valencia two mornings and two evenings each week as well. Donna had been told by her doctor to stop working and rest at home while she waited for the baby to come. It was a rough schedule.

My classes at Northridge went well. I always wore a jacket and tie the first couple of weeks of class and made sure students understood my expectations by providing them with a detailed syllabus, list of graded assignments, and set of rules. As the semester progressed, I left the tie at home and I introduced more flexibility and humor into my classes. I assigned my freshman classes an essay to read and discuss about education and its role in American society, and introduced them to Existentialism as a way to give them a shared vocabulary about taking responsibility for their own actions and education. As each class has a unique chemistry and mix of personalities, I customized my approach as needed. With the class I could be tough, but with individuals I always tried to be kind.

Once, I had a freshman student who refused to do any of the class work, refused to answer questions or even participate in groups. He sat through every class meeting with a wry smile on his face, as though he knew something the rest of the students did not. Though he was never disruptive or openly disrespectful, eventually I talked with him after class and invited him to my office so that we could speak candidly and in private. I asked him if he would like a cup of coffee and then I told him that it was clear to me that he was a bright and sensitive person, so I was curious why he attended class when it was obvious that he didn't want to be there. When he told me that he was in school only to please his parents, I nodded and told him that I understood why he might not find much value in formal education. "It's not for everyone, and that's perfectly okay," I said. I told him that I had had a similar response to much of my own education. Nevertheless, I explained that when he walked into my classroom in the role of a student, he had entered into a social contract. "Whether you excel or fail has nothing to do with me," I said. "My part of the contract is to work within social expectations to help students master a subject and to evaluate their progress. If a student can't work within those parameters, he is merely wasting his time and his parents' money. His protest accomplishes nothing and only hurts himself. If I were you," I told him, "I would simply go home and tell my parents I don't want to go to college and tell them what you really would like to do instead." He listened carefully to what I had to say. Then he thanked me and we shook hands. He never came to class again.

Sometimes, I dismissed an entire class that had shown up unprepared. When I came to class ready to discuss an assigned essay and saw that half the class did not have their book open, I knew there would be problems. I would immediately ask how many people had read the text and were prepared to discuss it. The two or three top students in the class would raise their hands, while the rest looked sheepish and fidgeted in their seats. "There's no point in holding class today, if you haven't come prepared. I get paid whether I teach today or send you off to read the assignment for next time, whereas you have cheated yourself and your classmates out of one of the days for which you or your parents have paid tuition. Please think about that, along with the reading for next time." Over the three years I taught at CSU Northridge, only twice did I dismiss an entire class. Both times it completely corrected the problem.

I quickly got a reputation at Northridge for being an effective teacher. My student evaluations were excellent, as were the letters from faculty peers who had sat in on my classes. The department's Director of Composition, who already knew my capabilities, made sure his daughter got placed in one of my Freshman Composition classes.

Meanwhile, I struggled to make sense of teaching at the junior college level. Most of the day students were simply trying to extend their high school experience. Few of them had much ambition or even the expectation of success. The night students were different. They were working people who, after toiling at bad jobs and enduring low wages and poor treatment by employers, were desperate to retrain in a field that would provide them with a more secure and happier existence. Most of these students were highly motivated and serious about learning. Unfortunately, the remedial writing course I was teaching had been designed by the lead composition teacher at the college with the day students in mind. Expectations were low, and the goal of the class was simply to get students to pass an exam that would enable them to take a regular freshman composition class.

The textbook for the class was a thin, spiral bound book entitled *The Paragraph Book*. I found it insulting to ask that adult students spend a semester learning what I had mastered in elementary school. I quickly ditched *The Paragraph Book* and made up my own materials, supplying my classes with photocopies of essays and other materials. Not surprisingly, my students were quite capable of learning, and those who applied themselves learned to write a five-paragraph essay rather than a paragraph.

I only lasted one semester at College of the Canyons. Though my supervisor never talked with me, and my students did better than the course average on the end of term exam, apparently I was not a team player. The English Department did not offer me classes for the spring semester. On my way out the door, I dropped off a letter to the president of the college. I recall that it was a doozy.

During this time, Donna and I were so poor that I could only afford to buy two pairs of pants, three shirts and one wool sports coat to wear to teach my classes. I remembered Mrs. Holman, my junior high school math teacher, who had only two dresses. Toward the end of the semester, one of my married students brought me a paper bag full of her husband's used dress shirts. "You need these more than he does," she told me. "He's got so many he doesn't care."

* * *

That same semester, our son was born at Kaiser-Permanente in Panorama City, less than a mile from our house. Donna had gone into labor the evening of October 14 while I happened to be home, and Eric was born the following morning. Though a bit shell-shocked, I was proud of Donna and grateful for the kind nurses and midwives at the hospital, who had helped to make the experience so positive. I remember I went home and took a shower, then drove to Northridge to teach my class. Though I hadn't slept, I remember feeling calm and relaxed. I looked forward to bringing my wife and child home the next day.

I had always told people, especially girlfriends, that I never wanted to have children. Of course, I had also proclaimed that I didn't ever want to get married. I suppose my reluctance on both accounts was a reaction to my own childhood. Because I had witnessed firsthand the effects of a disastrous marriage, I wasn't convinced that any marriage had much chance of success, nor that I would be particularly well suited as a partner. I felt similarly about raising children. It was an enormous responsibility and I didn't want to mess it up.

After we returned from France, Donna and I discussed birth control. She had been taking oral contraceptives for over five years and we were worried about the long-term effects. Though neither of us made any declarations at the time about being ready to have children, we decided to simply let nature take its course. Eventually, Donna told me she was pregnant. I don't know how I could have been surprised, but I felt like the pilot had just come onto the intercom to announce a change in my flight's destination. My emotional baggage was still stowed in the overhead compartment above me, so it took me a while to figure out exactly what I felt.

I remember a time a few months after my son was born, when I went out for pizza with a friend. It was the first time I'd been away from Donna and the baby, except to go to work. I was enjoying being in the world again and conversing with my friend. Then I caught sight of a young family at a nearby table. The couple had a child in a high chair and they were feeding it as they ate their pizza. Suddenly I felt overwhelmed by a wave of emotion. I didn't quite understand what I was feeling, only that the young child had triggered something inside me. I needed to go home immediately. I needed to be with my child. I remember feeling surprised at this nurturing instinct, but also relieved to have experienced it so distinctly.

* * *

That semester, I was still waiting for *La Fanfarlo* to be published. There had been a series of delays getting the book out. First the publisher struggled to get the original French text typeset. The production manager finally decided to photograph the original pages I had sent them, which was a photocopy I had made from the *Oeuvres Complètes*. He asked me to supply him with another, cleaner copy, which meant I would have to travel to UCLA to do the work. Though the book had been advertised for a fall release, and I had been told the galleys would arrive soon, the production delays continued. Finally, I received a phone call from someone at Creative Arts telling me the galleys would arrive by courier that day. For some reason, they needed me to send them back two days after I received them. After all the delays, I was furious to have so little time to proofread. A couple months later, I received a small box containing ten advance copies of the finished book. Though the book was handsome enough—they had used one of Baudelaire's ink drawings of his mistress, the actress Jeanne Duval, on the cover—the bright colors seemed garish and inappropriate for a serious literary work.

La Fanfarlo received a number of excellent reviews in national publications, in which my translation was universally praised, including a mention in the "Noted with Pleasure" section of *The New York Times Book Review*. A mystery admirer in the English Department posted that review on the office bulletin board for everyone to see. A couple of professors congratulated me, while the other ninety-five did their best to pretend I did not exist and hoped that I would soon go away. The book quickly went into a second printing, and I received a few more author copies. After that, I never heard from the publisher again, as they ignored my requests for royalty statements the contract had specified. Though they kept the book in print until they finally went bankrupt and out of business in 2004, I never received another nickel past the original advance. Still, I was among the lucky ones, apparently: according to *Publisher's Weekly*, some of the press' last authors had paid the publisher from $8,000 to $15,000 to co-publish their books, then lost everything in the bankruptcy.

I had another idea pinging around inside my head as well at that time: a descriptive bibliography of Unicorn Press publications. I had been carefully studying every Unicorn publication I could find and I thought it would be interesting to catalog the entire output of the press. So I contacted Alan Brilliant at Unicorn and asked him what he thought of the idea. He told me that he had done some preliminary work on an abbreviated bibliography for Special Collections at Brown University Library, which owned the Unicorn archives. He agreed that I would be a good choice to undertake a more professional and complete bibliography, and he invited me to come to Greensboro to meet with him and look over the press copies and records he had on hand. I planned a trip for the summer break and began to set aside some money for the airfare.

The following semester, the department assigned me three sections of Freshman Composition, which meant that I had to grade seventy student essays each week for fifteen weeks. Little did I know that those 1,050 student essays would play an essential role in the creation of *Water & Power*, my first book of short stories. I remember sitting at my desk in my shared office on the eighth floor of Sierra Tower with a tall stack of unread essays in front of me and a much shorter stack of corrected and graded essays in the corner. After hours spent marking up sentence fragments, run-on sentences, and subject verb agreement problems, I'd push the stacks of papers away from me and begin writing a story, usually whatever came first to mind. Most of the time, I used a first-person narration and just let my character talk. After writing three failed novels, it was a relief to simply let an invented character's speaking voice dictate the narration. Often, the stories came out so fast that I felt as though I were transcribing rather than writing. Once I got started on a story, I usually finished it in one sitting, writing until it reached its conclusion. Then I'd go back to grading the student essays. I continued to write stories in my office for the next two years. By then, I'd learned how to write fiction and had enough material for a book.

"Water & Power," the title story of the book, is of particular interest, as it unexpectedly foreshadows the paintings and other artwork I would undertake nearly twenty years in the future, as well as conclusions I would later reach about the collective past of our Paleolithic ancestors. The story concerns a man living in Los Angeles who, through a series of everyday misfortunes, neglects to pay his utility bill. Determined to deliver his payment in person to the water and electric company, he leaves his apartment, only to find that as he shuts the door behind him the modern world vanishes, replaced by a prehistoric reality teeming with creatures whose bones he had often seen in the museum at the nearby La Brea tar pits. Brought to ground at the story's conclusion by a huge saber-toothed cat, as the predator is about to sink his dirk-like teeth into the neck of his prey, the narrator plunges a sharp pencil into the feline's eye. That the narrator of the story uses his pencil, a symbol of technology, culture, and written language, as a substitute for the sharp teeth and claws he lacks, underscores the evolutionary advantages the development of symbolic thinking bestowed upon *Homo sapiens.*

Fortunately, most semesters I got to teach literature or creative writing courses as well as composition. Though I worked hard to prepare and organize each new class, I enjoyed the challenge. Among the most enjoyable classes I taught were a course in Science Fiction Literature, which I constructed with an emphasis on dystopian fiction, and an evening class in Advanced Narrative Writing. I also taught a summer session of Advanced Expository Writing, in which I had students read non-fiction by Joan Didion, Tom Wolfe, and other masters of the New Journalism and learn to incorporate the techniques of fiction into their own essays.

By 1985, Apple, Inc. had already released its new Macintosh personal computer and Laserwriter printer, which would revolutionize the printing industry. The university had set up a lab in the Engineering Department, and there I learned how to use the new computers to typeset the titles for the first issues of *Asylum.* The following year, I applied for a yearly university-wide faculty competition called the Meritorious Performance and Professional Promise Award, which I received for my proposal to use the prize money to buy a Macintosh computer with which to publish my literary magazine.

By then, my book of prose poems had been published by Unicorn Press and I was publishing my short stories in magazines around the country. The English Department began offering me classes in Creative Writing and Narrative Writing. In one of my beginning Creative Writing classes, I made the mistake of asking students why they were taking the course. One of them told me that he wanted to be like me. "A writer?" I asked. He shook his head, no. What he meant is that he wanted to get paid to teach a subject that didn't require him to learn complicated formulas, or memorize the periodic table or verb terminations for modes or tenses that don't exist in English, or even read plays written in Elizabethan English. He wanted to teach creative writing. I took his point. It was a damned easy class to teach.

One of the other students in that same class was a kid with red hair and glasses who, like Elvis Costello or Devo, cultivated a look that was so geeky it was cool. He turned out to be the rock star of the class, as he had an offbeat and understated sense of humor that no seminar in creative writing could ever teach. I worried about him being in school. The following year, I ran into him on campus. He looked a bit depressed. "What's wrong?" I asked. He told me that he'd just got a short story he'd written for his Narrative Writing class back from the professor, who had circled every typographical error in red ink. "Well..." I started to say, but he cut me off and asked if I'd read the story and give him my opinion of it. I agreed and we arranged for him to come to my office the following day.

"The Proofreader" turned out to be a brilliant story in which the author's intentional typographical errors play a significant role in the exposition. I couldn't believe his professor had been so inattentive or downright dense as to miss the originality and genius of the story. When Tim came to my office, I told him his story was so good that I wanted to publish it in my magazine, *Asylum*. I also suggested he drop out of school, or at very least ignore everything his professors told him before the university ruined him. I later reprinted the story in the avant-garde fiction anthology I edited, called *Unscheduled Departures*. The story was again reprinted in an anthology of young writers called *Voices of the Xiled*. Tim Hensley went on to become a writer of alternative comics, including the graphic novel, *Wally Gropius*.

Word got out among creative writing students that I was someone they should meet and talk to. Students from my own classes as well as ones I'd never met before came to my office to discuss a range of topics. One day a tall, serious young man with a beard came to introduce himself. "I'm Jordan Jones," he said. He told me he worked on the university literary magazine and he wanted to ask me what I thought of various post-graduate writing programs. I told him to skip them all, write on his own, and start his own magazine instead. Though he opted for a M.A. in English at UC Davis, he did go on to start his own magazine, *Bakunin*.

Over the summer, I taught a course in Intermediate Expository Writing. The class met every evening, five days a week, for three hours, over an intense three-week period. I made $3,000 for teaching the class, which at the time was a small fortune for me. The money allowed me to go to North Carolina to meet with Alan and Teo and begin work on the Unicorn Press descriptive bibliography.

In Greensboro, I stayed in Alan and Teo's sprawling suburban house. Located in an upper middle-class neighborhood, most of the house had been converted to a production facility for Unicorn Press, which occupied several large rooms that appeared to be part of an addition to the original house. A big, open room with sliding glass doors that gave onto the back yard garden contained the hand-cranked Vandercook SP-15 cylindrical proofing press, along with a large bank of oak type cabinets, drying racks, metal shelves, and work benches. There were two small offices connected to a pre-press table for laying out non-letterpress books. An attached back building, perhaps at one time a garage, had been converted to a book bindery, warehouse, archives, and shipping area.

I stayed several days and slept on a single bed among the archives. I talked with Alan as he went through the routine tasks of filling orders, answering correspondence, and planning new publications. His assistant, a poet named Sarah Lindsay, who had hand-set and printed *The Masked Ball*, had recently left the press, as had another long-time employee, so Alan was currently working alone.

Each day, I had lunch with my editor and pen-pal Teo Savory. Since she only had the strength to leave her bed for a limited amount of time each day, she arranged her work and social life around her lunches. She was in her eighties, and was roughly thirty years older than her husband, Alan. Though dying of lung cancer, she made a point of spending as much time as possible with me. Teo told me stories about her life: she had grown up in China, had studied music and had a music career in London. Later, she had worked in New York as an executive during the early days of television. With her knowledge of languages, she had championed and translated foreign poets at a time when there was little interest in foreign literature in the United States, and had edited the influential Unicorn French and Unicorn Germans series. She told me the history of the press, and expressed her vision of the future of Unicorn.

* * *

Back in Northridge, my office mate that year was a pompous ass who introduced himself as a philologist. Since the department had hired a structural linguist and an expert in transformational grammar to teach linguistics courses, the philologist had instead tossed off two novels that he somehow managed to publish with a commercial publisher. These novels, which even he dismissed as inconsequential, nonetheless resulted in his reincarnation as a writer. He was fond of giving me unsolicited advice. "Greg, you're a talented young guy, but you waste too much time with students pestering you in the office. You've got better things to do. Over the years, I've learned to get rid of them quickly. Three minutes is all you need."

From time to time, Dr. Philologist's friend, a specialist in Victorian literature who sported a pointy goatee and dressed in tweedy suits, came to visit him. Apparently, what he had to say was top secret and could only be spoken in whispers, at least whenever I was present. "Don't mind me," I told him once, "it's time for my constitutional anyway." Thereafter, whenever I caught a glimpse of his goat-like bearded face peering in from the hallway, I promptly vacated the office.

At that stage of my life and for the next twenty years, I possessed an almost inexhaustible energy. I slept very little and never felt tired. I drank coffee all day and most of the night, yet never had trouble sleeping when I did finally go to bed. I drank too much and worked too hard. I taught classes. I read voraciously. I wrote stories, poems, and book reviews. No matter how much I took on or accomplished, I always felt I could do more.

During my brief time teaching at CSU Northridge I published my work in little magazines with wonderful names like *Stifled Yawn, Open, Noospapers, Rhododendron, Third Eye, Vice Versa, Pinchpenny, Bakunin, Paper Radio, Lactuca, NRG, Scree, Titmouse, Wordsworth's Socks, Poetry Motel, Central Park, Pididdle, Fell Swoop, Caliban, Wormwood Review, Broken Streets, Planet Detroit,* and *Catalyst,* or academic journals like *New Delta Review, Florida Review, Poet Lore, Cream City Review,* and *Hawaii Review.* I wrote critical essays and reviews. I wrote prose poems and short stories. I wrote and illustrated a book of original Jungian fairy tales, which I incorporated years later into my novel *The Double.* I worked on translations of poems by Jean Follain and stories by Petrus Borel. I wrote a children's book for my son called *Crabby the Selfish Shell Fish,* and illustrated it with watercolor paintings. I printed a series of erotic prints and bound them into a book for my wife. I published little poetry chapbooks in experimental formats. An editor named Kimberly Cole published a collection of my literary essays and reviews entitled *Balzac's Dolls, and Other Essays, Studies, and Literary Sketches* and a small book of my short stories called *More Lies.*

At CSU Northridge, many of the teaching faculty in the English department were yearly contract workers. These adjunct instructors taught from one to three classes each semester. Though some of these shadow professors had taught at the university for fifteen years and were widely published, the tenured faculty largely ignored their presence. They did not attend department meetings nor socialize with the "real" faculty. Named as professors only on their annual appointment letters, they were most often dismissively referred to within the department as "part-timers." The School of Humanities considered four classes per semester full-time employment. Ironically, none of the tenured, full-time faculty in the English department taught more than three classes, as they were almost always awarded "reassigned time" for research instead of teaching another class. The lower salaries of the part-time faculty paid for this significant perk. In addition, the tenured faculty rarely if ever had to teach sections of the one course within the department required of all university students—freshman composition—which the department euphemistically called written expression.

Based on my teaching experiences, I began drawing an underground comic strip called "The Part-Timer," which satirized the pecking order in the English department, the pompous buffoonery and eccentric behavior I encountered there, as well as exposing the hopelessness and despair of academic contract workers. As I recall, I drew my unlikely hero, The Part-Timer, with a pair of striped, curly horns on his head, and his main adversary, The Chairman, with an upside-down chair posed on his head like a hat. Though I never duplicated or distributed my comic, I did share it with a few of my part-time instructor colleagues. We needed a good laugh.

When our son was nine months old, my mother told us we would have to leave the house we'd been living in, as she and her husband were ready to sell it. Donna had only recently found a new job and was working part-time for a leasing company in Encino, while I watched Eric after my morning classes. Though the move caught us off guard, we quickly found a split level apartment with two bedrooms in a brand new building across from the women's softball field at the university. We moved into it, though we knew it would soon fill up with students and was more expensive than we could really afford. After moving in, we learned of another disadvantage: the old house next door contained a machine shop in the detached garage that its owner operated at all hours of the day and night. We called him Buzz.

Since we were close to the open athletic fields at the university, I used to take Eric to walk and play on the huge grassy lawns, where he loved to look for golf balls. He was learning to talk at this stage and seeing him develop the capacity for language fascinated me. I taught him words in both English and French and he was never once confused or had the slightest difficulty distinguishing between the languages. He loved the word *"hibou,"* which always made him laugh.

Just before we moved, I began to apply for jobs outside of Los Angeles, in areas where the cost of living was lower. Donna and I knew that we could never afford to buy a house if we stayed in Southern California. I applied for an adjunct faculty job at CSU Chico and received a letter from the Chairman of the English Department there offering me a one-year contract. Though it was a chance to leave Los Angeles, the job offered no real security. I also applied for a full time, permanent job at a junior college in Merced, where I was one of three finalists to interview for the job.

On the day of my interview, I drove five hours to Merced only to realize that I had left my sports coat at home. I was a couple hours early for the interview, so I parked our Volkswagen van downtown and walked around the block to look for somewhere I could buy a jacket. Luckily, I found a men's clothing store and bought a lightweight gray sports coat with the emergency cash I had in my pocket. The interview went well enough, though I had the feeling the people on the panel thought I was too intense for the job. Finally, one of them asked me what I would miss most about my current job. "Access to a good research library," I told them. They looked at me as though I had told them I would miss my drug connection. On the long drive home, I replayed the interview in my head. I knew I had been too forthright. If I had been on the committee, I would not have hired me for that job, either. I knew it was time for me to do something else with my life.

My few friends among the faculty at Northridge tried to encourage me to go on to a Ph.D. in literature, but I resisted. I had never intended to go to graduate school and had little tolerance for letting others orchestrate my reading, or influence my creative or scholarly pursuits. I had played around with drugs as a teenager, but had never taken LSD, just as I had played around the academy without getting a Ph.D. In my view, both were simply too dangerous for someone with an excess of imagination and creativity.

In addition to writing fiction, I continued my work on the Descriptive Bibliography of Unicorn Press Ephemeral Publications, samples of which I had brought back with me from Greensboro. I had also begun writing and illustrating a companion volume to *The Masked Ball* called *Puppet Theatre,* which I hoped Unicorn Press would also publish. When I finished the manuscript, I sent it to Alan and Teo. They wrote back that they would love to publish the book, and invited me to come typeset and print it myself in Greensboro the following summer. I immediately accepted and started making plans.

Meanwhile, the eccentrics around the English Department, along with the politics and the absurd and artificial hierarchies and pecking order increasingly got on my nerves. My friend Pat had received his M.A. in Conducting and had formed a chamber orchestra. Like me, he was ambitious but broke. A job overseeing the university-wide Writing Proficiency Exam had come up, as the test was overseen and managed by the English Department, and I suggested he apply for it. He did and landed the job, which for him was a mixed blessing, since it involved working in the toxic English Department. Since he was between apartments, we invited him to use our spare bedroom in exchange for help with the rent.

Over my final semester of teaching, I corresponded often with Alan at Unicorn and eventually our plans changed to include the possibility of my staying on past the summer and taking over as editor of the press. Teo was, by now, very weak, and almost totally bedridden. Though she admired my writing and my magazine and she, herself, had been the one to propose me as her successor, she was nevertheless reluctant to relinquish her authority over the press, so I knew that it would likely be a difficult transition. Nevertheless, I had grown bored and restless with my low-status teaching job, and wanted more than anything to be at the center of the hub, working in literary publishing. I was certain that was the correct path for me.

For the next few months, Donna and I saved all the money we could. I wanted to bring some state-of-the-art computer equipment with me to Greensboro, where I thought it might help turn Unicorn Press into a more profitable operation. The equipment would also enable us to do freelance typesetting and design work. So I began to look for a good deal on a new Macintosh computer with an internal hard drive and a laser printer. Eventually, I found what I was looking for through an advertisement in the newspaper, and I arranged to check it out. Though the seller claimed to be an official Apple reseller, the deal seemed too good to be plausible. Since I had no way of determining the provenance of the equipment, I decided to stop asking questions and buy it, though I suspected that it might not qualify for warranty if it did not function properly.

In May, I wrapped up my classes at Northridge and turned in my grades. Though I would draw pay for the next three months, my twelve-month contract was over. I knew that I would not go back. In early June, Donna and I loaded the new computer and laser printer, along with whatever belongings would fit, into our Volkswagen van. We pointed ourselves east and set out on the road toward North Carolina.

* * *

Since my mother had been an elementary school teacher her whole working life and my father had been a professor of engineering at UCLA for several years during the time I was growing up, I had always told myself, along with anyone who asked, that I did not want be a teacher. Ironically, I would realize years later, after having my own "Hay for the Horses" epiphany, that "that's just what I'd gone and done." Though never a career professor, I taught English, lectured, and gave readings at universities and colleges. I informally mentored younger writers, editors, and publishers and showed people how to do letterpress printing. I taught martial arts at a Taekwondo dojo professionally in Northern California. In Virginia, I taught for a year at a women's college and I lectured about Paleolithic Art in conjunction with exhibits of my paintings. During the five years we lived in Ecuador, I gave private lessons in English as a second language, phonetics, writing, drawing, and painting. Even the books I'd written and published were, according to Horace's famous definition of literature, instructional. As I got older, I began to tell my students that they had an obligation to share what they had learned with others. It seems those of us who are meant to teach do it whether we intend to or not.

The Last Unicorn

> Up here I try not to think. But if I do, I make sure it's not about the pain and stiffness in my neck, nor the heat from the sun on my back and legs, nor the sweat trickling from my brow that I can't seem to wipe without getting paint on my face... nor my fear of falling fifteen to twenty feet off the ladder, nor the unsafe but only possible way in which to angle and block the ladder on this side of the house, nor anything else too immediate, but rather about my hopes and dreams.
> — "Under the Eaves" from *Water & Power*

WE MOVED TO Spain in 2018. During the first year, we lived in Alicante, where I made several large paintings. One was a rectangular canvas containing a number of squares and smaller rectangles, most of which in turn contain symbols. Some of these symbols come from alphabets, both real and imagined. Others are signs that hobos once left in towns close to railroad lines. They warn of mean dogs and intolerant sheriffs, or advertise a kind-hearted woman. Other boxes in the painting I filled with linear mazes and twisted wire forms. I titled this autobiographical work "California Job Case."

In letterpress printing, a California job case is a large, thin, wooden drawer divided into compartments and used to store movable lead type. Compositors pick individual pieces of type—minuscules, majuscules, numbers, punctuation, spaces, and symbols—to arrange into lines in a hand-held tool called a stick. Foundry type faces backwards, as in a mirror image, so that when coated with ink and imprinted on paper, it reads correctly. Originally called an italics case or double case, the California job case evolved in stages and appeared in west coast foundries in its current form as early as the 1850s. By the turn of the century, it had become the most popular case design used in America. Because these new wooden type cases combined lower case letters and capital letters into a single type tray, the California job case was more efficient, as it reduced the travel of the compositor's hand by as much as a half a mile per day.

A California job case contains eighty-nine individual compartments, which hold specific letters, spacers, ligatures, and quads in preassigned locations. Minuscules, punctuation, and lead spacers of various widths are on the left side of the case. Capital letters are on the right. Numbers and symbols are at the top. The position and size of the compartments for lowercase letters correspond to the frequency of their use. Like the keys on a keyboard, the most commonly used letters occupy the easiest positions for the typesetter to reach. The compartments themselves vary in size as well to accommodate the need for additional characters. The largest partitions contain the "e" and other vowels, while the "j", "k", "q", "x", and "z" characters fit into the smallest compartments.

Setting moveable type by hand is slow, methodical work. As the repetitious motions easily become tedious, not everyone enjoys the process. Nevertheless, some people find a Zen-like quality in setting type: though the job requires a certain amount of concentration, the mind can wander where the work takes it. Like keyboarding on a computerized system, much depends on the quality of the manuscript. Setting type for a good book can be a rewarding experience. Likewise, typesetting a book of one's own poems by hand, character by character, can teach a poet much about concision. Each letter occupies a space on the page. Each phoneme and morpheme has a purpose. I remember making a handful of editorial changes in the prose poems in *Puppet Theatre* as I set the type for the book. As I recall, most of these changes involved removing adjectives or other superfluous words from the text.

Prior to setting type for a new book, one usually breaks down a previously printed book and distributes the type into a job case. When I set the type for *Puppet Theatre* at Unicorn Press in Greensboro during the summer and fall of 1988, I distributed the type from my earlier Unicorn Press book, *The Masked Ball*, which poet Sarah Lindsay had typeset in 1986, using the same Kennerly 12-point type. The process of distributing type, while faster than meticulously setting it with proper spacing a line at a time within a stick, still requires concentration and practice. It's a good place to begin, as distributing the type teaches one the layout of the job case. I remember that by the time I'd finishing breaking down one book, I knew enough to start putting together the next one.

When there's enough lead type available in the specified size of the required font, the typesetter can begin work on a new project. The compositor picks up each individual letter and space from the job case and arranges these backward letters into lines. Whether or not the right-hand margin is justified, the edges on both sides will contain metal spacers to create perfectly uniform edges and form a block of type. Normally, about three lines of type can fit onto the stick before those lines must be transferred onto a metal type tray and secured with metal line spacers and magnets. When the typesetter has set enough lines to form an entire page, he or she labels the type for that page and ties up the block of type with string. Each metal tray holds four pages of type. The compositor temporarily stores these trays in a cabinet.

The proofing stage begins when the compositor has completed typesetting all the pages of the book. At this point, the printer slides each of the type blocks from the type tray onto the flat metal chase that rests on the bed of the press, then unties the string and locks the type block tightly within the chase, using strips of wood of various lengths and widths called furniture and mechanical wedges called quoins. Depending on the style of proofing press, the printer inks the type directly, or else inks the cylinder of the press, and then pulls several proofs on newsprint. Then, the type block for that page is tied up again, transferred to the type tray, cleaned of ink with solvent, and stored in the drawer. The printer repeats this process until he or she has proofs for each page of the book.

While the author and editors mark up the proofs with their corrections, the designer and printer use a set of proofs to make a layout dummy or mock-up for the book. The mock-up indicates trim, gutters, folds, and the exact placement of type blocks for both sides of the large sheets of paper that will make up the folded eight-page signatures. In the case of *Puppet Theatre*, which, like its companion volume *The Masked Ball*, includes my linocut block prints on the pages facing each prose poem, I included the illustrations in the layout dummy.

Working from the master set of proofs, which incorporates all the indicated corrections, the compositor corrects minor typographical errors and pulls a second set of proofs, sometimes off the press, using a brayer to ink the type and a soft barren to print an impression from which to check the work. After the author or editor has approved the final set of corrections, the printer may finally begin reproducing the book.

Puppet Theatre was printed four pages up, two sides, which means that each printed sheet, when folded, yielded eight pages. Because the facing linocuts had to be inked more heavily than the type and thus could not be printed at the same time as the blocks of type, *Puppet Theatre* required two separate pulls through the press on each side of every sheet of paper, plus an additional pull for the spot color on the title page. Thus, the edition of 500 copies required me to pull large sheets of paper through the hand-cranked Vandercook SP-15 cylinder proofing press 12,500 times to print the entire edition of the book. That making books by hand is a slow, methodical, and labor-intensive process explains much about Unicorn Press and its rather quirky history and development, as well as my experience there.

* * *

Alan Brilliant told me that he founded Unicorn Press in 1966 as a collaboration between himself and Jack Shoemaker, manager of the newly opened Unicorn Book Shop. According to Alan, Shoemaker had met a wealthy young man named Ken Maytag in a coffee shop in Santa Barbara and after a free-ranging conversation about literature, books, and the ideal book shop, Maytag, an heir to the Maytag Appliance company, put up the money to open the Unicorn Book Shop in Isla Vista, with Shoemaker as the manager. In addition to selling books, Shoemaker also wanted to publish work by Beat poet Gary Snyder and the Vietnamese Buddhist monk and poet Thích Nhất Hạnh, whose work Brilliant and his multilingual wife Teo Savory had seen published in French translations in an avant-garde French literary magazine. Shoemaker invited Snyder to read at the Magic Lantern Theater next door to the book store to help publicize and celebrate the opening of the Unicorn Book Shop in January of 1966. Along with Thích Nhất Hạnh, Snyder was among the first Unicorn Press authors.

The money to begin publishing letterpress broadsides and chapbooks also came from Ken Maytag. I remember Alan telling me how he and Shoemaker pitched the idea for the press to him. "It came down to a choice between a submarine or a unicorn," Brilliant told me. "It was right around the time the Beatles had released their song 'Yellow Submarine' and Maytag was toying with the idea of buying one himself. Ultimately, he chose Unicorn, though honestly it could have gone either way." Maytag was writing poetry, and a press would give him a publishing outlet for his own work. Also, he liked Gary Snyder and welcomed the chance to publish his work.

Richard Brautigan first read from *Trout Fishing in America* at the Unicorn Book Shop in October of the following year. Soon after, police raided the Magic Lantern Theater during the showing of an art film that contained full frontal nudity. When local authorities charged the operators with obscenity, they lost their funding and had to close the theater. Shoemaker left Unicorn in 1968 to start a press with poet David Meltzer, and when that venture failed, he went on to manage Serendipity Books in Berkeley and start Sand Dollar Books, in Albany, California, for a time the largest poetry book store in the United States. He also founded and edited a number of well-regarded commercial literary publishing companies located in Berkeley, including North Point Press and Counterpoint. Melissa Mytinger, another poet who clerked at the Unicorn Book Shop, and whose work the press published, later went on to manage Cody's Books in Berkeley and, as events director for Cody's, organized lectures and readings by distinguished authors for many years.

After Shoemaker's departure, Alan Brilliant and his wife Teo Savory bought Unicorn Press from Maytag, who had already lost interest in it. Alan Brilliant was the only child of immigrant parents. His mother was from Vienna, Austria, and his father from Odessa, Ukraine. He grew up in a rough neighborhood in Camden, New Jersey. Inspired by Camden resident Walt Whitman, he took an interest in poetry and graduated from Columbia University in 1957. During his time at Columbia and after, he worked for legendary bookseller Ted Wilentz at the Eighth Street Book Shop and at Corinth Books in New York City, then managed the Gotham Book Mart. In 1958, he met novelist and poet Teo Savory, a five-times divorced woman nearly thirty years older than himself, and promptly married her. They were together for the next thirty-one years, until Savory's death in 1989.

Though Alan always spoke highly of his parents and kept a photograph of them on the nightstand in his Spartan bedroom in the house in Greensboro, his parents did not approve of his marriage to a divorced woman. They felt so strongly about the marriage that they refused to speak to their son again until 1990, when Alan's elderly father finally visited him in Greensboro and they reconciled.

According to her own account, Teo Savory was born in Hong Kong in 1907, the daughter of a Portland, Oregon flour merchant who had moved to China to manage a family business there. She married a British citizen in 1929 and moved with him to London, where she studied at the Royal College of Music. She performed in musical theater, comedic opera, and theater during the time she lived in England. After her return to the United States, she married expat British playwright Gerald Savory in 1938. Though she divorced Savory, she retained the name for her literary career. She worked as a publicist for The American National Theater and Academy and the Woodstock Playhouse. She also worked in early television production and established a literary agency for writers of television scripts. Her first fiction appeared in print in 1948 and she met Alan Brilliant ten years later.

In the early 1960s, Alan and Teo moved west to Santa Barbara, California, where they lived a bohemian lifestyle. Teo once told me that during those years she and Alan had agreed to commit fully to literature, even if that meant making sacrifices and doing whatever it took to persevere. Henceforth, they had little patience for distractions such as working to pay the rent. Alan wrote poems, learned letterpress printing, and worked with Noel Young, a commercial printer who would found Capra Press in 1969, setting type and printing books by literary publishers such as Black Sparrow Press. Meanwhile, Alan and Teo lived in a series of cheap apartments and beachside motels, where Teo worked on the novels that Unicorn would later publish. During this time, she also translated work by French poets (including Guillevic, Supervielle, Queneau, Corbière, Prévert, Jammes, and Michaux) that Unicorn would issue in their influential Unicorn French series. Most summers they spent at the house Teo owned in the Berkshire Mountains of Massachusetts.

After Ken Maytag agreed to fund the publishing venture, Alan set up offices and a shop in a rental property on El Paseo, off State Street in downtown Santa Barbara. An internal courtyard formed by the surrounding buildings and an old adobe complex, the internal walking street had been restored and redesigned in the 1920s to reflect a Spanish style courtyard with offices and shops facing inward. The original design for El Paseo included two studio wings for artists. The white stucco studios, offices and shops had handmade red clay roof tiles, Moorish lamps, hand-hewn wooden balconies, wrought iron grills on the casement windows, and rough plank doors. The walkway itself had been paved with flagstone. At a remove from the noise of traffic, a fountain bubbled in the courtyard, around which businesses looked onto orange trees and flowering vines.

No doubt this architectural paradise had fallen into disrepair by the 1960s, though it nonetheless must have remained a desirable, centrally located property. For the next seven years Alan, Teo, a few skilled workers, along with a perpetual house party of drop-in guests, set type, sewed, collated and assembled, marketed, packaged and shipped chapbooks, broadsides, folios, postcards, the *Unicorn Journal,* and a host of creatively conceived ephemeral poetry publications Alan designed and Teo edited. Initially, Alan and Noel Young printed the majority of the work at Young's commercial letterpress shop.

Maytag's money and an abundance of cheap labor, combined with efficient and original designs, allowed Unicorn Press to flourish during this period. The press published an on-going series of poetry broadsides, three series of Unicorn Folios, poetry post cards and postcard sets, folded broadsides, and chapbooks by individual poets, as well as two beautifully designed pocket-sized series of case-bound books that introduced the work of French and German poets in English translations. Unicorn Press authors included Gary Snyder, Diane Di Prima, Robert Bly, Thích Nhất Hạnh, James Tate, Philip Levine, George Hitchcock, Margaret Atwood, David Meltzer, W. S. Merwin, Guillaume Apollinaire, Kenneth Rexroth, Jerome Rothenberg, Lawrence Fixel, Jack Hirshman, Teo Savory, Gunter Eich, Frederico García Lorca, James Laughlin, Bert Meyers, Jorge Luis Borges, Muriel Rukeyser, Paul Éluard, Kenneth Patchen, Alan Brilliant, Paul Celan, Jacques Prévert, Carolyn Stoloff, Antonio Machado, Anselm Hollo, Thomas Merton, Lenore Marshall, Madeline Gleason, Nathaniel Tarn, Robert Hershon, Melissa Mytinger, Lew Welch, Boris Pasternak, Langston Hughes, Diane Wakowski, and Charles Simic, among many others.

Nevertheless, Unicorn made little money selling three-dollar poetry chapbooks and sets of poetry postcards, or seven-dollar subscriptions for the folios, no matter how original the work or lavish the design and production. As rents went up in Santa Barbara and the communal appeal of sacrificing a living wage in order to do meaningful work dissipated, Unicorn struggled to pay the rent and keep publishing. In the end, seduced by the possibility of a part-time job for Alan teaching aspects of literary publishing to MFA students at the University of North Carolina, Greensboro, Alan and Teo left California. The teaching job fell through, but by then it was too late. They had already moved to Greensboro.

* * *

It's a long way from California to North Carolina. I know, because I drove both directions and I remember how much I hoped I would never have to cross the bleak, empty expanse of Texas again. In 1988, Alan had invited me to come to Greensboro to hand-set and print my second collection of prose poems and prints at Unicorn Press, which had already published the earlier, companion volume. So, Donna and I gathered up our toddler son, packed anything of use or value we owned into our Volkswagen Microbus and set off on an adventure. I also packed the computer equipment and desktop publishing software I thought would help modernize production, editorial, fulfillment, and marketing operations at Unicorn Press and help transform it into a more viable and stable publisher.

On the first day of our drive from Los Angeles to Greensboro, our Volkswagen struggled up the steep grade into Flagstaff, Arizona at thirty miles per hour. It coughed and sputtered as we looked for a motel. The next morning, the van miraculously started up and ran normally. We got on the highway and continued east. We drove for four days straight and didn't take any of the sight-seeing detours we'd planned, as we feared the Volkswagen's engine would fail. Instead, we headed straight for Greensboro and arrived several days ahead of schedule, the underpowered van coughing and sputtering once again. It was worn out from the trip, and so were we.

We spent our first two nights in Greensboro at a cheap motel that served coffee and Krispy Kreme donuts for breakfast. Stuffed in the center with insanely sweet cream filling, the donuts tasted good but made us jumpy and hyperactive. When we called Alan, he told us we could stay for a week at a friend's empty house if we were willing to cut the grass. The owner had left town and put the house up for sale, so it needed to look presentable. For the next few days, we slept on the floor of the empty house, worked at cutting the grass in the huge back yard in the evening when it wasn't quite as hot and humid, and looked for a place to live. We called about an ad we saw in the newspaper and went to look at a tiny two-bedroom brick house on Tower Road across from an elementary school. The owner, a southern gentleman named Zane Leake, took an instant liking to us. Mr. Leake, as we always called him, was a retired engineer and a widower. We rented the house for $250.00 per month, bought two beds from a mattress shop, and moved in right away. A week later, we came home one afternoon to find Mr. Leake hanging a rope swing with a wooden seat he had made for our son from an overhanging branch of the huge oak tree in front of the house.

People in Greensboro loved garage sales, so after the first weekend, we had accumulated enough used furniture for the entire house. Since the kitchen didn't have a refrigerator, I went downtown and looked for one at a used appliance store. After the shop delivered the refrigerator, we realized it was full of cockroaches. We sprayed poison everywhere, dismantled the refrigerator, and washed it out with boiling water. Then we opened a bottle of wine we'd bought at the local Food Lion grocery store. We were drinking wine from plastic cups in shorts and water soaked, dirty t-shirts when a man and a woman dressed in their Sunday best knocked on our door. They were from the Baptist church two doors up the street and had come to ascertain what kind of people had moved into the rental house. Apparently, they wanted us to join their congregation. Donna stood firmly at the front door and did not invite them into the house, which was completely blown up from our attempts at exterminating. Though Donna listened politely to what they had to say, I can only imagine what they thought of us. After that initial encounter, they never greeted us or acknowledged our presence. It was quickly becoming clear that North Carolina was, indeed, a long way from California.

Meanwhile, Alan loaned me a bicycle to ride the three miles to work. My first week at Unicorn I broke down and distributed the Kennerly type I needed for my book and learned the basic operations of the print shop. Alan taught me a little about the Vandercook press as well, and put me to work printing copies of dust jackets for the novel *Cora Fry*, using type he had set earlier and a zinc plate for the artwork. I found working the press satisfying and meditative.

Each day, I had lunch with Teo, though she was by this time so ill with lung cancer that she could barely sit up for more than a half an hour at a time. During the day, she frequently interrupted Alan's work with the bell that she rang when she needed him to help her get to the bathroom or regulate her oxygen tank. Shriveled and bent with age and illness, she croaked with a raspy smoker's voice. Though she could barely catch her breath at times, she continued to smoke unfiltered Pall Mall cigarettes. Despite her physical limitations, Teo remained a lively, engaging story-teller and conversationalist. Legally blind, she spent most days in bed listening to books on tape Alan brought her from the public library. When I asked Alan if my conversations with Teo exhausted her, he told me that she enjoyed having someone new and interesting to talk with.

At first, we spoke mainly about Teo's life and work. I'd read most of her novels and collections of stories as well as her translations of French and German authors published by Unicorn Press. Our relationship had started with my translation of *La Fanfarlo*, which gave us a special connection. She'd been among the first editors to encourage me and I viewed her as a mentor. During our talks, she sometimes told stories about the writers she'd known over the years. Once she told me about Margaret and Hans Rey, the authors and illustrators of the famous *Curious George* books that had been among my favorite stories as a young child. For a time, the Reys had been her neighbors. They told her how they had settled in Paris before the war, and how they escaped from the Nazis by riding cobbled-together bicycles out of the city in 1940. They took only one suitcase and the manuscripts and artwork for some of their *Curious George* books and traveled all the way to the Spanish border, then on to Portugal, where they booked passage to Brazil, then to New York.

Teo also told me about her friendship with Paul Auster, a writer she'd corresponded with about French poetry and translation many years before he'd become a famous novelist. She said that she admired his work and hoped that I would achieve similar success as a fiction writer. Sometimes I asked her about her memories of China and her career in musical theater in England. Once, she told me how she had been forced to sell the sailboat she had owned in New England in order to keep Unicorn Press solvent. It was the only time I saw her cry.

Eventually, Teo asked me to read my short stories aloud to her, so I read from the manuscript of *Water & Power* each day after lunch. Teo wrote well crafted, very traditional literary fiction, so I didn't know what she'd think of my surreal, unconventionally constructed tales. As I read, she listened carefully to each word and sometimes asked me to repeat a sentence. Sometimes she chuckled out loud. Occasionally, she stopped me to correct an error or to question my diction. When I finished reading the final story in the collection, she gave me her verdict. "I think Unicorn should publish this collection," she said.

At the end of my first week, Alan made me a formal offer of a full-time job at the press. Teo had agreed that I would take over from her as editor and Alan would continue as director of the press. Our duties would overlap constantly and I would be expected to learn every aspect of running the press. I would, of course, continue to work on *Puppet Theatre*, but would immediately spend time on other tasks at the press as well. For my work I would receive $500.00 per month, slightly below the already low North Carolina legal minimum wage. Alas, given the mortgage on the house, the air conditioning and utilities, Teo's medical bills and need of home nursing visits and constant care, Alan told me that was all the press could afford to pay me. He added that the press could also pay Donna an already budgeted flat fee for computer typesetting four books over the coming year, which would add a couple hundred dollars a month to our income. As I'd been making over three times as much teaching part-time at the university, the offer of a sub-minimum wage job flabbergasted me. While money had never been important to me, as a husband and the father of a young child, I could not afford to be reckless. I told Alan I'd talk it over with Donna and give it some thought.

Under Alan and Teo's phased plan, Alan would continue to handle contracts, accounting, and business correspondence, oversee fulfillment, and make cases and hand bind any of the newer hardback books that were sold. In addition to working on my own book, I would take over as editor on a couple new projects, complete pre-press work on a couple more, and generally learn everything I could about the business from both Alan and Teo. That evening, I was riding the bicycle home after work when a sudden electrical storm appeared out of nowhere. A huge wind, driving rain, and fierce lightning and thunder exploded around me as I raced to get home. The next day, we learned that a child had been killed by a falling tree branch on one of the streets I had transited. A few days later, I returned the bicycle to Alan and Donna began driving me to and from work.

When I met with Alan to discuss the job offer, I told him that even though the salary he had offered was insufficient for a family of three to live on, I would agree to work at the press on the condition that he would allow me to implement a strategy that would reinvigorate the press and put it on a better financial footing, thereby freeing up resources for higher wages after the first year. I proposed new marketing strategies and initiatives that would make use of my computer equipment and expertise to help generate and expand sales and income—money that would eventually allow us to hire the additional help we would need to expand operations. When Alan agreed wholeheartedly with my plan, I figured I might as well give it a try, as we'd come all the way from California and both Donna and I had already quit our jobs there. Still, I wondered if Alan and Teo were capable of the kind of changes I had in mind.

I immediately got to work designing a series of direct mail catalogs that we could use to clean and activate the dormant Unicorn Press mailing list. We also rented targeted mailing lists from commercial list compilers to experiment with the outcomes. My thought was that the press had a wealth of attractive backlist and inventory of titles that had not been sold for the past twenty years. These books could be used to generate income through direct, full price sales, the capital the press needed to increase its production and its reach into the marketplace. Within two weeks, I had used my computer and laser printer to produce the masters of several attractive, easily reproduced mail-order catalogs, aimed at different target markets. We photocopied these catalogs, collated and folded them, then stapled the pages inside the covers I had designed and printed on the Vandercook press, using my original linoleum blocks for art.

* * *

Over the next couple of months, I finished setting the type for *Puppet Theatre* and began pulling, then correcting the proofs. I laid out *Bienek: Selected Poems 1957–1987* and acquired the manuscript of *Tales of Lord Shantih*, an unusual mixture of prose poetry and Zen-like spiritual tales by Thomas Wiloch, an author I had published many times in *Asylum*. The manuscript was a perfect fit for Unicorn Press and it would be my first and only manuscript acquisition for the press. I also acquired a poem called "Three Unsighted Rodents" by Wiloch, which I illustrated with lino blocks and printed in an edition of 250 copies as a three-color poetry broadside—the first Unicorn poetry broadside since the early seventies.

Though I wanted to plan a new series of poetry broadsides, I held off for the moment. While I was excited to cross pollinate the Unicorn Press list, Teo had already begun grumbling. At one point, Alan told me that Teo worried that I would bring my *Asylum* authors to Unicorn. "In case you haven't noticed, I already have," I told him. Ironically, both Teo and Alan had been delighted with the manuscript of *Tales of Lord Shantih*. As proof of their commitment to the project, the book was printed and released in a letterpress edition the year after I left.

During my time in Greensboro, I also tried to improve the look and scope of *Asylum* magazine. I increased the number of pages for each issue in order to include more art and reviews. I also designed and published an issue with a two-color cover. After photocopying a drawing by Greg Ruggiero onto gray card stock, I then ran the covers through the letterpress to add an imprinted red title. Thinking about how to make creative use of materials to produce the greatest impact for my investment, I launched a new monthly broadside magazine called *Art Dog*. Designed using the front and back of a single sheet of pastel colored, letter-sized paper, I photocopied from 300 to 500 copies of each issue. An annual subscription cost $3.50 and came each month folded in a letter-sized envelope. I sent each contributor 30 copies and often included a copy with my correspondence. As a free bonus for *Asylum* magazine subscribers, I inserted three issues into each release of the quarterly. *Art Dog* featured short poems, prose poems, and very short stories. The format allowed me to add more experimental writers and works to my publishing project. Authors included Willie Smith, John M. Bennett, Tom Whalen, Kirby Olson, Greg Geleta, Michael Cole, and at least a hundred others whose names I no longer recall. I'm pretty sure that I published *Art Dog* for two or three years, though I'm not certain today exactly how many issues exist. Because of their ephemeral format, I imagine very few complete sets of *Art Dog* have survived, though I've seen individual issues offered for sale online by rare book dealers.

During this time, I also released *The Flood,* a chapbook by Stephen-Paul Martin, as a special issue of *Asylum* magazine. One of the editors of the New York City–based literary magazine *Central Park,* Martin was a scholar who specialized in avant-garde writing. One of only a handful of active critics and reviewers of experimental work, he was also an outstanding fiction writer. I'd met him a year earlier in Los Angeles, when he'd come to California for a vacation. I remember enjoying our conversation. We had similar tastes and interests, both as editors and writers. Over the years, we continued to collaborate and share enthusiasm for writers whose work we both championed. I would later publish two of his collections of short fiction, *The Gothic Twilight* and *Instead of Confusion,* through Asylum Arts.

Meanwhile, at Unicorn Press, bindery work had fallen far behind schedule, as Alan did not have enough time to bind even previously ordered books. Consequently, a stack of library and special bookstore customer orders sat unfilled. In past years, there had been two apprentices at the press. One worked on letterpress and editorial support, and the other worked in the bindery and helped with fulfillment. It was clear to everyone that we needed more help. It was also clear to me that customers did not care whether they received a machine made novel or a commercially printed and sewn book with a handmade case and a letterpress printed dust jacket. I suggested that time consuming hand work should be reserved in the future for books most likely to appeal to libraries, collectors, and fans of the press: poetry books, chapbooks and a revived broadside series. Given the situation, I argued that Carol Hebald's novel *Three Blind Mice,* which Donna had keyboarded and I had begun to lay out on the computer at home in the evenings, should be printed, bound and fitted with commercially printed dust jackets so that orders could be filled immediately.

About this time, Donna and I heard from a friend who'd been living in Brazil. She had moved there a year earlier to live with her boyfriend. Unfortunately, the relationship had not worked out, so she had decided to return to the United States. I had worked with Denise at California State University, Northridge, where we shared an office one semester. Like me, she had grown up in an eccentric family. Her father was a professor and professional orchestra conductor. Denise had earned a degree in International Relations with a specialty in Russian. Bright, ironic, and funny, she'd been a good friend to Donna and she adored our little boy. I mentioned her to Alan, who agreed that she might be an asset to the press. Donna and I wrote her to ask if she'd be interested coming to Greensboro.

* * *

At that point, Unicorn largely operated on grants from both the National Endowment for the Arts and the North Carolina Arts Council, as well as smaller grants from a number of other non-profit granting organizations in support of specific books. As I recall, the operating budget for Unicorn Press was around $70,000 per year, which at that point supported the publication of four new titles annually. As I later proved when I launched Asylum Arts Publishing in 1990, I could publish twice as many titles in bigger editions for half the cost. Though Unicorn operated largely on public funds under the umbrella of a 501(c)3 non-profit organization, clearly much of the money went toward supporting Alan and Teo, whose finances intersected constantly with those of the press. Alan had been juggling for years, running a kind of literary Ponzi scheme, as he moved money from one project to another and diverted funds meant for publishing to the more immediate need to provide care for his dying wife.

As I slowly learned the details, I became increasingly concerned. I realized that Alan and Teo had from its inception used Unicorn Press as a way to create and live a literary life. They believed that the nobility of their project justified whatever means they deemed necessary. They were literary anarchists with little regard for rules, laws, or regulations. Their situational ethics allowed them to solicit funds from the State of North Carolina and the Federal government, which they despised, as well as from private charities and non-profit organizations, then act in bad faith with what they received, providing false accounting figures and doctored receipts. They consistently cooked the books and asked for additional funds the following year. Despite their fraudulent behavior, they felt no guilt whatsoever.

For years, Alan and Teo had conceived and fostered an alternative worldview that eventually collided with reality. They had learned how to live through their wits and their creativity. In an interview with Darin C. Bradley published in *The Porch* in 2004, Alan said: "There seems to be a chasm between those of us (of whom I think there are many) who live our lives with values that are spiritual and community-minded and people-orientated… and those of us who seem to have some kind of obsession with this thing called money, which hardly even exists to me. I mean it's very hard to say hello to it, embrace it. I don't get it—it's simply an inability to understand the market economy or the way the world works…"

Once Alan laughed as he told me how he'd made fifty copies of an anthology, using a large format photocopy machine and good quality cream colored paper stock. He hand sewed the signatures and bound them in stiff coated stock wrappers printed on the Vandercook. He even printed a few dust jackets for the case bound copies he made. He submitted some of these books to the granting agency, the Library of Congress, and Small Press Distribution, along with the other books the press had produced that year, thereby fulfilling his financial obligation. For all intents and purposes, Unicorn Press had published the books, though not in the expected editions. No one ever thought to challenge his press records.

When I first came to work at the press, Alan showed me a big cardboard box on the floor next to the trash can. "Almost everything goes here, instead of the trash," he instructed me. Several years earlier, he had sold the press archives to the Special Collections Department at the Brown University Library. "Each year I send Brown the previous year's records and archives. They pay us by the pound." There were times when I was pasting up a book and I saw him take paper trimmings I had thrown into the bin and move these scraps into the archive box.

Years later, I had a conversation with someone at Serendipity Books in Berkeley about Alan, Teo, and the early days of Unicorn Press in Santa Barbara. That's when I learned that someone had caught Alan burning the press records at the dump during the Romero wildfire in 1971. Alan had always claimed that the early press records, including information about the sale of the press, had been destroyed in a fire in Santa Barbara. Though that turned out to be true, the fire was apparently a smaller, more controlled one he had started himself for expressly that purpose.

Denise sent a letter to Alan and received a positive reply. He invited her to come to Greensboro and work as an apprentice book binder and production assistant. As she made plans to move to North Carolina, I decided to confront Alan about the actual financial health and budget of the press. At first, he seemed accommodating and produced a handwritten summary of the grants received and estimated itemized expenses for the year. While he detailed costs for printing, typesetting, postage, advertising and marketing, and my own salary, he lumped the majority of expenses into a vague category labeled "miscellaneous operating expenses." He did not mention his own salary or the cost of mortgage payments, utilities, or Teo's medical care. When I told him I would need a more detailed accounting, he at first raised his hands palms up in front of him. "That's all there is," he said. I explained that I could not realistically plan for the future of the business, including new employees, nor assure myself that I could provide for my family, unless I understood exactly how his personal finances intersected with those of the press. Alan always spoke softly and slowly. By nature, he projected a calm and wry sense of wonder. Perplexed by my questions, I could see that he was becoming exasperated. When I asked him how much he intended to pay Denise, he told me $500.00 per month.

I reminded him that he had told me only three months earlier that the press could only afford to pay me $500.00 per month. Suddenly, that figure had doubled, as if the money had mysteriously appeared out of thin air. Clearly, he wasn't being straight with me and never had been. Blinded by my own confidence and idealism, and misled by Alan, I had put myself in an impossible situation. I later learned that over the years Alan and Teo had developed some strange ways of treating their associates, as they trusted only each other. Anyone outside of their partnership was a threat both to their existence and, in their view, to the existence of the press.

Ironically, though their intentions were positive, and their love of poetry pure, they routinely sacrificed other idealistic individuals in their utopian book community for an abstract and often self-serving greater good. The society they created was one in which, as Orwell wrote "all animals are equal, but some animals are more equal than others." While violating the public trust with their fraudulent misuse of grant money may have served as a kind of social protest or an act of quiet revolution, it's difficult to understand how taking advantage of the poets and idealists who worked for them served any noble purpose.

At least forty apprentices and helpers had worked with Alan and Teo at the press over the years, many of them in Santa Barbara. Early on, the press operated as a kind of hippy book commune, where young workers crashed in the shop and were paid, according to Teo, "in cartons of cigarettes and spirits." Those who later came to work in Greensboro tended to be graduate students or recent graduates of MFA writing programs. Some of these young poets printed their own books and stayed longer to learn more aspects of book making and publishing. As far as I can tell, they all had several things in common: a love of poetry, a love of books, an attraction to making books by hand, an idealistic and spiritual nature, and a lack of common sense and practicality. This combination of characteristics made them suitable prospects for the alternative universe of the Unicorn book culture. That so many people with advanced degrees had willingly worked for a salary lower than the prevailing legal minimum wage also points to the soul-crushing nature of work and the dearth of meaningful employment options in America.

In late September, Denise arrived with several suitcases and a number of boxes on route from California. She lived with us for three weeks. During that time, she spent a couple of days at Unicorn Press with Alan, learning about book binding. She hung out with us and listened to my complaints about Alan's deceptive behavior. She looked at some charming apartments in Victorian houses downtown that she couldn't afford on Alan's proposed salary. In the end, she left Greensboro without accepting the job. A victim of idealism, she'd been intentionally misled by Alan, and unintentionally misinformed by me. A mistake for which I've never completely forgiven myself, it was also one of the most important lessons I learned from my time at Unicorn Press.

After Denise left, my relationship with Alan and Unicorn continued to deteriorate. At one point, Alan told me that Teo had complained to him that I was spending too much time working on printing my own book and not enough on other press projects. Though I wanted to throw the type tray I was holding in my hands through the window, instead I reminded him that I worked many hours each evening at home on projects that were better and more efficiently addressed using a computer, which did not exist at Unicorn. I also told him that I found such unfounded accusations ignorant and deeply disrespectful. I set the type tray down and wiped the ink off my hands with a rag. Then I told him I was done with Unicorn. "I can't take any more of this," I said.

Donna found a job at Guilford College. I worked from home and cared for Eric. A week later, Alan called to say that he and Teo agreed that I should finish printing my book in the evenings, as it was nearly complete. If I operated the press between five and eight o'clock, we wouldn't have to interact at all. I did the work as quickly as possible and though Donna and I remained in Greensboro another five months, we didn't see Alan or Teo again.

* * *

The rest of our time in North Carolina was a mixture of poverty and frustration, made worse by a lack of connection and opportunity. We didn't fit into a society largely defined by race, class, and church affiliation. Aside from our kind landlord, we had no friends, no social contacts whatsoever. While Donna's job working half time in Admissions and Records and half time for the Dean of Students at Guilford College, provided us with health care benefits, her salary was less than half what she had earned for similar work in California. I spent my days at home, watching our young son and looking for a job that didn't exist. At night I wrote short stories and book reviews. We were poor and socially isolated.

At some point, our tired Volkswagen finally quit running. A mechanic had told us that the motor had poor compression and we knew that it was leaking oil. Overall, it was in bad shape. We sold the van for a couple hundred dollars. With the little cash we had left from the money we'd saved in California, we bought a new Toyota Tercel, a tiny front wheel drive car that got forty miles to a gallon of gasoline

We began looking at real estate as a way to keep ourselves engaged and entertained, often attending open houses on the weekends. While we could have never afforded to buy a house in southern California, at that time it was possible to buy an attractive old house in Greensboro for as little as $40,000. Once, a realtor gave us the previous week's Multiple Listing Services book, which contained photos, addresses and information about every house on the market in the entire greater Greensboro area. We used this book as a resource to explore neighborhoods and outlying areas and to feed our dream of someday owning a home.

One day, my mother called to inform us that my grandmother had passed away. Apparently, she had suffered a massive heart attack and collapsed on the street while walking to the market to buy strawberries. A friend of hers had planned to visit her later that afternoon and my grandmother had wanted to prepare a treat to go with the strong, boiled coffee she served. I imagined my grandmother baking a pound cake, then setting off to buy fresh fruit with which to make a compote. No doubt she carried a stick in her hand to ward off any bad dogs that approached her as she walked. She was eighty-six years old and strong as a bull. She'd always had a twinkle in her eye. I'd loved my grandmother and now she was gone. We didn't have the money to travel to California for the funeral. My mother told me I shouldn't bother.

After a sad, pathetic Christmas, forever remembered for the scrawny pine tree I cut down in the forest in back of our rental house, we began to plan a retreat back to California. I looked into applying for teaching jobs for the fall, but learned that the State of California was experiencing a severe budget crisis. When I talked to my father on the phone at Christmas, I told him my job in Greensboro had not worked out and we were coming back to California. He asked me about my plans and I said I wanted to publish literary books. He said he'd help me and told me to meet with him in Santa Maria when we got back to California.

We left Greensboro with a few possessions loaded in the back of our tiny car. A couple hours later, when we crossed the state border, Donna and I discussed how glad we were to see North Carolina in our rearview mirror. Our little Tercel purred happily down the highway. When we got to Texas, we stopped to buy Eric a cowboy hat and to visit the Alamo.

By the time Unicorn Press finally released *Puppet Theatre*, we had settled in Santa Maria. Alan sent me a box of author copies, several in paper wrappers with blue end sheets, and several more case bound with the dust jackets I had printed before I left. I wrote a short note back, thanking him for the copies and for the opportunity to make the book, which had been a memorable experience, regardless of how everything else had turned out. A while later, I heard that Teo had died that same year.

* * *

Poet Sarah Lindsay, a National Book Award finalist who handset and printed my book *The Masked Ball,* as well as two of her own books at Unicorn, says she "swept the floor and served tea at four" during her years at the press. It's a gracious and poetic way of saying she willingly participated in work that was meaningful but menial, Zen-like but ultimately unsustainable, at least for those who have responsibilities to children and people other than just themselves. In fact, her description of her stint at Unicorn Press closely mirrors my own experience there. It was challenging, educational, spiritual, at times frustrating, often absurd, and kind of fun while it lasted.

After we left North Carolina and I began publishing Asylum Arts books, I received a copy of *Tales of Lord Shantih* along with a letter from David Nikias, a young poet and artist who succeeded me at the press and was at the time still working with Alan. I was glad to see that Nikias had done some lovely minimalist linoleum blocks as illustrations and designed and printed a handsome edition of the book. Strangely, however, in his letter Nikias asked me some very pointed questions about Alan, his business dealings, and about my experiences at Unicorn. Specifically, he wanted to know if I had left because of what I'd found out about the press defrauding the North Carolina Arts Council on grants. Though I avoided details and accusations, I told him I'd left Unicorn due to low pay and my discomfort with Alan's creative approach to accounting.

A few months later, I received another letter from Nikias, in which he detailed Alan's abuses and financial shenanigans. Apparently, Nikias had filed a whistleblower complaint against Alan with the North Carolina Arts Council. I don't know how any of that turned out, though I remember reading somewhere that Alan had to pay back at least one of the grants. I know also that he'd been forced to sell almost everything he owned, including his house, his car, and the letterpress print shop.

Many years later, when we were living in Chico, California, I received an unexpected letter from Alan. It was a long missive, as many years had passed and he had much to say. He told me how he'd followed my career as a writer and how he'd enjoyed my successes with Asylum Arts. He told me about his own life as well. After Teo died, he met and married a female minister and moved with her to Texas, when she took a job leading a congregation there. Most importantly, he told me how sorry he was for the way he'd treated us when we were in Greensboro, and how much he regretted what had happened. I wrote back to thank him and wish him well. Whatever I've experienced, I've tried not to hold grudges. We all make mistakes and forgiveness offers grace and a chance at redemption. I always liked Alan and I learned a lot from him. While some of what I learned from him served me well over the years in my work as a literary publisher, I also learned a number of equally important lessons about what not to do.

During the time I worked at Unicorn Press, Alan frequently received boxes of books he had purchased at pennies on the dollar discounts from remainder houses. He had an amazing sense for books of lasting value and would search the catalogs for titles that would endure, then order multiple copies of several at a time, for a couple dollars total. These books he stored for the future. "This is my retirement account," he told me. "When I'm old, I'm going to open up a shop and live off these books."

Alan returned to Greensboro in 2008, where he opened his bookshop in the Glenwood neighborhood he loved. For several years he slept in the office. His bookshop hosted experimental music concerts and theater, poetry readings, political and community activist groups and meetings, and free university classes. Alan taught workshops for poets who wanted to make their own books and classes in social activism. In 1995, the Small Press Center in The Mercantile Library in New York awarded him a Ben Franklin lifetime achievement award. Active throughout his life as a poet, writer, and publisher and in the Peace and Justice Movement, Alan Brilliant was a unique and unusual person who strove to bring light into the world. He passed away at the age of eighty-six in 2022.

As for Unicorn Press, it still exists. Though the Vandercook proofing press and tall oak type cabinets are long gone, Alan continued to publish small poetry pamphlets with hand-sewn bindings. In Greensboro he met a young poet named Andrew Saulters, who was studying for an MFA at the University of North Carolina. Andrew would be the last of his apprentices. In 2016, Alan turned over the press to Saulters, who also teaches Freshman Composition part time at Guilford College. "It's sort of a cliché of the literary life that a young man in his thirties decides to start a small press," Saulters noted at the time, in an interview with a local publication. "You'll know many of these foolish characters before you die — I'm one of them, I guess — but I'm not starting a press, I'm reviving one." Saulters goes on to say he spends eighty hours a week making books and that he wants to buy a Vandercook SP-15, so that he can recreate the Unicorn Press of its heyday. I understand all too well the attraction of that particular dream. I wish him well.

Unicorns are legendary creatures from antiquity that by the Middle Ages had become symbols of rarity and purity. They were also thought to be ferocious and evasive. The only way to capture one was to charm it with the embrace of a female virgin—or perhaps a letterpress poetry book.

Do-It-Yourself Asylum

"Welcome to the anti-Paris, Roger."
— "The Conference" from *Modern Love and Other Tall Tales*

Light filters through the lens of a window, and when I squint and focus on it I can see toy cars driving past on the street. A little woman is walking a little dog, a little mailman making his rounds. And the sun, is it smaller, too? I wonder. If I stood up, I'd crash through the roof and have nowhere to live.
— "American Nightmare" from *Carnival Aptitude*

My first day in Santa Maria I saw a young man carrying a large, hand-made wooden cross on his back. Dressed in a white robe with a rope belt, he stooped and struggled under the weight of his burden, shuffling and jerking forward along the sidewalk in fits and starts like an old man walking a three-legged dog. I later learned that most days he hauled his homemade cross to the corner of Broadway and Main Streets, where he spent his time alternately supplicating or glaring at passing motorists. None of the morning commuters on their way to work paid him any attention. They'd seen it all before. Meanwhile, just beyond the fringes of the city, migrant workers picked strawberries or tended the broccoli fields. Later in the day, the air would fill with smoke and the smell of seared meat from giant portable barbecues made from cut and welded oil drums. It was that kind of place.

Neither Donna nor I liked Santa Maria. We hadn't wanted to live there. Nevertheless, we ended up buying a house that we hated in the center of the town and spending the next six years trying to get out from under the mortgage payments and the drudgery of our life there. In retrospect, I suppose we'd had our reasons for diving head first into that dry pool. After all, we had a child to raise, which required a certain amount of stability. In addition, I'd wanted to start a literary publishing business. Donna longed to be close to family. We were young, foolish, and open to compromise. Looking back, I admit I have no one to blame but myself.

The house we bought on East Las Flores Avenue was the only one we could afford. We used the money a distant relative had willed to Donna for the down payment. Built in the late 1950s to military specifications, the house resembled the rows of green painted barracks at Camp Roberts, visible from Highway 101, a few miles north of Paso Robles. With its squat appearance and flat roof, the house lacked any sense of architectural interest, personality or charm. Though purpose built on a foundation, it resembled a double wide mobile home, albeit one that had been built to last two hundred years and withstand tornados, hurricanes, earthquakes, and nuclear war. It had small, uniform windows, a single car garage set in a straight line past the kitchen, and utilitarian concrete steps leading to the front door. From the street, the yard sloped up, hilly and uneven, overgrown with juniper bushes. The wooden fence that enclosed the weeds in back of the structure leaned and dipped almost to the ground in places. Inside, the house had three small bedrooms and one bathroom. Like our big brick Cape Cod style house in Virginia years later, one of the bedrooms had been painted bright pink. The living room adjoined a kitchen just big enough to accommodate a small table and three chairs. The day we took possession of the house we ripped out the dirty carpet and waxed the oak hardwood floors. Then we started painting.

In many ways, the house on East Las Flores and the Man with the Cross were central to our experience in Santa Maria. They set the tone and explained the striving, the longing, and the frustration we endured. During the years we lived on the Central Coast of California, I wrote two short stories based on my experiences and perceptions that were published in my collection *Modern Love*. The first, called "Horny" concerns the religious fanatic with his cross at the corner of Broadway and Main. Late one night, I remember putting myself inside the character's head and taking dictation as he narrated his story in what I imagined were his own words. I also wrote a longer story called "The Conference" that takes place in a parallel universe version of what my life might have become if I had stayed in the house on East Las Flores in Santa Maria another fifteen or twenty years. In that story, a divorced, alcoholic writer named George Body lures a creative writing student to a fake summer writing conference at his shabby house in order to spend the student's tuition on beer. The unlikely scenario results in an explosion of imaginative fiction.

* * *

After our ten-month-long misadventure in Greensboro, Donna and I returned to Southern California broke, unemployed, and virtually homeless. We stayed for a week with Donna's parents in La Crescenta, then moved to the house at Oxnard Beach. Though my grandmother had passed away several months earlier, leaving the house empty, for us the house would serve as a temporary motel room for transient workers. We could stay a couple weeks until we found jobs and rented a place of our own. "The sooner the better," my mother insisted.

Before we left North Carolina, I had inquired about teaching some classes in the fall. I thought that we might find an apartment to rent in Ventura and I could drive into the San Fernando Valley to teach at CSU, Northridge, or teach classes at the junior college in Oxnard or Ventura, or at one of the private colleges in the area. However, almost all part-time university instructors at Northridge and other campuses in the massive California State University system had recently been terminated due to state budget cuts. With so many adjunct and part-time faculty out of work, there was no hope of finding a job teaching anywhere.

My father had offered to help me get started in business when I'd spoken with him at Christmas, so I called and arranged to meet with him at his company in Santa Maria. Neither Donna nor I trusted him, but we agreed that it made sense to at least hear what he had to say. Before the meeting, I prepared a business plan for a typesetting and graphic design micro-business I thought might provide the economic stability to allow me to branch into literary publishing.

During our meeting, my father barely listened to what I said or even looked at the proposal I'd brought with me. Often when I talked to him, I could feel his impatience when I spoke; some small visual tick, or worse—a reptilian coldness in his eyes—betrayed his total disinterest in what I had to say, no matter how important the subject was to me. As usual, he'd already prepared an alternative plan that better suited his own purposes. Years earlier, he arranged for his parents to sell their house in Pittsburgh and move to a mobile home park in Pacific Palisades. For years after that, he'd been making tempting offers to his younger brother, a skilled machinist, to come work at his company. My uncle had resisted, as his children were still finishing school in Pittsburgh and had little interest in moving west. When my father moved his company into the new facility he built in the industrial complex near the Santa Maria airport, he moved his parents to a mobile home park nearby. Eventually, his brother Darrell accepted his job offer, and he and his wife Nancy moved to Santa Maria and bought a house there as well. My father's attempt to bring me under his control by making me vice president of marketing at his company had fallen flat ten years earlier. It didn't surprise me that he would try again.

This time he offered me a position as a "Technical Publications Specialist." When I questioned whether the job had any real purpose or function in a microwave radar manufacturing business, my father explained that he'd recently bought $100,000 worth of new computer equipment from Sun Microsystems, including two repurposed Apple LaserWriters, and several high-powered engineering workstations joined in a local area network. This system would replace the company's old Hewlett-Packard PCs. The problem thus far was that the Sun machines required all input to be coded in Unix, including such basic business functions as writing a letter. At present, no one in the company except its president, my genius father, was capable of preparing a proposal or even typing up simple business correspondence. Before the company invested in more Sun workstations, my father wanted me to teach the secretaries and support personnel how to use the new machines. Since the job paid well and seemed to involve teaching, I agreed to give it a try, at least long enough to regain my equilibrium.

Before I began work, Donna, Eric, and I moved into a sterile and pretentious condo with a big open stairway leading to a massive master bedroom and two additional upstairs bedrooms in Orcutt, just outside Santa Maria. We found a used sectional couch at a garage sale and moved our bed and the few possessions we owned into the apartment. Eric attended a local parent participation preschool nearby, while Donna tried to manage yet another transition. Despite the chaos, she somehow kept the plates cycling through the air above her head from crashing to the floor.

When I started work, I found myself in a cubicle within in a room at the rear of the big building, a space I shared with two mechanical engineers and a draftsman. The two engineers were friendly, smart, and busy with their work. They understood that I had nothing to do with their projects. The draftsman, bright and friendly as well, sat behind a big table on the other side of the room, where he listened to Rush Limbaugh and other conservative talk radio programs as he worked. Fortunately, the engineers had already asked him to keep the volume low. According to the company's organizational chart, my father's second wife was my boss, though I rarely saw her and barely spoke to her the entire time I worked there.

My first week, I worked with the secretary from the marketing department, a woman named Rita, who had learned enough Unix command lines to allow her to type paragraph sections of manuscripts. Tables, titles, special characters, and dozens of other basic formatting instructions remained beyond her ability, which frustrated her to no end, as she'd already mastered word processing on several other systems, without the overly arcane instruction set inherent in Unix, a programming language never intended nor optimized for everyday office use.

I'd learned to set type blind on Compugraphic and Mergenthaler computerized phototypesetting equipment during the time I worked at the newspaper in San Fernando, so I was familiar with command line instruction sets. The Unix toolkit was bigger and more versatile, but at the same time unmanageably complex. Worse, Apple Computer's Macintosh had made all of these systems obsolete six years earlier, by replacing memorized command lines with a simple, intuitive graphical user interface and word processing and desktop publishing software that had already revolutionized the world of publishing and graphic design. Apple's operating system and graphic interface allowed for a "what you see is what you get" work experience that eliminated steep learning curves and greatly increased productivity.

At the end of the week, I brought my little Macintosh SE/30 to work and taught Rita how to use it in a couple of hours. Together we worked through a backlog of proposals and correspondence, which we printed out on the Sun LaserWriter, which still contained its original Apple drivers and capabilities. A week later, I picked up the first of the company's Apple computers, a Macintosh IIx that sat on my desk until I left the company a year and a half later. I set to work redesigning paper and electronic versions of the company's forms and the company procedure manual. Three more Macintosh computers soon arrived: one for Rita, one for the executive secretary, and one for the draftsman. My father also bought a top-of-the-line Mac and began playing with it. He eventually wrote a programming "cookbook" that allowed him to port all of his proprietary engineering programs to the Mac operating system.

By the end of my first year at Microwave Applications Group, The Macintosh IIci had become the standard issue computer within the company, while the Sun Microsystem machines had been relegated to a purely engineering function. I had established a number of local area networks for printer sharing, as well as an Ethernet network. Initially, I handled weekly backups to an archived tape drive. I eventually turned these routine functions over to the company's system administrator, who had previously controlled the data coming off a Hewlett-Packard mainframe computer. Initially, he had resisted all of the changes. Then, when it became obvious that productivity had increased, he argued to implement a PC-based desktop system. Within a few months everyone was more productive and finding their own creative solutions. The engineers kept their Unix-based Sun computers, and everyone else gleefully switched to a Macintosh.

Once I'd proved out the new computers and networked them, there was less for me to do at work and I began devoting much of my time at MAG to other projects. One was a special project for my father, who was president of the board of directors of the Santa Maria Symphony. The other was the founding of my literary press Asylum Arts Publishing.

My father had been a talented French horn player in his youth, though his parents did not allow him to pursue a career as a professional musician. For a time, he gave up playing the horn, though he maintained an interest in classical music. I still remember, from my childhood, the spooky cover of his Strauss *Death and Transfiguration* record album. I also remember that my father could whistle entire symphonies. After he started his company in Chatsworth, divorced my mother, and bought his own house in Northridge, he traveled to Europe, where he bought a custom, gold-plated French horn from a Swedish horn-maker. He started playing in concerts with the Burbank Symphony Orchestra.

When he moved to Santa Maria, he got involved in the local community orchestra. He played in the Santa Maria Symphony Orchestra and made big cash donations through his company. After a couple of years, he assumed the role of president of the organization's board of directors. Then he staged a coup to remove the cranky, elderly music director and conductor, with the goal of professionalizing the orchestra and improving the musicianship of the group.

About the time I began working at Microwave Applications Group, the orchestra's board of directors had just begun a national search for a new music director and conductor. My father asked me to assist him in the process by reviewing the materials from more than

100 applicants. Surprisingly, over half the applicants seemed vastly over-qualified for the position. Many had extensive experience and even international careers. Some had won major competitions and conducted well-regarded orchestras and operas in Europe. Since the Santa Maria organization had a modest budget for salaries and wanted someone who would ideally live in the community and devote his or her efforts and energy toward community outreach and activities, they preferred a young candidate in the early stages of his or her career.

Ironically, my friend and ex-roommate Patrick fit these qualifications, as he had recently completed an advanced degree in Conducting at California State University, Northridge. He concurrently worked as a music director at a big Catholic Church, as well as in a support position at the university. He also conducted New Music concerts at the university and had founded his own professional performance group, called the Bellerophon Chamber Orchestra, with which he had performed a number of concerts at churches in Northridge. He was struggling to get his conducting career going. I called him and suggested he apply for the job in Santa Maria.

During the time I worked for him, my father habitually stopped by my cubicle each day to check in with me. In retrospect, it was a thoughtful gesture. Sometimes he'd stay five or ten minutes, sometimes up to an hour. Though he preferred to control the conversation or talk about himself, occasionally he would make an effort to listen to my ideas and suggestions. Sometimes he would sit in a chair next to my desk and say nothing for several minutes at a time. Though I tried to fill up these awkward silences with anecdotes, questions, or monologues, I'd learned over the years that nothing helped. My father seemed perfectly content to stare absently into a distance only he could see. Though it was something he'd always done, I never got used to it.

Like other insecure and wealthy people, my father surrounded himself at work with sycophants. Whenever he falsely assumed that I agreed with him, I quickly let him know I didn't. Unlike everyone else in the building, I told him the truth, which usually disturbed him. Often, I got the feeling that when he looked at me, he was simply looking into a mirror. More than once, I stopped him mid-conversation to remind him that I was someone related, but nonetheless radically different from him. I insisted that we had little in common in terms of our experience and beliefs. "I'm not you," I'd remind him. My words seemed to startle him. Once, I got so frustrated with his inability to see me as a separate person that I told him to follow me outside, where I chewed him out in the parking lot. In the long run, nothing I did nor said to him made much difference.

A couple years later, my friend Pat mentioned that he'd had his fortune told by a woman who read Tarot cards. She had set up shop at Cafe Monet in Santa Maria and would be in town for three days. At his insistence, we went to the coffee house, where I paid for a reading and shuffled the deck. The woman read the cards with growing intensity, piling details up to form a profile with a distinctive history and psychology. While her predictions for the future were little more than vague generalities, her description of the past was accurate and full of insights. I let her continue without comment, though my stomach churned. When she had finished her reading, I thanked her. I told her what she had said was correct, yet at the same time completely wrong. She had read my father's fortune, rather than mine. I explained my relationship with my father and how I was trying to get him to see me as a person distinct from himself. I told her that the reading was spooky. When she offered to refund my money, I declined. "Clearly I'm working through some conflicts in my psyche right now," I said. My grandmother had never been able to read my cards, either. As a young child I had learned not to trust others or allow them full access to my emotions. I had created firewalls to keep people from getting inside my head. Over the years, I would come to realize that those barriers also walled off my heart.

* * *

I worked full time at MAG for a year, then half-time for another six months as I transitioned to running Asylum Arts Publishing. During the period I worked at my father's company, I tried to remain in the background. At the same time, I made friends with the other employees and made it clear that despite all the nepotism in the company, I had no interest in advancing my career there nor even working at MAG very long. People knew that I had other interests and goals, because I had told them. Nor did I hide the fact that I devoted a large part of my work day to tasks that had nothing to do with microwave phase shifter design and production.

Sometimes my father would ask me to edit a draft of a conference paper he had authored or the program notes he wrote for the symphony concert brochures. In addition to assisting my father with the symphony music director search, I spent time at work setting up the systems I would use for the literary publishing company I would launch in the coming months. As my work at MAG gave me the opportunity to research the latest business software, I acquired tools that would help me run my publishing company without the need for employees or expensive professional services. Since I could manage all pre-press work on the books myself, my major expense would be the printing, binding, and shipping costs. I would also need to develop a database that would allow me to track sales and inventory, print invoices and shipping labels, and develop mailing lists for marketing, promotion, and other purposes.

Unexpectedly, my research into computer programs and applications led me to hypertext fiction. Searching the Internet, I came across a mention of Michael Joyce's *Afternoon: A Story*, a kind of database enabled novel that introduced me to the possibilities inherent in a branching fictional text comprised of multiple user selected paths of interconnected narratives. Intrigued by the interactive possibilities inherent in these texts, I began work on an experimental text called *One Day: Thousands of Stories*, which I built using the HyperCard application. Unlike other literary hypertexts I'd seen, which activated readers and made them into participants via their constant choices, *One Day* included a deeper level of interaction, a feature which allowed readers to add text cards and new links to the story, thereby extending it indefinitely and unpredictably as it circulated. It was an open-ended literary system, an infinite series of potential narratives with a potentially endless number of authors.

Of course, without active participants, my open-ended story only existed in the theoretical realm. Unfortunately, few people at the time seemed interested in the intersection of fiction, theory, and technology. I remember I wrote to Michael Joyce, though I have no idea what I said or if he wrote back. I had the distinct feeling that there were only a handful of people who would know what I was trying to do and perhaps even fewer who might enter into the spirit of the venture. Many of the writers I knew through editing *Asylum* magazine still prepared manuscripts on typewriters and most had no interest in how computers could be used to create experimental narratives. I mailed a floppy disk of the beginnings of the story to two or three people who I thought might be interested, though I never got a response. So instead I wrote and published an essay in *Central Park* called "Hypertext and the Way We Read: Some Notes on Literary Progress," which described the text and situated it in the current landscape. It also included screen shots of some of the actual cards from *One Day: Thousands of Stories*.

Looking back on this work, I'm surprised literary hypertexts didn't catch on. I'm also surprised that writers are still producing the same kinds of novels they were writing hundreds of years ago. Clearly, art is slow to evolve. Leonardo DaVinci's notebooks are full of imagined flying machines and other futuristic inventions that would not be built for hundreds of years. The colors Van Gogh saw and painted did not make sense to people until many years after his death. A multimedia novel like *The Nambuli Papers* is still an oddity even close to twenty years after its publication. Likewise, the interactive, movable paintings I made in the late 1990s never caught on nor realized their potential. So, it's really no surprise that hypertext literary fiction in the form of computer games that participants enter into has not yet found its practitioners nor audience.

* * *

Meanwhile, my father and the board of directors had narrowed the field of potential applicants for the music director and conductor search down to the top ten prospects. Of those, they determined to invite three as guest conductors for the upcoming symphony concert season. I'd done what I could to narrow the field early on, by eliminating the most overqualified candidates—ones whose ambition and need for a reasonable salary would keep them from accepting the job. The rest was up to my father and the board. Pat had made the top ten. I thought that was an impressive accomplishment by itself. I was surprised and delighted when the full board chose him, based on a phone interview, to be one of the three finalists and invited him to guest conduct Beethoven's Eighth Symphony. The two other candidates would also guest conduct Beethoven Symphonies as part of the regular season's offerings.

One of the other candidates was a young woman from the Midwest and the third a middle-aged man named John Farrer, who conducted the Bakersfield Symphony Orchestra and also ran a summer music institute. Farrer knew how to present himself to a board of directors, and seemed particularly skillful in persuading my father that he was the natural choice for the job. He proposed to add the Santa Maria ensemble to his conducting schedule and commute from Bakersfield, as it was only two hours from Santa Maria by car. Though a part-time conductor who lived out of town was not what the organization had wanted, my father fell increasingly under his spell.

The board assigned Pat to guest conduct during the opening concert of the new season. During the rehearsals, he quickly developed rapport with the concert master and the orchestra. Well prepared and certain of his interpretation, he guided the orchestra through the work, praising and correcting in equal measure. The rehearsal itself seemed like a solid performance and I could tell he was winning allies among the musicians. In concert, the orchestra performed well under his leadership, and the audience responded enthusiastically to the symphony.

The Beethoven symphonies conducted by the other two candidates were also well received. After years of playing under the condescending and exhausted baton of the retiring music director, the musicians seemed delighted to work with any of the three candidates. In the end, the board members seemed split; the decision came down to a choice between Pat's energy, creativity, and total commitment, and the Bakersfield conductor's experience and predictable approach.

My father, who had initially supported Pat's candidacy, threw his vote solidly behind the older man, with whom he'd been in constant contact over the phone. He felt that he could exert more influence and even discuss what music to program with John, whereas Pat seemed unpredictable and less likely to let financial concerns dictate his decisions. In other words, my father correctly worried that Pat might not appreciate nor respect his self-created role as the powerful wizard who pulled the strings behind the scenes.

Despite my father's strenuous lobbying against Pat, the board selected him anyway, as he exactly matched the criteria they'd specified when they began the search. He accepted the job, moved to Santa Maria, and dove into the work, just as the board had hoped. My father decided to make the best of the situation for the time being.

* * *

For the first two books that I published with Asylum Arts, I chose a collection of short stories by Stephen Dixon called *Friends* and two plays by avant-garde playwright, poet, and writer Kenneth Bernard. Both had solid reputations as authors of serious, avant-garde literature. I'd published their work previously in *Asylum*. When I invited them to send a manuscript for me to consider for the press I was launching, both responded positively.

In one of his earlier story collections published by Johns Hopkins University Press, Stephen Dixon had presented an interconnected series of stories about a couple named Will and Magna. I'd read the book and particularly enjoyed those connected stories, so I was delighted when he sent me a number of other Will and Magna stories that had not gone into the original book. These previously uncollected stories became *Friends: More Will and Magna Stories*. Ken Bernard sent me the manuscript of two plays that had originally been directed by John Vaccaro and performed Off-Off-Broadway at the Playhouse of the Ridiculous. They made for a challenging and unusual book.

Both Dixon and Bernard were thoroughly professional authors and genuinely good people, and they helped me through the publication process. Dixon shared some of his earlier contracts and made good suggestions throughout, which helped me build the solid author/publisher agreement I used, not only for his book, but every book going forward. Both Dixon and Bernard shared mailing lists and contacts. They supplied lists of reviewers and libraries. Dixon even gave me a massive database of independent bookstores around the country.

I had already contracted for and begun production work on the next three books, when *Friends* and *How We Danced While We Burned* were released. I sent the books to a large list of reviewers with a press release and a letter introducing Asylum Arts and outlining its future publishing program. I was surprised and pleased when a syndicated reviewer chose to review Stephen Dixon's book. The review appeared in a number of national newspapers, including *The Washington Times*. Small press publications also took note of both books.

I quickly followed with Kendall Lappin's new translation of Gérard de Nerval's classic pre-surrealist text *Aurélia*, *Unscheduled Departures* (an anthology of short fiction that had originally appeared in *Asylum*), John Taylor's translation of a collection of short stories called *Toothpaste with Chlorophyll* by contemporary Greek writer Elias Papadimitrokopoulos, and my own short story collection *Water & Power*. Reviewers showered all four books with praise. *The Los Angeles Times*, *Library Journal*, *Choice*, *The San Francisco Chronicle*, and many other publications featured reviews of *Aurélia*. *Unscheduled Departures* received a good deal of attention, including a review in *Publishers Weekly* that resulted in multiple sales of reprint rights to a story called "Deportation at Breakfast" by Larry Fondation, which would be reprinted in five different anthologies and textbooks. More unexpected still, *Water & Power* attracted reviews in *The Review of Contemporary Fiction*, *The Los Angeles Times*, *The Saint Petersburg Times*, *The Washington Times*, *Newsday*, *The San Luis Obispo Tribune* and *Small Press*, as well as in literary magazines like *Small Press Review, Central Park,* and *Bakunin.* Out of the nearly two dozen published reviews, only *The Santa Maria Times,* whose reviewer puritanically objected to portrayals of drinking in some of the stories, had anything bad to say about the book.

As the critical success of these early books generated many library jobber orders and special orders from independent bookstores, I decided to pursue sales through personal visits to independent bookstores. That first year, I hand sold Asylum Arts books to Serendipity, Moe's and Cody's in Berkeley, to City Lights, Small Press Distribution, Green Apple, and Small Press Traffic in San Francisco, to Chaucer's and Earthling in Santa Barbara, to Ventura Books, to Phoenix Books and Earthling in San Luis Obispo, to Vroman's, Small World Books, Book Soup, Intellectuals and Liars, and Papa Bach's in Los Angeles.

In my second year, I published, in both cloth and paper editions, *Choose Your Own World,* a collection of prose poems by the legendary American surrealist writer, poet, and art critic Edouard Roditi, who had sent me the manuscript from his home in Paris. One condition Roditi made in his contract was that I also issue a signed and lettered edition of the book. To create the twenty-six copies of the special edition, I removed the dust jackets of the books bound in black cloth and affixed a small, square, black and white photograph of an eye with glasses above. I had used this photo in a letterhead for the press and had also previously printed it on postcards. I finished the book with clear mylar dust jackets, boxed up the books, and sent them to the author in France. Sadly, Roditi died while the books were en route to him and I had to cancel the lettered edition. Though I asked Roditi's literary executor to destroy the unsigned edition, I'm not sure what happened to those twenty-six books.

Along with Roditi's book, Kendall Lappin put together an anthology of his selected translations of classic French poems called *Gallic Echoes,* and contributed to the cost of having the book printed. Finally, I published two lively collections of short fiction by young writers: *Another Perfect Murder* by Danny Antonelli and *The Gothic Twilight* by Stephen-Paul Martin.

I had known Danny Antonelli at CSU, Northridge, where we'd both been undergraduates. The son of an Italian diplomat, he had gone to school in Europe, South Africa, and the United States. After graduation, Antonelli returned to Europe, living first in Portugal, then in Germany. He eventually became a disc jockey and radio host, as well as a song writer. He performed for years in a country western band in Hamburg, where he still lives.

Most of these books were well received by critics and reviewers, which increased my incentive to gain wider distribution for the press. I realized that I had done as much as I could working by myself to promote and sell the books I was publishing. What started as a small literary venture was quickly moving to the next stage of its development. Suddenly, I had some important decisions to make about the organization, status, and distribution of Asylum Arts.

At that time, I believed grants for artists were a distraction. Instead of spending time writing or doing creative work, the solicitation of grants demanded a different mindset. From what I'd seen, those who were good at writing grants were not particularly good at creating original literature and vice versa. Though in my late twenties I'd applied three times for National Endowment for the Arts grants in support of my writing, once for poetry and twice for specific translation projects, the whole process seemed like a literary lottery, so I stopped applying. Often, those who received the grants already had teaching jobs and were at best part-time artists. They used the money to buy new cars or travel to exotic places to help stimulate their imaginations during their summers away from teaching. I didn't need financial rewards and perks to stimulate my imagination or give me time and permission to write. In fact, I couldn't stop myself from writing.

As for grants in support of literary publishing, my experience with Unicorn Press had taught me that grant dependency and non-profit status entailed serious risks. Many presses that had started out as labors of love founded and operated by a passionate visionary, later became non-profit organizations run by a board of directors who replaced the founder, editor, and publisher with a staff of paid workers lacking the same degree of passion and commitment. As literary presses such as Unicorn, Copper Canyon, Coffeehouse, and others transitioned to 501(c)3 organizations, they sometimes struggled to maintain their identities and meet their new legal obligations. To me, the potential financial support and salary assistance was not worth the complications and obligations, as well as the loss of spontaneity, control, flexibility and joy.

I opted instead to run my press as leanly and simply as possible, even if it meant doing all the work myself without a safety net or even a pay check. I naïvely believed that the sacrifices I made would eventually pay off, and that if I continued to work as a writer, artist, and publisher, I would eventually succeed in one or more of these areas. I remember saying that the difference between success and failure was so little that all I needed was to reach a point where I could afford to pay myself five hundred dollars a month. Ironically, it wasn't until I began receiving Social Security last year that I finally realized that goal.

About this time, I began looking seriously for a full-service distributor with a dedicated sales force for Asylum Arts. My first choice and by far the best distributor for literary presses was Consortium Book Sales and Distribution, a company located in Minneapolis, MN that is still in business today. My second choice was Inland Book Company, founded by former Coordinating Council of Literary Magazines (CCLM) president David Wilk and located in Stamford, CT. Both offered data reporting, inventory management, warehousing, logistics, shipping, marketing, a dedicated sales force, seasonal catalogs, and other tools for getting books into bookstores, libraries, and ultimately readers' hands.

I sent both companies all the books I'd published to date, along with a complete set of all reviews, sales figures from Ingram and other library jobbers, bookstores and direct mail. I also sent detailed descriptions of titles already under contract and in production for the next two years of planned releases. I heard back quickly from Wilk at Inland, who offered to represent Asylum Arts. I thanked him and asked that he send a contract for me to consider. Meanwhile, I waited to hear from Consortium before signing with Inland. The people at

Consortium asked good questions and I supplied them with a great deal of information. Energetic, well organized, and thoroughly professional, Asylum Arts already had a growing reputation. I had demonstrated an ability to attract excellent authors and build a solid list of literary titles. Nevertheless, in the end, Consortium declined to add Asylum Arts to their list of publishers. My limited experience, lack of non-profit status, lack of employees, and lack of resources beyond direct book sales, made it difficult for them to predict long-range success for the press. Of course, they turned out to be right. Ironically, their pessimism and lack of belief not only predicted but also contributed to the failure of the press.

* * *

Once Consortium had declined to represent Asylum Arts, I immediately signed with Inland, arranged for a truck to pick up several thousand books to ship to Connecticut, and began preparing for the coming publishing season. At first, everything went well. I loved seeing the computerized sales reports that arrived each month. As much as I enjoyed seeing Asylum Arts books available in bookstores throughout the country, I liked the monthly checks even better.

Now that Asylum Arts had a distributor, I started making plans to add books by authors I admired. I had become friends with Lawrence Fixel, a San Francisco poet associated with Unicorn Press, and I hoped to someday publish a book of his prose poems. I wrote to George Hickcock, a poet I liked who'd published a book with Unicorn Press and had edited a magazine called *Kayak*. He wrote back to thank me for my interest and explain that he was now a painter. Ironically that's exactly what would later become of me as well. I seriously considered a book of stories by Jim Krusoe, a fine writer who I had known briefly when we both taught part-time at CSU, Northridge. I also wrote to Russell Edson and asked if he would allow me to reprint his book *The Very Thing That Happens,* which New Directions had let go out of print years earlier. I was surprised when he wrote back to decline, saying "I think anyone who wanted to read that book has already done so." At the time I couldn't comprehend Edson's attitude about publishing his work, though now, many years later, it makes sense to me. Fortunately, Fixel, Edson and Krusoe did contribute work to the new *Asylum Annual*.

The newly redesigned, large format 1993 *Asylum Annual* helped kick off the first Inland list. It featured a cover and a selection of photographs by Anne Arden McDonald, as well as work by Charles Bukowski, Russell Edson, René Daumal (in a translation by Jordan Jones), Daniel Quinn, and Tom Whalen. It also featured paintings by Sergio Ceccotti and P. J. Crook, collages by Kenneth Bernard, art criticism by Edouard Roditi and Eric Basso, and work by current and forthcoming Asylum Arts authors including Robert Peters, Elliot Richman, Kenneth Bernard, Cynthia Hendershot, Carolyn Stoloff, Samuel Appelbaum, Edouard Roditi, and Eric Basso.

In addition to Inland, which distributed *Asylum Annual* to the book trade, I had arranged for Ubiquity and Fine Print to distribute the magazine to periodical dealers around the country. The initial print run was 2,000 copies, which increased to 2,500 by 1995. I worked steadily to build a stable publishing operation that would produce the annual magazine and six to eight additional titles each year. I wanted to reach a point where I could eventually earn enough to keep the press functioning at that level and pay myself a small salary. Though on track to accomplish my goal within the coming year or two, I failed due to unforeseen circumstances.

After an initial grace period of a year and a half, Inland came apart in stages over the following two and a half years. First, they were late on their monthly payments. Then, they began paying quarterly instead of monthly, a strategy whereby they withheld half a year's payments from all their publishers. I think everyone knew that this delaying tactic would eventually result in a total collapse. In 1995, Inland informed me via a letter that they were filing for bankruptcy. After the court mandated liquidation of assets, Inland paid pennies on the dollar of the debts they owed to publishers. Worse, they destroyed all the books warehoused in Connecticut that publishers could not afford to pay to ship elsewhere.

Though low on cash, I calculated how many of each title I could realistically afford to ship back to California and warehouse myself. Without a distributor, I had no real hope of selling large quantities of books, even over many years. I wrote to each individual author and explained the situation. Inland had supplied me with the cost per carton to have books shipped out of their warehouse. I told my authors that from whatever remained after I shipped back my own stock, they could take as many copies of their own remaining books as they wanted. Most of the authors sent money to Inland in order to retrieve copies of their books. Nobody complained. We'd all been conditioned to accept the Darwinian nature of capitalism.

The catastrophic failure of Inland Book Company effectively wiped out Asylum Arts, along with dozens of other small publishers. At the time of their bankruptcy, Inland owed me tens of thousands of dollars. Afterward, I had no cash reserves, no distributor, very little stock on hand to sell, and no means of selling future titles I published. Despite these challenges, I had already entered into various agreements with authors to publish their books. Though I explained to them how much the circumstances had changed, none of them took me up on my offer to cancel their contracts. It was difficult to find a competent publisher for literary books, especially the kind of challenging work and genres in which Asylum Arts specialized. Some of these authors supported the press by offering to co-publish their own books. Under this arrangement, I would edit, design, typeset, promote and market their work, and they would underwrite the cost of printing, binding, and shipping the books.

Kendall Lappin had from the beginning proposed an even better offer. Not only did he pay for the production of the six books he published with Asylum Arts, he also gave me extra money to compensate me for my time. Such generosity kept the press going, in the best of times, as I folded all these funds back into producing new books. Among Kendall's books, three were among the press' bestselling titles: *Aurélia*, *Echoes of Baudelaire*, and *Dead French Poets*.

Eric Basso had also offered to pay for the printing, binding, and shipping of his life work. It was a huge publishing project, to be completed over a period of several years. I issued twelve of his books, two or three each year, over a period of five years, including the massive theatrical work *The Golem Triptych,* which took me nearly a year to typeset. The book included a complicated musical score by Basso, which my father skillfully typeset into musical notation using a computer program he'd learned to use as a hobby. It was the only time my father had any connection to Asylum Arts, and it was an unexpected and unlikely contribution. Among Basso's other books were collections of poems, including *Ghost Light, The Smoking Mirror,* and *Catafalques,* a novel called *Bartholomew Fair,* stories collected in *The Beak Doctor,* and a wonderful book of short plays called *Enigmas.*

Other authors, including Ken Bernard, Richard Martin, Elliot Richman, Sam Appelbaum, and Robert Peters also contributed to the health of the press by co-publishing books. Without these contributions, Asylum Arts would not have made it through the financial difficulties of Inland's last two years of operation, nor survived beyond the near total devastation of their bankruptcy.

During the ten years I published Asylum Arts, I maintained good relationships with nearly all the authors whose books I published. It was well known that I was a "writer's publisher," which is to say someone who'd been disappointed by his own publishers. Consequently, I worked to get the books I published into print within a year of signing a contract. I also valued communication, competence, design aesthetics, and honesty. Most of the authors were a pleasure to work with, though some were fussier than others. In general, I accepted input from an author about any aspect of the publishing process. It was, after all, their book. If an author had a strong opinion about a cover or some artwork, I tried my best to work with him or her. Most authors wrote or emailed, which I preferred. A few, like Carolyn Stoloff, called once a week or more. A perfectionist who had an opinion about every detail, hers was in the end a very fine-looking book, though it cost me a lot of time. Moreover, she could also be quite grumpy. Once while we were talking on the phone, she heard Donna whistling to herself in the background. "What on earth is that?" she asked me. "Who's that songbird?"

Because I copy-edited, designed and typeset every Asylum Arts book myself, with good time management I could greatly accelerate the process and get books out quickly. However, I was careful to make clear to the authors that although I would faithfully make any corrections and read through the proofs again myself, having set the type for the book, it was difficult for me to see the text with fresh eyes. Therefore, they would be solely responsible for proofreading their books. Even though I sent out proofs early and encouraged the authors to find friends and other writers to help them eliminate typographical errors, most of the books still contain typos. One short book of stories has so many errors I wonder if the author even bothered to read the page proofs.

By 1994, I'd been working for three years without pay. I'd published over two dozen critically acclaimed books that were selling well to libraries across the country and were available in bookstores. Readers could find *Asylum Annual* on newsstands throughout the country, as well as in bookstores. With a print run of 2,500 copies, it was the only Asylum Arts title I knew would make money each year. Nevertheless, when Inland fell behind on payments, operating the press went from very difficult to impossible.

At the depths of this crisis, I tried to save Asylum Arts by conducting a nation-wide search for a teaching job. On the recommendation of Stephen Dixon, I applied for a Wallace Stegner Fellowship in Creative writing at Stanford University, which I viewed simply as a temporary job. After sending my vita to over one hundred university English department jobs listed in *The Chronicle of Higher Education*, I was invited to interview for just one position: a temporary visiting writer job at a state university in Oklahoma. I went for the interview, but didn't get the job. Nor did Stanford offer me a Stegner Fellowship.

Throughout this period, I received dozens of inquiries each week, some by mail, others over the phone, from recent graduates of MFA programs, all of whom wanted to work for Asylum Arts. I would have liked to have told them, "I'm just a guy working alone and without a paycheck out of a spare bedroom in a shitty old house in a God-forsaken town." Instead, I thanked them for their interest, suggested they try one of the university or non-profit presses, and wished them luck. The irony eventually caught up with me, and drove me to write one of my best comic works, a long story called "The Conference," which Kate Gale and Mark Cull at Red Hen Press published in 2000 as part of my collection *Modern Love and Other Tall Tales*.

At the lowest point, I received an unexpected letter from Daniel Quinn, an author I'd published several times in *Asylum* magazine. From our correspondence, I knew that Quinn had been working on a novel for the past fifteen years. After dozens of revisions and changes of approach, he finally submitted the manuscript to a contest sponsored by Cable News Network founder Ted Turner, called The Turner Tomorrow Fellowship Award. A panel of celebrated writers, including William Styron, Wallace Stegner, Ray Bradbury, Nadine Gordimer, and Peter Matthiessen eventually selected *Ishmael* from 2,500 submissions worldwide. When Quinn won the controversial half-a-million-dollar award in 1991, it was the single largest cash sum ever given for a literary work. In addition, the publisher set aside $50,000 to market the book and film option. Quinn also received a hardcover publishing contract for his next three books.

The award proved to be controversial. Some of the judges, who were each paid $10,000 themselves, publicly stated that none of the novels by the dozen finalists was worth a half-million dollars. "All of us felt that not even a book of our own would deserve that much," said novelist Wallace Stegner, whose name graced the Stanford University fellowship which had only recently rejected my application. "We were agreed that there was not a worthy prize winner." While Styron, Matthiessen, and Stegner agreed that *Ishmael* was the best of the manuscripts, they didn't like that Quinn would receive such a large sum of money. Ray Bradbury disagreed: "If Kitty Kelley can make $5-million-to-$6 million, why not half-a-million for a real book?"

After the success of *Ishmael*, which was translated into multiple languages and became a worldwide bestseller, Quinn set out to write a sequel called *The Story of B*. He also collaborated with Tom Whalen, another small press author whose work had also appeared frequently in *Asylum*, on a comic and surreal book called *A Newcomer's Guide to the Afterlife.* Quinn told me how much he had liked the black and white photomontages I'd made for my book *Carnival Aptitude* in 1993. He asked me if I could use the technique to create a dozen surreal "photographs" of scenes from the afterlife and provide captions. The montages would serve as the illustrations for his book. His publisher, Bantam books, would pay me $500.00 for each illustration.

I made twelve illustrations for the book in a single day. I remember that I was ill with the flu and had a high fever. A couple of the montages I'd used in *Carnival Aptitude* seemed perfect for the project and I quickly wrote captions for them, then set them aside. Then, I spread my materials on the floor, where I picked out backgrounds and elements to cut out from other photos. I combined them and glued them together over a period of several hours. Because Bantam opted for cover art that falsely advertised the book as a sequel to *Ishmael*, they did not use the two images I'd made for the covers. Nonetheless, they paid me for all twelve of my montages, a total of $6,000. It was more money than I had made over the previous two years working full time at writing and publishing.

In early 1995, Asylum Arts was struggling for cash to publish its spring and fall lists. For the first and only time, I cut titles for which I had earlier contracted. By then, I was trying to pull whatever money I received from Inland's late payments out of the press in order to recoup some of my initial investment and plan for the future. In addition to *The Book of Orgasms,* a small-format book of prose poems by Nin Andrews, I had books by Eric Basso, Richard Kostelantez, Robert Peters, Elliot Richman, and Kendall Lappin ready to publish. I also had two titles that required me to invest more money into printing and binding: *The Asylum Annual 1995* and a post-punk dystopian novel. I had already invested a great deal of time in both books, as each was ready to print. Unfortunately, I only had the cash on hand to print one of them.

In the end, it was an easy choice. *Asylum Annual* had always made money. Also, if I canceled *Asylum Annual 1995,* I'd be disappointing nearly eighty contributors instead of disappointing an academic writer who had recently suggested I resolve my financial difficulties by applying to a Ph.D. program at his university and becoming a teaching assistant. I remember telling him over the phone that his suggestion degraded us both, as well as our profession.

For years I'd tried to get professors who taught in creative writing programs to support their own profession by asking academic libraries to adopt standing orders for books published by outstanding literary publishers, and by teaching some of these books in their own courses. My efforts were largely in vain. By 1990, the majority of submissions I received to the magazine and press were from full-time professors. My frustration with the system continued to grow. While I had been unable to secure even a part-time job teaching, much of my work and financial sacrifice in publishing books and a literary magazine benefited and advanced the careers of professional academics. As the ten-year run of *Asylum* magazine came to end, I realized that careerists had undermined and coopted my project. They'd dressed themselves in rags to gain admission to the asylum, then unlocked the doors. They pushed some of the original inhabitants out and hung gilded mirrors in the halls to better admire themselves as they pranced around. They used the magazine and press to pad their *curriculum vitae* in order to achieve step raises and get better teaching jobs. An avant-garde lasts only until it is recognized.

Once, a poet candidly revealed to me the strategy he'd used to win a prestigious $20,000 National Endowment for the Arts grant. In support of his application, he wrote a series of poems from the point of view of a working-class black woman. As there were no names attached to the manuscripts submitted by potential grantees, the judges had no idea the poems were actually written by a white male college professor.

Another professor whose book I'd scheduled for publication had found time to solicit a grant to publish his translation of selected poems by an obscure surrealist poet. Unfortunately, despite his expertise in securing grant money, he showed little commitment to finishing his translations. As I'd already announced and delayed the book twice, my patience boiled over. I cut that title as well. I told myself I was done publishing books for people who focused on academic careers and rewards rather than art. In my mind, my perceived failures were piling up without any hope of redemption. My response was to rant and at times treat people unkindly.

After a series of unpleasant, manipulative calls from the two authors whose books I'd cancelled, I began using the answering machine on my phone to screen incoming calls. Though both these authors clearly understood that Asylum Arts had lost its distribution and was failing financially, they refused to accept that I'd chosen the welfare of my family over their career-enhancing books. Both authors continued to leave messages, whining and arguing into the recorder until the tape ran out. When I listened to those voices on the phone, acid from my stomach crept up into my throat and my former idealism and enthusiasm turned into resentment and bile. In retrospect, I see that the rigors of literary publishing had caused me to lose my perspective. If I didn't adjust my attitude, I knew that I'd become bitter and vindictive.

By late 1995, having exhausted all other options, I placed an ad in *Publishers Weekly* and tried to find a buyer for Asylum Arts. I fielded several inquiries, sent out materials, took a few phone calls. Though a handful of potential buyers expressed admiration for the press and its list, the overriding concern was that "Asylum Arts is you." Without my vision and direction, no one knew what to do with it. One of these people, who introduced himself to me as BJ, was a publisher of a successful line of travel guides located in Davis, California. While he wasn't interested in buying Asylum Arts, BJ instead wanted to form his own literary imprint called HiJinx Press, using my expertise and connections. He asked if I'd work for him as a consultant and editor-at-large for a couple of years on a retainer. Thus, I helped launch and build HiJinx Press, even as Asylum Arts wound down and stagnated.

At first, the venture seemed promising. I contacted a number of authors I knew and asked if they had any suitable manuscripts. Geoff Clark sent me a gritty novel called *Jackdog Summer* and Stephen Dixon sent an unusual book of short, illustrated plays called *Man on Stage*, both of which the publisher enthusiastically accepted, along with a novel of mine called *Sacred Hearts*. Next, I acquired an anthology of short stories edited by Gilbert Alter-Gilbert called *Life and Limb: Tales of Peril, Predicament, and Dire Distress*, as well as novels by Joe Martin, John Richards, Mark Wisniewski, and R. M. Ryan.

BJ had in mind a unique concept for the aesthetics of the press. He wanted HiJinx books to have an edgy feel and he liked the idea of designing covers using neon colors and intentionally ugly, "grunge" fonts. Though I warned him that a little ugly goes a long way in design, with the exception of the anthology, he insisted on designing the books and covers himself. While some of the designs were barely acceptable, others were simply awful, most notably the cover of John Richard's novel *Working Stiff*. Though both the author and I objected to the design, BJ refused to change it.

Meanwhile, BJ had been neglecting his travel book business and revenues had fallen steeply. I'd been working for HiJinx less than a year before Donna and I moved from Santa Maria to Paradise. Several months later, BJ told me he could no longer afford to pay me my retainer. He asked if I'd stay on to help usher the rest of the books into print, and promised to pay what he owed me when he got some returns on the HiJinx titles. Like Inland, HiJinx Press turned out to be yet another financial disaster for me. I felt an obligation to help get the books I'd acquired into print, though HiJinx folded soon thereafter and I never received any further compensation for my work.

* * *

I've mentioned earlier that my father grew up during the Great Depression. As a child, he'd begged his parents to buy him a Monopoly game. Despite their financial difficulties, such a modest purchase remained well within their means. Nevertheless, they had repeatedly refused to accommodate him. Ironically, the only game I remember playing with my parents as a young child in Syracuse was Monopoly. Whenever my sister and I played together with our parents, I ended up crying, for each time we played I landed on my father's or my sister's Park Place or Boardwalk combined properties, which wiped out my future in a single roll of the dice. It happened so often that I finally refused to play anymore, as I was convinced that the outcome was predestined.

On vacations to Atlantic City or Virginia Beach, my parents took us to play bingo. I always lost my money right away, whereas my sister usually won enough to continue playing, and invariably came away with extra money. Despite what my parents told me about being a good sport, I could see that it just wasn't fair or right that a few people got all the money and the rest lost what little they had, so I gave up gambling and games of chance altogether. I learned early that money and luck were intrinsically connected. From my initial experiences with money, I concluded that it had no connection with fairness, reason, talent, hard work, nor justice. Instead, money seemed closely allied with cruelty, randomness, and disappointment. I learned early to distrust the foundations of our economic and social system, to distrust money, and to look for value elsewhere.

Very soon after my father started his business and divorced my mother, he became quite wealthy. Afterward, his favorite subject was how much money he had. Whenever I saw him, he would tell me about the latest government contracts that his company hoped to secure and about the massive profits he was making. He carried a special wallet just to hold his dozens of credit cards. When he made a purchase, he liked to theatrically flip open the wallet and let the cards cascade downward in their plastic sleeves, from waist level to the floor. "Which one would you like?" He'd ask the clerk.

He enjoyed telling me about the top-of-the-line Mercedes Benz and BMW cars he bought in Germany and had shipped to the port of Los Angeles, and the dozens of suits and shirts his tailor in Hong Kong made for him. He bragged about the custom-built, gold-plated French horn he commissioned a Swedish horn-maker to craft for him. He liked to detail all the gold he had hidden away in Swiss banks and in safe deposit boxes. He boasted about the cost of the big houses overlooking the Pacific Ocean he bought and remodeled, only to sell and build even bigger ones. Once, he described how he had filled in a perfectly good swimming pool in order to build an indoor lap pool for his wife.

Almost everything he touched turned to gold. He bragged about his investments in stocks and municipal bonds, which usually produced massive returns, though once he admitted to losing "the equivalent of a Rolls Royce" in a single stock market transaction. He once bought an avocado grove in Simi Valley, which he sold five years later for a huge profit when the state of California extended the 118 Freeway from the San Fernando Valley, through Simi Valley and on to Moorpark. He personally owned a big commercial building at the Santa Maria Industrial Park, which he rented to his own company for thirty years, then sold to the new owners of the company for an obscene profit.

In his late eighties, my father bought a Tesla electric car that cost more than the apartment Donna and I own in Spain. Though his body was bent and he could barely walk, he liked to startle passengers in his car by accelerating rapidly, so that the torque of the deceptively quiet electric motors pinned them to the back of the seat. After one brief experience, I refused to ride with him again.

When I was in college, I remember him telling me that I should never waste my time working for money. On that much I agreed. A few years later, however, after I'd chosen a career in the arts, he told me "Art's nice if you can afford it." Clearly, I couldn't afford it, but I persisted nonetheless. Meanwhile, my father dumped hundreds of thousands of dollars into support for local community orchestras he played in or founded, but never contributed to any of my artistic pursuits. Though he patronized restaurants and cafes in Santa Maria that featured my art and attended the opening of my one-man show at a gallery in San Luis Obispo, he never purchased any of my work. When I asked him if he liked what I was doing, he replied, "I'm not into that kind of art." Meanwhile, his wife collected expensive pseudo-Impressionist paintings and old master–style Dutch landscapes. She even designed the ground floor of their Avila Beach mansion as a gallery in which to display her collection of expensive kitsch.

Perhaps most annoying of all was how, later in his life, my father bragged about the ludicrous monthly payments he and his wife received from social security. Why the government would give two retired multi-millionaires over $100,000 each year was beyond my comprehension. Of course, I already knew why my father accepted and kept the money: he was fond of saying he'd earned it.

Ironically, neither he nor his wife did much actual work at the company, at least not on a day-to-day basis. Though my father had developed the theoretical concepts, designs, and computer programs that allowed for the manufacturing of the microwave phase shifters that went into various military radar systems, he rarely concerned himself with the operations of the company. His wife, a vice president who graduated from law school but never took the bar exam, drove her company car to work for twenty-five years and sat in her big office all day with the door shut, while my father sat in his office noodling with his computer programs, or pursuing his latest obsession—learning to typeset musical notation, researching the genealogy of his family, founding and running a symphony orchestra, planning trips to China, Hong Kong, Russia, India, and Europe, building ever grander mansions.

Despite his money, my father never seemed to have much fun. He owned a golf cart and belonged to a country club, but he was not athletic, didn't play well, and struggled to enjoy the game. Throughout his life he remained awkward around people and didn't care much for their company. Besides, music, he had few interests. I can't remember him ever having a single friend. Even family was, for him, an abstract concept devoid of any corresponding emotional component. He valued material things more for their ability to communicate success and status than for their beauty, comfort, or utility. I told him he should try to have more fun. When I joked that he should buy a tuna boat and go fishing, he didn't laugh. When I suggested he buy himself a Ferrari, he said, "I'm not into that. I like BMW sedans."

Besides money and music, the only pursuits and passions that truly inspired and motivated my father were sex and drinking, both of which he seemed to pursue with varying degrees of secrecy and deception. He particularly liked wine and cultivated an interest in collecting quantities of fine wines that facilitated his daily self-medicating sessions. As for sex, I've discussed his addiction earlier. The last time I saw my father, eighty-five years old, his mind pickled in a life's worth of excessive alcohol, he still had just enough focus to uncork bottles of good wine. He openly gawked at Donna and when she got up to use the bathroom, he told me how lucky I was to still be able to enjoy my wife's charms. Creepy to the end.

One night after Pat had got the job conducting the Santa Maria Symphony, we went to visit my father at his house in Arroyo Grande. When it was time to leave, my father walked us to my car, which was parked in his long driveway. The three of us were still talking and my father suddenly began a strange soliloquy. He paused mid-thought, as though he were searching for the right way to continue, but instead stared off into the darkness in silence, his face slightly contorted by some sudden fear of the unknown, as if death had tapped him on the shoulder. We waited for him to regain his composure, but he was lost. Finally, Pat said, "Well, thanks for the conversation. I've got to get back home." We got into the car and drove away, leaving him standing alone in the dark.

* * *

It's well known that writers, poets, musicians, and artists tend to be a little nuts, or in many cases completely bonkers. Research shows that creative people are at much greater risk than others of experiencing psychosis, manic-depression, and to a somewhat lesser extent schizophrenia. Poets are even more prone to disorders than the rest. Psychologist James C. Kaufman goes so far as to term the phenomenon that poets are less stable than other creative writers "The Sylvia Plath Effect." Creative artists of all kinds also tend to be outsiders who struggle with relationships, social integration and acceptance, and financial support. At the same time, psychologist Abraham H. Maslow suggests that creative people who spend their lives self-actualizing are actually the most mentally healthy, productive, and happy members of society. So are writers better adjusted than others, or are they hopelessly alienated? I think, perhaps, depending on the individual and the circumstances, that they can be both, sometimes within the same lifetime or even the same day. Perhaps the underlying problem is society—it's institutions, educational system, and values. Particularly in America, where creative work is undervalued and even ridiculed, creative artists often feel disconnected and constantly question their self-worth, along with the value of their work.

Many famous artists and writers have ended up in mental institutions or insane asylums, among them Vincent van Gogh, Allen Ginsberg, Antonin Artuad, Ezra Pound, Leonora Carrington, David Foster Wallace, Anne Sexton, Robert Lowell, Sylvia Plath, and Richard Brautigan. Others committed suicide or killed themselves slowly through alcohol or drug addiction. While the public is eager to vicariously experience real life stories of artistic "fine madness" and line up for blocks to see a traveling exhibition of paintings signed "Vincent," they have little patience for the artists who struggle to live among them. There's little doubt that if Jesus showed up again, the very same people who pack themselves into megachurches would happily crucify him for being an anarchist. Likewise, if Van Gogh offered to draw portraits of the people in line waiting to see his exhibit, they'd chase him away and tell him to "get a real job."

When I chose *Asylum* as the name of the literary magazine I started in 1985, I wanted the title to reflect my editorial preference for work that fell within the broad scope of something I thought of as "American Surrealism." What I really meant was work by contemporary poets, writers, and artists who happened to live within the culture of late capitalism and worked within the Romantic and Imaginative tradition. Later, when I began publishing books, I called my press Asylum Arts Publishing. By this time, I had broadened my concept of "Asylum." For implicit in the word was also the idea of community, inclusion and refuge. I wanted to provide an outlet for the kinds of creative works that were the most difficult and challenging to publish: poetry, short fiction, and avant-garde theater, as well as translations of classic pre-surrealist French literature. I wanted to offer neglected and interesting writers asylum.

What I had not really considered or understood at that time is that I, along with most of the people I published, operated outside the cultural boundaries of understandable and acceptable behavior. Collectively, we valued an alternative currency, ambled to a different beat, saw colors and strange visions that others didn't see, heard voices that narrated our stories and novels. Some were renegades and loners, others exiles and malcontents. I became a curator who looked for and expected the unexpected. When I found it, I happily put it into print.

Since the time we'd worked together on my translation of Baudelaire's *La Fanfarlo*, Ken Lappin had been, along with Eric Basso, among my most regular correspondents. When I launched Asylum Arts, Lappin told me that he'd been working on a translation of a French text that held special meaning for him, as it accurately describes a descent into madness, something he himself had experienced earlier in his life, when he'd been so stricken that he'd been institutionalized for a time. The work was Gérard de Nerval's classic pre-surrealist novel *Aurélia*. He wanted to know if I'd consider his translation for publication.

Researcher Andreas Fink at the University of Graz in Austria has found that the brains of hyper-creative people operate differently than the average person. Highly creative people constantly make connections between the external world and their internal thoughts and memories. Because that part of their brain is always switched on and operating, creative people often display schizophrenic, borderline manic-depressive tendencies. Fink found that the inability to suppress the area of the brain that has been linked to self-consciousness and memory retrieval, is seen most dominantly in two types of people: creatives and psychosis patients. This constant stream of thoughts and introspection is apparently vital to creativity. In *Touched with Fire,* her seminal book about "madness and creativity," Kay Redfield Jamison, a psychiatry professor at Johns Hopkins, reported that successful people were eight times more likely to suffer from a serious depressive illness.

* * *

I'd started making relief prints using linoleum back when Donna and I were living together in Oakland in 1980. The first were illustrations for my book *Circus Deluxe*. Over the years, I'd continued to make occasional prints, a few in wood, though most in linoleum. However, I'd never thought about creating editions of these prints. In Santa Maria, I spent a lot of time visiting bookstores, coffee houses and galleries throughout California, as I was always looking for interesting artists for *Asylum* magazine and to supply art for the covers of the books I was producing. Through Nick Campbell, a poet I'd known in Northridge years earlier and whose poems I'd published in *Asylum,* I met a number of painters and poets in San Luis Obispo.

Later, artists such as Bruce Salter and the photographer Anne Arden McDonald contacted me through the magazine. The writer and art critic Edouard Roditi introduced me to European artists, including the work of Greek painter Nikos Engonopoulos and Italian painter Sergio Ceccotti, whose works I later published in *Asylum Annual.* Closer to home, art critic and anthologist Gilbert Alter-Gilbert published a survey of Los Angeles "New Enigma" artists in the 1995 issue.

At some point, I showed a portfolio of proofs of my prints to the owner of a small art gallery called the L.A./Santa Fe Gallery in San Luis Obispo and she encouraged me to print editions of them to sell in her shop. I ordered a selection of hand-made papers and set to work printing hand pulled editions of forty different prints. It was physically demanding and meticulous work and I pulled the editions late at night, after I'd filled orders, spent hours typesetting forthcoming titles, answered correspondence, and worked through all the various tasks the press required during the day. Of course, I was also writing during this period, which I usually did first thing in the morning. As for sleep, I didn't really need more than five or six hours a night.

Once I had editions of my prints to sell, I did a one man show at the L.A./Santa Fe Gallery in San Luis Obispo and began placing the prints, mounted on foam core and bagged in archival plastic, in galleries in Ventura and Santa Barbara as well. I hung framed shows at Cafe Monet in Santa Maria, and at a restaurant in Orcutt. The prints sometimes brought in more money per month than the books I was publishing with the press, which inspired me to make new series of prints.

Because *Water & Power* had been so well reviewed and continued to sell reasonably well, considering the press had no real sales reps or distributor, I thought I should follow up this success with a novel. So I began work on "Christabel," an academic comedy set in a public university English department. The plot loosely followed that of the English Romantic poet Samuel Taylor Coleridge's unfinished Gothic poem by the same title. I included the 900 lines of "Coleridge" verse that I'd composed years earlier, though I intentionally left that version unfinished as well.

Academics in general, and those teaching in English departments specifically, have a well-deserved reputation for quirky, puerile, neurotic behavior. While not a *roman-à-clef*, "Christabel" did showcase some of the skewed personalities I'd seen on display in the English Department during my eight years at California State University, Northridge. An intellectual freak show, the faculty abounded with archetypical drunkards, whiners, satyrs, back-stabbers, blowhards, and lazybones. One professor had formerly been a nun, another an ex-Marine Corps officer. Others had launched parallel careers in real estate and watercolor painting. The faculty included the expected whisperers and screamers, feminists and macho men, sadists and masochists, poets and poetasters, phonies, pretenders, failures and fools. Politics and power struggles reigned supreme. Sexual energy and innuendo sloshed around like boozy stomach acid. Pecking orders, cliques, and enemies lists abounded. Professors secretly paired up with each other, with each other's spouses, or with their students. Graduate students openly slept with all of the above and everyone else. Meanwhile, the fifty part-time faculty members were too busy teaching composition and working as freelance writers and journalists to participate in the circus: nobody really knew or cared what they did.

When I'd completed the novel, I sent the manuscript to an editor named Kit Ward at Little, Brown. She wrote back to say she liked the book, but was leaving the company, as they were moving the operation from Boston to New York City and she didn't want to leave her home. She told me that she was launching a new literary agency in Boston, and asked if she could represent my work. Though I hadn't found a publisher, I'd at least signed with an agent. Kit shopped the manuscript around, though ultimately without success. Though she got close with one New York publisher, the editor wrote that they had just contracted for an academic comedy by another writer. Since it had only taken me three months to write the novel, I didn't really care. Though it had not appeared to be commercial enough for New York publishers, it was still too commercial to be of much interest to me.

I tried to interest Kit in a new book of short stories I'd already started called *Modern Love and Other Tall Tales,* but she was struggling to make a living and told me she needed me to keep writing novels. I told her I'd think about it, but that I was busy and my heart really wasn't into writing commercial literary fiction. I met Kit in Boston when I flew in to do a reading at Roger Williams University in Rhode Island. Over dinner, she told me that my work and my voice were original, which scared editors and publishers. "If you want my opinion," she said, "you should write what you want and continue to publish your books yourself. You shouldn't have to change what you're doing for me, or them, or anyone else." Though I hadn't wanted to hear it at the time, she'd given me good advice.

After our talk, I continued writing the short stories that would eventually become *Modern Love.* Among them was a reimagining of Mark Twain's characters Tom Sawyer, Huck Finn, and Jim. For me, Twain's bitter-sweet, tragicomic novel *The Adventures of Huckleberry Finn* has always been the most complete and accurate description of America. Both Huck Finn and Tom Sawyer are American archetypes. Self-reliant, self-aware, and independent, Huck's thoughts and his values are his own. He's not a product of the educational system, religious indoctrination, or other "civilizing" influences. Instead, he's pure of heart, creative, and resourceful. Unlike his friend Tom, he's immune to the mythology of America. While Tom cleverly charges his friends money to whitewash the fence his aunt has assigned him to paint, Huck escapes downriver in the company of a runaway slave, a man he comes to appreciate as a good person and a loyal friend. When Huck says he wants to light out for the territory, he means the wild wood, the prelapsarian wilderness, a time before civilization imposed the kinds of rules that destroyed equality, human dignity, and common sense. Unlike most of us, he's incapable of living a lie, even if it means going to hell.

I set my version of Twain's classic novel, which I called "The Further Adventures of Huck, Tom, and Jim," in contemporary Los Angeles, where Huck and Jim are now street people living under a bridge over one of the many dry, cement flood channels that make up the L.A. River system. I made Huck a male prostitute dying of AIDS and Jim a Vietnam War veteran who loves and cares for him. In the course of the story, Huck and Jim meet up with their old friend, Tom Sawyer, a failing capitalist who has come to Los Angeles to cash in on real estate only to find the bottom has dropped out of the market. I wrote the story in miniature chapters, which gives the work the feel of a highly compressed novel. When I'd finished the writing, I made a set of five linocut illustrations for the story. The story and illustrations appeared together in a magazine called *Artful Dodge,* which paid me $200.00 for the work.

By the time I'd finished the manuscript of *Modern Love,* Jordan Jones connected me with Kate Gale, a writer he'd known at California State University, Northridge. Kate and her husband Mark Cull had recently formed a literary publishing house called Red Hen Press and they asked to see my manuscript. They published *Modern Love* the following year.

At this time, I also began work on a short, surrealistic road novel I titled *Sacred Hearts.* The plot concerned two waitresses who try to track down the leader of a religious cult one of them thinks may be the child she abandoned in her youth. Though in the end I didn't give the manuscript to Kit to circulate, I later published the novel with HiJinx Press.

* * *

Because we never really felt at home in Santa Maria, Donna and I usually found an excuse to leave town on the weekends. Often, we simply put Eric and our dog into our little red Toyota and took a drive.

In those days, we loved to explore back roads. Though sometimes we had a specific destination in mind, we often just drove for the sake of driving. We took day trips to Lompoc, Solvang, Santa Barbara, Morro Bay, Cambria, San Simeon, San Luis Obispo, Atascadero, and Paso Robles. We drove hours on back roads just to eat at the Burger Barn in New Cuyama. We visited Donna's childhood friend Diane in in Pollock Pines, and her cousin in Sacramento. We took three or four trips to Sequoia and King's Canyon National Parks and went twice to Yosemite, where we rented a cabin with a wood burning stove for heat. While we were there, we took hikes to scenic viewpoints. We dressed in camouflage and played capture the flag, a game where we tried to sneak past each other in the woods. We spent hours catching lizards and tossing rocks into streams.

Sometimes we visited Donna's parents in La Crescenta, or I went alone to see literary friends in Los Angeles. On the latter occasions, I often stayed in Huntington Beach at the home of Robert Peters, whose *Selected Poems* I published. Like Charles Bukowski, Peters had been one of my early literary influences. Along with Russell Edson's *The Very Thing That Happens* and Bukowski's *Burning in Water, Drowning in Flames*, his first book of selected poems, *Gauguin's Chair*, had been one of my favorite collections during the time I'd been a student. I had first connected with Bob during my time at Unicorn Press, as he was also one of Unicorn's authors. In California, we became good friends. Bob described me as "a flaming heterosexual." On book distributing trips I sometimes spent the night at his house, as it was a long trip back to Santa Maria. I loved hearing his gossipy stories about all the poets who had stayed in the house when they'd been guest readers at the University of California, Irvine, where Bob was a professor of English who taught courses in Victorian Literature. A kind and gentle giant with a biting sense of humor, he knew more about contemporary American poetry than any living reviewer or critic. His informal reviews and essays on poets, collected in three volumes called *The Great American Poetry Bake-Off*, set the standard for non-academic poetry criticism. Asylum Arts also published a book of his literary criticism called *Where the Bee Sucks: Workers, Drones and*

Queens of Contemporary American Poetry, as well as his verse play *Mad Ludwig of Bavaria*. When Donna and Eric came with me to Los Angeles, Bob's partner Paul took the two of them to Disneyland for the day while Bob and I stayed behind to talk about books.

Donna and I also took longer trips up the coast to Oregon, where we hoped to live someday. Twice we came close to buying small, charming, Victorian-era houses, once in Oakland, Oregon, and another time in Elkton, though what we really longed for was a chance to live in Portland, where we would have had access to the universities, bookstores, and galleries. Though at the time it was still possible to buy inexpensive houses, lofts or studio space in emerging Portland neighborhoods, our mortgage in Santa Maria kept us from making the move.

Once, when I did a reading in Portland, we visited our friend Denise, who shared a house with her mother in Vancouver, just across the border in Washington. At the time, Denise was raising a young daughter as a single parent. Though none of us talked much about what had happened in North Carolina, we all knew that the failed experiment with Unicorn Press had ruined our friendship. For me, it was a painful reminder that when collaborating with others I needed to be more realistic and pragmatic; though willing to work for little or nothing myself, I could not let my enthusiasm and idealism overwhelm social norms and the common sense need to earn a living wage. My utopian vision of reinvigorating and modernizing Unicorn Press had resulted in a misadventure that had been a disaster for Denise, as well as for Donna and me. As the three of us talked over a glass of wine, our children clamoring for attention, I remember feeling that becoming adults had canceled our subscription to youth and innocence. In the process, each of us had shelved our sense of wonder and possibility. Though we have not stayed in touch, Denise remained in Vancouver, where she raised her daughter and worked as a school librarian.

Some weekends we visited my mother at the house in Oxnard Beach where she and her husband Phil now lived. They had remodeled the little pink and blue stucco beach house, adding a second story with a modern kitchen, wide plank hardwood floors, and a walk-in closet where my mother stored her ever expanding collection of antique dolls. During those visits, Phil showed Eric how to play old Atari 2600 computer games like Pong, Asteroids, and Pac-Man. The five of us also played card games and board games together. For unknown reasons, Phil encouraged Eric to cheat at every game. Though I didn't approve of teaching my child how to cheat, there was nothing I could say without causing trouble. My mother, so strict, proper, and unbending during my own childhood, apparently now found it entertaining to watch her grandson cheat at cards. Phil also introduced Eric to other games like Tetris and Super Mario Brothers that ran on the newer Commodore 64. Eric has loved video games ever since.

When we stayed in Santa Maria on the weekends, we rode bicycles together and went to Costco for hot dogs. We took walks on the campus of the junior college near our house, where Eric would scamper through the bushes hunting for lizards. We laughed during meals and played games we made up amongst ourselves. Burping out loud during a meal earned a "point." Using bad words also merited a point. Technically, each infraction cost a quarter, though I was the only one who ever had to pay. At home, I worked out of the spare bedroom, where I had a big maple wood table and a desk for my computer. I also had an easel where I painted.

Outside, I planted seasonal vegetables and sunflowers in the backyard garden. I cut the grass or weeded the garden while Eric hung upside down from a tree limb or sat on the steps out front playing Pogs with his friends. Eric filled his room with Lego sets, aquariums full of lizards he caught, and binders full of basketball trading cards. In those days he liked knock-knock jokes, Goosebumps and Redwall novels, and music by Mariah Carey and MC Hammer. He complained bitterly with his squeaky voice whenever the dog stepped on his crotch in the back seat of the car.

Once, Donna took Eric with her to attend a family reunion in Minnesota, while I stayed home to work. A couple weeks before their trip, I had found a hobby shop in San Luis Obispo that sold little boxes of the same tiny molded plastic soldiers I'd played with as a child.

I bought twenty dollars' worth—enough British, French, Polish and Austrian Napoleonic War solders, cavalry, and artillery to stage my own Waterloo. More importantly, I bought a set of model paints with which to completely transform the dull plastic figures. Each night while Donna and Eric were gone, I sat at the kitchen table and painted hundreds of uniforms, horses, and guns with tiny brushes until the armies of toy soldiers of which I had dreamed as a child finally appeared. Then I built a battleground on a full sheet of plywood, using drywall mud to create hills, fields, and roads. I painted the board with acrylic paints, built walls out of tiny pebbles, and decorated the terrain with trees made of bits of dry green moss we'd collected during one of our trips to the Sierra Nevada mountains. When Donna and Eric returned from their trip, Eric found a battle in progress on a table in my studio.

French artillery occupying the high ground bombarded British Highlanders, as the Imperial Guard advanced on their left front and flank. Elsewhere British dragoons and Scott's Grays skirmished with Polish Lancers and French cuirassiers, while French infantry advanced in a column along a road and Austrian soldiers waited in reserve behind the British infantry. My son and I played together briefly with the new toy, but it didn't seem to hold Eric's interest. When I asked him later if he liked the soldiers, he told me he did, but it was clear that he was being polite. He never showed the battlefield to his friends nor invited them to play with the hundreds of hand-painted soldiers. A week or two later I boxed up the armies and returned the board to the garage. A few years later, before we left Santa Maria, I tossed the decorated board into the back of my pickup truck, along with some rusty gallon cans of used house paint, a broken lawnmower, and other junk from the garage, and took it to the city dump. For years I saved the painted soldiers, horses, and canons, packed together in a wooden cigar box, in case Eric had a son himself someday.

* * *

I always thought that my friend Pat was an exceptionally talented person. The son of a midwestern factory worker who drank himself to death, I admired how he had overcome the limitations of his upbringing, left home at an early age, and worked to achieve something unexpected and extraordinary. At the same time, I recognized that his experiences had taught him to change his camouflage to fit his surroundings, in much the same way my own experiences had shaped my near complete distrust of authority. We were both stubborn, serious, driven people who refused to be denied. I remember the absurdity of Pat studying Calculus to prepare for an entrance exam for a Ph.D. orchestral conducting program, even though he knew that there was little chance that the prestigious Ivy League school for which he had applied would accept a musician with an Irish surname and a degree from a west coast state university. Though I would have rather thrown a brick through the institution's window than waste a minute studying math, I admired Pat's hell-bent determination. As I recall, he scored so highly on the test that he secured an interview. Then, after spending money he did not have on plane tickets, he flew to the east coast, where the selection panel condescendingly allowed him to answer their questions while they dismissed and undervalued his achievements. He returned to California burning like a blue flame, more determined than ever to prove them wrong.

As young and ambitious artists with similar insecurities, we had much in common. In Northridge and later in Santa Maria, we spent a good deal of time—most of it fueled by chain-smoked cigarettes, cups of late night coffee, or beer—defining and discussing the artist's role in society and justifying our sacrifices and self-importance. Fate and destiny often figured into these discussions. Over a period of several years, we each built bullet-proof, larger-than-life personas, which we half-seriously molded out of talent, hard work, bravado, and bullshit, fired with a searing blast of hot air. As we understood it, the only real currency was imagination, and art required one to exist in the no-man's-land between mythology and everyday life. Our purpose was, as poet Diane di Prima wrote in her autobiography, "to be great, whatever that means." Like many inexperienced and passionate people, our boundless enthusiasm and arrogance sometimes overwhelmed our peers. With Baudelaire, Blake, Beethoven, and Bukowski as models, we didn't much care how others perceived us. Nevertheless, I sometimes couldn't help satirizing both myself and Pat, as I did in two stories in *Modern Love*, "The Convention," and "Yllek, Fishing," the latter about the absurd and legendary exploits of a pompous turn-of-the-century French orchestra conductor named Kirtap Yllek.

While we worked on greatness, Pat and I also crafted home brewed beer during those years in Santa Maria. We cooked up big batches of raw ingredients and fermented our brews in five-gallon glass carboys. We brewed passable brown ale and pilsner, along with a good dark porter and a tasty wheat beer. Though we made many attempts at a Guinness-style stout, we never came close to replicating the original. It was a good hobby, both creative and relaxing. We brewed beer, drank, shared our professional frustrations, and collaborated artistically when we could.

In his second year of conducting the Santa Maria Symphony, Pat chose to program an ambitious work that required multiple vocal soloists and a chorus, as well as the orchestra: Carl Orff's *Carmina Burana*, a musical setting of two dozen bawdy, irreverent, and vulgar 12th century drinking songs. Written in Latin by students and clergy called Goliards, the original poems satirized the values and hypocrisy of the Catholic Church.

To help promote and celebrate the occasion, Pat and I collaborated on a manifesto called "Hac in Hora," which we published as an op-ed in the *Santa Maria Times* and *The New Times* in San Luis Obispo. I also designed a set of two posters, one of the text of the essay and the other advertising the concert. The extra media attention helped sell tickets and fill the hall. Pat hired soloists from Los Angeles and the resulting performance energized the audience and made the concert a memorable event. Throughout it all, my father, who insisted he didn't like Orff's *Carmina Burana* because he found it vulgar, pouted through the Symphony's success. Marginalized and upstaged, the president of the board had lost control of the orchestra.

Eventually, Pat met a practical, grounded girl also named Donna, who became his partner and wife. The four of us socialized often. Though they hosted a big public celebration afterward, they kept their wedding ceremony private: my own wife Donna and I were their only witnesses. After their wedding, they bought a house on Central Avenue and began renovating it. The first of their two children was born while they lived there.

After they finished remodeling the house in Santa Maria, Pat and Donna decided to sell the property so that they could use the profit to help fund the construction of a custom house on some rural property they bought in Colson Canyon, about a half hour drive from town. One day, Pat asked if I'd help him clear some brush off the building site and we set out with a trunk full of hand tools. The bare winter trees shivered in the weak sun and the brush huddled together in thickets of twisted vines. We'd been at work for a couple of hours, cutting and raking the debris into a big pile when someone drove up the road and parked below us. A young man exited the car and walked up the hill toward us. He asked what we were doing and who we were. Pat explained that he owned the property and was going to build on the lot. "Okay," he said. "You know, you're standing knee deep in poison oak. Can't see the red leaves this time of year, but those are the vines."

Though we'd been wearing boots, gloves, jeans and long-sleeved shirts, we knew it was probably going to be bad. We went home, put our clothes in plastic bags and then into the trash, showered, and treated our skin with something a pharmacist had recommended. By the end of the following day, some red bubbles started to appear, mostly on my legs and arms at first. Hiking in the Southern California foothills and mountains as a kid, I'd had many cases of poison oak. It was unpleasant, but nothing to worry about. Unfortunately, the following day I needed to load up my little Nissan truck and drive to San Francisco for the annual Bay Area Book Festival, where I had a booth for Asylum Arts.

During the book fair the welts, bubbles and redness increased. Aside from my face, genitals, and feet, the poison oak covered my body. The itching became unbearable. I remember driving home from San Francisco late on a Sunday night, with my forearm pressed against the cold glass of the passenger side window. The discharge from the weeping bubbles and welts coated the glass. It was all I could do to keep from scratching the skin completely off my arms.

The next day, I went to the doctor, who told me that I had a systemic allergic reaction. He gave me a cortisone injection and a prescription for cortisone pills. Even with strong medicine, the poison oak lasted about six weeks and reappeared in various areas for the next several years. Up to thirty years later, I'd occasionally see a tiny, localized outbreak.

While Pat's reaction to the poison oak was not as severe as mine, the oak turned out to be only the beginning of the bad luck surrounding the property in Colson Canyon. He'd originally wanted to use post and beam construction for the house, but he couldn't find a contractor who could work within his budget, so he hired a young builder to modify his design to a more traditional stick-built house made of two-by-four inch lumber. The permit process and the endless building inspections required by Santa Barbara County added unexpected costs and delayed the construction further. As the house took shape, various sub-contractors came to perform different tasks. One of them got into a shouting match with Pat over the quality of his work. Another employed a young man who looked like the identical twin of a serial killer, nicknamed The Night Stalker, who had murdered sleeping couples in their beds several years earlier in Los Angeles. The next day, Pat discovered a pentagram carved into a floor tile he was about to install. A few days later, Pat became seriously ill from a bacterial infection from drinking the well water out of the big tank on his property. When tested in a lab, the water in the tank showed contamination from human feces. Someone had purposefully defecated into his drinking water.

After he and his family had moved into the house, a neighbor told him that someone had hung himself from a tree on the property. A stray dog appeared one day and refused to leave, so Pat and Donna adopted him. A few weeks later another neighbor saw the dog with

Pat and accused him of stealing his pet. Though Pat had designed and built a lovely home and tiled it himself with beautiful slate floors, I hated visiting him there, as the place pulsed with bad energy. A year or so after Donna and I left Santa Maria, Pat sold the house and moved his family back to town. Though I'm not a superstitious person, I think that land was cursed.

Meanwhile, Pat had transformed the Santa Maria Symphony from a community orchestra to a professional regional symphony. One of the goals the board of directors had most desired of their new music director was that he improve the musicianship and sound of the ensemble. As time passed, Pat began to push players to practice their instruments more and improve their playing. He often brought professionals from outside the area to play in concerts with difficult solo instrumental parts that he felt were beyond the ability of the first chair players. Slowly he weeded out the less proficient musicians in order to create a more professional orchestra and a more satisfying experience for audiences.

This culling eventually extended to my father, whose playing, in spite of his fancy horn, was sometimes less than golden. Enraged when Pat assigned the principal French horn player to play a part he was having trouble executing properly during a rehearsal, my father responded by taking his football and going home: he resigned from the board, quit the orchestra, and withdrew all his financial support for the organization.

Two years later, the Santa Maria Symphony board had mismanaged the orchestra so badly that it fell into bankruptcy and the organization disbanded. When Pat couldn't find another conducting job, he pursued a different passion instead. He borrowed money from a bank and bought a twin-engine airplane, on which he gained enough hours to obtain a commercial pilot's license. Then he moved his family to New Mexico, where he worked as an instructor at a flight school, flew for regional airlines, and piloted air ambulances.

Years later, when my father revived the ghost of the poisoned Santa Maria Symphony and rechristened it the Santa Maria Philharmonic, the new board bowed to its benefactor-puppeteer and hired John

Farrer as their Music Director, a job he held for ten years. In 2014 California State University, Bakersfield awarded Farrer an honorary Doctorate of Fine Arts, citing among his accomplishments his "having conducted special programs for royalty, including the Duchess of Cornwall." Seriously?

* * *

Our son Eric attended pre-school in Orcutt. At first, we tried a Montessori school, but he didn't like anything about it, so we switched to a more traditional program. Eric was a bright child with a natural gift for memorizing facts and information, an advantage that accelerated his learning. When we moved into the house on East Las Flores, we sent him to kindergarten at the public school a few blocks from where we lived. Though we had concerns about the quality of education in Santa Maria, in the end, Donna and I enrolled our child in public schools because we were both products of them ourselves and we strongly felt that if he were to succeed in American society, he would need to experience the social norms and make his own choices about what he would come to believe, rather than be molded and shaped by an artist father who had largely rejected the tenants and values of that society.

I remember how I had taught Eric his first active vocabulary in both English and French, back when we lived in Northridge. While he'd already forgotten those words, such games were part of his everyday experience. Before Eric went to school, his play was indistinguishable from my art. He was precocious, bright and funny. He inserted himself into adult conversations, where his opinions and observations were part of the dialogue. I remember how Pat taught him to salute him when he came to visit. "Hail, Caesar," he'd say, pounding his heart with his fist. I modified the salute to "Hail, Geezer," which Eric loved even more.

Within a month of his starting school, I noticed an obvious decline in Eric's verbal abilities. He'd spent most of his life up until then around adults, participating in their conversations, and now that he was around children his own age much of the day it was as though he regressed to a lower level of verbal communication. His vocabulary declined, as did his concentration. At the same time, he seemed happy. It was clear that Eric craved attention and acceptance. A very social person, he liked nothing better than fitting in with his peers. There were times when I wondered if we had made the right choice, but given his personality, I don't think he would have responded well or been happy with home schooling or exposure to eccentric, genius tutors.

* * *

For years, my mother had studied piano with a woman who happened to be the mother of one of my sister's childhood friends. Marianne had been a child prodigy whose parents had dragged her around the country during the Depression to play concerts like a performing chimpanzee. Consequently, she had not enjoyed a normal childhood nor a normal relationship with her parents. Like my mother's parents, Marianne's had invested in her musical education in the hope that she would enjoy the same success as the immensely popular Shirley Temple. Marjorie and Marianne had in common a similar story of expectation, betrayal, and disappointment. Having received a full scholarship to Dusquene University for her violin playing, my mother had majored in music and played in the university orchestra. Under Marianne's tutelage, she became a proficient pianist. For many years, my mother took weekly lessons, and she and her teacher developed a close bond.

As Asylum Arts struggled to stay afloat, I sought a diversion from the constant stress and workload of writing, editing, and publishing. Instead of automatically reinvesting all the money I received from Inbook back into the press account, I used some to buy a piano. I asked my mother for advice about study materials and methods. I also asked if she would give me a few lessons to get me started. Over the next year, I worked through a three-book piano course recommended by Marianne. In general, my mother seemed to enjoy sharing her knowledge and her enthusiasm for the piano with me. The occasional lessons she provided also gave me an opportunity to connect with her as an adult.

I was delighted to be able to play ragtime and blues tunes, along with some easy pieces by Bach and Beethoven. However, as I learned enough to begin composing some simple pieces of my own, I realized that for me the joy in music was not the mastery of the instrument, but rather the act of creation. Though I did not have the proper background in music theory nor the training and musicality to play and compose by ear, which made writing music difficult, especially in comparison to the facility I had for composing in words, I still enjoyed bringing new sounds into the world.

My exposure to the music of Erik Satie further revealed what my time at the piano really meant to me. Music was a door that I could walk through if I abandoned myself completely to it and allowed myself to learn and then throw out the rules, and to develop the kind of intuitive instincts I had for writing and visual art. Otherwise, it was just a paint-by-numbers hobby in which one learns to play, like Jack Nicolson's character in the film by the same title, some variation of "Five Easy Pieces."

I recently watched some footage of Erik Satie and Francis Picabia dancing around a canon in René Clair's 1924 film *Entr'acte*. The movements they make in the film reminded me of the gestural "conversations" I had with Tony Liano in scenes from his silent film *The Lost Reel* in *The Nambuli Papers*. Everything connects.

When we left Santa Maria, there was no question of further piano lessons. I would continue to play the piano for the eight years we lived in Paradise, often improvising at the keyboard, but the learning curve was too steep, the time required too dear, and without the commitment, guidance, and tools to write my own music, I didn't make progress. When we sold our house in Paradise, I sold my piano as well.

* * *

I woke up with the weight of my laptop computer on my thighs. Then I realized that I'd been dreaming and the computer was actually in the next room, where I'd left it when I lay down for a nap. As I transitioned from sleep to wakefulness, suddenly everything became very still and quiet, as though someone had just shut a window and sealed out the street noise coming from outside. As I breached the surface of consciousness, I remembered that it was a tranquil Saturday afternoon. The world outside me was completely silent and the white noise roar I'd exited was my overactive subconscious mind.

When I'm working on a big writing project, I never really leave it. Though I may set it aside to eat, sleep, take a walk, converse with others, or attend to some entirely unrelated task, part of my mind is still engaged in the writing. Sometimes, I wake up with images or whole paragraphs of carefully constructed prose in my mind and must move quickly to set the words down before they evaporate from my memory. At those times, I prefer to write by hand straight into a notebook, which seems more direct and faster than sitting down at a keyboard. I often carry a notebook with me when I leave the house, in case something unexpected comes into my head.

When I began writing seriously in my early twenties, it took me a long time to complete an essay, a poem, or a story. During those years, I wrote a number of bad novels and the process was tedious and exhausting, like painting the outside of a house alone in the summer heat. At some point, however, I stopped editing myself as I wrote and let the words tumble out on their own, as fast as I could set them down. I found that I could write poems quickly. Often, they were complete rubbish. Sometimes they contained some lines or an image that I could ponder and give shape to later. On rare occasions, they astounded me with their completeness. To write fiction, I learned to simply imagine a character in my mind and let that person talk.

It takes a good deal of practice to build the skill and confidence to write well. To develop further as a creative writer, one also needs to read widely. I tried to avoid creative writing workshops and mentors. Instead, most of what I needed to know about writing came from close readings of contemporary American and modern French poets, surrealists, and comic writers like Mark Twain, Kurt Vonnegut, and

Stephen Dixon. Of course, dozens of other poets and writers also influenced my thinking, my aesthetic, and my philosophy.

Throughout my career, I've engaged in an experimental game I call speed writing. I'll assign myself a task—a collection of poems, a short story, a novel—and then give myself a predetermined time limit in which to complete the work. For an individual poem or story, it's usually a single sitting. However, I once wrote a collection of fifty comic poems, some of which I published in magazines like *Wormwood Review*, over a three-day period. I wrote my unpublished novel "Christabel" on a short deadline, while also working full time. I completed the script for the film *Seven Fallen Objects* in ten days, and the erotic novella *The Widow* in a single week. I've found that these tight deadlines increase my focus. I enter into a kind of brain-induced creative high that sometimes produces unusually original work.

Sometimes people ask me about my writing process. For most of my life I've enjoyed the illusion that I write almost effortlessly. Of course, I work for hours, days, weeks, months at the keyboard, so clearly there's work involved. However, when I'm tuned in, it's like taking dictation. That's not to say that what I write is good or has value. As I have no control over readers' responses, I don't really think about pleasing others. I write for myself. If I'm amused, entertained, shocked, or otherwise moved somehow by what I'm writing, then I keep going. That's how I write.

* * *

The third time we put our house on East Las Flores Avenue on the market, it finally sold. Each time we listed it, the price went down. By late 1995, housing prices in the area had fallen so low that despite having made mortgage payments for six years, we lost our entire down payment. Even worse, we had to give the bank an additional two thousand dollars to complete the sale. Nevertheless, we felt relieved to finally be free of the small house with outsized mortgage payments. We were tired of windy, dull Santa Maria.

During the time we lived on East Las Flores, we had done our best to fix up the house and try to make it better reflect our aesthetic. I'd repaired and painted the fence, laid in a flagstone patio, planted fruit trees, a climbing yellow rose bush, grass, and a lush garden in the back yard. We'd removed all the juniper bushes in front of the house, leveled the yard, and planted grass there as well. We'd painted and put up wallpaper inside, waxed and shined the oak floors. We'd decorated the house with an exquisite French art nouveau sideboard we bought in Ventura. Though well cared for, the house remained disturbingly utilitarian. Even the best-groomed skunk still stinks.

We rented a truck to move our belongings from Santa Maria to Magalia, in the foothills of the Sierra Nevada mountains above Chico, in the northern part of the state. I remember that Donna, Pat, and I wrestled my console piano over the threshold of the front door, across a sheet of plywood, and into the bay of the truck. We hired a professional piano mover on the other end to get the instrument into our new residence. He moved the piano by himself over rough terrain and seemingly impossible obstacles, using a collection of hydraulic lifts and other devices he'd made himself. He would move the piano three times over the coming years.

* * *

Prior to the time we left Santa Maria, a constant stream of failures had filled me with quiet rage. Disgust had risen from my spleen, filled my lungs and chest, and crept up my throat, so that the bitter taste of it constantly filled my mouth. I wanted nothing more than to lie down in the shade of tall trees and stare up at the sky for as long as it took for me to feel whole again.

Politicians, businessmen, and football coaches all seem fond of the expression "failure is not an option." What they mean, I think, is that whatever task, goal, or deadline they are currently confronting is so worthy, notable, and important that they feel they simply *must* succeed. Nevertheless, in spite the slogan, failure remains an option for those who abandon their free will, give up, or settle for something less than their true self demands of them. Failure thrives on lack of responsibility, on addictive behavior, on moral and ethical compromise, on self-delusion.

If we define failure as the absence of success, then how we measure success determines our own self-image. The society in which we live teaches us from an early age to pursue material wealth and status, which in of themselves have nothing to do with success. After all, even the most despicable thief, pimp, crooked politician, corporate raider, real estate developer, global polluter, white collar mafioso, or mass murderer can wear a thick gold chain around his neck, live in a hilltop mansion with a big swimming pool, posture on television, and drive an expensive car. On the other hand, if we treat others well, maintain a set of personal values and ethics that serve a higher purpose than material gain, and actualize our spiritual potential, are we not truly successful? If, throughout our lives we become wiser and more insightful, is that not success as well? If we dedicate ourselves to truth and knowledge, learn to speak other languages and appreciate other cultures, if we read and write books of worth, bring art or music into the world, teach others what we know, how can such a full and productive life be a failure? Perhaps in the end we should trust our better nature instead of pursuing the empty goals society imposes upon us.

If failure exists at all in a self-actualized life, it is only to teach us what not to do, how not to do it, or why we should not let others determine the measure of our worth. If we heed these lessons, even perceived failures make us stronger and more resilient, and help us to become wiser, truer versions of ourselves. Though at first we may think a perceived failure slams a door shut in our face, it often also provides us with new and unexpected opportunities. How we respond to adversity reveals much about us. If we define ourselves by our own values and standards rather than weighing our merits against social norms and yearnings, the fear of failure evaporates like summer rain on a hot sidewalk.

Of course, such wisdom comes more easily now, decades later, when the scars from long-healed burns have faded to white.

Literary Road Trips

> My brother and I spent the next several months traveling, with no particular destination or goal in mind. It was quite simple: we were young and curious.
> — "The Dark Brother" from *The Nambuli Papers*

> "What the hell," I said. "What have I got to lose?"
> — *Sacred Hearts*

MOST OF THE writers and poets I have known are busier than people imagine. Not only do they spend hours composing their stories, novels, poems, plays, and essays, some also work as editors, publishers, and translators. As there's little money to be made writing literary fiction and none at all in writing poetry, some try their hand at commercial or genre fiction, general non-fiction, or scripts for film or television. Others write children's books, journalism, or pornography. Some ghostwrite books for others or give workshops on how to write. Many work at odd and unrelated jobs. Charles Bukowski famously worked as a mail sorter for the U.S. Postal Service. Kurt Vonnegut owned a car dealership, while George Orwell had been a policeman. Before he was hired to teach at Johns Hopkins, Stephen Dixon worked as a bartender and a substitute teacher. Margaret Atwood had been a barista. Poet William Carlos Williams was also a physician, Wallace Stevens an insurance lawyer, and T. S. Eliot a banker. These days many writers and poets teach writing or literature at universities. Most try to patch together a living in whatever way they can that still affords them time to write. Some travel a good deal.

Over a twenty-five-year period, I traveled extensively. I drove to Los Angeles and San Francisco, Portland and Phoenix. I flew to New York, Boston, and Washington. I traveled to Rhode Island, Pennsylvania, and Maryland, to North Carolina, Virginia, and Colorado. I voyaged to Paris and Chartres to make a film, and to Les Eyzies to study cave art. I went places for lectures, for book selling and account servicing, for book fairs and job interviews. I met with artists, writers, agents, and publishers. I did research and radio appearances, classroom visits and writing workshops. But mostly I traveled for readings. I read my work in coffee houses and bars, at colleges and universities, at community centers, at arts centers, at literary centers. I read at bookstores and galleries. I read at libraries. I even read at a nightclub and a garden party.

Anyone who has ever participated in a poetry reading knows that there are two kinds. The successful ones are usually organized by an established reading series. They tend to be high energy undertakings hosted by independent bookstores, colleges and universities, literary and art centers, libraries, and galleries. The readers are paid for their time, often at rates similar to other professionals. They may even receive travel expenses or money to cover airline tickets. These readings tend to attract large, sophisticated audiences: the kind of people who laugh in the right places, exclaim out loud as though they're watching fireworks, linger afterwards to ask questions and have books they've purchased inscribed. Poets leave feeling energized by their connection with the audience.

The second type of reading, hosted by an inexperienced or uncommitted organization and plagued by inadequate planning and promotion, involves words that take flight and hang like frozen birds, suspended for a brief moment in mid-air, before they disappear forever into the black hole of a near empty room. If they are part of a book-selling tour, or the author lacks an appetite for irony or masochistic abuse, these kinds of readings can be soul-crushing affairs.

Having traveled a great distance, the poet arrives early. Hoping to recoup his gas money, he places stacks of his books on a table near the podium, then waits for the audience to arrive. Minutes before the event begins, a handful of other poets shuffle in carrying notebooks and sheafs of paper, anxious to share the open mic. One of them sits in the first row and stares, chin jutting forward, eyes wide and bright. The others lurk in the shadows near the door. After checking his watch for the third time, the host fumbles with a pack of chewing gum. He writes something on his palm in ballpoint pen, then begins his introduction. Dipping his knees slightly, like an opera singer digging to reach the highest note of an aria, he lists the unknown poet's numerous awards and publications in a single breath. "It's my pleasure and great honor to welcome…" he concludes. There's a sound like static in his ears as the poet walks from his chair to the podium. He stumbles as mud swallows one of his shoes. Grabbing hold of the lectern with both hands, he lurches forward. As he arranges his materials, a stiff wind blows some of his papers into the air, where they hang above him like words in a comic strip bubble. He grasps at a book, coughs into his fist, and taps the mic, which does not respond. When he opens his eyes, he sees folding chairs stacked against the wall in an empty room.

Such readings inspire feelings of rejection, shame, and disgrace for everyone involved. They remind us that poets struggle to be heard in our culture. They also affirm that, as long as poets are declaiming aloud in near empty rooms, imagination, self-expression, and the human spirit stubbornly refuse to die.

* * *

The most impressive live literary event I participated in was a group reading organized by Susie Bright and her publisher Simon and Schuster for *Best American Erotica 1993*, the first in the series of annual anthologies published over the next sixteen years. Held at musician Boz Scaggs' nightclub and concert venue Slim's in San Francisco, tickets cost $10.00 each. The house sold out, with over 500 people in attendance. I read my short story "Horny," about a religious fanatic consumed by guilt, who carries a heavy homemade wooden cross on his back and stands each day at the busiest intersection in town as a way of punishing himself for his fantasies about his neighbors. During the story, the narrator alternates between detailed descriptions of his sexual desires, and condemnation of himself and others for their impure thoughts. I had fashioned a costume made by sewing together half a button up dress shirt and half a t-shirt, which I changed into back stage. I remember talking with Bob Flanagan and his girlfriend, photographer Sherrie Levin, who took photos as I shaved off half my beard. When it was time for me to read, I went on stage with a kind of line down my center that represented the schizophrenic nature of my narrator: half clean-shaven face above a dress shirt, and half a bearded face above a t-shirt. I shifted each side into the light as the narrative moved between the point of view of the repressed religious fanatic and the unhinged sexual maniac. Afterward, I watched from stage right as Bob Flanagan opened his reading by performing a song called "Supermasochistic Bob Has Cystic Fibrosis" to the tune of the song "Supercalifragilisticexpialidocious," from the Disney musical *Mary Poppins*. It was a wild night.

* * *

In 1993, after the publication of *Water & Power*, I embarked on my first east coast reading tour. As my book had already received good reviews in *The Los Angeles Times, The Washington Times, Publishers Weekly*, and other publications, Geoff Clark had arranged for me to come to Rhode Island to meet with creative writing classes and give a public reading of my work. Roger Williams University paid for my airline tickets, as well as giving me a stipend of $2,000. Through various literary contacts, I set up other paid readings at a community college and a state university in Plattsburgh, New York, and at the Big Horror Reading Series in Binghamton, New York, as well as a lecture on the poetry of Charles Baudelaire at Clarion University in Pennsylvania.

I drove from Santa Maria to Los Angeles, flew to Boston and rented a car at the airport. The next day, I met with my literary agent, a former editor with Little Brown, who had formed her own agency when the company moved from Boston to New York City. She was currently representing the manuscript of a novel called "Christabel," a loose retelling of Coleridge's long, unfinished gothic poem by the same title. Over dinner we discussed my writing and the state of literary publishing. She wanted me to move away from short fiction and focus entirely on writing comic novels she felt she could sell. I told her I was sketching out a surreal feminist road novel, which would later become *Sacred Hearts*.

The following day I drove to Roger Williams University in Rhode Island, where I met Geoffrey Clark and his wife. I stayed at their home during my two-day visit. I remember they had an impressive Great Pyrenees dog named Bear. Geoff had grown up in Michigan's Upper Peninsula and attended the Iowa Writer's Workshop, where he studied with Richard Yates. Geoff wrote naturalistic stories and novels about class conflicts, masculinity, violence and sex, often based on his adolescent experiences. An ex-alcoholic, he got up early each day and ran ten miles, even in the worst weather. He was easy to like: soft-spoken, personable and sincere. I had published his story collection *Schooling the Spirit* through Asylum Arts and would later acquire and edit his novel *Jackdog Summer* for Hi Jinx Press. I visited two of Geoff's fiction writing classes, where I read and discussed my stories and my approach to writing. Students asked some interesting questions and we had some good laughs. Years later, Geoff told me that one of my stories, "Up Yours," had achieved a kind of legendary status among the creative writing students on campus, as they liked to drink to excess and read the story aloud to each other.

My reading took place in the Student Union. Due to word of mouth from the creative writing students, the multipurpose room was filled to overflowing. I remember the reading as boisterous and fun. When I returned to the campus three years later, I read at The Roger Williams Performing Arts Center, known on campus as The Barn. A black box theater built into a 1893 barn which had been disassembled and rebuilt by architecture students in the 1980s, The Barn was a beautiful and intimate space, perfect for a story-teller or performance poet.

Next, I drove through Providence toward Worcester, then up interstate 90 through Springfield to Stockbridge, where I had arranged to meet photographer Anne Arden McDonald. I had featured her arresting and surreal self-portraits, photographs she staged by building installations in abandoned factories and empty landscapes, places in which she performed for the camera. Part dance, part dream, her photos had been a perfect fit for the covers and inside pages of *Asylum Annual 1993*. In West Stockbridge she had an exhibition of her work in a gallery, where she gave a talk about staged self-portraits, both her own and the work of several Czech and Slovak photographers. After her lecture, we went to dinner. She drove to the restaurant in a car decorated with a forest of miniature figurines she had collected and glued to the dashboard. I found her conversation to be as unexpected, ephemeral, and dreamlike as her photos.

The next day, I headed north along the shore of Lake Champlain to Plattsburgh, New York, where I had two readings on consecutive days. Elliot Richman, a poet I had published in *Asylum* magazine, had invited me to read at Clinton Community College, where he taught in the English department. I stayed in the spare bedroom at his downtown loft. The next morning, the sky was steel gray and the temperature had dropped considerably. After coffee and breakfast out, we drove to the college, where I poked around the library and waited for the afternoon reading. The reading itself was fairly routine, though I remember snow falling as we walked outside. That evening we met with a few local writers and poets at a restaurant and talked over dinner.

The following day, I read from my fiction and prose poems to an enthusiastic audience at SUNY Plattsburgh. I waited for the reading in my host's English department office on campus, where we talked about translating literature. Suddenly he changed the subject and asked if I wanted to teach his Shakespeare class. They were halfway through *Macbeth*, he told me, and he was sure his students would enjoy hearing what someone else had to say about the play. When I declined, he looked disappointed. It was obvious that he didn't feel much like teaching. Sighing, he gathered up his books and headed off to class, while I stayed in his office and rested my eyes before the reading.

Next, I drove my rental car to Binghamton, New York, where I met Richard Martin for the first time. A hardscrabble poet with a natural affinity for philosophical musings on the absurd, he told me about Binghamton and the group of friends he'd known most of his life. He had grown up in a working-class neighborhood, where his father had owned a bar. Since then, he had lived a life full of crazy jobs, travel, poetry, domestic turmoil, friendship, and unusual experiences, all of which he had turned into a hilarious monolog. Among the funniest natural story-tellers I have ever met, he entertained me for hours as we talked. Later, we met up with three or four of his friends who had worked for years with him to run and promote the Big Horror Poetry Readings, a series he ran from 1983 to 1996. At this time, Dick had a job as a state writing specialist. He traveled to schools all over New York, helping administrators and teachers improve the writing programs and curriculum. A few years later, he would finish his career as a public-school principal in Boston.

The reading took place in a working-class bar—a neighborhood dive with air hockey, pool tables, and a television over the bar blaring out a Celtics game. One corner of the dark room had a small raised stage, where the occasional poet or singer-songwriter performed. Roughly two dozen folding chairs had been set up in front of the stage. "How's this work?" I asked. Dick told me there would probably be an equal number of people there for the poetry reading as there were regulars drinking around the bar. "It's fun," he said, "though sometimes it can seem a bit like parallel play."

Dick told me I'd be reading with Patricia Smith, a poetry slam champion who had recently released her first book, *Life According to Motown*. Dick would warm up the mic for me with a few poems of his own, then I would read for half an hour, followed by Patricia. It seemed like a good strategy to slowly turn up the heat in a room where, for half the potential audience, poetry was about as popular as frostbite.

The poetry crowd trickled in, ordered drinks, and filled up several rows of gray metal folding chairs. I met Patricia Smith and her husband, also a veteran of the poetry slam circuit. Both impressed me as relaxed and congenial. We discussed the reading order and Patricia's husband offered to recite one of his poems after Dick read, before I came on. The energy in the room was growing more intense. Finally, Dick approached the mic and welcomed the crowd.

Dick knew many of the people in the audience. Some were from the university, others part of various communities of local writers. A few had driven in from other places. He bantered a bit and told stories about the poems he skillfully read. The poetry slam poet then recited a short poem from memory, which he accompanied with expressive gestures and emphatic delivery. The audience gave him a warm applause. When it was time for me to read, I offered up a selection of surreal and humorous prose poems and short stories, closing with "Up Yours." Though a few people from the bar swiveled their stools in my direction, the Celtics still ruled the bar.

Then Dick introduced Patricia and she took the stage, her book in hand. She told the crowd she would be performing poems from her first collection, which she held up for people to see. Then she put the book back into her bag on the floor behind her. She stood at the mic for a few seconds, silently taking in the entire room. Finally, she abandoned the safely of the mic, stepped down from the little wooden riser and walked across the room to the bar, where everyone sat with their back to her, talking and watching the basketball game. The only black person in a sea of white bar patrons, she approached a big, bearded man in grease-stained jeans and a John Deere cap, tapped him on the shoulder, and yelled, "Hey mister!" The room froze. The pool balls stopped rolling halfway across the felt and the air hockey disk hung suspended half an inch above the table. The Celtic game magically switched itself off. "That's me up there," she continued, opening her poem with a reference to a James Taylor song. The guy in the John Deere cap smiled at her and nodded. Everyone at the bar swiveled toward her as she walked back to the stage, still reciting her poem from memory. The room was hers now: she owned it.

To say that Patricia Smith is a brilliant performer of her own work is an understatement. More accurately, that night at least, she was more like an illuminating presence—the human embodiment of poetry. As she recited her long and detailed poems from memory, her voice sang the words with an intonation at times as gentle as rain on a foggy window, at times as raw and powerful as a circular saw ripping plywood. Those fortunate enough to have been present for the reading knew that they had experienced a small miracle. Afterward, Patricia seemed at once drained and ecstatic. She told us she had acted purely on instinct, pushing the limits of her own confidence and commitment.

We were all so keyed up after the reading that no one wanted the experience to end. We talked and drank Rolling Rock beer at the bar until it closed, then went to an all-night restaurant and ordered breakfast. The sun was up by the time we finally left and said goodbye. Each of us went back to our lives knowing that magic does exist in the world.

Back at Dick's apartment, I slept for a few hours on the couch, then said goodbye and drove to Pennsylvania. The snow followed me as I arrived in Clarion. As my critical edition and translation of *La Fanfarlo* had made me something of an expert on Baudelaire, a professor of French literature had invited me to give a public lecture on the poet. Pushing the boundaries of common sense, political correctness, and good taste, I gave a semi-tongue-in-cheek talk on "The Feminism of Charles Baudelaire." I'm not sure what people thought of my talk, though the student newspaper published a short review of it later that week. Somehow, I had persuaded at least one person that Baudelaire was ahead of his time in his views about women.

* * *

Powell's City of Books in Portland, Oregon claims to be the biggest independent new and used bookstore in the world. Founded by

Walter Powell in 1971, the store operates out of a three-story building connected to other buildings that collectively take up a full city block in downtown Portland's Pearl District. The store is so massive that sections are color coded, as it's easy to get lost wandering around inside. Powell's remains open 365 days a year and claims that up to 10,000 people visit the store each day. They have an inventory of over four million books.

In the early 1990s, as I began publishing books under the Asylum Arts imprint, I corresponded with buyers at Powell's, who ordered Asylum Arts titles based on reviews in trade magazines like *Publisher's Weekly, Library Journal, Choice, Small Press,* and *Small Press Review.* They took the entire back list as well as the newest titles, liked what they saw, and established a standing order for new books. People who work at Powell's are known for recommending and hand selling books they've enjoyed themselves. They are readers first, and thus knowledgeable and capable booksellers.

The contemporary fiction buyer for the store familiarized herself with Asylum Arts. Her enthusiasm for *Water & Power* led to a personal recommendation and prominent display of the book in her section of the store, which resulted in multiple re-orders. Later, she selected me to be one of three featured readers at the grand opening of the new room the store was opening dedicated to small literary presses and magazines. Donna happened to be on vacation that week, so we loaded the truck with books and prints, and headed north to Oregon.

The night of the reading I displayed my prints in the new small press room. An overflow crowd had packed into a large open area and filled the surrounding stacks. Local poet Walt Curtis opened the reading. I read next, alternating prose poems from *The Masked Ball* and *Puppet Theatre* with stories from *Water & Power.* City Lights author Pamela Karol, whose pen name was "La Loca", closed out the evening by reading poems from her book *Adventures on the Isle of Adolescence.*

* * *

During the early and mid 1990s, I traveled to San Francisco every year to attend the Bay Area Book Festival, where, along with hundreds of other publishers from around the country, I rented a booth to display books Asylum Arts had published. The books featured distinctive black and white covers I'd designed, which stood out in the sea of colorful display booths, and attracted a lot of attention from people drawn to literature and art. I also displayed copies of my hand-pulled editions of linoleum and woodcut prints, which I sold alongside the books. My relief prints, shrink wrapped on foam core backings and priced between $25.00 and $75.00, sold well. The art sales more than paid the expense of attending the book fair, which offset the lackluster book sales.

Initially, I rented my own booth, though in later years I shared one with Jordan Jones and his magazine *Bakunin,* which helped reduce the cost of attending the event. Since the local Teamsters Union made the rules and controlled labor at convention centers in San Francisco, setting up for the book fair was always an intense, physically exhausting experience. Basically, you either paid union wages to have your boxes of books moved by teamsters from the building's loading dock, or else carried them by hand, one heavy load at a time, from a distant parking space through the huge building, to your booth. Hand trucks or wheeled dollies of any kind were forbidden. As the cost for setting up and moving materials for a small booth were greater than total sales from the event, I always carried the heavy boxes of books into and back out of the building myself, a task which demanded hours of backbreaking manual labor.

The book fair itself crackled with energy. Throughout the day, guests attended performances and talks by readers and lecturers, or panel discussions with authors, editors, and publishers. However, the main focus was books. With hundreds of publishers displaying their newest titles, readers could browse thousands of titles, talk with a favorite author and have a copy their book inscribed. In addition to meeting readers, the fair also gave me the chance to talk with writers and poets I'd published in the magazine over the years. I also met artists and writers who asked about submitting work to the press. Each year I found time to visit and converse with literary friends and editors like Susie Bright, or literary publishers like Bruce McPherson of McPherson & Company and Damon Krukowski and Naomi Yang, a pair of multi-talented, Harvard-educated rock musicians who had founded an outstanding press devoted to publishing translations of classic surrealist texts under an imprint they called Exact Change.

While exciting, standing for eight hours and talking to hundreds of people each day could also be exhausting. Nevertheless, book fairs provided an opportunity to get firsthand feedback directly from readers. Over the years, the only books that went into multiple printings were Kendall Lappin's translations of Gérard de Nerval's *Aurélia*, Baudelaire in *Echoes of Baudelaire,* and the anthology *Dead French Poets,* as well as my own book of short stories *Water & Power.* Though the marketplace had already told me that the most profitable Asylum Arts titles were translations of French literature and the *Asylum Annual,* it hurt to see firsthand just how little interest the books by contemporary poets the press had published generated.

According to statistics kept by Poets House, Asylum Arts was during that time one of the most prominent (measured by number of new poetry collections published each year) publishers of contemporary poetry in America for three years in a row. That number includes all commercial presses, university presses, and non-profit literary publishers. It's difficult to understand how a one-man operation, run out of a spare bedroom and existing in the margins of society, could be in such a position, especially in a country with hundreds of professional writing programs, each offering advanced degrees in poetry. Clearly Asylum Arts, along with other publishers of poetry, catered to a niche so small as to guarantee financial failure. In such an environment, independent literary publishers dismiss practicality and conventional wisdom. They abandon themselves to madness. "Sure, I'd be happy to publish your epic poem on the melting ice caps and the destruction of the environment… as soon as I obtain a grant from ExxonMobil."

* * *

At the lowest point of my career as a publisher and writer, after the disastrous bankruptcy of my distributor, Inland Book Company, I decided to look for a job teaching writing. I had somehow convinced myself that a regular salary was all I needed to repair Asylum Arts and the literary career I had worked to build. So, I gathered together a stack of recommendations by writers I admired, a handful of testimonials about my proven effectiveness as a teacher of writing, and a pile of photocopied reviews of my books, and sent these glowing papers, along with my *curriculum vitæ* and the most humble and sincere letter I could manufacture, to every English department advertising a full-time writing position in *The Chronicle of Higher Education*. I told myself some small university with a writing program might like to have a nationally distributed magazine and literary press in residence. When I failed to get a response, I began broadening my search. In the end, I tried everything, including junior colleges and offers to teach freshman composition part-time. When I finally secured a single invitation, the letter informed me that the interviews would be held during the annual Associated Writing Programs conference in Phoenix that spring.

Though I wasn't a member, the AWP had sent a flyer addressed to Asylum Arts. They were holding a book fair in conjunction with the conference and wanted to attract literary presses as exhibitors. Since I was going to Phoenix for the interview, I thought I might as well rent a booth, pack my truck full of books, and try to cover my travel costs through book sales. I drove straight from Santa Maria to Arizona and stayed in the cheapest accommodation I could find, a noisy, run-down motel next to the highway. By contrast, the conference was held at a swank hotel adjoining the university. The following day, the organizers assigned me a folding banquet table and a graduate student from the MFA program in creative writing to serve as my assistant. He was a bright, curious, and sincere young man who asked good questions about how to start and run a literary magazine and press. Unfortunately, few of the poets and writers in attendance gave the *Asylum Annual* or the dozens of Asylum Arts books more than a passing glance. In fact, the only publication that generated any interest from the conference attendees seemed to be a brand-new magazine called *Creative Non-Fiction*. "As opposed to what?" I asked the graduate student rhetorically, "uninspired non-fiction?"

The only positive memory I have of the AWP conference was meeting Peter Johnson, who was exhibiting a magazine he edited called *The Prose Poem: An International Journal* at the book fair. I had corresponded with Peter for a couple of years, as we shared an intense interest in the prose poem, and he had published some of my work as well as a review of *Carnival Aptitude* in his magazine. In person, I liked him immediately. He impressed me with his knowledge, his genuineness, and his common sense and decency. I also liked the conversational quality, the uneasy insights and the humor of his poems. Unlike many poets, he seemed comfortable in his own skin, deeply knowledgeable, and sure of his opinions. Since we both detested the posturing and pretension of the majority of the academic poets and writers, many of whom appeared to be using the AWP conference as an excuse to get drunk and try to sleep with each other's wives, students, and colleagues, we spent a good deal of time talking about books and ideas instead. Peter complained that his wife had retreated to their hotel room, as she was tired of middle-aged pick-up artists drooling over her. In a note I received from him years later, Peter related another story from the conference: "A gorgeous woman from Texas came up to my table and asked me to meet her upstairs. I told her I was with my wife. She asked if my wife was pretty. I said she's very pretty and sexy, and so the Texas woman said to tell her to come along. As the woman seemed intent on driving the conversation over a cliff, I told her, 'No thanks. One woman at a time is enough.'"

My job interview for the visiting writer position the following day was only slightly less farcical. All that I recall about it now was a question put to me by the chairman of the department, who asked (I'd be tempted to say with head-wagging jollity), "How do you feel about not having a Ph.D.?" I remember telling him and the rest of the hiring committee, including the outgoing writer-in-residence, that I felt just fine about not having a "terminal" degree in creative writing, because the books I'd written, translated and published over the past fifteen years had been by far more challenging, rigorous, and valuable than hoop dancing to earn the ultimate academic seal of unoriginality and approval. And since when, I added, did a creative writer or a literary editor need to have a fucking Ph.D. to do his job? Needless to say, I wouldn't be welcome in Oklahoma anytime soon. Apparently, I was categorically unqualified to be a visiting writer.

Ironically, I later learned that the previous year's writer-in-residence, actually *did* have a Ph.D. in creative writing. Moreover, he happened to be the author of a novel called *Mustang Sally,* an academic comedy that an acquisitions editor at a commercial press had only a few years prior accepted for publication just before reading the manuscript of my novel "Christabel." The editor had cited his reluctance to publish two similar novels as the sole reason why they passed on my novel. Not long after the trip to Phoenix, I ran across *Mustang Sally* at the Santa Maria public library and checked it out. It wasn't a very good novel, but then neither was "Christabel."

Thus ended my one and only experience at the AWP. Though I didn't attend any of the workshops or readings, I could easily imagine the satisfied and self-congratulatory atmosphere that surrounds such events. In those days, when I looked at a magazine like *Poets & Writers,* to use yet another example of professional malpractice, I was always surprised at the upbeat tone of the articles, which seemed designed to convey the message that "everything's fine out there; everyone's successful and happy." No one talked about a profession in crisis. No one wrote about the difficulties of selling literary properties, of making a living as a writer. No one discussed the shrinking literary market, the dearth of vibrant literary publishers. Nobody complained about the death of literary culture. No one published articles on the stillbirth of the vast majority of literary titles, the shredding and remaindering of books. No one publicized the depressing reality that even the winners of the Pulitzer and Nobel prizes for poetry, in spite of their large cash awards to the winning poets, sold only a few hundred copies of the poets' books, which were, in turn, heavily subsidized by the Academy of American Poets' membership dues.

It seemed clear that the profession had been coopted by university writing programs, that books and readers had been replaced by professors and students, degrees, prizes, and pedigrees. In this alternate literary universe, most authors simply accepted that few people would ever read the books they probably wouldn't even write. Back then, when I talked to writers, particularly those teaching in academic writing programs, I was always amazed at how little they knew or cared about the business of literature. Most of them had never made any attempt to live off their writing, nor would they ever consider doing so. After all, they already had a job teaching other would-be poets and writers how to eventually become, if they were good at politics and very lucky, teachers of poetry and writing.

There were always a few success stories to crow about and most writers and poets didn't want to hear that it was virtually impossible to make a living writing, editing, publishing, or selling the kinds of books we all professed to love so much. Certainly, it seemed more hopeful to read through pages of grants available to writers, to dream of making the right connections, to realistically pursue an MFA or Ph.D. program in creative writing that might lead to a coveted teaching position.

I recall that the back pages of *Poets & Writers* listed dozens of advertisements for low-residence MFA programs, seminars, and summer writing workshops. The guest faculty at these institutions and seminars often seemed to be the same group of insiders. Because most of these writers already had permanent jobs teaching at or directing MFA programs, most were double- or even triple-dipping. So, I suppose they'd found a way to make the politics and business of literature, if not the writing itself, pay far better than the books they promised their students would someday write.

* * *

Just after I published a collection of his poems, Elliot Richman received a grant that allowed him to drive across the country, giving readings along the way. When he reached California, he came to Santa

Maria, where I joined him on his tour. He parked his car in front of our house on East Las Flores Avenue and together we drove, with my Keeshond puppy sequestered in the enclosed back of my Nissan pickup, to Portland, then up the Columbia River. When we got to Idaho, the rural locals treated us like toxic invaders from a hostile planet. A New Yorker with thick glasses and long hair he wore in a ponytail, Richman attracted disapproving glares everywhere we went. Apparently, two men traveling together was suspect as well. We camped out each night along the way. The poet slept in his tiny blue tent, while I crawled into the back of my truck and slept with the dog.

One morning, after leaving a campsite, we stopped at a roadside diner for breakfast, where we sat at the counter and ordered coffee and cold cereal. Some fat rednecks sitting at the other end of the bar murmured something and laughed, though I didn't hear what they said. Later, Richman told me they'd said they were surprised that we ordered corn flakes instead of "Froot Loops." Though we'd already been on the road for forty minutes, I briefly considered turning the vehicle around and returning to the diner. I envisioned myself driving my truck through the plate glass window and smashing into the counter. "I'll have a bowl of Froot Loops," I'd say.

In Montana, we camped along the Little Bighorn River, visited the Custer Battlefield, drank beer at a microbrewery in Bozeman. Then we drove through Wyoming, Utah, Monument Valley, Las Vegas, and back to Santa Maria. After a week on the road, we agreed that although America was impressive for its vast forests, gleaming cities, and majestic open spaces, being a poet in our country was the shits.

A few years later, when we were living in Paradise, California, in the foothills of the Sierra Nevada mountains, poet Richard Martin asked me to set up some readings to help promote his second Asylum Arts book, *Marks*. Donna and I hosted Dick at our house on Sawmill Road. We put together a publication party for the book and introduced Dick to the local literary crowd, including Len Fulton, publisher of Dust Books and the *International Directory of Little Magazines and Small Presses*, and a handful of poets and artists from Chico, Sacramento, and the surrounding area. We screened a videotape of a documentary someone had made about faux artist Thomas Kincade, the kitschy "Painter of Light," whose paint by numbers landscapes blighted shops in malls across the country. The film documented a sales presentation Kincade had made at the banquet room of a Chico hotel the previous year, during which he cynically plucked money from starry-eyed seniors. Confronted by the filmmaker with questions about his operation and motives, Kincade became defensive and incoherent. The film was both uncomfortable and hilarious. We also screened Tony Liano's short film *Three-Cornered Hat*. Then Dick entertained us with a short reading from *Marks*.

The following day, I had set up a reading for Dick at a coffee house in San Mateo, which turned out to be a suburban haven for social climbing Bay Area escapees. The reading series was run by the editor of a small but well-regarded literary magazine. When we arrived, the editor greeted us and took us to a wine bar with prices that taxed my budget. She told us she'd made a reservation for us to have dinner together at her friend's upscale restaurant before the reading. Since we'd had a late lunch and weren't eager to pay for an unplanned gourmet meal, we politely declined, which for some reason infuriated our host. In fact, she didn't even bother to show up to the reading.

Worse, she hadn't promoted the event at all. When we arrived, there were three people in attendance. I felt terrible that Dick had been so badly treated and I took full responsibility for the fiasco. It seemed unfair that someone who had for years directed one of the best reading series in the country and was an expert on promoting and staging successful poetry readings would be asked to read to such a poor audience. Fortunately, poets tend to make friends with irony. A poet whose imagination dwelt comfortably in the realm of the absurd, Dick insisted we read as planned, despite the lack of interest. So, we read to each other, the barista, and the three people who'd come to hear our work. Afterwards, we ate some grub at a truck stop on the way back to Paradise. The food was lousy, even a little cold, but the waitress was working hard. More importantly, the freshly-brewed coffee was strong and hot.

The next day, we drove to San Francisco, where we'd arranged to meet Jordan Jones and Tony Liano for dinner before our reading at a cafe in North Beach. On the drive in from Paradise, Dick told me about writing a poem every day for a year, which got me thinking. Suddenly I envisioned a massive art project for the Internet, in which artists, poets, writers, musicians, and film makers would be invited to participate by reacting artistically to absurd clips taken from newscasts taped around the country and posted on a web site. The resulting social and political commentary, in the form of poems, stories, songs, videos, and artwork, would also be posted each day on the site, with links from the corresponding day's news clip. By the end of the year, the project would be a record of a society in turmoil, as the Bush administration was already gearing up for the post-9-11 invasion of Iraq.

When we met with Jordan and Tony, both were enthusiastic about the idea. Everyone contributed ideas about how to structure and organize the project. Tony agreed to research the hardware and software we'd need to grab the video clips off local television broadcasts. Jordan said he'd get to work setting up a web site. I would write press releases, a mission statement, and text for the web site. We all would put our contacts to work. By the end of the evening, the four of us were committed to doing The 365 Project, which was conceived and launched in a single day. I don't remember much about the reading, except that again the organizer didn't bother to show up.

After taking a day off to relax, we drove to Sacramento for a reading at The Book Collector, a downtown used book store with a special interest in poetry. The owner, Richard Hansen, was also the publisher of a series of tiny handmade books, called Poems for All, each of which featured a single poem. His idea was that poems could be distributed "like seeds," planted in public places for people to find and take nourishment from. Hansen had already published a number of my own poems in this format, and he had prepared two of Dick's poems to give away at the reading.

Jordan drove up from the Bay Area to help videotape the event. Richard Hansen had set up as many folding chairs as the room could hold. A few more people squeezed into the stacks. Dick got the audience laughing right away and kept them entertained throughout. He ended the evening with a brilliant reading of his poem "Poets Addicted to Moths."

* * *

On January 1, 2003, we officially launched The 365 Project. The first news clips Dick, Tony, Jordan, and I taped and submitted each day went onto the site the following day. From then on, we selected the winning clips by vote in groups of three or four days. In the first months, the clips reflected disturbing and surreal news and commentary from the Iraq war, along with freak show stories reported by local news stations, mind numbing quotes from George Bush, Dick Chaney, Donald Rumsfeld, and Ari Fleischer. Watching those clips in retrospect, we should have little confusion about how we arrived at the current state of cultural and political disintegration.

As the first poetry and art submissions went onto the site, we began planning trips to promote the project, one to southern California, the other to Washington, DC, New York City, and Boston. We scheduled readings and presentations at a gallery in Ventura County and at Beyond Baroque in the Venice Beach area of Los Angeles. Tony prepared a short video about the project, which we screened at the reading events.

In February, I flew from Sacramento to Washington, DC. On the flight I sat next to a thin, energetic woman who told me that aliens had repeatedly abducted her as a child. We'd been making small talk about our travel plans—she and her mother, who was sitting in the row ahead of us because they'd been late boarding the overbooked flight, were on their way home from a funeral—when she suddenly put her hand over her mouth. "Oh my goodness. I'm sorry for asking so many questions," she said. "I don't mean to be rude. Maybe you'd rather read your book or take a nap? It's just that I've got a habit of talking people up to pass the time."

I smiled and admitted I had the same habit.

Chuckling to herself, she said we'd ended up in the right seats after all then. "I listen to people all day long and never yet got tired of it." The key to good conversation is to be a good listener. If you're patient and let people have their say, they'll tell you some pretty interesting things, that's for sure.

I agreed with her. "Everybody has a story." That's when she told me hers.

"Most people don't believe me," she said, after she'd asked me if I was interested in hearing about her experience with aliens, "but that doesn't bother me much now. I'm used to it." She fidgeted with her necklace and studied my face for a moment before she continued. Then she took a breath and began.

"Up until the age of sixteen, they'd come for me," she said. "I'd be asleep in my bed and a warm green light would fill the room. Then off I'd go, up to their ship. It happened fast, almost before I could catch my breath. They came for me about every six months." I listened intently to what she told me. She spoke deliberately and when she paused, I waited for her to continue. "I'd have liked to think it was just a dream, but after a while I knew better because of the experiments they did on me. Didn't they, mama?"

An elderly woman with oversized glasses peeked her head above the back of the seat in front of me. "They surely did."

"I don't want to say all they done, but most of it wasn't nice. It made me so I'm not afraid of nothing now."

"Are you worried they'll come back for you again some time?" I asked.

"No, I'm not. Because I know for sure they won't. I know a lot of things I probably shouldn't." Then she told me a story about how she'd tried to warn the son of a family friend that if he didn't stop using drugs and committing petty crimes something bad would happen. "He laughed at me and walked away. I told him I would pray for him. Later on, that same day he died an unnatural death."

Just before the plane landed, the woman pulled her purse out from under the seat and gave me her business card. She owned a barbershop in Saint Louis where she cut men's hair. "I won't touch women's hair," she explained. When I told her she should write down her stories, she looked at me and said, "I'm telling them to you for a reason."

When the plane landed, I waited at Dulles airport for Jordan Jones, who lived in nearby Chantilly, close to the Civil War battlefield at Bull Run. I had a reading scheduled at the Writer's Center in Bethesda, Maryland the following day, where I also planned to discuss The 365 Project and invite the audience to participate. That evening the series organizer, who was the editor of a well-known literary magazine, called to say he wouldn't be able to attend the reading. Though my reading was set for early afternoon, he and his wife were throwing an Academy Awards party at their home later that same day, and he needed to prepare for the annual festival of Hollywood self-congratulation to be broadcast on television.

The following day we drove to Bethesda. In an act of distressing symbolism, Jordan and I found the doors to the Writer's Center locked when we arrived for my reading. A couple of minutes before the scheduled event, someone came to open up. When the one person who apparently hadn't been invited to the Academy Awards party showed up for the reading, I unapologetically canceled the event. Jordan snapped a photo of me lying as though crucified on the floor of the empty reading room. I felt like I'd been transported to the Mother Ship and subjected to some kind of twisted psychological stress test.

That evening Jordan and I drove to Randallstown, Maryland to visit the late, great writer Eric Basso, a virtually unknown literary figure who I had always thought of as the last of the great Modernists. We'd invited him to come with us to New York City to participate in the 365 reading event at a gallery in Soho where I had been invited to read by the director, through Paul Rosheim of Obscure Publications. I would share the billing with Kirpal Gordon. I planned to include readings by Jordan and Richard Martin, my co-editors on The 365 Project. Jordan and I agreed that it would be a fine gesture and a monumental opportunity to have Eric participate as well.

Basso had a reputation for being a recluse. For many years he had concentrated on writing his thirty-six full length plays, six collections of poems, two books of fiction, as well as a selection of critical essays, and two volumes of dreams. For part of that time, he stayed at home caring for his elderly and ailing parents. Once they both passed away, his reclusive behavior continued. He seemed uninterested in venturing into the world.

We'd already discussed the idea with Basso via email and phone conversations, and we knew that he was eager to participate. When we arrived at his house, he had laid in a huge stock of beer for the evening. By that time, I'd already known Eric professionally for nearly twenty-five years, as he was among the first writers I published in the single issue of a magazine I edited in 1980 called *Amputated Fingers*. Over the years, his poems, fiction, translations, and essays had appeared regularly in *Asylum* magazine. Asylum Arts had published five full-length collections of his poems, two books of fiction, and three volumes of plays, including the massive *Golem Triptych*.

While Jordan had connected with Basso when he moved from California to Virginia, I had never met him before, nor even spoken with him on the phone. Ours was a writer's relationship, based entirely on letters, and then emails. It was good to finally put a face to those many years of letters, and the three of us passed a very pleasant evening together. We made plans to meet at Union Station the following day and ride the train together to New York.

However, the trip did not unfold as planned, at least for Eric. Later that same night, Jordan received a phone call from Basso, who told him that he had been very drunk and had fallen down the stairs at his house and injured himself. His face looked particularly bad, he said. When Jordan asked if he'd gone to the hospital, Eric told him that he was fine, just a bit bloody and beat up. He said that he was sorry that he could not go with us to New York, and then he hung up. I have never doubted that Eric did fall down the stairs, though I strongly suspect it was at least partially by subconscious design.

The following day, Jordan and I boarded a train for New York. We called Eric from the train to check on him and he told us that his eye was black and blue and partially swollen shut and his lip cut and swollen as well. Aside from his injured pride, he said, he was really okay. It was a long train trip. To alleviate the boredom, I made up a series of gestures, which I used to confound Jordan. Always a good sport, Jordan played along, and I eventually taught him my new "gestural language," which I called "NoNohNon." I later incorporated NoNohNon into the Tidewriters section of my novel *The Nambuli Papers*. After a long day on the train, we finally arrived in Grand Central Station just as a fight broke out. I thought to myself, "Welcome to New York City."

For the next three days, everywhere we went, at any hour, there were too many people, all of them talking too loud, over even louder music. I left restaurants halfway through meals to seek fresh air and the relative quiet of the sidewalk outside. Perhaps I'd been living in the mountains of California too long, but I found New York City to be a brash and unforgiving place. Like other major cities, it was a place only the well-off could fully enjoy.

Our first day in the city, I had arranged to visit poet and painter Carolyn Stoloff, whose book *You Came to Meet Someone Else* I had published. I met her in her studio off Union Square and we talked for several hours. Later that evening, Jordan and I attended an off-off Broadway play by another Asylum Arts author, Kenneth Bernard. Afterward, Ken and his wife took us to a lovely, quiet Polish restaurant in their neighborhood. We enjoyed hours of relaxed conversation. While his work is among the most challenging and outrageous I published, Ken was calm and philosophical, intellectual and original, with a wry sense of humor. I always enjoyed both his company and his letters.

When we met Tony the next morning, both Jordan and I greeted him with a gesture in which the fingers of the right hand touch the forehead, then the arm extends outward with the palm up, a gesture that meant "Tony doesn't get it." For a few minutes, we gaslighted Tony with NoNohNon gestures, but he was too cool to be rattled by our nonsense and began to make up his own gestures in return. Suddenly, the language had taken off. We were conversing, though about what wasn't quite clear. We spent most of the day poking around the Metropolitan Museum of Art, then went out for pizza and beer.

The following day we went to the Guggenheim Museum. We had no idea the museum was staging an exhibit of large sculptures, along with drawings and screenings of parts of Matthew Barney's *Cremaster Cycle,* a series of five feature-length art films funded by the Guggenheim Foundation. The exhibit was made up of massive constructs that reflected a deeply personal symbolism which offered little in the way of context. The exhibit took up nearly the entire museum, which was filled with television screens and large installations made of plastic, metal, wax, and Vaseline. The massive scale of the sculptures, fabrications, and installations alone seemed overstated to the point of vulgarity. I could only imagine the cost of fabricating such nightmarish creations.

According to the Guggenheim Museum, *The Cremaster Cycle (1994–2002)* is a self-enclosed aesthetic system consisting of five feature-length films that explore the process of creation… Its conceptual departure point is the male cremaster muscle, which controls testicular contractions in response to sexual stimuli." No wonder the people I saw in the museum looked so dazed and confused. Nobody told them they'd be wandering around inside a giant scrotum.

Everything about the exhibit screamed excess and waste. The casual vulgarity of late-stage capitalism seemed to be the real theme, or at least that's how I interpreted the exhibition. I stood and watched the other visitors silently walking amongst the mounds of Vaseline, their eyes slightly bulging. They didn't know how to react, so they didn't react at all. Afraid they might come off as ignorant or unsophisticated, they didn't want to be the ones that made poor Vincent cut off his own damned ear. I, on the other hand, didn't care what people thought of me. I'd been making art my whole life and I knew that Marcel Duchamp had done a better job of satirizing the art world nearly a hundred years earlier when he titled his plumber's supply ceramic urinal "Fountain", signed it "R. Mutt" and brought it into the Society of Independent Artists exhibition in New York City in April of 1917. While there may have been something interesting and artistic about Barney's nine-hour art film binge, I couldn't get past the obvious fact that such self-indulgence would not have been possible without the funding of the Guggenheim's robber-baron resources. In fact, I couldn't help from feeling that the Guggenheim Foundation could have saved itself millions of dollars by dragging some stained and rusty plumbing fixtures out of one of the museum's basement restrooms instead.

Money, however, seemed to be the whole point. The show smelled like paper currency smeared in Vaseline. It offered up a mountain of blood, sperm, and shit-encrusted lucre burned on the pyre of corporate greed. I later learned that, in addition to the millions Barney had received from Guggenheim, his co-producer, Barbara Gladstone, owned a gallery that, according to *Forbes,* did 100 million dollars in annual revenue. An article in *The Economist* stated that the series of five *Cremaster* films was released as a limited edition of twenty sets of DVDs, which each sold for at least $100,000. In 2007, one disc (*Cremaster 2)* sold for $571,000. If the point of Barney's nine hours of self-indulgent personal mythology, sex, biology, and bodily functions and fluids had been to illicit sadness and disgust at the decadence of a culture capable of producing such a wasteful spectacle, then I suppose he had succeeded brilliantly.

Fast forward a few years to Art Basel in Miami, where Italian artist Maurizio Cattelan hangs three bananas on a wall. Apparently, there's no shortage of people willing to buy them for a hundred and twenty thousand dollars apiece and he quickly sells out the edition. As usual, the story briefly inspires a sense of dull shock and numb outrage. By then, I'm living in Ecuador, where bananas cost five cents each and people are lucky if they have a job that pays five hundred dollars a month.

Before I left the Guggenheim, I struck up a conversation with one of the museum security guards, a painter earning his rent and food money so that he could make art. We shared our opinions about the show. "So far you're the only person I've seen come through here who's had an honest, intelligent response," he told me. "Everyone else seems like they got off at the wrong subway exit and came inside thinking they were at the mall."

That night Tony, Jordan, Dick and I sat together in the lobby of the Chelsea Hotel and wrote a play in NoNohNon called "Tony Doesn't Get It" that parodied what we'd just experienced at the Guggenheim Museum. The following morning, we went back to the Guggenheim and performed the play on the sidewalk in front of the entrance. Tony's brother Rob, a documentary filmmaker living in New York, videotaped the event. In the video, The Narrator, played by Richard Martin, describes the play to the passersby as "A Sidewalk Play, written and performed in NoNohNon," and "A trip to the Guggenheim in the form of a counter-attack on the Artstocracy." The nine-minute video, written late the night before, performed on the street, and produced for free, further parodies the millions of dollars spent to produce Barney's nine-hour long set of art films on display inside the museum.

Later that day, we met up with Paul Rosheim, who had come from Minnesota for the reading. We discovered a bar called "Toad Hall," nearly across the street from the gallery and parked ourselves inside for several hours before the event. I remember multiple pitchers of Guinness, origami-folded dollar bills, temporary sculptures made from napkins, beer glasses, and ashtrays, and having a nonsensical, drunken argument with Rob Liano over absolutely nothing at all. Then, it was time for the reading.

We walked across the street and stumbled into the gallery, where we met the co-owner, a novelist and philosopher of science, who looked strangely familiar to me. We helped set up chairs for the reading and talked with Kirpal Gordon, Steve Hirsch, an editor at *Heaven Bone,* and bass player Peter Priore, who arrived just after we did. It was good to finally meet Kirpal, whose work I had admired in *Central Park, Open* and other magazines.

Kirpal Gordon opened the reading with a performance of his jazz-inspired poems, backed by Hirsch on drums and Priore on stand-up bass. His experiments and innovations with language, voice, and music created a sense of something new and exciting and his work was well-received. Then, Tony screened his video about The 365 Project and he and I took turns talking about the project and inviting the audience to participate in it. I read a few prose poems and turned the mic over to Jordan and Dick.

After the reading, I finally placed where I had seen the director of the foundation. Years earlier, she had submitted to Asylum Arts the manuscript of a novel about a hostess in a Geisha club in New York. In her cover letter and biography, she mentioned being a Ph.D. candidate in English who had worked at strip clubs as research for her novel. Rather bizarrely, she included a glossy photo of herself shot from behind, wearing nothing but high heels, and looking back over her shoulder. In an interview after her first books were published, she stated, "Believe me, it was my naked butt that got the attention and the writing that got the reviews."

Dick Martin flew back to Boston the next morning, while Jordan, Tony and I continued to explore the city. We walked through Times Square and ate donuts and pizza on the street. Tony took us to some of his favorite dive bars and treated us to a late-night meal at a fantastic Kosher deli. Then Tony flew back to San Francisco and Jordan and I continued on the train to Boston, where Dick had arranged one final reading for me at the West Roxbury Branch of the Boston Public Library.

It was snowing when we arrived in Boston. Dick had told us he'd pick us up at the station in his car and drive us out to the suburbs, where he lived. Unfortunately, due to a misunderstanding and our never having been in the station before, we exited through the wrong door and waited outside for Dick to arrive, while unbeknownst to us he had parked on the other side of the building. When Jordan called Dick, who'd turned around and gone home after waiting fifteen minutes for us, the two of them, both exhausted, blamed each other for the mishap. Finally, Dick came to get us a second time and we drove back to his house in silence.

Fortunately, the reading the next evening went much better than our arrival. The Pied Piper of poetry readings, Richard Martin consistently lured audiences to the events he organized. A large crowd packed into the public library, filling the chairs and lining the walls. A few minutes before the reading, Dick pulled me aside and gave me a private pep talk. "This is a pretty new reading series I've set up, so I'm still building trust with the community. Just go out there and wow them. Give it everything you've got." I delivered my poems and stories with as much energy and focus as I could, and the people in the audience rewarded me with their enthusiasm.

* * *

I once drove three and a half hours from Paradise to Berkeley and then back home again with only an hour and a half between the two trips. I had been invited to read at Cody's Books, but though I showed up on time and ready, I never got the chance. For years, I had maintained a strange relationship with Benjamin Saltman, a poet who had been my thesis advisor at California State University, Northridge. Intentional or not, we seemed to take turns slighting each other, though any sense of competition between us was likely unconscious. In recent years, we had both made an effort to be friends. We visited each other's homes and both enjoyed our relaxed conversations. I published Ben's essay on surrealism in *Asylum Annual* and Ben praised my books. We had finally arrived at a place where a genuine mutual respect existed between us. Still, I was surprised when the readings coordinator at Cody's contacted me. Apparently, Ben had specifically asked for me to share the billing with him at what he knew would be the last public reading of his life.

A full house had come to see Ben read his poems. His voice, quiet at first, seemed to gather strength as he continued. He smiled between poems and told witty stories to introduce some of the work. He appeared to be enjoying himself, so much, in fact, that his reading ran far beyond his allotted time. The host and much of the audience knew that Ben had a terminal illness and that this would be his last public reading. No one had the heart to stop him. By the time he stopped himself, only five minutes remained. A meeting had been scheduled for the room, so there was no way to extend the reading. Somehow, the reading that wasn't seemed a fitting end to our rocky relationship.

* * *

One literary road trip never took place, though I've always wished that it had. When we lived in Santa Maria, I conceived of an idea for a traveling literary vaudeville called "Show of Shows: The Asylum Arts Traveling Circus and Literary Vaudeville." I wrote a script in which a master of ceremonies introduces poets and writers who then give short readings from their work. Between literary guests, the master of ceremonies plays maudlin tunes poorly on a violin, insults the audience, and performs intentionally bad magic tricks and "miracles" with poorly-constructed props. My idea was to stage the show in bookstores and other venues around the country, where local Asylum Arts book authors and *Asylum Annual* contributors would join the cast of readers.

The first step would involve rehearsing and then videotaping an initial performance at a local coffeehouse, then using the edited tape to secure bookings at universities and bookstores around the country. When the show actually went on tour, I wanted to have a photographer and videographer with us so that I could produce a documentary film about the experience.

In addition to myself and Donna, I would have needed two permanent cast members to commit to participating in the whole reading circuit. I asked my friend Patrick, who had years of theater, opera, and musical theater experience, to be the master of ceremonies, and Danny Antonelli to play live musical interludes based on the songs from his CD *Dead End Streets*. Though I pitched the idea to both of them, neither expressed much interest in participating. To be fair, they both raised valid questions about the logistics and practicality of such a venture. In the end, however, as always, it was a question of money.

Throughout my life, most of my attempts to work on big projects with others have resulted in similar disappointments. That creative people let society limit their imaginations and undermine their goals always saddened me. No doubt I'm a fool, but I've always tried to pursue my passions independent of social expectations, simply for the joyful experience of doing something extraordinary. Perhaps that's why I have often failed so spectacularly.

* * *

In the winter of 2003, Donna and I traveled to France to work on the film *Tidewriters: The Lost Reel*, which Leaping Dog Press and BlueRain Films would issue on DVD, along with two books and a board game, as my multimedia novel *The Nambuli Papers*. It was the first time we'd been back to France since the eight months we had spent in Langlade in 1982. The locations for the film were in Paris and nearby Chartres, a day trip away by train. We arrived a week before film director Tony Liano, so we would have time to visit Paris again and spend time with Donna's cousin Kathy, who had lived for many years in the XVII Arrondissement. Both Kathy and her boyfriend Bertrand would have small roles in the comic silent film we were making.

Donna and I had spent a wonderful, romantic week enjoying museums, shops, cafes, and restaurants. Unfortunately, the day before she left to return to her job in California, I fell ill with a debilitating case of intestinal flu. Donna left for the airport early the next morning and I stayed in the hotel room, sick in bed the entire day. Meanwhile, Tony arrived at the hotel. When he saw that I was too ill to move, he took off with his film school friend Will, who was living in Paris with his French girlfriend, to shoot guerrilla footage of Yves Klein's paintings hanging in the Pompidou Center for our film. The following morning, Tony treated me to tea and toast, the first food I'd had in two days, at the Café de Flore on the Boulevard Saint-Germaine. Despite the unabashed snobbery of the famous café, I had to admit, though I'm normally a coffee drinker, I'd never had a better cup of tea.

Over the next four days, we shot most of the scenes we needed for *The Lost Reel*. The rest were done in and around San Francisco the following month. Tony and Will shot the intentionally grainy black-and-white footage on super 8mm film with an old hand-held camera. The film consists of rough outtakes from an unedited missing reel not included in a 1963 documentary about a fictional international art movement called the Tidewriters. The reel is presented with music and the voice over narration of the supposed original Australian film maker. In the film, I play Edmond Jouvret, the leader of the Tidewriters, an eccentric group of writers and artists who literally write their work in the wet sand at the seashore, only to witness it being erased by the incoming tide. In addition to scenes filmed on the beaches near San Francisco, Jouvret's Chaplinesque antics take him to Paris and Chartres.

One of the biggest challenges in shooting the film in Paris was keeping our locations free of any contemporary buildings, vehicles, or people in the background wearing out-of-era clothing. We solved the problem by shooting many of the scenes indoors or in parks, rather than on the street. As our reel was supposedly shot in the late 1950s, we wanted to include both timeless markers such as Notre Dame in the background, as well as era appropriate details. After much searching, we finally located a pristine Deux Chevaux parked on a side street in Chartres.

Ironically, our most difficult challenge turned out to be a pencil we needed as a prop for closeups of poet Bertrand Hébert smoking Gitanes and writing in hieroglyphics in a bar. On Sundays few shops are open and we couldn't find anywhere to buy a pencil. We walked all around the Latin Quarter and the only pencils for sale had "I love Paris" printed on them. Finally, I went to my hotel and asked the clerk at the front desk to loan me a pencil. He was strangely reluctant and made me promise to bring it back when we were done with it.

On the nonstop flight back from Paris to San Francisco, I sat next to a dreadlocked twenty-one-year-old Portuguese girl named Anna. She was reading a novel by a Brazilian writer, so I asked her advice about contemporary authors writing in Portuguese. She borrowed my notebook and filled a page with a list of names and titles. "These are just some of the better known ones," she said. Pulling a portable music player out of her striped wool bag, she asked, "Do you like music?" She handed me the headphones so I could sample a band with a strong techno beat while she wrote names of her favorite musicians on another page of the notebook.

As we talked, she took a tiny bottle of clear liquid from her purse and applied it to the metal ring that protruded from her lower lip. "It's important to keep piercings in that area wet," she said. "Saliva's not the best lubricant." Then she delivered a dissertation on the art, psychology, history, and sexuality of body piercing.

In addition to the metal on her lip, she showed me the rings, studs, and i-bars on her tongue, ears, and brow, but left to my imagination the ones in less-publicly-accessed spaces. She loved piercings, she told me. She'd been doing them professionally for two years, working at a body mod shop on the outskirts of Brighton and then doing them on demand in Paris. Piercings, she claimed, are addictive. "There's something about the process, you know, the pain, that's hard to describe. It's very intense," she said. "I like to do them for other people, and I like to have them done for me. But it's really important to get it right. You must make people comfortable, talk to them the whole time. It's so personal. And you better really explain how to care for it afterwards so it heals okay. You know, so many people don't know what they're doing or even why they're doing it."

She was going to California with plans to spend a year working at a tattoo parlor in Isla Vista, near the campus of the University of California, Santa Barbara. A friend of a friend she met in Paris knew the owner. "I spoke to him on the phone," she said. "He seemed very nice and told me I could sleep on the couch." She hoped that customs agents at the San Francisco airport wouldn't find or object to the large quantity of surgical needles in her luggage. "I don't know where I'd get needles," she said. "Besides, we like to use our own kind." The more she thought about those needles in her luggage, the more apprehensive she became. "What are they going to think? I hope they don't tell me to leave immediately," she said.

Though young enough to be my daughter, she was curious about the details of my marriage. "You know something about women, about life," she said when I told her I'd been married for close to twenty-five years. She had lived with different men in England and in Paris, but she wasn't sure she'd ever really been in love. "How is the sex now after all this time?" she wanted to know. I told her it was just fine. At some point, the flight attendants brought food and drinks and the lights had dimmed for a movie. It was a short ten hours, and before deplaning we exchanged email addresses. Months later, I heard from her. Denied an extension on her tourist visa, she had gone to India and completed a Transcendental Meditation program at an ashram. Now she was traveling alone on a bus into the mountains. "The people here are amazing," she wrote. That was the last I heard from her.

* * *

After I published *The Nambuli Papers* in 2003, I did two readings at Chico bookstores and another at a gallery. I also read at The Book Collector in Sacramento. Somehow one of the people in Los Angeles to whom I'd sent a copy of the book passed it on to a poet who organized readings at the Venice Beach branch of the Los Angeles Public Library. He had read the book immediately and loved it. Overflowing with enthusiasm, he contacted me and invited me to read at the library. Though it was a long trip from Chico to Los Angeles and he did not offer any compensation, I agreed, on the condition that he advertise the event and bring in a big crowd. He assured me that the venue was first rate. He made sure that the readings, which were held on Saturday afternoons, always appeared in *The Los Angeles Times*. He told me he was certain my event would attract a good crowd.

Some of what he said turned out to be true. The library was a relatively new building that included a large, dedicated room for meetings and literary events such as readings. When I arrived, I saw a man wearing a fencing mask standing by the front door waiting. I was surprised to see the reading coordinator was so taken with the playful, absurd spirit of the work as to reenact a motif taken from Dr. Crocker's character in the book and film. Unfortunately, though he was clearly a fan, he hadn't done much to promote the reading. Inside were at best half a dozen people and a video camera on a tripod. "I'm going to tape the reading," he told me.

Though disappointed, I nonetheless put on the best performance I could muster for the seven people in attendance. I performed "It's Like the Eiffel Tower" in NoNonNoh gestures, entertained with short selections about the life and times of turn-of-the-century magician

Aristide Nambuli, and screened *Tidewriters: The Lost Reel*. Nevertheless, I was glad when it was over.

Though I was offered two hundred dollars to read from my work at Riverviews Artspace when we first moved to Lynchburg, Virginia, I politely declined. Donna and I lived in a loft in the same building, and I didn't think conservative, religious Lynchburg was ready for what I had to say. I supposed by then I'd calmed down a bit as well. Like many performers, I'm a shy person who had to learn to overcome his inhibitions. Despite the adrenaline rush, I never really liked to perform in public. In recent years I've been blissfully quiet, and then distantly removed, as we've lived for a decade in Ecuador and Spain. These days, I'm content to stay close to home. My "Show of Shows" is over.

Almost Paradise

> Using my flimsy suitcase to make a sandwich board, Buli set me to walking up and down the main street of the town, advertising the west coast's first school for Chinese Boxing, which he now called Nam Bu Lee Kung Fu.
> — "The Dark Brother" from *The Nambuli Papers*

> Arson investigators also found similar metal gas cans in the mountains near the site where they had discovered the charred remains of the missing girls. The authorities suspected I'd started the forest fire to cover up my crime.
> —"The Angel Tree"

THE TRUNK OF a giant Ponderosa pine tree once sliced through the roof and walls of my house and landed in bed next to me. The top of the tree destroyed the pickup truck parked on the driveway outside. If the tree would have landed a foot to the left and crushed me, no one would have heard it fall. The tree would have eventually decomposed, along with the house and my body, leaving only a few bones as yet unburied or carried away by animals or the wind. If no one had been there to hear it, and no one remained who remembered me, did the tree really fall? Though we can't hear the screams of people crushed by buildings that crumble in earthquakes and wars, nor the voices of those maimed in accidents and dying in hospitals, nor the cries of prisoners, of the homeless, the abused, the trafficked, the unloved, the ignored and the forgotten, science tells us that, whether or not we hear them, the vibrations of sounds float in the air and may be recorded by other means. Sometimes when we least expect it, they echo in our hearts.

It was early December and I had been living alone in the mountains, when a freak storm brought hurricane force winds, lightning, and driving rain that flooded many low-lying areas in California. As the wind howled through the tall trees outside and the sky exploded with thunder and lightning, I went to bed in the little mobile home feeling as though I were backpacking solo, my tent pitched on the exposed granite cliffs of a mountain peak.

Sometime during the night, I woke to the sound of a terrific crack, followed instantly by an explosion so loud it temporarily deafened me. It felt like someone had tossed a grenade into the room through the window. Though everything happened in a split second, time felt suspended, and the moment seemed to stretch out like some kind of slow-motion movie effect. I could feel the air being sucked out of the room as shards of broken glass showered the bed. I instinctively raised my arm to protect my face as the vibration and noise of the explosion echoed in my ears. Though aware of the storm raging outside, everything seemed perfectly still and silent, as though the darkness around me had somehow erased me from the scene. Then I felt my heartbeat and my breath. I moved my hands and feet tentatively. When I checked my body for injuries, my hands came in contact with the rough wet bark of the tree trunk that had crashed through the roof and was lying inches away from me on the bed. Miraculously, it hadn't touched me.

When I heard the dog whimpering nearby, I sat up. My hand shook as I reached down and gathered the dog, who had been sleeping next to me on the floor. She was unharmed as well. Then I dressed, somehow located a flashlight, and exited the house, holding the dog in my arms. Shining the flashlight ahead of me, I stepped over and through the tree branches that covered the wooden porch. When I reached the driveway, I saw that one of the giant Ponderosa pines on the hill above the house had snapped and fallen onto the house and across the hood of my pickup truck. I walked part way up the hill to the carport where I had parked my jeep.

On the street above, I found a fire engine parked in front of another residence where a tree had also bisected a house. After checking with the firefighters, I drove to the town of Paradise through the pouring rain. Then I traveled down the empty Skyway to Chico, in the valley below. I recall how the wind buffeted the jeep, how slowly I had to drive, how I had to fight to keep the vehicle on the road. I pulled into the parking lot of an all-night restaurant around 4:00 in the morning, went inside, and ordered breakfast. Just before daybreak, I called Donna in Santa Maria to tell her what had happened.

Donna and I had wanted to let our son finish the school year before we completed our move to Northern California. After spending a week of vacation with me riding mountain bikes and exploring fire roads in my jeep, Eric returned to Santa Maria, where Donna had arranged to stay temporarily with a friend. We had already moved our possessions to the property in Magalia, where, according to our plan, I would live until late December and attend martial arts classes in Chico until they arrived. Located on a street with roughly a dozen other houses, the little mobile home we had bought perched on the side of a steep and narrow fold filled with tall pine trees. Below, a tiny creek trickled along a seam in the fold.

At first light, I drove back to the property to retrieve our homeowner's insurance policy and the paperwork I'd need to file a claim. Through the rain, I could see the wind blowing the top-heavy trees from side to side in a seemingly unnatural arc, like windshield wipers in motion, or something out of a bad dream. I left the dog in the jeep parked on the street above and walked down the steep driveway to the house, where in the daylight I could see the devastation clearly for the first time. The trunk of the tree had snapped like a pencil, crushing the mobile home. How it fell at such an odd angle I'll never know. I climbed over a huge cluster of broken branches and foliage from the top of the destroyed tree to access the door to the house. I wondered how I had navigated such a dangerous route in the darkness, wind, and rain, with the dog in my arms, only a few hours earlier. My heart raced as I searched the filing cabinet inside and I grabbed the papers I needed. I ran back up the driveway to the jeep and headed down to Chico with my heart pounding.

Thus began our ten years in Paradise.

* * *

I spent the next two nights sleeping on the floor of the martial arts school, as I was low on cash and didn't know what the future would bring. Within a few days, the insurance company sent a check for some advance money to help me get settled and I moved into a motel in Paradise. My father sent me a check for $1,500 to help with immediate expenses, while Kendall Lappin, a man I'd never met, sent another $3,000.

The first thing to do was clear the fallen tree. I hired some out of work loggers to cut up the slash and haul it away. They sawed the trunk into big rounds, which they stacked on the driveway to be split later for firewood. Ironically, my neighbor, whose house was above mine, immediately laid claim to this giant stack of wood, and had it moved to her wood shed up the hill. Since the tree had originally been on her property, she believed the wood rightfully belonged to her and she did not hesitate to ask permission to retrieve it. As far as I was concerned, she was welcome to take the cursed wood. If I could have lifted the rounds myself and thrown them up the steep hill, through her front window and directly into her fireplace, I would have gladly done so.

The insurance company sent an adjuster to look at the property and begin repairs. Donna arrived at the end of the week and together we began looking for a house with a yard for the dog that we could rent. We visited the site of the accident and tried to salvage whatever we could. We also worked on an inventory of losses to submit to the insurance company. As we dug through the waterlogged and destroyed clothes, books, artwork, photo albums and other treasures we had stored in the bedroom closet, I realized just how unimportant possessions were. The biggest loss was Donna's wedding dress, which she'd kept in a plastic zipper bag in the closet. The bag had ripped and water had seeped in so that mold destroyed the cloth. As there was no way to salvage the dress, she had to part with it. Another casualty was my Seagull acoustic guitar. Though it had been in a hard case, it suffered some damage to the bridge and top. Our insurance paid for our losses and even to repair and restore the guitar and Donna's prized James Thurber drawing. It didn't matter much now; they were just things in a world full of things. When Donna asked me how I was feeling, I told her that I felt calm and happy. I'd been given another chance to learn how to live my life, and I had resolved to reset my priorities. She remembers being surprised when I told her the accident might have been the best thing that ever happened to me.

When the insurance company informed me that my policy did not cover the damage to my vehicle, I talked to the owner of a local body shop, who gave me a good price to put the little truck back together again. He located the parts in a junkyard and replaced the entire front end. Then he repainted the vehicle gray. Though the engine occasionally clicked loudly due to a sticky valve lifter, I drove that truck for the next ten years.

While our insurance eventually paid to repair the broken structure, we never returned there to live. Months later, when Donna went with me to check the repairs, we found a ten-foot section of tree top planted like a giant spear in the earth in front of the house. It seemed like folly to ignore such a warning. We talked to a realtor about selling the property later that same day.

* * *

Though we struggled to find a place that would accept a dog, we finally signed a year lease and moved into a rental house in lower Paradise, where we slowly began to adjust to our new surroundings. Donna accepted a job working at the local Parks and Recreation District, our son began school, and I took a position as an administrator working part-time for the City of Chico Arts Commission. My job was to help oversee the city's selection process for a public arts project in the lobby of the Chico Municipal Center building. Eric and I continued taking martial arts classes in Chico twice a week. One day, Donna surprised me by saying she wanted to take the classes as well.

I was also still working without pay for HiJinx Press in Davis. I did, however, receive some money for the design and typesetting of *Life and Limb: Tales of Peril, Predicament and Dire Distress*, a big anthology edited by Gilbert Alter-Gilbert. In 2001, HiJinx published my novel *Sacred Hearts*, which, along with the other HiJinx titles, the publisher failed to promote. Consequently, the books sold poorly.

During this time, I also began to take on work as a freelance book designer. I typeset and designed *Clown at Wall: A Kenneth Bernard Reader* for Confrontation Press at Long Island University. I also designed and set the type for a number of poetry books for Cahuenga Press, a poetry cooperative in Los Angeles, including books by Harry Northrup, Holly Prado, Jimm Cushing, Ann Stanford, Phoebe McAdams, and Cecilia Woloch. I worked as a free-lance editor on a number of other literary projects, designed a linocut logo for a new press, and sold my collages and prints as cover art for other books. Though Asylum Arts remained partially dormant, I tried my best to use my skills to continue working within the profession.

My son and I began playing video games together while we lived in the rental house in Paradise. It's something he's always enjoyed and something we've done, off and on, ever since. We were also enjoying our martial arts classes together. At our yellow belt testing, we executed a form that ended in a deep back stance, with the left hand moving to an open hand outside block while the right hand pulls slowly back from the left elbow to a knife-hand position at the sternum. I had drawn an eye in black ink on each of our left palms, so that when we performed the form together, the eyes on our palms faced the judges.

After we'd sold the property in Magalia, we bought a house in Paradise, on Sawmill Road. Situated on half an acre, the house included a large, separate shop building with two attached garages behind the house, an apple orchard, a handful of pine trees, two giant oak trees, and a cherry tree that gave us more fruit than we could eat for two months each summer. After we'd pulled the carpet off the hardwood floors and moved into the house, we cleaned up the workshop, which the previous owner had used for small engine repairs. We put up drywall and insulation, and installed a wood stove for heat. I used the garage to store the inventory of Asylum Arts books. I also installed overhead track lighting in the studio to make up for the limited light that came through the small windows. We called the newly-remodeled building Asylum Arts Studio.

Once I had sufficient space for a proper studio, I looked for an inexpensive Vandercook press. I drove to Santa Barbara to consider a letterpress printer's shop that I'd seen advertised on the Internet. The equipment included a large format automatic sheet-fed proofing press with an ample selection of moveable type in lovely oak cabinets. Though tempting, the press cost more than I could afford. It was also large for the space and too expensive to move.

Eventually, I located a smaller, hand-cranked Vandercook Universal 4 proofing press, along with enough moveable type to make poetry broadsides, though not books. The owner had bought the press from California Polytechnic University, San Luis Obispo, where it had once served students in the art department. The old press had been in storage for years and appeared to be in questionable condition for printing type, but it was nearly free and came with dozens of tins of printer's ink in every color. The owner also offered to deliver and install it into my studio. I thought I could clean it up so that it would serve for making editions of my prints.

Over the next eight years, I printed dozens of advertising and poetry broadsides on that little blue Vandercook, as well as larger editions of linocuts, including some of my first two-, three-, and four-color prints. I also printed a series of poetry greeting cards featuring my linocuts and French poems translated by Kendall Lappin. When Eric Lorberer and Kelly Everding, editors of *Rain Taxi,* came to visit us in Paradise, together we printed one of my linocuts and the type for the cover of a chapbook by Paul Metcalf that they published. I designed and printed a broadside to commemorate the publication of Samuel Appelbaum's book *Chtcheglov* and printed hundreds of special Asylum

Arts broadsides commemorating the 1998 Bay Area Book Festival, which I gave to visitors to the Asylum Arts booth that year. I also let visitors to my studio pull a souvenir broadside during the annual Open Studios Tour organized by the Chico Art Center.

After I'd resigned from my job working for the City of Chico Arts Council, I took on more freelance design work, including a massive art catalog edited by Gilbert Alter-Gilbert. I'd known Rick Gilbert several years and had published his art criticism in *Asylum Annual*. I'd also edited his anthology *Life and Limb* for HiJinx Press. An art critic, translator, and anthologist, Gilbert was a fountain of knowledge and literary trivia. Like Eric Basso, he was also, to a large degree, an autodidact. Like BJ from HiJinx, he could talk on the phone for hours. He had a special devotion to obscure foreign writers, hobo lore, and zoos. I remember that, during the time I lived in Santa Maria, Rick drove from Los Angeles to Santa Barbara to visit the zoo with my young son and me. The full-color art catalog was a complex project. It had taken Rick three years to put the deal together. I finished the pre-press work in roughly a month, then waited for Rick to write the introduction so that we could send the book to press and get paid. When he finally sent me the introduction two months later, the draft was still in a rough state. I didn't mention my edits, nor send him the corrections for fear that we'd be delayed another two months. In the end, however, we both felt good about the project, as we were handsomely compensated for our work.

For the next several years, I continued to run a scaled-back version of Asylum Arts, as I felt an obligation toward the books I'd published and their authors. Because I no longer had access to sales representatives, national distribution depended on non-profit organizations such as Small Press Distribution and big library jobbers such as Ingram. To limit my financial obligations, I published fewer books and chose these projects carefully. In Paradise, I published just a dozen new Asylum Arts titles over eight years. Most of these books were co-published, which meant that the authors underwrote the cost of printing and binding their books, while I edited, typeset, designed, and marketed them. Despite this arrangement, I made nothing from my labor.

I collaborated mainly with authors I had published previously and with whom I had a good working relationship. These authors understood the challenges facing independent literary publishers and consistently supported my efforts on their behalf. Nevertheless, in spite of the quality of the books, I felt that Asylum Arts had become an unsustainable project. After twenty years of publishing literary books, I sold the press in 2005. It was a relief to finally unburden myself.

* * *

I began training in martial arts because my son had wanted to continue the Taekwondo classes he had started in Santa Maria. I took Eric to visit two different dojangs in Chico that taught the same style he'd been practicing. The first school we visited belonged to a lean and dangerous looking man. We watched one of the classes and neither of us cared for the instructor's teaching style. Afterward, the owner sat down with us in his office to discuss the program, hoping to lock us into a contract. A phone call interrupted him halfway through his sales pitch. From his side of the conversation, it was clear that he was discussing motorcycle parts. We'd seen a big Harley Davidson parked out front. After he hung up the phone, I told him we wanted to check out one other school before making a decision.

The second school was smaller and more relaxed. The owner taught the class himself. His students were a near equal mix of men and women. A handful of older students mixed seamlessly with college-aged students. They all displayed positive attitudes, courtesy, and respect for each other. Best of all, they seemed to be having fun. They laughed and smiled. They celebrated each other's successes. We liked what we saw. At our meeting with the owner, he casually invited us to come and give the classes a try for a week without any obligation. He talked me into coming as well. "Just wear loose clothing like sweat pants," he said. "If you're there with him, your son will be more comfortable."

We started in the beginner class the following week. We were hooked from the first moment. After class, we signed up for three months and bought our white uniforms. My son happily showed me how to tie my white belt. When Eric returned to Santa Maria, I continued the classes on my own. I was horribly out of shape and for the first two months the beginner classes pushed me to the limit of physical exertion. I was often so exhausted after class that I needed to sit down and drink water for half an hour before I felt like driving home. For years I'd been eating poorly, drinking coffee day and night, barely sleeping, drinking too much, and smoking whenever I drank. I was stressed out, overweight, and completely out of shape. After two months, my new white uniform was permanently stained light brown by the toxins and nicotine that I sweated out.

The day after the tree fell onto our house in Magalia, I contacted the owner of the school, as I didn't know anyone else in the area to ask for help. He quickly put me in touch with people who could cut up and remove the debris and he gave me a key to the school so that I could sleep on the padded floor of the Hapkido room until I arranged other accommodations. I stayed there until the insurance company gave me money for a motel. I was grateful for the friends I had already made in the school, as people expressed a genuine concern and many offered whatever help they could provide. It was a good group of people.

When Donna and Eric joined me again in Paradise after Christmas, we moved into the house we had rented and Eric resumed martial arts classes with me. One Saturday morning, we drove to Chico for a morning class. Afterward, Eric suggested we climb the rope that hung from the tall ceiling of the building. It was not a thick, soft climbing rope like I had climbed in junior high and high school gym classes, but instead a thinner rope with a slightly slick, rough surface. I helped Eric climb about halfway up, then lifted and set him down on the mat, where he stood next to me, waiting for me to try. I was already tired from the class and hadn't climbed a rope since high school. In those days, I could move up a rope rapidly hand over hand with little effort. So, I grabbed hold of the rope and began climbing.

I didn't realize that my weaker strength to weight ratio would make the climb so difficult. Though I managed to struggle to the top of the rope, my hands could barely squeeze the rope tightly enough to maintain my grip. My arms strained as I started moving down. Suddenly, my grip failed and I began sliding rapidly down the rope. While I didn't fall, the rope shredded my hands. The owner of the school applied first aid and sent me home with instructions on how to treat the burn. I never saw a doctor and my hands healed quicker than I would have expected. While I had hurt myself badly and wounded my pride, I learned an important lesson. I was no longer young. I needed to build strength slowly. If I planned to someday become a black belt, I would have to train for it intelligently and with patience.

A month later, we attended our first rank testings at the school, where we saw the school's three assistant instructors complete the public part of their test to receive their first-degree black belt. We watched them perform ten complicated forms in a row, including several they were randomly asked to do backwards or wearing a blindfold. We watched them perform a series of precisely choreographed moves with a long wooden staff, a wooden baton, and nunchaku. We saw them disarm and subdue attackers with Hapkido throwing techniques and joint locks. We saw them break boards with spinning kicks and jump spin kicks. We saw them leap over three students positioned on all fours and break a board with a flying side kick. We saw them break blocks of concrete with a hand strike. It was like an action movie unspooling before our wide-open eyes. We left feeling exhilarated and overwhelmed by what we'd witnessed. How would it ever be possible for us to do what we had just seen?

Donna eventually signed up for classes at the school as well, though by then my son and I had graduated out of the beginner class. Though we were at different levels, we all enjoyed our classes and the new friends we made at the school. Over time, we began to train harder, stretch several times throughout the day, and practice more at home. We also worked on eating a healthier diet. I gave up drinking alcohol and coffee and started running to improve my stamina.

I stayed at the school for over five years, long enough to impress another generation of new students who attended my black belt testing. I broke dozens of pine boards with flying sidekicks, jump spin kicks, axe kicks, punches, and knife hand strikes. I demonstrated forms and weapons routines. I broke a concrete block. While it felt good to finally have the test behind me, after three days of running, climbing, and diving head first over obstacles, demonstrating knowledge and proficiency in Taekwondo forms, Hapkido and Arnis at each rank, sparring with the other candidates and the black belt instructors in the school, the public performance felt anti-climactic.

For two years, I also taught classes. My last year at the school I worked full time as the head instructor of the adult program. Though I increased the adult enrollment by twenty percent during my tenure and earned the trust of the students, I became increasingly uncomfortable overseeing a program that continued to raise prices while offering fewer classes to students. Nor did I appreciate that the owner sometimes expected me to demonstrate loyalty to the school over loyalty to my family. It came as a big surprise and shock to my students when I resigned and left the academy due to my ethical and philosophical differences with the owner.

There's a lot I could say about my experience in martial arts, both positive and negative. In the end, much depends on the integrity of the school, its owner, the instructors, and the staff. While martial arts schools exist in theory to empower people and improve their health and quality of life, they are also businesses driven by profit. Like other businesses that exist to make a profit promoting health, sanity, and well-being, the lust for money often undermines the mission.

* * *

After my short-lived career as a martial artist, I began filling up the void with art projects. I devoted myself to drawing every day, and began work on *The Nambuli Papers,* an illustrated set of stories about a turn of the century Parisian magician and escape artist. Like Jesus in the gospels of *The New Testament,* Nambuli himself had left no writings, no pictures of himself, and few records of his time on earth. Consequently, the stories about Aristide Nambuli are narrated by different people who had encountered him during his brief but memorable life. My experiences with martial arts also figured into the book. I had often seen self-proclaimed "grand masters" employ astounding levels of hyperbole when describing their background and professional accomplishments. They routinely mythologized their teachers and training, as well as other aspects of their lives.

As an instructor, I had met dozens of martial arts school owners and masters in various styles of martial arts at professional conferences held by an "educational funding" company that took a cut of student fees at schools in trade for acting as a clearinghouse, accounting firm, and collection agency. The company also helped owners make their schools more profitable, thereby further enriching itself. Their tactics encouraged owners to over-promise and under-deliver on services, and to overcharge students for special seminars, programs within the school, and equipment. At their conferences, both company representatives and school owners presented seminars on how to attract and maintain control of entire families of new students and how to make and keep students psychologically dependent and loyal to the school and its master. They discussed how to structure a program so that senior students became sources of free labor to teach classes, how to establish and maintain unbending loyalty within their schools, and a host of other business strategies that stood in stark opposition to the pledges and values students typically recite at the beginning and end of each class.

The martial arts school owners I met seemed strangely comfortable existing within a self-contradictory world in which many of them routinely deceived, abused, and lied to their students. Some were so self-involved and self-important that they invented entirely new styles of martial arts and turned their schools into cult-like centers of self-aggrandizement and adulation. I found their tendency to confound fiction and truth both disturbing and dangerous. As the same tendency seemed to be spreading into other areas of society, most notably the political realm, I wanted to write a book that explored the subject. Thus, I modeled the personality of my magician and escape artist Artistide Nambuli on these self-mythologizing martial artists.

Later, when I wrote the final, extended version of the Nambuli stories, I added a long narrative by Nambuli's albino twin brother, who describes their traveling magic and medicine show through the American west. Always looking for new sources of easy income, at one point Nambuli hatches a plan to offer classes in "Chinese Boxing" to local townspeople and their children. The scene parodies the games instructors use to teach martial arts to young children with limited attention spans.

Obscure Publications published the first version of *The Nambuli Papers* as a chapbook that included ten of my whimsical pen and ink drawings. Publisher Paul Rosheim later released a second installment entitled *The Tide Writers*, which introduces a fictional group of writers and artists who created temporary, ephemeral works of art, many written or drawn in the sand at the beaches in southern France. These two chapbooks were the seeds that later grew into the expanded 2003 multimedia novel *The Nambuli Papers*.

After completing the two chapbooks, I began writing another novel called *The Double: Doppelangelgänger*, in which I employed doubling as the organizing principle. I constructed the book as a kind of textual collage, using short stories I had written earlier, a handful of Jungian fairy tales, and a narrative about a man whose life is suddenly upended by his encounter with his destructive doppelgänger. I divided the book into two sections, a main narrative and a set of stories listed in an appendix. I also divided the pages of the narrative so that other stories appear as footnotes at the bottom of some pages. Both photomontage and linocuts serve to illustrate the book, yet another doubling. Doubles of all kinds abound within the text itself so that the book in some way resembles an Oulipo textual experiment.

Jordan Jones had just launched a new literary venture called Leaping Dog Press and asked to see the manuscript of *The Double*. I sent it to him and he enthusiastically agreed to take on the project. When Leaping Dog released the book in 2002, in both paperback and hardbound editions, the novel received an outstanding review by Jim Dwyer in *Library Journal*, which stimulated sales to libraries. *The Review of Contemporary Fiction*, *Rain Taxi*, and other literary journals published reviews of the book by Irving Malin, Anitra Budd, Stephen-Paul Martin, and Kirpal Gordon.

I had conceived the book as a kind of existential comedy and I was pleased when a writer whose work I respected wrote to say he had laughed so hard and uncontrollably reading the book that, in his words, he "blew snot." While many people enjoyed the strange humor in the novel, the book also caused strong negative reactions in some readers. A psychologist friend told me she found the narrative so disturbing she couldn't read it. I also received an interesting letter from another writer to whom I had sent the book. Though we'd never corresponded before, he wrote me a long letter detailing why he found the book so powerfully unsettling. Apparently, something similar had happened to him in his own life. When he was young, he had taken a new job and moved back to his home town, where he encountered a childhood friend whose husband had died suddenly and unexpectedly. The writer ended up marrying the widow. He then lived in the other man's house, socialized with the other man's friends and family, and even played the same music on the dead man's piano. Strangest of all, the job he had taken was the vacancy left open when the other man had died.

This letter surprised me, not only for the strangeness of the story it related, but also because it triggered in me a sudden awareness that my novel was really a retelling or perhaps revisiting of something that had happened in my own life. I have written elsewhere in this book about my brief but intense friendship and relationship with a young poet named Rachel Sherwood, who died in a car accident at the age of twenty-five and how I consequently became involved with another young woman who seemed for a time to take on the personality and life of the dead poet. Because the situation was so emotionally wrought, complicated and inexplicable, none of the small group of people involved at the time knew quite how to interpret or even discuss what was happening. From my point of view, I knew what I was experiencing was strange and even a bit creepy, but, like Gail, for whom the situation was no doubt a hundredfold more bizarre, I did my best to ignore what couldn't be explained. That Rachel lived on for a time through Gail, resuming her friendships, reliving her relationships, and eventually marrying the man who had been her boyfriend and a passenger in her car the night of her accident, was simply too odd to contemplate. Yet the story stayed buried within my psyche for years, waiting to be told.

There's one more story to tell about *The Double*. While a graduate student at California State University, Northridge, I had taken a seminar on the works of John Steinbeck taught by Louis Owens, a young professor who later taught at the University of New Mexico and the University of California at Davis. He was a talented scholar of Native American writing, an expert in the works of Steinbeck, and a dynamic teacher. He later became a well-regarded and successful fiction writer whose novel *Nightland* won the 1997 American Book Award. While I had lost contact with him, when Jordan had the bound galleys of the book ready to send out to reviewers, I sent Owens a copy, along with a letter asking him if he'd read my book and offer a quote or "blurb" that we could use on the back cover.

Always generous and professional, he responded within the week. Along with Harry Mathews, Stephen Dixon, Daniel Quinn, and Raymond Queneau's English translator Barbara Wright, Owens offered me a quote to use to promote my novel. *"The Double,"* he wrote, "is one of the most original, dizzyingly enjoyable rides in recent literature. Seldom have I come across a piece of fiction that is so deftly and cleverly written, a work that made me puzzle and laugh on every page. This is a radical achievement, a novel deserving of a wide audience." I later learned that Louis Owens committed suicide the same week he read my book and wrote his blurb. From what I could discern, no one had any idea why he had shot himself in the head in a stall in the public restroom at the Albuquerque airport.

* * *

One day, my publisher Jordan Jones forwarded me an email from someone who had contacted him looking for a way to get in touch with me. The email came from a filmmaker in San Francisco who had stumbled upon my book *Carnival Aptitude* in a used bookstore and had fallen in love with some of my short narratives. He wanted to know how much money I would require for the film rights to "Three-Cornered Hat," which he wanted to make into a short film to be professionally produced and shot on 35mm film. I wrote back and gave him my phone number. The following day he called and we talked. Thus began a friendship based on creative collaboration.

The filmmaker, A. D. "Tony" Liano, had grown up in Chicago, graduated with a MBA from Northwestern, and began his career as a marketing executive at Microsoft in Seattle. There he met his wife, Jodi, a Microsoft recruiting executive. Though both of them were well compensated professionals with bonuses and stock options, neither felt fulfilled by their work. After they married, they decided to leave Microsoft, cash in their stock options, and retrain for new careers.

While Jodi went to culinary school in San Francisco, Tony headed to film school in New York City. When I first met them, they were living in a house they'd bought in North Beach. Jodi was working as an instructor at Tante Marie's Cooking School, writing her first cookbooks for Williams-Sonoma, and occasionally developing recipes in the kitchen of The Food Network in New York. Tony had just completed a full-length Americana documentary called *Barberland,* and was making short films, directing commercials, and developing larger projects.

I think we settled on two hundred dollars for the film rights to "Three-Cornered Hat," though it could have been less. I've always believed the creative process is its own reward, and I thought it would be exciting to see how a director and actors interpreted the story for film. The film was shot at a Tudor style house in an upscale Berkeley neighborhood. Tony invited me to visit the set, and Donna and I drove down from Paradise early on a Saturday and arrived around noon. We met actors Al Liner and Luis Saguar, along with the cinematographer and the rest of the crew. Jodi had prepared food and set up a catering table.

The film itself concerns a home owner who sees a pirate digging a hole in his backyard to retrieve a treasure. After a struggle, the homeowner kills the pirate with his shovel, buries him in the hole, puts on his three-cornered hat, and consults the pirate's treasure map, which leads him into his neighbor's yard, where he begins digging a hole and is in turn confronted by his neighbor…

Tony had ordered copies of *Carnival Aptitude* for the entire production crew, so when I arrived people were excited to meet me. There was even talk of producing other tales from the book. Someone suggested they should start at the beginning and work their way through the book. Though such ideas were unrealistic, I appreciated their enthusiasm. Donna and I enjoyed the day immensely, and we looked forward to seeing Tony and Jodi again.

When Tony sent me a copy of the film transferred to VHS format, we were amazed at the quality of the production. Though only eight minutes long, the film is a finely polished little jewel. *Three-Cornered Hat* has been broadcast many times on public television stations around the country and has been featured at festivals of short films.

* * *

I had always loved the rough and expressive graphic work of Vincent Van Gogh. After failing miserably as an evangelical minister serving a community of coal miners in northern France, Van Gogh had spent three years teaching himself how to draw from life, sometimes hiring prostitutes in The Hague as models. I bought a book of his complete drawings and set to work copying some of them and also drawing from set ups I made in my studio. A few months later, I took drawing and painting classes in the Art Department at the university in Chico. As Donna worked in the Alumni Office on campus, we arranged to have lunch together on the days I drove down for my classes. Though I soon grew bored with the classes, some of what I learned helped me years later, when I gave art lessons to students in Ecuador.

Through practice in gestural drawing, I discovered the utility and eloquence of unbroken lines. I saw that scribbles could convey as much narrative information as short stories. I also began to see and appreciate a full spectrum of intoxicating, psychedelic colors. At times these previously unregistered colors overwhelmed my senses. Sometimes they seemed to possess tactile, olfactory, and sonic qualities that lurked just beneath the surface of their being. I remember the spring colors, particularly the grass and the yellow ochre mustard growing at the base of the flowering trees that exploded in the almond orchards that lined the road as we drove from Paradise to Sacramento. Though paint companies have invented hundreds of imaginative shades of blue, words fail us constantly and the sky remains beyond description. Looking out the window of the car made my chest swell and filled me with joy. I didn't need psychoactive drugs to help me make connections.

As I began painting seriously in my studio, I set out to discover a new way of presenting two-dimensional art. It was during this time that I began to make what I called moveable or interactive paintings. The concept of a traditional (non-electronic) image that can be manipulated by the viewer to create many potential paintings from a single work came from a desire to actualize the motion implicit in abstract expressionist painting. Using slide puzzles as my initial inspiration for a moveable, interactive picture plane, I began fashioning painted square tiles of hardboard into core images which contain the seed of millions, even billions of potential paintings. I mounted these painted tiles with magnets onto sheet metal frames so that they could be pulled off, rotated and freely manipulated. In even the simplest configuration, the nine positions of the tiles multiplied by each of the four possible orientations of the squares results in a huge number of potential abstract arrangements. When I named my show "Millions of Paintings," I wanted to be sure I was not exaggerating, so I asked my father if he could figure out the potential number of paintings that could be made from one of most simple paintings: nine tiles, each rotated four different orientations in their various positions spread over the nine slots. He gave me a mathematical formula that proved it that would be impossible for a person working twelve hours a day combining the tiles to exhaust the number of potential combinations in one lifetime.

The moveable surface of the paintings allowed for an on-going liberation of textures, colors and images while maintaining traditional mediums and forms of painting. The ability to break up and rearrange the picture plane also helped facilitate a rich interplay of styles: from a single representational image, I created both a solvable puzzle and a dynamic series of neo-Cubist, Futurist, or Abstract Expressionist type paintings. As representational images metamorphose into abstractions, these iconoclastic paintings confront the traditional distinctions between representational and abstract subjects and approaches, while simultaneously bridging the gap between artist and viewer.

Because the works were meant to be scrambled and manipulated to form a host of potential paintings rather than a single static image, representational depictions were always of secondary interest. Though those paintings that did contain representational images were essentially puzzles, the shattered surfaces of more abstract arrangements invariably produced more interest. For this reason, I sometimes incorporated surface depictions that were overtly sexual into the paintings as an unblinking challenge to the primacy of the image.

At this time, Susie Bright, who had published my writing in her annual *Best American Erotica* series, commissioned me to write an erotic literary novella for a book entitled *Three the Hard Way*, published by Touchstone Books, a division of Simon & Schuster. To make the paid work more interesting for myself, I placed two conditions on what I would write. First, I had to complete the project in a single week. Second, it had to be experimental or nontraditional in form. I responded with a novella entitled "The Widow" that interwove two separate, but connected narratives, one the manuscript of an erotic novel written by a wife and the other the responses to her work penned by her husband. The two stories unfold simultaneously on pages divided roughly in half in order to create a rich interplay between the two narratives. Though erotic, the text I created was philosophical, formally experimental, and multi-layered, not unlike my moveable paintings. My point in either case was that human sexuality could be celebrated in art, as part of a bigger more complex and complete psychology.

Pornography depends upon an unbroken gaze to achieve its prurient effect, whereas art naturally dissolves into something deeper.

Because it was advertised and promoted as a book of erotica, readers knew exactly what to expect. In a review in the *New York Times Book Review*, Amy Sohn praised "The Widow," writing, "The novella-within-a-novella is deliberately hackneyed, but on the bottom half of the pages we get the husband's perspective, as he discovers his wife's book on the computer and wonders whether he has neglected her. The surprisingly sweet ending is moving and arousing at the same time."

The paintings were also unpredictable and surprising. When a gallery owner displayed a scrambled image from one of my erotic moveable paintings in the window of a gallery in Chico during a show of the work, a passerby complained about the content and asked the owner to remove the painting. I can only wonder how many hours that person had spent gazing at the painting and trying to mentally arrange the pieces. In the end, the gallery owner told the man he had a dirty mind and refused to remove the work from the window.

Some of the paintings referenced other artists and paintings. In one I replaced the couple in Renoir's *Dance at Bougival* with the faces of Donna and myself. Another was comprised of copies of nine different German Expressionist paintings. Portraits and faces also figure into my moveable paintings. I painted a series of small portraits of myself, Donna, our son Eric, and our dog Skip, which we hung in our house in Paradise. If someone was acting up, they'd soon find their face rearranged, sometimes with pointed dog ears. A larger portrait I painted of Donna, comprised of thirty-six tiles, easily metamorphoses into whimsical Cubist iterations.

In addition to puzzles, some of the paintings functioned as poetry generators, games and Exquisite Corpses. One large painting was built around images with Xs and Os, so that the painting could be used to play TicTackToe. Another had three figures, a woman, a fish, and a violin, which could be arranged so the fish head appeared on the woman's body and the woman's face on the violin.

In a period of intense activity between 2000 and 2003, I produced around thirty interactive paintings of various sizes and configurations.

The paintings had from nine to thirty-six tiles, all of them square. The size of the tiles varied, with the biggest being twelve-inch squares and the smallest three-inch squares. Some included painted letters, which could be rearranged to create different texts. The paintings were exhibited at Cory's in Chico and at the Doyen Gallery in Thousand Oaks. Ten of the paintings are now in private collections, though regrettably I never photographed or documented some of them. I destroyed a handful of the paintings, donated others to Larry Basset's public art collection, and gave a couple to friends when we moved. The remaining moveable paintings remain in storage in Virginia.

* * *

As my son Eric progressed through school and made friends in Paradise, it became increasingly clear to him that his father was different from those of the other kids. I had never insisted that Eric participate in my world, nor encouraged him to follow my path. As he entered middle school, my approach to life must have seemed increasingly incomprehensible and mysterious to him, for it didn't match what he saw around him. His friends' fathers drove trucks or roofed houses and bought speed boats to play with on the weekend. Eric instead grew up surrounded by books and art, poets and artists. Nevertheless, Donna and I wanted him to be free to ignore these influences if he chose. We wanted him to find his own direction. Though we tried to model good behavior, especially through martial arts training, for better or worse we allowed our son a great deal of freedom to make his own mistakes and learn from them.

I remember going with Eric to Paradise High School to register him for his first semester freshman classes. For years, I had heard from people at the martial arts school that the high school in Paradise was a particularly troubling environment, full of drugs and budding juvenile delinquency. Still, nothing had prepared me for the palpable sense of chaos that permeated the campus. Though almost devoid of students, the offices, classrooms and open quad resonated with teenage angst and bad energy. At first, I shrugged it off as a reaction to not having been on a high school campus since my own adolescence, but as bad as my high school seemed to me at the time, I knew on a deep, instinctual level, that this school was a hundred-fold worse. I wanted to leave, but there was nowhere else to go. Chico High School, a half hour drive away, was just as bad.

As an adolescent, I'd had virtually no parental supervision. I'd barely spoken to my father during my last two years of high school. I knew how easy it was to make a fatal mistake or do something that would irrevocably change the future for the worse. I tried to talk to Eric. I remember telling him that at this stage of existence every decision he made, even the small ones, had the potential to affect the rest of his life.

Before his final year of high school, I suggested that Eric finish school early and take a year off before going on to university studies. He had already completed most of his requirements, including Advanced Placement English and math courses, and I worried that he would be bored in school, which in my experience was not a good idea. There were worse fears than wasting time in school. The past year, one of his friends had committed suicide and another had died of a drug overdose.

I told my son I'd help facilitate any educational project or adventure he was passionate about. If he wanted to study martial arts for a year in Japan or Korea, we'd go together. If he wanted to buy a sailboat and sail it to Hawaii, we'd learn how to do it. If he wanted to build a cabin or walk the Pacific Crest Trail, I was ready. He sighed as he shrugged off my offer. "I just want to finish my last year of high school with my friends," he said.

Soon after high school graduation, Eric joined the Air Force on a delayed enlistment. When I tried to talk to him about the career options available in the Air Force, he rolled his eyes. "There are some exciting opportunities," I enthused. "What about Public Affairs, Signals Intelligence, Space Operations, Photojournalist, Physical Therapist, Paralegal, Operations Intelligence, Cryptologic Language Analyst, Broadcast Journalist?"

"I don't care," he said. "I'll just let them assign me something when I go in." He spent the next eight years loading and supervising the loading of bombs and armaments onto planes and drones on flight lines at bases in Florida, Alaska, Guam, New Mexico, and Idaho, a job he thoroughly detested.

* * *

During the ten years we lived in Northern California, I sometimes backpacked alone in the Sierra Nevada mountains. I always invited my son to come with me, but he told me he hated camping and hiking. Some of these trips were short weekend jaunts and others involved more challenging circular routes. In the summer months, the mountains radiated dry heat and buzzed with mosquitos. Still, the spectacular vistas and solitude attracted me. Though dangerous to walk alone in the wilderness, it felt good to get away from civilization. Coming home again made me appreciate the love and companionship I sometimes took for granted, as well as the comfortable life I had.

Once I had Donna drop me off at a trailhead in Mount Lassen National Park, where I walked through a large part of the park on the Pacific Crest Trail. In the six days I was hiking, I saw only two other people and one large brown bear. The bear I had come upon suddenly as I rounded a bend in the trail. He was about thirty yards away, fishing in a stream. I stopped and stood very still. We stared at each other for a minute, and when he dipped his paw back into the steam, I began to step backward slowly, increasing the distance between us. At one point, I stopped and took a couple of pictures of him with the disposable camera I had brought with me. Then I walked off the trail and made a wide detour around the bear. When the sun went down, I cooked my dinner and tended my fire as long as I could keep my eyes open. It was a clear night and a sky full of stars broadcast their mystery through the darkness. Alone in the wilderness on a planet lost in an infinite universe, my consciousness amounted to less than a speck of dust. Surrounded by dark forest and night sounds, I kept my fire burning bright.

* * *

Throughout the decade we spent in Paradise, I continued to work with Eric Basso pursuing a project that had been set into motion years earlier: Eric had wanted to put the majority of his collected writings into print and had set aside money from his inheritance to help offset the cost of this huge undertaking. The books were done as a co-publishing venture. Though Basso never compensated me for my own in-kind contributions, which included design, typesetting, editing, and marketing, he underwrote the printing and shipping costs of all these books. While in Santa Maria, I had already published several volumes of his poems, all of his fiction, and the majority of the plays he cared most about, including the massive *Golem Triptych*. In Paradise, I continued to issue his collections of poetry. Jordan Jones would later publish *Decompositions: Essays on Art and Literature, 1973–1989* and *Revagations: A Book of Dreams, 1966–1974, Volume I*, after he took over Asylum Arts.

I continued to work with Kendall Lappin during this time. I published his final anthology of translations, *Dead French Poets Speak Plain English* in 1997, along with his *Memoirs of a Translator of Poetry* in 1999. I also published a series of poetry note cards based on his translations of classic French poems. Some of these cards included my original artwork, and one I printed by hand on my Vandercook letterpress. Throughout this time, Lappin continued to assist me financially with these projects. He insisted on paying me for my time as well as the expenses I incurred. A couple times he unexpectedly sent me a check for $3,000. When I asked him why, he wrote back to say that he had more money than he knew what to do with and no family to give it to. He told me he wanted to distribute some of this money where he thought it might do some good.

At some point, Kendall began to act irrationally and erratically. His letters became increasingly paranoid. He thought other translators were scheming to undermine his efforts and reputation. Though we had never spoken on the phone before, he called me unexpectedly and we had a pleasant conversation. A couple weeks later he called again, this time to accuse me of disloyalty to him. It was sad to hear him so lost and unmoored. I reminded him that we had known each other and worked together in harmony for many years, accomplishing goals we both felt were valuable and important. I asked how he could possibly think that I would work against him, when I had been his friend and main collaborator. He seemed genuinely moved by what I said and apologized profusely.

A month later, he sent me three checks over the course of one week, each one for $10,000. I knew something was terribly wrong, so I set the checks aside. Over the years, Kendall had always told me he was financially well off, had no family aside from his wife, and that she had more than enough money to live in comfort for the rest of her life. Now, however, I began to question whether what he'd told me was true. Within days, I received a phone call from an attorney in Annapolis that answered this question.

The attorney explained that he had worked for Kendall and his wife Dorothy for many years. Apparently, Kendall had experienced a rapid decline and was not well physically nor mentally. He had just been admitted to a hospital for treatment. The attorney also told me that Kendall and Dorothy were not wealthy and that Dorothy would need the money in the coming years. I said that I had suspected something was wrong and had not cashed the checks. He asked me to return them to him and I did.

Soon thereafter, I learned from Dorothy that Kendall had passed away. Two years later, I received a large envelope from the same attorney. Inside was a copy of Dorothy's will. She had passed away, too, and left me $20,000.

* * *

Following the terrorist attack on September 11, 2001, the world looked as though it had suddenly spun out of control. Overwhelmed by what had happened, few people understood the implications of the government's response to the attack. Despite some organized protests against the unnecessary war in Iraq, there seemed to be little concern about the loss of personal liberty embodied by a far-ranging legislation called The Patriot Act, a set of new laws rushed through Congress before legislators even had time to read the massive tome. I could hardly believe that thousands of pages of complicated legal jargon increasing police powers and surveillance of citizens, at the expense of basic rights formerly guaranteed by the Constitution and Bill of Rights, appeared overnight and passed into law faster than it could be read.

In conjunction with my publisher Jordan Jones, poet Richard Martin, and filmmaker A. D. Liano, I conceived of a participatory on-line artistic response to these events. Called *The 365 Project*, we published social and political commentary, in the form of poems, stories, songs, videos, and artwork, on a web site each day, under corresponding news clips. We hoped that the project would provide a record of a society in turmoil.

Beginning with the first day of the year, I began to post photographs of the "Backyard Sculptures" I made each day, using found objects—fallen fruit and leaves arranged into patterns, portraits, spirals, and mazes. I cut grass into patterns and placed a mirror in odd places to unexpectedly reflect the sky. I wrapped tree trunks in newspaper and painted them. I made sculptures out of firewood from the woodshed and bits of sod placed on furniture. I hoisted paintings from my studio, shoes, and lawn furniture with fishing line pulled over the high branches of trees and hung them against the sky. I made a semi-transparent fence by stretching a long roll of plastic sheeting around the trunks of pine trees. I created a money tree out of dollar bills attached to the branches of a leafless apple tree.

During January and February, I also wrote hundreds of emails and letters to poets and writers, inviting them to contribute work to the web site. Most ignored my invitation, though some did write back to say they didn't own or know how to use a computer or didn't have an Internet connection. Others didn't like the idea of publishing their poems online. Still others told me they couldn't write in response to a subject or theme they didn't choose themselves. The most common excuse, however, was that most of the poets, writers, and artists I had contacted felt strongly that they did not want to address political or social issues in their work. Though I'm usually at ease with irony, in this instance their response mystified and infuriated me. I wondered how these poets and writers defined their role and purpose in society.

After seven months, we abandoned the multi-discipline artistic project due to a lack of interest. I found that I was posting half of all the responses to the new clips myself, frantically writing poems, stories and non-fiction pieces in different styles and publishing them on the site under a dozen different names. *The 365 Project* had lasted just over 200 days. The overwhelming apathy within the artistic community taught me another hard lesson about America.

* * *

Even as one big project wound down, I was already working on an extended, multimedia version of *The Nambuli Papers*. I wanted the novel to be something completely new and original, both in conception and in format. Instead of using line drawings, as I had in the original Obscure Publications chapbook, I decided to make both Nambuli and the Tide Writers as real as possible by using historical photographs and even film. Though clearly a parody of artistic excesses and a Dadaist inspired art movement, I wanted the entire work to nonetheless seem plausible. While never intended to pass as a hoax, *The Nambuli Papers* became a kind of "mock hoax."

I extended the first-person narratives about Aristide Nambuli, added new sections, and included a center section of black and white historical photographs for which I wrote captions that tied them to the narrative. I also added a section about Aristide's twin brother, an albino who became a famous circus clown. Then I wrote a separate book about the Tide Writers that included poems written in French, English, and NoNohNon, as well as a "scholarly" introduction and history of the group and its members. I developed a script for a silent documentary film about the Tide Writers called *The Lost Reel* that Tony Liano directed and filmed with an old handheld super 8 camera. We shot the film over two weekends at the beach and in San

Francisco, and during six days in France, with locations in Paris and Chartres. I played the fictional novelist Edmond Jouvret, while Donna was the fictional painter, Claire Ribbonet. Tony played the real-life painter Yves Klein, and Jordan, the fictional Dr. Crocker, who, for some reason, always wore a fencing mask. Other cast members included Donna's cousin Kathy and her boyfriend Bertrand, both of whom live in Paris, a painter friend Tony had met in film school, his French girlfriend, and some friends of friends we used as extras.

In its published form, *The Nambuli Papers* contains two paperback books and a DVD case with a DVD of *The Lost Reel* and other works, as well as game pieces and instructions for a board game called *Don't Hate the Game*. The books and DVD come wrapped in a printed and folded game board, with the entire package shrink-wrapped for sale. I also designed and produced a limited edition of the book housed in a wooden box. The author, filmmaker, and publisher signed each of the 26 copies, lettered A-Z. Along with the book, DVD, and game, the box contains tactile elements such as a bag of sand, a marble, a tarot card, a glass eye, and other strange and unexpected surprises that figure into the narrative.

Perhaps the review of the work that comes closest to my own feelings came from Kirpal Gordon, who wrote: "Boyd's not content with playing what's already been played. One senses that he hates clichés. He's restless with the known; he's intent on stretching the form; he's looking for ways to open up the song to greater improvisation. He wants to liberate our imaginations and I can think of no mission more relevant to the climate of our nation at this moment in our history."

* * *

While I was working on my backyard sculptures, writing for The 365 Project, and extending *The Nambuli Papers* into its final form, Tony Liano began adapting some of the poems we'd published on the web site as short films shot directly onto videotape. I drove to San Francisco to help him make the video of my poem "War Stinks." We stopped people on the street in various parts of the city and asked them to read a line of the poem. Then Tony edited the footage together to form a strangely moving short anti-war film.

Fired up by the first poetry videos, Tony decided to ask other Bay Area filmmakers to make similar short videos based on other poems from the site. He wanted to weave these short poetry videos together into a feature film with some kind of unifying narrative. He asked if I'd do the writing. It was a daunting task, but I agreed, and set to work on the script of a semi-autobiographical black comedy set at a dinner party. Tony reworked the stage play I'd written into a script for a feature film he produced and directed. Shot mostly at a sound stage in the film production facilities at the Presidio, he called his film *Seven Fallen Objects*.

I drove to San Francisco to visit the set twice during the two weeks of filming, once with Donna and once alone. I remember being surprised how many people were working on the film. In addition to the six actors, there was a small army of cinematographers, assistant directors, sound engineers, art directors, make-up artists, costume and set designers, still photographers, grips and production assistants. I found the whole experience exciting and a bit surreal, as the characters and plot had only recently tumbled from my imagination onto paper. Suddenly, my eccentric black comedy was being recreated and brought to life in front of me. I reveled in the wildly imaginative set design, along with the actors' fully-formed character portrayals and Tony's bold vision and direction.

The film stars Al Liner, an actor who also appeared in *Three-Cornered Hat*. In the film, Al plays George Body, a misunderstood and down-on-his-luck poet and painter, who suffers through an evening of dinner party conversation so toxic that it literally kills him. In the end, he collapses face down onto the plate before him on the table, as the other guests ignore his body and fuss over dessert.

After Tony had finished editing the film, he arranged a private screening at a local theater for the cast and crew, along with their families and friends. It was the first time I'd seen the film and seeing it on the big screen exceeded all of my expectations. During the screening, I sat next to Al Liner, whose amazing performance seemed to surprise him more than anyone. For months afterward, Tony continued to edit the film. I'm not sure whether or not he attempted to enter it into any festivals. It was an odd, hybrid work that didn't fit into any expected genre or tradition. Whenever I talked with him, Tony seemed restless and bored. He told me he was looking for new material for another project. Eventually, he proposed that I write down a story idea I had told him about called "The Angel Tree."

Equal parts murder mystery and literary allegory, "The Angel Tree" is a Faustian tale that concerns an ambitious young photographer who sells his soul to the Devil in trade for success in his art. The Devil helps him stage a series of shocking photographs of innocent looking young girls with wings on their backs hanging by their feet from the branches of a giant live oak tree as the Devil himself struts around naked, holding a whip. In the photos, the Devil has a grotesque, triangular-headed tail and a massive, hammerhead penis. After a wildly successful first show, the unraveling photographer struggles for inspiration and hires an amateur porn actress to accompany him on an unsuccessful and dangerous shoot during a wildfire that's burning out of control in the nearby foothills. In the end, the Devil claims his reward, as the photographer finds the lifeless body of his angelic folk singer girlfriend swinging upside down from a tree. He watches in horror as a wall of flame engulfs the landscape.

The draft I wrote portrayed various characters as representing the Seven Deadly Sins. When I finished the novel, I gave it to Tony to read. Enthusiastic about the project, he suggested we look at some possible film locations in Chico and the foothills above. He also wanted to visit Los Osos, as I had shown him photos of the twisted ancient oak trees in the state park there. Though we did make those trips together, we never began work on a script. As my story was too ambitious and required too many settings, Tony told me it would be too expensive to produce as an independent film.

Though Tony went on to produce at least one other independent film and direct commercials, our artistic collaborations were over. A few years later, he took a job working for Sony Pictures on web and other Internet-based entertainment. Knowing my interest in short narrative forms and surrealist themes, Tony commissioned me to develop and write an original series of five-minute works for video, which formed a program I called *Midnight Carnival*. Though the program was never adapted and produced, Sony paid me for the rights. A few years later, Tony and his wife Jodi, an author of cookbooks, and instructor of gourmet cooking classes, opened a culinary school dedicated to the training of professional chefs in San Francisco.

* * *

After graduating from high school, our son Eric struggled with the transition to adulthood. For most of his school years, he'd been a good student, so we had always assumed he would go on to university studies and choose a profession based on his interests. Instead, he enlisted in the Air Force. Donna and I attended his graduation from Basic Training in San Antonio and saw that military discipline had already done him some good. Eventually, he decided to make a career of the Air Force, completed an online degree program, applied for Officer Training School, and received a commission. He continues to serve as a career officer. We are proud of his accomplishments.

Once Eric had left home, I sold Asylum Arts Publishing to Jordan Jones for eight thousand dollars. Jordan and I rented a truck and moved the tens of thousands of books I'd been storing in my garage and studio to a commercial storage unit in Milpitas, near San Jose. Soon afterward, Donna and I put our house on Sawmill Road up for sale. When the house sold, we realized a handsome profit, enough to allow us to pay cash for a two-bedroom condo next to Bidwell Park in Chico. After ten years of driving up and down the Skyway between Paradise and Chico, Donna was pleased to be able to walk across town in ten minutes to her job at the university.

Before we moved to Chico, we sold most of our possessions, including our furniture, at a giant garage sale. I gave the Vandercook proofing press to an artist in Chico whose husband was off fighting a war in Iraq. She told me she needed something to keep her mind occupied while he was away. I sold my piano but kept my guitar, though I'd played it very little since it had been repaired.

In Chico, I no longer had access to a studio. Instead, I set up the small second bedroom as an office. However, I didn't accomplish much there. I spent most of the year playing video games and looking at historical houses for sale online. I was burned out from my literary career and disappointed that nothing had come of The 365 Project and the two books I had published the previous year. Though *The Nambuli Papers* received good reviews in literary journals and a long article in the local paper, aside from critics and other writers, who sent letters and emails expressing their amazement at the sheer moxie and originality of the book, relatively few general readers got to experience the novel. The feature film I had authored for Tony Liano was never officially released. Susie Bright's *Three the Hard Way* had sold well, and my novella, "The Widow," had been particularly well received. Yet when I queried editors at Touchstone and Simon & Schuster about my manuscript "The Angel Tree," they didn't bother to respond. Though my work had made money for them and had been reviewed positively in the *New York Times Book Review,* they showed me no respect. Though I was good at creating innovative work that critics and reviewers praised, I consistently failed to connect with commercial publishers who could have helped me reach a larger audience.

By summer, we were already making plans to leave California. We sold our condo completely furnished to the first person who saw it—a realtor who'd just divorced her husband. When Donna told me about a young man she'd worked with at CSU, Chico who played guitar, I gave him the Seagull. "Please play it or give it to someone who will," I told him when he came to pick it up. In mid-November Donna quit her job and we put my archives and a few valued possessions on a wooden pallet and into temporary storage. Then we drove to Oxnard to spend a final, disastrous Christmas with my mother. We left California the day after Christmas and started the new year in Virginia.

* * *

On November 8, 2018, Donna and I were living in Spain, preparing for our move from Alicante to Palomares, when we heard that a fire started by a faulty electric-transmission line and driven by a strong east wind had wiped out the town of Paradise. Within the first four hours, the fire had killed eighty-five people and destroyed nearly 18,000 structures, among them our former house and studio on Sawmill Road. Ninety-five percent of the town burned to the ground. It was the deadliest and most destructive wildfire in California history.

Seen from above on Google Earth, the town no longer exists. All that's left of the house and studio on Sawmill Road is the four-foot-high stone facade and the stonework around the wood burning stove that had been in the living room. Like everyone who lived in Paradise, we'd known about the danger of wildfires and the lack of sufficient escape routes. I had even envisioned the hell of a wild fire burning out of control through the foothills and wrote it into the ending of "The Angel Tree" just before we left Paradise. Years later, like the narrator in the novella, I realized that I had set down in words something that would have been better left unseen.

Living in the Past

"What really terrifies me is the ghosts of all the men who were killed by this weapon. I just know they'll come floating through one of the downstairs windows one night, let's make it on the eve of the 125th anniversary of the battle of Chancellorsville, and I suppose they should really come through the swamp cooler into the attic—that's where ghosts usually originate—then downstairs to take the gun and massacre us all with it while we sleep. And it will be the strangest case the homicide cops have ever seen—no evidence of the gun having been recently fired and the slugs they dig out of our bodies will be 125-year-old hunks of lead."

— "The Gun" from *Water & Power*

I'M NOT REALLY sure how we chose Virginia as the destination of our cross-country move. Neither Donna nor I had a job there, nor did we have any relatives or friends who lived in the area. We simply got into the car and drove toward an unknown future, a future that turned out to be deeply rooted in the past. I'd always been attracted to history and old things in general, and we somehow got the notion to look for an historic house for sale in Virginia. Years earlier, when we had lived briefly in North Carolina, we drove to Virginia to see Colonial Williamsburg and some of the Civil War battlefields around Richmond. On that same trip, we passed through a town called Crew one morning. The light that day in Crew lit the old houses and fields so that the town and the surrounding landscape resembled a series of Impressionist paintings. The clarity of the light was what painters sometimes refer to as "French light," and we never forgot that morning in Crew. Maybe that was reason enough to go.

On our way out of California, on Christmas Day, 2006, a drunk driver sideswiped us at high speed on the highway just outside of Palm Springs. I remember looking at the big wind turbines that dotted the hills on side of the highway. Donna was driving and I glanced over my shoulder and saw a car coming up fast from behind. It seemed like it would crash into us from the rear, but the driver suddenly veered toward the left lane to pass. He misjudged his speed and his car clipped us as it moved past, jolting us in our seats and sending us off course. The other car continued forward, now out of control. We watched it spin three circles in front of us as if in slow motion, then crash into the concrete center divider. Donna guided our car onto the shoulder of the highway. Her hands still gripped the steering wheel tightly as I reached over and turned the ignition key, shutting off the engine.

Someone traveling behind us had seen the accident and pulled behind us to check our condition. He waited half an hour for the Highway Patrol to arrive in order to provide an account of the accident. The other car still straddled the left lane. A couple other drivers pulled over and tried to slow down the approaching traffic. Though no one had been injured, both cars were destroyed. The police arrested the drunk driver, who we learned had been driving illegally on a suspended license.

Earlier that same morning, Donna and I had left my mother's house, where we had spent our worst Christmas ever. Angry that we were abandoning her by moving out of the state, my mother had been so openly hostile toward us when we arrived that we gave up our plan to spend the holiday at her house and got a hotel room nearby. In the days that followed, she continued to lash out at us in a stream of illogical, mean-spirited diatribes so precisely delivered that they almost seemed rehearsed. I was used to her negative treatment, but when she unexpectedly turned on Donna, who had always been kind and loving toward her, it was too much for me. After a pathetic Christmas breakfast, we got into our car and left. Though I refused to fight with her, I had made it clear to my mother that she had finally gone too far.

Though it took some time to sort out the insurance and find a used car we could buy, three days later we resumed our journey, and made our way across the country. Bruised emotionally from my mother and physically from the accident, we drove cautiously, unsure of ourselves in the Subaru we had just purchased. We stopped briefly in Chattanooga, Tennessee to visit Lookout Mountain and then again to see the Shiloh Civil War battlefield and a nearby property we had seen in a magazine advertising historic homes. Eventually we arrived in Virginia.

At first, we considered living in Roanoke, but we ended up in Lynchburg instead, though we despised the name. We learned eventually that the city had been named after its founder, John Lynch, who ran a ferry across the James River beneath the bluffs where the town would be built. Lynch petitioned the General Assembly of Virginia for a charter to establish a town and in 1786 his petition was granted. A pacifist Quaker, Lynch freed his own slaves during his lifetime and consistently supported the antislavery movement.

Though not yet available, we looked at some loft apartments that were under construction in one of the old brick factory buildings downtown. Then we rented a two-bedroom apartment near Randolph College. Over the coming months, we looked at dozens of houses for sale in the area. Most were older homes in attractive neighborhoods in Lynchburg, though some were in outlying areas.

Unlike the California housing market, which combined stunningly high prices with unappealing ranch style architecture, Virginia offered a wide selection of affordable, charming older houses. Some needed too much work to restore, others seemed too big for just the two of us, and the best were out of our price range. Still, we enjoyed looking. We eventually made a low offer on a large house in an established neighborhood directly across from Randolph College. It had a second-story sunroom that would have made a terrific studio. However, the owners did not accept our offer. They contacted us a month later to tell us they had reconsidered, but by then it was too late, as we had already chosen a different house.

My favorite property, a two-story brick house on two acres of land, perched atop a little bluff overlooking the road to Roanoke. Called Locust Grove, the house had been built in 1797. It had three tall brick chimneys, a red tin roof, and a small barn built of rough-hewn logs. Roughly halfway between Roanoke and Lynchburg, a half hour drive to either, we worried that the house was too isolated. After all the years of commuting in California, neither of us wanted to spend an hour or more each day driving.

When Donna accepted a job as a secretary to the dean of Student Affairs at Sweet Briar College, a women's college close to the town of Amherst, we decided to look for a house there, as the town was only a seven-minute drive to the Sweet Briar campus. A community of about 2,200 residents, Amherst offered a handful of interesting choices, including a small, single-story brick house also built in the 1790s. Though attracted to that property for its history, we agreed that it was overpriced and needed too much work, so we instead chose a large, ramshackle brick Cape Cod style house with a beautiful slate roof.

I began work remodeling the house with the help of two brothers named Ram and Javier. One was a mason by trade and the other a skilled handyman who had recently retired from a career as an Army Ranger non-commissioned officer. Together, we gutted and completely remodeled three bathrooms, refinished the antique pine floors and staircase, worked on the drainage and landscaping, repaired the plaster, painted the entire house, and installed a large cast-iron wood stove that vented through the fireplace in the living room.

I had researched colors typically used inside houses during the colonial period, and I painted the rooms of the house with paint I bought from a company that offered a special Colonial Architecture color palette. On weekends, Donna and I took day trips to visit large antique centers, where we acquired some country style furnishings. When the decorating was complete, we had a comfortable Virginia home. With its shiny pine wood floors and staircase, and its brick fireplaces and black and white tile bathrooms, the house emphasized its connection to the past.

By local convention, our house was known as "The Brown House," after the name of the builder and original occupants. We knew that the house had been built in the 1940s, though we eventually learned from a neighbor that the staircase and wide pine floors in the house had been salvaged from a demolished 1820s house. Our neighbor, a wealthy seventy-eight-year-old gentleman named Paul, had invited me to his home to talk one day after I told him I was passionate about history.

Paul was the unofficial historian of Amherst. His family had lived in Virginia since colonial times. He once showed me some letters written by British General Edward Braddock during the French and Indian War, which he pulled from a drawer in his massive roll top desk. He also had a diary written by his grandfather, who'd been a physician during the Civil War and had worked in town and later at Sweet Briar College. Embarrassed by his grandfather's views on race, he didn't allow me to read from the diary. As a boy, Paul had grown up with a housekeeper who had been born a slave and remembered the war in great detail. Another time, he told me how he'd attended the opening of *Gone with the Wind* with Robert E. Lee's grandson in Richmond.

The past lives on in Virginia. On weekends, Donna and I explored the different historic districts in Lynchburg on foot and went to the historical society to ask questions. Over time, we visited Appomattox, only half an hour from Lynchburg, as well as the Civil War battlefields at Fredericksburg, Petersburg, Chancellorsville, Spotsylvania Courthouse, The Wilderness, Mechanicsville, Winchester, Brandy Station, and Sailor's Creek. We took an overnight trip and drove to Gettysburg in Pennsylvania. On a trip to visit our son in New Mexico, we stopped in Vicksburg, Mississippi. We also visited Colonial Williamsburg, Jamestown, Yorktown, Lexington, Richmond, Monticello, the University of Virginia in Charlottesville, Mount Vernon, and the Frontier Culture Museum in Staunton.

Much of the Civil War was fought in Virginia and battlefields are scattered around the state, especially between Washington, DC and Richmond, the capital of the Confederate States of America. A century and a half later, there remains among the population a great deal of veneration of Confederate generals such as Robert E. Lee and "Stonewall" Jackson. It's not unusual to see portraits of Lee in homes, bars, restaurants, and other public places. In general, whites accept without question such displays of "Southern pride" and "heritage," while blacks tactfully ignore them. On the other hand, I never saw a single portrait of Abraham Lincoln, who remains a controversial figure for some white Virginians.

The old road that connects Amherst with Lynchburg passes through a town called Madison Heights, a zone of commercial properties—strip malls, fast food restaurants, gas stations, grocery stores, and big box stores like Walmart and Home Depot. Not far from Taco Bell, Dixie Outfitters, a "Southern Pride" establishment, offers Confederate flags, t-shirts, bumper stickers, and other Lost Cause propaganda. A prominent Confederate battle flag flies proudly above the building.

On its web site, Dixie Outfitters includes a "True History" section with an archive of "historically accurate" articles contending, among other things, that the Civil War was fought over tariffs, not slavery, that Abraham Lincoln was "an infidel," that Communists supported Lincoln and the Union, and that a quarter of the troops fighting in the Union Army were Prussians from Germany. Offering up a twisted and salty pretzel of legal "thinking," the website gives detailed instructions to students contesting bans on "Southern symbols," including a form letter to send to school boards, informing them that they may be practicing "discrimination against Confederate Americans under the Civil Rights Act of 1964."

Imagine the pain and suffering of "Confederate Americans" and "Nazi Americans" who school officials prohibit from showing up to class wearing an offensive shirt imprinted with a racist hate symbol.

* * *

While it is often said that history is written by the victors, in the case of the United States, history often seems to be written by sore but powerful losers. While ignoring the complete subjugation and near destruction of Native Americans, history textbooks also portray George Armstrong Custer as an outnumbered hero who died a tragic death at the hands of savages, rather than an overly aggressive nincompoop who foolishly divided his command and rode into a hornet's nest. Likewise, Americans prefer to cite impressive wins against the North Vietnamese Army in set battles, rather than remember the chaotic evacuation of Saigon, broadcast live on television.

Perhaps the most remarkable and consequential case of losers controlling the historical narrative concerns the "Lost Cause" ideology surrounding the Confederate defeat in the American Civil War, a conflict which has, for all intents and purposes, never come to an end. From the Lost Cause perspective, the War of Succession was not a traitorous and illegal uprising, but a just and heroic undertaking to maintain a set of culturally superior antebellum values and an entire way of life. It maintains that the South fought the war to defend states' rights in the face of overwhelming "Northern aggression," while minimizing or even completely denying the central role that slavery and white supremacy played in causing the war. It even leaves the door open for a future attempt at succession.

According to University of Virginia History professor Gary W. Gallagher, "The architects of the Lost Cause acted from various motives. They collectively sought to justify their own actions and allow themselves and other former Confederates to find something positive in all-encompassing failure. They also wanted to provide their children and future generations of white Southerners with a 'correct' narrative of the war."

While the distortion of historical fact began even before the war had ended, the first systematic attempt to rewrite history appeared in print a year after Lee's surrender at Appomattox Court House. Edward Alfred Pollard, a Virginia journalist and editor of the *Richmond Examiner* during the Civil War, was a staunch supporter of Southern succession and the Confederacy. After the Union Army occupied

Richmond in 1865, Pollard was arrested for publishing pro-Confederate and pro-slavery tracts and articles in which he referred to emancipation as a war crime. His book *The Lost Cause* appeared in 1866. In the book, he describes slavery as a key to the nobility of the South, which he considered to be a more advanced and evolved social order. A later book, *The Lost Cause Regained,* published in 1868, introduces for the first time the idea that the war had not been fought over slavery, but to protect states' rights.

Another of the original Lost Cause myth-makers was Lynchburg native Jubal Early, a Confederate general and self-described "unreconstructed rebel." An outspoken proponent of white supremacy, which he justified through his interpretations of Christian religion, Early characterized former slaves as "barbarous natives of Africa," who acted "in a civilized and Christianized condition" only as a result of their enslavement.

Alternatively, an 1868 report by U.S. Army general George Henry Thomas identified these efforts by Early, Pollard, former Confederate President Jefferson Davis, and others to falsely recast the Confederacy in a positive light. "This is, of course, intended as a species of political cant," he wrote, "whereby the crime of treason might be covered with a counterfeit varnish of patriotism, so that the precipitators of the rebellion might go down in history hand in hand with the defenders of the government, thus wiping out with their own hands their own stains; a species of self-forgiveness amazing in its effrontery, when it is considered that life and property—justly forfeited by the laws of the country, of war, and of nations, through the magnanimity of the government and people—was not exacted from them."

Around the time of the First World War, The Lost Cause movement again gained momentum, as the last Confederate veterans began to die and groups such as the Daughters of the Confederacy and the Sons of Confederate Veterans pushed to preserve their memories in a positive light. A second wave of support and activity occurred during the Civil Rights Movement, in reaction to growing public support for racial equality. By funding and building monuments to the Confederacy and revising school history textbooks, the Lost Cause movement pushed a racist agenda on future generations.

A Rebel soldier during the Civil War, sculptor Moses Jacob Ezekiel created a series of statues of Confederate heroes which both celebrated the Lost Cause and became a model for Confederate monuments erected in the early 20th century. No monument exemplifies the Lost Cause narrative better than Ezekiel's Confederate Memorial in Arlington, where the woman representing the South appears to be protecting the black figures below. According to his descendant Judith Ezekiel, who has headed a group of his descendants calling for its removal, "This statue was a very, very deliberate part of revisionist history of racist America." According to historian Gabriel Reich, "the statue functions as propaganda for the Lost Cause."

One of the most influential popularizers of the Lost Cause was D. W. Griffith's 1915 production *Birth of a Nation,* a film glorifying the Ku Klux Klan. Based on a novel by Baptist minister and professional racist Thomas Dixon, the movie shows masked cavalry as the reluctant heroes of the Reconstruction period, as they preserve white supremacy and Southern culture. The movie portrays the KKK as defenders of Southern culture and Southern womanhood against rape and destruction at the hands of freed Blacks and Yankee carpetbaggers.

Finally, Margaret Mitchell's 1936 novel *Gone with the Wind* and the 1939 film based on the book, also adds to the Lost Cause legend. As David W. Blight writes in *Race and Reunion: The Civil War in American Memory,* "One of the ideas the reconciliationist Lost Cause instilled deeply into the national culture is that even when Americans lose, they win. Such was the message, the indomitable spirit, that Margaret Mitchell infused into her character Scarlett O'Hara in *Gone with the Wind."*

Today, in the wake of the Black Lives Matter protests, statues of Confederate generals and statesmen are finally being removed by local government or pulled down by protesters. The Confederate battle flag has been removed from state flags and banned by the United States Marine Corps, the U.S. Navy, and NASCAR, and the names of Army installations located in Southern states and named after Confederate generals are also under renewed scrutiny. Nevertheless, based on the actions of the seditious mob that attacked and desecrated the Capitol in Washington, DC on January 6, 2021, smearing the floors with feces and waving Confederate battle flags inside the chambers of the House of Representatives and the Senate, one wonders if Americans will ever give up on the Lost Cause.

* * *

After we moved into the newly remodeled house in Amherst, Donna showed me an advertisement from Sweet Briar College for a job overseeing their Writing Center. I applied for the job and received an invitation to interview for the position. After I'd answered questions about my education, specific training in the teaching of writing, and experience, the Academic Dean of the college asked me if there was anything else that I'd like to share with the hiring committee. At that point, I began unpacking some of the books I'd authored and translated, as well as the magazine I edited for ten years. "As a professional writer and editor, I think I'd bring a unique perspective to the job," I said. The dean looked over several of the publications and passed them around the table. Then he asked if I might prefer to teach a class in writing in the English department instead. When he offered me a position on the spot, I accepted, though I could see that the chairperson of the department was not pleased.

Long before it became a women's college with charming Georgian Revival architecture, the 3,250-acre Sweet Briar campus existed as an antebellum plantation. Elijah Fletcher, the plantation's proprietor, had owned more than a hundred slaves. After the Civil War, former slaves and descendants of slaves continued to work for pay and live at Sweet Briar. Even today, descendants of the slaves owned by the family still work at the college. Fletcher's daughter Indiana married James Henry Williams in 1865. Their daughter, Maria Georgiana "Daisy" Williams, was born in 1867. After Daisy died at the age of sixteen in 1884, her father expressed a wish in his will that a school be established in her honor. When Indiana died in 1900, she bequeathed

Sweet Briar plantation to become a school "for the education of white girls and young women." The college took legal action to alter Indiana Fletcher Williams' will in order to admit the first African-American student in 1966.

With only two weeks until the start of the new semester, I quickly selected and placed an order for the books I would use in the course and set to work preparing a syllabus for my class. Though I would be teaching expository writing to entering freshmen, the department had stipulated that the course would be based on readings from literary texts. Most instructors chose novels that gave each section of the course a loose theme. I chose dystopian literature, with books by Ursula LeGuin, Kurt Vonnegut, Margaret Atwood, Philip K. Dick, and Anthony Burgess.

Though I wasn't happy about the literary focus the English Department had imposed on the course, which I felt worked against the goal of improving writing skills across the curriculum, I nevertheless enjoyed being back in the classroom after so many years away from teaching. I appreciated the students' energy and I wanted do my best to make their initial experience at the college challenging and memorable. I felt that teaching at a small liberal arts college might somehow be less fraught with annoying hierarchies and personality conflicts than what I remembered about teaching at a large state university.

Certainly, the food was better. On the days I taught, Donna and I would enjoy lunch at the cafeteria, usually in the company of one or more of her colleagues. Unlike the English Department, where I kept a low profile during the hours I spent in a shared office, Donna's co-workers formed a more congenial group. Unused to the rich Southern food, we both gained weight that year.

Halfway through the semester, the chairperson of the English Department left a note in my mailbox informing me that she planned to attend one of my classes in order to evaluate my teaching. I replied that she was welcome to come at her convenience. After she had made and cancelled three consecutive appearances, I forgot about the evaluation. One morning, I walked into my class to find her lurking in a chair at the back of the room. In my experience, students always seemed to put forth their best effort during such evaluations. They instinctively knew that it was a performance, and they invariably did their best to make me look good. Even students who rarely participated in class discussions raised their hands and offered opinions. Though I hadn't prepared anything special for the lesson, that day we discussed an early poem by Margaret Atwood and compared some of the themes to what we'd already studied in *The Handmaid's Tale*. My students' enthusiasm, energy and universal engagement made for a charged and exciting discussion. Nevertheless, my passing the audition only seemed to further infuriate the chairperson, who met with me later to discuss my teaching and seemed at a near complete loss for words.

The following semester, the dean asked me to teach a course in Journalism, a minor administered by the English Department. When students complained to me throughout the semester that the minor program seemed ill defined and difficult to navigate, as the department offered the classes infrequently, I wrote a proposal for revamping the minor, which I submitted to the department chair. My proposal incorporated updating the curriculum to reflect new technology and journalistic approaches, along with some rather obvious changes, such as awarding students academic credits for their work on the campus newspaper.

During the semester, my students each published an online blog about a particular subject. I assigned students to cover events on campus and write news stories or reviews about them. I worked with each student to conceive and produce a long essay about some unusual aspect of the local or college culture or a profile of one of the uncelebrated workers on campus. One student chose to profile a cafeteria worker who spent hours each week receiving kidney dialysis. Another wrote about the dismantled eighteenth-century historic manor "Tusculum" that Sweet Briar College had stored in hundreds of pieces in a barn on campus, with the unrealistic and never to be realized plan to reconstruct it as a museum. Some of the students produced first-rate work.

While I enjoyed teaching at Sweet Briar College, mainly for the good interaction I had with my students, I wasn't always pleased with the attitudes I encountered. The backward-looking traditions of the college seemed to exacerbate the rigidity of some of my students' thinking. It bothered me that the college's antebellum past dovetailed neatly into a present where nearly all of the students and faculty were white, while nearly all of the groundskeepers, maintenance workers, janitors, and kitchen workers were black. That the students often actively resisted feminism discouraged me as well. The college and its students seemed rooted in the past and out of step with the present. It seemed clear to me that a women's college that offered students the opportunity to board their own horses at its famous equestrian facilities served more as a means to preserve the status quo of a culture of privilege than as an agent to promote positive change in society.

At the end of my year of teaching, I attended a party with Donna honoring faculty who were retiring, moving on to other jobs, or not returning to the college. I learned during the event that I was among those who were leaving. As no one had bothered, or perhaps had the nerve, to inform me that I wouldn't be rehired, the separation initially came as unwelcome news. However, when I had time to think more clearly, I felt fortunate to be free, as the job required a good deal of preparation and time and paid very poorly. In fact, I had spent all of my earnings from teaching that year on a root canal and crown. I later learned that the following year the chairperson implemented all of the suggestions for the Journalism minor I had proposed. For several years I kept in contact with a handful of students and attended their graduation four years later, as I had promised them I would. However, I've never since considered teaching in any professional capacity.

* * *

Near the end of my time teaching at Sweet Briar College, I injured myself while exercising at home. I was doing pushups in the living room and I remember hearing a loud popping sound as my shoulder gave out and I crashed to the floor. When I struggled to my feet, I found that I could no longer stand up straight. My right shoulder seemed to sag several inches lower on that side of my body. The pain increased throughout the day, to the point where it was uncomfortable to stand, walk, sit, or lie down. The next day, I made an appointment to see a chiropractor. After the chiropractor had examined me, she said that my injury would require a great deal of rehabilitation and physical therapy. She likened the injury to the kind of trauma more common as a result of a serious car accident or fall.

Sally, the chiropractor, started me on a regime of bi-weekly adjustments and exercises that I could barely attempt at first. For months, the treatments continued and the constant pain in my neck and shoulder, along with the numbness in my fingers was unsettling and depressing. Slowly, she added more exercises and insisted that I try harder to maintain my posture between adjustments. One day, she told me I should stop painting, stop sitting at the computer, and stop reading, as these positions and their associated repetitive motions put too much stress on my neck, shoulder, and spine and were in fact impeding my recovery. I told her I could not stop painting, as that was the only thing giving me the purpose and joy I needed to deal with the constant pain and discomfort. We argued and she insisted I wouldn't get better if I refused to listen to her.

I worked harder at the exercises, willing myself to heal. Sally gave me a new exercise with resistance bands to help build muscle strength to hold my posture in the correct position. For two years, I worked with bands and exercise balls, and had regular adjustments. I tried acupuncture and began taking tai chi classes. Slowly the pain receded and my flexibility and range of motion increased. Though I eventually recovered, I have needed periodic chiropractic adjustments ever since and my body is prone to relapses. I cannot carry weight, lift heavy objects, or do work that requires repetitive motions. Though only fifty-one years old at the time of the injury, I would never be the same again.

* * *

Our second summer in Virginia, we traveled to Alaska to see Eric and his wife Sabrina. They had recently married and settled into an off-base apartment together in North Pole, just outside of Fairbanks, where Eric was stationed. I had always wanted to visit Alaska, so even though I was still working toward recovering from my injury, we nonetheless undertook the long flight from Washington DC to Seattle, then another long flight to Fairbanks. The immensity of the flat, open spaces surprised us as we flew over vast expanses of tundra.

Our first day in Alaska, Eric guided us around the Air Force base and showed us some of the aircraft on which he worked. As we drove across the base, we saw moose grazing at the edge of the forest. Later in the week, we drove several hours to Denali National Park and back. Like the Sierra Nevada mountains in California, the scope of the landscape in Alaska overwhelms the viewer. It's simply too much to take in.

In June, the sun remained in the sky most of the night, which took some getting used to, even with blackout curtains in the bedroom. Both Eric and Sabrina seemed happy to have light and warmth instead of the sub-zero temperatures and near total darkness of the Alaskan winter. Even in summer, Fairbanks seemed grim: hostile, desolate, and hopelessly isolated. Some of the people we met appeared eccentric and ill at ease around others, as though their interaction reflected the harshness of the environment.

The morning after our trip to Denali, I received a phone call from my mother in California. She was calling from a hospital bed and wanted me to know that she'd suffered a massive heart attack and would have open heart surgery in a couple of hours. The doctor did not seem overly optimistic about her chances, she said. Caught off guard, I didn't know quite what to say. I'd had a falling out with her when we left California and I had spoken to her only once briefly in the two years since. When I told her I would come to California as soon as I could arrange it, she said I should finish my visit with my son first, as my sister was on her way and there was really nothing anyone could do now anyway.

One of the few serious subjects on which I'd conversed with my mother over the years had been death. A willful person, she was terrified to think that she might end up in a situation where she had no control over her own life. On many occasions she had stated that her preference was to die a dignified and natural death rather than be maintained on life support. She had always made it clear that she expected my sister and me to allow her to die if fate were to place her in such circumstances.

I eventually arranged to fly to California in time to relieve my sister, who was starting a new job in Colorado. When I arrived at the airport, Linda drove me to Oxnard, where we stayed at our mother's house. A Nurse Practitioner with over thirty years of experience in medicine, Linda told me on the way that the surgery had not gone well and our mother was in a coma. When the surgeon opened her chest, he saw that her heart was severely damaged. The surgery lasted ten hours and, though her condition remained hopeless, he had patched her up as best he could. "He should have let her die on the table in the operating room," Linda said. Now the surgeon wanted to keep her alive for as long as possible so that the surgery wouldn't count as a failure on his record.

"Do they really keep score like that with patients?" I asked.

"Actually, they do. For heart surgeons, outcomes are important because it's a life-or-death kind of intervention. If you've got a bad track record, then you probably won't have many patients."

Even death is about money. Because my mother had extensive insurance coverage, her extended care produced profit for the hospital and the doctors who treated her, while prolonging her suffering. When my sister flew back to Denver, our mother was still in a coma. After briefly regaining consciousness and indicating that she did not want to be maintained further on life support, my mother died thirty-six hours after entering hospice. All told, she'd been in the hospital close to a month. After her surgery, her jerry-rigged heart leaked and her other internal organs immediately began to fail. Despite the doctors' constant stream of nonsense and magical thinking, there had never been any chance she'd recover.

* * *

By August of 2008, I had barely moved past the responsibilities of selling my mother's house and my duties as executor of her will. I'd been to California twice over the summer. On the final trip, I drove her car back alone across the country to Virginia. The long hours of driving gave me time to think, to review and take stock of my own history. By the time I arrived home, I was mentally and spiritually exhausted.

One unexpected consequence of my mother's death was the sudden release of many formerly repressed feelings. After her death, I was overcome, not by grief, but by anger. Over the years, my mother had carefully constructed the myth that my father had been solely responsible for any problems or neglect my sister and I experienced as children and young adults. Finally, I could see past her deflection and acknowledge the damaging effects of her personality as well. As I reviewed my childhood and my relationship with my mother, I realized that she, too, had been negligent and abusive, that she, too, had been responsible for her behavior and actions. Though repressed and buried deep within my psyche, the past had finally bubbled up to the surface.

In the midst of all this psychic turmoil, on the morning of August ninth I woke up with an idea strongly imprinted on my brain: Cave Art. I'm not sure where this thought came from or what it meant, exactly, but the feeling it generated was so compelling that I found it impossible to ignore. It was as though someone or some thing was trying to transmit important information through a language I didn't speak or understand. I showered and drank some coffee, then drove directly to the library at Sweet Briar College. I piled every book I could find on cave art onto a table in the basement and spent the day reading about Paleolithic art. The following day, I bought some paper and began a series of pastel studies based on these images. I remember I set up a table on the screened porch in the back of our house in Amherst and made dozens of pastel drawings of individual figures and groups of animals from the books I'd borrowed from the library. I based many of the paintings I would make over the coming months and years on these studies.

Though I still had no idea what I was doing or why, I ordered a number of large canvases, a gallon of modeling paste, and some pearl mica, pumice stone gel, glass bead gel, iron oxide, and sand. Then I set to work on a series of heavily textured paintings in acrylics and minerals. My first efforts were among the best paintings I have done. I had already decided to make the paintings as large as possible, ideally monumental in size. Initially, I worked mainly with 3 x 4 feet and 3 x 3 feet canvases. I based the first paintings on my interpretations of a group of four horse heads in the Chauvet Cave, along with a number of individual horses or bulls from Lascaux.

At the same time, I delved into the literature concerning Paleolithic art, beginning with books by Paul Bahn and Jean Clottes. Later, I read major studies by R. Dale Guthrie and David Lewis Williams. I even read Jean Auel's novel *Clan of the Cave Bear*, followed by her progressively tedious sequels. My research revealed that paleontologists—scientists, anthropologists, and art historians—knew little about the animal images that our ancestors had made for tens of thousands of years, aside from what could be measured, counted, described, or carbon dated, while fictional depictions seemed implausible and tainted by the contemporary world view of their authors. Though I felt certain that the origins of art contained universal and profound lessons for humanity, the purpose and meaning of the images remained a mystery. I'd stumbled upon a Rosetta Stone, but I needed a lexicon that didn't exist, a code to interpret what I had before me.

In late September, Donna and I noticed that the loft apartments at Riverviews Art Space in Lynchburg had come onto the market for the first time. A seven-story brick building constructed in the 1880s as a warehouse for the shoe-making industry in Lynchburg, the building had been abandoned for many years until a local group formed a non-profit organization to buy and rehabilitate it into lofts and studio space in which artists could live and work. The organization converted the building using historic tax credits, which were only available to a single owner, which meant the lofts must be rented out for the first five years. While current renters received the first option to buy into the new association, a number of units remained without offers.

We made an appointment to look at each of the apartments still available for sale and used some of the money my mother had left me to purchase a 1,200 square foot loft. Aside from the bathroom and a small entry hall, the entire loft, including the kitchen, consisted of a single open space, with high ceilings, rough wood floors, wooden pillars and ceiling beams, and a bank of ten-foot-high windows on one side. We selected a unit on the third floor of the building with a view of the James River, some old factory buildings, and the Blue Ridge Mountains.

I moved my studio from the house in Amherst to the loft, where I worked on my own versions of prehistoric European cave art. The expansive studio allowed me to create an eighteen-foot-long painting based on the "Hall of the Bulls" in Lascaux. Executed in oil paints on a roll of five-foot-by-eighteen-foot canvas, the painting took up an entire wall in the loft. I also made two very large paintings in oils based on images from the Chauvet cave.

* * *

The following summer, Donna and I took a trip to France specifically to visit sites where we could see Paleolithic art first-hand. We had arranged to stay at the home of British archeologist Steve Burman and his wife Judie, in the Dordogne, only a few miles from the Lascaux cave and the town of Montignac. In Charlottesville, on our way to the airport, we stopped at a mountaineering shop so I could look for a pair of shoes. I told the salesman that I needed shoes that would keep me from slipping on wet rocks while we were visiting caves in France. "You wouldn't want to get hurt there," he said. "Those socialist countries don't have good health care." I told him we had friends who were doctors in France and that, according to the World Health Organization, France has the best health care in the world, whereas the United States is far down the list because acceptable levels of care are beyond the means of all but the wealthiest of our citizens. I don't think he believed a word I said, but the shoes he sold me did the job.

After a few days in Paris, we rode the train to the Dordogne, where Steve met us at the station. Each day that week Steve took us to see cave art, mostly in the Vézère Valley around Montignac and Les Eyzies. We visited Rouffingnac, Cap Blanc, Font-de-Gaume, Les Combarelles, and Castel Merle, and the National Museum of Prehistory. He also took us to see the caves at Cougnac. In addition, we visited some local castles and historic towns in the region, including Sarlat, and enjoyed the excellent food and wine. Each night, Steve and I would stay up late to discuss what we'd seen that day, along with the theories put forth by various scholars.

When Steve took us to Les Eyzies to see the National Museum of Prehistory, I experienced a dizzying sense of *déjà-vu*. Like the hotel and other buildings in Les Eyzies, the museum is built into the limestone cliffs and there's a magnificent view of the Vézère River winding through the narrow green valley below. As I stood on the museum's terrace and gazed over the panoramic view of the valley, the river, and the lush surrounding landscape, I remember feeling a sense of tranquility and connection. It was as if time had come unbound. "I know this place," I said out loud. Afterward we visited The Cro-Magnon Rock Shelter, a small outcropping in the cliff next to the hotel, where burial remains of the first modern humans had been uncovered in 1868. A chapel for our species, a simple brass plaque commemorates the site. We were the only visitors.

While each of the decorated caves has its own unique art and geology, two of the most impressive exist within half a mile of each other, just outside of Les Eyzies. Font-de-Gaume cave is extraordinary for the polychromatic paintings, dated 16,000 years before present, found within its narrow passages. It is the only Ice Age cave in France with polychromatic paintings still open to the public. Along with large numbers of paintings of bison, horses, and mammoths, there are also paintings of deer, ibex, reindeer, cave bears, cave lions, and wooly rhinoceroses. Font-de-Gaume also includes an extremely rare representation of a Paleolithic dog.

The other decorated cave within walking distance of Les Eyzies is Les Combarelles, which contains roughly 600 animal figures, most of them engraved during the late Magdalenian period, about 10,000 years before present time. A few include black outlines drawn over the rock walls. Many of the engravings are superimposed, one or more on top of existing figures. A large percentage of the engravings feature finely detailed and accurately drawn animal figures, though most can only be seen in exactly the right light and from a sharp angle. Given the wealth of artwork, the guides only have time to offer close views and explanations of a few selected images. To their credit, they try to make each tour unique. In the off season, an extended visit can be arranged. One of the most striking images portrays a single, well-defined cave lion.

Steve also took us to Castel Merle, where he introduced us to the self-described *"paysan-préhistorien"* René Castanet, whose family owned and farmed the land where excavations of ten "abri" or rock overhangs, have uncovered Neanderthal artifacts and evidence of habitation as well as Cro-Magnon engravings on the walls. Castel Merle provides evidence of continuous human occupation for over 85,000 years. During our visit, René displayed near boundless enthusiasm and willingness to share his knowledge of prehistoric art and artifacts. In response to our conversation and our interest, he generously spent hours guiding us through his personal museum of artifacts that he and his father had unearthed from the digs on their land. Though the majority of the artifacts from Castel Merle are in the National Museum of Prehistory, the Castanet family had kept some particularly interesting items for themselves. René happily shared everything with scholars and visitors alike. Over the years, René also taught himself to knap flint and recreate some of the complex spear tips, knife blades, and other Stone Age tools. His explanations of how to fashion and use these tools and the stories behind the discovery of the original artifacts made for a memorable afternoon. When I told Monsieur Castanet that I would like to interview him further for a book I wanted to write on Paleolithic art, he smiled at me. "You better hurry," he said, "I won't last forever." He was eighty-five years old at the time.

René was out of town on the day we returned to Castel Merle, two years later, but we again saw the fantastic Musée Castanet, at the time in one wing of René's house. Passing through a courtyard littered with piles of flint chips from René's flint knapping, we found the door to the museum ajar, its priceless treasures there for anyone to enjoy. The Musée Castanet was a miniature version of the National Museum of Prehistory in nearby Les Eyzies, with the added bonus that the glass cases are unlocked, the specimens available for handling. A hand axe or a scraper makes much more sense when one can feel its weight and how it fits into the hand. Most beautiful are the ivory, bone, shell, and tooth necklaces. Most mysterious the carved lunar calendar.

I did eventually write a short book called *The Cave Art Notebooks* based on the observations and drawings I had made during our various trips to cave art sites in France over the years. It seems to me that there exists a strong connection between the prehistoric art and the people who continue to live on the land around these sites. The guides I've talked with have been people who have grown up and lived within a few miles of the sites. They display a remarkable degree of pride in their collective past. Other local people have become artists, flint knappers, teachers, or professional or amateur archeologists. In his dual role as a farmer-prehistorian, René Castanet typified that connection. Sadly, he passed away in 2013, before I had the chance to talk with him again.

* * *

During the time we spent in France with Steve and Judie Burman, we learned about the history of the Dordogne region of France. We also learned about the medieval pilgrim route, the *Chemin de Saint-Jacques,* from one of Steve's free-ranging discussions. While more widely known and followed in Spain these days as the *Camino de Santiago,* the idea of a historical pilgrimage through Europe appealed greatly to Donna. Though I was surprised that she would choose to undertake a physically challenging trek across France and Spain that would take two months or more, it sounded like a wonderful adventure. I threw myself behind the idea wholeheartedly.

We both knew that such a trip would be difficult and life-changing at our age. At first, we thought that Donna could take a couple of months off work during the summer or find a ten-month job on campus, but those ideas turned out to be unrealistic. To do the trip properly, she would have to quit her job. We decided to use the Camino as a way to simplify our life and move toward a new phase. We would plan our trip mindfully and see where it took us. We gave ourselves two years to make the arrangements.

Our first task was to sell our house in Amherst and move into the loft apartment in Lynchburg. By then, we had replaced all the windows and doors in the house. We also needed to remove the oil-fired furnace and fuel tank and replace them with a modern heating and air conditioning system. Finally, we had a roofing contractor replace the flashing around the chimney, which fixed a problem we had with water getting into the basement. I repainted the basement and back porch. Then, we gave away some extra furniture and staged the house as a four-bedroom family home. Our realtor appeared happy with what we had done and assured us that a house so well remodeled and staged was a rare find on the market.

Though we sold the house quickly, the offer was well under the amount we had hoped for, given the labor and money we had invested in the renovation. Nevertheless, after careful deliberation, we accepted it. The house felt like a completed project. It was time to do something else. A week before we moved, we organized a garage sale and sold half our furniture to our Amherst neighbors. We also gave some of the nicer antiques to friends we'd met at Sweet Briar College. Donna hired a co-worker from the college and his cousin, who both lived in Amherst, to help us move our remaining possessions to the loft at Riverviews in Lynchburg.

For many years, downtown Lynchburg had been in a sad state of decay and disuse. At the time we lived there, the majority of old shoe industry buildings and warehouses still remained empty, along with some of the commercial properties on the main street of the city. Though the downtown revitalization had already begun, it would be several years before the city completed the expensive upgrades to electrical and plumbing systems that would allow for the complete urban renewal that has since taken place.

Though the downtown still lacked a grocery store and pharmacy, it had a tall office building, the only modern skyscraper in the city, a couple of hotels, the municipal social services building, a parking structure, and more than a dozen good restaurants. In addition to Riverviews, repurposed historical buildings included the Craddock-Terry hotel and two connected restaurants, a children's museum called Amazement Square, several other large buildings converted to loft apartments, some small shops, a couple of coffeehouses, and the Depot Restaurant, which operated out of the old Lynchburg rail station.

As we didn't have curtains or blinds on the ten-foot-tall windows of our loft and no walls nor designated bedroom, we designed curtains for our canopy bed and hired a seamstress to make them. We placed the bed against a wall on which I had hung a six foot by nine-foot oil painting of the Chauvet horses. We also hired a cabinetmaker to build a closet in the entryway. We found a giant antique Persian rug at a downtown Lynchburg estate sale outlet and arranged our living room furniture on top of it. One weekend we drove to the Ikea store in northern Virginia, where we bought black bookcases and dressers, and hauled back the boxes in our Subaru Forester. A unique and beautiful space, the loft was an ideal live-in studio. My paintings of horses, bulls, bison, mammoths, bears, and lions covered the tall brick walls, and the eighteen foot Hall of the Bulls oil painting spread across the wall behind the easels and tables where I painted.

During the day, light from the tall bank of windows filled the loft. Looking down from the third floor of the building, we could see a wide section of the historic downtown spread out before us. Directly across the street, a city parking lot adjoined the Lynchburg Social Services building, while giant metal ants crawled up the side of the Amazement Square Children's Museum on the corner of 9th and Jefferson streets. Further away, smoke rose from the tall stacks of the pipe factory next to the railroad tracks that ran alongside the James River. Matchbox cars and trucks transited the bridge that connected Lynchburg to Madison Heights. Farther off, a three-story, eighteenth-century brick mansion hovered on a grassy knoll above the factory. In the distance beyond, the gentle curves of the Blue Ridge Mountains nestled against the sky.

At night, the streetlights below cast a soft glow through the windows, which created a kind of torchlight effect on the walls. I always loved waking up during the night surrounded by the large animal figures on the walls of our cavernous loft. In the defused and flickering light, the horses and bison seemed to be running across the walls. Surrounded by these totems, the apartment felt like a safe, comforting, and sacred space. I didn't understand how those simple paintings could elicit such strong emotional responses in me and others, but I suspected they had something important to tell us if we listened carefully. When I assembled photographs of the three giant oil paintings I'd done in different stages of completion into a volume called *Shoe Factory Grotto,* the book had no text. The paintings would eventually reveal their meaning, but not yet.

Like the Riverviews Artspace Gallery on the ground floor of the building, the high ceilings, rough hardwood floors, aged brick walls, tall windows, and massive wooden pillars and beams of our loft provided a striking backdrop for my large, colorful paintings. Regional design and lifestyle magazines twice published photos of our studio and apartment, the first time as part of a profile of me and my work and the second time as illustrations for a feature story on loft living.

Each year Lynchburg holds an Annual Downtown Loft Tour to raise money for the Free Clinic. Owners of unique downtown properties open their lofts to visitors for the day. We participated in the loft tours twice and enjoyed talking with the roughly two hundred visitors. Among our guests one year were my chiropractor and friend Sally and her husband Bill. A brilliant but troubled man, Bill was a retired Harvard-trained medical doctor. He'd grown up in rural Virginia and had lived in Amherst County most of his life. In his youth, he learned to hunt deer and had remained a hunter throughout his life. For years he'd been the Amherst town physician, who also attended to students living on the Sweet Briar College campus. Before med school, he'd served as a helicopter pilot in Vietnam. A sensitive man, the war had taken a huge toll on him. He lived each day as a recovering alcoholic.

A man of few words, Bill made obligatory small talk for a few minutes before planting himself on the leather couch. Four hours later he was still seated there. Over the course of the afternoon, I'd watched him stare at the paintings with his hands clasped over his stomach. Occasionally, his gaze wandered out the window for a while, before returning to the animals. "I've never seen him so calm and peaceful," Sally told me. When it was past time to go home, she had to work a bit at getting him to leave. We shook hands and he thanked me on the way out. I invited him to come back any time.

My father once visited us in Lynchburg as well. He spent several hours seated on the same leather couch, yet never commented on nor even seemed to take note of the giant paintings that surrounded him.

* * *

From downtown and many other places in Lynchburg, it's easy to spot the massive Liberty University monogram glaring down on the city from its position near the top of Candler's Mountain above the campus. Created in 2007 by Southern Baptists, who cut down three acres of forest on the mountain side and bulldozed the area flat, the monogram uses 200 tons of white stone to form a background. Red brick chips fill in the areas between the approximately 1,200 Japanese Barberry and other flowering plants that make up the giant letters "L" and "U." During the time we lived in Lynchburg, an unknown group once rearranged the brick chips so that the "L" in the monogram became an "F" overnight, and in the morning the mountainside proclaimed: "F U." Shortly afterward, the university erected a fence around the monogram.

Founded by televangelist Jerry Falwell in 1971 as Lynchburg Baptist College, Liberty University is one of Virginia's largest institutions of higher education. Though Liberty enjoys tax-exempt, non-profit status, the university's distance and online learning programs are wildly profitable, as tax-payer dollars support them in the form of federal educational student loans and programs such as Pell Grants. The university claims it generates over a billion dollars in economic impact to the greater Lynchburg area annually. As the biggest employer and economic engine in the Lynchburg region, Liberty University exerts a great deal of influence over public policy in the city, especially regarding development of its sprawling campus. Aside from its divisive politics, the university also creates controversy in other ways. While some love the jobs and money the institution attracts to the area, others bemoan the poor planning, tangled traffic, and bullying tactics of the university. While no one complains about the bland, well-behaved students, city residents remain deeply divided by Liberty and the Falwell legacy.

In 1956, twenty-two-year-old Jerry Falwell received a degree from the unaccredited Baptist Bible College in Springfield, Missouri, and promptly returned to Lynchburg to found the Thomas Road Baptist Church with thirty-five members. That same year, he began broadcasting his sermons on the *Old-Time Gospel Hour*, a nationally syndicated radio and television ministry. With the publicity from his broadcasts, Thomas Road Baptist Church grew into a megachurch. During the 1960s, Falwell spoke against civil rights activist Martin Luther King, Jr. and the desegregation of public-school systems by the U.S. federal government. He also founded a Christian school in Lynchburg which was described in 1966 by the *Lynchburg News* as "a private school for white students."

In 1978, when an IRS ruling took away tax-exempt status from all-white private schools like Falwell's in Lynchburg, he formed a political action and lobbying organization called the Moral Majority. Falwell and other white evangelicals insisted that their schools were Christian academies, not segregation academies. Over this racist attempt to derail school segregation, the Religious Right asserted its power and joined forces with political conservatives.

During the 1980s the Moral Majority became one of the largest political lobby groups for evangelical Christians in the United States. The Moral Majority promoted itself as representing a "pro-life," "pro–traditional family," "pro-moral" and "pro-American" political perspective. During his time as head of the Moral Majority, Falwell consistently supported Republican candidates and conservative causes.

A couple months after we arrived in Lynchburg, Jerry Falwell died, leaving his two sons to manage Thomas Road Church and Liberty University. I read in the news the other day that Jerry Jr., president of Liberty University, and his wife Becki, apparently enjoy a rather liberated sexual lifestyle in which Becki has sex with younger men while her husband watches. Meanwhile, students at Liberty University are restricted by published university rules from doing more than holding hands until they are married.

Recently, a young Liberty student who played in a rock band with Jerry and Becki's son, accused Becki of seducing him during an overnight stay in their home. Apparently, Becki snuck into the guest bedroom and gave the Falwell son's bandmate a blowjob while Jerry was out of town. Jerry's been busy as well. He posted photos of himself drinking in a nightclub and clowning around on a yacht with his pants unzipped and his arm around his wife's pregnant young friend. He has since resigned as president of the university, after receiving a ten-million-dollar severance package. Of course, the hypocritical Liberty libertine has denied any wrongdoing. "There wasn't any cause," he said, for his resignation. "I haven't done anything."

* * *

During the time we lived at the loft in the Riverviews building, Donna and I began to plan and train for our walking trip across France and Spain. We used the extensive trail system that passed within a block of our building to take long walks each day. One direction took us along the James River and across to the Percival's Island Natural Area and the other direction climbed up the bluff and followed the canyon of the Blackwater Creek Natural Area. We always found the people in Lynchburg to be friendly and polite. It's common practice to greet everyone you meet. Some days I walked for miles alongside chatty strangers who engaged me in conversation. Once, deep within the Blackwater Creek trail system I encountered a man and a woman in distress. I discovered the woman lying on the ground, barely conscious and having a drug and alcohol induced seizure, while the man, clearly intoxicated, hovered over her in a state of confusion. Eventually I calmed him down and got him to agree that we should call for emergency medical help. I waited with them until the paramedics arrived on a special all-terrain vehicle.

During our time living at Riverviews, we met some wonderful people who lived in the building, including a photographer who had asked at one of the loft tours if she could take some pictures of my paintings. Afterward, we talked for a while and she asked me a lot of questions about my artwork and my books. I remember talking to her for half an hour about *The Nambuli Papers*. A couple of days later, she gave me two CDs, one with the professional photos of my paintings she had taken and the other a video she had made of the interview she had conducted with me. I was surprised to see the video, as I had completely forgotten that she had asked my permission to film.

That was my introduction to Susan Saandholland, who has become a good friend and collaborator over the years. A psychotherapist with a practice in Roanoke, Susan had chosen to keep her art completely separate from her other profession. She pursued her career as a photographer and artist under a different name in a different city. Over the years, she has documented my paintings, videotaped a talk I did at the Academy of Fine Arts, and helped produce a series of interviews with me for the Greg Boyd Asylum Arts and Unicorn Press Collection at the University of California at Santa Barbara Library Special Collections Unit.

Before we left for Ecuador, I sold most of my cave art–inspired paintings. The show at The Academy of Fine Arts resulted in the sale of seven paintings. Our friends Susan and Rick from Charlottesville purchased nine more. Our neighbor at Riverviews bought five large canvases for a house he had just finished building. Larry Bassett, the owner of an upstairs loft, bought two for his collection of work by local artists. Sally, my chiropractor, whose husband had been so calmed by the paintings when they visited the loft, purchased eight others for her clinic in Amherst. Several other Riverviews residents and friends bought individual paintings. I gave two to Susan Saandholland to thank her for photographing and documenting the work. I rolled up the large format oil paintings and put them into storage, along with a dozen remaining paintings and my literary archives. Eight years later, when I came to Lynchburg to pack and ship the archives to the UCSB Library Special Collections Unit, I took three paintings off their stretchers and rolled them into tubes to take with us back to Spain. The remaining paintings I donated to Larry Bassett's collection, which had grown into a rotating art exhibit displayed in municipal buildings in Lynchburg. Heritage High School in Lynchburg has recently taken over Larry Bassett's collection.

* * *

When people in Spain talk to me about the United States, they generally view it as a progressive and moderate society. Like most American citizens, Spaniards seem to know more about our myth-making than our actual history. Consequently, they don't understand much about our politics. Though we hate to admit it, the United States of America has a history of institutionalized racism, intolerance based on twisted religious beliefs, gun violence, and political corruption fueled by greed and irresponsible, under-regulated capitalism. Those influences continue to deeply affect and undermine our society. Unless we face the past honestly and commit to change, the United States will never escape the toxic legacy of "The Lost Cause."

Sore Feet and Miracles

> I don't know for sure that flowers bloomed out of season everywhere we went or that Sheila sometimes had a tattoo of a rose on her breast. I can't prove that she healed with her touch a dog that had been hit by a car along the highway or whispered to a deaf man in the bus station and made him laugh. At this point, I'm not even sure about the angels I saw jump from the overpass in Bakersfield.
> — *Sacred Hearts*

For many years, Donna and I had dreamed of walking, village to village, across France. On a trip to visit cave art sites in the Dordogne, some friends had told us about the Camino de Santiago de Compostela, a medieval pilgrim route that traverses France and continues over the Pyrenees and across Spain to the northwest coast. One of the most important Christian pilgrimages during the Middle Ages, The Way of Saint James is a network of footpaths that lead from various parts of Europe to the shrine of the apostle James the Great in the cathedral of Santiago de Compostela in Galicia, Spain. According to legend, the remains of the saint were buried there after he was martyred in Jerusalem in 44 A.D. and his body transported by boat to Spain, where earlier he had been the first to preach the gospel in Iberia.

These days, many people continue to follow the Camino as a spiritual journey, though it is also increasingly popular with hikers and cyclists. Over the years, the scallop shell, common on the shores in

Galicia, has come to symbolize the Camino de Santiago. Contemporary pilgrims often attach the shells to their backpacks.

In the spring of 2011, we set off on this journey, planning to walk the 960-mile route from Vézelay in France to Santiago de Compostela in Spain. Along the way, we'd stay in pilgrim hostels, inexpensive hotels, bed and breakfast inns, and with local people who provide hospitality for pilgrims. After having lived in France for eight months just after our wedding, Donna and I had always talked about living there again when we had fewer responsibilities and obligations. A walking trip across the country seemed like a great way to research how practical that idea might be. Though we had not yet formed any clear plan, we thought that we might be able to find an inexpensive place to live in the Dordogne, close to the cave art sites, or else in a small town near the Camino, where we could open our home to pilgrims.

After arriving in May, we spent a few days in Paris adjusting to the time change. We visited L'Orangerie to see Monet's water lily paintings. Then we took a day trip with Donna's cousin Kathy, who has lived in Paris for over thirty years, to see Monet's home and gardens at Giverny. In springtime, the famous gardens explode with blossoms. The vegetation and the carefully recreated paths, ponds, and bridges invite guests to enter into a living, organic version of the artist's paintings. A few days later, we took the train to Vézelay, where we would begin our walk.

Near the town of Arcy-sur-Cure, we visited the Grottes d'Arcy, a large cave with two underground lakes and some prehistoric drawings of animal figures done in charcoal or red ochre. On the way back, we met a man who was returning home from the *boulangerie*, his dog trotting beside him. He showed us a shortcut along the river and told us a few stories along the way. When we came to the town, we sat for a while on a bench near the bridge beside the river, where I filled a notebook with Conté crayon drawings of the prehistoric animal figures we had just seen.

In the walled town of Vézelay, the starting point of our pilgrimage, and the site of a Franciscan monastery, we received our credentials (a kind of passport that allows pilgrims to stay in the official hostels). We wandered around the ramparts of the town and visited a shop staffed by monks and nuns from the various orders. Late in the day, we attended part of a mass at the basilica. We set out into the lush surrounding countryside the next morning.

The first night, we slept in a small hotel in a rural village, the next in a hostel in a much bigger town. The hostel experience disappointed us for a number of reasons. At our age, we need a good night's sleep and we quickly realized that we would be more comfortable staying in hotels and *chambres d'hôte* where we could have our own room whenever possible, instead of sleeping head-to-head with strangers in a big room full of cots.

During a hard rain, we took shelter in a covered bus stop in a village between Bazoches and Saint-Révérien. There we met a little man who seemed genuinely delighted when we told him we were Americans. He had been the town's postman all of his working life. Now he was one of only a handful of old-timers who still lived in the village. He told us of his memories of American soldiers liberating France. He said he will never forget these men. He told us one of his daughters married an American and lives in Boston. When the rain let up and we walked away, he seemed sorry to see us go.

On the road again, we enjoyed the painterly French light. Later, we passed through some deep forests, then climbed a steep hill to another village, where we spent the night in a municipal pilgrim refuge housed in the same building as the school and mayor's office. An official from the town let us into the room and stopped by later for a glass of wine and some conversation. That evening, I relaxed by drawing the village church in my notebook.

The following day, we arrived at our next destination hot, dirty, and exhausted in the early afternoon. When we entered the hotel where we had planned to spend the night, we found the restaurant below crowded with local people, many of whom turned to look at us. One of the owners, who was busy finishing the lunch service, brought us cold drinks and told us to sit down. When we excused ourselves for our ragged appearance, she reassured us. "This is a very congenial place, she told us. We're all friends here." An hour later, she took us upstairs to our room and told us when we should come back for dinner. The only other guests were a German couple a few years older than us, who were riding their bicycles back to Germany from Spain. The owner insisted that the four of us sit together and enjoy the meal and conversation. At one point, both the owners and the cook joined us for a drink. Though we'd been speaking English with the German couple, everyone switched to French. As the young owner had assured us earlier, it was a congenial place.

After a week of walking, we came to Nevers, the first city we'd seen in a week. We had already walked 100 kilometers. At the hotel, the receptionist looked at our backpacks and insisted we pay in advance. After a shower and a change of clothes, we went to a restaurant downtown, where we ordered a hamburger and listened to a recording of Eric Clapton singing "Tears in Heaven." The following day, we visited the gothic cathedral and palace. The cathedral had been refurbished recently with new stained-glass windows designed by six different contemporary artists. We loved the contrast between the medieval stonework and the colorful modern designs.

Despite my lifelong rejection of organized religion, it seemed only right that we open ourselves to the full experience of the pilgrimage. Consequently, while in Nevers we visited the *Espace Bernadette*, the place where Saint Bernadette is "buried" (fully preserved in a glass coffin), on the grounds of the Sisters of Charity congregation. As a child, I remember seeing the 1943 movie *The Song of Bernadette* about the life of Bernadette Soubirous, a fourteen-year-old girl whose neighbors and community had scorned her for having experienced visions of The Virgin Mary while playing with her friends in a grotto near Lourdes. Years later, she suffered uncomplainingly through a painful illness and death while living as a nun at the Sisters of Charity in Nevers. It was a moving story and it had stayed with me.

Just inside the entrance, we struck up a conversation with one of the volunteers who was welcoming guests and answering questions. When we told him we were pilgrims, he asked about our journey and Donna mentioned her blisters. To our surprise, he offered to examine her feet, as he was a nurse by profession. Donna felt much better after he reassured her that she was doing exactly what she should to care for the blisters.

After visiting the museum and chapel, we walked through the gardens. Surrounded by high walls, the tranquil *Espace Bernadette* seemed far removed from the city that surrounded it. After lunch, we strolled along the medieval ramparts of the city and came across a gorgeous rose arbor near the old tower gatehouse. The arbor made Donna happy, in spite of her blisters, and she took photos with the inexpensive digital camera we had purchased for the trip. Donna took so many excellent photographs with that camera during our journey that we later collected them in a book that documented our trip.

Outside of Nevers, we stayed at Magny-Cours, site of a Formula One racetrack. As a treat, we spent the night at a hotel next to the racecourse, where we enjoyed a luxurious room with a huge, soft bed. In this part of France, we often passed handsome cream-colored cows. Local restaurants frequently featured beef as a main course. At the hotel restaurant in Magny-Cours, we ate steak for dinner, with raspberry tart and flan for dessert.

The next day, we came across the first pilgrims we'd seen along the trail: first a lone German man, and then, a few minutes later, a Dutch couple. After introductions and talk about life on the Camino, we took off walking together through the forest, all of us still carrying on various conversations in a mixture of French, English, and German. After several minutes, the trail dipped and disappeared into a shallow creek. One by one, we removed our boots and waded across the rocky stream. The German crossed first, then came back to help the others. He even carried Donna's pack across for her. On the other side, we congratulated each other on the successful crossing, took photos, and celebrated with chocolate. Then, the Dutch gentleman noticed something through the trees: a small concrete footbridge that remarkably none of us had seen. Clearly, it was more important for us to share the crossing than to see the bridge. We all had a good laugh and took more pictures.

That same afternoon, a big storm caught us in the middle of nowhere. It was Donna's birthday, and we were walking through a deluge. An hour later, we arrived completely soaked at our *chambre d'hôte*, a big, modern house in a tiny village, where our hosts dried our boots in an incubator they used for hatching chicks. After a delicious home-cooked dinner and a couple hours of conversation, they opened a bottle of champagne so that we could all celebrate Donna's birthday with a toast and some dessert. The next day, we walked along the Canal de Berry, one of the most scenic sections of the trail in France.

We followed the canal to a town where we spent the night and ate dinner in the restaurant downstairs. The only other client was a foreigner like us, though we didn't speak to him. The next morning, Donna called to reserve a room in a little hotel farther along the route and the owner said they were closed that night but she would leave the door open for us. She said that the restaurant was also closed but we could eat in the room, so we packed some bread, cheese, salami, and chocolate for a picnic. When we got to the hotel and entered the room, we found a cooler on the table with a wonderful meal, including dessert and wine waiting for us.

The next day, along the trail we encountered the same man we'd seen at the restaurant a couple days earlier. He told us his name was Louis, and he was walking from Holland to Santiago to honor the memory of his wife, who he'd recently lost to illness. As his walking pace was faster than ours, we arranged to meet again that evening at the bed and breakfast in Châteaumeillant where we had both planned to stay. The house, painted with pink accents, also featured a pink bedroom. The owner, Madame Chabbert, asked us to buy bread for dinner when we went out for a walk around the town. When we didn't ask her to reimburse us for the bread, she became more friendly. She served us a rum and fruit juice aperitif, followed by a delicious meal. After coffee, we sat in her parlor and listened to her stories for hours.

In the morning, a woman reached over her fence to give us handfuls of cherries she'd just picked when she saw us walking by her house. While some of the people who live along the Camino ignore the pilgrims, others make an effort to help them on their journey.

Following the Camino route in France on the *Voie de Vézelay* challenged our map-reading ability at times, as the printed directions in our guide didn't always correspond to the signs posted on trees, light posts, and fences. At times of confusion, the topographic maps we carried helped us stay on track. Better still were the directions we got from local people. Poorly or incorrectly marked trails and inaccurate instructions meant that each new day brought surprises, detours, changes, and confusion. In the Dordogne, we once traveled seven miles without seeing any signs and ended up walking alongside a major highway until we could find a safe place to cross, join a road, and follow it into a town where we could then pick up the Camino trail again.

Though the maps and guides were updated each year, the routes changed constantly due to local politics and a general lack of coordination and communication, as regional clubs and groups administered and maintained each section of the trail. Some towns wanted pilgrims to pass through and spend money at cafes and shops, while others preferred to be off the route. Land owners moved their fences and opened up new pastures. Trees fell and foot bridges got washed away in floods. Sometimes, when the Camino intersected with or joined one of the national trail system routes, we found multiple, often contradictory markers. We spent a lot of time staring at maps. Sometimes we got lost and wandered for miles in the wrong direction.

On the trail between Gargilesse-Dampierre and Crozant, we missed a turn because someone had left a pile of freshly cut timber in front of the trail marker as we passed through a hamlet. We then wandered four or five kilometers along a forest path and dirt roads through the hills in the wrong direction. Hopelessly lost, we flagged down the first and only vehicle we had seen and asked for directions. The driver, a young woman on her way to work, looked at our map and told us we were far off course. She pointed to the back of her little Renault camionette. "Get in," she said, "I'll take you back to where you should be." When she dropped us back in the hamlet, we told her that she was an angel. As she drove away, we saw the marker behind the wood pile near a stone barn covered in climbing vines with red flowers.

On the way out of Crozant, we followed a set of markers that showed post-Impressionist paintings from the Crozant School of artists who had painted views of the landscape around the town, particularly along the Sédelle. The old watermills along the creek are particularly beautiful. Dozens of small *châteaux* dot the landscape. Most are privately owned. Among the most picturesque sights were the ruins of medieval fortresses near La Châtre, Gargilesse-Dampierre, and Crozant.

Between Crozant and La Souterraine, we crossed cultivated fields, wandered back roads, and passed through deep woods. For lunch, we stopped at a tiny restaurant in a hamlet, where the fixed price meal was stewed rabbit and noodles (though the owner kindly offered to fry a steak for Donna instead of the bunny). Late that afternoon, we came across a wooden box and a homemade wooden bench and chair in the middle of nowhere. Inside the box, we found a notebook wrapped in plastic and a pen for pilgrims to write messages to each other. A lot of them, like us, thanked whomever had placed the bench there.

After walking another 110 kilometers over a five-day period, our feet had become really sore. From razor-sharp thorn bushes, to cars speeding recklessly around blind curves, to close encounters with cows, bulls, sheep, horses, and donkeys, to wet and rocky stair-step steep trails, to furiously barking village dogs, to nearly invisible electrified fences, to clothes-invading beetles, we'd encountered our share of hazards along the way. Perhaps the most dangerous was the triangular-headed viper that slithered rapidly across the trail a footstep in front of Donna's boot.

Exhausted after hours of walking, we limped into Bénévent-l'Abbaye. We had reserved a room in the only hotel in town, a converted mansion that had formerly been a private residence with large rooms, high ceilings, and windows that overlooked the town. Best of all, our room had a bathtub where we could soak our tired feet and muscles. For a couple of days, we became tourists instead of pilgrims and we enjoyed visiting the church and shops in town. While relaxing at a local tea room, we heard cars honking in front of the church and we ran outside, along with the owner of the shop, to watch a wedding procession. The beautiful bride smiled happily and waved as we took her picture.

Our next stop was Saint-Léonard-de-Noblat, a very old town with an oddly configured church that holds the tomb of the saint for whom the town had been named. Saint-Léonard-de-Noblat was one of the most venerated saints of the late Middle Ages. He converted to Christianity along with King Clovis, at Christmas in 496. According to legend, Léonard then became a hermit in the forests near Limoges. Through his prayers, the queen of the Franks safely bore a male child, and in recompense Clovis gave Léonard royal lands at Noblat, thirteen miles from Limoges. There he founded the abbey of Noblat, around which a village grew, named in his honor. Also, according to legend, prisoners who invoked him were released or saw their chains break before their eyes. Many came to him afterwards, leaving their chains and irons in the church as an offering. Some remained with him, and he gave them parts of his vast forest to clear and farm so that they could live an honest life. Even today, the basilica bears witness to hundreds of testimonials from former prisoners.

We arrived in Saint-Léonard-de-Noblat around noon, ate lunch at a cafe, and visited the church. It was moving to read the testimonials from so many prisoners who had visited the church to give thanks for their release. Though usually not one for prayers, I nevertheless offered up my wish that every political prisoner held anywhere in the world would be released. More specifically, Donna lit candles for two Americans who had recently been detained in Iran and for a young Israeli soldier who had been taken prisoner while patrolling the West Bank. We were happy when we learned that all three were released within a month.

Several kilometers outside of Limoges, we stayed in a bed and breakfast housed in a sixteenth-century priory. The owners came to pick us up on the road to Limoges, after we called to say we couldn't find the house. When we arrived, they brought tea and cookies on a tray to our room. After a shower and a change of clothes, we sat in the lovely garden behind the house. Later, the owners told us about the property.

After the French Revolution, the monks who had lived in the priory abandoned their agricultural enterprise and the estate passed into private ownership. It was eventually purchased by the Chastagner family, proprietors of one of the better-known Limoges porcelain manufacturers. While Chastagner porcelain is no longer produced commercially, the heirs are in the process of reintroducing classic designs in handmade artisan quality originals created in the studio attached to the priory. Amid all this history, we enjoyed an amazing dinner, a quiet, restful night, and a typical French breakfast.

The next day, we arrived in Limoges, roughly 420 kilometers from where we had started in Vézelay, and about a quarter of the way to Santiago de Compostela. We found Limoges to be an attractive, modern city, with *trompe-l'œil* paintings on the sides of buildings in the shopping district, and a wealth of museums, most notably the National Porcelain Museum. At the Museum of Fine Arts, we saw paintings of the exact scenes we had passed through the previous week.

We also visited *Les Halles,* the big indoor market in Limoges, which reminded us of the old photograph of my grandfather, August Pusateri, in his fruit and vegetable stall at the city market in Pittsburgh. Whereas that black and white Depression-era photograph seems stark and foreboding, the colorful market in Limoges, filled with special gourmet foods and museum worthy produce, symbolizes the joy that French people express through their love of well-prepared food.

* * *

In the months before we began our trip, I tried to break in a pair of expensive hiking boots, but they gave me a never-ending series of blisters. No matter how patiently I worked at bending the leather to my will, those boots simply didn't suit my feet. Instead, I considered using low-cut trail shoes, but in the end chose a pair of light hiking boots that provided support for my ankles while having enough flexibility to keep my feet happy. While the boots never gave me a single blister, they caused me other problems.

Though we tried to limit the weight of our packs to under twenty pounds, there were times when we carried more. Walking all day over a combination of rough, rocky terrain and pavement, even the light weight of my pack put additional stress on my feet, as my boots lacked the stiffness and thick-soled construction of more traditional hiking boots. Consequently, on the days we walked long distances, the soles of my feet began to ache every step I took past twenty kilometers. I remember first feeling a burning sensation, as though I were walking barefoot on hot coals, followed by occasional piercing pain like stepping on a sharp rock or a nail. There were days when I felt as though I limped for hours down the road and into whatever town or hamlet had been our destination for the night. For most of the trip, Donna had blisters and I had aching soles. We both spent a lot of time soaking and massaging our feet.

No matter how tough the going had been the day before, nor how ragged and exhausted we'd felt when we arrived at our destination, the following morning we'd get up early, stow our gear in our backpacks, eat breakfast, and head out onto the trail with joy and enthusiasm. Buoyed by the night's rest, fresh croissants and bread, strong coffee, and the cool morning air, we cherished the first kilometers of each new day. Our legs felt capable and our spirit willing. Wrapped in clean socks and moleskin, even our feet were content, at least for the moment.

Next to our shoes, the most important items we owned were our breathable raincoats and waterproof pants. We invested a lot of money in those rain jackets, and we were glad we did, as it seemed we used them at least half the days we walked in France. It was an unusually wet summer. On days when it did not rain, the sun beat down on us. There were times when we put on rain pants and took them off again two or three times during a single morning.

As we traveled along the Chemin de Saint-Jacques through France, we found very few places to sit along the way. Most days, we ate our lunch or rested sitting on the ground. Occasionally, we'd come across a bench or a picnic table in one of the towns or villages we passed through. Once, we found a couple of wicker chairs that the owner of a house had put out in front of his property. "Pilgrims. Take a rest here!" a sign read. Elsewhere, people had carved a bench out of a fallen tree or set out sections of sawn tree trunks as stools. For long distance hikers, even the smallest gestures matter.

On our journey, we learned not to take simple things for granted. When you are hungry and worn out, each meal is a cause for thanks and celebration. When you are hot and sweaty, your clothes covered in dust, a communal shower in a hostel or shabby hotel feels like a day spa. When you have walked from early morning until evening, a shared fruit cocktail and a quiet conversation with a stranger in the salon of a private bed and breakfast, or a meal cheerfully cooked and served in a cafe can be a balm for the spirit. A pleasant waitress can be a blessing and fresh bread in the morning a sacrament.

Even a bad meal can be good on the Camino. Once, at a cheap hotel near the end of our walk, we sat down to a breakfast of dry and chalky cookies. The instant coffee tasted like bitter, brackish water, but at least it was hot. Though we knew damned well that the food was awful, we couldn't help from feeling thankful for it anyway.

* * *

When we got to Limoges, we had planned to take a break from our walk and join our English friends Steve and Judie for another cave art tour. From Limoges we took a train to Brive-la-Gaillard, where Steve met us at the station, then drove us to our hotel in Les Eyzies, a village known as "the Capitol of Prehistory." The limestone cliff above the Abri Cro-Magnon, where the first complete Cro-Magnon skeletons had been discovered, forms part of the back wall of the hotel in which we stayed. The old chateau and National Museum of Prehistory are a few hundred feet down the road.

The next day, we visited the caves at Font-de-Gaume and Les Combarelles, both an easy walk from the village of Les Eyzies. Then we went with our friends to the Lot Valley. After a visit to the decorated cave at Cougnac, we toured Pech Merle, which is the most astounding of the caves I have seen. The entire subterranean complex seems to be a living being. The rock surfaces give the illusion at times of being soft living tissue or internal organs; one sees limestone nerves, muscles, brains. One narrow passage is indicative of the birth canal. Elsewhere, one notes a white stalactite that resembles a phallus.

While known for the painting of the famous "spotted horses," Pech Merle contains a far more impressive natural attraction. In one of the cavernous rooms an enormous, complete horse head and neck jut out from the ceiling, dominating the space below. How anyone can enter this huge gallery and fail to see what can only be described as "The Horse God" is beyond my comprehension, yet the guide and the entire tour group walked past without ever looking up. Likewise, few people remark on the many folded concretions that clearly resemble mammoths. While the original artists engraved or outlined in black or red the natural shapes of animals they saw on the limestone concretions, there are no doubt hundreds more unadorned animal figures to be found within the natural formations of the cave.

Pech Merle is also notable for its human depictions, both the "wounded man" and the various female representations and "bison women." Is the man pierced by multiple spears a metaphor for physical decay, suffering, and death? The underground has long been associated with the unconscious in literature. What kinds of insights did the Cro-Magnon cave artists bring back with them to the daylight?

The following day, we drove to the Pyrenees Mountains to see the painted caves at Niaux and Gargas, among others. I kept another notebook along the way, and recorded both sketches I made of the art we saw and writings about my impressions. Unlike many of the other caves we've seen, Niaux has been left in a "raw" state, which means it is almost entirely unlit. Visitors instead carry their own flashlights through a series of huge caverns leading to the "Salon Noir" nearly a kilometer from the entrance. As one enters the decorated gallery, the guide asks visitors to extinguish their lamps. Finally, after a moment of total darkness, the painted wall is dramatically revealed by battery powered spotlights.

The caves at Gargas are notable for the dozens of black and red ochre hand prints on the walls. Throughout the Gargas cave I identified dozens of unpainted animal figures formed by the limestone concretions on the walls. Close to Niaux, in the town of Tarascon, there's an interpretive center that includes facsimiles of prehistoric artwork from several sites. While photography is not permitted in the decorated caves, museum visitors are allowed to photograph the carefully rendered recreations of the artwork. We also visited Le Mas-d'Azil, a huge river tunnel inhabited throughout prehistory.

* * *

After a week of looking at cave art, we headed back to Limoges. The following morning, we took off on foot in the general direction of Spain, passing through the towns of Aixe-sur-Vienne, Chalus, La Coquille, and Thiviers. One day, we walked nineteen kilometers in the rain without ever finding a place to stop and rest: no bench, no wall, no tree stump. We finally sat down in the middle of a gravel path and ate some dried fruit.

I never understood the fascination with zombies in popular novels and movies. In these stories, it's common for hordes of half-decayed ghouls to claw their way out of graveyards to attack travelers who have the bad luck to be passing through zombie-infested small towns. To me, the entire notion of zombies or undead seemed silly—until we arrived in the town of La Coquille.

One might think that a town named "La Coquille" (which means seashell, the symbol of the pilgrimage) would be a welcoming place for those arriving on foot. Instead, we found a town full of negative energy and unsmiling, unhappy people. After an icy reception at the only hotel in town, an unhelpful and cursory response to our question about Wi-Fi hotspots at the mayor's office, and a disdainful snort at the pizza restaurant when we asked to sit outside, we realized that the entire town had been taken over by zombies. After washing down a tasteless pizza with equally tasteless wine, we hurried back to our hotel room and double locked the door behind us. In the movie version, I would have dozed nervously in an arm chair facing the door, a shotgun across my lap.

In the morning, we watched rain drip from the roof across the ugly courtyard outside the dining area of our hotel. Over a breakfast of stale bread and questionable jam, we discussed hastening our departure by taking a train or a taxi out of town. Instead, we put on our rain gear, pulled our hoods over our heads, and took off on foot. A couple of kilometers from town, the negativity dispersed. The only way to escape from the zombies was to walk along the narrow path of the Chemin de Saint-Jacques. We were lucky: instead of being trapped for eternity in the train station, our mouths filled with dust, our limbs torn asunder and strewn rudely around us, we escaped to the land of the living. On the outskirts of the next town, Thiviers, we met an old man who shook our hands. "Pray for me in Santiago," he said.

As we walked through rural France, we were often struck by how much the country has changed since we lived in Langlade in 1982. With increasing levels of prosperity, the European Union, and the influence of American popular culture, we seem to be heading toward a homogenous and increasingly mindless monoculture. Nevertheless, walking through the woods and cultivated fields, past ancient ruins, castles, water mills, and fortified farms, there are times when it is easy to imagine nothing has changed since the Middle Ages, since Roman times, since prehistory. The roads themselves feel timeless, the route traveled by pilgrims for over a thousand years, and before them by Roman legions, who laid stones over the footpaths blazed thousands of years earlier by bands of migrating hunter-gatherers. Traversing a forest one day, lost in our own thoughts and lulled by the rhythm of our footsteps, we were surprised by a deep roar that seemed to fill the woods around us. Suddenly a passenger train appeared on a partially hidden embankment above us to the right, startling us back into the present.

We stayed two days in Thiviers, as it was one of the towns we had wanted to investigate as possible places to live in the future. However, like Bénévent-l'Abbye and La Souterraine, we couldn't imagine ourselves settling in such a place permanently. In spite of the appealing medieval architecture, the town felt claustrophobic, dull, and lifeless.

Rural France seems to be dying a painfully slow death, as young people continue to leave for better opportunities in the cities.

One day, Donna took our dirty clothes to the laundry and returned to the hotel with a surprise date for a guided tour of a medieval church in one of the neighboring towns. While waiting for the clothes to dry, she had met a woman from a nearby town and had conversed about a range of topics, including the complex history of the local church. The following day, we met Noelle in Sorges. As she had authored a monograph on the history and architecture of the church, she gave us a detailed tour. Forty minutes later, her husband arrived and they invited us to join them for dinner at the lovely farmhouse they had restored.

Thus, we spent a completely unexpected and memorable evening with two delightful, intelligent people who opened their home and their lives to complete strangers. They cooked bison sausages and served us a peach wine aperitif. During the meal, Michel told us that his father had been a soldier from the United States who had been part of the Normandy landing. He knew his name only because his mother had given him a pocket-sized government issue French phrase book with his father's name in it. For the past few years, Michel had been searching, with the help of an American investigator, for connections to his family there. Six years later, we heard from Noelle and Michel again, via an email sent to my web site. We wrote back and began a conversation in which Michel told us about locating his family in the United States. He had five half-sisters living in Utah. He and Noelle had gone to see them and some of his sisters had visited them in France. We were happy for him to have finally solved the mystery of his past and found his missing family.

Near Cornille, we spent a night in a fortified farm complex. That morning, we again lost our way in a forest. We had missed any trail markings and we had not seen any roads or landmarks that were on the map for the past hour. We walked until we passed what looked like a Boy Scout Camp. When we came out of the wood, we stumbled onto the exact address of the *chambre d'hôte* we were looking for, surrounded by forest and connected only by a dirt road. The house itself was very rustic, with a thick square tower. Our room reminded us of the apartment in which we had lived in Langlade years earlier. The owner, a *vicomtesse*, was a local potter.

We spent July fourteenth, Bastille Day, in the city of Périgueux. Among the festivities was a singing competition, complete with a table of judges. The competition took place in a square next to the cathedral. Most of the contestants were excellent, though one girl forgot the words to her song and asked to begin again. The judges stopped her halfway through her second attempt. Predictably, she couldn't accept that she didn't advance to the final round and sang next to the tent in which the judges were deliberating. The French love fireworks on the fourteenth of July as much as Americans do on the fourth. In Périgueux, they shoot them off over the river. Beneath our hotel window, people gathered on the bridge to watch the show.

Originally a Gallo-Roman city called Vesunna, Périgueux is known for its beautiful Romanesque cathedral and medieval quarter. The city also has ruins of a Roman amphitheater, a temple dedicated to a Gallic goddess, and what must have once been a very swank villa. The latter can be seen enclosed in a glass structure containing both the ruins of the villa and a museum of artifacts uncovered in and around the site. We found the architecture of the largely glass museum impressive by itself.

While we were in Périgueux, Steve and Judie drove up from Montignac and took us to see a nearby castle. Afterward, we enjoyed couscous at an outdoor restaurant. The next day we took off on foot again. After passing through Saint-Foy-la-Grande, we took a side trip to Bergerac, an attractive city on the Dordogne River. In addition to multiple statues of the famous character, Cyrano de Bergerac, the narrow streets of the old section of town include many pretty squares, churches, and buildings.

During the summer months, every French city, town, village, and hamlet has its own festivals and fairs. In Saint-Sever they even have one based on a local type of cake. These evening market celebrations often include sausages laid out on long tables in baskets. French butcher shops make sausages from just about anything, including bison, wild boar, donkey, elk, and duck.

As we closed in on the Spanish border, it rained hard every day, all day long. Though miserable, we slogged on, thinking the next day would be better, but it never was. Sometimes people in cars took pity on us and pulled over to ask if they could give us a ride into the next town. They had no idea how wet we were. We always declined, telling them we'd ruin their upholstery. When we finally arrived, we found the towns and villages flooded. The summer festivals had all been canceled or postponed because of the rain. On we walked, through soggy forests, along muddy trails, on blacktop splashed with driving rain. One day, we entered a town with ankle-high water pooled on the empty streets. The people looked sad and disappointed. Posters advertising events for their fair hung in the shop windows. The stage on the main square floated over a pond of dirty water. We looked at each other and knew part of our camino was coming to an end.

From Saint-Sever to Orthez, we continued walking through driving rain. We arrived at our destinations completely soaked from head to feet, took a hot shower, ate, went to bed, got up in the morning and did it again. We came to understand firsthand an expression one hears along the Chemin de Saint-Jacques: *La pluie du matin n'arrête pas le pèlerin* (the morning rain doesn't stop the pilgrim). We tried to tell ourselves that hot, sunny weather would be worse.

One day, as we were sitting under a sliver of shelter somewhere in the middle of nowhere, we met a young man from Holland who approached us out of the rain smiling and waving a half empty bag of potato chips. He joined us in the shelter and we offered him some dried fruit as we waited for the rain let up a little. Like most Dutch people, he spoke good English, as well as French, Spanish, and German. He told us he was walking from Holland to Santiago de Compostela following a set of strict, self-imposed rules. He carried no money and no phone and walked a predetermined set of stages averaging about thirty kilometers a day. To eat and sleep, he depended on the kindness of strangers and of local mayors, farmers, and clergy. Though he accepted small donations of food or money to cover the cost of a night at a hostel or refuge, he asked for nothing, offering instead to perform chores in trade. We walked through the rain with this polite, articulate, and well-educated young man until we came to a restaurant, where we bought him the first real meal he'd had in three days, as he'd been living on bread and sardines, along with that bag of chips he'd found on a park bench.

Over lunch he explained why he'd set out on the camino. Though he only gave us his first name, which I don't recall after all these years, he told us he was from an extremely wealthy family. After finishing graduate school, he'd been groomed for a top management position in the family business. Now, at the age of twenty-eight, he was about to assume responsibility for part of the operation of a large multinational corporation. Before he stepped into this role, he had wanted to take some time to reflect on his life and his values and to gain further insight into humanity, society, and himself. He had wanted to walk across France and Spain as a humble pilgrim with no money and no position in society. When we asked him what he had learned thus far, he laughed. Though I don't recall exactly what he replied, I remember his answer was both enigmatic, soulful, and deep.

After the meal, we gathered up our packs and rain gear. As it was still raining hard, Donna and I decided to spend the night at a hotel in town, but Super Pilgrim slipped his pack onto his back and set off down the road, his head covered by the hood of his jacket. He had another twelve kilometers to go. Before he left, we gave him the food we had in our packs and a little money for the hostel in Orthez.

Though we continued as far as Orthez, approximately 600 kilometers from Vézelay, the rain had broken our spirit. Donna's cousin Kathy had called a week earlier to offer us the use of her apartment in Paris while she visited family in the United States. At the time, we had told her we'd give it some thought. As we'd finally had enough of slogging through the mud with the hard rain in our faces, we decided to take advantage of free lodgings in Paris. From Orthez, we got on the train to Bordeaux, where we spent two days exploring the city, then continued on to Paris.

* * *

We had explored Paris on several earlier trips. Each time we had visited different museums. Since we had two weeks in Kathy's apartment, we made a list of some of the lesser-known attractions and museums in the city and went to see one each day. We saw the Chagall ceilings at the Opéra. We visited the Père Lachaise Cemetery, the Parc de Buttes Chaumont, the Passage Jouffroy, the Paris bird market, and Les Arènes de Lutèce. We walked along the Promenade Plantée and the Canal Martin. We looked for antiques at the Marché aux Puces. We ate lunch at the rooftop *terrasse* of the Galleries Lafayette. We visited the Musée des Arts et Métiers and the Musée Carnavalet. We went to a bookstore where I talked with the owner I'd dealt with back when I was running Asylum Arts. He agreed to send me a copy of the typescript of the first part of Edouard Roditi's autobiography. I bought some pastel sticks at the Sennelier shop across from the Seine.

In general, Americans tend to love French culture (art, food, perfume, fashion, monuments, history, etc.) but often dislike and misunderstand the French. Most Americans expect the French to be more like the British, who despite some quaintness, are for us more comprehensible. In reality, however, the French are an alien people, with a singular connection to their land and their own unique traditions and institutions dating back hundreds and sometimes thousands of years.

These days, France is itself in a state of transition, as it tries, with varying degrees of success, to assimilate a large number of second- or third-generation citizens from Africa and the Middle East. One day on the Métro, I saw a young woman dressed modestly from head to foot in black and wearing a headscarf and a t-shirt printed in large white block letters that read: "F C K" Then, in smaller print: "the only thing missing is u."

I wonder how much of our world we really understand.

* * *

We had prepaid for a two-week intensive Spanish language course in Pamplona. After two months of unseasonably cloudy, wet and cool weather in France, it was sunny, clear, and very hot in Spain. We found Pamplona to be a beautiful city, perfect for walking. From the old city ramparts, one can see the Pyrenees mountains in the distance. We stayed in the historic downtown. Our hotel room overlooked a convent, where one day we saw some young nuns in habits take turns riding a pink bicycle around the courtyard.

Weekdays we had four hours of intensive Spanish language classes each morning. The first day we wandered out of the building in a daze and agreed not to speak French again until we left Spain. Overall, the teachers at the school were excellent. Though we tried to practice what we learned in our classes with waiters and the hotel staff, after two weeks we understood very little and could speak even less. Nevertheless, it was a good introduction to the language.

Ever since Ernest Hemingway published his novel *The Sun Also Rises* in 1926, Pamplona has been famous for the running of the bulls, which occurs as part of the festival of San Fermin in early July. Throughout the year, shops in the historic area offer bull-related souvenirs. Tourists visit the two bullfighting museums, the bullring, and a statue honoring those who participate in the *encierro*.

We loved Spain. The people smiled and laughed easily. They seemed relaxed and affectionate. While we had trouble getting used to eating lunch at 2:00 or 3:00 in the afternoon and dinner at 10:00 or 11:00 at night, we did find ourselves taking siestas and staying up later and later. On Saturday nights, in parks all over town, bands and disc jockeys play loud dance music until 3:00 in the morning. Everyone, young and old, ventures into the streets. Even on weeknights, what seems like hundreds of little bars teem with customers. The narrow streets swarm with people moving from bar to bar. In the main square, the Plaza de Castillo, musicians play traditional music as dozens of people join in the folk dances. Everywhere you look there are people, dogs, babies in strollers, children, elderly couples, families, lovers and friends enjoying themselves and each other. Dignified and without inhibition, controlled and chaotic, the Spanish stay up late.

After we finished our language course, we left Pamplona, not on foot, but on the train, not headed up a steep grade and onto the treeless, sunbaked plains, but to the museums, restaurants and beaches of Barcelona. We had enjoyed walking through France. It was an amazing and fulfilling experience. However, after three months on the road, we were physically exhausted. So, we abandoned the Camino and set out on our own, with no prescribed route.

Barcelona is an amazing city. We went to the Picasso Museum and to the beach, ate Mexican food and drank Guinness at an English pub. It's that kind of place. A fan of Art Nouveau, I looked forward to seeing Antoni Gaudí's famous unfinished cathedral-size church in Barcelona, the Sagrada Família. According to the tourist web sites, the church is the number one attraction in a city that does not lack for interesting sites. Tourists swarm around the church from every angle, cameras in hand, while the edifice itself, sheeted in webbing and scaffolding and bristling with cranes, is still a work in progress. Though it's a fascinating structure, it seems to have somehow gone conceptually astray. Like the Winchester Mystery House, one wonders if it will ever be finished, or ever quite make sense. Despite some reservations, I admit that I like it, if only for its obvious eccentricity, even if it does look like something built by an enormous army of barn swallows, mud daubers, and African termites.

After a week in Barcelona, we headed back into France, where we visited Carcassonne. In 1979, Donna and I had been to the famous walled city, arriving in the early hours of the morning, after a twelve-hour train trip from Rome. Along the way, I'd consumed a cheese sandwich that had turned in the intense heat and given me a powerful dose of food poisoning. So, I never really saw much of the city. It was good to get a second chance.

Next, we traveled to Narbonne, then took a bus to the ocean, where we found ourselves an inexpensive rental a few steps from a wide, sandy, five-mile-long beach at Saint-Pierre-la-Mer. The weather and the water were warm and we enjoyed both the beach and the community. It was fun to be at a resort frequented almost entirely by French people. Since the official French vacations end on September first, when the kids go back to school, the only people left were older couples like us. We found it life-affirming to see so many older people relaxing on the beach, frolicking in the sea, eating in the restaurants, and shopping at the outdoor market.

After a week at the beach, we traveled to Nîmes. We arrived in time for the Feria des Vendanges, a festival that celebrates the grape harvest. From there, we went to the village of Langlade to see the process first-hand. A couple months after our wedding, we had spent eight months there at the home of friends who own a vineyard and winery. The family has played an important role in the life of the village for at least 700 years. In 1982, there were 200 inhabitants. Our experience then had given us a taste of authentic rural French life.

Thirty years later, the village has expanded to 2,000 inhabitants. The formerly abandoned stone town houses have been renovated, the ancient windmill restored. There are now shops and a thriving boulangerie in the village. Langlade has also become a bedroom community for upwardly mobile people who work in Nîmes or Montpellier. Rows of tacky stucco "villas" with swimming pools and garages now adjoin the village.

We spent five days in Langlade with Lis and Eliane. Most of the time, we tried to stay out of the way and help where we could with the preparations and processes of the vendange. Lis had hired a crew of mostly Moroccan laborers to pick the grapes, while her partner Michel and a friend of his drove the tractor and did much of the heavy labor. The entire crew ate lunch together in the house each day.

One day, Donna and I took off to revisit some of the local sights we remembered from the time we had lived there so many years earlier. We walked to the ruins of a pre-Roman Gallic town in the hills, where we sat under some olive trees and looked out over the valley below. Though Langlade had changed, the landscape remained the same. We felt thousands of years in the rocks under our feet. A dry breeze rustled through the scrub pines.

That evening, Lis took us to buy chèvre, or goat's milk cheese, from a local man who raised goats. A big white mare followed him around the property. The goats came to him when he called. Dozens of them surrounded us, nuzzling and rubbing against us. They were as clean as cats, as friendly and tame as dogs. Though I've never liked the bitter bite of goat cheese, the fresh little white rounds made from the milk of these happy animals tasted smooth, creamy, and delicious, a perfect complement to the full-bodied red wine Lis produced in her historic winery.

A week later, in mid-October, we were back in Virginia, wondering what we would do next. I had a one man show of my cave art inspired paintings forthcoming at the Academy of Fine Arts during the month of January, so I got to work making a new series of paintings and preparing for the show. At the same time, after four months on the road in Europe, our life in Virginia seemed one dimensional and uninspired. Donna paced around the apartment and took long walks. We both sensed somehow that we'd already moved on.

* * *

As I look back upon our Camino now, I can see how deeply the experience changed us. Afterward, Donna and I were never quite able to return to our previous lives in the United States. Our experience had made us question our values. We had begun a journey that required us to move forward rather than backward.

Donna had worked for many years to support us financially. Now, I wanted the two of us to spend our time together, learning another language, enjoying new experiences, and meeting new people. Though we looked into downtown real estate with the idea of opening a gallery, there were no opportunities for people with our limited means. Donna halfheartedly looked for a job and for once didn't immediately find a good match. We took a trip to Florida to visit Donna's cousin and along the way saw our son, who was temporarily stationed for training at a base in Birmingham, Alabama. While in Florida, we looked at a small house that was for sale in Saint Petersburg, in a neighborhood popular with artists a few blocks from the ocean. We were glad when the property turned out to be more expensive than we could realistically afford.

After my show at the Academy of Fine Arts in Lynchburg closed in February, we researched Spanish language schools in Latin America and decided to take a two-month immersion course in Cuenca, Ecuador, which had a reputation as both a beautiful city and a place where people spoke a pure, clearly enunciated Spanish. Before we left for Ecuador, my chiropractor offered Donna a job managing her new clinic in Amherst when we returned. We told ourselves it was a good opportunity, but I don't think either of us really believed we'd go back to live in Amherst. We've never been good at retracing our steps.

Instead, we sold our car and most of our possessions and went to live in Ecuador. Two years later, we sold our loft in Lynchburg. Over the years, we slowly gave up whatever possessions we still owned in the United States. On one of our trips back to Lynchburg, I dispersed my entire library. Later I donated my archives and the future rights to my books to the University of California, and gave what remained of my artwork to non-profit organizations in Virginia. In Spain, a few years later, we would let our driver's licenses expire and become vegetarians.

The Camino is a state of mind, a metaphorical journey that has no real beginning nor end. Here are a few things I learned along the way: Keep your mind and your heart open. Teach what you know and learn whatever you can. Accept and embrace change. Remember that everything is a gift, if you know how to unwrap it. Be humble and grateful. Make wisdom your goal. Love everything and everyone. Do the best you can. Put one foot in front of the other. Breathe deeply. Walk in the light with your eyes open.

Santa Ana de los Cuatro Rios de Cuenca

> It was dawn in the desert
> west of Santa Fe,
> when Pablo pulled over
> to roll a smoke and pray.
>
> — *Alien Pizza*

ONE OF OUR neighbors on the Avenida 12 de Abril kept guinea pigs stacked in cages in her front yard. In Ecuador, these animals are considered a delicacy, and she raised them to sell for holiday meals. Whenever we walked past her house, she smiled and waved at us through the metal gate. If she happened to be close to the street, she greeted us warmly, though at first we couldn't understand a word she said. Sometimes we'd see her wandering around town. She wore her long, silver hair in a braid and dressed in dark, ankle-length skirts, so she was easy to recognize. Sometimes we'd see her walking along the banks of the Tomebamba River, a bundle of grass with which to feed her animals slung over her shoulder. Though elderly, she was uncommonly tall for an Ecuadorian woman and she carried herself with dignity. Once, I offered to transport the bundle back to her house. She set it down on the sidewalk and smiled. When I lifted it onto my shoulder, I found that it was surprisingly heavy and I wondered how she managed to carry it so far by herself. Back then, Donna and I referred to her as *vecina,* though between us we called her Mrs. Cuy. Later we learned from friends who lived nearby that her name was

Rosita. She was well known in the neighborhood for her stamina, her devotion, and her friendliness.

Over the years, we often talked with Rosita. After we moved downtown, we saw less of her, though she always greeted us with a smile and a traditional kiss on the cheek whenever we encountered her on the street. One reason we had trouble understanding her was that she never opened her mouth when she spoke. We suspected she was missing some teeth. In time, we learned to decipher some of the words that accompanied her elaborate gestures—enough to allow for simple conversations, which always seemed to involve superstition, distrust of government, and devotion to God, who she referred to as *"Deocito."* Like everything else in Ecuador, we never fully understood Rosita, though we nonetheless came to value her kindness, her uncomplicated spirit, and her open heart.

* * *

On our first trip to Ecuador, we flew into Quito, a city of more than a million and a half people, located high in the Andes Mountains. At 9,360 feet, it is the highest capitol city in the world. After getting our passports stamped with tourist visas and picking our luggage out of the carousel, we took a taxi to a surprisingly upscale and modern Howard Johnson hotel not far from the airport. Though we'd made a reservation online with our credit card, the receptionist asked us to pay for the room in cash when we checked in. I remember that we sat in our room upstairs drinking bottled water and gazing out over the city. The tops of many of the surrounding buildings had rebar sticking up from the roof, ready for another floor to be added sometime in the future. We both had a headache, which is a symptom of the altitude sickness visitors to Quito or Cuenca often experience. Neither of us slept well. In the morning, we ate breakfast at the restaurant in the hotel. Most of the male guests wore suits and the women dresses. The food seemed well prepared but strange. Donna ordered black tea with milk and the waitress brought her a cup of hot milk with a tea bag in it. On the way out, we saw a uniformed guard in the lobby carrying a submachine gun.

After breakfast, we took a taxi back to the airport and boarded a flight to Cuenca. Like the old Quito airport, the airport in Cuenca is located close to the center of the city. Both cities fit within valleys surrounded by high mountains. I watched out the window as the plane descended over the surrounding peaks, then circled in a big arc above the city, before it dipped low, passed over a river, cleared the surrounding buildings, and finally touched down. A driver hired by the Spanish school we would be attending waited for us to exit the baggage claim area. He held up a sign with our name on it. The driver helped carry our bags to his car, then took us to an apartment-hotel alongside the Tomebamba River, where we would stay during the two months we studied Spanish in Cuenca.

The first person we met at the Hotel Otorongo was a friendly woman with a round face who worked as a factotum. Sometimes, we saw her in the office performing the duties of a receptionist. Mornings, we'd see her wearing an apron and working as a chambermaid. When she wasn't cleaning, answering the phone, or checking guests into or out of the hotel, she kept busy by repairing broken kitchen utensils or small appliances. She told us her name was Sara, though what she said sounded like "Zara" to our ears. We later learned that she'd worked at the hotel her whole life. The current owner's parents had hired her when she was a teenager. She had helped care for their children, one of whom was now her boss. Though not well paid, nor even much appreciated, she considered herself lucky to have a steady job.

After we stowed our suitcases, we wandered out to look for a place to eat lunch. We had no idea where we were going, so we walked along the big street that ran parallel to the river. It was midafternoon and the few businesses we passed seemed closed. The houses on the street had bars on the windows and high fences and walls. A few dogs barked at us from behind metal gates. When we came to an intersection with a bridge over the river, we crossed the street and walked back toward the hotel. Eventually, we saw a handmade sign written on a sandwich board in front of what looked like a house with a metal fence and open gate in front. The sign read: "Cafe. Brownies." Hoping for a sandwich or some kind of light lunch, we timidly entered the gate.

Like many Ecuadorian businesses, the house doubled as a commercial enterprise that operated on the ground floor, with the living area above. Inside, we found three empty tables. We sat down and a tiny Ecuadorian woman greeted us. When we asked for a menu, she looked at us sadly and told us that she only had coffee and brownies. Donna grimaced, as I ordered one of each. The woman disappeared into what must have been her household kitchen and prepared a cup of instant coffee. She brought it to me in a cracked cup with a lumpy, tasteless brownie on a mismatched desert plate. I chewed the brownie and sipped the hot liquid in silence. After I'd finished eating, the woman charged us a dollar and we left, wondering on what planet we had landed.

Back at the hotel, we asked Sara for a map and told her we needed to buy food. She pointed out a grocery store and a supermarket on the map and marked the best routes with a pen. It seemed like a long walk to the supermarket, so we headed off to the smaller store. There we bought as many groceries as we could carry: bread, butter, jam, canned tuna, eggs, bananas, oatmeal, cookies, chips and a big jug of bottled water. We spent the rest of the weekend huddled inside our hotel room reading books and eating tuna sandwiches and fried eggs with tea and toast.

* * *

On Monday morning, we plotted a course on our map and walked from our hotel along the Tomebamba River, up the steep stairs at the Plaza del Otorongo, past the San Sebastian Church, down Calle Simón Bolívar to Parque Calderon and the Catedral de la Inmaculada Concepción. Then we headed down Calle Luis Cordero to the school where we would study Spanish for the next eight weeks. The scenic walk took nearly half an hour. Our classes began at eight in the morning and lasted until noon. Though there were few people on the streets at seven thirty when we set out, by noon the city bustled with cars, buses, and pedestrians. At first, we marveled at just about everything we saw. Sometimes Donna took pictures along with way. Once, she stopped to take a photo of a dog with his head hanging out of a hole in the cement blocks of an upstairs porch of a tiny, narrow house on Calle Simón Bolívar, half a block from the San Sebastian church.

Our class met Monday through Friday. The tuition we paid allowed us to have our own dedicated teacher. Though a handful of young people from Europe attended the school, the majority of students were retired North Americans. While the secretary and the administrators spoke English, most of the teachers did not. Because wages are so low in Ecuador, our semi-private classes cost roughly the same for two months of instruction as it had cost for two weeks of group lessons in Spain.

We later learned that a wealthy Swede owned the business, along with another school in Quito. He also owned a yacht that took tourists around the Galapagos Islands. Spanish lessons at the school cost $9.00 per hour for the two of us. While the dozen or so young teachers, most of whom held university degrees, worked for the national minimum wage, the most experienced teachers earned $2.50 an hour.

Located in a three-story Spanish colonial style house with a central courtyard, the school had nearly two dozen small rooms used as individual classrooms for private lessons. Halfway through the morning classes, students gathered in a big room on the second floor that served as a library and break room, where they enjoyed coffee or herbal tea and ate five-cent bakery rolls. Once a month, the school hosted a cultural program in the courtyard, during which professors dressed in traditional clothing and performed Ecuadorian music and folk dancing.

Our teacher was six months pregnant when we began our class. Unlike the other instructors, who often took their students for walks around the city and visits to museums and shops where they could practice their Spanish, our teacher didn't want to leave the school, so we stared at each other across a wooden table in one of the little rooms for four hours each day for eight weeks. Though we struggled to understand Spanish, Donna and I diligently worked through the text book with determination. Our knowledge of French grammar helped us with concepts such as reflexive verbs, though French vocabulary constantly came to mind and confounded us whenever we tried to speak.

At first, we found our teacher humorless and dour. She delivered the lessons mechanically, without creativity, and provided little encouragement. She rarely smiled and we wondered if she even knew how to laugh. Though she pointed out every error, she never complimented us for correct answers or work well done. Instead, she pushed us to memorize lists of words and verb conjugations. She gave us hours of homework each day and tested us constantly like a stereotypical schoolmarm. Sometimes she gave us a task to do in class while she read what appeared to be a comic book or graphic novel. For the first couple of weeks, we didn't care much for her, though we knew it was ultimately our responsibility to study hard, work together, and learn as much as we could in order to make the experience valuable for ourselves.

Over time, as she got to know us, mainly through our writing, Bibi began to warm up to us. I would try to amuse her with funny stories and surreal narratives when she asked us to write about our lives. In turn, she began to tell us stories about her own life, or about Ecuadorian customs and superstitions. She loved ghost stories and all things macabre. She tried to shock us with tall tales and funeral customs. She told us how no one in Cuenca was cremated because corpses needed to be sawed into pieces, as the furnaces were too short to burn the entire body at once. She told us about a university friend who had suddenly, and without saying goodbye, disappeared into a convent where the nuns practiced a strict vow of silence and isolation. She told us about her husband's job at the General Tire factory in Cuenca, and how workers there had been maimed horribly or even killed by the machinery.

Little by little, her stories became more personal. She complained about living in the same house as her in-laws. She explained how she had considered herself a strong, independent woman, a feminist, when she was a student at the university. She described in detail the traditional Ecuadorian confinement rituals after giving birth: new mothers are sequestered in a bedroom for forty days and are cared for and served by the family so that they have no distractions from feeding and bonding with their babies. We were surprised to learn that during this time the new mothers are fed only chicken, rice, and vegetables and bathe infrequently. In time, our teacher talked about her disappointments and her unhappiness. She had married young and already had a seven-year-old daughter and a four-year-old son.

After six weeks of total language immersion, our comprehension had improved to the point where we understood much of what we heard, at least when spoken slowly by people whose voices were familiar to us. Still, we could only manage basic responses, as our ability to speak lagged far behind our comprehension. As a teacher, a lecturer, a writer—someone used to expressing ideas and opinions—listening was not a skill I had practiced much. In Ecuador, I had no choice. I learned how to listen. While it frustrated me at times, especially initially, when I felt at a loss for words myself, I realized that being a good listener instead of a self-important windbag opened a path toward spiritual growth, empathy, and wisdom.

Listening carefully built patience and humility, and demonstrated respect and concern for others. During the five years we lived in Cuenca, we made many friends, most of them humble, stoic people: chambermaids, bakers, construction workers, secretaries, artists, students, and teachers. Despite their stoicism, they were candid and open-hearted. The majority of them confided in us regularly, in ways they couldn't with their families. They gave me insights into their culture and shared their hopes and dreams. They also helped me to become a more complete and healthy person.

About a week before our classes ended and we left Cuenca, our teacher unlocked the door to our little classroom, switched on the overhead light, removed her coat and scarf, unpacked her books, and sat behind her desk, just as she had so many other days. However, instead of asking to see our homework or telling us to open our textbooks to a particular page, Bibi stared at us for a moment across the desk. "I don't really know how to express this," she said, "but there's something very important that I want to tell you." Though normally controlled and rigid, her voice shook with emotion, which made us shift slightly in our chairs. We looked at her and nodded for her to continue.

What followed was an unexpected emotional deluge. She admitted that when we first met she was suffering. She felt trapped in her own body, a body that to her seemed controlled by the attitudes of the culture and the people around her. She told us that the day we came to the school to begin our classes, she had been so distraught that she had not known whether she would be able to speak to us, let alone offer us any instruction. She had not even known whether she would return to the school the following day. "But over the weeks something happened," she said, wiping the tears from her eyes. Then she told us that she wanted to thank us for what we had done for her.

Donna and I looked at each other, then at her. We started to respond, but she stopped us. "Please let me continue," she said. Then she explained how through our actions and attitude we had modeled patience, kindness, and friendship. More importantly, through our interaction with and support of each other we had demonstrated how a man and a woman could foster growth and love, how they could act in harmony and enjoy each other's companionship. It was clear to her that we loved each other deeply, that we were the best of friends. We had given her hope that she and her husband could also learn to love each other. "I know it's all going to be okay now," she said. "I wanted to thank you."

Her confession was so raw with emotion that it left us shaking. When she finished talking, we stood up and the three of us hugged each other. I don't recall what we said to her, though we continued talking for hours. It didn't seem to matter that our Spanish was limited and rudimentary. What had happened and the connection we had made seemed beyond words. Looking back now, I can see that our experiences and relationships in Ecuador were often like that.

* * *

Back in Lynchburg, we felt disconnected and strangely uprooted, as though we'd left what we had begun in Ecuador unfinished. Donna and I both felt strongly that we should return to Cuenca and live there for a while. So instead of taking the job with our friend Sally, the chiropractor, as planned, Donna told her that we wanted to move permanently to Ecuador, where the cost of living was low enough that we could live off her small pension from the state of California, our savings, and our investments until we were old enough to receive social security. It took us several months to make the arrangements, organize the paperwork for our visa, sell our car and possessions, and rent our loft in Lynchburg. By October, we were on our way back to Ecuador.

When we returned to Cuenca, we again stayed in the Apartamentos Otorongo while we looked for a more permanent rental. One of our neighbors at the hotel had recently moved a few hundred yards down Avenida 12 de Abril into an apartment in a large historic house on the fenced property of an old watermill, now an upscale restaurant called *Los Molinos del Batán,* roughly a hundred yards from the Plaza del Otorongo along the Tomebamba River. She told us the owner was currently renovating the upstairs apartment next to hers and planned to rent it when the work was complete. We went to peek through the open door of the apartment and talked to the workers who were doing the renovation. They put us in touch with the owner, who lived in a big house just up the street. The following day, the owner showed us the apartment, which was quaint and funky. It had views of the river and a metal spiral staircase that led to a garret that I could use as a studio. Though small, the apartment had a new, modern kitchen and a remodeled bathroom. It was only a ten-minute walk to the center of town.

For some reason, neither Donna nor I could understand anything Anita, the owner, said to us. Nevertheless, with the help of her daughter, who spoke a few words of English and whose Spanish was slightly more intelligible to us, we managed to rent the apartment for $250 per month. As soon as we had signed the rental agreement, we began shopping for furniture. Our most important and best purchase was a comfortable bed from a company in Cuenca that made excellent mattresses. We also bought a stylish wrought iron and glass dining table with four chairs, a small couch and love seat, and a refrigerator for the kitchen. The rest of our furniture and decorations came from the *Plaza Rotary,* where vendors sold inexpensive, unfinished wooden tables, chairs, and chests. We bought a few pots, pans, and kitchen items from a department store called Coral. Later, we collected a set of beautiful ceramic dishes from the seconds stacks at *Artesa,* a producer of ceramic crockery and houseware designed by Eduardo Vega. We also acquired some restaurant-quality silverware and cooking utensils from a gringo-owned Thai restaurant that had gone out of business.

The large house at *Los Molinos* had been divided into four apartments, two upstairs and two downstairs. All four apartments were owned by siblings from the same family, who also owned the land and the restaurant next door. The two buildings were surrounded by a large, fenced in green space, which doubled as a parking lot for the restaurant. A guard controlled the gate during business hours and watched over the property at night. While gringos rented the two upstairs apartments, the chef from the restaurant and her family lived beneath us. Restaurant workers also lived in the other downstairs apartment.

Though charming and well-situated, the apartment was not without problems. During hard rains, the roof leaked so badly that we had to put plastic buckets and pots from the kitchen on the floor to catch the water in three or four places. When a family rented the restaurant for a wedding party, the music and dancing ended only when the sun came up the next day. We once went a week without a hot shower, as our water heater, though new, mysteriously malfunctioned. Another time, our landlady forgot to pay the electric bill and we were without lights or hot water for two days. Nevertheless, we loved living at *Los Molinos.* In time, we came to know our neighbors, the owners, the guard, and all of the restaurant workers, which made it seem like we were living in a tiny hamlet within the city.

During our first months in Cuenca, we devoted much time and energy to the complicated process of securing a residency visa and obtaining our *cedula,* or national identification card. In Lynchburg, we had researched and contacted an Ecuadorian immigration lawyer to help us navigate the mass of paperwork and documents we needed to submit to the government. At first, everything seemed to go well. We retrieved copies of whatever missing documents we needed and assembled them into a thick file. However, because it was difficult to make appointments at the ministry, by the time our lawyer arranged for us to hand in our documents, the law changed suddenly so that the apostille on our birth certificates was two days past the new, shortened expiration date. The bureaucrat behind the counter folded her arms and smugly refused our application. Though I was frustrated and furious, our lawyer stoically accepted the verdict. "These things happen," he said. "Don't worry. They aren't so small minded and literal in Quito. I'll send the applications and your passports there and my associate will take care of everything."

Three weeks later, our passports arrived with the visas already in place. All we needed now was a document and a stamp from the Cuenca office for our *cedula* application. Though the bureaucrats in Cuenca were not pleased that we had obtained our visas in Quito, there was nothing they could do about it. They stamped the documents and sent us off to pay the fees. A couple months later, we had our pictures taken and received our *cedula* cards. We had become legal residents of Ecuador.

During the year that we lived in the apartment on Avenida 12 de Abril, I filled the apartment and studio above with paintings and drawings. For the first month, Donna and I took more classes at the language school. Eventually, Bibi quit her job there, as she and her husband had bought a house outside of the city and she wanted to spend more time with her new baby. Donna arranged to take cooking lessons, where she learned how to make Ecuadorian dishes, while I continued to study Spanish with other teachers at the school. Each Saturday evening, I walked down the street to the *Apartamentos Otorongo,* where I sat for an hour or two in the office and practiced my Spanish with Sara. I had also begun giving our friend Angelita English lessons on Saturday afternoons. I soon extended the offer to Sara's son

Cristian, who came once or twice a week to our house for an hour of instruction.

One day, a couple of recent University of Cuenca graduates showed up at our door. Xavier, the owner of the *Apartamentos Otorongo,* had sent them to me after they'd asked if he knew any native English speakers who might be able to help them study for the Test of English as a Foreign Language (TOEFL) exam, as they were planning to apply for a state sponsored Master's Degree program in Belgium that was taught in English.

Paul had studied economics and Maria-José philosophy. They told me they had each learned some English in high school and at the university. They were also enrolled in an intensive test preparation course. Nevertheless, they felt they needed more help passing the test, especially some directed practice with writing. They offered to exchange lessons in Spanish, but I knew they were busy with their studies and jobs. I told them that since I already had a teacher and I could speak Spanish every day with my neighbors and friends, I'd be happy to tutor them for free.

In our first meeting the following weekend, Paul did most of the talking. He was serious, knowledgeable, and passionate about economics. At the same time, he could be funny and self-effacing. He spoke English well. Maria-José was more of an enigma. Like many Ecuadorian students, she seemed shy and reluctant to speak. It was difficult for me to evaluate her level. The following week Paul called to say he had accepted a job at a bank and no longer had time for our class. He said he hoped that I would continue to work with Maria-José. In any case, he wanted us to remain friends. I told him that I would happily work with Maria-José and that the four of us should plan to have a meal together soon.

When Maria-José arrived that Saturday, I found that she was perfectly capable of conversing in English. Though not as fluent as Paul, she seemed determined to improve. She told me that she had been translating passages from Bertrand Russell into Spanish and planned to rewrite her thesis, then translate it into English for publication in a scholarly journal. Impressed by her self-motivation, I laid out a plan to help her improve her score on the TOEFL. Over the coming weeks, I taught her how to recognize and respond to various types of test questions and to structure her essays accordingly. Each week, I gave her a list of topics based on past test questions, and put her to work writing a timed essay every day. During our class sessions we reviewed her essays and discussed ways to improve her responses. I encouraged her to use simple, direct sentences, then showed her how to join these sentences to form compound and subordinated structures.

The first time I analyzed her writing, Maria-José looked like she would die. Like most capable students, she had an inflated view of her competence. Consequently, she had not realized how hard she would have to work to achieve her goal in such a short time. Though I could see she was holding back tears, she bit her lip and listened to my critique. The following week, she followed my instructions and produced a more coherent set of essays. She worked hard at the tasks I assigned her. By the end of the summer, she was ready to take the exam. Maria-José improved her score by ten points, which allowed her to apply for one of the spots in the study abroad program. A couple months later, she was accepted into the program. She spent the following year in Belgium, where she earned a Master's Degree, then returned to Cuenca and taught at the university.

* * *

Meanwhile, I found my own studies equally challenging. When I had more or less mastered the basics of Spanish grammar, my teachers turned their attention to helping me improve my ability to express myself. They took me on long walks around various neighborhoods of the city. We talked while we walked. Knowing my interests, they also took me to museums and asked me my opinion on paintings and sculptures. I went to visit local artists, where my teachers encouraged me to ask questions and engage in long conversations about art and the challenges of making a living in the arts. Through these conversations, I learned that Ecuadorian artists are uniformly generous and gracious to guests and other artists. Unlike Americans, they do not compete with each other. Because it's so difficult to earn money in Ecuador, artists tend to be very supportive of each other's work and activities.

On one occasion, I arranged to visit one of Cuenca's most famous sculptors, Eduardo Segovia, at his home and studio. Segovia worked mainly in ceramics, with special emphasis on sculptures of whimsical animals. When the artist had finished showing me his studio and his work, we went into his home, where his wife prepared a traditional tea from plants she picked out of her garden. We talked for a couple of hours about art, his travels and exhibitions in Europe and the United States, and life in Cuenca. Then he took me to see his collection of paintings. Over the years, he had traded his own sculptures for art made by other artists. I have never seen a more engaging personal collection of art. Though he offered to trade one of his own works for a painting of mine as well, soon after my visit to his home I bought one of his sculptures at a show and displayed it prominently in our house. I remember his delight at seeing it when he visited us there.

On another occasion, one of my teachers, a young man named Santiago, took Donna and me on a tour of the university of Cuenca. One of the better public universities in Ecuador, the university serves around 12,000 students. Among the highlights of the trip was the library, which was a great source of pride among the students. Though each of the several floors of the building contained large open spaces full of tables and chairs for students to gather and study, the stacks were comprised of short metal bookcases distributed at the fringes of these rooms. When I asked to see the section that contained Ecuadorian literature, we found only a few low shelves of books.

The University of Cuenca library contains 63,000 books. By comparison, the main branch of the Lynchburg Public Library holds just over 200,000 titles, whereas the research library at the University of California, Los Angeles, where I researched my Master of Arts thesis, as well as the introduction to my translation of *La Fanfarlo*, contains over twelve million volumes. These statistics sadden me, for books represent knowledge. Despite the Internet, carefully edited and peer-reviewed physical books and articles remain the primary tool of scholars. Without good libraries, students often rely instead on unvetted and often inaccurate information they find in online sources.

As few people in Cuenca can afford to buy books published outside of Ecuador, only a couple of full service book stores exist in the city. Due to the high cost of books, particularly imported textbooks from foreign publishers, university students taking a course together usually pool their resources to buy a single copy of the course textbook, which they photocopy and distribute to smaller study groups that in turn share each of the photocopies. While the Internet has made some research materials more affordable and more readily available in electronic formats, the most current research remains beyond the financial means of all but the wealthiest Ecuadorian students. High school students face similar challenges with textbooks. Even primary school pupils often work out of antiquated textbooks or from photocopied texts.

* * *

While it's possible to buy sliced bread in loaves or even French style baguettes from a supermarket, Ecuadorians prefer the rolls baked throughout the day in neighborhood bakeries and sold for a nickel apiece. These rolls come in various sizes, shapes, and flavors, each with a colorful name. *Rodillas de Cristo,* or Christ's knees, for example, are white bread rolls with a spot of cheese baked onto a depression in the center. Also popular is *pan de yuca, pan de chocolate,* and *pan dulce. Guaguas de pan,* or bread babies, decorated as little figures, are popular on November 2, Day of the Dead. Ideally, bakery rolls are best selected from the rack and eaten warm from the oven. While delicious when fresh, they are less appealing when they sit for hours in open baskets at the bakery.

When we lived in the apartment next to the restaurant, there were no bakeries nearby, so we often bought our bread downtown on our way home from classes or while running other errands. Our favorite bakery downtown was a dark hole-in-the-wall on Calle Tarqui. Like most small businesses, the bakery had no name, for named businesses with a sign incur an additional municipal fee. The baker, Victor, was usually elbow deep in flour or dough. Though he was a man of few words, he always seemed pleased when we came into his shop. Whenever we asked him *"¿Como está?"* he'd reply *"Estoy trabajando."* His wife sometimes worked at the counter. In contrast, she was a friendly chatterbox who spoke with the famous singing accent of Cuenca.

On days we didn't go downtown, we usually bought bread at one of the bakeries on Remigio Crespo. One day, we took a short cut where we passed a small bakery operating out of the ground floor of a three-story house. We wandered in and met a woman who told us her name was Martina. A friendly person who loved to talk, Martina seemed delighted that we had discovered her bakery. "If you come here to buy your bread, you can practice speaking Spanish with me," she laughed. When we left, we told her we'd see her again soon.

Though we didn't buy our bread from her every day, we talked with Martina three or four times a week. We especially liked the chocolate donuts her husband occasionally made. Over the next several weeks, we learned that she and her husband rented the space and the bakery equipment from her husband's uncle, who lived with his family in the house above, while Martina and Damian lived in a small apartment with their two adolescent children. Each day they got up early in the morning, took a taxi to the bakery, and began making bread. Their children walked to school. Most days Damian and Martina finished working and cleaning up at the bakery around nine o'clock. They worked six days a week.

The first time we met Damian, he barely spoke. When Martina took us into the production area of the bakery to meet him, he seemed shy and not particularly interested in interacting with gringos. Later, we learned that he had recently returned to Ecuador after having worked construction jobs in New York City for eight years. In time, Damian and I became friends. Years later, we spent a pleasant afternoon together drinking coffee and conversing in English. It was the only time we ever spoke English together.

One day, Martina introduced us to her son Bryan, and her daughter Karen, who were students at a Catholic high school. Bryan was enthusiastic about improving his English and Martina asked if I might have time to give her kids lessons twice a week during their summer break. I agreed to give it a try and see how they liked it. The first time they came to our apartment the two siblings squeezed together on the couch. They seemed almost to be holding onto each other for support. I thought Karen might faint each time I asked her a question. It was difficult to get her to say more than "yes" or "no." Nevertheless, by the end of our first lesson, Bryan seemed to be enjoying himself. He liked that I gave him as much time as he needed to think through and structure his responses. Halfway through the lesson, Donna served chocolate chip cookies still warm from the oven. When they left, Bryan shook my hand. Karen had yet to make eye contact.

Over the course of the next few weeks, I learned about Bryan's interests and a little about his sister as well. As they became more comfortable hearing and speaking English, they began to relax and I encouraged them to share their opinions with me. In time, we began to laugh and have fun. When their vacation ended and they returned to school, I missed seeing them.

Meanwhile, the bakery put Damian and Martina under a great deal of stress. Martina told us that they had taken a bank loan to finance the operation. Eventually, she shared her concern that things were not going well for the business. After nearly a year, they still were not making enough to pay their living expenses, the loan payment, and the rent for the bakery. She didn't know how much longer they could continue.

* * *

After Donna and I quit taking classes at the language school, I decided to continue my Spanish lessons more informally. I looked online for a private teacher who would be open to working with me on improving my conversational skills and building my vocabulary. I sent email inquiries to three potential teachers and spoke to two of them over the phone. I decided to try a man named Julio, who taught

English part-time at the university and gave Spanish lessons out of his home.

Julio lived a couple blocks from the María Auxiliadora church in a rented house he shared with his son, his estranged wife, and several cages of colorful parakeets. He often held class in the open courtyard of the house. He was fond of dictating texts for me to write and having me read aloud from Ecuadorian history books or books of local legends. He gave me phrases to memorize and homework to write. Mostly, though, he just liked to talk.

Because he had a car, Julio sometimes took Donna and me on field trips. We once spent a lovely day touring the Cajas National Park in the mountains high above Cuenca and had lunch at an old rustic tavern. On the way home, he insisted we stop to fish for trout at a commercial fishing resort, as he had planned to prepare trout for dinner when he returned home. The pond turned out to be a kind of cement swimming pool stocked with hundreds of fish. The owners gave us sticks with fishing line and a hook attached, baited with sticky cornmeal. When we dipped the hooks into the water, the fish instantly bit. Patrons paid by the fish. Another day, he took us to Gualaceo and Chordeleg, and once to meet his mother, Estrella, in Sígsig, where he had grown up. Surprisingly, Estrella was a natural blond, which was rare in Ecuador, though for some reason less so in Sígsig. He also took us to the thermal pools at Baños. Once he even brought me to see a private zoo that a wealthy friend, who played on his soccer team, owned on some steep, terraced property in Turi. I later read that the government had confiscated most of the rare birds and animals we had seen, as it was not legal for individuals to own these creatures privately.

Outside of our classes, Julio sometimes practiced his English with me. Though he could speak English well, he struggled with writing. Consequently, he used me as a resource to help him arrive at and understand the correct answers to the confusing and often nonsensical department-wide exams he had to give his students at the end of each semester, and for jobs he got through the university, translating texts from Spanish into English.

Julio had studied English at the University of Cuenca with a man who had come to Ecuador in the 1970s, when Cuenca was still an isolated Andean city. His sole qualification for teaching English language and literature had been a Doctor of Jurisprudence degree from a law school in the United States, which at that time had been enough to land him a job as the head of the English language program at the university. According to Julio, the ex-attorney relied heavily on Shakespeare plays as texts for his courses.

Julio loved American culture. He had relatives who lived in Minneapolis, including a brother who made a good salary working in a factory there. His brother had married a woman from Mexico, bought a house, and raised his children in Minnesota. Julio had visited them there, and had also spent a week in New York City. Sometimes he talked about going to live in the United States himself. "I could teach Spanish," he would tell me. His big dream, however, was to travel around the southwest and visit the Indian reservations. He loved western movies, but favored the Indians. "Maybe we'll go on a road trip together some day," I told him. I gave him a copy of *Bury My Heart at Wounded Knee* that I bought in the U.S. during our Christmas trip. I don't think he read it.

One day, Donna and I wandered into one of the two good bookstores we'd found in Cuenca, where I bought a thick anthology of work by contemporary Ecuadorian poets. Among the poems I liked best were sections of a long poem about the city of Cuenca called *Sinfonía de la ciudad amada* by Jorge Dávila Vázquez, who taught at the University of Cuenca. After I'd finished translating the sections that had been reprinted in the anthology into English, I asked Julio about Dávila and he told me he would try to set up a meeting. A couple weeks later, Julio took me to the poet's elegant apartment, located on Grand Columbia, in a brick high-rise building that overlooked the Tomebamba River. Before meeting him, I did some research on Dávila and learned that he was among a handful of the most famous living writers in Ecuador.

Dávila met us at the door and greeted me warmly. He seemed happy to converse with a writer from the United States. On the other hand, he was openly dismissive of my teacher, and made it clear that Julio was not a part of the conversation. For the next hour, Julio sat quietly in the corner, as the two of us talked about a range of subjects. Though I struggled to express myself at times, Dávila was charming and patient with my Spanish. He told me that he had little doubt that I would improve my conversational skills rapidly through our friendship. Then he inscribed and presented me with several of his books, including an illustrated edition of *Sinfonía de la ciudad amada*. In return, I gave him a copy of *The Masked Ball*, which he couldn't read. We joked that he could simply enjoy my linocut illustrations. Knowing that he spoke French and had studied in France, I also gave him a copy of my bilingual edition of *La Fanfarlo*.

* * *

One day while Donna and I were walking home from downtown, we saw a "for sale" sign in the window of the little house on Calle Simón Bolívar where Donna had taken the photograph of the dog's head poking through a hole in the bricks of the upstairs terrace. It was a remarkable building for both its narrow size and for being next door to the large, modern *Ministerio de Desarrollo y Vivienda* government building that was set back farther from the street than the surrounding houses and buildings, which all had shared walls and butted up to the sidewalk. We crossed the street and looked at the photographs on the windows of the shop beneath the house, which happened to be a little real estate office. We saw that the building, which included both the shop and the house above, was listed for $64,000.

Without a second thought Donna walked into the office and asked a man sitting bored behind a desk what he knew about the house. "Do you want to see it?" he replied. He walked outside and directed a loud stream of Spanish at the window above him. A few seconds later a voice called back to him. Then a door we hadn't noticed buzzed open. "Let's go," the man said. We followed him up the steep wooden stairs to a tiny landing, where a young man stood at the entrance to the house. "His father is sleeping upstairs, but we won't bother him if we look," the realtor told us.

The house was so tiny that it was next to impossible to comprehend the interior spaces. Opposite the entrance was a closet, in which they'd temporarily locked the dog. Couches filled most of the first floor, except for a closet-sized room with a bunk bed inside. A wooden internal stairway led to the second floor, which consisted of a decrepit bathroom with a toilet, sink, and shower, and a bedroom not much bigger than the double mattress upon which an older man lay sound asleep. An exit door led to a terrace that served as an outdoor kitchen. From the terrace a set of dangerous, exposed metal stairs led to the flat roof, from which there was a near panoramic view of the city.

While the house shocked us with its filthy outdoor kitchen, its lack of space, and its overall deplorable condition, it did have some admirable qualities. Foremost among them was its location on the main street of the historic district of the city. Another attractive feature was the view, both from the windows, the terraces, and particularly the roof. Finally, the commercial space downstairs offered options for growth and creativity. Though we'd have to remodel and upgrade the entire building, construction costs were low. That night, we reminded each other how often we had said that investing in foreign real estate would be risky and foolish. We laughed at our impulsiveness and went to bed. In the morning, however, the house remained in our thoughts. As the coffee dripped into the pot and the pancakes bubbled on the pan, we agreed that life should be an adventure. We set the pancakes, maple syrup, and coffee on the table. Halfway through the second stack, we decided to buy the house.

We wisely engaged Nelson, our attorney, to handle the details of the sale. Marcello, the realtor who had showed us the house, represented the sellers. For some reason, Nelson intimidated and terrified Marcello. Within a week, we had signed a *"promesa de compraventa"* and paid the sellers three thousand dollars as a down payment. Because three siblings had inherited the house, and each of them had debts connected to the property that needed to be paid before the house could be legally sold and the deed transferred, the sale turned out to be a long and complicated process.

The transaction dragged on for many months, and despite occasional reassurances from Marcello or Nelson, it appeared that we were making little progress. Many times, Donna and I walked by the house and questioned the wisdom of our choice. On a good day, it seemed as though we'd bought a gingerbread house in a haunted forest. On a bad day, it looked more like a ruined doll house someone had left in the street next to a dumpster. After nearly seven months, we began to think we might lose our down payment.

Then, we received an unexpected call from Nelson's assistant, who told us the sale would take place later that week. The owners had already vacated the house. Both parties would go to a notary, where we would sign the papers. We would need to bring several thousand dollars in cash to give to the sellers, which would facilitate their ability to finalize the remaining documents and prepare the deed. They, in turn, would hand over the keys to us and we would take physical possession of the house. At the same time, we gave Nelson a check for the rest of the money for him to deposit into an escrow account and hold until all conditions had been met for the deed to be transferred. Only after the deed had been registered in our names, would Nelson release the funds to the sellers.

As soon as we received the keys, we walked directly from the lawyer's office to the house. Donna took a photo of me standing on the sidewalk as I opened the entry door for the first time. Then she took a series of pictures of the uninhabitable little house we now owned. While there were many modern, comfortable homes in Cuenca, it saddened us that a large percentage of the people lived in such substandard housing. The wooden floors were rough and uneven, the tile in the bathroom broken, and the fixtures ancient. Unshielded florescent tubes were bolted to the low ceilings. The cracked windows were dark with years of accumulated diesel exhaust from the buses that roared down Calle Simón Bolívar all day long. We saw few electrical outlets. The bathroom smelled awful. The house had no kitchen.

The view from the roof was as spectacular as we remembered, though we immediately noted a construction project in progress directly behind the house. While only half complete, it looked like an office building or small school, as there were two stories around an open courtyard. We wondered how this new structure would impact our property. Later that week we asked Marcello if he knew anything about the project, but he told us he had no information.

Over the coming weeks, we spent much of our time cleaning and envisioning what we might make of our new home. We looked at modular kitchens and had a salesman take measurements. When a contractor talked to me about remodeling the house, he told me that he could do the work at night without permits to save money. He said he could upgrade the electricity, install a kitchen, remodel the bathroom, put in overhead lights, refinish the floors, replace some of the windows, and paint the house for six thousand dollars. I thanked him for his estimate and told him I'd think about it. I didn't believe a word he said. During this time, we also had Nelson draw up a rental agreement for a one-year extension of Marcello's real estate office in the shop beneath the house. We were careful to note that the contract would not be renewed after the one-year period ended, as we hoped to use money from the sale of our loft in Lynchburg to renovate the shop.

Next, I contacted two architects. Both came highly recommended and spoke English. The first wanted to add another floor to the building. His plans were elegant and ambitious, but ultimately unrealistic, given the twenty-five-thousand-dollar estimate he provided. I figured the actual cost would easily be double that amount. Esteban, the second architect, presented us with a more streamlined and thoughtful design. Esteban had studied, lived, and worked for several years in North Carolina. He liked to use local materials whenever possible, and he was familiar with urban apartments and "tiny houses." A contractor as well as an architect, Esteban provided us with a detailed and itemized list of the extensive work he would undertake, along with the costs of the permits, plans, materials, and labor. The total cost of the project was sixteen thousand dollars.

We began by hiring him to draw up a complete set of blueprints for the house. According to the design, he would gut the existing structure, tear down the internal walls, and extend the upstairs interior space by reducing the size of the terrace. He would rewire the building and replace all the plumbing in the house, build a new, steel reinforced roof and new subfloors, re-plaster and paint, and install new dual pane wooden windows, lighting fixtures, cabinets, and flooring. The kitchen and living room would take up the lower floor, while the bedroom, bathroom, and walk-in laundry and closet would be upstairs. The plans also called for a rooftop studio with handsome sliding lateral wood slat panels over glass. Once we had signed off on the design, he submitted the plans to the city for approval.

The initial response from the city was that we should tear down the existing building and construct in its place a single-story structure of approximately 350 square feet, as the house was located in the historic district and, according to the historic architecture commission, a small adobe-looking structure would blend into the original buildings and look more authentic. Of course, no one had bothered to check that the buildings on either side of ours, as well as across the street, were all from two to four stories tall. After Esteban presented photographs of the house and its surroundings, the planning commission approved an extensive remodel, though they denied permission to build anything larger than a windowless storage shed on the roof. Despite our disappointment, we decided to push forward with the project.

A couple weeks later, Esteban invited us to a house warming celebration for a house he had recently built for clients in the mountains near the town of Biblián, about an hour's drive from Cuenca. We drove with Esteban's sister, who was also an architect. Ironically, she worked for the City of Cuenca, as an expert in historical property, though she had not reviewed her brother's application for a permit to remodel our house. Built of bamboo and red brick, with much of one side open panels of glass that gave onto an expansive view of green fields and mountains, Esteban's design made for a remarkable house. We stayed for several hours, as a large group of the new owner's family, the laborers who had built the house, and Esteban's family celebrated the completion of the project with a feast and many champagne toasts. On the way home, I asked his sister questions about the architectural history of Cuenca.

Esteban scheduled work to begin on our house just before Christmas. We still owned our loft in Lynchburg, which we had rented out for the year. After buying the house in Cuenca, we were several thousand dollars short of the money we needed to pay for the renovation. As we had already made plans to visit my father and my sister in California, we told Esteban that we would pay half the money when we returned from our trip. In California, our son Eric and his wife traveled from Guam, where he was stationed, to join us for the holiday. I returned to Cuenca alone to pay the architect, while Donna flew to Lynchburg to sell the gold coins we had in a safe deposit box to help with the remainder of the costs. We also began making plans to sell the loft in Lynchburg in the spring.

* * *

While Donna traveled to Virginia, I met with the architect. Afterward, I walked by the house and saw that workers had started the demolition over the Christmas holiday. When I came back outside after looking at the destruction, our next-door neighbor accosted me on the street. Angry that no one had informed her about the work, she wondered why we had started the day before Christmas. Her husband was not well, she told me, and the noise and dust had caused problems for them. Though upset, she told me that she understood that as the new owner it was completely within my rights to improve the property. She just wished someone would have informed her first. I felt very badly for her and apologized for the misunderstanding. I told her that we'd been out of the country when the work began and that I had assumed the architect would have already spoken to her. When I gave her his card and told her that I would ask him to come talk to her about the project, she seemed relieved and we left on much better terms.

A couple days later, Martina and Damian invited me to their apartment for breakfast. They suspected I might be bored and lonely without Donna. It was only the second time I had been to their apartment. The first time Donna and I had gone for coffee, we were surprised that the family of four lived in what amounted to two rooms: in addition to a tiny kitchen and bathroom, the entire apartment consisted of a living area with a dining table, and a bedroom divided into two by a false wall constructed of freestanding closets.

Recently, a new business had opened in the commercial space directly beneath the apartment. Two young men were operating an illegal fast-food restaurant, serving hamburgers made on a grill without proper ventilation. Each evening, the exhaust from the grill rose up and enveloped the apartment above in thick, greasy smoke, as loud reggaeton music geared to the young clientele played until midnight.

I walked to their apartment on a quiet Saturday morning. Martina made coffee and served *quimbolitos,* steamed corn cakes made from corn flour, eggs, butter, sugar, and raisins stuffed inside large green canna leaves. Though I arrived early, both Bryan and Karen had already left for the day, busy with study groups for their school projects. In retrospect, I'm sure Martina and Damian had planned the day so that there would be time for the adults to talk. Apparently, Donna and I had gained their trust to the point that they had decided to share the events of their life with us. For me, our friends' story is an essential narrative, one that in many ways has helped shape my understanding of the world. Though uniquely their own, it's a familiar tale for people living in Latin America, as it concerns ordinary people caught in a global economic riptide.

After I had answered their questions about my trip to California and the demolition work that had started on the house downtown, Martina began to talk about her life. She told me that when she was fifteen years old her father had sent her and her sister Gaby to live by themselves in Cuenca and paid for them to attend a private Catholic high school so that they could receive a superior education to what was available in their small rural town. After graduation, she met Damian, who worked with his family in agriculture in Jima. She told me that after they married and became the parents of two children, they struggled to make a living, as Damian worked as a baker in a *panadería* in Jima.

At that time, Ecuador had fallen into financial crisis and the currency collapsed. High inflation and high unemployment had all but destroyed the economy and people began to change their *sucres* for dollars on their own. The government petitioned the International Monetary Fund to officially make the switch from the *sucre* to the dollar in 2000. Like many Ecuadorians, Damian and Martina worried about poverty and wondered what kind of life their children would have, growing up in Jima. During this period, hundreds of thousands of young Ecuadorian men left the country to look for work in the United States, Canada, and Spain. Over the past ten years, many have now returned, though there are still entire villages where young and middle-aged men are strangely absent.

Though it was a tough decision, Martina explained that they had finally agreed to borrow enough money from relatives to finance Damian's trip to Mexico, and to pay for the guide, or *coyote* who would bring him across the desert and arrange his transportation to New York. As Damian's brother already lived in New York City, he could live with him while he looked for work.

Damian then told me about his trip and how he had followed the *coyote* through the desert at night to cross the border. He talked about his fear of being robbed, murdered, and left dead in the desert. He talked about his fear of being caught by the authorities. He talked about his eight years in New York and how he had lived in an apartment with other men from Ecuador who had each left their families behind to find work in the United States. He told me how he had worked for an Italian American contractor who maintained a crew of illegal construction workers from around the world that he would pay in cash at the end of each week. Damian claimed his employer was a good man who respected his workers and had learned enough Spanish to communicate and even joke with them. During this time, Damian had worked hard, learned quickly, and earned a good wage at his job.

After work, he took English classes at night school. He sent most of his earnings to Martina back in Ecuador.

Meanwhile, Martina invested this money in a series of failed business ventures in Cuenca. One day, she got a call from Damian, who had been admitted to the hospital for emergency appendicitis surgery. Martina flew immediately to New York. Once they had paid the hospital whatever additional money Damian had set aside, they were allowed to leave the country. After eight years in the United States, Damian returned home sick, penniless, and unemployed.

For a while, the two adults and two children shared an apartment with cousins, where the entire family lived in a single bedroom. Martina and Damian started a neighborhood business where they cooked and delivered lunches to businessmen who worked in downtown offices. This business also failed. Then they arranged for a bank loan, co-signed by both sets of in-laws, which allowed them to rent a modest apartment and open the bakery.

When we met Martina and Damian, they were trying to repay personal loans, as well monthly payment to the bank. Selling rolls for a nickel apiece wasn't profitable enough to keep pace with their debts. One by one, Damian sold at a loss the small herd of dairy cows he'd sent his father money to purchase and keep for him as an investment. After the bakery failed, Damian found a job working for a gringo who was remodeling a small, three-story house in downtown Cuenca. He hired Damian to work on the electrical, painting, and plumbing, as well as to install an absurdly tiny interior elevator in the building. The job lasted nearly a year and our friends eventually set aside enough money to move into a bigger apartment just off of Remigio Crespo.

Over the next few years, Donna and I hired Damian to paint our house and to revarnish the wooden windows. We also hired him to install tiles on the risers of the stairs leading from the street to the house. For a while, Damian worked with one of his cousins doing painting and electrical work. It was difficult to find work as a painter in Cuenca, as there were hundreds of contractors who would bid low on jobs then use poor quality materials and water down the paint. It wasn't uncommon to see thin, watery paint being applied with a broom.

* * *

When Donna retuned to Cuenca, I took her to see the progress on the house. Workers had removed the small windows and opened up the space inside by demolishing the interior walls. Even piled full of rubble, the apartment looked bigger. For the next month I monitored the progress. Sometimes I went inside and talked to the workers or the project manager. A couple of times, I saw Esteban and he explained how the work was progressing. Once, I went into the house after the workers had stopped for the day and saw that they had left a large hole in the roof above the interior stairs. As it rained nearly every day in Cuenca, I couldn't understand why they would not put plastic sheeting up at the end of the day. I called Esteban and told him.

Several days later, when I walked by the house, Marcello rushed out of the real estate office and began speaking to me frantically. Apparently, his office had been flooded from above in a heavy overnight rain storm, when water from the hole in the roof had coursed down the interior stairs, then leaked through the uncured cement subfloor and dripped onto his desk below, ruining his computer. I let Esteban know, and he agreed to give Marcello one of the computers from his office, which was an upgrade for the realtor. It also allowed Esteban to buy a new Macintosh for his office. It seemed as though the story would have a happy ending, though Donna and I had no idea that we would end up paying the additional cost, even though I'd warned Esteban about covering the hole in the roof.

By the end of January, the house began to show noticeable changes. Workers had finally sealed and tiled the roof. New wooden windows enclosed the interior spaces. Workers had installed recessed lighting and laid tile in the bathroom and kitchen. A few days later, they removed most of the trash and debris and began to install the laminate flooring. I saw the wooden kitchen cabinets and closets, still wrapped in plastic, stacked against the walls. A week later, the house was complete. Esteban hosted a party for us and for some of the tradesmen who had worked on the project. We were amazed how Esteban's design had converted a dark, claustrophobic apartment into a light-filled open space with a modern kitchen and ample bathroom. We particularly liked the built-in closets and bookcase, the big pantry and work counter in the kitchen, the way he had incorporated skylights and recessed lighting into the house. A final surprise was the drop-down metal stairway he had designed and fabricated to create an interior access to the roof.

We hired a young man named Emilio to help us move our furniture and household goods to the new house. He and his cousin packed everything we owned into the back of a pickup truck. Because the stairs from the street were so steep and narrow and the angles so sharp, they pulled the queen-sized mattress up the side of the building with a rope and brought it into the third-floor bedroom through the door to the terrace. As we were leaving the apartment next to *Los Molinos del Batán,* the waiters and kitchen help came outside to say goodbye. *"Que pena,"* they said, sad to see us go. They wished us luck and made us promise to visit them.

A week after we had moved into the house, a local television station sent a crew to shoot a feature on the house and to interview Esteban about his innovative and unusual renovation. Despite the overall excellence of the design and construction, we did encounter one serious flaw. We discovered that the rooftop drains Esteban had engineered were too small to effectively drain the roof during the strong downpours that Cuenca often experiences. During a particularly heavy rain that lasted several hours, we noticed water seeping onto the wall near the ceiling of our bedroom. When we checked the roof, we saw that dirt and debris from the roof had clogged the drains and the roof had filled up like a shallow swimming pool. Donna and I worked for an hour in the driving rain to unplug the drains and remove the water from the roof, bailing with a bucket, which we poured over the edge and onto the sidewalk below. The next day, we called Damian, who came with his cousin to install a larger set of drains. Damian also found some metal workers to fabricate a new set of handrails for the steep stairs leading from the street up the house.

* * *

That summer, after we sold our loft in Lynchburg, we decided to continue the renovation of our little building and we asked Esteban to prepare plans for a gallery space in the shop on the street level. At the same time, we asked Nelson, our attorney, to draw up and officially serve our tenant Marcello a legal notification that we did not intend to renew his rental agreement. Without such a document and someone to serve it, we would have never been able to evict him from the shop below our house, as the laws strongly favor tenants who have rented past the first year.

Marcello had been a problematic renter. The first couple of months, he had paid his $150 monthly rent on time. However, he soon began to find excuses for being late. It got to be an annoying game he played. He seemed to spend a lot of his time at the office watching football on television or videos on his computer. Sometimes he appeared to be drunk. Once when I came to collect the rent, he told me his wife was ill. He promised to pay us what he owed when she recovered. In the ten months he'd been renting from us, we calculated he'd paid us only half of what he owed. Our Ecuadorian friends weren't the least bit surprised, and even sympathized with Marcello. We determined that being landlords was not for us.

After Marcello received the papers from Nelson, he left a month before the contract ended, moving into the empty shop beneath the house directly next door. Despite the awkwardness of owing us money we all knew he would never repay, we nonetheless remained on good terms, which was natural. After all, we were neighbors.

Esteban designed a commercial space that matched the upstairs and unified the entire building. He replaced the street-level windows and metal grills with solid glass blocks that appeared opaque from the outside yet let in light and created interesting prismatic patterns on the inside of the gallery. He built handsome dual-paned wood and glass doors in the front of the shop. He tore out the old wooden mezzanine and replaced it with a fabricated metal structure with a matching staircase and sufficient headroom. He installed a half bath that matched the bathroom of the apartment upstairs, a built-in stainless steel work table, and a full storage closet. The work had proceeded slowly in comparison to the house, but after three months, it needed only a new exterior security door.

Unfortunately, the city had just passed a new ordinance aimed at eliminating over time the ugly pull-down metal doors commonly used to secure commercial properties. The city planners wanted to replace metal doors in the historical section of the city with wooden doors that would blend more harmoniously with the colonial architecture. Unfortunately, local builders had no experience making wooden security doors. Esteban added an additional two thousand dollars to our quote. Then he designed a solid wood accordion door, with four folding panels joined by hinges. Though his carpenters and cabinet-makers labored for a month, they could not make the design function properly. They revised the door over and over, moving the position of the locks and hinges. Finally, they gave up. Another contractor came to build a less complicated design, which only worked after I insisted Esteban add metal braces and shims that would convert the four-panel design into two relatively sold panels. By the time the shop finally opened, another three months had passed. In the end, however, the finished studio-gallery gave me a modern, handsome and utilitarian space in which to work.

* * *

In late 2012, Jordan Jones and Susie Bright each wrote to me about a project they had in mind. They wanted to collaborate on publishing a collection of my selected stories in audio book and e-book format. Susie, who had recently begun editing a series for Amazon's Audible Books division, would oversee production of the audio book, while Jordan's Leaping Dog Press would publish the electronic book version in Kindle format. I remember telling each of them that I had no objections to the project, though I didn't have time to participate directly. I told them that I trusted them to do whatever they wanted with the story selection, editing, design, and other aspects of the publication. After some discussion, Jordan and Susie decided to release the book as *Horny: Stories Selected and New*. They asked me to select two previously unpublished stories for the book, and I sent them "Symphony for Severe Thunderstorm" and "Alternating Currents of Excitement and Dread," two stories from my unfinished manuscript of "The Tidewriter Anthology," an uncompleted follow-up to *The Nambuli Papers.*

With so much going on in my life in Ecuador, I felt disconnected from the publication of the ebook and audio book in 2013. Susie had chosen Christopher Kipiniak to interpret and narrate my stories. While I could appreciate his effort and professionalism, listening to someone else narrate stories I had performed myself at readings over many years seemed odd and even a bit surreal. As for the e-book, I miss the smell of ink, the weight in my hands, and the pleasure of turning the pages. I miss seeing the physical book on my shelf.

* * *

After navigating all the paperwork needed to open a business in Cuenca, I finally opened my studio-gallery in the shop beneath our house. Though I didn't put up an official sign for the gallery, I mounted one of my old wooden oil painting palettes on the wooden security door so that it was visible as a kind of guild marker whenever the doors were open. Informally I called the space "Galería 14-54", which was the street number of the building.

Finding good quality art supplies in Ecuador, particularly paints and paper, was next to impossible, as the government imposed steep tariffs on almost all imported goods. As a result, stores in Cuenca offered either poor quality materials from China or, at best, off-brand student-grade paints. As printmaking was apparently not part of the Ecuadorian art tradition, I never found a source for linoleum, wood blocks, or print-making papers and inks. Even marginally acceptable quality drawing paper was in short supply and unbelievably expensive. Consequently, I made only one print during the five years we lived in Ecuador. Whenever Donna or I visited the United States or Europe, we would always bring back quantities of paper and paints. Fortunately, I found a stationary store where I could order custom made sizes of stretched canvases from local manufacturers at reasonable prices. Donna and I carried them across town together when they were too big to fit into a taxi.

After talking to Ecuadorian artists, I had no illusions about making money from my art. I had already done a show of a dozen of my cave art–inspired paintings in the lobby of one of the most exclusive high rise apartment buildings in the city without selling a single painting. Though the managers of the building were enthusiastic about having my art in the lobby and asked if I'd continue to provide new paintings to swap out every couple of months, I had declined, as I had nowhere to store unsold large canvases.

When I opened the gallery, I didn't bother to keep regular hours. If the right people happened to walk by when the doors were open, they'd come inside to look and talk, which meant that interactions with visitors tended to be spontaneous and often quite interesting. I liked when artists I knew, or artists new to me would visit. As Cuenca is a popular tourist destination, and there were half a dozen hotels nearby, tourists frequently visited as well. Over time, tourists purchased all of the easily transportable work I had on hand—dozens of prints and acrylic paintings on paper mounted on foam core, and all of the hardbound copies of my illustrated letterpress books I had brought from the United States.

Sometimes, Ecuadorians wandered in and asked me to teach them or their children how to draw or paint. Sometimes, they would ask me for English lessons. As I didn't charge money for my lessons, I told them I already had too many students and I didn't have time for more. Other people would come in to sell me pencils, food, or random items they bought in bulk. Some would simply ask for money, others for a loan. The latter usually involved stories about how they had traveled to work in Cuenca, and their employers had failed to pay them upon completion of the job. They asked me for bus fare home. When I wanted to paint without interruption, I closed the security doors behind me and locked them from the inside.

* * *

During our five years in Cuenca, Donna and I grew increasingly close to Damian, Martina, Bryan, and Karen. We frequently visited each other's homes, shared meals, and celebrated birthdays and holidays together. Sometimes Martina brought lunches she had cooked to our house. We laughed together, drank coffee from Loja, and enjoyed homemade cakes and cookies Donna and I baked. I made pizza and carrot cake, while Damian prepared tacos he had learned to make in New York. We attended the children's graduations and confirmation ceremonies, and got to know our friends' extended family, particularly Martina's sister Gaby, her husband Marco, and two young sons. We visited the town of Jima, where both Damian and Martina had been raised. We listened to their problems and tried to provide whatever suggestions and support we could. They were our family in Ecuador and we treated them accordingly. We will forever keep them close in our hearts.

The summer after I opened the gallery, I taught Bryan and Karen each morning for six weeks. It was a chance for them to practice their English while learning more about art. Karen had just graduated from high school and Bryan had one more year to complete before he could begin his university studies. Karen planned to take the exam for entrance into medical school at the University of Cuenca, though only a dozen new students, from all over the country, were admitted to the program each year.

I taught them how to draw and introduced them to painting, music, and literature. We met at the gallery each weekday morning and worked for four hours. I bought them each a plastic tackle box and stocked it full of good quality pencils, Conté crayons, charcoal sticks, and other drawing supplies, as well as a set of brushes, ink pens, and ink I had brought back from Madrid on our previous trip. Some days we spent the entire session drawing or painting. I often played classical music for them, or introduced them to songs with interesting lyrics we could discuss in English as they worked on their drawings or painted. Some days, we split the time between art instruction downstairs in the studio-gallery and conversation, reading, and literature upstairs. In either case, we always took a break halfway through for a snack.

I structured the English lessons around conversation, working initially from a list of general topics that got progressively more engaging. I also taught them about world history and the history and development of the Spanish language, a subject about which they knew nothing. We read short stories and poems in English as well. I remember in particular that we read Raymond Carver's short story "A Small Good Thing," out loud and discussed it in detail.

At the end of the summer, Karen took her exam, while Bryan went back to school. Unlike the United States, where students must first complete a four-year course of study in pre-med, biology, or another subject, exceptional high school graduates who pass a battery of competitive tests may qualify for medical school. Thus, the top performing students in Ecuador sometimes go directly from high school into a five-year program in general medicine. However, seventeen-year-old Karen was not accepted on her first attempt.

Disappointed, Karen resolved to take an in-depth test preparation course, study anatomy, chemistry and math on her own, then attempt the exam again the following year. I suggested that she continue her studies with me three mornings a week as well. I felt that, if she improved her English, she would have more educational and employment opportunities and would also discover her strengths and interests in the process. Throughout the year, I worked with her on English grammar and writing, as well as literature and teaching methodology. We read Kurt Vonnegut's novel *Cat's Cradle* aloud, and discussed it together. We also read and discussed poems by Langston Hughes, William Stafford, Kim Addonizio, Gary Snyder, Gregory Corso, Joy Harjo, Edwin Arlington Robinson, Amy Gerstler, Charles Simic, Robert Blake, Charles Bukowski, Lawrence Ferlinghetti, Sharon Olds, and Russell Edson, along with song lyrics by Bob Dylan, Paul Simon, Leonard Cohen, and John Lennon. Halfway through the year, she began giving English lessons to her young cousins after school.

Despite her earlier disappointment, Karen held onto her dream of becoming a doctor. She told me her goal was to become a heart specialist in Cuenca and perform surgeries for wealthy gringos. In August, Karen again took the national university admissions test, as did her brother, who hoped to begin studies in Telecommunications Systems Engineering. When Bryan scored in the top tier and was accepted into his major and Karen again failed to qualify for admission, the entire family struggled with disappointment. Instead of celebrating his own success, Bryan felt guilty for achieving what had again eluded his older sister.

Despite her family's financial struggles, Karen decided to wait another year and take the test a final time. For a while, Martina and Karen tried to make chocolate candies on sticks to sell to shops, but in a city full of cottage industries based on food, the competition smothered their efforts. Instead, I offered Karen a part-time, temporary job as my assistant in the gallery. Her job was to keep the gallery clean and help with sales and related chores. Over the next several months, she practiced and improved her English, studied literature and painting under my tutelage, learned how to run a gallery, and helped to stage an exhibition.

Among the useful scraps I'd saved from the remodeling of the shop was a spool of stiff, black, coated wire. One day while we were talking together, I brought the wire out, snipped a length, and began bending it into an abstract sculpture. Like the story about a brown paper bag I had written thirty years earlier, I've always enjoyed challenging myself to find inspiration in the most ordinary things. I saw no reason why a discarded spool of wire could not become the subject of a future exhibition of paintings at the gallery. I wanted to prove to Karen that there was no real mystery lurking behind the transformative power of creativity. Like anything else in life, art depends upon desire, confidence, hard work, and a healthy sense of playfulness. Though Karen did not yet know it, our noodling with bended sections of wire would soon evolve into a two-person show called *Wires / Cables*.

Each day for the next few months, Karen and I each drew one or more of the wire sculptures we'd made. Learning how to convey depth and perspective provided Karen with a challenge that greatly improved her draftsmanship. Next, we began work on more finished concepts, including some large-scale paintings in acrylics. I gave Karen three canvases of various sizes and told her to paint two of the canvases with photorealistic representations based on photographs we'd taken. The remaining canvas would be her chance to conceptualize something more expressive and original. I also gave her a wooden pencil box and a wooden pot with a lid to decorate with a painting of the wire sculptures. In addition, we selected one of her drawings for the show. Meanwhile, I also made paintings of various sizes.

We varnished the finished paintings, built simple wooden frames for them, and hung the show in the gallery. We designed a flyer for the exhibition and printed artist statements and a description of the work in both Spanish and English. Karen sent press releases to newspapers and online publications to advertise the opening. We put flyers in restaurants popular with foreigners and emailed invitations to Ecuadorian friends. We baked cookies and bought cheap wine and plastic cups.

The evening of the opening, we had a good turnout. We were lucky that people arrived at the tiny gallery at different times throughout the evening, as we'd hoped. Though several people expressed interest in individual paintings, the only work we sold that night were two of my cave art–themed pastels unrelated to the subject of the show. Nevertheless, I was pleased with the reception. Over the coming weeks, Karen sold one of her small paintings and I sold two of mine. Of the three large paintings I'd made, one I gave to our neighbors as a house warming gift for their newly renovated house, and the other two were included in the sale of our house when we left Cuenca. After the show closed, I published a catalog of the show called *Wires / Cables* through a print-on-demand service, and ordered copies for Karen and myself.

Once the show had run its course, we turned to translating and producing a small bilingual anthology of Ecuadorian poets called *The Other Shore*. I showed Karen how to design and lay out a book and we produced photocopies from the master and covers from our original art on gray cover stock, then hand sewed the bindings. When the book was complete, I told Karen I needed to get back to my own projects. I hoped that she would use some of what she had learned and that she would eventually find her place in the world.

* * *

Cuencanos love parades, music, dancing, and fiestas, which occur at regular intervals throughout the year. It's not uncommon, especially in the weeks after Christmas, to see several small parades a day, each representing a particular parish or organization, each with its own band of hired musicians. To us it seemed like there were so many minor religious celebrations, there had to be more than one for each week of the year. At first, we asked what people were celebrating, but we soon realized many of our friends had only a vague idea themselves.

Secular festivities abound as well. Of particular note are the *jornadas deportivas* staged by various schools. Because of our friendship with Bryan and Karen, we attended two of the *jornadas deportivas* hosted by the Hermano Miguel La Salle Catholic School in Cuenca. It was a day of friendly competitions between classes built around a yearly theme. Students in various classes and grade levels invested huge amounts of time designing and building elaborate floats and models, sewing uniforms, and crafting costumes, all in the hope of outdoing their classmates and winning a prize, which was generally a cash award used to throw a pizza party for the winning classes. These outlandish and often surreal affairs included a teenage fire-eater, dangerous pyrotechnics, and the zip line descent from a rooftop to the surface of the blacktop playground of a student Michael Jackson impersonator dressed in gold lame jumpsuit and a wig.

Celebrated with surprising intensity and gusto in Cuenca and throughout the Ecuadorian Andes, Carnival takes place just prior to the beginning of Lent. The holiday features parades, neighborhood and work-related parties, family feasts, and food fights. A huge concert gathering and public foam-and-water fight in Parque Calderon marks the official start of the celebration in Cuenca, though the related public games, water fights, and rowdiness can last the entire week. It's not unusual for passengers in cars driving on city streets to target pedestrians with water balloons. Troublemakers sometimes pour buckets of water onto unsuspecting pedestrians from open windows, doorways, or rooftops. *Espuma,* or foam that resembles shaving cream, sold in large spray cans, is another, more extreme alternative, as is flour. People returning from the big celebration at Parque Calderon are often coated from head to toe in a thick, disgusting sludge of foam, water, and flour.

Our first experience with Carnival was at the language school, where the teachers, staff, and administrators, along with a handful of younger European students, gathered in the courtyard to take turns soaking each other with a hose. We shook our heads as we watched the normally reserved, shy, and dignified Ecuadorians pour water out of their shoes. The women wrung out their long black hair and folded their arms across their chests over their wet clothing. Most of them walked home through the city soaked to the skin.

Donna disliked Carnival and stayed indoors much of the week. She wasn't the only one. Plenty of Ecuadorian women also dislike the "playful" yet aggressive attacks; they see them as merely a socially sanctioned excuse for bad behavior and disrespect. While the government mildly discourages people from throwing water and foam on unsuspecting tourists, gringos, and the elderly, most young people consider anyone walking the streets fair game.

In contrast, our favorite local holiday was *3 de noviembre,* the day the city of Cuenca celebrates its independence from Spain. In addition to outstanding folk dancing performances and a street devoted to food stands, the city hosts a week-long exhibition of folk artisans from all over South America, who set up booths along the Tomebamba River in open-sided canvas structures they rent from the city. For us it was a chance to meet artists from all over Ecuador, as well as from Columbia, Peru, Bolivia, and Chile. It was also a good time to shop for sweaters, as indigenous vendors came with clothing bundled in drop cloths, which they spread out along the sidewalks that run the length of the river.

Once, near the *Puente Roto,* we encountered a young Ecuadorian folk artist who showed us dozens of paintings in oils on leather made by himself and members of his family. The paintings portrayed the people, scenery, and animals of Ecuador. Each colorful painting depicted a miniature world full of details and stories. We bought a small painting, though it was difficult to choose just one.

With more than 70,000 participants, the *Paseo del Niño Viajero* is the largest parade in South America and one of the biggest religious festivals in Ecuador. Each year on December 24 the procession passed directly under the picture windows of our house on Calle Simón Bolívar. A celebration of children in general and the Christ child more specifically, the tradition started in Ecuador in the 1960s when a Christ Child statue, since known as *Niño Viajero,* was brought back from Rome, after having been blessed by the pope. Beginning at ten o'clock at the San Sebastián church, the procession moves through the city to the church of San Blas. It takes most of the day for the thousands of participants to complete the walk, which is meant to depict the journey of Mary and Joseph to the town of Bethlehem. Part parade, part pageant, the procession includes hundreds of horses, many carrying children in fancy dress and decorated with food and candy, along with cars, trucks, and motorcycles transformed into floats covered with roasted pigs, bottles of liquor, flowers, and fruit, hundreds of people dressed as the Three Wise Men, Shepherds, Angels, and Santa Claus, babies and young boys in traditional garb with mustaches drawn onto their faces with black ink markers. Groups, clubs, parishes, schools, many with their own bands and musicians playing, stilt-walkers, street performers, folk dancing groups, people impersonating characters from the Bible, shepherds driving flocks of sheep, farmers leading llamas or livestock, all flow down the streets of Cuenca, while brass bands, military bands, rock groups on the back of trucks, recorded music, and radio and television announcers create a cacophony of sounds. It's a spectacle in which much of the city participates.

New Year's Eve is another crazy time in Cuenca. While fireworks are popular all year round in Ecuador, and are often used to enhance celebrations such as weddings, graduations, school functions, sporting events, and even religious holidays, nothing compares to New Year's

Eve, when thousands of neighborhood pyromaniacs throughout the city light up the sky in every direction with a constant barrage of fireworks that lasts well over an hour. We usually enjoyed the show from our roof, which gave us a near 360-degree view of the city. The noise, smoke, and constant explosions of color were unlike anything I'd ever seen. Meanwhile, at ground level, we could see dozens of bonfires, including one at the corner of Bolívar and Estévez de Toral, where some of our neighbors jumped over the fire as others shot off a seemingly endless supply of fireworks. Along with traditions like wearing yellow underwear to ensure prosperity, and walking around the block carrying a suitcase for those who hoped to travel in the coming year, making bonfires in the street and jumping over them at midnight, remains a popular tradition.

* * *

For a large city, Cuenca always felt safe and secure. While it's important to be aware of your surroundings, and to avoid certain areas at certain hours, the same can be said of any city. While petty crimes like theft, robbery, purse snatching, pickpocketing, and burglary are common, the murder rate is very low. Shootings and gun related violence are almost non-existent. Driving, however, endangers everyone each day. Even being a passenger in a taxi or on a bus can be a harrowing experience. Bus drivers are among the worst offenders. When they come to a stop, they dump people out as quickly as possible, and rarely wait for all the passengers to board before taking off again. Because the exits can be steep, the old and infirm sometimes end up sprawled in the street as the bus rushes away, spewing a thick cloud of toxic black exhaust behind them.

A walk in Cuenca can easily become a surreal, nightmarish experience. Unlike Europe or the United States, motor vehicles rather than pedestrians have the legal right of way, except in marked crosswalks with traffic lights. Whenever we crossed a street, we moved like cockroaches scurrying to hide under a refrigerator. In addition to the cars and buses, the sidewalks themselves pose dangers. When it rains, the red tiled walkways downtown become as slick as ice-skating rinks. Deep, uncovered holes in the sidewalk are common, as are thick, threaded metal bolts sticking out from the ground where a now absent pole once supported a sign. Metal racks that hold trash cans and metal bars on windows project out from buildings and fences at eye level. Barbed wire appears in unlikely places. Dogs guarding fenced yards aggressively rush at pedestrians as they walk past. In the crowded downtown streets people burst out of shops at full speed without looking to see who might be passing in front of them. Individuals suddenly turn around mid-stride. Couples stop suddenly to begin a conversation in the middle of the sidewalk. No one looks where they are going.

In time, one can adjust and acclimate to cultural differences. The high elevation, the city's proximity to the Northern Volcanic Zone and position within the so-called Ring of Fire represent a more serious threat. The most terrifying experience we lived through in Cuenca was the 2016 earthquake centered in the coastal region near Manta. We were sitting in our living room at home talking with Bryan, who had come to visit us after his classes at the university, when the temblor occurred just before 8:00 in the evening. We heard a noise and felt a strong jolt, immediately followed by a rolling motion that shook the house. The shaking seemed to last around two minutes, though it was probably less. It felt as though we were in a tiny boat on the ocean. There was nowhere safe to go within the house, so we rode it out together in place.

I'd experienced the 1972 Sylmar earthquake as a child, when I lived in the San Fernando Valley near Los Angeles. Later, both Donna and I had attended California State University, Northridge, which was heavily damaged in another catastrophic earthquake in 1992. We felt the temblor far up the coast in Santa Maria, where we lived at the time. We were surprised to learn that the apartment building in which we had lived a few years earlier had collapsed.

Though my memories of the Sylmar earthquake are similar to what we experienced in Cuenca, the latter seemed more intense because we were upstairs in a building only anchored on one side to the surrounding buildings. Afterward, I always felt anxious when I went to bed on the third floor of the house, knowing that the concrete roof above my head had been repaired rather than completely rebuilt.

* * *

There exists a strong connection between Ecuador and the United States, as hundreds of thousands of Ecuadorian immigrants live and work in New York City, Minneapolis, and spread throughout the rest of the country. Many of these people, most of them young men, came to the U.S. to seek work during the Ecuadorian financial crisis of the early 2000s. The majority of them learned to speak English and sent much of their pay back to their families in Ecuador. Some have returned, though many continue to live in the U.S. People in Cuenca often say that New York City is the fourth largest city in Ecuador, as more than 300,000 Ecuadorians live there. Because so many Ecuadorians have relatives in the U.S., they tend to have strong positive feelings toward the country and toward North Americans in general. Unlike in Mexico and most other countries in Latin America, the word "gringo" does not have a pejorative meaning in Ecuador. It simply means a North American, a non-Spanish European, or an English-speaker from anywhere else in the world, such as Australia or New Zealand.

In sharp contrast to Ecuadorians living in the U.S., most of the 4,000 or so gringos who live in Cuenca are retired, well educated, and fairly wealthy by Ecuadorian standards. Those originally from the United States typically do not speak more than a few words of Spanish, though if asked, many of them would say they are nearly fluent. Their reluctance to study a new language may have something to do with their age. According to a joint study undertaken by the city of Cuenca and the United Nations Development Program, the average age of expats living in Cuenca is sixty-six. Over 80% have a college degree and the average monthly household income is slightly over $3,000.00. By contrast, 65% of Cuencanos are under the age of thirty-five, and the average monthly household income is under $500.00.

The majority of gringos in Cuenca tend to keep to themselves, as most can't communicate easily with their neighbors. While North Americans in Cuenca generally integrate into Ecuadorian neighborhoods, many live in clusters of high-rise apartments the locals refer to as "Gringolandia" for their relatively high concentration of gringo residents. Given their limited Spanish, most gringos socialize with other English speakers. They often participate in clubs, social events, charities and parties organized for and hosted by foreigners. Many also enjoy eating out together in groups at restaurants, particularly pizza parlors and upscale cafes offering hamburgers. Despite their high average age, many seem to drink to excess.

There are several publications in Cuenca, both online and in print, that cater to gringo readers. The online forums and news outlets are notable for the vicious bickering and character-assassinations of the participants, who routinely argue about every news story or subject, no matter how innocuous, twisting the subject to fit their narrow political points of view and then defending themselves and their supporters against a barrage of attacks from other readers.

While most of the gringo residents behave themselves, some certainly qualify as "ugly Americans." Once, Donna and I were having lunch in a restaurant with a fixed menu of $2.50 per person. The owner offered well prepared and presented food, and had recently remodeled and decorated the dining area in an attractive, modern style. While she worked to prepare meals in the kitchen, a group of five North Americans entered and seated themselves at a table near us. In general, Ecuadorians tend to be reserved and quiet during meals outside the home. Suddenly, loud and boisterous foreign voices filled the room. When the server did not immediately come to take their order, two of the newcomers went behind the bar and began mixing their own drinks. "The owner knows us. She won't mind," they explained to their friends at the table. We exchanged a horrified look with the Ecuadorian couple at the next table.

Another time, I took Damian and Sara's son Cristian, who were painting the outside of our house, to a neighborhood restaurant. Over lunch we had been discussing the upcoming Ecuadorian election, when three retired Texans sitting at the table behind us began talking about the evils of socialism. At the same time, they bragged about the benefits of the cheap, government subsidized gas they used for cooking and the refunds they received from Ecuadorian government each month on the Value Added Tax. Next, they enthused about the nearly free Ecuadorian health care they had received, including an open-heart surgery. Still, they complained bitterly that "socialism" had ruined the United States. Listening to them, I didn't know whether to laugh or cry.

It's easy to make friends in Ecuador. People who once lived and worked in the U.S. sometimes approached us in the park and engaged us in unexpected conversations in English. University students in English classes asked to interview us on camera for their class projects. If Spanish-speaking gringos show up to cultural events, reporters from the newspapers take their picture and solicit their opinions. Though a few superstitious indigenous people reportedly stare and hiss at gringos on the street, and taxi drivers and shopkeepers sometimes apply a "gringo tax" or charge "gringo prices," to tourists and non-Spanish speakers, there's a certain status automatically afforded to foreigners, who are generally perceived as wealthy and well educated.

After starting his studies at the University of Cuenca, our young friend Bryan met a retired arts administrator from New York City. They spoke in English several times and exchanged emails. The American eventually invited Bryan to coffee. It was the first time Bryan had ever met someone for coffee and he was happy to be doing something so special and adult. While the two of them were conversing, a well-dressed Ecuadorian woman got up from her table nearby and interjected herself into the conversation, speaking in Spanish to Bryan. "How do you have gringo friends?" She asked. "I would like to know some North Americans and be seen with them here. Unlike you, I am middle class, yet you are here having coffee with this man. I want to know how that is possible," she told him. He told us later that he felt as though she had belittled and embarrassed him in front of his friend. Her rudeness had ruined his experience.

* * *

Through the social criticism inherent in my writing, I had always hoped to have some positive impact, to help inspire people to greater awareness, to make the world a better place. It wasn't until I lived in Ecuador that I discovered a more potent and healing way to exert my influence. I learned that the small acts of kindness and caring—classes I gave to young students, or the cookies we baked for others—had more immediate meaning and impact than the words in my books.

My experiences in Ecuador taught me that my knowledge, perspective, and attitude could be a lifeline in the lives of the people with whom we interacted each day. Cuencanos looked up to me, literally—I was a foot taller than most of them. It surprised me to see how I towered above others on the street, when I saw my reflection in a shop window. Donna and I were well educated and comparatively well-off North Americans of European descent. We spoke Spanish and could teach others to speak English. We lived in a house and worked in a studio filled with books and art. People listened carefully to what we said.

From our first days in Ecuador, our experience was centered around the people we met. Whenever someone asked us what we liked about their country, we always answered, "the people." We made an effort to treat everyone with kindness and respect, which, in a society still consumed by social hierarchies, made an impression upon our friends and neighbors. Though we entertained visitors from the United States, we rarely spoke with other foreigners. Instead, our friends in Cuenca were Ecuadorians. We learned about the culture in which we lived, shared meals, holidays, and special occasions with our friends. We participated in the daily life of our neighborhood and the community.

* * *

The block of Calle Simón Bolívar where we lived, between Estévez de Toral and Coronel Talbot, was dense with houses above the street-level shops. Businesses included two small markets, a bakery, two bazars—shops that sold everything from toys to stationery, to clothes and gifts—a photography studio, a dentist's office, a public notary, an upscale Italian restaurant, a pharmacy, a taxi stand at the corner, a shop that sold compact discs of pirated movies, an ice cream stand, a large government building housing the *Ministerio de Desarrollo Urbano y Vivienda*, Marcello's tiny real estate office, the Posada de Angel and Cuenca Suites hotels, a Catholic orphanage and nursing home, and later my own art gallery. The day we moved into our house, I met the Mother Superior and director of the Hogar Miguel León, the entrance to which was located directly across the street. No doubt she had monitored the renovation project and was curious about the new owners. While we were unloading our possessions from the pickup truck, she happened to pull up in a taxi. As she approached me, I greeted her respectfully. We shook hands as she introduced herself. "I hope you plan to take care of us," she said. I told her I planned to be a good neighbor.

Our little block was like a small town. Neighboring shopkeepers sometimes met on the sidewalk to pass the time together when business was slow. We made a point of patronizing the local stores and chatting with the neighbors. We made friends with the guards at the *Ministerio* and gave them cookies we baked. In return, they looked after our property and kept it free of graffiti. The hotels offered special rates when our friends and relatives came to visit. Our neighbors knew that I was an artist, that I taught English, that our friends were Ecuadorians. They also looked out for us and were glad to help whenever we had questions.

Eventually, we learned what the building under construction behind us would become. For months it had been a mystery and source of speculation for the whole neighborhood. Finally, a sign went up that read: Cuenca Suites. Soon thereafter, we met a young Dane named Simon and his Ecuadorian wife, Rebecca, who would live in one of the apartments with their two young daughters and manage the facility for Rebecca's family, who owned the original historic property. They gave us a tour of the new apartment hotel, which was built on two levels, in a colonial style, with thick wooden posts, tile roofs, wrought iron railings, and an outdoor walkway overlooking an internal courtyard with a fountain. When Simon and Rebecca asked what I thought they might do to make the space warmer and more appealing, I told them that they needed some color in the courtyard, a focal point for the eye. They had already been to my studio and gallery and admired my work, so I offered to make them some large paintings to hang in the hotel. Over the next year, I made five large paintings, including two giant oil paintings of local subjects. When we left Cuenca, I left a number of other paintings with Simon and Rebecca, including some of my cave art–inspired works, which they used to decorate some of the rooms throughout the hotel.

Eventually, Simon and Rebecca bought a house of their own several blocks from the hotel. They remodeled the inside extensively, from their own plans. Simon did most of the work himself over several months. Somehow, he managed to turn a dingy two story 60s house divided into multiple small rooms into a modern, European open concept showcase, with a grand staircase and a towering atrium. To help celebrate the new house, I gave Simon one of my more colorful abstract paintings from the "Cables" series to hang in the dining room. My last major artistic project in Cuenca was a three-meter square abstract painting called "Clockwork Poem" that I created specifically for the upstairs landing of their house.

* * *

Like all countries, Ecuador is a product of its history, a history which, along with the rest of Latin America, intersects with that of Spain. Columbus discovered the New World in the same year his sponsors, the Catholic Monarchs King Ferdinand II of Aragon and Queen Isabella of Castile, completed the *Reconquista,* or restoration of the Visigothic Kingdom over territories that had been controlled and ruled for centuries by Muslim Moors. The surrender of Granada, the last of the Muslim emirates in Spain, on January 2, 1492 subtly affected what would later become Latin America.

What is today known as the city of Cuenca, was originally a Cañari settlement called Guapondelig, founded around 500 AD. The Inca Empire absorbed the Cañari city in the late 1400s and renamed it Tomebamba. When the Spanish arrived, the local inhabitants destroyed the city and disappeared into the surrounding mountains. Gil Ramírez Dávalos founded the Spanish settlement of Cuenca on April 12, 1557 and named it after Cuenca, Spain. The city grew steadily during the colonial period. Cuenca achieved its independence from Spain on November 3, 1820.

I had always wondered how relatively few Spaniards had conquered and maintained control over most of South America, Central America, and Mexico, and how native people had been so quickly and completely assimilated into Spanish culture. The short answer is religion. In return for their good work pushing the Moors out of Europe, the pope rewarded Ferdinand and Isabella with the rights to the vast, yet unexplored territories of the New World. He also gave the Spanish monarchy a mandate to convert the native population to Catholicism.

As the Spanish had lived for close to 800 years in a land of mixed races—Moors, Blacks, Semites, and Caucasians, religion rather than race distinguished and separated them. In the New World, Spanish soldiers conquered the indigenous people, while the Roman Catholic clergy converted them. Spanish *conquistadores* and their officers secured alliances by marrying women from royal Indio background, while soldiers, traders, and functionaries sired offspring with local women, both in and out of wedlock, producing a new generation of *Mestizos,* or mixed-race Spaniards.

During the Spanish Inquisition, when the remaining "New Christians," or converted Moors and Jews, were expelled from Spain, the Spanish developed an obsession for demonstrating the "purity" of their blood in order to prove that they were not "tainted" by exposure to earlier, non-Christian family ties. The twisted obsession appeared as well in the colonies, where complicated charts for *casta* or lineage took form. An intricate set of rules resulted, which codified social standing in much of Latin American culture. In Spanish colonial law, mixed-race *castas* were classified as part of the *república de españoles* and not the *república de indios*. Indigenous Amerindians existed outside the Hispanic sphere.

Ironically, after winning their independence from Spain in the early 1800s, Hispanic elites within Latin American society continued to consider the degree of acculturation to Hispanic culture and the *sistema de castas* to determine a person's place in society and to justify their own high social standing. Even today, in contemporary Ecuadorian society, indigenous people who want to improve their social standing and standard of living, typically move to a city, give up their traditional garb and language, and enroll their children in the educational system. Still, many citizens prefer the traditional lifestyle, language, and values and choose not to fully enter into Hispanic culture.

Another fascinating aspect of how history has impacted Ecuadorian society concerns the unusual structure of the short-lived Inca Empire, which lasted roughly a hundred years and stretched across the Andean region from Ecuador to Chile. It was the Incas who the Spaniards encountered when they arrived in South America. Centered in Cusco, Peru, the Incas chose Quechua, still spoken today by indigenous people throughout the Andes, as the lingua franca of their empire.

According to Gordon Francis McEwan, in his book *The Incas: New Perspectives,* the "most unusual aspect of the Inca economy was the lack of a market system and money." With only a few exceptions, trade as we know it did not exist in the Inca Empire. "Each citizen of the empire was issued the necessities of life out of the state storehouses, including food, tools, raw materials, and clothing, and needed to purchase nothing." Since there were no shops or markets, "there was no need for a standard currency or money, and there was nowhere to spend money or purchase or trade for necessities," writes McEwan. Also noticeable is the communal ownership of some land in rural communities, as well as the government mandate that communities provide and care for the sick and elderly.

The Inca government centrally controlled planning, production, distribution, and allocation of commodities. Internally, there was little to no market economy. In the event of shortages of non-vital goods, an area would correct the problem through colonization instead of barter or trade. In cases of shortages of essential goods, the state mandated resource exchanges between provinces.

A kind of hybrid socialist monarchy, the most notable difference between the Incan taxpayer and the European serf was that the Inca paid their taxes in labor. In return, the ruling class provided workers with food and clothing out of state warehouses. Tapping the large labor force, the Inca built impressive sites like Machu Picchu, irrigated the Andes for farming, built a huge network of roads that spanned the empire, and conquered much of the continent.

With the Inca model in mind, it's little surprise that people who live within indigenous and rural communities in Ecuador are often asked to provide shared labor for local public works projects. They also tend to live more communally, in harmony with nature. They usually lean to the left in their political affiliations.

These days, like much of Latin America, Ecuador suffers from a relatively weak economy. The country has little manufacturing and few good paying jobs outside of high-level professional activities. The only real safety net is the willingness and often limited ability of extended family to absorb the costs of feeding and sheltering family members who lose their jobs or experience unexpected health problems or other hardships.

Though an expensive or highly competitive university education helps, it is by no means a guarantee of success or financial security. In fact, many degree holders remain underemployed and often work outside of their academic fields. Only business owners, doctors, particularly specialists with foreign degrees or internships, engineers, high-status architects, or pilots trained by the military (often sons of wealthy families), can reasonably expect to command a good salary. Being an employee in Ecuador is often a horrible experience, a kind of demeaning servitude, especially for temporary or minimum-wage workers. Even highly desirable government jobs are often performed under temporary or time-limited contracts. Since the government itself often violates national labor laws in its treatment of its employees, it rarely enforces these laws in the private sector. Along with poverty, alcoholism, and underemployment, domestic violence, government corruption, and petty crime persist in Ecuadorian society.

* * *

We first met Angelita at the *Apartamentos Otorongo,* where she worked cleaning rooms six hours a day, six days a week. After her shift at the hotel, she would run across town to the private residences of wealthy foreigners, whose high-rise apartments she would also clean. Angelita came from an indigenous family in Tarqui, a village just outside of Cuenca. She had two young children she raised and supported by herself, as she had left her abusive husband several years earlier. Her parents and siblings did not approve of such independence and barely spoke to her. Her only friend was a Canadian woman she had worked for who had helped her when she left her husband.

Industrious and driven to create a better life for her children, Angelita worked long hours doing physical labor without complaint. Some days she ate potato pancakes from a plastic container as she hurried across town. She lived frugally and saved her money. Her dream was to buy a house for herself and her children.

Soon after Donna and I moved into the apartment next to *Los Molinos del Batán,* Angelita became my first Ecuadorian student. She asked me to help her with her English on Saturday afternoons. She also wanted to introduce her young children to people from other cultures who might influence them positively. When we first met them, Juanito and Anita seemed shy and withdrawn. Juanito would sometimes fall asleep on the couch while we talked.

During the summer months, while her children were home from school, Angelita asked if I would give them art lessons, as both Juanito and Anita admired my paintings and had expressed an interest in learning how to draw. I knew that the children would be locked in their apartment with little to do while their mother was at work all day, so I agreed to give them lessons during the afternoons. I taught them some basic techniques and put them to work drawing fruit and crockery from life with pencils and charcoal. For such young children, they had remarkable concentration and patience. Their work improved steadily.

Three years later, Angelita purchased a townhouse that was under construction in the foothills surrounding Cuenca. The contractor cut corners on construction and did not provide proper documentation for the property. Nevertheless, after months of bureaucratic delays, Angelita eventually received a legal deed and permission to connect to the municipal water system, which allowed her to finally take possession of the property. Though it was a long trip by bus into town, Angelita and her children were delighted to have their own home. When we left Cuenca, I gave her one of my large paintings for her house. Both Ana and Juan attended an international high school and went on to study at the University of Cuenca. Angelita sometimes sends us cheerful notes.

* * *

The Central Intelligence Agency of the United States government, which has a long history of meddling in Ecuadorian politics, enjoys a legendary status in Ecuador. Inside the Ecuadorian parliament building in Quito, there is a mural by Ecuadorian painter Oswaldo Guayasamín entitled *"Imagen de la Patria,"* which features, among its many parts and panels, a grinning skull in a military helmet emblazoned with the letters "CIA." On the street, it's common to see people wearing baseball caps with FBI or CIA embroidered on them. Average Ecuadorians routinely blame strange events, particularly anti-government political scandals and protests, on the machinations of *"La Cia."*

Following the Cuban revolution in 1959, the CIA spread throughout Latin America to counteract the influence of communist labor unions, student groups, and socialist governments. In the early 1960's, the CIA pressed Ecuadorian President José Maria Velasco Ibarra and Vice President Carlos Julio Arosemena Monroy, his successor, to break diplomatic relations with Castro's government in Cuba. When each refused to help isolate Castro, both were successively removed in CIA-backed coups by the country's military forces. Ecuadorians also believe that the CIA was directly responsible for the May 1981 plane crash that killed President Jaime Roldós Aguilera in the province of Loja. Roldós Aguilera had refused an invitation to Ronald Reagan's inauguration and maintained friendly relations with the Sandinistas in Nicaragua and the Cuban government. He was also planning to reorganize the Ecuadorian oil industry, threatening the interests of transnational oil corporations working in the country.

When President Rafael Correa took office in 2007, the CIA again intensified its efforts in Ecuador. During his tenure, Correa shut down the U.S. military base in Manta, deported a number of suspected CIA operatives and fired others who he claimed had infiltrated national police, military, and intelligence agencies. Nongovernmental organizations such as USAID and the National Endowment for Democracy (NED), along with the nonprofit organization *Fundamedios,* which monitors "threats to media freedom" in Ecuador, helped disseminate CIA-sponsored propaganda. Meanwhile, the NGO *Participación Ciudadana,* which specializes in "investigative journalism" authored by the CIA, received hundreds of thousands of dollars in aid to help undermine the Correa government.

On a more personal level, one of my teachers told me he had been bullied by a CIA operative in Cuenca. For many years, he had taught English at a cultural center with obvious ties to the American embassy and the U.S. government. When he was fired suddenly and replaced by a less experienced teacher at a lower rate of pay, he asked to see the director, a North American he suspected was a CIA operative. The director told him to shut up and leave or he'd have him killed. My teacher showed me a photocopy of the letter he wrote to the U.S. embassy in Quito detailing his assertions. He told me he'd never received a reply.

* * *

Our friend Sara once told us a story about her attitude toward money and status. When her son Cristian was in high school, he asked her to buy him a pair of "designer label" jeans, which in Ecuador probably cost well over a hundred dollars. Her response was that she always bought him label jeans. "These?" he asked, confused.

"Yes," she responded, "they're F-L Jeans and they only cost ten dollars."

"F-L?"

"*Sí mijo: F-L, Feria Libre.*" She had bought them, like everything else, at the central market in Cuenca.

El Arenal, Feria Libre is in some ways the beating heart of Cuenca. It typifies the kind of commerce common throughout the country, which is to say self-employed, cottage industry. A good percentage of Ecuadorians work for themselves, many of them growing, transporting, cooking, preparing, and selling food. A massive complex of covered and open-air market stalls and huge parking lots, the *Feria Libre* sprawls over seven acres near the intersection of Avenida de las Americas and Remigio Crespo. Like the eight smaller Mercados in the city, the *Feria Libre* sells fruits, vegetables, meat, fish, and dried goods. What sets it apart, aside from the massive scale, are the live animals that are also for sale, including pigs, *cuy* (guinea pigs that are a popular local dish), chickens, and goats, all of which are sold for food, along with the small birds, puppies, and kittens sold as pets.

At least half the massive enclosed space is devoted to a dizzying internal maze, a kind of medieval city of narrow alleys between tightly packed miniature shops offering a variety of goods, including cell phones and electronics, cookware, cheap aluminum pots and pans, clothing, shoes, underwear, toys, backpacks, products for the home, leather goods, wooden vessels and utensils, perfume, plastic vessels and storage containers, hats, sunglasses, knives, and mystery products bought in bulk from who knows where. Everything seems to cost *un dolarcito*. It's also possible to get a bargain haircut and a shave. Of course, shoppers can also visit the large food court to drink fresh fruit and vegetable juices, eat breakfast or *almuerzos*, often *secos*, a kind of stew served over rice, at one of the dozens of utilitarian restaurants that sell inexpensive lunches and fast food presented on plastic plates.

For the uninitiated, a visit to any of the local Mercados can result in a kind of sensory overload. In the meat section, large cuts dangle from hooks as butchers hack away at animal parts piled on work benches. The claustrophobic interior space and the iron-rich smell of the blood that pools at their feet, near the drains on the concrete floors, can be overwhelming. Piles of cardboard boxes or wooden crates full of plucked, headless chickens, their starfish-shaped yellow feet still attached, are stacked along passageways. Miles of sausages hang from the rafters like macabre Christmas ornaments. At the Feria Libre I once saw a ten-foot-tall hill of fish that looked like it had been dumped from a large truck directly onto the concrete floor. Like Annie Dillard's descriptions of the fecundity of nature in her book *A Pilgrim at Tinker Creek,* the sheer volume of fresh food on offer at the Feria Libre can be disorienting.

Competing stalls specialize in potatoes and sell dozens of different varieties. Vendors stand in front of giant piles of bananas and plantains brought in from the coast. Sara once told me that growers export and sell the best bananas abroad. One of my teachers at the language school instructed me about the different varieties of bananas. *"Bananas de seda* are the best," he said. Pineapples also come from the coast and are inexpensive and delicious. Avocados were another special treat for us, as they are plentiful year-round and relatively inexpensive compared to the U.S. Ecuadorians love fruit juices, and many people own a good quality blender, which they consider essential kitchen equipment. In addition to orange juice, other popular fruit drinks are made from mangos, coconuts, strawberries, blackberries, and cantaloupes. Along with the expected fruits, the *mercados* offer many exotic fruits rarely seen in north American markets, including *maracuyá, babaco, cherimoya,* and spiky little balls with a soft, pulpy center called *achotillo.*

At the edges of the *mercados* and in stores surrounding the *Diez de Agosto Mercado,* other *vendadores* sell bulk goods by weight out of wooden barrels: dried beans, grains, various shapes of pasta, and chunks of unsweetened chocolate. Others concentrate on household goods like oils, detergent, and paper goods. Throughout the city, food is plentiful and ever present.

Each of the municipal *mercados* features a section of booths that sell spices and herbal remedies. Folk medicine remains popular in the Andes region of the country, and the women who sell these herbs serve as a kind of alternative pharmacy. They are happy to tell clients suffering from specific ills how to brew up infusions that they believe will cure just about anything. Most locals blame the changeable weather in the mountains for a range of physical problems, a view that is sometimes reinforced by medical practitioners.

At street level of both the *Diez de Agosto* and *Nueve de Octubre mercados,* female indigenous healers exorcise demons and treat virtually any ailment for paying customers on Tuesdays and Thursdays. During these cleansing sessions, the healers gently beat the afflicted with bunches of herbs and mysterious combinations of plants and vegetation, blow smoke at them, rub a raw egg over them to absorb the evil, and sometimes even spit a spray of strong alcohol in their faces. Given its location on Calle Larga, tourists often come to take photographs at the *Diez de Agosto Mercado.* Sometimes they subject themselves to a cleansing.

By their own admission, Ecuadorians are superstitious people. I like to joke that I've never met an Ecuadorian, or rather one from the Andes region, who has not seen at least one UFO and several ghosts. Emilio, a friendly taxi driver who had helped us move from our apartment to our house, and who sometimes brought us to or from the airport in Guayaquil, often entertained us during the three-hour drive with ghost stories and legends that had transpired in the surrounding mountain communities. Our first Spanish teacher also used to delight in telling us real-life ghost stories that had happened to her. She told us as well that when her daughter was little, she developed a stomach disorder and started to lose weight at an alarming rate. Though she took the child to see numerous doctors, none could properly diagnose or solve the problem. Finally, she brought the girl to the *mercado* for a cleansing. The following day, her daughter displayed no symptoms. She had been miraculously cured. "I know it's hard to believe," she told us, "but it's true."

We often shopped for produce at the *Diez de Agosto Mercado* downtown, though the smaller *Tres de Noviembre Mercado* was closer to our house. Trust was a big factor in choosing which stalls and particular venders to patronize. Over time, the *vendadores* would come to recognize you as a regular customer, which had distinct advantages. Loyalty eventually resulted in better quality produce, more prompt service, and the occasional *yapa*, or extra items given as a premium or reward. Donna had her favorites for potatoes. She had two other vendors she patronized for different kinds of vegetables. I usually bought the fruit, as I had developed a good relationship with one of the young women who operated a large stall that offered every kind of fruit available. Though it was a big stand, with a constant stream of customers, whenever she saw me waiting, she gave me a big smile. When it was my turn, she always greeted me as *"Joven,"* (youngster) which made me smile as well.

* * *

My last teacher in Cuenca was a woman named Lucía. In addition to introducing me to essays and short stories by the Spanish writer Rosa Montero, she also recommended documentaries, films, and television programs I could watch online, including a Chilean investigative journalism program I found fascinating. I watched films produced in Ecuador, Columbia, Chile, Mexico, Cuba, Argentina, and Spain. Lucía also introduced me to the controversial and hilarious Peruvian author, personality, and talk show host Jaime Bailey, whose scandalous exploits, offbeat humor, and novel opinions we both found entertaining.

Bailey's nightly television show aired on Spanish-language television from Miami, where he has lived for many years. The Spanish speaking guests ranged from rappers and actresses, to former politicians, to authors and journalists. Once a candidate for president in Peru and now a U.S. citizen, Bailey loves to discuss politics. In both his books and his live television show he offers his opinions, his disgust, and his self-mockery in equal measure.

In addition to working on my grammar, Lucía constantly engaged me in conversations on topics she knew interested us both: literature, politics, film, and current events. She also used me as a resource to improve her own teaching and general knowledge. Her thorough subject knowledge, her intellectual curiosity, and her ability to customize curriculum to the needs and interests of individual students made her an excellent teacher. Her sense of humor and open heart made her a good friend as well.

* * *

Though she knew only a handful of words in English, our friend Sara nonetheless had an amazing ability to understand and communicate with guests at the hotel where she worked. While most of her interactions with foreign guests were routine, Sara could anticipate the needs of guests and communicate nonverbally. When we moved from the hotel to our apartment along the river, a few blocks up the same street, Sara suggested I come to the hotel office to practice my Spanish with her on Saturday evenings when it was quiet and she had nothing to do but babysit the front desk. For the next year I spent an hour or two in the office of the hotel each Saturday evening. At one point, she asked if I'd help her son Cristian with his English, and I agreed. By the end of the year, Cristian had moved on to other concerns and Sara herself had replaced him as my student.

After we moved to our house downtown, I stopped going to the Hotel Otorongo on Saturday evenings to converse with Sara. However, since we were only few blocks from where Sara lived, she continued her English lessons once a week on Sunday afternoons at our apartment. I had told her that one hour a week was not enough to make real progress with the language, but that's all the time she could spare from her busy schedule. Though Sara struggled with English, I could see that what she really needed was friends who would listen to her without judgment.

A bright, intuitive person, I couldn't understand why she had so much trouble learning English. During the three years she was my student, Sara asked me to repeat the same basic grammar lessons over and over without ever memorizing nor mastering the concepts. "I just can't seem to concentrate," she told me. "I'm always tired and there are too many other things to worry about. My brain just can't remember the words." Like her co-worker Angelita, Sara was so busy working and taking care of others that she barely had time to eat or sleep. Despite her lack of success with English, she told us repeatedly how much she enjoyed coming to our house. She told us that before meeting us, she'd never had friends. Her lessons provided her with an excuse to relax, socialize, and enjoy a cup of coffee.

After three years of instruction, Sara could barely form a coherent sentence. Then one day she seemed to have a breakthrough. Instead of relating the week's events in Spanish as she usually did, for a period of about half an hour she communicated entirely in English. I couldn't believe it, but encouraged her to continue her narrative. When she finished, we looked at each other in disbelief. She had no idea how she had managed it, nor did I. Though she never duplicated the performance, her sudden fluency was nevertheless a kind of a miracle.

* * *

When Pope Francis visited Ecuador in July of 2015, we watched, along with millions of people in Ecuador and around the world, the processions and the huge public mass Francis performed at the Bicentennial Park in Quito on television. For weeks prior to the pope's arrival, there had been stories in the local newspapers about the gifts that Ecuador's president, Raphael Correa, and others would present to the pope. Made by artisans from the Azuay communities of Gualaceo, Chordeleg, and Sígsig, many of these gifts were items the pope would wear and use during his appearances in Quito and Guayaquil.

As usual, U. S. media coverage of the Papal visit portrayed Ecuador, its people and its government, in a negative, slanted, and largely inaccurate manner. According to an article by David Wright of ABC News, "At the start of a weeklong visit to his native continent, Pope Francis arrived to a red-carpet reception at Quito's main airport, where Ecuador's socialist president Rafael Correa greeted him on the tarmac. But as the pope's motorcade proceeded into the city, many along the sidelines voiced their disapproval of Correa, giving him thumbs down." Wright himself deserves a "thumbs down" for his blatantly biased and misleading reporting. Indeed, anyone who directly witnessed, watched Ecuadorian television coverage of the event, or lived in the country during this time would find such propaganda laughable. Despite recent political squabbles with indigenous groups and a proposal to increase inheritance tax which was vehemently opposed by the upper middle class and the wealthy, Correa had recently won reelection by a wide margin. His party controlled the National Assembly, and Correa himself enjoyed overwhelming popular support among Ecuadorians, particularly from the people on the street. In fact, the only real "thumbs down" came from a tiny class of highly vocal, wealthy elites who owned and funded the opposition news outlets the Ecuadorian president had restricted once their stories had been proven to be directed and often written by the CIA.

An opinion piece in the *Wall Street Journal* went so far as to accuse Ecuador's president of wanting to "co-opt Pope Francis." Not content with attacking Correa and socialism, the U.S. media also suggested that the pope's ideas on wealth distribution and social justice were naive and dangerous. The ending of David Wright's ABC News article quoted above, absurdly attempts to frame the pope not only as a misguided hippy, but as a potential user of a "controlled substance": "As a young man, Pope Francis lost part of one lung due to an illness, and church officials acknowledged some concern about altitude sickness. According to Vatican officials, the pope has expressed an interest in trying a local remedy popular among indigenous people in the Andes mountains: coca leaves... But coca leaves are illegal *in much of the developed world* [italics mine], banned as a controlled substance because they are the raw ingredient of cocaine."

Among the most Catholic nations in Latin America, nearly eighty percent of the Ecuadorian population identifies as Catholic. Abortion is all but illegal in the country, and according to a 2014 Pew Research Center survey, 84% of Ecuadorian Catholics object to it as morally wrong. Ecuador also has the highest teenage pregnancy rate in South America, with 8% of women between the ages of fifteen and nineteen giving birth.

About 7% of the population claims to be agnostic or atheist, while a little over 10% identifies as Protestant or Evangelical. Protestant charities and missions, along with other Christian-variant religions imported from the United States, most notably the Jehovah's Witnesses, are continually making inroads into Ecuadorian society. According to the Jehovah's Witnesses web site, there are now over 100,000 "ministers who teach the Bible" in Ecuador. While some of these operations may be well intended, they often seem like the cultural equivalent to an invasive species that disrupts important ecosystem processes.

The Jehovah's Witnesses and other religious groups often attract converts and followers by offering direct financial assistance, food, and medical aid to downtrodden members of poor communities. When their level of charity surpasses whatever relief and aid can be offered by the local Catholic parish, the poorest people in the community gravitate toward these new, competing religions, not out of any religious fervor, but as a matter of survival. In the town of Jima, we saw a JW Kingdom Hall operating out of an old storefront. We learned from our friends that elders from the headquarters organization in Guayaquil had expressed interest in buying a piece of property on which to construct a permanent Kingdom Hall and social center. For the past several years, local land owners had resisted, refusing to sell their property to them. No one wanted to be the one who betrayed the Catholic Church and centuries of local heritage and tradition. No one wanted to face the collective scorn of the community.

Begun in 1885, the massive red brick Cathedral of the Immaculate Conception, or New Cathedral, is the spiritual and physical center of Cuenca. With its twin towers and iconic blue and white tile domes, the cathedral is the city's primary landmark and is easily identifiable from the surrounding hills. The cathedral faces the large public square called Parque Calderon. Across the square sits the smaller, white El Sagrario church, also called the Old Cathedral.

In 1565, the El Sagrario Church was built in what today is the historical center of the city. Like the other original buildings of the city, the materials used in its construction were simple and readily available: stone, sand, wood, and brick. Today, the old cathedral serves as a museum and is also used for occasional concerts performed by the Cuenca Symphony Orchestra.

The towers and the main arch beneath the stained-glass rosette of the New Cathedral form part of the arched promenade that covers the walkways in front of the buildings on the streets that border Parque Calderon, except for the Old Cathedral. Vendors sell candles and religious souvenirs from a colorful stand at the bottom of the steps that lead to the entrance to the cathedral. Inside the vestibule, a handful of elderly beggars silently solicit alms. Though many residents live in poverty, there are very few beggars in Cuenca, as most people, even those with handicaps, prefer to supplement family incomes by selling pencils, candy, baked goods, or fruit door to door or on the street.

Like many residents of Cuenca, Donna and I, either together or separately, would often go into the cathedral to stand or sit for a while in the cool tranquility of the sacred space. Sometimes Donna lit a candle for our son at one of the side altars. Sometimes I lit one as well, usually at the altar of the *Dolorosa,* if only to bring a little more light into the world. It was something we had learned to do on our walking trip through France, where we had visited so many churches.

Our Ecuadorian friends were all devout Catholics. I often asked them about local saints and about the significance of local religious holidays. I was careful to treat their faith with respect. When they asked about my own views on religion, I told them I had been raised a Catholic, but had been an agnostic since adolescence. I told them I was interested in Eastern religions, mysticism and spirituality, and that I rejected the dogma, politics, and troubled history of Western religions. I told them I preferred socialism to capitalism and that I liked the new pope. Though my head was full of unusual ideas and new information, they viewed me as a good person, and they trusted me with the education of their children.

Though I love the blossoms and buds of spring, the way the trees put on a handsome new coat of foliage, I've always disliked the holiday we call Easter, especially the ironically named "Good Friday," which seems more a disturbing meditation upon human cruelty and death than a celebration of fecundity and rebirth. As a child, the Catholic obsession with the details of "The Passion" of Christ seemed more barbaric than holy. I couldn't get past the horrific and detailed descriptions of the sadistic tortures so fundamental to the "stations of the cross." I remember that my mother once made my sister and me sit through several hours of Good Friday rituals at a Catholic Church while we were on vacation in San Francisco. The unrelenting horrors of the crucifixion disgusted and repelled me. I simply couldn't accept the portrayal of life as devoid of beauty and goodness and filled instead with pain and suffering. Years later, when I studied the history of Japan at the university, I remember how my Japanese professor giggled nervously as he tried to explain how Japanese people view Christianity. "We just don't understand why Christians worship a bloody, tortured man nailed to a cross," he said. "It seems barbaric to us." Though I could appreciate the good intentions of Christianity, like the Japanese, I naturally rejected what seemed to me a cult of sadism and death.

In Cuenca, as in other Latin American countries, the Passion of Christ is routinely reenacted in the streets. On Palm Sunday, people carry palm fronds. On Good Friday, they walk from church to church to hear about each "station of the cross." The Hogar Miguel León orphanage opposite our house displayed an elaborate table and decorations outside the entrance each year. I don't know which specific torture it was in charge of explaining, as I tried to ignore the whole event. It was just one evening per year.

The same year our friends' daughter Karen graduated from high school, she also celebrated her Confirmation. We were invited to attend the ceremony, which took place in the gymnasium of the La Salle Catholic School. Karen chose her aunt Gaby to be her sponsor. Near the end of the program, the Bishop of Cuenca addressed the new members of the church. While I don't recall the exact theme of the talk, I remember the elegant manner with which he spoke. Later that year, we also attended Karen's graduation, held in the same building. Afterwards, we went to a party hosted by relatives of Damian's we'd never met before. Bryan was assigned the task of making sure we didn't feel completely alienated.

* * *

Through most of our first four years living in Ecuador, we paid little attention to the news coming out of the United States. Since we didn't watch television, we got most of our news from our online subscriptions to *The Washington Post* and *The New Yorker*, along with the BBC, CNN, and *The Huffington Post*. From what we saw, the U.S. remained hopelessly divided and the politics increasingly toxic. Even social media, which had at first seemed like a promising way to reconnect with people from our past, especially for expats, began to sour as increasingly rigid social and political opinions, often based on faulty information and propaganda, overwhelmed much of the discourse. By 2015, the coming presidential election made it impossible to ignore the news coming from the U.S. By then, social media had become so negative and muddied by politics, that we canceled all our accounts and completely withdrew from it.

That summer and fall, I followed news of the protests of the Standing Rock Sioux against the Dakota Access Pipeline in North Dakota, which had been rerouted near the Standing Rock Sioux Reservation after authorities deemed a proposed route near the state capital too risky for Bismarck's water supply. The tribe objected to the pipeline for similar reasons. They felt that allowing the pipeline to cross under Lake Oahe and the Missouri River threatened their only supply of clean water. What began as the Sacred Stone Camp grew into several large camps in the area, which collectively became the largest gathering of Native Tribes in the past hundred years. Protests at the pipeline site drew indigenous people from throughout North America and the rest of the world, along with other supporters, who all agreed to let the Sioux elders lead the non-violent protests and civil disobedience.

By late September, representatives of over 300 Native American tribes and an estimated 3,000 to 4,000 pipeline resistance supporters resided in the camp. Arrests first occurred when people chained themselves to heavy machinery.

In early September, the Dakota Pipeline company hired a small army of private security guards as the company used bulldozers to dig up part of the pipeline route that was subject to a pending injunction motion. The land contained possible Native graves and burial artifacts. When unarmed protesters approached the bulldozers, the guards used pepper spray and guard dogs to attack them. At least six protesters were treated for dog bites, and an estimated thirty others were pepper-sprayed. Police from seven neighboring states were sent to reinforce the local police effort against protesters. During November, when the temperature fell below freezing, police sprayed the protesters with water cannons. Police have also acknowledged using sponge rounds, bean bag rounds, stinger rounds, teargas grenades, pepper spray, Mace, Tasers and a mysterious and unnamed sonic weapon.

As events at Standing Rock played out, Donna and I watched in horror as squabbling Democrats undermined common sense by offering up a well-qualified but entitled, divisive, and unlikeable candidate much of the country despised. Meanwhile, Donald Trump was busy laying waste to what little remained of common sense and decency in American politics. We watched in horror as people expressed their disgust for both political parties. Aided by Russian trolls, Americans gave their attention to Trump's clownish reality television campaign, in which the Republican debates devolved into a twisted remake of *Survivor*. Then, Trump postured and posed at a Republican Convention with a party platform so bizarre and contradictory, many Republican insiders quit in disgust. In November, election night turned into an election nightmare.

For the first three months of Trump's presidency, I slept poorly, wracked by apocalyptic dreams. One of Trump's first acts was to issue an executive order to speed up approval to construct the pipeline, on the basis of creating more jobs. The order provoked a new wave of protests and response from leaders of the Sioux tribe. The number of protesters arrested had by then surpassed 700. On February 3, activist Chase Iron Eyes and more than seventy peaceful protesters were arrested for "inciting a riot" during a police raid ordered by the Trump administration. The felony charge can result in up to five years in prison. In early February, Trump authorized the Army Corps of Engineers to end its environmental impact assessment and proceed with construction. The pipeline was completed by April.

* * *

By January of the following year, Donna and I had decided that we would slowly begin the process of leaving Ecuador, perhaps in stages. We'd spent the previous two summers exploring Spain and we thought we'd like to live in Europe for a while. By March, we'd decided to put our house on the market. We didn't expect that it would sell quickly, as the steep stairs were a disadvantage, particularly for older gringo buyers.

The following month, on a routine trip to the dentist, I learned that a filling in one of my molars had failed and the tooth required a root canal operation. In the course of the procedure, something went wrong and I found myself in a sudden and unexpected world of pain and confusion that resulted in oral surgery to remove the tooth and patch a hole open to my sinus with synthetic bone. After the surgery, I experienced a severe sinus infection, followed by overwhelming pain throughout one side of my face, particularly behind my left eye.

Luckily, I found a young ear, nose, and throat specialist who recognized that I was suffering from nerve damage that had switched the pain receptors on permanently. He told me that he had fallen through a plate glass window several years earlier and had damaged the nerves in his hand so badly that he didn't think he'd ever be able to perform surgeries again. Then he prescribed the same drug that had restored his proper nerve function. He was confident that it would work for me as well. He increased the dosage slowly over the next several days until the pain had completely disappeared. Though I hated the effect of the drug, which made me feel like I was swimming underwater, particularly when I was outside on the street, I was overjoyed and thankful to be free of pain.

Two months later, I was off the medication and feeling close to normal again. I realize now that the whole ordeal took a toll on me. Hoping to relax and recover at the beach, we arranged a trip to Spain for September. However, there would be no relaxation in our immediate future, as we sold the house suddenly and unexpectedly in early August.

The buyer, an independent computer programmer, had lived for years in Venezuela, where he'd married a local woman. After his divorce, he'd lived in New York City for a while, but missed South America. While a guest at Cuenca Suites, he mentioned to Simon and Rebecca that he was looking to buy a house in Cuenca. They told him ours was for sale.

When he knocked on our door, I showed him the house. He asked me how much I wanted for it and we negotiated a price on the spot. We sold the house completely furnished, the kitchen stocked, some of the art still on the walls. The rest of our possessions we gave to our Ecuadorian friends or donated to the thrift shop a couple blocks away.

Before we left Cuenca, we tried to connect with our friends again. We met Lucía for lunch one day. The next, we invited Sara to join us for a hamburger. Another day, our friends Blanca and Belen took us to a famous barbecue restaurant just outside of the city. We invited Maria-José and Paul to breakfast. Finally, just before Emilio took us to the airport in Guayaquil, we took our friends Damian, Martina, Bryan, and Karen to the San Sebas Cafe. It was heartbreaking to leave them behind.

We spent the next six weeks in the United States finalizing the paperwork at the Spanish embassy in Washington, DC. We also flew to Idaho to visit Eric, Sabrina, and our baby granddaughter. The pace was crushing. Less than two days before we were scheduled to fly to Madrid, we learned that the postal service had misplaced the Priority Mail packages that contained our passports with the Spanish visas inside them. We rented a car, drove from Washington, DC to Lynchburg, and with the help of a dedicated postal service manager, tracked down the packages just in time to make our flight the next day.

It's been several years now since we left Ecuador. These days we try to stay in contact with our friends in Cuenca through email and video calls. They tell as that much has changed since we left. In the aftermath of the pandemic, tens of thousands of desperate people from neighboring Venezuela have come to Cuenca, further disrupting an already dismal job market. Meanwhile, Columbian drug cartels have taken control of major port cities and drug related violence has spread throughout Ecuador.

In 2020, we let our Ecuadorian visas expire. When we left Cuenca, we never expected that we might not return to visit the people and country we had come to love so deeply.

Vista del Mar

> I take off my shoes and throw them in the river. I take off my clothes and light them on fire. I cut off my hair with a pair of scissors. I shave off my beard with a razor. A man crosses the bridge on a bicycle. As he pedals by, he says "good morning."
>
> — "Bonjour" from *Carnival Aptitude*

As a young man, I loved the rugged beauty and isolation of the mountains. The back country represented the last frontier, a place I could go to escape the limits and rules of society. I spent a good deal of time backpacking in the Sierra Nevadas in California, and Donna and I lived for eight years in the foothills of those same mountains. In Ecuador, we lived in the Andes at an elevation of 8,000 feet. The weather was so changeable that people said there were four seasons in a day. Though we lived in the third largest city in the country, it often felt like a village, as the mountains isolated the population from the rest of the world.

During the years we lived in Ecuador, Donna and I began taking summer trips to Spain. We found it a relief to leave the mountains and relax at sea level. The shops in Madrid offered clothes and shoes that fit, art supplies I couldn't find in Cuenca, and bookstores filled with affordable paperbacks. We traveled to Barcelona, Valencia, and Alicante. We visited Sevilla, Cordoba, Granada, and Almería. We enjoyed the art and architecture, the good food and wine.

Most of all, we liked the Spanish beaches. During the day, the sun and the sea breeze caressed our skin and the water cooled us when we got too hot. We liked the relaxed atmosphere, the colorful clothes, and the boisterous people. Though we'd been to the beach in Barcelona on an earlier trip, we set out to find an uncrowded and inexpensive vacation spot. We tried Torre del Mar, near Malaga, Santa Pola, near Alicante, and Vera Playa on the Costa de Almería.

During our vacations in Vera Playa, we got up early, ate breakfast on the patio outside, then relaxed on the beach until noon. Sometimes we walked for miles along the unbroken stretch of sandy beach between the towns of Villaricos and Garrucha. When the sun reached its apex, we returned to our apartment to prepare lunch. Afterward, we read under the big umbrella on our porch or napped inside during the warmest part of the day. In the evening, we returned to the beach, staying sometimes until nine o'clock. Then we mixed pitchers of *tinto de verano* and ate *tortilla,* olives, and crackers with hummus on the porch. When the sun finally set, we worked through the stacks of books we'd brought with us from Madrid.

The sea attracted and seduced us. It had a healthy, calming effect. Our vacations passed quickly. In paradise, days blend together. The blue of the sky above the deeper blue of the sea, the shining white village on the hill in the distance, the colored umbrellas and tanned bodies, focused our attention on the present. The joy of simply existing in the moment produced a kind of hypnotic bliss that manifested itself in a permanent smile. We were always sad to leave and looked forward to the next trip. Though we loved our friends in Ecuador, our life in the Andes felt considerably more demanding, as it required the strength and endurance of youth.

* * *

When we moved permanently to Spain, Donna and I arrived with four suitcases between us. Aside from a few paintings, a box of photographs, and some plastic tubs containing my literary archives, which we stored in Virginia, those suitcases contained everything we owned.

After a couple of days in Madrid, we boarded a train to the coastal city of Alicante, where we'd decided to stay for a year while we determined where we wanted to live permanently.

Our first task was to activate our visa. After our experiences dealing with the Ecuadorian bureaucracy, we expected the process would be easier in Spain. However, no one at the Spanish Embassy in Washington had informed us that we had only thirty days from the time we entered the country to complete the paperwork, nor that we'd need a phone, a bank account, and a rental contract for housing in order to acquire the municipal documents needed to apply for a national identification card. It was two weeks before Christmas, a terrible time to try to accomplish any business. Though we got a cell phone immediately, opening a bank account proved problematic. Without an address, we couldn't open an account, and without an account, we couldn't rent an apartment.

A few days before Christmas, we wandered into a law office and asked if they could help us with our immigration paperwork. Though the employees were starting to leave for their annual Christmas lunch, the owner noted our anxiety and promised to have a specialist in immigration law call us later that day. When the lawyer called, we arranged a meeting. Alejandro, a baby-faced eccentric in his late twenties, told us that he lived with his parents and didn't drive. We walked together to a bank, where he helped us open an account using his parents' address. Then he focused on scheduling appointments at the city offices to get our documents. Because the immigration office in Alicante already had a three-month-long backlog of prior appointments, Alejandro took us to the nearby city of Elche to finish the visa registration.

Through a real estate agent, we found a centrally located apartment on the top floor of a four-story building a block from the El Corte Inglés department store and across the street from a Mercadona supermarket. While bigger than we needed and more expensive than we could afford, the apartment was conveniently located and we didn't have time to be picky. The living room had high ceilings and a wall of large windows for light. It looked like a good place to paint.

The owners agreed to let us move some furniture into the apartment before the lease took effect. Our first purchase was a well-used studio easel that I found in an art supply store several blocks away. I rolled it home and took it up the elevator to our empty apartment.

Next, we bought a bed from a local mattress store, and sheets, pillows, blankets, dishes and kitchenware from El Corte Inglés. The rest of our furniture and household goods came from Ikea. The order arrived in boxes and we spent the week after Christmas assembling bookcases and chests of drawers. We bought some wool rugs to warm up the living room, but the apartment still seemed bare, with stark white walls more suited to a hospital than a home. I ordered some stretched canvases online and bought acrylic paints and brushes.

When my canvases arrived, I worked on a series of paintings with themes from Greek mythology that combined Escheresque constructions with images of some of the wire sculptures I'd made in Cuenca. One of these paintings, "Pegasus," featured my wire sculpture horse entangled within an impossible cube floating in a cloud-filled sky. I also made some abstract paintings, including a large canvas called "California Job Case."

After I found a store in Madrid and two online sources where I could buy Rives BFK paper imported from France, I made relief prints as well. I carved a dozen small abstract lino blocks and then followed them with a series of ten portraits of German Expressionist painters and print-makers. My first two years in Spain, I made nearly a hundred new prints.

While painting at my easel one morning, I noticed a car double-parked on the street below, near the trash and recycling receptacles across the street from our building. A middle-aged couple began unloading boxes of books, which they left on the sidewalk near the recycling bin. I watched from the window until they finished and drove away. Then I rode the elevator down to the lobby, walked outside, and crossed the street. The books proved to be a treasure trove of modern and contemporary Spanish literature. I'd been making a list of Spanish authors and novels I should read. I found at least a dozen books from my list among the discarded books, as well as another dozen that looked interesting. By the time I left with my own box of books, three or four other people had joined me on the sidewalk to look through the titles. Aside from the drunken tourists and the bachelor and hen parties, it was one of the few times I saw happy people in Alicante.

Our year in Alicante was uneventful for the most part. We had chosen the city for its beaches, restaurants, shopping, and because it was a transportation hub with a nearby airport and fast, direct trains to Madrid, Valencia, and Barcelona. However, the same features that made Alicante a good choice on paper, made it difficult to meet people and integrate into daily life. The casinos, shopping malls, pleasure boat harbor, El Corte Inglés department store, tapas bars, Starbucks coffee, beaches, fast-food restaurants and seaside promenade made for a constant stream of tourists and foreign visitors. Local people generally didn't bother much with people like us, who seemed to be merely passing through. We doubted we would renew the lease on our apartment.

During our year in Alicante, we traveled up the coast to Dénia, Gandía, Valencia, and Sagunto. At first, we liked Sagunto for its giant hilltop fortifications and Roman theater, as well as its proximity to Valencia. However, our second day there we were less enthusiastic. Aside from the Roman theatre and fortifications, there was little to do. The town seemed to lack services, and even the nearby beaches failed to impress us.

When we asked ourselves what had most attracted us to Spain, we thought about our vacations at Vera Playa. We'd chosen Alicante instead because we had been afraid that living year-round in a beach community, away from the stimulation and services of a big city might be dull in the off season. Nevertheless, we decided to look at apartments on the *costa de Almería*. After the three-hour bus ride from Alicante, we looked at apartments in Vera, Garrucha, Vera Playa, and the village of Palomares. As we wanted to live within walking distance to the beach, we eliminated the town of Vera, which had the most affordable real estate, but was eight kilometers from the sea. We also eliminated Garrucha, which in some ways seemed like a smaller version of Alicante. We preferred an apartment with two bedrooms, but the ones for sale in Vera Playa were beyond what we could comfortably afford. We did, however, find a small apartment with two bedrooms, a view of the ocean, and a rooftop deck, in Palomares, a fifteen-minute walk to the seashore.

* * *

Outside the front window of our apartment on Calle Los Ramos, we can see a giant Araucaria tree that our neighbor's father planted seventy years ago. For generations the Ramos family had farmed this land. Today, a tiny lot next to the apartment complex still contains some remaining orange and olive trees. On the few surrounding streets there are other apartment buildings. Up the hill, a handful of wealthy people own big houses that overlook the sea. In the house behind us three generations of Muslim agricultural workers live together. The big house on the corner contains a restaurant with a bar downstairs, where local workers eat breakfast and drink coffee or beer on their mid-morning break. Across the road, fields planted with lettuce, broccoli, cauliflower, or watermelon stretch nearly all the way to the sea.

During the pandemic, the bar and restaurant on the corner closed, as no one could leave home except to buy food. Paco, the chef, began selling produce on the terrace out front. Though we had often eaten lunch at the restaurant, or had coffee or a drink at the bar, he'd been too busy talking with the locals to pay much attention to us. When Donna started buying produce three or four times a week, Paco had more time for conversation and he learned that we were his neighbors rather than tourists or summer residents. Since then, he has treated us as friends. On Saturdays, when the restaurant is closed, the owners' son and his Spanish punk-rock bandmates practice their music downstairs. I don't know what they call their band, but I've named it Piper at the Gates.

A few months after we moved in, the ceramic tile floor in our hallway began to crack and shatter, leaving holes and a mess of broken tile. When we learned that the tile could no longer be matched, we decided to replace the flooring in the apartment with more attractive and contemporary tile. Our realtor suggested we call a contractor named Diego to help us with the installation. After his crew installed the new floor and the painter finished repainting the walls, Diego's sister Juana came to deep clean the entire apartment.

Donna and I had just returned from a trip to the U.S. and we were exhausted as we watched her work. A tall young woman with Diego's wry sense of humor and the wiry, muscular body of a professional athlete, Juana mopped, scrubbed, and polished every surface, whether tile, glass, porcelain, wood, plastic, or metal. She attacked the accumulated dust and dirt with an astonishing degree of zest and vigor. When she finished, she started over and did it again. She mopped and scrubbed the floor four times before it finally met her standards. As she cleaned, she quizzed us about our trip, our interests, our life. "Where did you learn to work like that?" We asked her. "Does your whole family have that kind of energy?"

She laughed. "You should see my mother," she said.

* * *

Palomares means "dovecotes" in Spanish. Our neighbor Pepe told us that at one time many people in the village, including his grandfather, raised pigeons. Though much of the local crop was tomatoes in those days, his family also grew bananas. Between our apartment building and the restaurant on the corner, there's a small fenced in plot of land with orange and olive trees, several dozen exotic hens and roosters, and a rustic dovecote full of pigeons. A man named José Ignacio arrives in his car each morning to feed and tend to these birds. He cleans the yard and releases the doves to fly around the neighborhood. Often, he sits in the shade of an orange tree and reads his newspaper among the chickens. In the evening, he returns to lock the doves safely in the little shed, while the hens and roosters settle themselves in the low branches of the squat trees, where they roost during the night. Though José Ignacio gathers the eggs each day to sell to local restaurants and cafes, his birds seem more of a hobby than a business.

When we first moved into our apartment, we heard the roosters crowing at all hours of the day and night. Now we hardly notice them. Once, in the middle of the night, I heard the birds shrieking. I didn't know what to make of it, so I rolled over and went back to sleep. We learned later that someone had cut the lock on the gate and stolen three or four of José Ignacio's prized chickens. More recently, a fox jumped the wire fence around the property and destroyed half the flock.

When I began writing and illustrating little story books for my granddaughters, I wanted to share with them something of their grandparents' life in far-away Spain. So, I wrote about Pepe's daughter Desiree's little dog Lula and about José Ignacio and his birds. To protect his identity, I made up a character I named Señor Sanchez, who loved his chickens and doves. When the doves told the chickens about seeing the ocean from the sky, the chickens became depressed and stopped laying eggs. Then Señor Sanchez cured them by putting them into his car and driving them to the beach. As I composed the story, it came to me in Spanish, though I later translated it into English for my granddaughters.

I used an online service to lay out the text and the artwork for these books and published them. I ordered copies of *A View of the Sea* in English to be sent to my granddaughters in the United States and copies of *Vista del Mar*, the Spanish language version of the book, to give to Desiree and José Ignacio. The day after I gave the book to José Ignacio, Donna and I were surprised when he showed us his national identification card. We saw that his name really is Señor Sanchez.

* * *

When we moved to Ecuador in 2012, we put the few possessions we still owned into a climate-controlled storage unit in Lynchburg. Among these possessions was my complete collection of Unicorn Press broadsides, folios, postcards, chapbooks, the manuscript of my descriptive bibliography of these ephemeral publications, my correspondence with Alan Brilliant and Teo Savory, and the original manuscripts, mockups, designs, printed sheets, linoleum and zinc blocks, from my two Unicorn Press books, *The Masked Ball* and *Puppet Theatre*. I also had eight cartons of letters, reviews, publications, manuscripts, contracts, designs, artwork, magazines, and books pertaining to my own work as a writer, graphic artist, publisher, literary translator, and artist, including a complete run of *Asylum* magazine and copies of every book I'd published with Asylum Arts.

Having lived abroad for eight years, it seemed like a good time to donate these materials to an academic research library, where they would be available to the public and to scholars of contemporary American literature. During our year in Alicante, I began to think of libraries that had a connection with Unicorn Press and Asylum Arts. I started with the University of California, Santa Barbara Library Special Collections Unit, as both Unicorn Press and Asylum Arts were founded in Santa Barbara County and I had spent most of my life in California.

I sent a detailed description of the collections to the director of the Special Collections Unit at UCSB, and I quickly received an enthusiastic response. By the end of the month, I had signed an agreement to donate the works to the University of California. The archive would be called "The Greg Boyd Asylum Arts and Unicorn Press Collection." More than a year passed before I could physically return to Lynchburg to organize, pack, and ship the materials to the library.

In March of 2019 Donna and I finally traveled to Lynchburg, where we spent ten days. We stayed in a loft at Riverviews Artspace owned by our friend and occasional collaborator Susan Saandholland. Sue hosted us, brought us food, invited us to meals, helped me document my collection in photographs, and shot hours of interviews with me on video. I also connected with Larry Bassett, another friend from Riverviews who had, over the past ten years, used an inheritance to purchase and curate an extensive collection of art, mostly by local artists. Larry had purchased two of my cave art paintings for his collection. When we left the United States, I gave him a couple boxes of my books to distribute. Since then, he had worked with the city of Lynchburg to put art from his collection into municipal buildings and agencies such as Housing and Social Services, where it is available for local residents to enjoy.

I donated my remaining cave art works, including three giant oil paintings, to Larry's collection. In addition, I gave him some of my framed prints and two moveable paintings. I also gave Susan Saandholland a large cave art painting, a framed print, all of my remaining books and art books, and the art supplies and paper I'd kept in storage. While I was busy organizing, labeling, and packing the archives for the library in California, Donna digitized the thousands of photographs she had left in storage. When we finished, we packed our suitcases full of books and artwork and headed back to Spain.

* * *

We returned to Palomares with two big tubes containing my Chauvet Cave Lions and Lascaux Horse paintings. I remounted the canvases and hung them in our apartment. Then I set to work editing the raw video interview footage that Susan Saandholland had shot in Lynchburg. I produced nine short videos. In one I provide an overview of the "Greg Boyd Asylum Arts and Unicorn Press Collection." Other videos present an oral history of Unicorn Press and my experiences there. Three videos make up a series called "The Cave Art Notebooks" and address my experiences and perceptions while visiting cave art sites in France. I also made a video about my moveable, interactive paintings, a video about my prints, and a video in which I unroll my eighteen-foot-long oil painting based on the "Hall of the Bulls" at Lascaux.

After I'd finished the videos and sent them to the UCSB Library, I began work on a series of art books that serve as complete catalogs of my cave art paintings, relief prints, moveable paintings, and photomontages, as well as a monograph on cave art with illustrations from the notebooks of drawings and texts I'd made during visits to cave art sites in France. I wrote introductions to each of these books, and used an online publishing company to lay out the books and make copies for myself and the library. These books are also available online.

During this time, I also wrote a "children's book" for adults called *Alien Pizza,* a poem about immigrants, illustrated with eerie green and black linocuts. I experimented with making original videos, including a forty-minute collaborative film I completed with Susan Saandholland in 2022, based on my book of prose poems *Carnival Aptitude.* Over a two-year period, I also wrote and illustrated two dozen children's books for my two granddaughters. I used many different techniques to make these little books look and feel different from one another, including linocuts, color linocuts, painted paper cut-outs, collage, watercolor, colored pencil, ink, photography, acrylic, and even cut-up fruit. Some of the books include rhyming poetry for text. Others are prose stories. One book is haiku. The most ambitious is a story called *Gina's Dream,* which features four- and five-color reduction linocuts of cave art animals.

A couple of times, we received back little videos of the girls "reading" the books I sent to them, especially the ones that are about themselves. In the videos, they carry the books around with them, or sit and turn the pages. Coco memorizes the text and "reads" to Eric. In another video, Kiwi points at herself on the back cover. "That's me!" she says, amazed. I've always said that books are powerful magic.

I believe some of the best books are written for children and young adults. Throughout my life books like *Curious George, Green Eggs and Ham, The Little House, Where the Wild Things Are, Mike Mulligan and His Steam Shovel, Ferdinand the Bull, The Wind in the Willows, The Adventures of Huckleberry Finn, A Connecticut Yankee in King Arthur's Court, The Prince and the Pauper, The Call of the Wild, The Hobbit, Animal Farm, Of Mice and Men, The Old Man and the Sea, The Iliad, Treasure Island, The Illustrated Man, The Good Earth, Robinson Crusoe, To Kill a Mockingbird,* and *The Catcher in the Rye* have exerted a tremendous influence on my thinking and my development. As a young child, I loved that there were stories about an intellectually curious little monkey named George. It was as if Margaret and H. A. Rey conceived these books just for me. Such books have impacted how I write as well as how I think about the world. Books for children can be funny, poetic, and profound. I've strived to incorporate the same qualities in everything I write.

* * *

Our apartment is located not quite half a mile from the Mediterranean Sea, at an elevation of about fifty feet above sea level. When we walk toward the ocean, we usually see two or three cargo ships anchored offshore waiting their turn to unload goods at the port of Garrucha and take on loads of gypsum from the quarries in nearby Sorbas and Rodalquliar. From the top of the rise, on clear, sunny days, the huge ships appear to be clustered together about a hundred yards from the shore. However, as we approach the beach, we realize that the ships are, in fact, separated by great distances and anchored far out to sea. Like Plato's parable of the cave, the ships demonstrate that what we perceive at any given moment can easily mislead us: sometimes the information we receive is faulty or incomplete. If we keep an open mind, our perspective may shift or broaden so that it offers a more accurate view—one that completely alters our conclusions.

Human history is full of folly. As we consider the world around us, life seems more complicated than ever. The problems we face appear insurmountable and cataclysmic. Perhaps they are. Or perhaps chaos, greed, and stupidity simply define the state of human existence, which has always been tenuous. Imagine the Visigoths overrunning Rome, Genghis Khan, the Viking raids, slavery and serfdom, the warlord society of feudal Europe, the bubonic plague, the vast corruption and greed of the Catholic Church, the Crusades, the Inquisition, the wars of religion, the world wars, the civil wars, the Wars of the Roses, the Punic Wars, the Trojan War, the French and Indian Wars, Queen Anne's War, King George's War, King Phillip's War, the War of the Three Henrys, the Napoleonic Wars, the War of Jenkins' Ear, the Hundred Years' War, The Seven-Years' War, The Six-Day War, the War of a Thousand Days, the War of 1812, the Mexican-American War, the Indian Wars, the Korean War, the Vietnam War, the

Gulf War(s), the Great War, the Phony War, the Pastry War, the Black War, the Dirty War, the Cold War, the African slave trade, The Great Depression, the American Revolution, the French Revolution, the Industrial Revolution, the Mexican Revolution, the Russian Revolution, the Sexual Revolution, Revolution Number Nine. We are born, we live for a while, and we die. What we do in between matters. Either we dedicate ourselves to imagination and creation or succumb to greed and destruction.

Economies, social classes, religions, nations, political systems, and their related systems of education, indoctrination, and control are human constructs that seem to defy the natural order. They are self-serving, manipulative devices used to enable some at the expense of others. They make existence appear more complex than it is, which in turn distracts and excuses us from our bad behavior. Our way of living consistently rationalizes irresponsibility and selfishness. Worse, it robs us of our imagination and any semblance of free will. Without imagination, we march in step to familiar music we didn't choose for ourselves. Without imagination, we never live fully nor reach our potential. People feel lost, alienated and discontent. They drink and take drugs. They overdose on religion, sex, technology, shopping, and work. They long to be rich, famous, and powerful without realizing that such shallow goals compromise their soul. They try to fill up the black hole that has swallowed them.

Reviewing my life's work, preparing catalogs of my art, and writing the introductions to those catalogs and the text of *The Cave Art Notebooks,* led to me to put into words some conclusions about what I have learned in the course of my life. Artistic expression has always been what sustained me and gave meaning to my existence. I've come to believe that it's also what makes us human.

Imagination, which encompasses our ability to think and express ourselves symbolically, first manifested itself through art and language. While other species fashion and use simple tools they've been making for millions of years, humans have progressed from stone hand axes to computers in a relatively short time. Other species use sounds to communicate, but only humans have mastered the symbolic nature of language. The Neanderthals who inhabited the earth for some 300,000 years prior to the appearance of our own species, produced no art of their own, aside from an occasional hand print. Consequently, they were quickly displaced and assimilated by competing *Homo sapiens*.

In Darwinian terms, symbolic thinking is our biggest evolutionary advantage, the key to our development and our success as a species. Ironically, symbolic thinking also represents our biggest challenge and danger. Throughout our history we have used our brains to assure our survival. Unfortunately, our ingenuity has also led to the creation and implementation of systems and social structures that end up limiting us, as rigid economic, religious, and political systems tend to suffocate our imagination.

Humanity took a bad turn when we began to manipulate the world around us. When we cleverly planted seeds and fenced in animals, we also unwittingly invented private property and war. Complex social structures and hierarchies followed at a rapid pace. These inventions helped pervert, control, and restrict the imagination, increasing the absurdity and unnaturalness of our existence. Over the past several thousand years, we've misused our intellect to enable personal privilege, and in the process created societies and cultures built on insane and unnatural ideas and foundations. We've come to accept these radical changes without question. In modern societies we're taught to rationalize, normalize, and accept all manner of nonsense, including patriarchal religions, institutionalized racism, kings and queens, dictators and presidents, nations, political and economic systems, and the latest fashions, fads, and dangerous technological innovations.

Economics provides an example of our misuse of creativity. In effect, the whole idea of an economy, particularly one based on symbols, seems inherently flawed. Yet these days we've gone beyond a reliance on silos full of wheat and vaults full of rare and shiny minerals. Now we base our ability to feed, clothe and shelter ourselves on speculation, faux currencies, and "futures" that don't even exist.

Technology represents another trap when we mindlessly accept it without first determining for ourselves its potential negative effects and impact. The last time I visited the United States, I constantly encountered well-dressed functionaries wandering along the sidewalks of Washington, DC, staring at their outstretched palms, as just a few blocks away, a delusional maniac raged in the White House. I witnessed other professionals talking to themselves as they ate lunch alone in restaurants. I noted with dismay that the majority of people in public places ignored the people and events around them and instead focused their attention on tiny, backlit digital screens. Obsessive reliance on and connection to technology dehumanizes people and turns them into comical automatons. One could easily imagine such dysfunctional and distracted living cartoons walking in front of a bus or falling down an open manhole.

Our notion of politics seems equally flawed. It's instructive to note that during the Spanish Civil War, the only thing the Fascists and the Communists agreed upon was the need to eliminate the Anarcho-syndicalists in Catalonia, who briefly created a fully functional, self-governing, class-less society with no traditional economy. In his book *Homage to Catalonia,* George Orwell wrote that "Many of the normal motives of civilized life—snobbishness, money-grubbing, fear of the boss, etc.—had simply ceased to exist. The ordinary class-division of society had disappeared to an extent that is almost unthinkable in the money-tainted air of England." Tellingly, in the end, the Socialists and Communists who were fighting to preserve the Republic were more successful in wiping out their Anarchist allies than in winning the war against Franco and the Fascists.

In "Politics is Like Trying to Screw a Cat in the Ass," one of his underground newspaper columns from 1968, American poet Charles Bukowski expressed similar disdain for the smoke-and-mirrors illusions of politics: "The difference between a Democracy and a Dictatorship is that in a Dictatorship you don't have to waste your time voting." Ironically, Bukowski also referred to Palomares in the same article. He mentioned the 1966 "broken arrow" incident in which a hydrogen bomb had been lost in the ocean just off shore: "that last bomb—the god damned thing had gotten itself wedged on the edge of a sandhill far down in the sea… meanwhile, all the poor people in that coast town were tossing in their beds at night wondering if they'd be blown to hell, courtesy of the Stars and Stripes... Palomares. yes, that's where it happened: Palomares. and you know what they did next? the American Navy had a BAND CONCERT in the town park in celebration of finding the bomb."

My neighbor Pepe lived a short walk from where three hydrogen bombs landed in Palomares in 1966. Though only five years old at the time of the accident, he has vivid memories of airplane parts raining down on his family's tomato fields. His older sister joined a group of curious teenagers who walked toward the ocean to see where wreckage from the two planes that collided had landed. There they came across an unexploded nuclear bomb. The next day American soldiers arrived in trucks and jeeps and built a camp near the dry Almanzora River.

*   *   *

When I was a child, it was still possible to make a fire on the beach and enjoy a cookout next to the sea. Sometimes my mother fried the sand perch or sea bass that my father and I caught surf fishing in the evening. More often, we let part of the fire die down, then used a shovel to drop packets of potatoes, carrots, onions, and ground beef wrapped in aluminum foil into the hole, then covered them with red hot coals. After dinner, we toasted marshmallows and made s'mores out of graham crackers, chocolate bars, and marshmallows.

As the sun dipped into the sea, an ink wash spread across the sky, darkening until it looked like black velvet dotted with tiny diamonds. In those days, there were very few electric lights in the area, so the stars shone brightly. My sister and I would study the constellations and try to pick out the astrological zodiac. I couldn't often find the connected groups of stars, but I nonetheless loved how the Greek myths and legends had ended up in the sky above us. Often Linda and I would simply stare up at the night sky until we saw a shooting star. "Did you see it?" I'd ask.

"There's another one over there," she'd reply, pointing to a different spot. I imagined they were everywhere, streaking across the endless void, as lively and beautiful as the pod of dolphins we'd once seen riding the surf together along the shore.

Ten years ago, Donna and I visited our son when he was stationed at Holloman Air Force Base in Alamogordo, NM. I remember that he took us to the New Mexico Museum of Space History. Afterward, we stayed to watch a movie about the Hubble Space Telescope at the adjoining IMAX theater. Projected onto the big dome of the theatre, the images shot through the telescope took my breath away. As I tilted back in my seat and witnessed the birth and death of stars, the deep field galaxies and black holes, the explosions of prehistoric color from the expanding universe, tears rolled down my cheeks. To borrow a phrase by C. S. Lewis, I found myself "surprised by joy."

Contemplating these images calms me. I've since downloaded images recorded by the Hubble Telescope onto my computer and I cycle through them from time to time. Apparently, the newer, more advanced James Webb space telescope now parked in deep orbit a million and a half kilometers from Earth is already sending back pictures documenting the birth of the universe. Somehow, I find the vast reaches of time and space reassuring. Surely there is more to life than what we can consciously comprehend.

* * *

In these days of instant electronic communication, there's little need for physical cards or letters delivered by the postal service. In fact, aside from the occasional package, the only mail we receive in Spain consists of advertising circulars or *facturas* from the water company (though our bank automatically pays the actual bills). Nonetheless, I dream that I find my mailbox full of letters from old friends and correspondents. As I pull the envelopes from the narrow box, I recall the *Asylum* magazine post office box in Santa Maria. As I turn the key to close the door to the box, I notice some familiar handwriting on the letter on top. I know it's from Eric Basso before I even see the name Decius on the return address. Of course, "Decius" was Eric's e-mail address rather than his mailing address, but dreams rarely respect such logic and distinctions. Eric and I had corresponded over a period of forty years, exchanging hundreds of letters and later emails. I learned only recently that he had passed away in June of 2019. The last I'd heard from him was an email I received from him while we were still living in Alicante. "The fire in Paradise," it began. "I wasn't sure if you were still living there, and am wondering, are you all right? I wrote back to remind him that we'd left Paradise fifteen years earlier and now lived in Spain.

The dream about letters from former correspondents reminded me that I haven't yet mentioned the literary friends and collaborators who've passed on. As my literary career blossomed early, I was usually the youngest contributor in the magazines and anthologies that featured my work. As an editor and publisher, the poets and writers I published were often twenty to forty-five years older than me. Edouard Roditi, Lawrence Fixel, and the translator Kendall Lappin had been the elder statesmen and guides in my literary universe. Charles Bukowski, Stephen Dixon, and Russell Edson were each strong literary influences of mine as well as star contributors in my magazine and press. Though also a good deal older than me, I viewed Eric Basso, Robert Peters, and Daniel Quinn as brilliant writers, friends and peers. All of them are gone now, and deeply missed.

I used to own thousands of books and so much art I didn't know what to do with it all. Now Donna and I live in a tiny apartment and have very few possessions. During my first years in Spain I returned to making small editions of relief prints and writing and designing books for children. While it's crazy to make an edition of five copies of a seven- or eight-color reduction print, I don't care—for me the joy is always in the doing. The pandemic changed everything. With each passing day now, I have less interest in reaching an audience. The work I've done seems trivial in comparison to the larger issues facing us all. Now I enjoy playing my guitars. I like to spend time with my wife, take walks on the beach, read, converse, and discover and support young musicians and poets I find on the Internet. I gave the University of California the copyrights to my books and manuscripts after

I'm gone. I've given away what remained of my paintings in the U.S. and Ecuador. Eventually, I will find a way to give away whatever's left.

* * *

As a child, I sometimes walked during the summer months along the beach in the early morning in the company of my grandmother. We would get up at sunrise and sneak out of the house, leaving the others asleep in their beds. We called our walks beach combing, as we always brought along a bucket to collect any treasures that washed onto the shore: un-chipped white sand dollars, bits of sea glass, large, colorful albacore shells good for crafts, flat rocks perfect for skipping in the shallows, sea shells, lost coins, and whatever else might catch our eyes. Those early morning walks on the beach with my grandmother, the hours I spent diving into the waves and body surfing, and the time I spent with my friends at the beach, made me feel like the King of Silver Strand. They are by far my favorite childhood memories.

If I found a well-formed shell on the beach, I'd clean it and present it to my sister, who had started a shell collection, which she meticulously labeled with the scientific names of each type—*Cassidae, Strombidae, Pinnidae, Donacidae, Olividae, Cypraeidae, Veneridae, Pectinidae, Naticidae, Mitridae, Haliotidae*—then placed on the book shelf in her bedroom. Once, I found an expensive Seiko watch in the dry sand above the tide. Like the dozens of fossilized black sharks' teeth I had collected on a trip to Florida one summer and brought home with me, the alternative currency of whatever I put into the bucket gave me a feeling of satisfaction and prosperity.

In Spain, fifty-five years later, I've taken to walking the beach during the winter months, when there's no one around. I pick up the occasional Euro coin, rocks with interesting patterns that remind me of cave art drawings, or heart-shaped stones. I try to breathe deeply, to take note of what changes the tide makes and what small treasures it deposits on the beach each day. I try to see what's in front of me in all its detail and majesty.

In December of 2019, I worried that I might be seriously ill. My heart was racing and I felt weak and uncharacteristically apathetic. I'd gained weight, I wasn't sleeping well at night, and my spine always felt out of adjustment. I worried constantly about the toxic and dangerous political situation back in the United States. I worried about travel. I worried about my prostate, my teeth, my erections. Everyone I met told me I needed to relax, but I was tightly wound and couldn't seem to uncoil. I felt my energy slipping away from me. For the first time in my life, I felt old.

Donna and I had planned to spend Christmas with our son, his wife, and our two young granddaughters, who were living at the time in Colorado. Though we had not wanted to travel during the holidays, our daughter-in-law insisted, only to irrationally rescind our invitation several weeks before our scheduled flight. Though initially astounded, angry, and disappointed, in the end I felt a great sense of relief; I knew that there was a chance that if we would have gone to Colorado, I might have spent the holiday in a hospital in Boulder, or worse, that I might not have survived the trip. Given my racing heart and unsettled state of mind, Donna called to cancel our airline tickets while I made an appointment to see a doctor.

I slept almost constantly for the next three days. My heart still beat abnormally fast, and the doctor confirmed that I was suffering from acute stress. When the blood tests came back normal, I determined to forgo medication and address the problem myself. I began meditating at home and took long daily walks on the beach. I got on the floor and stretched each day. I gave myself permission to do nothing at all, to let my mind wander and relax. I took hot baths and long naps. I drank less coffee, ate less sugar, avoided alcohol. I went to bed before midnight. I stopped checking news sites throughout the day and reduced my time at the computer.

By late January I was feeling better. My heartbeat was within the normal range and my blood work and cholesterol levels were good for my age. One day Donna showed me a book she had read about the health benefits of a vegan diet. We both agreed to give it a try and see how we felt. A week later, I began writing this narrative, which has turned out to be an exorcism of formerly repressed memories and emotions.

When the Covid-19 pandemic drove us indoors for months at a time, I worked on the book, baked bread, researched and tested out new vegan recipes and ingredients. I walked up and down the stairs, and exercised on the roof, where I could look out and see the ocean as I walked or ran. I started relearning some of the forms I'd practiced when I studied and taught Taekwondo twenty-five years earlier. Though the situation in the United States still disturbed me, I tried not to worry about abstractions. Over time, I became more aware and accepting of my physical limitations and my mortality.

As a young person, I realized there were distinct and recognizable stages of life, though I didn't think much about how those stages would manifest themselves or what they would mean to me in the future. Nevertheless, I tried to define the characteristics and acknowledge the importance of the particular stages in which I found myself. I knew, for example, that the transition from childhood to adulthood involved risk and confusion. Therefore, I gave myself over to experimentation, rebellion, failure, and joy. In my twenties, I took the time to wander as mindfully as I could through a forest of choices. I worked at making up for my poor education, at forming a deep and lasting emotional bond with my wife, at starting a career and a family. I began serving a life-long arts apprenticeship. During my thirties and forties, the power phase of my life, I slept little and labored constantly. I pushed myself to work without boundaries or limits, to experience the full measure of my creativity, whatever form it might take. In my fifties, I opened myself to new experiences, knowledge and practices. I gave up writing, publishing, and design and became a full-time painter and student of Paleolithic art. After our son enlisted in the Air Force, Donna and I moved to Virginia, walked across France, then settled for five years in Ecuador. I learned to speak, read, and write Spanish. I learned to listen and to place greater value on people than accomplishments and possessions.

In my sixties, I've come to other realizations. I see that will, ambition and striving are of little importance. I understand and accept that my work is of no interest and has no meaning for most people, nor does it change anything for the better. My earlier ambition and striving for acceptance now seem desperate to me, and it's a relief to let go of such egotism. Meanwhile, like the brittle, yellowed pages of a favorite book pulled off the shelf many years later, I'm shocked at how my body has aged and declined. In the mirror, my white hair seems to belong to someone else—my grandfather. Sometimes I search for Spanish words I've already learned and forgotten. I find that I'm content to sit in the sun and read or simply mine memories. When I move along the sidewalk on my way to the beach, cars seem to rush past at impossible speed. In my dreams, my teeth feel loose against my tongue—when I touch them, they fall from my mouth like the stones I tossed into a river as a child.

Some things we can never understand. Others we know all too well. To know that we are locked into an inevitable cycle is the human condition. No matter that we've done our best, we realize that we have failed in exactly the ways we hoped to avoid. There's no point in assigning blame or feeling guilt. Human psychology and emotions are complex. Our relationships often seem less than what we hope for. Each of us is lacking in some way. Since we cannot change our condition and must simply accept it, instead of despair, we must forgive ourselves and each other. Instead of pining for what has been lost, what could be, or what could have been, we must do what is still possible. We must do the best we can.

Ultimately, others will decide whether anything I have produced has value. Was I perceptive, original, and humorous, or was I selfish, odd, and overly intense? Was I a good person, a good father, a good friend? It's not for me to say.

* * *

The Indalo is a common symbol in the area of Andalucía in which we live. Based on a Neolithic rock carving found inside the Los Leteros Cave in the Sierra de María-Los Vélez Natural Park, the figure of the Indalo depicts a man holding an arc over his head. Thought to represent a hunter with his bow extended, a religious idol, or a rainbow, the symbol may have been used as protection against evil spirits. In recent times, the symbol has become associated with the province of Almería and is often seen on the houses, apartment doors, or cars of local residents.

During one of my spells of print-making in Palomares, I carved a design that shows the Indalo with stick figures of a man and a woman on either side. The masculine symbol includes a shorter appendage between the legs and the feminine symbol two circles on the chest. Beneath the three symbols I carved, in capital letters TOTGAD WOTOM: Too old to give a damn what others think of me. After proofing it in black ink, we mounted a copy of the print on the door of our apartment.

* * *

Aside from Donna, the first person with whom I shared parts of this book was my sister. Over the years, Linda and I had talked extensively and in great detail about our childhood memories and experiences. These discussions helped us both sort out our complicated and contradictory feelings toward our parents. Sometimes after our talks I made notes about what Linda had told me. Two years my senior, she remembers more than I do about our early childhood. When I began writing this book, I asked her a number of specific questions, all of which she answered in detail. When I sent her a draft of the sections pertaining to our childhood, she responded with additional memories and precise insights into the psychology and history of our parents. Her insights and the details she provided helped give shape and depth to the narrative.

I also shared some of the text with my oldest friend David, to whom I had mentioned I was writing about our time in high school. When he asked to read "Scissors on the Beach," he refreshed my memory in several places and gave me some insight into his own experiences with and perceptions of my parents. He's also told me about his own life during the more than forty years since we've seen each other.

Through our correspondence I've been pleased to learn that the bright and original boy I first met in the third grade has become exactly the kind of man I'd hoped he would be.

I relied as well on another old friend who read and helped correct parts of the narrative that took place in Santa Maria, California. Without Patrick's detailed memories of those days, I would not have been able to fairly or accurately describe an important chapter my life. I've often said that history is important. If we hope to make sense of the world, we must study the past and come to an understanding of how it has shaped the present. Each person also has a unique history, and these personal trajectories influence everything that follows.

* * *

It's summer now and we're free to enjoy the beach. This morning, Donna saw a nine- or ten-year-old boy playing in the ocean. She pointed him out to me. "He's boxing the waves," she said. I spotted him jumping in the water. I watched him for a while, but he'd already moved on to other games. Nevertheless, his behavior, which Donna had witnessed and described, reminded me of how I, too, had spent happy hours sparring with the tops of waves at Silver Strand Beach, when I was a nine- or ten-year-old boy. I remember now how I used to watch local boxing matches broadcast live on Wednesday nights from the Olympic Auditorium in Los Angeles on my grandmother's portable black-and-white television. I learned how to throw punches in combinations—left jab, left jab, right cross—body blows, hooks, and uppercuts, and I practiced these techniques in the ocean during the summer months.

I also liked to dive into, over, or beneath the breaking waves and big walls of white water. "I'm like a fish," my grandmother would often say when she swam in the sea. My sister and I were dolphins. We'd jump and dive together, over and over, with a pure joy that's impossible to describe. I learned how to body surf by watching older kids swim to catch waves and ride them toward the beach. Sometimes my father would go into the water and ride the waves as well. As with everything he did, he had his own unconventional method, his own awkward style. Instead of paddling with the wave as it broke and then dropping into it and riding the curl, he would position himself directly beneath the lip of the wave as it folded, then face the shore with his arms extended straight out in front of him, palms pressed together, like Superman flying. He usually rode the white water all the way to the shore. I tried out his style from time to time and though it looked ridiculous, I had to admit it worked.

Because the waves at Silver Strand were famously thick and powerful, the rides were always fast. When the surf was big, it wasn't uncommon for swimmers and body surfers to get caught underwater and turned over several times in the churning white water we called "the washing machine." I remember being stuck underwater holding my breath for what seemed like minutes at a time. Afterwards, I stumbled onto the shore feeling beat up and frightened. After a few minutes' rest, I went back in the water again. In those days, we used to get terrific sunburns. It was uncomfortable, but no one realized the danger back then. Advertisements for Coppertone suntan lotion featured a cute little girl with a bright red bottom. Sun block didn't exist.

For vacationers and retired people, during the summer months, the beaches of Quitapellejos, Cala Marques, and Vera Playa can sometimes resemble a dream. When they wake up in the morning, visitors pick a spot directly in front of the ocean on which to set up umbrellas and lounge chairs, then return to their apartments to eat breakfast. They'll come back when the sun is higher and the spotless blue sky stretches dome-like over the shimmering sea. By then the sand will be hot underfoot and the cool, calm sea will beckon. In the distance, the white town of Mojácar sparkles above the sea at the foot of the mountains. On the beach, naked bodies glisten, stride along the shoreline, or bob among the ocean swells. As the season deepens and the days seem to repeat, one enters into a smiling, contented trance. In such an environment, it's easy to feel that I have become once more the King of the Silver Strand.

In our corner of Andalucía, it's possible to swim in the ocean half the year. Even in January, when the water is too cold for bathing, there are clear, windless days when the weak winter sun invites you to take off your coat and lie down on the sand, your shirt and jeans piled beneath your head as you warm yourself for an hour on the near deserted beach.

These days, Donna and I often take a nap in the afternoon. The siestas are cultural, we tell ourselves. In the summer it's too hot in Spain to do anything after lunch but rest. In truth, we're also tired, which has more to do with age than culture. This afternoon Donna awoke from our nap before I did. She sat up in bed and watched a little sailboat out the window as it moved across the ocean, not far from the shore. When I opened my eyes, she pointed it out to me. I searched for sails against the immense sky. When I located it, the boat looked vaguely familiar. It reminded me of the red hulled plastic toy with the cloth sails I played with in the bathtub as a child, or a watercolor painting of a sloop on an emerald sea. Then in a sudden wave of recognition, I recalled a dream in which I'd once caught a brief glimpse of eternity.

Palomares, Spain, March 2020–May 2022

Addendum

Begun in the second month of the global Covid-19 pandemic, *Planet Hazmat* was my first attempt at writing my autobiography. The text recalls and describes a world that has become increasingly more toxic and dangerous throughout my life. It's a factual and brutal narrative, devastating in its joylessness. It doesn't soften the truth or spare people's feelings. We are all guilty through our complicity. *Planet Hazmat's* purpose here is to serve both as a reflection of my mental state when I began my autobiographical project and as a measure of my psychic and spiritual evolution.

When I first showed my sister a draft of *Planet Hazmat,* she told me that my poisonous little book would likely make people in the United States unhappy and angry. I'm sure she was right, though I replied that I didn't care, as my job is to tell the truth. Of course, in an "Information Age" populated by elected leaders with personality disorders, paid Internet trolls, corporate propagandists and social saboteurs working for hostile foreign governments, my insistence on "truth" probably seems quaint.

I began writing *Planet Hazmat* only a few weeks after suffering a kind of physical and emotional collapse. I had always known that I would eventually write such a book, but I had no idea when. Suddenly, the time had come; writing about my life seemed a way to exorcise past demons and gain some insight, acceptance, and peace of mind.

Planet Hazmat

ABOVE THE ROOFTOP terrace where I walk my ovals and figure eights, an unbroken expanse of blue dominates the landscape below. Past the sprawling lettuce fields, the deeper hue of the sea hems the brilliant sky. Though late morning, no cars circulate on the streets between the village and the sea. Despite the sunny weather, the sandy beach half a kilometer away appears empty. It's mid-March, 2020 on the *Costa de Almería*. From pictures I've seen, I know that in Madrid and other cities, public places appear eerily deserted as well—empty parks and plazas, quiet boulevards and sidewalks. Schools and universities remain closed throughout the country and most people are now working from home or not at all. A while ago, the Spanish government issued an emergency decree forbidding non-essential workers and everyone else from leaving their residences, except to buy food, empty the trash, or seek medical treatment.

The mandatory lockdown doesn't bother me much, as I'm still recovering from a physical and emotional collapse I suffered in the months before the pandemic began. My resting heart rate had increased to an alarming level and I was having difficulty sleeping. Negative thoughts and emotions overwhelmed me and I felt worn out, apathetic, and unwell. Apparently changing countries and continents three times over a period of seven years had been more taxing than I'd realized. Living in a world that has become increasingly toxic and dangerous had gradually increased my anxiety. In addition, the hostile political climate in the United States and the uncivil and abusive state of social media had further contributed to my stress. Meanwhile, busy with my projects, I had failed to realize that I had become as toxic as the world in which I'd been born, raised, and educated—the world that had shaped my values, the world in which I lived. When I went to the clinic, the doctor took one look at me and told me I needed to relax. On subsequent visits, he assured me my blood work revealed nothing amiss. Relieved, I began the process of meditating, dieting, exercising, and sleeping my way out of my stress-induced illness.

Each morning, I climb the metal spiral staircase to the roof of my apartment, where I spend an hour exercising, breathing deeply, and surveying the world beyond. I keep hoping to see someone on one of the other rooftops, someone I might greet with a wave of my arm from the distance, but no one ever appears. The tranquil winter months, after the tourists and vacationers return to their urban homes, have never seemed so empty, so silent. Even the air seems thin and brittle. For some reason, this morning the stillness reminds me of the moments just before the wail of the early warning sirens the authorities used to test each month when I was growing up in Cold War era Los Angeles.

For close to two months, I've been hiding like a hermit crab inside the protective shell of my apartment. During this time of forced isolation, without conversations in cafes, meals in restaurants, walks on the beach, without errands to run and friends to visit, without bus trips to Almería to shop for books, without the routines and distractions of the physical world, I've become even more introspective than usual. When I'm not monitoring the latest news about the virus and its social implications, my psyche sometimes sends me on errands to fetch back pieces of the past. I think about how my personal history relates to the present. It's a broad subject that includes everything I've experienced in my life. At times, my mind makes strange and random associations. For example, as I walked around the perimeter of the roof this morning, two photos developed in the chemical bath of my consciousness. One of the images I'd seen on the Internet recently, and the other bubbled up from my childhood.

The first picture portrays a young boy and girl standing in front of their farmhouse in Palomares, Spain. The uncredited photographer captured the image in August of 1966, seven months after a United States Strategic Air Command B-52 bomber collided with a KC-135 tanker plane while refueling above the coast of Almería. As a result of the mid-air accident, three hydrogen bombs fell onto the village below, one of which buried itself on impact in the garden of Miguel Bonillo, whose children are shown posing with the family donkey. The other photo is a picture of myself at about the same time, standing in shorts and holding Frisky, my Shetland Sheepdog, on a leash. I'm standing in a field in Chatsworth Park, at the northern border of the sprawling city of Los Angeles, California.

We know from experience that memories can be imprecise, inaccurate, and difficult to grasp. Sometimes a photograph is all that's left of the past, all that connects us with our distant and hazy recollections. Before my parents moved to southern California from New York when I was eight, one of my favorite places was the "French Fort," a stockade of log walls and block houses that overlooked Lake Onondaga in Syracuse. I still remember the stairs to the catwalks and the cannon in the courtyard. I think a secret tunnel ran under the wall, joining the barracks to the woods above the lake, but that could be something I dreamed up myself or else remember from Tom Sawyer's Island at Disneyland. The French Fort helped to awaken in me an imagination that thrived on all things historical, including television portrayals of Daniel Boone and movies like *Drums Along the Mohawk* and *The Last of the Mohicans*.

When my wife and I visited Syracuse in 2005, it was the first time I'd been back in forty years. In our rented car we located my old house and Bear Road Elementary School. Later, we parked the car downtown and took a walk on the Syracuse University campus. The next day, we set out to look for the French Fort, but found in its place, or rather a couple miles up the road, a small and unimpressive log enclosure alongside the new "Saint-Marie Among the Iroquois" museum. When I asked the college intern working in the visitor center what had happened to the French Fort, she stared blankly as I described what I remembered.

Then the museum director, a neatly-dressed woman about my age who had overheard the conversation and must have occasionally fielded similar questions, stepped out of her office and told us to follow her. She dug through a closet and produced a framed photograph of the impressive log stockade I remembered so well. "That's it, all right," I said. "So, what happened to it?"

I'm not sure the director sighed, but she could have. Maybe she simply drew in a breath before speaking. "The 1933 structure wasn't historically accurate," she explained, "so they tore it down in 1988 after archeologists discovered the actual foundation of the original 1566 Jesuit stockade. What you see outside today is what we believe the French settlement really looked like."

We thanked her for her time and for her explanation and walked out to look at the reconstructed settlement, which included a couple of plain log structures and a homely log chapel with windows open to the air, surrounded by a rectangular eight-foot-tall stockade. That the settlement lasted less than two years didn't surprise me. An uncomfortable home, a shabby church, and a hastily and poorly designed and constructed fort, it seemed of little value. Warned by friendly Indians that a hostile war party was coming to massacre them all, I imagine the French were only too happy to abandon the dreary outpost on Lake Onondaga and escape back to Quebec or even to France from whence they'd come. I couldn't help thinking that things might have turned out differently if they would have just stayed in the 1933 stockade with the high walls, the stout blockhouses, and the cannon I remembered so well.

In spite of the home movie playing in my head, I'm sure that the museum director had told me the truth and that the research engendered a necessary historical correction. However, for me the collision of memory and revision also resulted in a disturbing sense of loss. The 1933 log stockade, historically inaccurate though it had been, also had its own history. WPA workers had constructed the romanticized fort during the Great Depression. Over many years it had become a part of the memories of countless people, creating, in effect, a parallel history that unseen hands had suddenly erased both from physical existence and the historical record. We all have a personal history that intersects with the larger narrative. In this instance, the child in me couldn't help from feeling that a band of marauding revisionist historians had razed my memory and salted the ground. At the same time,

I know only too well that much of what I'd been taught as a child qualifies as myth or propaganda rather than truth.

I've since learned that soon after our visit in 2005, the visitor center had been closed due to mismanagement and budget concerns. Ironically, given its location on the shore of a lake known for its pollution, the museum building had been rented to a soil and water business for use as an office. Tragically, Lake Onondaga is an environmental disaster, one of the Environmental Protection Agency's 1,659 National Priority List Superfund sites.

Refusing to be bribed into silence by the offer of casino licenses, the Onondaga Nation has brought lawsuits for illegal land grabs and damage inflicted on the environment against the City of Syracuse, Onondaga County, and the State of New York, as well as Honeywell International, Clark Concrete Company, Hansen Aggregates, and Trigen Syracuse Energy Corporation. According to the tribe, Onondaga Lake is roughly four and a half miles long and one mile wide. It is the site where the Peacemaker brought the Seneca, Cayuga, Onondaga, Oneida, and Mohawk Nations together, and where these warring nations agreed to set aside their differences and form the Haudenosaunee Confederacy—the first representative democracy in America. Lake Onondaga thus became a sacred place. Sadly, after two centuries of dumping untreated sewage and over 165,000 pounds of methyl mercury into the water, these days it is better known as the most polluted lake in America.

A related trope from childhood comes to mind. For many years, network television stations all over the country aired a memorable series of public service messages. Beginning in 1971, the Keep America Beautiful campaign produced these highly popular, hard-hitting commercials. Long regarded as public service message classics, these days they are also well known for the ironic circumstances of their creation.

Better known as the "Crying Indian" anti-pollution public service message, the original commercial featured an actor who called himself "Iron-Eyes Cody." Dressed in Native American garb, Cody appears in the videotape paddling a canoe down a pristine inland waterway. His paddle dips near a piece of floating trash as he approaches civilization. Suddenly factories appear on the shoreline, spewing black smoke. The lake or river has become a toxic mess. Iron-Eyes pulls his canoe onto the shore and stares stoically at the highway just above the beach. A single tear runs down his cheek as a passing motorist discards a bag of trash that explodes at his feet.

It turns out that the commercials were actually funded and produced by big bottling, beverage and packaging corporations, in an effort to combat new state laws aimed at prohibiting single use, non-refundable glass bottles. The corporate sleight-of-hand relied on misdirection to shift the blame for litter and pollution away from their own irresponsible manufacturing and marketing practices. By indoctrinating consumers to assume responsibility for the problem, they cleverly absolved themselves. Later, corporations like Exxon got in on the greenwashing with their "People Do" commercials, which attempted to control public relations damage after the Exxon Valdez Alaskan oil spill. One marvels at the cynicism of corporations that have spent millions to produce or fund "public service" messages that were never anything more than self-serving public relations schemes.

The Crying Indian "Iron-Eyes Cody" disappoints as well. An Italian-American actor who played Native American roles in more than 200 Hollywood films, Cody was born in Louisiana and baptized Espera Oscar de Corti, the son of Sicilian immigrants. He played Chief Iron Eyes in Bob Hope's film *The Paleface* and throughout his life was known to dress in stereotypic Native American costumes offstage, including braided wigs, leather tunics with fringes, and beaded moccasins. Despite the evidence on his baptismal record revealed late in his life by his sister, Cody nonetheless continued to claim his father was Cherokee and his mother Cree.

As for the commercial, sources say Cody refused to squeeze out the required tear, telling the director that crying was uncharacteristic of a true Native American. So, the prop master solved the dilemma by applying a drop of glycerin—a phony tear worn by a phony Native American for a phony public service announcement benefitting the interests of the corporations behind it. America the Beautiful.

The living museum and visitor center on the shore of Lake Onondaga are now back in operation, this time under the direction of the Onondaga Historical Association, which has renamed the site yet again, Skä•noñh—Great Law of Peace Center—and repurposed it with a Native American focus. Meanwhile, history and memory continue to spin through time and space, randomly disappearing into one black hole and popping out of another.

Planet Hazmat

A week after we'd visited the French Fort in Syracuse in 2005, my wife and I were still in upstate New York when Donna learned that her elderly father had fallen and had been hospitalized with a broken hip. She took the next available flight directly from Syracuse to Los Angeles and arrived at the hospital just after her father's surgery. The following day, I flew to Sacramento and returned home to get our dog out of the kennel where we'd boarded her during our trip. When my father-in-law passed away several days later, I drove from Northern California to Los Angeles to help Donna with the arrangements.

As I drove down Interstate Highway 5, somewhere in the Central Valley the traffic slowed to a crawl due to an overturned tanker truck. I'd told Donna I expected to arrive in Claremont soon after dark, so I decided to take my chances on the back roads. I left the highway at the next exit and set out to find a road that would take me in a direction parallel to the highway. I hoped to go around the bottleneck and rejoin the highway further south. After a few twists and turns, I found myself in a landscape that reminded me of driving through Nebraska with my parents in 1965.

It was a July evening and the summer light brought everything into sharp focus as I drove along miles of two-lane road lined with what appeared to be identical ten-foot-tall stalks of perfect corn. The giant size of the stalks, planted in close proximity to each other, made an unforgettable impression. Impossibly uniform and robust, shockingly and vividly green, they looked as artificial as plastic flowers. I slowed the car and studied the massive trunks, the perfect husks. It looked as though they had been planted by a John Deere mothership from a distant galaxy.

I later learned that corporate farmers had grown this corn from genetically modified seed developed by Monsanto to be resistant to its own glyphosate weed killers. Monsanto, or whatever multinational corporate name they hide behind these days, calls the poison-tolerant seeds "Roundup Ready." Monsanto's introduction of a system based on modified seeds followed by herbicide treatment allows farmers to eliminate space needed for mechanical tilling. Instead, they position planted rows closer together, increasing yield.

I remember the name Monsanto from my childhood because it had a close relationship with the Disney Corporation. I first saw Monsanto's "House of the Future" when my parents took my sister and me to New York City to visit the World's Fair in 1964. When we moved to California, we saw it again in Anaheim, where Walt had commissioned a similar plastic house as part of "Futureworld" at Disneyland.

More than twenty million people viewed the attraction, which Monsanto created to demonstrate the versatility and functionality of plastics. Inside, they showcased early versions of newfangled technological wonders like the microwave oven. When the House of the Future closed in 1967, demolition crews were unable to dismantle the plastic house using the usual wrecking balls, cutting torches, chainsaws, and jackhammers. They finally resorted to choker chains to crush the-structure-that-refused-to-die into smaller parts, though the house resisted so forcefully that the half-inch steel bolts used to mount it to its foundation broke before the plastic did.

Despite its Disneyfied public face, environmentalists have long vilified Monsanto as "the most evil corporation on Earth." Since its founding in 1901, Monsanto has been responsible for the introduction of a number of highly toxic substances, including polychlorinated biphenyls (PCBs), which even today environmental health professionals consider one of the worst chemical threats on the planet. Widely used over a fifty-year period as lubricants, hydraulic fluids, cutting oils, waterproof coatings, and liquid sealants, PCBs are potent carcinogens, exposure to which can cause reproductive, developmental, and immune system disorders. Though governments around the world eventually banned PCBs, traces still exist in just about all animal and human blood and tissue cells everywhere on the planet.

As early as the 1930s, documents introduced in court showed Monsanto had been fully aware of the deadly effects of their products, but criminally hid them from the public. In addition to PCBs, Monsanto also introduced and manufactured the commercial herbicides Dioxin and Roundup, Agent Orange, aspartame (a neurotoxic in the form of an artificial sweetener), genetically modified Synthetic Bovine Growth Hormone (rBGH), produced from a genetically modified E. coli bacteria, and a host of toxic, self-pollinating genetically modified seeds that are systematically wiping out the planet's bee population.

In America, we are quick to embrace new commercial applications of science and technology. At the same time, most of us naively trust that our government will protect us from the unforeseen dangers of these new products. While recent advances in medicine and the invention and widespread implementation of vaccines, along with modern farming methods and the threat of "mutually assured destruction" have eradicated a number of significant diseases, helped control famine, and for the most part limited wars to regional conflicts, the irresponsible use of under-regulated technology remains the single biggest threat to the long-term survival of every species on the planet, including our own.

In addition to the forthcoming catastrophic effects of climate change, nuclear proliferation and dirty bombs, and the ongoing poisoning of the environment, we should give some thought to the irresponsible development of robots and artificial intelligence. We've already seen what can happen when technology develops faster than the ethical and practical constraints needed to monitor and control its negative effects. Nevertheless, if history teaches us anything, it's that we aren't great at taking advice from history, which is just a more polite way of saying we're profoundly stupid.

Author and educator Adam Robinson wrote a book called *How Not to Be Stupid*, in which he examines how people come to make what they would later describe as stupid mistakes. In his view, stupidity is not the opposite of intelligence. Rather, it is the overlooking or dismissing of conspicuously crucial information. In other words, stupidity results when we ignore or refuse to accept essential facts and information, when, whether by accident, groupthink, information overload, stress, hurry, a lack of competence, or just plain carelessness, we fail to act on information we already know is true and essential.

When my parents moved from Syracuse to Los Angeles in the summer of 1965, we arrived in mid-August, a day or two after the Watts Riots began. For a while, we lived in a motel on Ventura Boulevard in Tarzana. Whenever we left our air-conditioned room, a wave of intense, dry heat blasted us. Stepping outside was like opening the door of an oven. My mother seemed depressed and cried for hours at a time. She developed dark half-moons under her eyes.

On television, we watched as 14,000 California National Guard troops joined nearly 2,000 Los Angeles Police and Sheriff's Department officers in Watts. The live reports showed buildings on fire and cops in helmets beating and arresting people. Apparently, snipers had shot at fire trucks to keep them away from burning buildings. The police responded with overwhelming force. In a live television interview, LAPD Chief William H. Parker compared the police operation to fighting the Viet Cong in Vietnam. Meanwhile, U.S. Marines had secretly launched Operation Starlight, the first major U.S. assault of the war, against a Viet Cong regiment in Van Tuong village, twelve miles north of the Chu Lai Airbase.

I'm not quite sure why—perhaps they felt that they needed to get into a house quickly before the new school year began—but my parents purchased an ugly, run-down tract house in a working-class neighborhood in Canoga Park in the San Fernando Valley. Instead of the swimming pool my sister and I had hoped for, the house had a cement pad that all but covered the small back yard. The cement absorbed the summer heat and kept the house stiflingly hot, even at night. Despite temperatures that could climb as high as 115 degrees, the house lacked air conditioning.

Looking back, my parents' choices didn't make much sense. My father was an electrical engineer with a Ph.D. from Syracuse University. At that time, in that place, he could have walked into any number of big aerospace corporations and named his own salary. My mother had a Master's degree in education and had taught in the public schools in New York. Both my parents had a good earning potential. I'm not sure why they settled for such an inexpensive house in such a depressing neighborhood. Maybe they both knew their marriage wouldn't survive the Summer of Love.

One of our neighbors in Syracuse had been stationed for training in Southern California during the Second World War. He remembered the orange grove filled San Fernando Valley as a lost Garden of Eden where the weather was always sunny and warm. We quickly found, however, that even paradise has problems.

In addition to the oven-like dry heat in the summer months, the torrential rains that sometimes came in winter, the wild fires in the canyons, and the mudslides in the hills, we learned about smog. Photochemical smog is a kind of air pollution produced by vehicular emissions from internal combustion engines and the release of industrial smoke and fumes. These pollutants react with sunlight and form secondary pollutants, which then combine with the primary emissions to form a thick brown haze which burns the eyes and lungs. According to health experts, air pollution can cause severe sickness. Exposure over time can result in shortened life span or premature death.

The World Health Organization estimates that worldwide air pollution causes around twenty-five percent of all fatalities from lung cancer, heart failure, stroke, and pulmonary disease. Prior to the Clean Air Act of 1970 and the formation of the Environmental Protection Agency, signed into law by Richard Nixon, Los Angeles was the reining smog capital of the world. Photographs from the 1960s reveal downtown office workers wearing gas masks and a brown layer of pollutants so thick that it obscured tall buildings. I still remember the smog alerts that cautioned against exercising or playing outdoors, and the burning sensation in my lungs when I took a deep breath.

A short walk from our house on Acre Street, surrounded by empty fields of tumbleweeds along the "S" turn on Nordhoff Street, a significant cluster of large buildings housed aerospace related industries, including Rocketdyne and Atomics International. Though we never gave these companies much thought, an informative book called *Environmental Monitoring at Major U.S. Research and Development Facilities,* published by the Department of Energy in 1976, identifies these seemingly innocuous facilities as housing some rather unexpected and disturbing operations: "building 001 containing uranium fuel production facilities, and building 004, containing analytical chemistry laboratories, and a Co60 gamma irradiation facility."

Six miles away, hidden in the folds of the Santa Susana hills, these same companies operated the ominous Santa Susana Field Research Laboratory, a 2,850-acre facility, where they developed and tested ten experimental nuclear reactors. In July 1959, an early prototype Breed nuclear reactor at the field lab suffered a partial meltdown. When workers tried and failed to repair it, their superiors ordered them to open the reactor's large door, releasing radiation into the air, thereby contaminating the nearby communities of Simi Valley, Chatsworth, and Canoga Park.

Several weeks after the meltdown, the Atomic Energy Commission issued a statement admitting that there had been a minor "fuel element failure," while at the same time falsely claiming that there was "no release of radioactive materials" into the environment. I imagine the unfortunate writer employed by the U.S. government sitting at his desk as he carefully crafted this outright lie. Today, such skill at deception would likely result in a better paying job as a press secretary or as the host of a current events talk show on a cable television network.

In addition to the Breed Reactor core meltdown, at least three of the other experimental nuclear reactors operated by Atomics International and the United States Department of Energy at the Santa Susana lab suffered partial meltdowns, release of fission gases, or damage to fuel rods. Though some scientists have estimated the radioactive elements released during these events was 400 times greater than the amount released during the highly publicized Three Mile Island incident years later, Atomics International and the government kept the accidents secret for decades.

An uncredited still photo from Dario Mellado's documentary film *Nuclear Cowboys* shows what appears to be three Atomics International executives in suits and hard hats watching from a safe distance at the Santa Susana Field Laboratory as a geyser of radioactive gas escapes into the air. Mellado's documentary features former Atomics International employees who recount how the company approved the release of high concentrations of radiation over parts of Los Angeles during a two-week period. They also discuss the routine illegal burning of chemicals in sodium pits, which released radiation into the air for decades.

Along with the experimental reactors and sodium burn pits, other related nuclear facilities on the site included a plutonium fuel fabrication facility, a uranium carbide fuel fabrication facility and what has been called the biggest "Hot Lab" in the United States. This hot lab was used to cut up irradiated nuclear fuel rods shipped in from sites all over the country. In 1957 a fire in the lab got out of control and, according to an official government publication called the *Sodium Graphite Reactor, Quarterly Progress Report, January-March, 1957*, resulted in "massive contamination."

Along with the experimental nuclear reactors, the Santa Susana Field Lab facilities also included several large rocket engine test stands, where Rocketdyne conducted thousands of rocket fuel tests over a forty-year period. This extensive research facility, better suited to the desert of New Mexico or Nevada, existed only a short distance from a semi-urban population that numbers over a million people.

Toxic waste from burn pits and chemical labs, as well as solvents used to clean the rocket engines, were stored in fifty-gallon barrels that workers often disposed of using firearms to blow them up on site. Once the barrels exploded, they released their contents into the air. Hundreds of other barrels were left scattered on the ground in various places throughout the surrounding hills.

As a child and adolescent, I used to enjoy hiking with friends through the surrounding hills. Sometimes one of our parents would drop us off at Chatsworth Park or Bell Canyon and we would walk all day through Upper Las Virgenes Canyon in the hills behind the Santa Susana Field Research Laboratory until we ran into Highway 101, near Agoura. Though we never wandered into the Burro Flats Painted Cave, which features the oldest pictograms in California, many times, both around Chatsworth Park and in Las Virgenes Canyon, we did stumble upon collections of fifty-gallon barrels. We had no idea that they contained toxic waste. Sometimes security guards in Ford Broncos or pickup trucks tried to chase us off the property, which made for an exciting game, as we knew that if we ran from them through the hills, climbing over rough terrain, they'd have to leave their vehicles and follow on foot.

According to information published by Boeing, which now owns and manages the decommissioned laboratory site, the area is "home to abundant wildlife, endangered plant species and Native American cultural resources" as well as nearby movie ranches where Hollywood directors shot hundreds of westerns and other films. On the Boeing website, one finds a "Visiting Santa Susana Factsheet" that goes so far as to encourage potential visitors to participate in a guided tour of the former field laboratory.

The factsheet presents a carefully constructed alternative reality: "A handful of decommissioned rocket engine test stands dot the landscape," it wistfully states, "relics of the testing that powered moon landings, satellite launches and national defense." Though some minor accidental spillage "resulted in the release of chemicals onto the ground, which contaminated areas of soil and groundwater on-site," it was all much ado about nothing, for "numerous health studies conducted over many years collectively reinforce that past operations have not affected the health of area residents." Of course, Boeing is happy to confirm that "visitors participating in bus tours and guided walks are safe."

Despite the misleading information from Boeing, studies of employees at the Field Lab and residents who lived nearby conducted by the UCLA School of Public Health and others between 1988 and 2002, reveal high rates of certain types of cancers. Part of Chatsworth and Canoga Park, as well as most of West Hills and Simi Valley are within five miles of the laboratory. The 1997 study showed up to a sixty percent greater chance of cancers for area residents.

The widespread use of highly toxic chemicals to power over 30,000 rocket engine tests and to clean the test-stands at the site afterwards resulted in massive contamination of soil and ground water. The ongoing nuclear research and four known nuclear accidents, contributed further to the toxicity of the entire area. After the state of California asked NASA, the Department of Defense, and Boeing to clean up the site, all but Boeing complied. Instead, in October 2007, Boeing announced that it would give the nearly 2,400 acres of land that is currently the Santa Susana Field Laboratory to the government of California for future use as a state park. At the same time, Boeing has waged a decades-long legal battle against the state to avoid cleaning up its portion of the former field laboratory.

In the 1950s, the Gee-Whiz, Can-Do attitude of American scientists and researchers represented a danger to society and the planet, the consequences of which we are still feeling today. I remember the snarky, "factual" voice-over narrations that blared from television commercials and news broadcasts, from documentaries and school filmstrips throughout my childhood. Always that of a self-assured male, the voice was that of Mr. Know-it-All or his sidekick Don't-Worry-About-It. That the same attitude continues to exist, projected and amplified by the public relations of a huge corporation currently known for system failures resulting in fatal crashes of its 737 Max passenger jets, as well as its recent failed Starliner space capsule test, strikes me as both absurd and unforgivable. In his novel *Cat's Cradle*, Kurt Vonnegut wrote about a childishly irresponsible scientist named Felix Hoenikker. While puttering in his corporate lab, Hoenikker invents a compound called Ice-Nine, which accidentally destroys all life on the planet. If there's a real-world version of Felix Hoenikker, he's probably working at Boeing. Of course, he could also be found in the labs of Monsanto, Dow Chemical, ExxonMobil, and thousands of other companies.

My father, who, with his slide rule, pocket protectors, rolls of computer punch tapes, social awkwardness, selfishness, lack of interest and commitment to his family, and near total inability to communicate human emotion, has always reminded me of Vonnegut's emotionally disconnected and socially irresponsible scientist. To say he was distant and abstract would be overly charitable. Denied tenure in the Engineering Department at UCLA, he left academia to found his own engineering and manufacturing firm. His company became a subcontractor to Westinghouse and other aerospace concerns working to fulfill contracts with the Air Force and Navy. The company produced my father's own proprietary designs for microwave phase shifters used in military radar systems arrays on projects such as AWACS and the B-1 Bomber.

After divorcing my mother and abandoning his two children to marry his secretary, my father eventually won a lawsuit against his former partner, who had been robbing the till. Then, he became quite wealthy. For the rest of his life, he surrounded himself with mostly competent sycophants who oversaw the daily operations of the company, freeing him to play his French horn in community orchestras, and to indulge in his darker hobbies. Contracts with European and Indian companies and invitations to present papers at international conferences gave him plenty of opportunities to travel. He had a tailor in Hong Kong who made all his suits. He personally picked out his Mercedes Benz and BMW sedans and had them shipped directly from Germany. He acquired bigger and better mansions. When his wife wanted an indoor swimming pool, he had the existing outdoor pool filled in and replaced.

A couple years before he abandoned his family, my father took the photograph I mentioned earlier of me when I was a young boy, standing with my dog in Chatsworth Park. Shot in the bright summer sun, the film seems overexposed, as if the sun had exploded just as the lens captured the image. The colors in the nearly sixty-year-old photo have faded: the spotless sky behind me is dull gray-blue, the trees burnt mud, the grass a hot olive drab. I'm wearing a button up shirt tucked into khaki shorts with cargo pockets, a blue Cub Scout belt, gray socks, and black shoes. My chin is tilted slightly downward. I'm staring directly at the camera, holding onto the dog's leash with both hands. As yet, I hadn't quite learned how to smile.

In those days, kids rode their bicycles as far as they could go and played freely in any undeveloped places they could find. My friends from the neighborhood and I used to build forts and bunkers in the empty fields by the railroad tracks, not far from Atomics International. Later, my Pop Warner football team, the Chatsworth Chiefs, practiced in Chatsworth Park. Members of my High School Cross Country Team ran along the roads that wound through Box and Bell Canyons, close to the toxic field laboratory.

By the time I was a teenager, I was already indoctrinated into the ubiquitous American car culture. During these years, the internal combustion engine mesmerized me with its power and possibility. In our culture, motor vehicles represent personal freedom and the transition to adulthood. They also promise danger and speed. I entered into the economy early and voluntarily, as a result of my desire to purchase a car. By the time I graduated from college, I'd already owned eight different automobiles and four motorcycles. Under the influence of teenage hormones, alcohol, drugs, motor sports, and popular culture, I sometimes operated these vehicles in ways that endangered myself and others. It's a wonder I survived adolescence.

In those days, it was still possible to fill the tank of a car with leaded gasoline. Of course, no one worried about gasoline additives back then. Whenever I tanked up my 1955 Chevy hotrod, I looked for the highest-octane leaded gas I could find. Meanwhile, over the previous sixty years, so much lead had been deposited into the soil and onto city surfaces that an estimated sixty-eight million children unknowingly suffered from toxic levels of lead absorption. Each year, thousands of Americans died of lead-induced heart disease. Worse, lead affects cognitive functions, which, in effect, made us all measurably dumber. Neuroscientists have suggested that chronic lead exposure resulted in a significant dip in IQ scores during the leaded gas–era. Other researchers have also suggested that nervous system damage due to exposure to lead may have increased violent crime rates in the 20th century. In any case, statistics tell us that crime dropped to unheard of levels in the 1990s, a generation after abortion became legal and the government finally banned leaded gas at the pump.

At the same time, I was unwittingly making myself dumber, advertisers and social icons encouraged me to suck carcinogenic smoke out of paper tubes. According to the American Lung Association, there are approximately 600 ingredients in cigarettes. When burned, cigarettes create more than 7,000 chemicals. At least sixty-nine of these chemicals are known to cause cancer, and many are toxic. Among the chemicals in cigarette smoke are acetone, ammonia, arsenic, benzene, butane, cadmium, carbon monoxide, formaldehyde, lead, and tar. While consumer products that contain these chemicals have warning labels that identify them, cigarettes do not. Certainly, no sane person would willingly ingest these toxins, would they?

According to the Centers for Disease Control and Prevention, one in every five deaths in the United States, or nearly half a million preventable fatalities each year, are attributable to smoking. Since 1964, when the U.S. Surgeon General first stated that cigarette smoking caused cancer, government estimates show that tobacco has killed more than twenty million Americans, a number fifteen times greater than the number of Americans who have perished in all wars combined. Yet these toxic narcotic delivery systems still exist, heavily taxed but only marginally regulated.

For the past sixty years, the tobacco companies have continued to wage expensive and lengthy legal battles to preserve their perceived first amendment right to intentionally lie and mislead the public in order to make money killing other people. In recent years, for example, they have filed a dozen lawsuits, appeals, and challenges to U.S. District Judge Gladys Kessler's ruling that ordered them to quit lying about the health risks of their "light" or "low tar" products. The tobacco companies "have marketed and sold their lethal product with zeal, with deception, with a single-minded focus on their financial success, and without regard for the human tragedy or social costs that success exacted," Kessler wrote in *United States of America v. Philip Morris USA*. The tobacco companies responded by hiring an army of public relations experts, attorneys, and soulless scientists to contest every morpheme and comma of the ruling.

Other corporations now use the arguments, delaying tactics, and legal strategies pioneered by the tobacco companies to avoid responsibility for negative impact throughout society, most notably to cast doubt on the scientific consensus underlying global warming and climate change. By recasting scientific facts as a "debate," oil companies, car manufacturers, and builders of pipelines continue to promote and maintain an economy that extracts and burns fossil fuels, a scenario we already know threatens human existence over the long term.

Not far from Chatsworth Park, just off the old Santa Susana Pass Road, Charlie Manson lived at the Spahn Movie Ranch with members of his "family" in 1969, during the time they were planning and carrying out the Tate / LaBianca murders. I remember my parents worried that the Manson family might have been responsible for lifting our Volkswagen Beetle and turning it sideways in the driveway during the night, though it seemed more likely a prank played by some drunken high school football players. Only a few years later, no one remembered Manson. I recall attending an off-road motorcycle race held on the Spahn Ranch property. Later, when I was teaching at California State University, Northridge, my wife and I worried about another Los Angeles serial killer, Richard Ramirez, known then as The

Night Stalker, who preyed upon sleeping couples who lived, as we did, in single-family dwellings within a five-minute drive of a freeway onramp. Though we didn't have air conditioning, throughout that long hot summer we slept with our windows closed and locked, a claw hammer resting handle up on the floor next to the bed.

In those days. the rugged hills around Chatsworth above Porter Ranch remained accessible to hikers and off-road motorcycle enthusiasts. When I got my learner's permit at the age of fifteen, I used to ride my 100cc Honda Enduro motorcycle all over those hills, on land owned by the Getty Oil Company. Growing up in Los Angeles, it always surprised me how many oil pump jacks, or "nodding donkeys" I'd see in the hills and throughout the city. Now that I've had time to think about the consequences of all that oil, I find it increasingly difficult to understand how our society continues to operate on the false assumption that one hundred plus years of burning massive amounts of dead organic matter long buried beneath the ground has not harmed nor altered the environment.

As teenagers, my friends and I sometimes visited Oak Mountain, another area of interest and concern in Chatsworth. A winding road led up Brown's Canyon to the military installation on the summit. From where the road ended, we could see the entire San Fernando Valley, the Pacific Ocean, and on a clear day much of the Los Angeles Basin. Of course, the soldiers on duty at the secure entrance were not happy to see us and made us turn our vehicles around. Once they forced us at gunpoint to exit the car, then ripped the insignia off the military jacket one of my friends had bought at the Army-Navy Store a few miles away in Reseda.

Visible from below as a large white golf ball, the Nike Missile Base, designated LA-88, was surrounded by a tall chain link fence topped with barbed wire and patrolled by soldiers with guns and guard dogs. Until it closed in 1974, this base housed Ajax and Hercules anti-aircraft missiles, the latter tipped with nuclear bombs, meant to protect Los Angeles, and more specifically the aerospace infrastructure, by blowing Soviet bombers out of the sky just before they could drop their deadly payload on Rocketdyne, Atomics International, Hughes Aerospace, Lockheed, North American, McDonnell Douglas, the Jet Propulsion Laboratory, the Santa Susana Field Laboratory, Rockwell, the Rand Corporation, Raytheon, and my father's fledgling startup company, among hundreds of other small suppliers. If the idea of exploding nuclear devices in the atmosphere within a fifty-mile radius of a major population center seems a bit kooky, well, there you have it.

Planet Hazmat [539]

My mother's second husband, Philip Casey, enlisted in the Navy at the age of seventeen and served on a LST (Landing Ship, Tank) during World War II. After a brief stint of post war railroad work in Arizona, he enlisted in the Army and saw combat as a foot soldier on the Korean Peninsula. After that war, or conflict, as it is still known, as neither war nor peace have ever been declared, the Army sent him to Japan, then to Nevada to participate in live tests of hydrogen bombs. He once showed me a photo of himself published in Howard Rosenberg's 1980 book *Atomic Soldiers: American Victims of Nuclear Experiments*. In the photo he is "decontaminating"—with a broom—soldiers who had just been exposed to a nuclear bomb detonation in the Nevada desert. Other photos from the book show troops huddled in slit trenches ready to charge into the radiation as an enormous mushroom-shaped cloud forms during the detonation of a hydrogen bomb in the desert, or sailors on a nearby naval vessel watching the awesome power of a test bomb blast in the Pacific.

Recently declassified Pentagon documents reveal that the United States government deliberately exposed as many as 400,000 U.S. soldiers and sailors to massive doses of radiation in exercises they participated in during nuclear bomb tests at the Nevada nuclear test range, Bikini Atoll, and elsewhere during the 1950s. Designed to help soldiers overcome their fear of radiation, the exercises gave them "an emotional vaccination" to the effects of a close-range nuclear blast, so that they could effectively operate on a post-nuclear battlefield. Such nonsense reminds me of an interview Republican candidate George H. W. Bush gave to the *Los Angeles Times* during the California primary election against Ronald Reagan. Asked if he believed we could survive a nuclear exchange with Russia, the former head of the CIA answered that all citizens needed to do was dig a hole and pull something heavy, an entry door, for example, over them before the blast. Such is the logic of nuclear warfare.

Before the implementation of the Partial Nuclear Test Ban Treaty in 1963, the United States, Soviet Union, Great Britain, France, and China detonated over 2,000 above ground, atmospheric, underwater, and underground nuclear bombs at test sites around the world. Several of these tests convincingly demonstrated the dangers of nuclear fallout on the general population.

One 1957 "Plumbbob" atmospheric test in Nevada sent a cloud of radioactive fallout on a path over Reno to San Francisco, where it hovered for a couple of days before intercepting the jet stream and moving east. Over the next several days, fallout rained down onto much of North America all the way to the Eastern Seaboard. Medical experts have estimated that the twenty-eight detonations that made up the Plumbbob test series, during which 18,000 U.S. service members participated in nuclear maneuvers, may have added as many as 20,000 thyroid cancer deaths in the years since, along with many additional leukemia deaths. Perhaps the most striking evidence came from the film *The Conqueror*, shot in 1956, only a few miles from the Nevada Test Site. Several "dirty bombs" had been detonated in the area just a year prior, in 1955. Of the 220 cast and crew members who worked on the shoot, 91 developed cancer and 46 had died by 1980, most famously John Wayne and Susan Hayward.

In the 1950s, both the United States and the Soviet Union prioritized their capacity to deliver the high-yield hydrogen bombs they had been testing. Both countries already possessed large numbers of long-range bombers. Since nuclear armed bombers could neutralize defenses and wipe out civilian populations, U.S. armed forces needed to respond quickly to incoming threats. The construction of early-warning radar stations in conjunction with a large number of nuclear-armed bombers seemed the best strategic deterrent to a surprise attack by the Soviet Union.

The U.S. military established Strategic Air Command, or SAC, just after the end of the Second World War as a separate command of the U.S. Army Air Forces to oversee the nuclear-armed bomber operations. At this time, the United States also signed a number of treaties to establish additional bases around the world. The new bases gave the U.S. the ability to aerially refuel the SAC bombers so that they could reach targets within the Soviet Union. Under the new treaties, Spain, a country the U.S. Department of State strongly discouraged citizens from visiting due to the repressive fascist government of Francisco Franco, agreed to allow U.S. forces to establish bases on the Iberian Peninsula.

By the 1960s, both rocket and radar technology had improved. Intercontinental ballistic missiles with multiple warheads and Polaris nuclear submarines with missiles, made bombers obsolete. Nonetheless, the U.S. military maintained a small number of B-52 bombers, flying in pairs, constantly in the air until U.S. radar systems could accurately provide advanced warning of a Soviet missile attack.

In 1961, operation Chrome Dome kept twelve B-52s armed with three or four thermonuclear bombs continually flying from bases in the U.S. toward the Soviet Union. The bombs had predetermined targets and the planes flew one of three different routes. One route crossed the Atlantic Ocean, refueled over Spain, and then circled the Mediterranean Sea. Between 1961 and 1968, bombers loaded with nuclear weapons were flying over America's allies twenty-four hours a day.

Ever efficient, military bureaucrats studied the possibility of an accident due to the program. Their estimate turned out to be fairly accurate. In 1961, a B-52 broke up in flight near Goldsboro, NC and its unarmed bombs dropped from the plane. Two months later, another B-52 with two nukes on board crashed near Yuba City, California. The following year, a Chrome Dome bomber collided with a tanker plane and dropped two unarmed nuclear bombs on Kentucky. All of which brings us, finally, to Palomares, Spain, where I live, and what occurred here roughly fifty-five years ago.

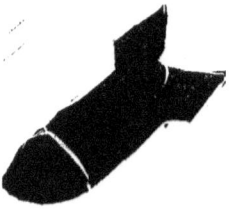

To residents of the village, the morning of Sunday, January 16, 1966 must have seemed like any other day in the tiny seaside agricultural community. The sky was clear, with the good visibility typical of the microclimate that makes this corner of the Spain the sunniest place in Europe. What wasn't normal was that three hydrogen bombs, along with the flaming wreckage of two United States Air Force planes, would fall onto their tomato fields and houses. At about 10:20 a.m., 31,000 feet above Palomares, the seven-man crew of a B-52 Stratofortress carrying four 1.5-megaton hydrogen bombs, prepared for aerial refueling. As they approached the waiting KC-135 tanker, the boom missed the fuel port opening and instead hit the plane with enough force to snap off the bomber's left wing. An explosion spread fire up the boom to the KC-135's full tanks of jet fuel. While the B-52 broke up in midair, the tanker dropped like a fiery comet and exploded at 1,600 feet, killing all four crew members.

Five of the bomber crewmen successfully escaped the B-52, though one died when his parachute burned or failed to open. The remaining two never made it out of the plane. The unarmed hydrogen bombs broke free from their rack and tumbled down from the sky.

At 10:22 a.m., the bombs and wreckage from the planes fell onto the village below. At that time, Palomares was a farming community of roughly 2,000 people in the impoverished region of Almería. Residents had often watched the daily refueling operation in the sky above and a number of villagers witnessed the midair collision. Huge sections of burning airplane pieces fell from the sky. The bomber's landing gear smashed down eighty yards from an elementary school. One of the burning engines from the tanker plane punched into the ground behind the house of Julio Ponce Navarro.

A ten-foot-long, torpedo-shaped hydrogen bomb landed in front of Pedro de la Torre Flores, who had been standing near the fields watching debris fall from the sky. The bomb's conventional explosives detonated upon impact, blowing the 83-year-old man to the ground. Though Flores had the wind knocked out of him, he was otherwise uninjured. Another bomb landed in the Cabezo Negro Hills on the other side of the village, where its conventional explosives also detonated. Miraculously, no one in Palomares was injured by the bombs and burning debris.

At the time of the accident, fishing boat captain Francisco Simó Orts was maneuvering five miles offshore. Orts saw the explosion in the sky and followed the descent of six parachutes. He noted the position of the two that landed in the water not far from his boat, approximately five and a half miles from shore. Spanish fishing boats rescued the three survivors who dropped into the sea soon after they entered the water. The captains of these vessels took the rescued crewmen to a hospital in Aguilas, where the fishermen lived. Villagers found the final survivor near Palomares. He was still strapped into his ejection seat, and suffering from a broken shoulder and burns.

According to official documents, historical records, and the corresponding publications based on them, five of the deceased crewmen landed directly in the tiny Palomares village cemetery, including all four crewmen from the tanker plane. Another dead man landed in his ejection seat a hundred yards away from the graveyard. The body of yet another deceased airman lay a short distance up the hill. That all seven corpses touched down within or very close to the small Palomares cemetery seems not only eerie, considering that the wreckage from both planes spread out over a sixteen-square-mile area, but also very unlikely. My own interviews with eyewitnesses in Palomares contradict the published historical record. In fact, these first-hand accounts indicate that many other details from the official version of these events are also laughably inaccurate—a clear case of a closely coordinated public relations spin and damage control by the fascist regime of dictator Francisco Franco and the United States government. Thus, the official history has the people of Palomares helpfully preparing coffins for the seven charred bodies which had all conveniently dropped in or near the village cemetery, the only place their horrific appearance wouldn't upset anyone.

Though none of the bombs that fell on Palomares triggered a nuclear explosion, the two bombs that detonated conventional explosives on impact spewed radioactive plutonium dust around the surrounding area. While alpha radiation from plutonium does not generally enter the body through the skin, it can be ingested or inhaled into the body. Most dangerous when inhaled, in large enough amounts it can cause immediate radiation sickness or future incidences of cancer.

While once again it's difficult to confirm the accuracy of the published historical record, according to what I've read, a breeze carried the toxic plutonium dust away from the village. Apparently, it was one of those windy days that sometimes ruin an otherwise warm and sunny morning on the *Costa de Almería*. The two bombs whose conventional weapons exploded fell near the hills or onto a tomato field, away from any houses. Also, the emergency parachutes on the two bombs did not work properly, so instead of landing gently, the bombs fell at high velocity and buried themselves in the ground before detonation, reducing the amount of the plutonium expelled into the air. Four days after the accident, authorities informed residents of the village that they would be tested for radiation. Within two weeks, more than a thousand people had been tested. According to the records, no one suffered radiation poisoning, and tests on urine samples indicated that only low levels of plutonium dust had been internalized.

After the accident, the American military set up a camp near the dry Almanzora riverbed, a five-minute walk through the seasonal lettuce and watermelon fields from my apartment. At that time, only one house existed in the area. One of my neighbors lived there with his parents, his grandparents, and his sisters. Though only five years old, he remembers walking across his family's tomato fields each day to the American camp, where soldiers and airmen gave him chocolate bars, chewing gum and tins of Spam. When the Americans grew weary of babysitting him, they drove him home in a Jeep. Though the U.S. military efficiently recovered and removed three of the four H-bombs within twenty-four hours of the accident, my neighbor's older sister nonetheless remembers that she and a group of her curious teenage friends had first gone to inspect and touch one of the bombs.

Within two weeks of the accident, about 750 people were searching for airplane parts, testing for radioactivity, and decontaminating the sites where the hydrogen bombs had landed. The military personnel on shore then turned their attention to the cleanup, while the search for the missing fourth bomb became a U.S. Navy ocean salvage operation. For several months, a fleet of thirty-four surface ships and two mini-submarines searched the ocean off of Palomares. However, it wasn't until the Navy enlisted the help of fishing boat captain Francisco Simó Orts that they finally located and recovered the submerged weapon.

At the time of the accident, both the United States government and Spanish dictator Francisco Franco tried to mislead the media about the nuclear aspect of the event. The U.S. had been concerned about the missing bomb, as well as the implications of revealing a potentially catastrophic international incident. For his part, Franco wanted to protect the Spanish tourism industry. Ironically, a young American reporter named Andre del Amo, who was working in Spain for the United Press International wire service, broke the story two days later when he helped translate for a military police officer who was trying to move local residents away from the scene of the wreckage in Palomares. When the reporter asked him if the authorities were worried about the bomb, the military policeman told him everything.

Meanwhile, workers sealed off the 630-acre area affected by plutonium fallout. After reaching an agreement with the Spanish government, workers removed the most highly tainted soil and replaced it with fresh topsoil. They plowed under another 640 acres. In addition, workers burned 3,970 truckloads of vegetation, which turned out to be a bad idea, as the smoke from the fires spread the plutonium further.

While U.S. authorities had said that they would restore Palomares to the condition it was in prior to the accident, they did not keep their promise. The hasty cleanup work and repairs took only eight weeks to complete and ended when the government shipped some of the contaminated soil back to the United States and buried it at the Atomic Energy Commission's Savannah River Facility in Aiken, South Carolina.

For many years thereafter, the U.S. government paid Spanish doctors to test residents of Palomares annually to monitor the long-term effects of radiation. The agreement with the U.S. government recently expired, though the Spanish government continues to offer free medical checkups for residents willing to travel to Madrid. In 2015, U.S. Secretary of State John Kerry met with Spanish Foreign Minister José Manuel García-Margallo and agreed that the United States would pay to dig up and remove an additional 490 acres of plutonium tainted soil from Palomares and transfer it to the United States. Thus far, the United States has not kept that promise either.

These days Palomares remains a quiet agricultural community. The fields around my apartment building produce a variety of crops, including lettuce, watermelons, zucchini, and broccoli. Most of the year it's quiet and calm here. In summer, tourists arrive from all over Europe, drawn by the naturist community and resort, the long, wide beaches, the sunny weather.

In early August, at the former site of the American camp, near the spot where the third hydrogen bomb landed, and where American soldiers and airmen later stacked the fifty-gallon drums of contaminated soil before loading them onto the ship that transported them to South Carolina, in normal times portable stages and tents go up for an annual music festival. Called "Dream Beach," the five-day-long electronic and dance music event attracts over 100,000 young fans. No doubt the local authorities will cancel Dream Beach this year, as it's just too dangerous to pack so many people together in such a confined space.

From the bedroom window of the apartment in which I am now writing, I can see the beach and the stand of trees where festival attendees pay to set up their tents to camp. I can walk in fifteen minutes to the beach where, a couple of days after the nuclear accident, the U.S. Ambassador to Spain, Angier Biddle Duke, famously took a dip in the sea to demonstrate the safety of the site. Another five minutes of walking along the beach brings one to the sprawling naturist community of Vera Playa.

I imagine that in time the threat of the Covid virus will eventually end or at least diminish to the point where it's more or less safe to leave the house. Sooner or later, big pharma will find a profitable vaccine against Covid-19. Yet it already seems clear that our lives will never quite be the same again. Nature and the cosmos are sending us a message, giving us a preview of disasters and cataclysms to come if we don't realistically begin to rethink our values and priorities, reconfigure our economic models and reduce the toxicity of our environment. I know that others, too, have been wondering how much longer we can continue to ignore what all of us already know—that despite being on the verge of self-extinction as a species, we persist in a state of collective denial rather than actively working to change our mindset and behavior to reflect the emergency we face. Based on my own observations, I'd say we are quick to forget and slow to evolve. I'd also say we are careless and stupid.

I've written elsewhere about the human tendency to create fictional worlds and narratives, a proclivity that, when misused, inevitably leads to widespread misinformation, manipulation, and the systematic erosion of truth. The widespread and casual acceptance of untruths may, in fact, be the most pressing concern of our times. That we live in an "information age" full of conspiracy theories, "alternative facts," superstition, scapegoating, and bold-faced lies says much about the current state of our civilization. A lack of transparency, combined with poorly researched and impossible-to-accept official explanations for world-shaping events such as the John F. Kennedy assassination, the events of September 11, 2001, the subsequent Anthrax attacks, and Iraq's fictional "weapons of mass destruction" have resulted in a decline in general trust in public institutions and government, as well as in journalism, science, scholarship, and expertise.

Ironically, though I know better, I'm guilty as well. I simply can't resist the temptation to tell stories. As we age, sometimes we become eccentric and irrational in our thinking. In the last years of his life, my ninety-two-year-old father-in-law, a pragmatic man who had taught geology at California State University, Northridge, sometimes prattled a bit about extraterrestrials. In a similar vein, I recently outlined a short story about an advanced alien race that comes to Earth to save the planet from destruction by humans. The aliens have been monitoring and studying humans for thousands of years. They decide to appear to us as fictional humans from the future who have traveled through a time warp. It seems like something we might understand.

So, they appear as characters from a popular 1960s era television show—the starship captain, his pointy eared first officer, the chief medical officer, the ship's engineer. As the starship orbits the planet, the officers beam down to meet with world leaders at the United Nations. The United States, North Korea, and Somalia boycott the meeting, as the U.S. mobilizes its military and nascent Space Force. In a passionate, emotional speech broadcast world-wide, the alien captain tells leaders that technology is killing the planet because it has outpaced our understanding of ethics. "We are all interconnected," he insists. "Though we may not like mosquitos, they serve as food for fish and reptiles. Without them, these species would die off, which would lead to…" He presses his hands to his head. "You tell them," he says to the first officer.

Joining the tips of his fingers so that they form an arch before him, the first officer begins speaking. "Your behavior is illogical," he says. "According to my calculations, in a matter of days this planet will reach the point of irreversible and inevitable self-destruction."

"Oh, for Christ's sake, man, give them something they can understand," says the ship's doctor, pushing the first officer aside. "Your planet is racing toward a black hole at warp speed," he yells into the microphone. "Damn it, man, can't you see that if you don't slow down, the ship's Lithium Crystals will explode, scattering radioactive debris across the universe?"

"Fascinating," the first officer responds, arching his eyebrow. "What the doctor is attempting to communicate is that the needs of the many outweigh the needs of the few."

"Precisely," adds the captain, stepping forward again. "We're here to help," he continues, with a crooked smile. "Under the legal jurisdiction of the Interplanetary Federation, we're implementing Resolution 0927, The Impulse Power Initiative. Henceforth all electronic devices on this planet—computers, cell phones, even the power grid—along with internal combustion engines, petroleum products, nuclear reactors, and chemical labs and factories have been permanently disabled." Suddenly the lights switch off, the cell phones fall silent, and airplanes drop out of the sky like wind-up birds whose mechanical hearts have unexpectedly quit beating in midair.

It seems there's no way to avoid toxicity. It's in the air we breathe, the water we drink, the food we ingest, the ground under our feet. Toxicity exists in both physical and psychic form. Both are the by-products of a culture of greed, destruction and deceit. We hear that people are toxic, relationships are toxic, politics is toxic. These days few of us are naive enough to think our government is not toxic. Yet if the best we can do is to carry on in an uneasy state of denial and ignorance, who will take responsibility and institute positive change?

Meanwhile, the news seems to get worse daily. People matter-of-factly accept a pre-manufactured reality; they willingly surrender control of their lives to antiquated belief systems and a corresponding economic and political systems that keep the majority in a state of spiritual, economic, and intellectual poverty. Truth no longer matters. Selfishness abounds. Personal responsibility, courtesy, and common sense are in short supply. Tribalism, race, and religion continue to divide us. Yet even as the social fabric unwinds, we willingly ingest the poison. Our destructive lifestyle is a drug we've been conditioned to enjoy.

According to online health sources, the sooner one recognizes the symptoms of poison, the better the outcome. The lasting effects of the toxin vary, depending on the substance, amount, and type of exposure. In serious cases, poisoning can result in brain damage, a coma, or death.

These days and at my age, I just want a few more years in which to feel the warmth of a sun made dangerous by the depletion of the ozone layer or take a dip in the Plutonium Sea. Maybe there's a limit to how much absurdity, stupidity, and toxicity we can internalize before our brains simply shut down. Nothing else could possibly explain life on Planet Hazmat.

Palomares, 2020

About the Author

Throughout his life, Greg Boyd has celebrated creativity as a writer, editor, publisher, designer, illustrator, gallery owner, and exhibiting artist. Over the years, he has traveled widely and taught and lectured on subjects ranging from Advanced Narrative Writing, to Paleolithic Art and Taekwondo. His books include works of fiction, poetry, multimedia, nonfiction, and literary translation. Some of his writings have been adapted for film, including an original screenplay produced as the feature film *Seven Fallen Objects*. Boyd's paintings, interactive paintings, relief prints, and illustrated, hand-set letterpress books have been exhibited in galleries and alternative art spaces. His prints and photo-collages have appeared as illustrations in and on the cover of books, magazines, and recordings.

Coyote Arts Titles

Gilbert Alter-Gilbert, editor. *Pipe Dreams: The Drug Experience in Literature*
Greg Boyd. *Brotherton's Travels: Memoirs*
Jefferson Carter. *Free Hugs: New and Selected Poems*
Joe Martin. *Rumi's Mathnavi: A Theatre Adaptation*
Lawrence Millman. *Goodbye, Ice: Arctic Poems*
Lawrence Millman. *Outsider: My Boyhood with Thoreau* (illustrated by Geoff Halverson)
Elias Papadimitrakopoulos. *Toothpaste with Chlorophyll | Maritime Hot Baths* (translated from the Greek by John Taylor; illustrated by Alekos Fassianos)
Eric Paul Shaffer. *A Million-Dollar Bill: Poems*
Eric Paul Shaffer. *Free Speech: Poems*
Eric Paul Shaffer. *Green Leaves: Selected & New Poems*
Christopher Spranger. *The Book of Tasks, Volume I: Atlantean Undertakings*
Christopher Spranger. *The Comedy of Agony: A Book of Poisonous Contemplations*
Leslie Stahlhut. *The Secret of the Old Cloche: Agatha Christine Mystery Stories*
John Taylor. *What Comes from the Night: Poems*

Forthcoming Coyote Arts Titles

Eric Basso. *Fictions: The Beak Doctor: Short Fictions, 1972–1976 & Bartholomew Fair*
René Daumal. *The Anti-Heaven* (translated and with an introduction by Jordan Jones)
Kendall Lappin. *Dead French Poets Speak Plain English & Memoirs of a Translator of Poetry*
Joe Martin. *Parabola: Shorter Fictions*
Gérard de Nerval. *Aurélia, followed by Sylvie* (translated by Kendall Lappin and with an introduction by Eric Basso)
Eric Paul Shaffer. *Second Nature: Poems*
Leslie Stahlhut. *Borderlands of the Heart and Other Stories*
Leslie Stahlhut. *The Hidden Staircase: Agatha Christine Mystery Stories, #2*

www.ingramcontent.com/pod-product-compliance
Lightning Source LLC
Chambersburg PA
CBHW030507080526
44586CB00011B/103